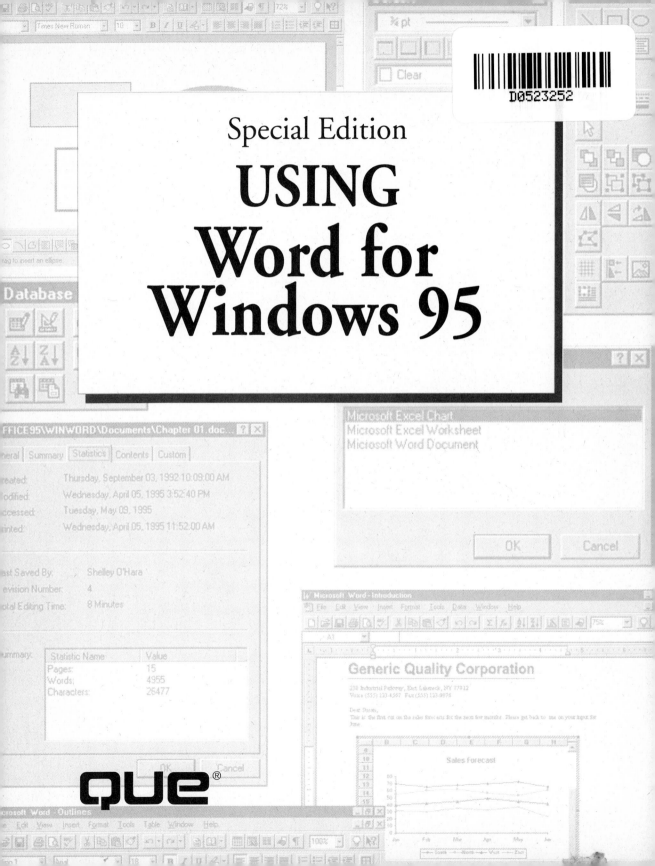

Special Edition
USING
Word for
Windows 95

que®

Special Edition

USING
Word for
Windows 95

Written by

Ron Person
Karen Rose

que®

Special Edition Using Word for Windows 95

Copyright© 1995 by Que® Corporation.

Library of Congress Catalog No.: 95-070633

ISBN: 0-7897-0084-0

97 96 95   6 5 4 3 2 1

Interpretation of the printing code: the rightmost double-digit number is the year of the book's printing; the rightmost single-digit number, the number of the book's printing. For example, a printing code of 95-1 shows that the first printing of the book occurred in 1995.

Screen reproductions in this book were created using Collage Plus from Inner Media, Inc., Hollis, NH.

Credits

President
Roland Elgey

Vice President and Publisher
Marie Butler-Knight

Associate Publisher
Don Roche Jr.

Editorial Services Director
Elizabeth Keaffaber

Managing Editor
Michael Cunningham

Director of Marketing
Lynn E. Zingraf

Senior Series Editor
Chris Nelson

Acquisitions Editor
Deborah Abshier

Product Directors
Lorna Gentry, Kathie-Jo Arnoff, Stephanie Gould, Lisa D. Wagner

Production Editors
Susan Ross Moore, Lisa M. Gebken

Editors
Judi Brunetti, Gail Burlakoff, Silvette Pope, Caroline D. Roop, Andy Saff, Linda Seifert

Assistant Product Marketing Manager
Kim Margolius

Technical Editors
Bruce Wynn, MS Windows Certified Professional, Joseph Risse, Janice A. Snyder, Robin Schreier, Michael Watson, Steven Wexler, President, WexTech Systems, Inc., Donald Doherty

Technical Specialist
Cari Skaggs

Acquisitions Coordinator
Tracy M. Williams

Operations Coordinator
Patty Brooks

Editorial Assistant
Carmen Phelps

Book Designers
Ruth Harvey, Sandra Stevenson

Cover Designer
Dan Armstrong

Production Team
Angela D. Bannan, Chad Cooper, Terri Edwards, Joan Evan, DiMonique Ford, Barry Jorden, Daryl Kessler, Beth Lewis, Julie Quinn, Kaylene Riemen, Bobbi Satterfield, Paul Wilson, Jody York

Indexer
Carol Sheehan

Composed in *Stone Serif* and *MCPdigital* by Que Corporation.

About the Authors

Ron Person has written more than 18 books for Que Corporation, including *Special Edition Using Excel for Windows 95*, *Web Publishing with Word for Windows*, and *Special Edition Using Windows 3.11*. He is an author of *Special Edition Using Windows 95*. He has an M.S. in physics from The Ohio State University and an M.B.A. from Hardin-Simmons University. Ron was one of Microsoft's original twelve Consulting Partners and is a Microsoft Solutions Partner.

Karen Rose has written five books for Que Corporation, including *Using Microsoft Windows 3*, 2nd Edition; and *Using Word 6 for Windows*, Special Edition. Karen has taught for the University of California, Berkeley Extension, and Sonoma State University. Karen is the owner and publisher of *Little Red Book Press*, publishers of hand-bound books.

Acknowledgments

The expertise, knowledge, and production that go into a book like *Special Edition Using Word for Windows 95* requires teams of talented people. A book of this size and detail can be updated only through conscientious and dedicated work from each person. To meet incredibly short deadlines, while covering Word in the depth it deserves, everyone missed weekends and worked long nights—and on a number of occasions, all night. Thank you for your work and skill.

Que, the world's largest publisher of computer books, continues to stay ahead of the competition through the energy and skills of its people. We appreciate their grace and humor while under pressure.

Don Roche, **Susan Moore**, **Debbie Abshier**, **Lorna Gentry** and **Michael Cunningham** did one of the smoothest jobs I've ever seen of managing the high-speed turnaround on this book. They stayed ahead of the project through every twist and turn and had alternative plans for every unexpected corner. The development and editing teams worked the long hours necessary to get this book through development and editing. Their contributions and long hours give the book that distinctive Que style.

Thanks also to **Joyce J. Nielson** for compiling the Index of Common Problems.

Thanks to the software consultants, professional writers, and technical editors who helped revise *Special Edition Using Word for Windows 95*. However, the responsibility for errors that may have slipped through their knowledgeable gaze lies solely with us.

There were weeks of 16-hour days and months of missed weekends with family in order to finish this book on time. We appreciate the work of these people:

Carlos Quiroga is the owner of Pacific Technical Documentation, a high-technology writing firm in Windsor, California. Carlos worked long hours and numerous weekends to insure a quality revision. His efforts contributed significantly to meeting our deadlines.

Lorry Laby has considerable experience as a software trainer and technical writer. Lorry teaches Word for Windows at Santa Rosa Junior College and trains municipal governments and businesses in Word for Windows and WordPerfect in northern California.

Elaine Marmel has written numerous books for Que and Alpha, including *Word for Windows 2*, Quick Start and *Using OS/2 Lotus SmartSuite*. She is currently writing the first of a new series of introductory-level books, *The Big Basics of Excel for Windows 95*. Elaine is an independent technical writer in Tampa, Florida.

Shelley O'Hara has written over 25 computer books and is one of Que's best-selling authors. Shelley is well known for having written most of Que's *Easy* series. Shelley is an independent technical writer and consultant in Indianapolis. Shelley's high productivity and clear writing style are always impressive.

The Techniques from the Pros chapters add valuable depth to this book. Thanks to Christine Solomon, Ted Kennedy, and Steve Wexler for their contributions. All of us who use Word for Windows appreciate tips passed on by professionals.

We'd Like to Hear from You!

As part of our continuing effort to produce books of the highest possible quality, Que would like to hear your comments. To stay competitive, we *really* want you, as a computer book reader and user, to let us know what you like or dislike most about this book or other Que products.

You can mail comments, ideas, or suggestions for improving future editions to the address below, or send us a fax at (317) 581-4663. For the on-line inclined, Macmillan Computer Publishing has a forum on CompuServe (type **GO QUEBOOKS** at any prompt) through which our staff and authors are available for questions and comments. The address of our Internet site is **http://www.mcp.com** (World Wide Web).

In addition to exploring our forum, please feel free to contact me personally to discuss your opinions of this book: on CompuServe, I'm at 75703,3251, and on the Internet, I'm **lgentry@que.mcp.com**.

Thanks in advance—your comments will help us to continue publishing the best books available on computer topics in today's market.

Lorna Gentry
Product Development Specialist
Que Corporation
201 W. 103rd Street
Indianapolis, Indiana 46290
USA

Contents at a Glance

Everyday Word Processing

Creating Envelopes & Mailings

Formatting Documents

Mastering Special Features

Contents

2 Getting Started in Word for Windows   37

3 Creating and Saving Documents   75

6 Using Templates and Wizards for Frequently Created Documents   **173**

7 Using Editing and Proofing Tools   195

8 Previewing and Printing a Document   227

II Formatting Documents   249

9 Formatting Characters and Changing Fonts   251

12 Working with Columns   377

15 Mastering Envelopes, Mail Merge, and Form Letters

18 Creating Bulleted or Numbered Lists   547

19 Organizing Content with an Outline   571

21 Building Forms and Fill-In Dialog Boxes   639

22 Working with Math and Equations   677

V Publishing with Graphics   697

23 Inserting Pictures in Your Document   699

24 Framing and Moving Text and Graphics   727

25 Drawing with Word's Drawing Tools   755

VI Handling Large Documents   845

28 Inserting Footnotes and Endnotes   847

29 Creating Indexes and Tables of Contents   863

30 Tracking Revisions and Annotations   901

31 Adding Cross-References and Captions   917

32 Assembling Large Documents   937

VII Using Word with Office and Networks   957

33 Working with a Group of People   959

34 Using Word with Office Applications   971

VIII Customizing with Word   1015

35 Customizing and Optimizing Word Features   1017

36 Customizing the Toolbar, Menus,
and Shortcut Keys   1033

37 Recording and Editing Macros   1053

IX Techniques from the Pros   1077

38 Desktop Publishing   1079

39 The Power of Field Codes   1115

40 Creating Online Help and Manuals   1135

Introduction

Word for Windows is the best-selling word processor available for Windows. In competitive reviews, Word for Windows has received the highest rating from every major reviewer and magazine. Its features range from those of an easy-to-use word processor to those that make it the most powerful and customizable word processor.

Why You Should Use This Book

This book and its previous editions are among the best-selling books on word processing in Windows. It is not just a rehash of the manual by writers who aren't familiar with Word for Windows. This book has in it the knowledge that comes from time spent on the front lines of business—helping individuals, departments, and corporations learn how to work effectively using Windows software. Our work has included helping business people who are just getting started with word processing to teaching corporate developers how to program in the Word and Excel application languages. We have seen the confusion caused by some areas in the manuals and have expanded and clarified these areas. We've tried to include tips and tricks that have been learned over time—many of which are either not in the manuals or difficult to find.

Word for Windows 95 is an important upgrade from Word for Windows 6. Word for Windows 95 has many features that make it easier to use, it's significantly faster than Word 6, and it takes advantage of Windows 95 features such as enhanced drag-and-drop and improved Open and Save As dialog boxes. Throughout the book, new features specific to Word for Windows 95 are marked by a New Feature icon (shown at the right of this paragraph). If you used Word for Windows before, watch for these icons so that you can quickly learn about new features. If you used a previous version of Word for Windows, you should read Chapter 1, "Word Processing Power in Word for Windows 95." It will give you a visual catalog of the major new features in Word for Windows 95.

Special Edition Using Word for Windows 95 includes extensive sections on how to get the most out of WordArt, Microsoft Graph, Equation Editor, and Microsoft Query—applications you can use to create publishing titles, create charts and graphs, insert equations, or retrieve data from external databases. You will also learn how to integrate Word for Windows 95 with other Windows and Office 95 applications. You can paste, link, or embed data from another Windows application into your Word document. And it includes four Techniques from the Pros chapters written by well-respected Word and Office consultants.

Why You Should Use Word for Windows

Many reasons exist for choosing Word for Windows as your word processor, including its wide array of features, accessibility, power, and ability to exchange data and graphics with other Windows applications. For those of you standardizing on a word processor, the choice of Word for Windows is an easy one. For those of you already using one or more word processors, Word for Windows can increase productivity and decrease support costs. Because of its capability to coexist with other word processors, you can begin a gradual transition toward Word for Windows.

Word for Windows Has Accessible Power

Word for Windows is the most powerful word processor, but it has features that make it the easiest to use and easiest for which to get help.

Most people do not need or use advanced word processing features regularly. On most days, you want a convenient word processor that doesn't get in the way. Word for Windows toolbars, shortcut menus, and excellent online help make it one of the easiest word processors to learn. You can also customize the screen display and menus to make the program even more straightforward and easy to use. Although Word's advanced features don't get in the way, they are there to handle any type of specialized work you need, such as drawing on a document, outlining, importing, or linking to mainframe database, desktop publishing, and much more.

Word makes advanced features that you only use occasionally easy to learn. The toolbars shown in figure I.1, for example, enable you to click a button to choose the most frequently used commands, such as opening or saving files, inserting bulleted lists, making tables or columns, or formatting for bold with centered alignment. You can even customize the toolbar to fit your needs by adding or removing buttons for specialized commands.

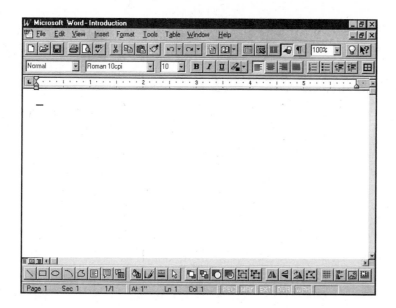

Fig. I.1

Select text and
click buttons on
toolbars to execute
many commands.

Word for Windows Works in the Windows 95 Environment

If you know any other Windows application, you already know how to use
Word for Windows' menus and commands, choose from dialog boxes, use
the Help window, and operate document windows. Another advantage of
Windows is that you can easily transfer data between applications, embed
graphics or text in a Word for Windows document, or link graphics or text
between applications. Figure I.2 shows a Word for Windows 95 document
linked to Microsoft Excel 95 charts and tables. You can easily switch between
the two applications.

Word for Windows gives you access to Object Linking and Embedding (OLE).
With OLE, you can embed text, graphics, and charts into a Word for Windows document and not have to worry about misplacing the file that the
text, graphics, or charts came from. The data is embedded along with the
result. Double-click an embedded object, like the chart in figure I.2, and the
appropriate application immediately loads the object so that you can edit it.
Word works with both OLE 1.0 and OLE 2.0 so that you can embed or link
with older or the most up-to-date Windows applications.

Word for Windows Shows You Results

Word for Windows enables you to zoom from a 25 to 200 percent view of
your document—exactly as it will appear when printed. You can edit and

format text or move framed objects while you are in any zoomed view. If you are using TrueType fonts, you are guaranteed to see what will print. Word has the features necessary to do most desktop publishing. Figure I.3 shows a document zoomed out to show two pages.

Fig. I.2
You can paste, link, or embed data from other Windows applications so that your word processor gives you the ability to integrate data from many different sources.

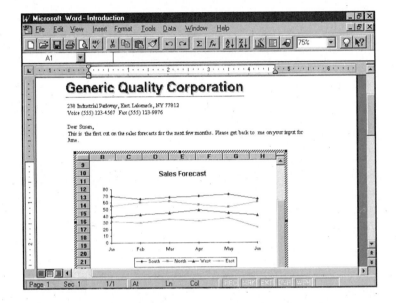

Fig. I.3
Word has the commands and buttons to do desktop publishing that satisfies most business and personal needs.

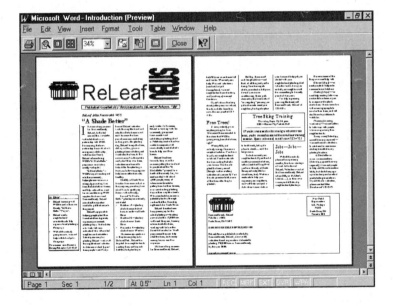

Word for Windows Reduces the Need for Technical Support

Word for Windows 95 contains extensive help files you can use to get an overview of a procedure. To get help, just press the F1 key or click the ? button and then click the item you want to learn about. When the Help window appears, you can click topics you want additional information about. Press Alt+F4 to close the Help window. In fact, anytime a dialog box or alert box appears and you want more information, just press F1. If you are working in a macro, you can even move the insertion point inside a macro statement (code) and press F1 to see detailed help about that specific statement. When you need more extensive help or tips and tricks, you'll find it in the procedures and tips in this book.

Word for Windows Helps WordPerfect Users

Word for Windows not only does a good job of translating WordPerfect documents and graphics, but it can also help you learn Word for Windows. When you install Word for Windows, or at any later time, you can turn on the capability to use WordPerfect menus and navigation keys. While the WordPerfect help system is on, you can press a WordPerfect key such as Ctrl+F8 for fonts and the WordPerfect Help dialog box, shown in figure I.4, will appear with the appropriate WordPerfect menu. (Figure I.4 shows the highest level WordPerfect menu.) Use the same keystrokes you would use in WordPerfect. When you finish making menu choices, Word for Windows displays a note describing what to do, or actually makes the Word for Windows menu and dialog choices for you. As you watch it make the correct choices, you learn how to use Word for Windows.

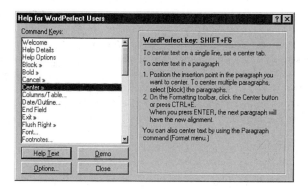

Fig. I.4
WordPerfect users can retrieve their WordPerfect documents and get help with commands.

If you are a professional typist who likes a clean, clear screen to work on, you can choose View, Full Screen to remove the menu bar, status bar, scroll bars, ruler, and toolbars so that the Word for Windows screen is clear. Pressing Esc or clicking the Full Screen button returns the screen to its original view.

Working with Word for Windows 95

Word for Windows 95 has features that fit many working environments. Even beginning and intermediate operators can customize Word for Windows to fit specific job needs. This section includes several examples of the many types of documents you can produce with Word for Windows.

Word Processing in Daily Business

Word for Windows makes repetitive work very easy. As a professional typist doing daily business work, you can use some of the following Word for Windows features:

- Automatically format standard types of documents with the AutoFormat command.

- Use template wizards to guide you through building brochures, newsletters, letters, and so on.

- Create forms that contain drop-down lists and check boxes to replace your office's printed forms.

- Use Print Preview or Page Layout views to see results before you print.

- Use the mail-merge capabilities that guide you through mailings and labels.

- Automatically generate envelopes.

- Use templates to hold repetitive documents, formatting styles, macros, text you want entered automatically, and shortcut keys.

- Choose the symbol for foreign languages or special characters (like trademarks) from a table.

- Insert tables that look like spreadsheets by clicking a toolbar button.

- Format numbered and bulleted lists by clicking a single toolbar button.

- Add toolbar buttons for the commands you use frequently.

- Include Portrait (vertical) and Landscape (horizontal) pages in the same document.

- Automatically spell check documents as you type and suggest correct spellings.

Word Processing for Legal and Medical Documents

Legal and medical documents present unique word processing requirements. Word for Windows is built to handle these specialized situations:

- AutoText to eliminate typing long words and repetitive phrases
- Outliners, which are among the best available
- Tables of authorities and automatic cross-referencing
- Annotations, hidden text, and revision marks
- Numbered lines with adjustable spacing
- Inserting graphics or pictures
- Drawing directly on the document with drawing tools

Word Processing for Scientific and Technical Documents

When you write scientific or technical papers, you need to include references, charts, tables, graphs, equations, table references, footnotes, and endnotes. Word for Windows 95 will help your technical documents with the following:

- An Equation Editor that builds equations when you click equation pieces and symbols
- Drawing and graphing tools built into Word for Windows 95
- The capability to insert many different types of graphics files as well as AutoCAD files
- Spreadsheet-like tables for data
- Mathematics in tables
- Embedding or linking with Excel, the leading Windows worksheet

Word Processing for Financial Documents

Your initial impression of a financial report comes when you turn the cover. Word for Windows gives you on-screen tables, similar to spreadsheets, and links to Microsoft Excel and Lotus 1-2-3 for Windows worksheets and charts. You will find the following productive features:

- Commands and structure very similar to Microsoft Excel

- The ability to operate Microsoft Excel or Lotus 1-2-3 and Word for Windows simultaneously and switch between them

- The ability to embed Microsoft Excel worksheets so that they can be updated within the Word document

- The ability to link Microsoft Excel or Lotus worksheets so that changes in the original worksheet appear in the Word document

- Row-and-column numeric tables that can include math

- The ability to use Microsoft Query to download and link to mainframe or server data

- Borders, shading, and underlining to enhance columnar reporting

- Tables and charts linked to other Windows applications

Word Processing for Graphic Artists and Advertising

Until now, testing page layouts and advertising design required two applications: a word processor and a desktop publishing program. Word for Windows combines both. Although Word for Windows doesn't have all the "free-form" capabilities of a publishing application like QuarkXPress or Aldus PageMaker, Word for Windows 95 still gives you many features, such as the following:

- Wide range of graphic file import filters

- Access to the Microsoft ClipArt Gallery

- Text wrap-around graphics

- Movable text or graphics

- Borders and shading

- Parallel or snaking columns that include graphics

- Print Preview or an editable Page Layout view that zooms 25 to 200 percent in VGA resolution

- Compatibility with PostScript typesetting equipment

- Linking of body copy and graphic files into a single, larger master document

- Drawing directly in the document

- Automatic captions and callouts that are tied to the graphic or position

Word Processing for Specific Industries

Word for Windows 95 is a fully customizable word processor. Therefore, industry associations, custom software houses, and application developers can tailor Word for Windows features to fit the needs of specific vertical industries or to integrate with their own custom applications. For example, they can create custom menus, toolbars, and shortcut keys that operate existing commands or run programs written in Word's extensive WordBasic programming language. To aid developers, Word for Windows includes the following:

- WordBasic, an extensive macro programming language with more than 400 commands

- A macro recorder and editing tools

- Customizable toolbars, menus, and shortcut keys

- AutoText for industry-specific terms

- Customized templates to package documents with customized features

- Personal and foreign-language dictionaries

- Control of Word features and documents from programs written in Excel, Access, or Visual Basic

- Integration and data exchange with other Windows applications

How This Book Is Organized

Word for Windows 95 is a program with immense capability and a wealth of features. It can be straightforward and easy to learn if approached correctly. This book is organized to help you learn Word for Windows 95 quickly and efficiently.

If you are familiar with Word for Windows 6, you should scan the table of contents for new features and look through the book for pages marked with the 95 icon that marks new features. Many of the Word 6 commands have been moved so that they are more accessible to the average user and so that Microsoft Excel and Word have a similar menu structure.

Special Edition Using Word for Windows 95 is organized into the following parts:

- Part I: Everyday Word Processing

- Part II: Formatting Documents

- Part III: Creating Envelopes and Mailings

- Part IV: Mastering Special Features

- Part V: Publishing with Graphics

- Part VI: Handling Large Documents

- Part VII: Using Word with Office and Networks

- Part VIII: Customizing with Word

- Part IX: Techniques from the Pros

Part I helps you learn the fundamentals of Word for Windows 95 that you will need for basic letters, and gives an overview of the new features in Word 95. Even if you are very familiar with Word 6, you will want to look at Chapter 1 to get an overview of Word's most powerful features and learn about the new features available in Word 95. Chapters 2 through 6 describe the basics you will need to know for opening, creating, editing, and saving documents. Chapter 7 describes proofing tools such as Word's spelling checker, thesaurus, and grammar checker. Chapter 8 closes Part I by showing you how to preview and print your document.

Part II shows you features that help you format the document. You begin by learning how to format characters in Chapter 9. Chapter 10 then describes how to format lines and paragraphs with such features as alignment, indentation, and borders. One of the most useful chapters in Part II is Chapter 11, "Using Styles for Repetitive Formats," which tells you how to take advantage of the many benefits of using styles for documents with repetitive elements such as headings, titles, and so on. Chapter 12 describes how to use multiple columns if you need to create newsletters, brochures, or scripts. Finally, Chapter 13 describes how to set overall page layout with such things as margins, page orientation, numbering, and type of paper.

In Part III, you learn how to automate mailing lists and bring data into Word from outside databases. In Chapter 14, you learn how to use Word's built-in database features or link Word to data files stored on disk, in a network server, or on the mainframe. Chapter 15 describes how to use that data to create form letters, envelopes, and labels. You will also learn how to use Word to send e-mail and faxes.

Part IV describes the many special features that make Word the industry's most powerful word processor. Chapters 16 and 17 will teach you about tables, spreadsheet-like grids that help you organize text, lists, numbers, and even graphics. In Chapter 18, you learn how to use bullets and numbering to organize thoughts into easily read lists. If you do a lot of writing and you want your thoughts to be well organized, read Chapter 19's discussion of Word's excellent outlining features. Other chapters such as 20 through 22 describe how to automate your documents with field codes and build forms that make data easy to enter.

If you want to use a word processor to do work similar to desktop publishing, Word is the one you should use. Part V describes how to use Word's built-in drawing tools and how to import graphics created in drawing programs. Chapter 23 shows you how easy it is to insert pictures from other programs or from one of the clip art collections. Chapter 24 shows you how to frame text or graphics so that you can make anything movable on-screen. You can drag items anywhere on the page and the text wraps around it. Word even comes with its own drawing tools as described in Chapter 25, so creating graphics in Word is very convenient. Chapters 26 and 27 describe the programs—WordArt and Graph—included with Word for Windows. These programs enable you to create fancy titles and banners, or build charts like those created by a program such as Excel.

If you write contracts, build large manuals, print a book with many chapters, or work with theses or formal term papers, you should turn to Part VI. You can make the contents of your documents easier to find if you use the indexing, table of contents, and cross-referencing features described in Chapters 29 and 31. Chapter 32 shows you how to build large documents—like books—from smaller chapter-sized documents. And since all good writing involves editing and revisions, Word's revision features, discussed in Chapter 30, will help you track revisions and edits and who made them.

Part VII shows you the advantage Word has when working with other applications in the Windows environment. Although this is a short section, Chapters 33 and 34 show you how to use Word with other applications and work with networks—two very essential tasks in the workplace. You can copy and paste, link, or embed data between Windows applications. You also learn how to work in a group of people that share documents. Chapter 34 also presents an overview of sending faxes and e-mail from within Word.

Even if you don't know how to program, Part VIII shows you how to customize Word to work the way you want and look the way you prefer. If you want to customize how Word works or looks, look to Chapter 35 for options that let you customize Word the way you prefer to work. Chapter 36 describes how to customize Word's features using the Tools, Options command. In addition, it shows you how easy it is to reorganize Word's menus, add new commands to toolbars, and add shortcut keys to cut down on your work. Chapter 37 describes how to automate Word and add new features through the use of the macro recorder. Word has a powerful built-in programming language that you can use even as a beginner.

Part IX includes chapters that describe how top-level consultants in office automation are using Word. Chapter 38 gives you tips on how to use Word to do many of the desktop publishing jobs faced by individuals and small businesses. The automating capability of fields, covered in Chapter 20, is further explored in Chapter 39. Many companies are creating their own online manuals and help files using Word. Chapter 40 describes how one company used Word and Doc-to-Help to create online policy and business manuals that not only helped its employees, but won a major national award.

Conventions Used in This Book

Conventions used in this book have been established to help you learn how to use the program quickly and easily. As much as possible, the conventions correspond with those used in the Word for Windows documentation.

Letters pressed to activate menus, choose commands in menus, and select options in dialog boxes are underlined: File, Open. Names of dialog boxes are written with initial capital letters, as the name appears on-screen. Messages that appear on-screen are printed in a special font: Document 1. New terms are introduced in *italic* type.

Two different types of key combinations are used with this program. For combinations joined with a comma (Alt, F), you press and release the first key and then press and release the second key. If a combination is joined with a plus sign (Alt+F), you press and hold the first key while you press the second key.

A special icon is used throughout this book to mark features new to Word for Windows 95.

The code continuation character ➡ is used to indicate that a breaking code line should be typed as one line. Here's an example:

```
        ToolsOptionsSave .CreateBackup = 0, .FastSaves = 1,
➡ .SummaryPrompt = 0, .GlobalDotPrompt = 0,
➡ .NativePictureFormat = 0, .EmbedFonts = 0, .FormsData = 0,
➡ .AutoSave = 0, .SaveInterval = "", .Password = "",
➡ .WritePassword = "",
➡ .RecommendReadOnly = 0
```

Even though the preceding example runs across six lines, the code continuation character tells you that the code fragment should be typed as one line. The code continuation character is your cue to continue typing a code fragment as one long line.

You find five other visual aids that help you on your Word for Windows 95 journey: **Notes**, **Tips**, **Cautions**, **Troubleshooting**, and **cross-references**.

Note

This paragraph format indicates additional information that may help you avoid problems or that should be considered in using the described features.

Caution

This paragraph format warns the reader of hazardous procedures (for example, activities that delete files).

Tip
This paragraph format suggests easier or alternative methods of executing a procedure.

Troubleshooting

This paragraph format provides guidance on how to find solutions to common problems. Specific problems you may encounter are shown in italic. Possible solutions appear in the paragraph(s) following the problem.

Special Edition Using Word for Windows 95 uses margin cross-references to help you access related information in other parts of the book. Right-facing triangles point you to related information in later chapters. Left-facing triangles point you to information in previous chapters.

Part I

Everyday Word Processing

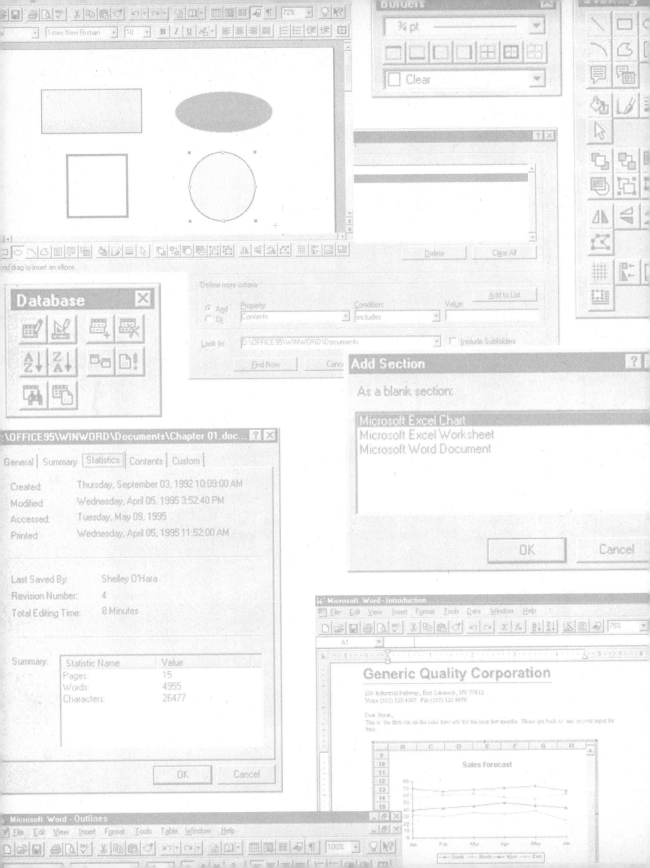

Chapter 1

Word Processing Power in Word for Windows 95

Word for Windows 95 combines ease of use with power. Microsoft has tested Word for Windows in its usability laboratory to find ways to make Word's features more accessible to you; it has many features that make what used to be arduous or impossible tasks much simpler.

This chapter catalogs some of the most important features in Word for Windows 95 that will add to your word processing power. Most of the changes and new features in Word 95 are also presented. If you are an experienced Word for Windows user, browse through this chapter to find what's new and what powerful features have been added.

Changes in Word for Windows are of two types: those that enhance existing features or make them easy to use, and new features that add to the power of Word.

Better Access to Features

Microsoft understands that powerful features aren't important unless you can use them. In Word for Windows 95, the features you use most often are very accessible and easy to use.

TipWizard

▶ See "Getting the Tip of the Day," p. 65

Applications such as Word for Windows are becoming easier to use with drop-down menus, tabbed dialog boxes, and toolbars, but when you become very proficient in certain tasks, you probably find yourself wishing for faster, more productive ways to work. Although you use the Search button in Help to learn about Word's many shortcuts, a more enjoyable way to discover them is by activating the TipWizard feature (see fig. 1.1). As you work in Word, the TipWizard will assist you and provide tips about more efficient ways to complete the tasks you are carrying out or point out new and related features. You can click the Show Me button to get more detailed information about the tip. The TipWizard will also display a different shortcut each time you start Word. When you've learned everything there is to know about Word, you can turn off the TipWizard.

Fig. 1.1
You can learn helpful tips about Word with the TipWizard.

Shortcut Menus

▶ See "Saving Time with Shortcut Menus," p. 51

With drop-down menus that lead into tabbed dialog boxes, you can quickly get at hundreds of options. You use some of these options and features more frequently than others, however. For this reason, Microsoft provides *shortcut menus* (see fig. 1.2). Shortcut menus appear when you click the right mouse button on text, an object, or a screen element, such as a toolbar. The shortcut menu appears (right under the pointer) depending upon which item you clicked. Although it takes a little while to remember that it is not always necessary to return to the main menu, using shortcut menus soon becomes automatic for you.

Fig. 1.2
Shortcut menus appear when you click the right mouse button on text, objects, or screen elements such as toolbars.

Tabbed Dialog Boxes

Word has so many different features and options that there is no way they can all be available from the menu. Instead, Microsoft keeps the menus short and makes hundreds of options available in dialog boxes. Because there are so many available options, they are grouped together into tabbed "cards" within the dialog box (see fig. 1.3). You can switch between different groups of options by clicking the tab or pressing Alt and the appropriate letter to choose a different tab.

▶ See "Working in Dialog Boxes," p. 57

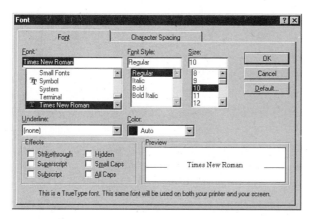

Fig. 1.3
With Word's tabbed dialog boxes, you have quick access to many options.

Wizards to Guide You

Wizards guide you through the process of creating special or complex documents (see fig. 1.4). To open a wizard, choose File, New, select the tab for the type of document you want to create, and select a wizard. Word comes with wizards that help you create documents such as a fax cover sheet, brochures, calendars, legal pleadings, business or personal letters, résumés, and complex tables with fancy formatting.

▶ See "Using Templates and Wizards for Frequently Created Documents," p. 173

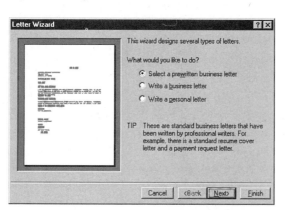

Fig. 1.4
Wizards guide you through producing complex documents.

Everyday Word Processing

▶ See "Control-
ling Your
Document's
Appearance
On-Screen,"
p. 123

Full Screen View

Some typists are distracted by menus, toolbars, and scroll bars. If you are such a typist, work in Word's Full Screen view. To display the full screen, just choose <u>V</u>iew, F<u>u</u>ll Screen (see fig. 1.5). Return to the previous view by pressing Esc or by clicking the Full Screen button.

Fig. 1.5
The Full Screen
view makes your
document look
like you are typing
on a white page
that fills the entire
screen.

Company Name
Address
City, State Zip
Telephone * Fax

FOR IMMEDIATE RELEASE

June 7, 1995

Contact: Chris Fields
(206) 555-5555

West Coast Sales Introduces the Tater Dicer Mark II

West Coast Sales recently announced the introduction of the Tater Dicer Mark II—a new way to dice potatoes and ensure both freshness and uniform potato cubes.

The Tater Dicer Mark II was developed by West Coast Sales in response to customer demand for a reliable way to produce potato cubes.

The Tater Dicer Mark II incorporates the latest dicing technology and is constructed entirely of stainless steel. The Tater Dicer features precision tooled parts for consistent cube size.

The Tater Dicer Mark II has a suggested list price of $149.99; it can be purchased directly from West Coast Sales or through commercial kitchen suppliers.

West Coast Sales has been producing quality tools and accessories for commercial kitchens for over 30 years. Founded in 1961, West Coast Sales has consistently provided improvements and innovations in kitchen tools. Other products include the Laser Date DePitter and the Pyrotechnic Apple Masher.

—30—

Automatic Corrections

With Word's AutoCorrect feature, you can type a word or abbreviation, and Word will automatically replace it with the text or graphic you specified in the AutoCorrect dialog box (see fig. 1.6). This can make legal and medical typing more productive—type an abbreviation, and it automatically converts to the correct word or phrase. You also can set AutoCorrect to automatically correct mistakes you frequently make such as changing *hte* to *the*, or capitalizing the first letter in a sentence.

AutoCorrect in Word 95 has several enhancements. It now has a much bigger list of built-in corrections and abbreviations and will correct capitalization if you accidentally press the Caps Lock key. You can also create a list of exceptions. Then AutoCorrect will not make changes to words in the exception list. If you reverse a correction AutoCorrect makes, it will remember this and not make the correction again.

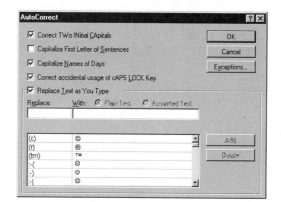

Fig. 1.6
You can "teach" AutoCorrect what mistakes and abbreviations you want it to recognize so that it will automatically replace the mistake or abbreviation with the text you specify.

Copy and Paste Formatting

When you need to reapply multiple formats, reach for the tool that looks like a paintbrush. The Format Painter button on the Standard toolbar enables you to select text that has formatting applied. Then click and drag the text you want reformatted. When you release the mouse button, the copied format is applied.

▶ See "Copying Formatting," p. 267

AutoFormat

The AutoFormat feature enables you to type a document and then apply a standardized set of formats to the document with a single command. Using a set of rules about what defines a heading, title, body copy, figures, tables, and so on, Word examines your document and applies styles to each element. You then can manually redefine each style or use the Style Gallery to change the overall appearance of the document.

▶ See "Formatting a Document Automatically," p. 339

AutoFormatting in Word 95 has several new features. You can now apply autoformats as you type. For example, if you type an asterisk followed by text, Word will automatically make the text a bulleted item and add bullets to additional items in the list as you type them. Type a number before the first item in the list, and AutoFormat will create a numbered list. AutoFormat can also automatically create headings and borders, and replace ordinals (1st) with superscript (1st) and fractions (1/2) with fraction characters ($\frac{1}{2}$).

Style Gallery

If you want to create a standardized appearance in your documents with more ease, use the Style Gallery (see fig. 1.7). The Style Gallery is a collection of formatting styles that are applied as a group to an entire document. You can actually see a sample of what the active document will look like as you select each different style in the gallery.

▶ See "Using the Style Gallery," p. 347

Fig. 1.7
The Style Gallery enables you to change the appearance of your entire document by changing entire collections of formatting styles.

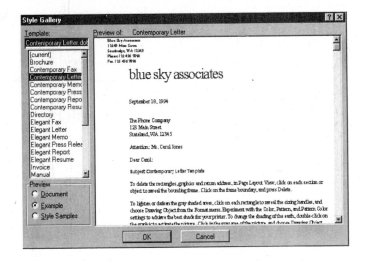

Easier Column Formatting

▶ See "Creating Columns," p. 380

Newspaper or snaking columns make text more readable. They give the eye a shorter distance to travel to see part of a sentence. By choosing Format, Columns, creating columns is very easy (see fig. 1.8). In Word 95, you can even create unevenly spaced columns.

Fig. 1.8
The Columns feature makes columns very easy to apply. You can even create unevenly spaced columns.

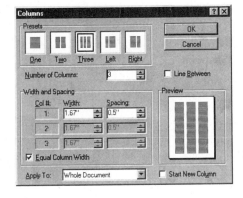

Customizable and Movable Toolbars for Quick Access to Commands

▶ See "Using the Toolbars," p. 53

Toolbars give you quick access to commands. Word has several toolbars which you can move and reshape on-screen (see fig. 1.9). By either choosing

View, Toolbars or right-mouse clicking a toolbar, you can display or hide a toolbar. Dragging in a toolbar's gray area moves it while dragging an edge reshapes it.

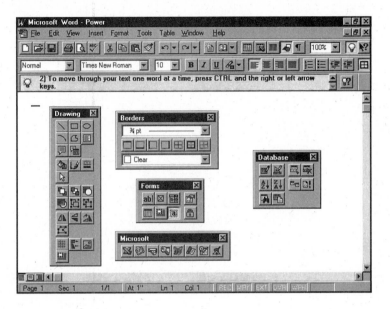

Fig. 1.9
Word's large number of movable toolbars gives you quick access to your most frequently used commands when using a mouse.

More Power

Word is one of the most powerful word processors. With it, you have varied capabilities, such as the ability to link to mainframe databases and acquire all the desktop publishing features of a publishing program.

Working with Other Windows Applications

Word has great flexibility and power when working with other Windows applications. In addition to its ability to copy and paste or link to data in other Windows applications, Word includes OLE automation. This means that you can edit or modify embedded objects from applications, such as Microsoft Excel 95, from within your Word document. Notice that in figure 1.10, the Word menu and toolbar reflect the Excel chart object that is selected in the document.

Fig. 1.10
Word works well with other Windows applications. You can edit data from OLE 2 applications such as Excel 95 while staying in your Word document.

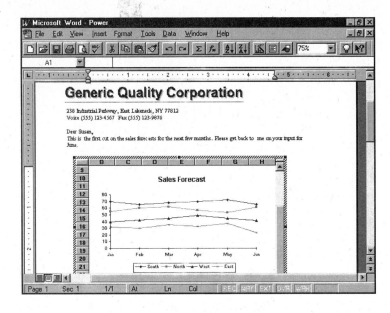

Inserting or Linking to External Databases

▶ See "Embedding Data," p. 986

Whether you work for a major corporation or a small business, you probably have information in a database that you use with Word for Windows. For example, you may need that information to print mailing labels, send form letters to customers, or create a new price sheet or catalog. Word has the ability to get information from most databases found in PC, SQL Server, or mainframes (see fig. 1.11). Word also works with Microsoft Query, the application that lets you search and retrieve information from within relational databases.

Fig. 1.11
You can insert or link to selected data on PC, SQL Server, or mainframe databases.

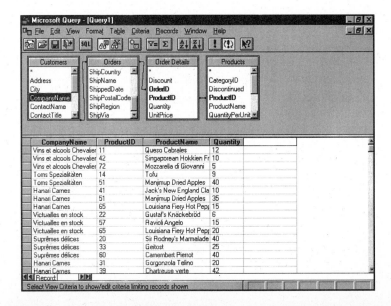

Manage Data with the Data Form

Mailing lists and product information are easy to maintain with Word's Data Form (see fig. 1.12). You can use the Data Form to find records and edit them in Word.

▶ See "Creating Your Mail Merge Data," p. 450

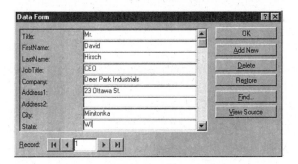

Fig. 1.12
Use Word's built-in Data Form to find, edit, or delete information in one of Word's data sources.

Customizable Toolbars

If you frequently use a command or feature and need quick access to it, you can assign it to a custom tool on your created toolbar or an existing toolbar (see fig. 1.13). You can even draw your own button faces and assign macros to buttons.

▶ See "Customizing and Creating Toolbars," p. 1034

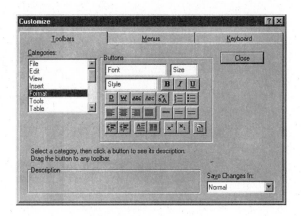

Fig. 1.13
You can customize existing toolbars or create your own toolbars.

Everyday Word Processing

Better File Management

▶ See "Searching for Files," p. 115

It doesn't take very long before you have hundreds of documents on your disk and finding a specific document becomes tedious and frustrating. Word's new Open dialog box (see fig. 1.14) includes commands that let you find files by using different characteristics and managing your documents much more easily than in Word 6. You can find and then open, print, move, copy, delete, and preview files, all within the Open dialog box.

Fig. 1.14
Finding and managing files from within Word is much easier with the new Open dialog box.

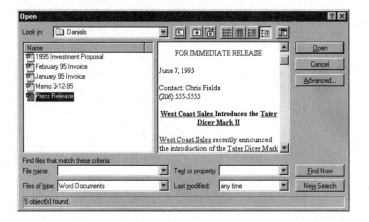

Forms That Include Pull-Down Lists, Edit Boxes, or Check Boxes

▶ See "Building Forms," p. 643

Word processors seem to lend themselves to doing forms, yet they can't manage to fill in the blanks on forms. Consequently, many businesses continue to inventory hundreds of pounds of preprinted forms. Word helps reduce the cost of storing and printing forms with its forms feature, shown in figure 1.15. In a normal word-processing document, you can now insert edit boxes, check boxes, and drop-down lists. You don't have to have to know how to program—all you have to do is make selections in a dialog box.

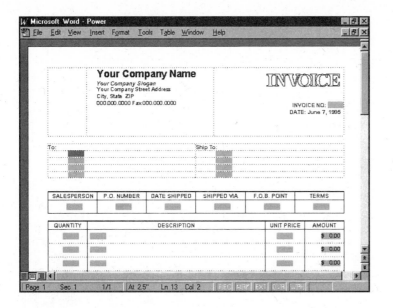

Fig. 1.15
Word's forms feature enables you to easily put edit boxes, check boxes, and drop-down lists within a normal document.

Improved Mail Merge

Mail merge is often looked at as a difficult task in word processing, yet it's something that many small- and medium-sized businesses do frequently. Word uses the Mail Merge Helper (see fig. 1.16), a series of dialog boxes that guide you through merging data into form letters, envelopes, and labels. You can even choose the layout for the types of envelopes and labels.

▶ See "Merging Mailing Lists and Docu-ments," p. 470

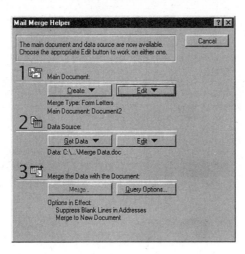

Fig. 1.16
The Mail Merge Helper guides you through the whole process of merging data with mail-merge documents.

Improved Envelope and Label Printing

With Word's envelope feature, creating an envelope is as easy as typing in a document (see fig. 1.17). Select standard-sized envelopes and labels or create custom settings (see fig. 1.18).

Fig. 1.17

The <u>L</u>abels tab contains lists of layout definitions for most standard business labels.

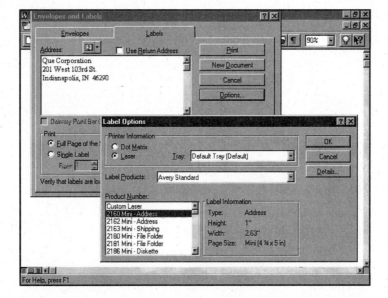

Fig. 1.18

The envelope options enable you to position addresses on different-sized envelopes as well as automatically print postal delivery bar codes.

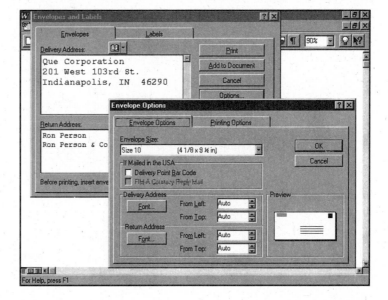

Improved Indexing and Tables of Contents or Authorities

If you work with major reports, proposals, or legal documents, you will find Word's indexing, table of contents, and table of authorities features very powerful (see fig. 1.19). You have more formatting options, and these features are easier to use. For more information on these features, turn to Chapter 29, "Creating Indexes and Tables of Contents."

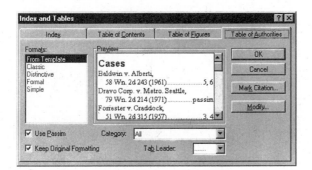

Fig. 1.19
The formatting and features in Word's indexing and table generation capabilities are improved.

Cross-References

One of the time-consuming jobs in proposals and authoritative documents is cross-referencing tables, figures, and comments. With a little guidance, Word takes care of the job for you. You don't even have to move back and forth in a document to see what you want to cross-reference. Word keeps track of different types of content and topics and presents them to you so you can select the topic you want to cross-reference.

▶ See "Creating Cross-References," p. 920

Drawing Directly on the Document

Word's Drawing toolbar is loaded with drawing buttons that allow you to create graphics directly in Word (see fig. 1.20). Also, there are now three graphics layers into which you can put your drawing or imported graphic. You can put drawings under the text to get a watermark-like effect, within the text so the text wraps around the graphic, or over the text as an overlay.

▶ See "Displaying and Understanding the Drawing Toolbar," p. 756

Everyday Word Processing

Fig. 1.20
With Word's drawing tools, you can draw directly in a document. You even have a choice of putting your graphics behind, with, or in front of text.

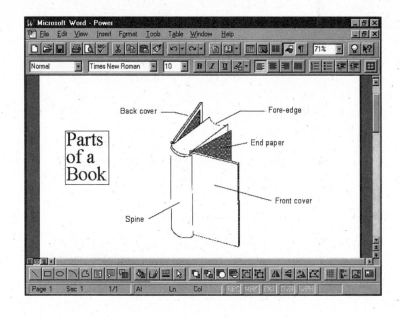

Drop Caps

▶ See "Starting Paragraphs with a Drop Cap," p. 278

Drop caps are large letters that designers use to make you aware of a new chapter or section (see fig. 1.21). They look fancy and attractive, and can enhance the look of your documents. In Word, choosing Format, Drop Cap enables you to easily format a character as a drop cap and to precisely control its position in the text.

Fig. 1.21
Publishers use drop caps to make new chapters and sections obvious. They are now a choice on the Format menu.

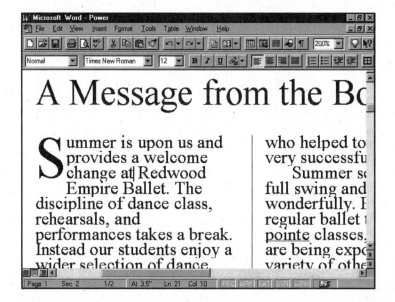

Callouts Attached to Objects

Anyone doing technical documentation or training materials on a word processor wishes to use callouts. *Callouts* are text boxes that explain elements of a picture or drawing, as you see in figure 1.22. Those documentation and training writers can put away their desktop publishing programs and stay in Word. Callouts in Word are easy to insert and can be formatted and attached to locations on-screen so they stay with the object they describe.

▶ See "Adding and Changing Callouts," p. 792

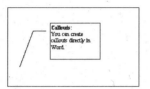

Fig. 1.22
With the callout feature, trainers and technical writers can create their documentation directly within Word.

Organizer for Managing Macros, Styles, AutoText, and Shortcut Keys

The Organizer in the Templates and Add-ins dialog box makes a simple task of moving macros, styles, AutoText entries, or shortcut keys between documents (see fig. 1.23). If you have a feature in one document that you want in another document, call in the Organizer.

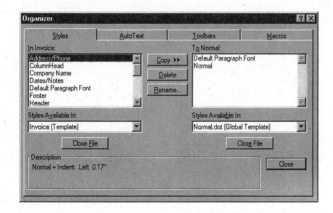

Fig. 1.23
If you like a feature in one document, use the Organizer to move it to any document you want.

▶ See "Transferring Template Contents Using the Organizer," p. 182

Everyday Word Processing

Improved Compatibility

Word has many filters and converters to import word processing documents, worksheets, database records, and graphic files. Word also has compatibility options that take into account the different ways non-Word programs handle special features. Because you are probably not familiar with the nuances between programs, Word recommends settings when you import a file from another application.

New Features in Word 95

In addition to the many outstanding features presented in the previous sections, Word has introduced some powerful and useful new features.

Spell It

Spell It is the ultimate spell checker. It checks your spelling as you type. When you select this option, a wavy red line will appear under any word you type that isn't in the dictionary (see fig. 1.24). When you click the word with the right mouse button, you are presented with a list of alternative spellings from which you can select the correct spelling.

Fig. 1.24

Spell It automatically checks your spelling as you type and presents you with a list of alternative spellings when it detects a mistake.

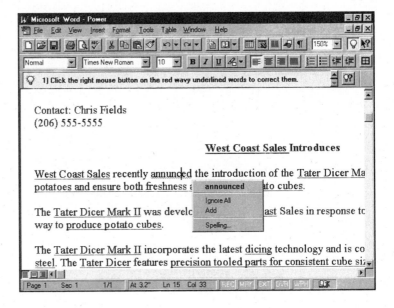

Highlighter

Just as you use a highlighting pen to emphasize text in your paper documents, use Word's new Highlight tool to highlight text with color on-screen (see fig. 1.25). This is a great way to mark important text for yourself and others using the document online.

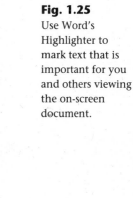

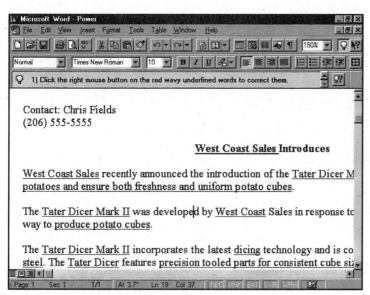

Fig. 1.25
Use Word's Highlighter to mark text that is important for you and others viewing the on-screen document.

Find and Replace All Word Forms

A new option in the Replace dialog box allows you to enter one form of a word and have Word find and replace all forms of that word. For example, if you ask Word to replace *make* with *create,* it will also replace *makes* with *creates* and *made* with *created.*

New Templates and Wizards

There are many new templates in Word, and many of them come in three styles: contemporary, professional, and elegant. Word's templates and Wizards are organized by categories in the File New dialog box (see fig. 1.26).

Fig. 1.26
Word 95 comes
with many new
templates and
organizes the
templates and
wizards by
categories.

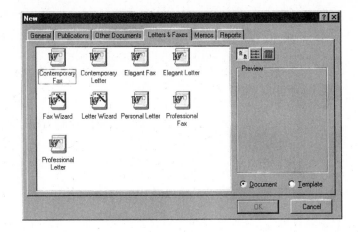

Answer Wizard

A new way to get help in Word is to use the Answer Wizard. Using your own words, you can type questions that ask the Answer Wizard for help on certain tasks. The Answer Wizard then displays a list of topics related to your question so you can quickly find the answer (see fig. 1.27).

Fig. 1.27
The Answer
Wizard lets you
ask questions in
your own
language and then
gives you the
answers.

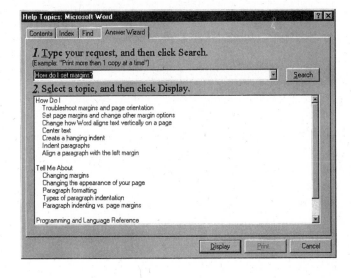

WordMail

This powerful new feature integrates Word 95 with Exchange E-mail, so that you can create and send e-mail messages and faxes from within Word. You can also access the Exchange address book from Word as you compose your messages.

Address Book

The Address Book enables you to keep lists of people to whom you frequently send e-mail, faxes or printed documents. You can use the address information stored in the address book to store different e-mail addresses, mailing addresses, phone numbers, and so forth. The information can then be merged into letters or e-mail and fax documents. ❖

Chapter 2

Getting Started in Word for Windows

The basics of using Word for Windows 95 are the same for using any other Windows program. If you are familiar with another Windows application, such as Microsoft Excel, you may not need to read this "basics" chapter (or perhaps a quick scan is all you need). If you are a new Windows user, however, you will find this chapter important for two reasons: you will become comfortable navigating Word for Windows, and you will have a head start on the next Windows program you learn.

In this chapter, you learn how to control not only Word for Windows menus and dialog boxes but also the windows that contain Word for Windows and its documents. By the time you finish this chapter, you will be able to use the mouse and the keyboard to choose commands from menus, select options from dialog boxes, access the extensive help system, and manipulate windows on-screen. Beyond these basic tasks, you should be able to organize Windows so that you can access and use multiple documents at once or "clear away your desktop" so that you can concentrate on a single job.

In this chapter you learn how to:

- Start and exit Word for Windows
- Choose commands and select from dialog boxes
- Operate Word for Windows from the keyboard or mouse
- Manipulate windows

Starting and Quitting Word for Windows

To activate Word for Windows, follow these steps:

1. Click the Start button in the taskbar at the bottom of the screen.

2. Move the mouse pointer over the Programs command. The Programs menu appears.

3. Click the Microsoft Word item.

Figure 2.1 shows the Programs menu with the Microsoft Word item selected.

Fig. 2.1
Start Word by selecting the Microsoft Word icon in the Programs menu.

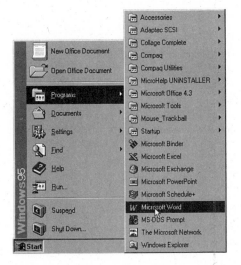

You can also start Word for Windows 95 by choosing a document file from the Windows Explorer. To start Word for Windows and load the document, double-click the file name for a Word for Windows document (DOC), or select the file name and press Enter. You can also start a document you have used recently by clicking the Start menu, moving the pointer over the Documents command, and then clicking the document you want loaded into Word. If Word is not running, it will start and load the document. If Word is running, it will load the document and activate Word so that it is on top of other windows.

Close—or "quit"—Word for Windows when you are finished working for the day or when you need to free memory for other applications. To quit Word for Windows, follow these steps:

1. If you are using a mouse, choose File, Exit or click the Close button in the top-right corner. (The Close button looks like an X.) If you are using the keyboard, press the shortcut key combination Alt+F4 or choose File, Exit by pressing Alt, F, X.

2. If you made changes to any document, Word displays an Alert box asking whether you want to save your current work. Click the Yes button or press Enter to save your work, or click the No button to quit without saving.

To learn how to use the mouse and keyboard for carrying out commands and other procedures, see "Understanding Windows and Word for Windows Terms" later in the chapter.

Understanding the Word for Windows Screen

One advantage of Windows applications is the capability to run several applications and display them on-screen simultaneously. Chapter 34, "Using Word with Office Applications," describes how to run Word for Windows and other Windows or DOS applications together and transfer information among them. This capability can save you time when you transfer data into or out of Word for Windows, create automatically updated links from Word for Windows and other Windows applications, or embed Word for Windows data into other Window application documents.

Each Windows application, like Word for Windows, runs in its own application window. Because some application windows can contain multiple document windows, you can work simultaneously with more than one document. Figure 2.2 shows the Word for Windows application window with two document windows inside.

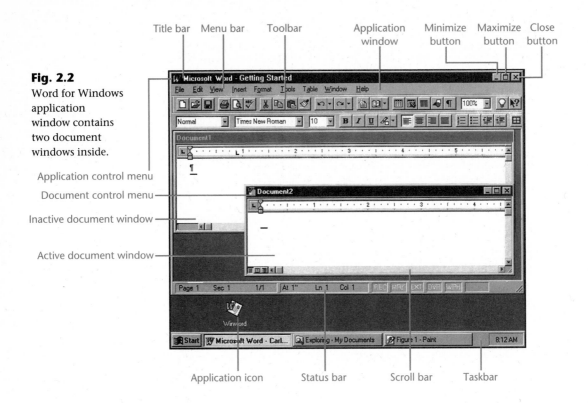

Fig. 2.2
Word for Windows application window contains two document windows inside.

Title bar   Menu bar   Toolbar   Application window   Minimize button   Maximize button   Close button

Application control menu
Document control menu
Inactive document window
Active document window

Application icon   Status bar   Scroll bar   Taskbar

Table 2.1 lists and describes the parts of a Word for Windows screen shown in figure 2.2.

Table 2.1 Parts of Word for Windows and Windows Screens	
Part	**Description**
Application window	The window within which Word for Windows runs
Application icon	The taskbar button of a running application
Document window	The window within which documents are displayed
Application Control menu	The menu that enables you to manipulate the application window
Document Control menu	The menu that enables you to manipulate the active (top) document window
Active document window	The window that accepts entries and commands; this window is shown with a solid title bar and is normally the top window

Part	Description
Mouse pointer	The on-screen arrow, I-beam, or drawing button indicates the current location affected by your mouse actions
Inactive document window	The background window which does not accept commands other than to be activated; this window is shown with a light-colored or patterned title bar
Insertion point	The point where text appears when you type
End of document marker	The point beyond which no text is entered
Title bar	The bar at the top of an application or document window
Menu bar	A list of menu names displayed below the title bar of an application
Toolbar	A bar containing buttons that, when chosen with the mouse pointer, produce a function or action
Minimize button	An underscore at the right of a title bar that stores an application as an application button in the taskbar at the bottom of the screen; equivalent to the application Control Minimize command
Maximize button	A box at the right of a title bar that fills available space with the document or application; equivalent to the Control Maximize command
Close button	A box at the right of a title bar that closes the window or dialog box
Restore button	A double box at the right of a title bar that restores an application or document into a sizable window; equivalent to the Control Restore command
Scroll bar	A gray horizontal and vertical bar that enables the mouse to scroll the screen; a scroll box in the bar shows the current display's position relative to the entire document
Status bar	A bar at the bottom of the screen that shows what Word for Windows is prepared to do next; watch the status bar for prompts, explanations of the current command, buttons under the mouse pointer, or guidance
Indicators	These display modes of operation on the status bar, such as REC when a macro is recording, OVR for Overtype mode, or EXT when the Extend mode is on

Everyday Word Processing

Figure 2.3 shows the elements within Word in more detail. The document window, Document 2, has a solid title bar, indicating that it is the active document window. You can have multiple document windows open at the same time. Most entries and commands affect only the active document window. Inactive windows are normally behind the active window and have a lighter colored or cross-hatched title bar.

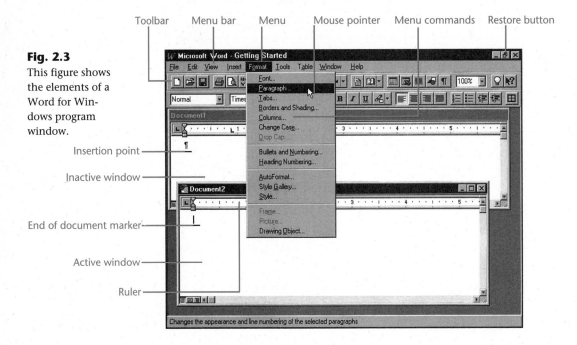

Fig. 2.3

This figure shows the elements of a Word for Windows program window.

The components in a Word screen are described in table 2.2.

Table 2.2 Parts of the Word Screen	
Part	**Description**
Active window	The document window that accepts entries and commands. This window has a solid title bar and is normally the top window
Inactive window	Window that contains documents that are loaded, but are not affected by commands. These windows have a light-colored title bar and are normally behind the active window
Menu bar	A list of menu names displayed below the title bar of an application

Part	Description
Menu	A drop-down list of commands
Command	A function or action chosen from a drop-down menu
Toolbar	A bar containing buttons that gives quick access to commands and features, such as the spell checker, bold, italic, edit cut and edit paste, styles, and fonts. A toolbar can be moved to different locations and reshaped to a different orientation
Ruler	A bar containing a scale that indicates tabs, paragraph indents, and margins in the paragraph where the insertion point (cursor) is located. The ruler can be used with the mouse to format paragraphs quickly
Mouse pointer	The on-screen pointer that shows the mouse location
Insertion point	The point where text appears when you type
End of document marker	The point beyond which no text is entered
Split box	Dark bars at the top of the vertical scroll bar that you can drag down to split a window into two views of the same document

Using the Mouse

The mouse is an optional piece of hardware that attaches to your personal computer and enables you to move the on-screen pointer as you move the mouse with your hand. In Word, you can control the program with mouse movements or with keystrokes, but most users will find that Word is easier to learn and to use with the mouse. Some Word actions—such as drawing graphical objects—require the use of a mouse; other actions—such as moving text—are significantly easier when you use a mouse. All menu commands and many other features are all accessible through the use of the keyboard. You will find that combining mouse actions with shortcut keys is the most productive way to work.

You can run the Mouse program and switch the left and right mouse button controls. This is useful if you are left-handed. To find the Mouse program, start the Control Panel from the Main group window of the Program Manager. See your Windows documentation or *Special Edition Using Windows 95* from Que for more information about using the Control Panel functions.

The mouse pointer changes appearance depending on its location. You usually see the mouse pointer as an arrow when it's in the menus or as a vertical I-beam shape when it's placed over a text area of your document. When you use the mouse pointer for drawing graphical objects or for embedding objects on a document, its shape changes to a *crosshair* (a thin cross). Each shape signals to you what action you can perform at that location.

Table 2.3 shows and explains the different shapes of the pointer.

Table 2.3 Mouse Pointer Shapes		
Pointer Appearance	**Screen Location**	**Function**
	Menu Scroll bars Objects or selected text	Select commands Scroll through document Move, size, or select objects
	Left edge of text	Select lines or paragraphs
	Selected text with mouse button depressed	Mouse moves selected text
	Text	Type, select, or edit text
	Window corner	Resize two sides of window
	Window edge Corner or side handle of selected frame or object	Resize single side of window Resize selected picture, frame, or object picture
	Window center object edge	Move window or object
	Top of table	Select column
	Left or right edge of any cell in a table	Widen or narrow column
	Split box	Split window into two panes
	Anywhere	Get help specific to next item selected
	Help window	Select help items
	Anywhere	Wait while processing

Understanding Windows and Word for Windows Terms

All Windows applications, including Word for Windows, require the same keyboard and mouse actions to select what is changed on-screen or to give commands. By learning the actions named in table 2.4, you will know how to operate menus and select items within any Windows application.

Table 2.4 Windows and Word Actions	
Action	**Description**
Select	Highlight or mark a section of text, menu name, command, dialog box option, or graphical object with the keyboard or with mouse actions.
Choose	Execute and complete a command. You may execute some commands when you select the menu command. Other commands execute when you choose OK from a dialog box.
Activate	Bring an application or document window to the foreground. When you are working with more than one application or more than one document within Word, the active window is the window you are working in.

Pointing Device Actions

Mouse and trackball techniques are simple to learn and to remember. These techniques make using Word for Windows much easier. In fact, for such work as moving and copying text, scrolling through a document, and drawing and embedding objects, a mouse or trackball is nearly indispensable. Table 2.5 describes the pointing device actions that you use in carrying out Word operations.

▶ See "Selecting Text with the Mouse," p. 141

Table 2.5 Mouse Actions	
Action	**Description**
Click	Place the tip of the mouse pointer or lower portion of the I-beam pointer at the desired location and then quickly press and release the left mouse or trackball button *once*. This action chooses a menu or command, moves the insertion point, or selects a graphical object so that you can work with it; this action also places the insertion point in text boxes.

(continues)

Table 2.5 Continued

Action	Description
Right-click	Position the tip of the mouse pointer in the desired location on a document or toolbar and then click the right mouse or trackball button. This action displays a menu appropriate to the item on which you clicked.
Double-click	Position the tip of the mouse pointer or the lower portion of the I-beam pointer at the desired location and then quickly press the left mouse or trackball button *twice*. This action is often a shortcut for carrying out a command or opening a dialog box from the Word screen. In Word, you can select a word by double-clicking anywhere in the word.
Drag	Position the tip of the mouse pointer, center of the crosshair, or the lower portion of the I-beam on an item; then hold down the left mouse or trackball button as you move the mouse pointer. This action selects multiple items, cells (in a worksheet), or text characters, or moves graphical objects.

▶ See "Selecting Text with the Mouse," p. 141

Some mouse actions have a different effect when you hold down the Shift or Ctrl key as you click, double-click, or drag with the mouse or trackball. As a general rule, holding down the Shift key as you click selects text between where your insertion point was, and the location where you Shift+click. Holding down the Ctrl button and clicking or double-clicking also has different effects, depending on what is selected when you carry out this action. You will learn about using the mouse in combination with the keyboard in the appropriate sections throughout the book.

Keyboard Actions

The keyboard is most useful for entering text and numbers, performing fast operations with shortcut keys, and operating with portable or laptop computers that don't have a mouse or trackball. Don't forget, however, that the best way of operating Word for Windows and other Windows applications is through the combined use of mouse and keyboard. Table 2.6 lists and describes the keyboard actions that you will use in Word for Windows.

Table 2.6   Keyboard Actions

Action	Description
Type	Type, but do not press the Enter key.
Enter	Press the Enter key.
Alt	Press the Alt key.
Alt, letter	Press the Alt key, release it, and then press the underlined letter or number shown. The active letters that appear underlined on-screen are underlined in this book.
Letter	Press only the underlined letter shown in the menu, command, or option.
Alt+letter	Hold down the Alt key as you press the underlined letter.
Alt, hyphen	Press the Alt key, release it, and then press the hyphen key.
Alt, space bar	Press the Alt key, release it, and then press the space bar.
Tab	Press the Tab key.
Esc	Press the Esc key.

Throughout this book, you see combinations of keys indicated with a plus sign (+), such as Alt+F. This combination means that you must hold down the Alt key while you press F. After pressing F, release both keys. (This book shows capital letters, as with the F, but you don't need to hold down the Shift key unless indicated.)

Keystrokes that appear separated by commas should be pressed in sequence. Alt, space bar, for example, is accomplished by pressing and releasing Alt and then pressing the space bar.

If you have a mouse, try using both mouse actions and keystrokes to perform commands and tasks. You soon will find that the keyboard works well for some commands and features and that the mouse works well for others. A combination of mouse and keyboard usually is the most efficient. The Quick Reference card bound inside the back cover of this book shows both keyboard and mouse shortcut methods.

Everyday Word Processing

▶ See "Formatting Paragraphs with Shortcut Keys," p. 293

The keyboard also is useful for many shortcut keys. These shortcut keys are listed in the appropriate areas throughout this book.

The 12 function keys give you a shortcut method for choosing commands that you normally choose from a menu. Some function keys use other keys in combination. When two or more keys are listed with a plus sign, hold down the first key(s) as you press the second key.

Notice that key combinations are listed on the right side of some drop-down menus. These key combinations execute the command immediately, without going through the menu and menu item. Instead of choosing Edit, Clear, for example, you can press the Delete key.

> **Note**
>
> If you are working in Word for Windows and forget a function key or shortcut key combination, choose Help, Microsoft Word Help Topics, and then select the Contents tab. In the Contents tab select Reference Information, then Keyboard Guide. Click the type of keyboard shortcuts you are interested in. Remember that you can print a Help Topic window of keyboard shortcuts for later reference by clicking the Options button and then clicking Print Topic.

Choosing Commands

Word for Windows uses the same menu-selection methods used by all Windows applications. You can control commands with the mouse, keystrokes, directional keys, or shortcut keys. You often can mix your methods of menu selection by starting with one method and finishing with another.

> **Caution**
>
> You cannot use a shortcut key while a menu is pulled down or a dialog box is displayed.

Notice that some commands in a menu may be gray. These commands are unavailable at that current point in Word operation.

Commands in the menu that are followed by an ellipsis (...) need more information from you before they execute. These commands display dialog boxes that ask you for more information.

In Word for Windows, you can back out of any drop-down menu or dialog box by pressing Esc. If you are using a mouse, you can back out of a menu by clicking the menu name a second time or by clicking the Cancel button in a dialog box.

Reading and Editing Document Summary Information

The Properties command makes it easy to view general, summary, statistical, or version information that relates to a Word document, an application, or a file item in the Windows Explorer. You can also add detailed information to Word documents. For example, you can add a more descriptive title; add subject, author, manager, and company name information; and even customize the information you want to view.

Figures 2.4 through 2.6 show the various types of Property pages accessed using the Properties command.

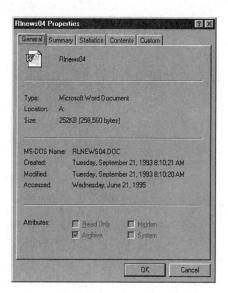

Fig. 2.4

Choose File, Properties to display the Properties sheet of an open Word document.

Fig. 2.5
Clicking an
application icon
with the right
mouse button and
choosing Proper-
ties displays the
Properties sheet
of the selected
application.

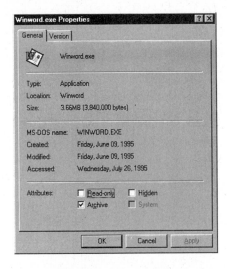

Fig. 2.6
Clicking a folder
item in the
Windows Explorer
with the right
mouse button
then choosing
Properties displays
the Properties
sheet of the
selected item.

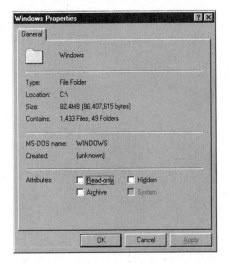

Some property dialog boxes have several options that can be selected for a customized configuration. Figure 2.7 shows the Taskbar Properties sheet with its selectable options.

Everyday Word Processing

Fig. 2.7
Clicking the right mouse button between the taskbar buttons and choosing Properties displays the Taskbar Properties sheet.

Saving Time with Shortcut Menus

You can save yourself time by using shortcut menus. *Shortcut menus* display the most frequently used commands that relate to the selected item or object.

To display a shortcut menu, click with the right mouse button on the item or object for which you need a shortcut menu. If you are using a keyboard, select the item and then press Shift+F10. For example, to open a shortcut menu that applies to text, select the text you want to work with, and click with the right mouse button on the text.

Shortcut menus appear under the mouse pointer or at the top left of the document window, if activated by the keyboard. Select a command by clicking it or by pressing ↑ or ↓ key and then pressing Enter. To remove a shortcut menu, click outside the menu or press the Esc key.

Figures 2.8 through 2.10 show a few shortcut menus, and the captions indicate the items with which the menus appear.

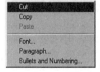

Fig. 2.8
A right mouse click on selected text displays a shortcut menu for text.

Fig. 2.9

A right mouse click on a selected object displays a shortcut menu to quickly manipulate the object.

Fig. 2.10

A right mouse click on a toolbar displays a shortcut menu for other toolbars.

Choosing Commands with the Keyboard

When you are familiar with the Word for Windows menus, you can perform the following steps to type commands:

1. Press Alt to select the menu bar.

2. Press the underlined letter in the menu name; for example, press **F** for File. The menu drops down.

3. Press the underlined letter in the command name; for example, press **O** for Open.

Tip

You do not need to wait for the menu to appear when you type commands.

Hold down the Shift key as you click the File menu and you will see a helpful command, Close All. Choose Close All to close all open documents. You will be prompted to save documents that have changed.

Using Drag-and-Drop Commands

You can save a great deal of time in Word for Windows when moving or copying text if you learn how to use *drag and drop*. Drag-and-drop commands are executed using the mouse and enable you to do with a simple mouse action what might require many keystroke steps. For example, to move selected text you only need to select the text, then move the pointer into the selected text and *drag* the selection. You will see a gray insertion point indicating where the text will be inserted. Position the insertion point and let go of the mouse button to *drop* the text. If you want to make sure you can use drag-and-drop commands, choose Tools, Options and select the Edit tab. Within the Edit tab, select the Drag-and-Drop Text Editing check box.

Troubleshooting

When I try to choose a command from a menu, it is grayed out.

When a menu command is grayed out, it means the command is not available at that time for some reason. For example, until you have used Edit, Copy or Edit, Cut to move text to the Clipboard, Edit, Paste will be grayed out and unavailable. You must carry out some other action before you can use a grayed out menu command.

Using the Toolbars

The toolbars in Word for Windows give you quick access to frequently used commands and procedures. Buttons on toolbars can only be used with a mouse (or similar pointing device). To use a button on a toolbar, click the button that represents the command or procedure you need. You decide which toolbars are displayed and where they appear on-screen. Toolbars are always accessible because they float above document windows.

In Word for Windows, you can display and work with more than one toolbar at a time. Word for Windows has eight predefined toolbars, described in the following list:

- *Standard toolbar.* The Standard toolbar contains the buttons most frequently used during document creation, file handling, and printing.

- *Formatting toolbar.* The Formatting toolbar contains buttons used for formatting fonts, setting alignment, applying numbering or bullets, applying format styles, and formatting borders.

- *Forms toolbar.* The Forms toolbar contains buttons to help you insert edit boxes, check boxes, lists, and tables. You also can change the properties of a form field and lock the form when you are finished.

- *Database toolbar.* The Database toolbar contains buttons to help you sort lists, edit a database, add or delete columns from a database, start mail merge, and insert data from a database outside of Word for Windows.

- *Drawing toolbar.* The Drawing toolbar contains buttons for drawing, filling, reshaping, and grouping objects in the document.

- *Borders toolbar.* The Borders toolbar enables you to quickly apply borders and change their thicknesses.

- *Microsoft toolbar.* The Microsoft toolbar contains buttons so you can quickly start and activate other Microsoft Windows applications.

- *TipWizard toolbar.* The TipWizard toolbar displays context-sensitive tips and a ShowMe button to give a more detailed explanation of the tip.

Word for Windows comes with many buttons that are not on the predefined toolbars. To customize predefined toolbars, you can drag off the buttons that you do not need and drag on the buttons that you do need. This is described in Chapter 36, "Customizing the Toolbar, Menus, and Shortcut Keys."

If someone has used Word for Windows before you, the predefined toolbars may be modified. Additional custom toolbars may be available to you that previous users have created or that have been created to assist you with specific tasks.

Getting Help on Buttons in the Toolbar

To see what a button does, move the mouse pointer over the button, pause, then read the name of the button in the ToolTip that pops up.

When you need help using a button, click the Help button, if available, and then click the button you want help with. If the Help button is not visible, press Shift+F1 and click the button you need help with. A Help window appears to show you how to use the tool. Press Alt+F4, choose File, Exit, or choose the Close button in the upper-right corner to close the Help window.

Displaying or Hiding Toolbars

You can choose View, Toolbars or right-click a toolbar and choose Toolbars to display and hide toolbars on-screen.

To display a toolbar, follow these steps:

1. Choose View, Toolbars to display the Toolbars dialog box shown in figure 2.11.

2. Select the toolbar that you want to display. Toolbars with selected check boxes will be displayed.

3. Choose OK. Word for Windows displays the toolbar you selected. The toolbar is displayed in the last position in which it was used.

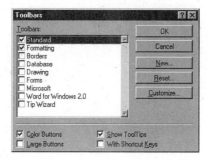

Fig. 2.11
Choose View, Toolbars or the shortcut menu to view the Toolbars dialog box.

To display a toolbar if you are using a mouse and a toolbar is currently displayed, follow these steps:

1. Right-click in the toolbar to display a shortcut menu.

2. Click the name of the toolbar you want to display.

You can hide a toolbar in three ways:

- Right-click the toolbar to display the toolbar shortcut menu. In the shortcut menu, displayed toolbars appear with a check mark. Click the name of the displayed toolbar that you want hidden.

- If a toolbar is in a floating window, you can close it by clicking once on the window's Control menu icon (a small box) to the left of the toolbar's title bar.

- You can close a toolbar by choosing Ⅴiew, Ⅰoolbars. When the Toolbars dialog box appears, deselect the toolbar check boxes you do not want displayed, and choose OK.

Word for Windows records the toolbars and their locations. When you restart Word for Windows, the toolbars you last used will be available to you.

Moving, Resizing, and Reshaping Toolbars

You can move and reshape toolbars to fit the way you want to work. Toolbars can be *docked* in a position along an edge of the window or they can *float* free in their own window. Docked toolbars are one button wide or high. You can reshape toolbars that float in a window and drag them wherever they are most convenient to use. Figure 2.12 shows floating and docked toolbars.

Fig. 2.12
Toolbars can be docked or float free.

Docked toolbar ——

Floating toolbar ——

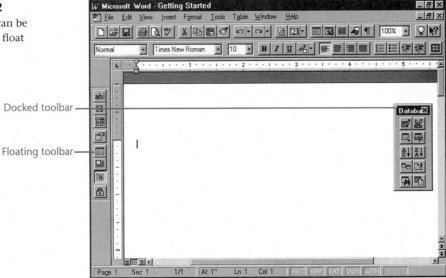

To move a toolbar, click the gray area around the edge of the toolbar and drag. If you drag the toolbar to an edge of the window, the toolbar docks against the edge. A toolbar is ready to dock when its gray outline becomes thinner.

Toolbars docked against a left or right edge may be too narrow for buttons with a drop-down list to display, such as the Style button. While docked against a left or right edge, these toolbars replace wide drop-down lists with buttons. Clicking a button displays the appropriate dialog box.

Toolbars also can float free in a window. To move a floating toolbar, click the gray area along one of the wide edges and drag. You can resize a floating toolbar window by dragging on a border. To return the toolbar to a dock, drag the floating toolbar's title bar to an edge of the screen and then release.

If you use a monitor with higher than VGA resolution, the normal size of buttons may be too small for you to see easily. You can manually switch between normal buttons and larger buttons by choosing View, Toolbars, selecting the Large Buttons option, and choosing OK.

Toolbars that have colored buttons will appear in color if you selected the Color Buttons check box in the Toolbars dialog box. When it is deselected, color buttons appear in shades of gray.

Working in Dialog Boxes

In drop-down menus, commands that require additional information are followed by an ellipsis (...). Choosing one of these commands displays a dialog box in which you enter needed information. Format, Font, for example, displays the dialog box shown in figure 2.13. This dialog box contains tabbed sections—the tabs showing across the top of the dialog box. Each tabbed section contains a different type of formatting.

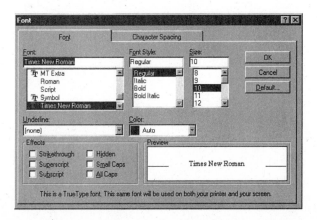

Tip
You can dock a floating toolbar by double-clicking it in the title bar or gray area. You can also float a docked toolbar by double-clicking it in the gray area.

▶ See "Customizing and Creating Toolbars," p. 1034

Fig. 2.13
The Font dialog box contains tabbed sections with text boxes, check boxes, and lists.

Everyday Word Processing

Dialog boxes contain different types of items. These items are described in more detail in the sections immediately following. The following list will help familiarize you with Word for Windows dialog box items:

- *Tab*. Multiple sections of a dialog box. Only one group at a time is displayed, and each group contains related options.

- *Text box*. A box in which you can type and edit text, dates, or numbers.

- *Option button*. A button that gives you one choice from a group of options. These are sometimes called radio buttons.

- *Check box*. A square box that can be turned on or off.

- *List box*. A list or drop-down list that scrolls to display available alternatives.

- *Command button*. A button that completes or cancels the command; some buttons give you access to additional options.

- *Spin box*. A box with up- and down-arrowhead buttons which increase or decrease the number in the box.

Selecting a Tab in a Dialog Box

A dialog box like the one shown in figure 2.13 may contain more than one tab. The tabs appear within the dialog box as though they are cards within a card file—all related options are on the same card. For example, all options relating to formatting fonts are in the Font tab of the Format Font dialog box. The titles of each section appear across the top of the dialog box as if they were tabs on filing cards.

To select a tab with the mouse, click the tab title.

To select a tab by keyboard, you can do one of two things:

- Press Alt+*letter*, where *letter* is the underlined letter in the tab's name.

- Hold down the Ctrl key and press the Tab key until the tab title you want displayed is selected.

Selecting Option Buttons and Check Boxes

Figure 2.13 shows check boxes, which appear as squares. Figure 2.14 shows groups of option buttons that appear as circles. You can select only one option button from within a group, but you can select one or more check boxes.

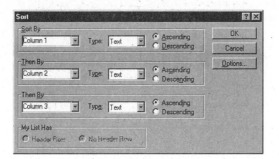

Everyday Word Processing

Fig. 2.14
A dialog box can
contain groups of
option buttons.

Check boxes are square boxes that you can turn on or off and use in combination with other check boxes. A check box is on when a ✓ appears in the box.

To select or deselect a check box, click the check box that you want to change. From the keyboard, press Alt+*letter* where *letter* is the underlined letter in the name of the check box.

To select an option button using the mouse, click the button. To clear an option button, you must click another in the same group. A dot within the option indicates that the option is on. Remember that you can select only one button in a group, but one is always selected.

To select an option button from the keyboard, hold down the Alt key and then press the underlined letter of the option group you want. Alternatively, press Tab until an option in the group is enclosed by dashed lines. After you select the group, press the arrow keys to select the option button that you want from within the group.

When you are using a keyboard and making a succession of changes in a dialog box, pressing the Tab key is probably the easiest way to move between items in the box. The active item is enclosed in a dashed border or is highlighted and contains the flashing insertion point for text editing. To change a check box that is enclosed by the dashed line, press the space bar. To change an option button in a group enclosed by the dashed line, press the arrow keys.

Tip
Shift+Tab moves
through option
buttons in the
reverse direction.

Editing Text Boxes

You use text boxes to type information, such as file names and numbers, into a dialog box. You can edit the text within a text box the same way you edit text elsewhere in Word for Windows.

The following mouse actions are used to select multiple letters, a word, or words or formula terms:

Select	Mouse Action
Multiple letters	Drag across letters
Single word	Double-click word
Multiple words	Double-click word; hold down button, then drag over adjacent words

To select text with the keyboard, press the Alt+*letter* combination for the text box. Press the ← or → key to move the flashing insertion point and then type the text you want to insert.

Delete characters to the right of the flashing insertion point by pressing the Delete key. Delete characters to the left of the insertion point by pressing the Backspace key.

Note

Keep in mind that the insertion point and the I-beam are not the same. The *insertion point* is where typing or deletions will take place. The *I-beam* is the mouse pointer—it moves when you move the mouse. The insertion point moves to the current I-beam location only when you click the left mouse button.

To select multiple characters using the keyboard so that you can delete or replace characters by typing, perform the actions listed in table 2.7.

Table 2.7 Text-Editing Actions

Mouse Action	Result
Click I-beam in text	Moves the insertion point (flashing cursor) to the I-beam location
Shift+click text	Selects all text between the current insertion point and the I-beam
Drag	Selects all text over which the I-beam moves while you hold down the mouse button

Keyboard Action	Result
←/→	Moves the insertion point left/right one character
Shift+arrow key	Selects text as the insertion point moves left or right
Ctrl+←/→	Moves the insertion point to the beginning of the preceding/next word
Shift+Ctrl+←/→	Selects from the insertion point to the beginning of the preceding or next word
Home	Moves the insertion point to the beginning of the line
Shift+Home	Selects from the insertion point to the beginning of the line
End	Moves the insertion point to the end of the line
Shift+End	Selects from the insertion point to the end of the line

To insert text in a text box using the mouse, click the I-beam at the location where you want the text, and then type the text. If you use a keyboard, press the Alt+*letter* combination or the Tab key to activate the text box, and then press one of the cursor-movement keys shown in table 2.7 to position the insertion point. Then type your text.

Text you type replaces the selected text only when you select the Typing Replaces Selection check box from the Edit tab of Tools, Options.

You can copy and paste in edit boxes within dialog boxes. This can be useful with commands such as Find or Replace. To do this, select text using the techniques described here, then press Ctrl+X to cut, Ctrl+C to copy, or Ctrl+V to paste. You can even copy and paste between dialog boxes or from a document into a dialog box.

Selecting from List Boxes

In some cases, Word for Windows will give you many alternatives from which to select. The Font tab in the Font dialog box, for example, shows you lists of fonts (refer to fig. 2.13).

Some list boxes show only the current selection in what appears to be a text box. To see the entire list of alternatives, you must pull down the list. Figure 2.13, for example, shows the Underline drop-down list in the up position. Figure 2.15 shows the same list dropped down to make the selection easier.

Fig. 2.15
The Underline list
is a drop-down
list, which makes
choosing a
selection easy.

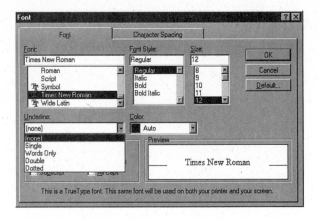

To select an item from a list box, follow these steps:

1. If the list is not displayed, click the down arrow to the side of the list or activate the list box by pressing Alt+*underlined letter*.

2. When the list is displayed, click the arrowheads in the scroll bar to scroll to the name you want. Then click the name you want to select.

   Alternatively, select the name you want by pressing the ↑ key, ↓ key, Home key, or End key.

3. Choose OK.

In most dialog boxes, you can double-click a name in a list box to select the name and choose OK in one operation. You cannot double-click a name in a drop-down list box.

Before you click a command button such as OK, make sure that the name you want to select from the list box is selected (highlighted), not just surrounded by a dashed line.

Command Buttons and How to Close Dialog Boxes

Command buttons usually appear at the upper-right corner or down the right side of dialog boxes. You usually use these buttons to execute or cancel a command. With a mouse, you can click a command button to choose it.

From the keyboard, you can choose a command button in three different ways:

■ If the command button contains an underlined letter, press Alt+*underlined letter*.

- If a button is bordered in bold, press Enter to choose the button. In most cases, pressing Enter will choose OK. Choose Cancel by pressing Esc.

- You can select any command button by pressing Tab until the button is bordered in bold, and then pressing Enter.

Getting Help

Windows and Word for Windows have Help information to guide you through new commands and procedures. Word's Help files are extensive and explain topics that range from parts of the screen to commands, dialog boxes, and business procedures.

To get help in Word or a Windows application, choose a command from the Help menu or press F1. You can also click the Help button, and then click the item of interest. Choosing Help, Microsoft Word Help Topics or pressing F1 will display the window shown in figure 2.16. From this window, you can learn how to use Help, or you can see the contents of all Help topics. Notice that you can access or control Help information in different ways:

Tip
You can print the contents of most Help windows by choosing Options, Print Topic from the Help window toolbar.

- You can select a topic from the list in the Contents tab.

- You can select the Index tab and select a topic.

- You can select the Find tab and search for a topic.

- You can select the AnswerWizard tab, type any word or words, and search for a topic.

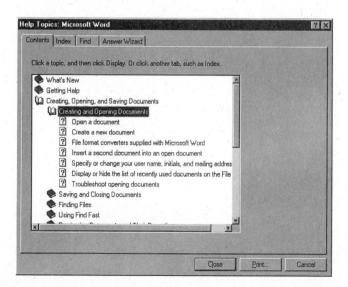

Fig. 2.16
The Help Contents window lists the topics you can get help on.

Command buttons are located under the title bar in a Help topic window and help you move through the Help topics. Choose a button by clicking it or by pressing Alt+*letter*. The following command buttons help you move through information:

Button	Action
Help <u>T</u>opics	Shows the index or contents of Help at the highest level
<u>B</u>ack	Returns to the preceding Help topic. With this button, you can retrace the topics you have viewed back to the initial Help Index
<u>O</u>ptions	Displays a list of options used for adding notes, copying and printing the topic, changing the font, keeping the Help dialog box open and displayed over other active windows, and changing system colors. Click an option or press the underlined letter to select the topic

Within Word's dialog boxes, you can get help on the dialog box contents by clicking the ? button, located at the top right of the box. When the pointer changes to a question mark, click the element of the dialog box with which you need help. A pop-up help window describes the part of the dialog box on which you clicked, as shown in figure 2.17.

Fig. 2.17
Get help in dialog boxes by clicking the question mark and then clicking an item in the box.

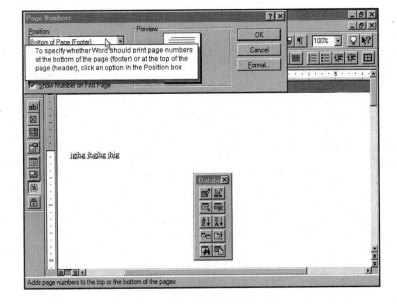

Getting the Tip of the Day

Often we get so involved with daily tasks we forget to look for ways to improve our work or to improve our skills. Word comes with a feature called Tip of the Day that is a painless way to learn a few of the many shortcuts in Word.

Figure 2.18 shows the TipWizard box that appears when you click the TipWizard button. The Tip of the Day box reveals one of Word's shortcuts. If you want to see the next tip in Tip of the Day, just click the up and down buttons at the right edge of the TipWizard box.

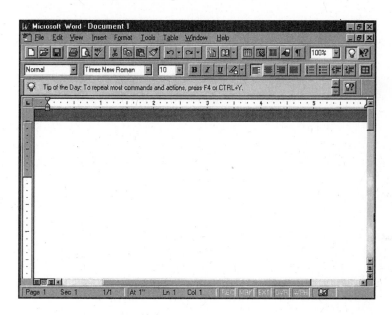

Fig. 2.18
Tip of the Day appears when you click the TipWizard button so that you can learn Word's many shortcuts.

You can display the TipWizard box at any time by clicking the TipWizard button on the Standard toolbar. You can turn off the TipWizard box by clicking the TipWizard button a second time. You also can turn the TipWizard box on or off by right-clicking any toolbar and then clicking TipWizard in the shortcut menu.

By default, the TipWizard box displays when you first install Word. If you do not want the TipWizard box to appear when Word starts, choose Tools, Options and click the General tab. Deselect the TipWizard Active check box and choose OK. To turn the TipWizard on so that it appears when you start Word, just select the TipWizard Active check box.

Everyday Word Processing

I

Searching for a Topic in Help

The Find tab enables you to search for specific words and phrases in Help topics. To use Find, choose Help, Microsoft Word Help Topics, then choose the Find tab. The dialog box shown in figure 2.19 appears.

Fig. 2.19

The Find tab in Help is used to search for specific words or phrases.

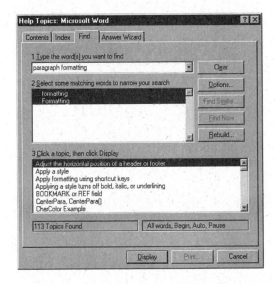

Type a word in the second drop-down list box. The top list will display matching words or phrases that you can select to narrow the search. Select a topic from the bottom list and click the Display button.

You also can click the Options button to select additional search options, or click the Find Similar button to display a list of similar topics.

The Rebuild button creates a list of every word from the help files. The list must be created before you can use Find Now.

The Index tab enables you to search for a specific word by typing the first few letters of the word. To use Index, choose Help, Microsoft Word Help Topics, then choose the Index tab. The dialog box shown in figure 2.20 appears.

Type a few letters of the word you want to find in the first text box. The second box displays matching words and phrases that you can select to narrow the search. Select an index entry you want from the second box and click the Display button.

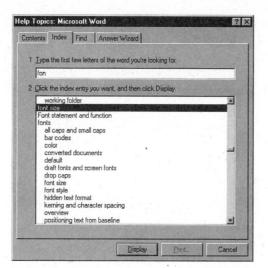

Everyday Word Processing

Fig. 2.20
The Index tab in
Help is used to
search for a
specific word.

Jumping between Help Topics

Hot words or *hot phrases* appear within the actual Help text. These words or
phrases have a solid or dashed underline and are displayed in green, meaning
that the word or phrase is linked to additional information. Words or phrases
with definitions appear with a dashed underline.

To jump to the topic related to a solid underlined word, click the word or
press Tab until the word is selected and press Enter.

To display the definition of a word that appears with a dashed underline,
click the word or tab to the word and press Enter. Click again or press Enter
to remove the definition.

Getting Help in Dialog Boxes

You can get help for any dialog box or error message that appears in Word for
Windows. Figure 2.21 shows the Help message that appears when you click
the <u>H</u>elp "<u>P</u>" button at the top-right corner of a dialog box and then click the
specific item you want information about. You can also move the pointer
over an item in the dialog box and right-click to display help about that dialog box item.

Fig. 2.21

A help message for dialog box items appears when you click the ? button and then click the item or right-click the item.

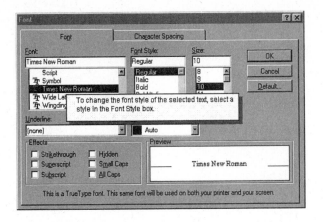

 To learn what action a command performs or how a button or portion of the screen works, press Shift+F1 to change the pointer to a pointer with an over-laid question mark. You can then click a command or screen element to learn more about it. You can also change the pointer to this help pointer by clicking the Help button on the Standard toolbar and then clicking the command or screen element. Pressing Esc returns the pointer to its normal appearance and mode of operation.

Troubleshooting

When I press Shift+F1 to display the question mark cursor so I can get context-sensitive help, a Help for WordPerfect Users dialog box appears.

The Help for WordPerfect Users option is turned on, which is why you get this dialog box instead of the question mark cursor. To turn off this option, choose Tools, Options, and select the General tab. Deselect the Help for WordPerfect Users option and choose OK.

Annotating, Copying, or Printing Help

You can add your own notes to tailor the Help system to your specific needs using the Annotate command. The Copy command enables you to copy the text of a help topic and then paste it into a document. You also can print the text of a help topic by choosing Print Topic.

To add notes to a help topic, click the Options button in a Help Topic window, choose Annotate, type in your notes in the Annotate dialog box, and then choose Save. Notice that a paper clip symbol appears before the text of the help topic. Clicking this symbol accesses your notes.

To copy the text of a help topic, click the Options button, and then choose Copy. The help text is now copied to the Clipboard, enabling you to paste it into a document.

To print the text of a help topic, click the Options button, choose Print Topic, set up the desired printer options, and then choose OK.

Closing the Help Window

Because Help is an actual application, you need to close its window when you are done. To remove the Help window, click the X mark in the top-right corner; or press Alt, space bar, and then C for Close, or press Alt+F4.

Manipulating Windows

When you use Word for Windows, you can display and run more than one application in Windows or use multiple documents while you are in Word for Windows. Seeing that much information on your screen can be confusing unless you keep your windows organized. Just as you organize folders and papers on your desk, you can organize your Windows applications and Word for Windows documents.

▶ See "Working with Multiple Documents," p. 90

You will see two types of windows on-screen:

■ An application window contains an application, such as the Windows Explorer, Microsoft Word for Windows, or Excel.

■ A document window contains a Word for Windows document. You can open multiple document windows within the Word for Windows window.

Switching between Applications

You can work in an application or document only when its window is active. The active window has a solid title bar. In most cases, the active window is also the top window. In a few instances, however, such as during the process of linking documents together, the active window may not be on top.

If you are running Word for Windows with other Windows or non-Windows applications, you can switch between application windows by activating the application whose window you want. If the taskbar is not displayed at the bottom of the screen, move the mouse pointer to the bottom of the screen. The taskbar appears, displaying the applications that are currently running. Choose an application by clicking its button in the taskbar. If you are using a keyboard or cannot find the taskbar with the mouse, press Ctrl+Esc to make it appear.

You also can cycle between applications by holding down the Alt key and pressing Tab. An application bar displays icons for each open application. Pressing the Alt+Tab key moves a selection box between icons. Release Alt and Tab when the box encloses the icon for the application you want active.

A convenient method of switching between office-related applications is by enabling the Microsoft Office Shortcut Bar, as shown in figure 2.22.

Fig. 2.22
The Microsoft Office Shortcut Bar gives you quick access to other Office applications and features.

▶ See "Using the Microsoft Office Shortcut Bar for Multi-Application Users," p. 972

The Microsoft Office Shortcut Bar enables quick access to applications such as Microsoft Word, Microsoft Excel, Schedule+, and the Microsoft Binder. The Microsoft Office Shortcut Bar is only available if you are using Office 95. It is not available with a stand-alone copy of Word.

To enable the Microsoft Office Shortcut Bar, perform the following steps:

▶ See "Using Microsoft Office Binder to Group Documents," p. 1003

1. Click the Start button in the taskbar at the bottom of the screen.

2. Move the mouse pointer over the Programs command.

3. Move the mouse pointer over the startup command.

4. Move the mouse pointer over the Microsoft Office Shortcut Bar, and then click.

Switching between Document Windows

Because Word for Windows makes working with several documents easy, you frequently may have more than one window on-screen. Each document window may contain a different document. You can affect only the active document window, however. From within the Word for Windows window, if you can see the window, you can make it active by clicking it with the mouse pointer. If you cannot see the document window, move the other document windows so that you can see it.

To switch to another window from the keyboard, choose the <u>W</u>indow menu and then press or click the number of the document window that you want to activate. The name of each document appears in the menu. You can cycle between document windows by pressing Ctrl+F6.

Minimizing, Maximizing, and Restoring Windows

For complex jobs you may need to work with more than one application and each application may have more than one document. Working with a lot of applications and documents can become visually confusing, so Windows supplies a way for you to work with multiple windows at a time and to get unused windows out of the way but keep them quickly available.

Tip
If you can't see the Windows taskbar, press Ctrl+Esc. The Start menu and taskbar will appear.

Applications and documents use three control buttons at the top right corner of each window or title bar. When a document window fills the application, then the document's control buttons move to the right edge of the application's menu bar.

To gain more room on the desktop, you can store open applications by minimizing them so that they become small buttons in the taskbar at the bottom of the Windows desktop. To *minimize* an application, click the Minimize button at the right end of the application title bar. When an application minimizes to a button on the taskbar, it is still open but out of the way on the screen. Click the application button on the taskbar to reopen the application window.

To minimize a document window so it is out of the way but still open, click the Minimize button at the right side of a document window's title bar. The Minimize button looks like a small bar. If the document window fills the application window, then the document's Minimize button will be at the right edge of the menu bar. A minimized document becomes a small taskbar at the bottom of the application window. Click the Restore or Maximize buttons on a minimized document to restore the document to a window or fill the inside of the application window.

Restore applications or documents into a window by clicking the Restore button. This button looks like overlapping windows.

Fill the Windows desktop with an application by clicking the application's Maximize button. The Maximize button looks like a single large square window. Maximize a document so that it fills the inside of an application window by clicking the document's Maximize button.

Note

Double-click the title bar of an application to maximize or restore it. Double-click the title bar of a document to restore it to a window.

Tip

Press Alt, spacebar to open the application's Control menu. Press Alt, hyphen (-) to open the document's Control menu.

Moving a Window

With multiple applications or multiple Word for Windows documents on-screen, you will want to move windows for the same reason that you shuffle papers on your desk. You can move a window with the mouse or the keyboard by following these steps:

- If you are using a mouse, activate the window that you want to move. Drag the title bar until the shadow border is where you want the window to be located. Release the mouse button to fix the window in its new location.

- From the keyboard, select the application or document Control menu by pressing Alt, space bar for the application Control menu or Alt, hyphen for the document Control menu. Press **M** to select <u>M</u>ove. A four-headed arrow appears in the title bar. Press an arrow key to move the shadowed outline of the window. Press Enter to fix the window in its new location, or press Esc to retain the original location.

Sizing a Window

You often want to see only part of an application or document window. The following steps show you how to change the size of the window by using the mouse or the keyboard.

To resize a window with the mouse, drag the window edge or corner to the location you want, then release the mouse button.

To resize a window from the keyboard, follow these steps:

1. Activate the window.

2. Press Alt, space bar for the application Control menu or Alt, hyphen for the document Control menu.

3. Press **S** for S̲ize.

4. Press the arrow key that points to the edge you want to reposition.

5. Press the arrow keys to move that edge.

6. Press Enter to fix the edge in its new location, or press Esc to cancel.

Closing a Document Window

When you finish with a document, you should close the window to remove it from the screen and to free memory. If you made a change since the last time you saved the document, Word displays an alert dialog box, shown in figure 2.23, asking whether you want to save your work before closing. Choose Y̲es if you want to save your most recent changes before closing a document.

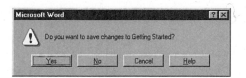

There is an important difference between closing a document window and closing the document. If more than one window is open on a document, you can close a window without closing the file. However, if there is only one document window or if you choose F̲ile, C̲lose, you close the file and all document windows that show that file.

To close the active document window using a mouse when more than one window is open on a document, double-click the document Control menu icon on the left side of the document's title bar (when the document is in its own window), or click the Close button on the right end of the menu bar.

To close the active document window by keyboard when more than one window is open on a document, press Alt, hyphen to choose the document Control menu, and press **C** for C̲lose.

Tip

The Size feature is not available if the window is maximized.

▶ See "Saving a Document," p. 91

Fig. 2.23

An alert dialog box prompts you for a specific action.

Everyday Word Processing

To close the file so that all windows using a document close, follow these steps:

1. Choose File, Close.

   The window closes if no changes have been made to the document since the last save.

2. If you made changes to the document after the last save, a dialog box appears asking you to confirm whether you want to save your changes.

   In the dialog box, click the No command button if you don't want to save the changed version of the file, or click the Yes command button to save your changes.

▶ See "Closing a Document," p. 104

3. If you chose Yes and the file has not been saved before, a Save As dialog box appears. Enter a new file name and choose Save.

To close all visible documents, hold down the Shift key as you choose the File menu. The Close All command will be available in place of Close. Choose Close All to close all visible documents. ❖

Chapter 3

Creating and Saving Documents

Word processing basics begin with creating a new document, typing the text, and saving the document. You need to know how to accomplish these basic tasks before you learn about the more advanced tools that Word for Windows 95 offers for working with your documents. In this chapter, you learn how to create a new document, open an existing document, and how to save your documents. You also learn how to work with more than one document at the same time.

In this chapter, you learn to do the following:

- Open an existing document

- Create a new document

- Work with more than one document at a time

- Close and save your document

What You Need to Know about Creating and Saving Documents

When you are working on a document in Word for Windows, the document is stored in the memory of your computer. This memory is often referred to as *RAM*, or *random-access memory*, and it is a temporary location for the programs and documents you use when you are working with your computer. When you exit a program or turn off your computer, whatever was stored in memory is removed. For this reason, you need a permanent storage location for your programs and files. Floppy disks and hard disks are used for this purpose. They are magnetic media, much like the cassette tapes that are used to record music, on which information from your computer can be stored for as long as you want.

When you first open Word for Windows, you are presented with a blank document. You can begin typing text into this document right away. Until you save the file, the work you do is only temporarily stored in the computer's memory. Eventually, you need to save this document onto a disk, either the hard disk in your computer or a floppy disk, by choosing File, Save. When you first save the document, you need to give it a name, which you do in the Save As dialog box. From then on, you have the choice of saving the file with the same name, or saving it with a new name, which you can do by choosing File, Save As.

Understanding File Names

The first time you save a new document, you must give it a name and assign it to a disk drive and folder. With previous versions of Word, you were limited to an eight-character file name, with a three-character extension. With Windows 95, you can now use longer file names. Keep these guidelines in mind when naming files:

- For the file name, you can type as many as 255 characters, including spaces.

- You can use letters A through Z (uppercase or lowercase), numbers 0 through 9, hyphens (-), underscores (_), and exclamation points (!).

- Legal characters include !, @, #, $, %, `, &, (,), _, -, {, and }. Use the exclamation point or another legal character as the first character in a name when you want the name to be first in the alphabetical listing of names.

- You cannot use the following characters:

  \ ? : * , " < > |

- Word for Windows provides its own extension, DOC. You can override this default when you name your file by including a period and an extension. Using the Word for Windows default extension is better, however, because the extension helps you to identify each file's type and eases the task of opening files. (By default, Word for Windows lists only files with the DOC extension in the Open dialog box.)

Understanding Folders

When you save a file on the hard disk of your computer, it ends up in a folder on your hard disk. Folders are analogous to the file drawers and file folders you use in your office to help you organize and locate your paper files. You can locate files more easily if you store related files together in a folder. For example, you could store all the business letters you create in Word in a folder named \BUSINESS LETTERS and all your proposals in a folder named \PROPOSAL.

> ### Caution
>
> Don't store the files you create in the folders where your program files are stored. If you ever have to reinstall or upgrade Word, you could lose any files you stored in the program folders. Also, because many files are already in the program folders, you will not have as much room to store your own files if you use these folders. Create your own folders and folders within folders for storing your files.

The first time you use File, Open or File, Save As, Word for Windows assumes that you want to open or save a document in the Word for Windows folder. Instead, you usually want to open or save a file in one of your own folders. For example, you may have a folder named C:\WINWORD\PRIVATE. You must tell Word for Windows where the file you want to open is located or where you want to save a file—whether that location is a different folder, a different drive on your hard disk, or a disk in drive A or B. To switch folders or drives, use the appropriate list boxes in the Open and Save As dialog boxes, as discussed in the following paragraphs.

The selected folder appears in the Look In drop-down list (see fig. 3.1). You can display this list to select another drive.

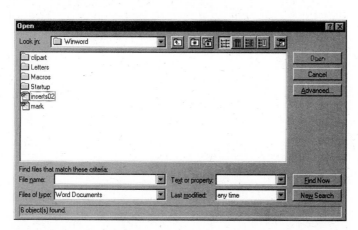

Fig. 3.1
You can change drives and folders in the Save As dialog box or the Open dialog box.

The list box includes all the subfolders in the current folder. You may see different folders in the dialog box, depending on the folders you have set up on your system. An icon that resembles a file folder represents each folder. If you want to open a file in a subfolder, you first must open the folder. You can do so by double-clicking the subfolder icon.

To change disk drives or folders in the Open dialog box, follow these steps:

1. Display the Look In drop-down list and select the drive you want.

2. To select a folder, double-click the folder icon. You also can click the Up One Level button to move up one level in the folder structure.

3. Select the file from the list. Or type the file name in the File Name text box.

4. Choose Open.

You can use the same procedures as just described in the Save As dialog box to change drives and folders when you are saving a file.

Setting the Default Folder

When you first choose File, Open or File, Save As, you see a listing of files in the \WINWORD folder. Because you should reserve this folder for the Word program files and store the files you create in Word in other folders, you will have to switch to some other folder to find the file you want. After you have switched folders in the Open dialog box (or the Save As dialog box), that folder becomes the current folder until you close Word, and whenever you choose File, Open or File, Save As, the files in the current folder are listed.

You can change the default folder, which is the folder that appears when you first choose File, Open or File, Save As. Making the folder where you store the files that you use most often your default folder can save you some time when you open and save files.

To change the default folder, follow these steps:

1. Choose Tools, Options.

2. Select the File Locations tab. The File Locations folder is displayed (see fig. 3.2).

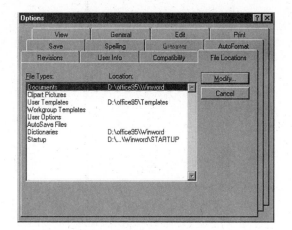

Fig. 3.2
You can change
the default folder
for Word for
Windows docu-
ments.

3. Select Documents in the File Types list.

4. Choose Modify to display the Modify Location dialog box.

5. Select the folder you want to use as the default from the list box or type
   the full path name for the folder in the Folder Name text box.

6. Choose OK and then choose Close.

Opening an Existing Document

The great advantage to word processors is that you can use the same files
repeatedly. You can return to the same document as many times as you want
to print it, edit it, or add new material to it. Or you can open an existing
document and use parts of it in a new document.

You are not restricted to opening files created by Word for Windows. When
you install Word, you are given the option of installing one or more conversion files that enable you to open files created by other programs, for example, WordPerfect. Word's conversion capability allows you to view and
edit a document created by another user using a different program or to convert documents you created on another word processor as you make the transition to Word for Windows.

You can speed up the process of opening a file by automatically opening
Word and a document at the same time from My Computer or Windows
Explorer.

What You Need to Know about Opening a Document

Opening a document involves locating the document in a drive and folder and knowing what type the file is. Word for Windows, by default, lists only files that end in the extension DOC in the Open dialog box. The program also can open template files (which have the extension DOT) and files created by other programs (which have various extensions). To open a file with an extension other than DOC, you must specify the extension you want to list by choosing the file type in the Files of Type box in the Open dialog box or by typing the extension preceded by the characters *. in the File Name box and then pressing Enter.

You can use wild cards to help you locate the type of file you want. An asterisk (*) means any character or characters, and a question mark (?) means any single character. If you want to locate all files that end in the extension EXT, for example, type ***.EXT** in the File Name box. If you want to list files with any name that end in any extension, type ***.*** in the File Name box.

Opening a Document

Choose File, Open to open an existing document. Switch to the drive and folder where the file is stored, and then select the file from the list of files in the Open dialog box.

To open an existing document, follow these steps:

1. Choose File, Open, press Ctrl+O, or click the Open button on the Standard toolbar (the second button from the left). The Open dialog box appears (see fig. 3.3).

Fig. 3.3
Select the file you want to open in the Open dialog box.

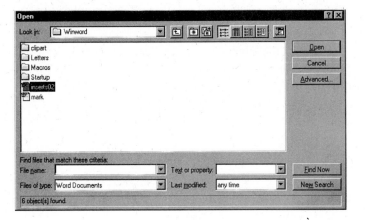

2. If necessary, select a different disk drive in the Look In drop-down list (see "Understanding Folders," earlier in this chapter).

3. If necessary, select a different folder in the list (see "Understanding Folders," earlier in this chapter).

4. If necessary, select a different file type in the Files of Type box.

5. If you want to prevent changes to the original document, click the Commands and Settings button in the dialog box toolbar and click Open Read Only from the menu.

   This option prevents the use of File, Save, which replaces the original version with the changed document. Documents opened with Read Only must be saved with File, Save As and a new file name.

6. In the File Name text box, type the name of the file you want to open, or select the file you want to open from the list.

7. Choose Open. As a shortcut for steps 6 and 7, you can double-click the file name to open it.

If you want fast access to a frequently used folder or file, you can create a shortcut and keep it in the FAVORITES folder. You can then select the shortcut and open the folder or file without having to figure out where that file or folder is stored.

To add a file or folder, select it in the Open dialog box. Then choose the Add to Favorites button. To open the file or folder, click the Look in Favorites button.

> **Note**
>
> You can use the Open dialog box to search for files. For example, you can find files using summary information, file information, or any string of characters that appears in the file. After you find a file, you can open, print, view, copy, or delete it. For details about the search features, see Chapter 4, "Managing Documents and Files."

Opening a Recently Used File

Word remembers the last several documents you have used and lists them at the bottom of the File menu. You can quickly open any of these documents by selecting it from the list.

Tip

After you open a file, you can quickly return to the place in the document where you left off when you last closed the file. Press Shift+F5, and the insertion point moves to where it was when the file was last saved.

▶ See "Searching for Files," p. 115

To reopen a recently closed file, follow these steps:

1. Choose File.

2. Select the file name from the bottom of the menu by clicking the file you want to reopen or typing the number of the file you want to reopen.

> **Note**
>
> You can specify how many files appear in the list at the bottom of the File menu by choosing Tools, Options and selecting the General tab. Select or type the number of entries you want to appear in the list in the Entries spin box next to the Recently Used File List check box and choose OK. You can specify as many as nine files.

Opening Non-Word for Windows Files

Word for Windows can open files created by other programs such as the Windows Notepad (or any other application that creates a text file), WordPerfect, Word for DOS, WordStar, Works, and others. You use File, Open, but then you must identify the file type so that Word for Windows can convert the file into its own format. (Word for Windows proposes the file type it thinks the file should be, which is usually correct.)

To open non-Word for Windows files, follow these steps:

1. Choose File, Open, or click the Open button on the Standard toolbar.

2. Select the drive and folder containing the file you want to open.

3. Display the Files of Type drop-down list, and select the type of file you want to open.

4. From the list of files, select the file you want to open.

5. Choose OK.

If there is no converter for the file, the Convert File dialog box appears. Select a substitute converter from the list and choose OK. The other option is to run the Word for Windows setup program. You will have the chance to install additional converters found on Word for Windows installation disks.

Opening a Document While Starting Word for Windows

From My Computer or Windows Explorer, you can start Word for Windows and open a file at the same time. This is handy if you use these tools to help you find a file and you want to immediately open the file.

To open a file from My Computer or Windows Explorer, follow these steps:

1. Display the window containing the Word for Windows document you want to open.

2. Double-click the file with the mouse. Word for Windows starts and displays the document you selected.

   You can also open a document from the Office toolbar on the desktop.

▶ See "Opening Documents and Applications from the Office Shortcut Bar," p. 974

Troubleshooting

When I choose File, Open and switch to the folder where my file should be stored, I don't see the file listed.

If you selected to display only certain file types, you may not see the file listed. Be sure that Word Documents or All Documents is selected in the Files of Type list.

Whenever I try to open a particular document in Word, I get a dialog box asking me for a password. How can I access this document?

Someone must have saved the document as a protected file. This means you must know the password that was assigned to the document to open it. Find out from others who have worked on the document what the password is.

Opening a New Document

When you first start Word for Windows (see Chapter 2, "Getting Started in Word for Windows"), you see a blank document, ready for typing (see fig. 3.4). This new document is named Document1 to indicate that the document is the first one you have created since starting the program.

Fig. 3.4

A blank document is ready for you to begin entering text.

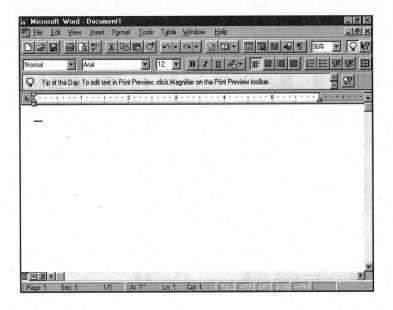

If your new document isn't the first one you have seen since starting Word for Windows, however, the document is numbered accordingly: the second new document is called Document2, the third is Document3, and so on. Even if you save and close Document1, the next new document in the current working session is numbered Document2.

You can create a new document in Word in three ways. New documents can be based on three different types of *templates*. These templates contain frequently used text, formatting styles, macros, and custom settings. The three different templates that documents can be based on are the following:

- NORMAL.DOT, which contains the default settings for standard documents

- Custom templates that come with Word (such as Professional Fax) or that you create that contain predefined text, formatting styles, macros, and custom features necessary for a specific type of document

- Template wizards, which are templates combined with intelligent dialog boxes that guide you through the process of completing the document. Wizards come with Word (Calendar Wizard, for example) or they can be built by individuals familiar with WordBasic

The following sections describe how to open documents based on these three different templates.

Understanding Templates

When you create a new document, Word bases the new document on a template. Unless you specify otherwise, Word uses the Normal template, NORMAL.DOT, as the basis for your new document.

A *template* is a predefined set of formatting characteristics, such as type style, margin width, tab settings, and so on, and can also contain boilerplate text, such as a letterhead. Word comes with templates for creating standard business letters, memos, fax cover sheets, and many other types of documents. These templates save you the trouble of having to type standard text, such as the To, From, and Subject fields in a memo, and they help you produce documents that are formatted consistently from one to the next.

You also can create your own templates. For example, you may want to base your document on a special template you have created called Letters that includes formatting to match your company's letterhead. Unless you choose otherwise, however, Word for Windows bases new documents on the Normal template. You can think of NORMAL.DOT as the global template, which contains the settings that are used by default for new documents.

Creating a New Blank Document

When you want to start writing in a blank document, you will often use the NORMAL.DOT template as a basis for the new document. Opening a document based on NORMAL.DOT is very easy.

To start a new document, follow these steps:

1. Choose File, New or press Ctrl+N. The New dialog box appears (see fig. 3.5).

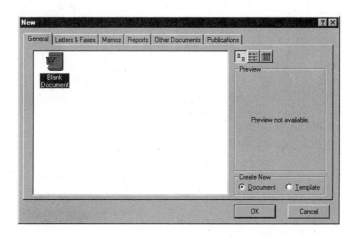

Fig. 3.5
Start a new document from the New dialog box.

2. Choose OK.

You also can start a new document by clicking the New button (the first button on the left of the Standard toolbar). A new document based on the Normal template is opened.

Creating a New Document from a Template

Tip
You can change
how the templates
are listed in the
New dialog box
using the buttons.
You can select List,
Details, or Large
Icons as the view.

When you use File, New to open a new document, the New dialog box appears on-screen (refer to fig. 3.5). In the New dialog box, you see tabs for different template types. By default, the General tab is displayed, and the Normal template is selected (the template that a new document opened with the New button is based on). You will probably use the Normal template for most of your documents. However, you can choose one of the other predefined templates if you want, or you can choose a custom template that you have created. Select the tab to see the available templates. You also can preview a template to see what it contains.

To open a new document based on a template, follow these steps:

1. Choose File, New. The New dialog box appears (refer to fig. 3.5).

2. Select the tab that contains the template you want to use or preview.

3. To see a preview of a template, select it in the list (see fig. 3.6).

Fig. 3.6
Preview a template
by selecting it.

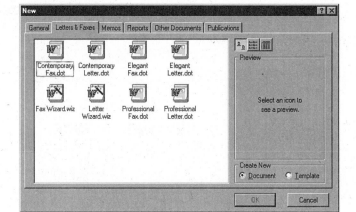

4. If you want to use this template, choose OK.

Creating a New Document with a Template Wizard

When you display some of the tabs, you will notice that some templates include Wizard after the name. Wizards provide on-screen guidance as you create a new document. For example, if you choose the Fax Wizard, you are guided through the entire process of creating a fax cover sheet. All you have to do is follow the instructions in the dialog boxes as they appear on-screen. A series of buttons along the bottom of the wizard dialog boxes enable you to move from one dialog box to the next.

To create a new document using a wizard, follow these steps:

1. Choose File, New.

2. Select the tab that contains the type of document you want to create.

3. Select the wizard you want to use from the list. A sample appears in the Preview box.

4. Choose OK. A Wizard dialog box appears, as shown in figure 3.7.

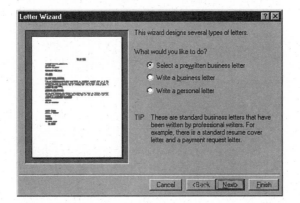

Fig. 3.7
Wizards guide you through the process of creating a new document.

5. Follow the steps in the Wizard dialog box, using the buttons at the bottom of the dialog box to move from box to box.

> **Note**
>
> Most of your documents will probably be based on NORMAL.DOT. If you don't like the predefined settings in the Normal template, you can modify them so that all new documents based on the Normal template use your preferred settings and you don't have to change them for each new document. For example, if you want to use different margin settings or a different font, you can change these settings in the Normal template. For more information on how to modify a template, see Chapter 6, "Using Templates and Wizards for Frequently Created Documents."

▶ See "Changing a Template," p. 186

▶ See "Recording a Macro," p. 1058

Troubleshooting

I opened a new document using one of the templates that comes with Word and typed in some text that I always want to appear in documents using this template. I saved the document, but when I open a new document using this template, the text I typed doesn't appear in the document.

To edit a template, you must work directly with the template. Choose File, Open, switch to the TEMPLATE folder, and select Document Templates in the Files of Type box. Select the template you want to modify in the File Name list box and choose OK. Edit the template to your liking and then save it. Now, whenever you open a new document template based on this template, the changes you made will apply to the new document. See Chapter 6, "Using Templates and Wizards for Frequently Created Documents," for more information on templates.

Working in a Document

After you open a new or existing document, you need to know how to work with that document. This section introduces some of the basic concepts and procedures you need to know to work in a document. Many of the concepts and procedures discussed in the following section will be familiar to you if you have worked with other word processors. If you have never used a word processor, you need to become familiar with these basics before you start working with a document in Word for Windows.

When you create a new document in Word for Windows, you see a blank typing screen (except for the helpful tools at the top, bottom, and right). A vertical bar—the insertion point—flashes at the top left. Below the insertion point is a horizontal line called the *document end mark*. When you begin typing, your characters appear on-screen to the left of the insertion point, which moves to the right as you type.

If you have never typed in a word processor before, you immediately become aware of one difference from typing on a typewriter: you don't have to press the Enter key at the end of every line. You continue typing past the end of the right margin, and Word for Windows wraps sentences around to fit within the margins.

Press the Enter key only to mark the end of a paragraph or to insert a blank line. Pressing Enter inserts a paragraph mark. (Normally you don't see paragraph marks on-screen; if you want to see them, see Chapter 10, "Formatting Lines and Paragraphs.")

Everyday Word Processing

There are two important reasons for pressing Enter only when you want to end a paragraph. First, if you add or delete text from the paragraph, the word-wrap feature ensures that the paragraph stays intact. If you press Enter at the end of each line and then add or delete text, each line ends where you pressed Enter, whether it's at the beginning or middle of the line. Second, as you learn in Chapter 10, a paragraph is a special set of text with its own useful formatting commands, such as alignment, indents, line spacing, and tabs.

When you type text on-screen, you can use all the characters on your keyboard. Besides the normal characters you see on your keyboard, however, Word for Windows offers many special characters, including bullets, typesetting quotes, wide dashes, and many others. For details about entering these characters, see Chapter 9, "Formatting Characters and Changing Fonts."

When you type in Word for Windows Insert mode, you add text to an existing document between the existing words. In some cases, you may prefer to type in the Overtype mode so that new text types over existing text.

If you want to switch from the insert mode to the Overtype mode, press the Insert key on your keyboard or double-click the OVR indicator in the status bar. OVR becomes dark in the status bar at the bottom of the screen. Press the Insert key a second time to return to Insert mode. If your status bar isn't displayed, you don't see a screen message reminding you that you're in Overtype mode. (To display the status bar, choose Tools, Options and select the View tab. In the Window group, select Status Bar so that a check mark appears in the check box.)

If you prefer to use the Overtype mode all the time, you can customize Word for Windows to use Overtype mode as the default (see Chapter 35, "Customizing and Optimizing Word Features").

Caution

Be careful when working in Overtype mode. It is very easy to forget to return to Insert mode; you could end up typing over text you didn't want to replace.

You can move to a location where you were previously working in your document by pressing Shift+F5. Word remembers the previous three locations of the insertion point, so you can return to any of these locations by pressing Shift+F5 until you get to the location you want. When you first open an existing document, pressing Shift+F5 returns you to where the insertion point was located when you closed the document.

▶ See "Selecting
the Correct
View for Your
Work," p. 124

▶ See "Moving
in the Docu-
ment," p. 135

▶ See "Selecting
Text," p. 141

Troubleshooting
Whenever I try to enter new text, the new text I enter overwrites the text that was already in my document. How can I prevent this?
This happens when you are in Overtype mode. Press the Insert key to return to Insert mode. When you type in Insert mode, the new text is inserted after the insertion point and any existing text is moved to make room for the new text.

Working with Multiple Documents

In Word for Windows, you can work with several documents simultaneously. Each new document you create or each existing document you open resides in its own document window on your screen. (For details on the difference between the program window and document windows and on moving and sizing windows, see Chapter 2, "Getting Started in Word for Windows.")

One benefit to working with multiple documents simultaneously is that you easily can copy or move text between them. This feature eases the task of creating two different versions of one basic document or borrowing from an existing document as you build a new one.

To work with multiple documents, you simply open additional new or existing documents, as discussed in the previous sections. As you open successive documents, they appear in document windows that hide the previously opened documents. To work with these hidden documents, you can switch between them in this full-screen mode, or you can arrange the windows so that you can see at least a portion of each of them. Only one window can be active at a time. The window on top, with the different-colored title bar, is the active window. It displays the document in which you are working.

To arrange multiple document windows, choose Window, Arrange All. Word for Windows reduces the size of each window so that you can see them all on-screen. You can resize or move these windows using normal Windows techniques.

To switch between full-screen document windows, follow these steps:

1. Choose Window, which lists all currently open files.

2. Select the name of the file to which you want to switch.

Everyday Word Processing

As an alternative to using the <u>W</u>indow menu to switch between open documents, you can click the window you want to select, or use Ctrl+F6. Press Ctrl+F6 repeatedly to cycle through all open documents. This method is the quickest when you have only two files open. To restore any window to its full-screen size, click the Maximize button at the top right of the window, or choose Ma<u>x</u>imize in the Control menu.

To open a second copy of the current file, the one in the active window, follow these steps:

1. Choose <u>W</u>indow, which lists all currently open files.

2. Choose <u>N</u>ew Window.

When you open multiple copies of the same file, the first file name in the title bar ends with :1, the second with :2, and so on. You can switch between these windows in the same way you switch between any document windows, but any edits you make to one are made to all, and you can save the document from any of the windows displaying that document. If you close the document choosing <u>F</u>ile, <u>C</u>lose, all copies of the document are closed. To close just one of the windows for the document, select the Control menu for that window (click the control menu bar or press the Alt+Hyphen keys) and choose <u>C</u>lose. Or double-click the Control menu icon.

> **Note**
>
> You can open a second window and then change the way you view that document in the new window. In this way, you can have two different views of the same document. For example, you can view the document as an outline in one window and view the document normally in the second window.

▶ See "Selecting the Correct View for Your Work," p. 124

Saving a Document

By now, you probably have heard the lecture advising you to save your document frequently. Saving your work stores the work as a file on disk. Until you save, your work exists only in your computer's memory. Thus, if the electricity goes off, even for a very short time, everything in your computer's memory is lost—including your work.

Saving frequently also reduces the time required for Word for Windows to store your work on disk. In effect, you save time by saving often.

After you have saved a file, you can save it again with the same name, or save a new copy of the file with a different file name and storage location. You can attach summary information to the file when you save it, which makes it easier to find the file when you want to work on it again.

You can tell Word to automatically save your document at specified time intervals and to make a backup copy of your file each time you save a document. In this way, if you have forgotten to save a file and your power fails or some other problem occurs, you will at least be able to recover some of your lost work.

You can save a document created in Word for Windows in other formats so that you can transfer the document to other computers that do not have Word installed. For example, you can save a document as a WordPerfect file to give to someone who uses WordPerfect. You can also save a document as a protected file to limit access to the document and prevent anyone from altering the document unless you give them access to it.

The first time you save a document, you give it a file name and decide on what disk and in which folder you want to store it. After you have saved a file for the first time, you can save it again with the same file name, or you can save it as a new file with a different file name. This is what you would do if you wanted to save successive drafts of a document as you worked on it.

Creating Long Names for Files and Folders

Folders and files with long names can be used on older Windows and DOS systems. The *FAT (File Allocation Table)*, an area on the disk that stores file information, has been especially modified to store both old-style 8.3 file names as well as long file names.

Windows 3.1 used an 8.3 filename convention where eight characters were used for the first part of a file name; a period was inserted to separate the parts of the file name; and then three letters were used for a file's extension. The file extension usually indicated the type of data in the file and the application that created the file.

Caution

Beware of using MS-DOS based or previous Windows versions of file management software or file utilities with files that have long file names. The software or utilities will probably not correctly recognize long file names and will destroy the long file names. The data in the files may remain usable.

In Windows 95 you can have file and folder names up to 255 characters long, and the names can include spaces. This long file name is stored in an extended location in the FAT of the disk. This extended location does not hamper the normal 8.3 name also stored in the FAT.

Caution

Long file names cannot use the following characters:

/ \ : * ? " < > |

When you use a long file name, Windows automatically creates a file name fitting the 8.3 convention. This 8.3 file name is saved in its normal location in the FAT so that older Windows and DOS systems can still use the 8.3 file name.

You can see the MS-DOS file name that will be used for a file by right-clicking the file name in the Open dialog box and choosing Properties. Click the General tab. The long file name is at the top of the box, and the MS-DOS name appears near the middle.

Some of the rules involved in converting long file names to 8.3 file names include:

- Blank spaces are deleted before truncating long file names.

- File names where the first characters fit in eight characters or less are left unchanged.

- File names involving multiple periods, such as PROPOSAL.SMITH.DOC, will use the file name to the left of the first period and the extension to the right of the last period.

- File names longer than eight characters, but having a first word that is eight characters long and is followed by a space use the first word as the file name.

- File names that are created by truncating long file names end with ~#, where # is a number.

- No truncated file name will duplicate a file name existing in the same directory. ~# will be placed as the seventh and eighth characters and the # will be a number used to differentiate files with the same names.

If you use a DOS command from the command prompt, such as dir to list a directory containing files with long names, you see the normal file information as well as the long file names. The long file name is displayed in the far right column when using the DOS dir command.

Creating a Folder When Needed

As the number of files you create in Word increases, you may want to come up with some system for organizing files. The easiest way is to set up folders on the hard disk that contain related files. For example, you might have a folder for letters and another for memos.

One of the new features of Word is the capability of creating a new folder right from the Save As dialog box. This feature saves you the hassle of having to first create the folder in Windows and then save the file to the new folder. You will most often use this feature when you are saving documents, although the Create New Folder button is also available in the Open dialog box.

Follow these steps to create a new folder from the Save As dialog box:

1. Choose File, Save As. You see the Save As dialog box.

2. Change to the folder where you want to place the new folder. For example, if you want to place the folder within the WINWORD folder, change to that folder.

3. Click the Create New Folder button in the dialog box toolbar. You see the New Folder dialog box (see fig. 3.8).

Fig. 3.8
You can create a new folder right from the Save As dialog box.

4. Type the folder name. You can type as many as 255 characters, including spaces.

5. Choose the OK button.

Saving Your Document

The first time you save a document, you must name it and decide where you want to store it.

To save and name a file, follow these steps:

1. Choose File, Save As or press F12 or choose the Save button on the Standard toolbar (the third button from the left). The Save As dialog box appears (see fig. 3.9).

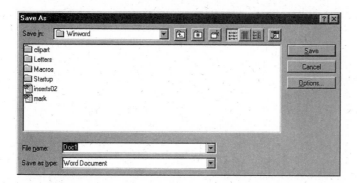

Fig. 3.9
Use the Save As dialog box to name a file and assign where you want it stored.

2. Type a file name in the File Name box. Word will assign the extension DOC. (See the section "Saving for Other Word Processors or Applications" later in this chapter for information on saving the file as another document type.)

3. In the Save In list, select the drive where you want to save your file. Use this option to save your file to a disk in drive A or B, for example, or to save the file to a different drive on your hard disk. (See "Understanding Folders," an earlier section in this chapter.)

4. In the list box, select the folder where you want to save your file. (See "Understanding Folders," an earlier section in this chapter.)

5. Choose OK.

6. If you have selected the option to display the Properties dialog box when you first save a file, fill in the dialog box when it appears and choose OK (see "Saving Documents with Descriptions to Make Documents Easier to Find," later in this chapter). You can bypass the dialog box by choosing OK without entering any information.

You can change the default folder that is listed when you first choose File, Save or File, Save As. See "Setting the Default Folder," an earlier section in this chapter.

> **Note**
>
> If you are familiar with folder path names, you can save a file into another folder by typing the path name and file name in the File Name box of the Save As dialog box. To save a file named REPORTS into the CLIENTS folder on drive C, for example, type the following path name and then choose OK:
>
> **C:\CLIENTS\REPORTS**

Saving Files with a New Name

You can use File, Save As to save a named file with a new name, which creates a backup of your file. If you have a file called LETTERA.DOC, for example, you can save your file a second time, giving it the name LETTERB.DOC. You then have two versions of the same file, each with a different name. You can save the new version of your file in the same folder as the original, or in any other folder or drive.

Revising your file before saving it with a new name is a common practice. You then have the original file and the second, revised file, each with a unique name. Using this method, you can store successive drafts of a document on disk. You can always return to an earlier draft if you need to.

To save a named file with a new name, choose File, Save As, change the file name in the File Name box, change the drive or folder if you want, and then choose OK.

> **Note**
>
> You can use File, Save As to make sequential backups of important documents. The first time you save a file, name the file with a number, such as FILE01. Then each time you save the file again, rename the document with the next higher number: FILE02, FILE03, and so on. The file with the highest number is always the most recent version. When you finish the project, you can delete the files with low numbers.

Tip
Be sure to name the files FILE01 and FILE02—including the zero—so that the files stay in numerical order in dialog box lists. If you don't, FILE11 is listed before FILE3 because files are listed alphabetically and numerically.

Saving Documents with Descriptions to Make Documents Easier to Find

Information that describes a document is called a *property*. For example, the file name, date created, and file size are all file properties for a Word document. You can also save summary information using the Properties sheet.

Summary information includes descriptive notes that can ease the task of organizing and finding files later, after you have created many files. You can attach summary information to your document when you first create the file, while you work on the file, or when you save the file.

To add summary information to a document, follow these steps:

1. Choose File, Properties. The Properties sheet appears, with the Summary page selected (see fig. 3.10).

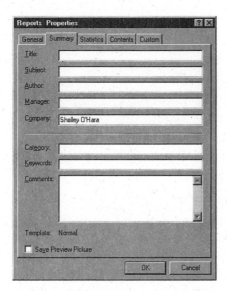

Fig. 3.10
Use the Summary tab of the Properties dialog box to attach useful information to your documents.

2. Fill in any of the fields with descriptive text. Include as much (up to 255 characters) or as little information as you like.

3. Choose OK.

The Statistics tab in this dialog box tells when you created the document; when the document was most recently saved; and how many pages, words, and characters the document contains.

To view the statistics for a document, follow these steps:

1. Select the Statistics page in the Properties sheet. The Statistics page appears (see fig. 3.11).

Everyday Word Processing

I

Fig. 3.11

The Statistics page provides detailed information on your document.

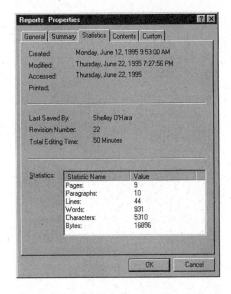

2. Take note of the statistics that interest you.

3. Choose OK.

If you want to be prompted to enter summary information when you save a file, you can select an option to display the Properties sheet whenever you choose File, Save As. Choose Tools, Options and select the Save tab. Select the Prompt for Document Properties option and choose OK. Now, whenever you first save a file, the Properties dialog box appears. If you don't want to enter summary information for that file, choose OK to bypass the dialog box.

Whichever method you choose, including summary information is a wonderful time-saver. In Chapter 4, "Managing Documents and Files," you learn how to use this information to locate misplaced files or files whose names you don't quite remember. You can include any text as many as 255 characters in any of the summary fields. No naming or character restrictions exist.

Filling in the Summary tab may seem like a nuisance, but try the box before giving it up. When you learn how to use the powerful find features, you see that summary information helps you find files much more easily.

Saving without Renaming

Every time you save a document with a unique name, you create a new file on disk—a good way to keep backups of your document. Not all files are so important, however, that you need multiple backups. In that case, you can save the document to its existing file name, replacing the current version of the file.

Remember that when you save without renaming, you erase and replace the existing file with the new file.

To save without renaming, choose File, Save or press Shift+F12, or click the Save button on the toolbar (the third button from the left).

Saving Many Documents at Once

If you have several documents open at once, you can save them all simultaneously by using File, Save All. The Save As dialog box appears for any documents that have not been saved before.

Files you normally don't see, including glossary and macro files, also are saved when you use this command.

Automatically Saving Documents

You can tell Word for Windows to automatically save your documents at specified intervals. AutoSave files are saved with a name different from your file name, but always with the ASD extension. AutoSave files are saved in the TEMP folder specified in your AUTOEXEC.BAT file. Normally, this is the \WINDOWS\TEMP folder. You can change the folder in which AutoSave files are saved by following these steps:

1. Choose Tools, Options and select the File Locations tab.

2. Select AutoSave Files from the File Types list and choose Modify. The Modify Location dialog box appears.

3. Specify the drive and folder where you want AutoSave files to be stored and choose OK. You also have the option of creating a new folder for your AutoSave files in the Modify Location dialog box.

4. Choose Close to close the Options dialog box.

Fig. 3.12
You can specify
several save
options in the
Save tab.

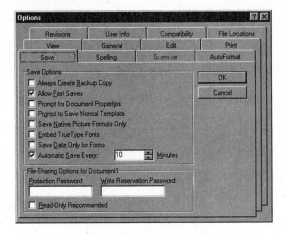

To turn on automatic saving, follow these steps:

1. Choose File, Save As, or press F12 and select Options, or choose Tools, Options and select the Save tab. The Save tab appears (see fig. 3.12).

2. Select the Automatic Save Every option.

3. Select or type the time interval, in minutes, between automatic saves in the Minutes spin box.

4. Choose OK.

As you are working in your document, Word periodically saves your document. A message in the status bar indicates that your file is being saved.

If a power failure or other problem causes Word to shut down while you are working on a document, and you have selected the automatic save option, you can recover everything that was entered up until the last automatic save. The next time you start Word for Windows, any files that were open when Word shut down will automatically be reopened. Any recovered file will be displayed in a window with (Recovered) next to the document name in the title bar.

Creating Automatic Backups

You can tell Word to create a backup copy of your document every time you save it. When you choose this option, Word saves the previous version of the document as a backup file and gives it the same file name as the original, but with the extension BAK.

To create a backup copy of your document, follow these steps:

1. Choose File, Save As, or press F12 and select Options, or choose Tools, Options and select the Save tab. The Save tab is displayed (refer to fig. 3.12).

2. Select the Always Create Backup Copy option.

3. Choose OK.

If you lose work because Word shuts down due to a power failure or some other problem, you can open the backup copy. You must save a file more than once before a backup copy is created. The backup copy is stored in the same folder as the original document.

Saving with Fast Save

You can speed up the process of saving a file by selecting the Allow Fast Saves option. With this option selected, Word for Windows saves faster because the program saves only the changes, not the entire document. Fast saves occur only with Save, not Save As. If you have selected the Always Create Backup Copy option (see previous section), you cannot use the fast save feature because backups can be made only with full saves.

To turn on the fast saves feature, follow these steps:

1. Choose File, Save As, or press F12 and select Options, or choose Tools, Options and select the Save tab. The Save tab is displayed (refer to fig. 3.12).

2. Select the Allow Fast Saves option.

3. Choose OK.

> **Note**
>
> When you select the Allow Fast Saves option to save time when saving files, the files you save take up more disk space than those created using a full save, because Word must keep the original file plus the changes. To free up disk space, choose File, Save As, choose the Options button, clear the Allow Fast Saves check box, and choose OK twice when you make your final save for the document. This will create a smaller file.

Saving for Other Word Processors or Applications

When you save a file in Word for Windows, by default the document is saved in Word for Windows format. Word for Windows, however, enables you to save your file in many formats. You may need to save a file into another format, such as WordPerfect format. At other times, you may need to save the file in Text (ASCII) format so that you can import the file into a different type of program.

To save your file in a non-Word for Windows format, follow these steps:

1. Choose File, Save As, or press F12.

2. In the File Name box, type the file name without an extension.

3. Select the file format from the Save as Type list box.

4. Choose OK to save your file.

Word for Windows assigns an appropriate extension to the file name.

Word for Windows displays only the types of files for which converters have been installed in the Save as Type list box. If the word processor you need doesn't appear, reinstall Word for Windows using the custom installation option. You will be given the chance to install converter files without reinstalling all of Word for Windows.

Saving a Document as a Protected File

If you share files or your PC with other users, you may want to prevent people from opening some files or modifying others. To prevent users from opening a file, you can assign a *protection password*. The next time you open the file, you must type the password. Another option is to assign a *write reservation password*, which allows anyone who knows the password to open the document and make and save changes to it. A user who does not know the password can open the file as a read-only document. They can read the document but cannot make and save changes to that document.

You can also assign the Read-Only Recommended option to a document. When a document with this option assigned is opened, a dialog box appears advising the user to open the document as a read-only document to which changes cannot be saved. However, the user does have the option of opening the document normally and saving changes to the document. For maximum protection, therefore, assign a password to the document.

You can also limit changes to a document to *annotations*, which are comments in a document that are viewed in a separate annotation pane and marked revisions, which can be incorporated into the document only by a user who knows the password. See Chapter 30, "Tracking Revisions and Annotations," for details on protecting a document with annotations and revisions.

If you have created a form in a Word for Windows document, you can protect the document against all changes except entries into the form fields. See Chapter 21, "Building Forms and Fill-In Dialog Boxes," for details on how to protect a form.

To assign a password to a document, follow these steps:

1. Choose File, Save As, or press F12 and select Options, or choose Tools, Options and select the Save tab to produce the Save dialog box.

2. To assign your file a password, select either the Protection Password or Write Reservation Password text box and type a password.

   As you type, you see only asterisks—no written record of your password exists anywhere. Your password can consist of as many as 15 characters, including letters, numbers, symbols, and spaces.

3. Choose OK. Reenter the password in the Confirm Password dialog box and choose OK.

4. Choose OK at the Save As dialog box to save the file.

> **Caution**
>
> When a file is password-protected, no one can open that file without the password—including you. Don't forget your password.

To change or delete a password, follow the same procedure, but delete the existing password (which still appears only as a string of asterisks) and type the new password (or not, if you want to remove the password).

To assign the Read-Only Recommended option to a document, follow these steps:

1. Choose File, Save As or press F12 and select Options, or choose Tools, Options and select the Save tab (refer to fig. 3.12).

2. Select the Read-Only Recommended option.

3. Choose OK.

▶ See "Protecting
and Saving the
Form," p. 647

▶ See "Protecting
Documents for
Annotations
Only," p. 914

Troubleshooting

*Periodically, Word saves the document I am working on. I find this annoying, because it
distracts me when I am entering text into the document.*

You need to turn off the AutoSave feature in Word. Choose Tools, Options, select the
Save tab, clear the Automatic Save Every option, and choose OK.

*I made some changes to a document and wanted to save the document with a new
name. When I clicked the Save button on the toolbar, the document was saved with the
same name and I lost my original document.*

To save a document with a new name, you must use File, Save As to open the Save
As dialog box, where you can enter a new name for the document. The Save button
on the Standard toolbar opens the Save As dialog box only the first time you save a
document. After that, it saves the document with the same file name you gave it
when you first saved it.

Closing a Document

After you finish working on a document and save the file, you may want to
close the document, especially if you have several documents open.

 To close a document, choose File, Close. If the document is in a window, you
can close it by clicking the Close button to the right of the title bar or by
double-clicking the Control icon at the top left corner of the document window. When a document is maximized to full screen, the Control icon appears
in the menu bar to the left of File. Be careful not to double-click the application Control icon in the top left corner of the Word window, or you will
close Word.

If you have made changes since you last saved, Word for Windows asks
whether you want to save your changes. Respond Yes to save them. (If you
haven't named the document, the Save As dialog box appears, and you must
name the file.) Respond No to discard changes. Choose Cancel to cancel the
close, or choose Help to access the Word for Windows Help window. ❖

Chapter 4

Managing Documents and Files

Although word processors undoubtedly offer a tremendous advantage over the typewriter for producing written documents, one fact remains: you accumulate Word files as fast as you gathered paper files before the advent of the word processor. Word for Windows 95, however, can help you to find and manage these files, using the options in the Open dialog box.

From the Open dialog box, you can sort the files in the list and preview any file without opening it in Word. Furthermore, you can view information about a file.

You can accomplish many other file-related tasks from the Open dialog box—open, print, copy, or delete the files. The capability to work with multiple files is a powerful feature and a great time-saver. Finally, you can search for files by file name, location, author, date, summary information, or contents.

In this chapter, you learn to do the following:

- View files and file information
- Manage files
- Find files

What You Need to Know about Managing Documents

The best way to keep track of files is to set up some type of folder structure and use this structure to organize your work. For example, you can set up one folder for your proposals, one for letters, and another for each project you are currently working on. Using this structure, you can place your work files in the appropriate folder.

After you have decided where to store your files, you still need to locate them when you need to work with them again. If you haven't worked with a document for a long time, you can easily forget its name or location when you want to reopen it. You can use the view features in the Open dialog box to display a document's contents, or find other information about a document.

If you can't find the file you want by browsing, you can use the Open dialog box's find features to search through the files on your computer. You can search by name, date, contents, or other criteria. When you execute a search, the matching files are listed in the Open dialog box. Then, in this list, you simply find and open the file you want. You can also use the find features to group similar files together, so that you can work on them all at the same time.

Viewing Documents and File Information

Even though a file has a descriptive file name, you may not be able to figure out what that file contains. If you are uncertain about a particular file, you can display additional information about it. For example, you can display a detailed view of the file, which lists the file size and date; these details might help you recognize the file. Or you can display a quick view of a document's contents. Finally, you can display a document's properties.

Viewing file information and previewing files can help you manage your documents. For example, you can preview a file before you open or print it, so that you know you are working with the right document. Or you can view file information to find out which is the most recent version of a document you have been working on.

The Open dialog box lists the files in the current folder. If you have performed a search (you learn how later in this chapter), the dialog box lists those files that match the criteria you entered. When you see the file you want in the list, you can select it to display information. To select the file, click the file name with the mouse, or press the Tab key until the *focus* (the dotted border) is in the list box. Then use the up- and down-arrow keys to select the file.

This section describes how to sort a list of files, preview a file, and view file information.

Changing the View in the Open Dialog Box

By default, files are listed by name in the Open dialog box. To change to a different view, use the buttons in the dialog box. You can select List, Details, Properties, or Preview. Figure 4.1 shows the list of files in Details view, which lists the file name as well as other information (the size of the file and the date it was last accessed.)

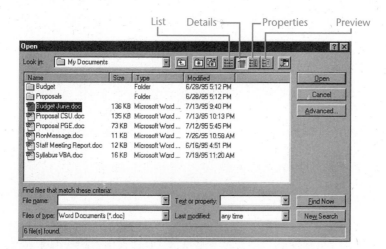

Fig. 4.1
Use the buttons in the Open dialog box to control how the files are listed.

Displaying a Quick View

Among the most useful features in the Open dialog box is the capability of previewing a document. When you search for files to work with, it is very helpful to view the contents of the files before opening them. In Word, there are two ways to view files from the Open dialog box without opening them. You can click the Preview button to see a miniature preview, or you can use the Quick View feature to open a window that shows a larger view of a file.

You can display a preview of the selected document by clicking the Preview button in the Open dialog box. Previewing is useful if you want to quickly examine a document to make sure you are opening the correct one. Preview only enables you to see the top or first page of the document. If you want to be able to scroll through a document to see other areas, you should use Quick View. Quick View is described later in this section.

When you click the Preview button, the right side of the Open dialog box becomes a display screen showing you the top of the document, as shown in figure 4.2. Notice that the file being previewed is a Word template. You can preview any document for which Word has an installed conversion filter.

Tip
Dialog boxes that are similar to Open, such as Insert Picture and Insert File, also contain a Preview button.

Everyday Word Processing

Fig. 4.2
Preview enables
you to quickly see
a document before
opening it.

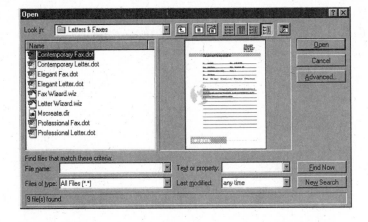

 If you want to see more of a document, scroll through its pages, or open a file belonging to another application; you will want to use Quick View to do this. Quick View is a program separate from Word, yet it can run from within Word's Open dialog box. Figure 4.3 shows a Quick View window being used to view the Excel file, FORECST02.XLS.

Fig. 4.3
Use Quick View
when you want to
scroll through the
file or open a file
from another
application.

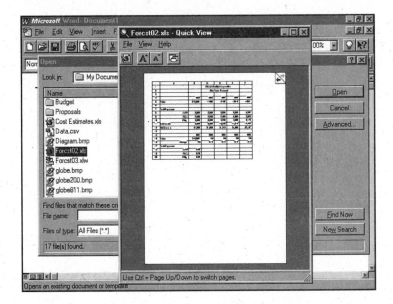

To display a quick view of a file, follow these steps:

1. In the Open dialog box, select the file you want to view.

2. Right-click the file name, and then choose Quick View. You see the contents of the document in a separate window (refer to fig. 4.3).

If the Quick View command is not visible on the shortcut menu, Windows 95 does not have the Quick View conversion filters necessary to view this file type.

You can view the document in two ways, full window or Page view. Page view is shown in figure 4.3. Change between full window and Page View by choosing View, Page View. To change pages while in Page view, click the corner tabs at the top right corner of the pages. While in full window view, change pages using the scroll bars. You also can pressing Page Up and Page Down to scroll through the document.

After reviewing the file, click the Close button to close the Quick View window. If, after previewing the document, you decide that you want to open the document for editing, you can. Either click the Open File for Editing button in the toolbar, or choose File, Open File for Editing.

Viewing File Properties

In the Open dialog box, you can use the Properties button to display a short list of some key document information (title, author, template, revision number, application, pages, words, characters, line, and paragraphs). You can display file properties for the selected file in the Open dialog box. You can view, for example, the summary information you entered, or other file information, such as statistical data about the file. In the Properties sheet, you can display different information by selecting the following tabs:

- *General tab.*   Displays the name, type, location, size, creation, modify, and access dates, and the file attributes (see fig. 4.4).

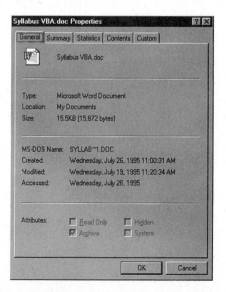

Fig. 4.4
Use the General tab to display general information about the selected file.

■ *Summary tab.* Displays the Summary information, including title, author name, subject, keywords, and comments you enter in the Properties sheet.

■ *Statistics tab.* Displays statistics about the file (see fig. 4.5).

Fig. 4.5
Use the Statistics tab to display the file statistics page.

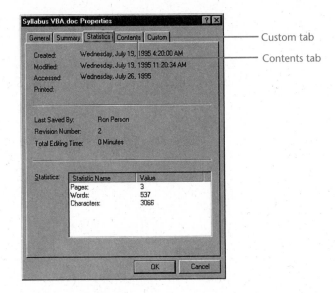

Custom tab

Contents tab

◄ See "Saving Documents with Descriptions to Make Documents Easier to Find," p. 96

To view file properties, follow these steps:

1. In the Open dialog box, select the file you want to view.

2. Right-click the file, then select Properties from the menu that appears. Or click the Commands and Settings button, then select Properties.

3. In the Properties sheet, select the tab you want to display. When you finish viewing the information, choose OK.

Editing and Adding File Properties

If you didn't add summary information to a document when you created or saved it (refer to Chapter 3, "Creating and Saving Documents"), or if you want to edit the summary information for a file, you can do so from the Open dialog box.

To edit or add summary information, follow these steps:

1. In the Open dialog box, select the file that you want to work with.

2. Right-click the file, and then select Properties from the menu that appears. Or click the Commands and Settings button and then select Properties.

3. Select the Summary tab, and then fill in or edit any of the text boxes. Include as much information (up to 255 characters in each text box) or as little as you want.

4. Choose OK.

Sorting File Lists

If the list of files in a folder is long, you may want to sort the files in the list. You can sort by file name, size, file type, or date last modified.

To sort a list of files, follow these steps:

1. In the Open dialog box, click the Commands and Settings button.

2. From the menu that appears, choose Sorting. The Sort By dialog box appears (see fig. 4.6).

3. In the Sort Files By drop-down list, select one of the following sorting options:

Option	How Files Are Listed
File Name	Alphabetically by file name
Size	Numerically by file size
Files of Type	Alphabetically by file type
Last Modified	Chronologically by the date files are saved (most recent date first)

4. Select a sort order: Ascending or Descending.

5. Choose OK.

The files in all folders in the Open dialog box are sorted.

Tip

If you have already opened a document, you can view and edit properties by choosing File, Properties.

Fig. 4.6
In the Sort By dialog box, you can select how you want to sort and list files.

◄ See "Opening a Document," p. 80

◄ See "Saving Documents with Descriptions to Make Documents Easier to Find," p. 96

I

Everyday Word Processing

Managing Files

You can accomplish many tasks with the files listed in the Open dialog box. You can open, print, copy, or delete a file or a group of selected files—all from this dialog box. Being able to select more than one file at a time from the list is a tremendous time-saver. For example, if you want to print several files at once, you can select them and issue one print command. This approach is much simpler and quicker than opening each file, one by one from within Word, and printing them separately. You can use the same approach to copy or delete groups of files. Being able to do something to several files simultaneously, as well as being able to preview the contents of a file without having to open it, makes the process of managing your files much smoother and easier.

Displaying and Selecting Files for File Management

Before you issue various commands to manage your files, you need to display the file or files you want to work with. If the files are in the same folder, you can simply change to that folder. If the files are in different folders, you can use a search to group the files together. Searching for files is covered later in this chapter in "Searching for Files."

When the files are displayed, you can select one or more of the files with which you want to work. To select a file with the mouse, click the name of the file you want, or press and hold down the Ctrl key while you click multiple file names (see fig. 4.7). If you want to select several sequential files, press and hold down the Shift key while you click the first and last file you want. Press and hold down the Ctrl key and click a second time to deselect any file you select by mistake.

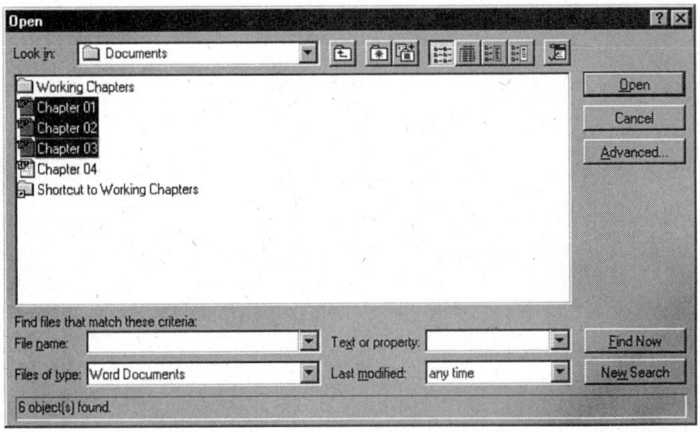

Fig. 4.7
You can select multiple files in the file list.

To select a file with the keyboard, press the Tab key until the focus (the dotted border) is in the file list box. Then use the up- or down-arrow key to move to the file you want to select. To select multiple files that are not contiguous, hold down the Ctrl key, use the arrow keys to move to the file you want to select, and press the space bar. To select multiple contiguous files, press the up- or down-arrow key to select the first file. Next, press and hold down the Shift key while you press the up- or down-arrow key to extend the selection.

Printing Files

You can choose File, Print to print the open document. If you want to print several documents with the same printing parameters simultaneously, however, use the Open dialog box. If all the files you want to print are in the same folder, you can simply display that folder. If the files are in different folders, you can use a search criterion to find and group the files you want to print.

▶ See "Controlling Printing Options," p. 244

To print documents from the Open dialog box, follow these steps:

1. Select one or more files you want to print.

2. Click the Commands and Settings button, and then choose Print from the submenu. You also can right-click the selected files and choose Print.

3. In the Print dialog box, choose OK.

Word opens the files, prints them, and then closes them. For more information about printing, see Chapter 8, "Previewing and Printing a Document."

Copying or Moving Files

You can use the Open dialog box to copy selected files from one location to another. Similarly, you can use this dialog box to move files.

To copy files, follow these steps:

1. In the Open dialog box, select one or more files you want to copy.

2. Right-click the files, and then choose Copy in the shortcut menu that appears.

3. Use the Look In drop-down list to select the drive or folder where you want to place the copy.

4. Right-click the drive or folder, and then choose Paste.

Files, with their original name and extension, are copied to a new location.

If you want to copy files to a floppy disk, you can use the Se_n_d To command. Select the files to copy, and then right-click one of the files. From the shortcut menu that appears, choose Send To, and then select the disk drive.

The process of moving a file from one folder to another or one drive to another is similar to that of copying a file. To move files, follow these steps:

1. In the Open dialog box, select one or more files you want to move.

2. Right-click the files, and then choose Cut from the shortcut menu.

3. In the Look _I_n drop-down list, select the drive or folder where you want to move the file.

4. Right-click the file list box, and then choose _P_aste.

Deleting Files

You can also delete files you no longer need. In Windows 95, when you delete a file, that file is moved to the Recycle Bin—a holding spot for deleted files. If you make a mistake, you can open the Recycle Bin and retrieve the files you've deleted. You can also choose to empty the Recycle Bin when you want to permanently get rid of the files.

The following steps show you how to delete files:

1. In the Open dialog box, select the files you want to delete.

2. Right-click the selected file(s) and choose _D_elete. A dialog box asks you to confirm the move to the Recycle Bin.

3. Choose _Y_es to delete the files; choose _N_o if you don't want to erase them.

If you accidentally delete a file, you can retrieve it from the Recycle Bin: on the desktop, double-click the Recycle Bin, select the files you want to undelete, and choose _F_ile, _R_estore.

◀ See "Working with Multiple Documents," p. 90

> **Note**
>
> You cannot delete an open file, nor can you delete a file from which you cut or copied text during the current work session.

Searching for Files

If you can't find the file you want after browsing through the drives and folders, you can click the Find Now button in the Open dialog box. Word offers powerful search capabilities that enable you to search for files by file name, location, author, and the date the files were created or last saved. Alternatively, you can use the information you entered in the Properties dialog box. You also can search for specific text that occurs in a document.

With the Find Now button, you can bring together a list of related files or find a specific file. The search can be narrow; for example, you can look for a particular file with a familiar file name. You also can search for a group of files that match whatever criteria you specify. The more you narrow the search, the fewer the files you will find.

Using Search Options in the Open Dialog Box

The bottom half of the Open dialog box contains text boxes in which you enter common search criteria. For example, you can use these text boxes to search for a file name, last modified date, file type, or text or property. You can also combine these options—for example, search for all files that start with B that were modified last week. If these options don't help you locate the file you want, you can build more complex search criteria by clicking the Advanced button. These search options are covered in the rest of this section.

After Word finds files that match the criteria you specified, it displays a list of their names in the Open dialog box. You can preview any file to make sure that it is the one you want, and then open, print, copy, or delete the file. To act on several files at once, you can select them first and then issue one of the commands that act on these files. You can select a group of files, for example, and then copy them to a disk to back them up, or print several files at once without opening the files in Word.

◄ See "Understanding File Names," p. 76

◄ See "Understanding Folders," p. 77

Searching for a File by Name

You can search for a file by name if you know its name (or at least a partial name). Follow these steps:

1. In the Open dialog box, enter the name (or partial name) of the file in the File name text box. You can use the ***** and **?** wild cards. An asterisk (*) represents any string of characters; to search for all files that start with CH, for example, simply type **CH***. A question mark (?) represents any one character; you can search for **CHAP?.DOC** to find all files named CHAP1.DOC, CHAP2.DOC, CHAP3.DOC, and so on.

Everyday Word Processing

2. Change to the drive that you want to search using the Look In drop-down list. Select the folder by double-clicking it in the file list. If you want to search the subfolders in the selected folder, click the Commands and Settings button and then choose Search Subfolders from the menu that appears. There should be a check mark next to this command for it to be activated. Selecting the command again turns off the check mark and the feature.

3. Click the Find Now button in the dialog box. Word searches the current folder, displays the names of any matching files, and indicates the number of objects found, at the bottom of the dialog box, figure 4.8 shows a list of all files that start with C.

Fig. 4.8
You can see the results of a search for all files that start with C.

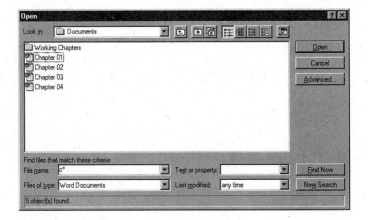

If you didn't find the files you want with this search, you can clear the search results by clicking the New Search button. Then you can start again. To cancel a search in progress, click the Stop button which appears in place of the Find Now button.

For instructions on how to view file information and preview the files in the list, refer to "Viewing Documents and File Information" earlier in this chapter.

Searching for Specific Files or Different File Types

By default, Word searches for Word files in the current folder, but you can search also for a specific file or different types of files. If the files are compatible with Word, you can open or print them; you can copy or delete the files you find, even if they are not compatible with Word.

To search for different file types, take these steps:

1. In the File Name text box of the Open dialog box, type the name of the file for which you want to search. If you just want to list all files of a certain type, leave the file name blank.

2. Display the Files of Type list, and select the type of file for which you want to search.

Searching by Date Modified

You can search for files based on the date you last modified the file. This feature is convenient, especially when used with other search criteria (covered in later sections). You can search for files created last week, for example, that contain the words *bank* and *letter.*

To search for files by date modified, follow these steps:

1. In the Open dialog box, enter a full or partial file name. You can also leave the file name blank to search for all files in a certain range of dates.

2. Display the Last Modified drop-down list, and select the time interval: Yesterday, Today, Last Week, This Week, Last Month, This Month, or Any Time (the default).

Searching by File Properties or Text in the File

One of the greatest advantages to including summary information in all Word files is that you can search for files by text contained in any of the summary information fields. You can add a title to a document, for example, and then use it to search through files.

To search by text or properties, follow these steps:

1. In the File Name text box of the Open dialog box, enter a full or partial file name (optional). You can also leave the file name blank to search for all files with certain text or properties.

2. In the Text or Property text box, enter the text you want to search for.

Using Advanced Search Options

By clicking the Advanced button, you can narrow the list of files you are searching for. You do this by specifying additional criteria, such as the file creation or save date, author name, summary information, or specific text strings (such as a word or phrase).

◄ See "Saving Documents with Descriptions to Make Documents Easier to Find," p. 96

Tip
Try to think of a unique word or phrase so that you limit your search. If you use a common word or phrase, the search takes longer, and the search results will include too many files.

Everyday Word Processing

◄ See "Saving
Documents
with Descrip-
tions to Make
Documents
Easier to Find,"
p. 96

You can create one or more search criteria. For example, you can tell Word to find all files that contain the words *health insurance,* created by the author *Smith*. When you select A<u>n</u>d, Word must match all the criteria you enter. When you select O<u>r</u>, Word can match either set of search instructions.

When you create a set of search instructions, you enter two to three parts to build the criteria. First, you select the property you want to search. You can select from many different properties including application name, author, category, company, keyword, last printed date, contents, and more.

Second, you select the condition to match. Depending on the property, the conditions will vary. For example, if you select the last printed date, you can select these conditions: yesterday, today, last week, this week, last month, this month, any time, anytime between, on, on or before, on or after, in the last.

Finally, for some conditions, you enter the value. For example, if you want to find all files printed yesterday, you don't have to enter a value. On the other hand, if you want to find all files printed on a certain date, you need to enter the date in the Values text box.

Here are some additional examples of different search instructions:

```
Author=begins w K
```

This example would list all files that have authors with a name that starts with K.

```
Contents includes phrase book proposal
```

This example would list all files that contained the phrase book proposal.

```
Number of words more than 1,200
```

This example would list all files that contained more than 1,200 words.

Follow these steps to create a set of search instructions:

1. In the Open dialog box, click the <u>A</u>dvanced button. You see the Advanced Find dialog box (see fig. 4.9).

2. To select which folders are searched, display the Look <u>I</u>n drop-down list and select the drive. You can also type the path to search directly in this text box. To include subfolders in the search, select the Searc<u>h</u> subfolders check box.

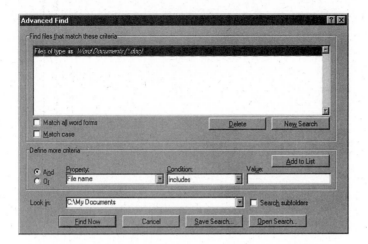

Everyday Word Processing

Fig. 4.9
Use the Advanced
Find dialog box to
further narrow
your search.

3. Select the type of criteria: And or Or.

4. Display the Property drop-down list, and select the property you want
to match.

5. Display the Condition drop-down list, and select how you want to
make the match.

6. Enter the value to match in the Value text box.

7. To add this set of search instructions to the list, click the Add to List
button.

8. Follow steps 3–7 to build the next set of instructions.

9. Select Match Case to match upper- and lowercase exactly. To match
word variations, select Match All Word Forms.

10. When you finish all your search criteria, click the Find Now button.

You can continue to add the criteria you want until the list is complete. The
more narrow the criteria, the fewer the files found. If you want to delete a
criterion, you can do so by selecting it and then clicking the Delete button.
To clear all the criteria, click the New Search button.

Some combinations of criteria won't work. In this case, you'll see an error
message. Review the message and then make the appropriate change. For
example, you cannot search for files that start with both B and C because that
search criteria doesn't make sense.

Saving Search Criteria

If you have entered a set of search criteria and want to reuse it for future searches, you can save the criteria with a name. When you want to reuse the criteria, you select the named set of criteria and then initiate a new search.

To save search criteria, follow these steps:

1. Set up the search criteria you want, as outlined in the preceding sections.

2. Click the Save Search button in the Advanced Find dialog box. The Save Search dialog box appears (see fig. 4.10).

Fig. 4.10

You can name a set of search criteria, save it, and reuse it.

3. In the Name for this Search text box, type a name for the search criteria.

4. Choose OK.

5. To start a search with these criteria, click Find Now.

To reuse saved search criteria, follow these steps:

1. In the Advanced Find dialog box, choose Open Search.

2. From the list that appears, select the search you want to execute.

3. Choose Open.

4. Choose Find Now.

Troubleshooting

I tried a search and didn't find the file I wanted. Now the file list is blank.

If you perform a search and no matching files were found, the file list is blank. To redisplay all the files that were listed before the search, clear the search instructions by clicking the New Search button.

I tried a search and didn't find the file I wanted. I'm sure the search should work.

Keep in mind that you can combine criteria. Be sure that you have entered only the criteria you want to use. For example, suppose that you started by searching for a file by name and entered a file name. When you didn't find the file, you tried searching by date. You still can't find the file. Remember that both the name and date criteria will be used if they are both entered. You may need to clear—in this example—the file name criteria and use just the date.

When I choose File, Open, I don't see all my files listed.

Keep in mind that Word remembers the last set of properties you entered. For example, if you selected to display a different file type using the Files of Type list box, the next time you use the Open command, that file type will still be listed. Change the options back to what you want displayed.

I

Everyday Word Processing

Chapter 5

Editing a Document

As you begin working with Word for Windows, start by gaining a solid under-standing of the basics. For example, several different options exist for viewing your document: you can work very fast in Normal mode, or you can slow down and zoom in to do detailed work by choosing the Page Layout view and enlarging it up to 200 percent. You can move around in your document in many ways, using the mouse and keyboard techniques. You should under-stand one of the most important principles in working with Word for Win-dows: *Select, then do*. You can move and copy text and objects from one part of your document to another, from one document to another, or even from one application to another.

In this chapter you learn the important features that will help you edit a document. There are also many editing shortcuts throughout the chapter. In this chapter, you learn how to:

- Control document windows and the display

- Select, edit, and delete text

- Insert frequently used text

- Check spelling and hyphenation

- Move and copy text and graphics

Controlling Your Document's Appearance On-Screen

In Word for Windows, you can display your document in the way that best fits what you need to do. As you work, you can use Normal view to see the body text as it will print, use Outline view for outline expansion or

▶ See "Working
with the Master
Document,"
p. 945

▶ See "Preview-
ing Pages be-
fore Printing,"
p. 234

contraction, and use Page Layout view to see the entire page exactly as it will print, including columns, headers, footers, and page numbers. You can use Master Document view to ease the creation and reorganization of long documents. Full Screen view can be set to display only your document text, excluding all other screen elements. In all these views you can type, format, and edit. (A sixth view in File, Print Preview shows thumbnail pictures of how pages will print, but you cannot edit in this view.) The sections that follow describe the various Word for Windows views.

You also can add or remove screen elements, such as scroll bars and the status bar, in these views. Screen elements are controlled by selections you make by choosing Tools, Options (see the section "Modifying the Screen Display" later in this chapter).

Figure 5.1 shows the screen modified to provide access to the menu bar and a maximum of typing space.

Fig. 5.1
The Word for Windows screen has been modified to display the menu bar and a maximum of typing space.

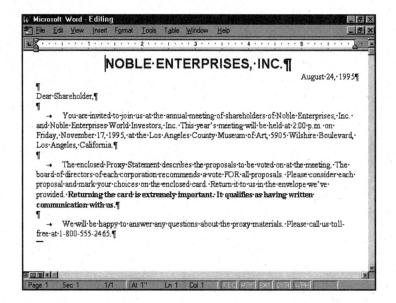

Selecting the Correct View for Your Work

The work you do will help you choose the best screen view. If you are a production typist, you may desire as much on-screen typing space as possible. If, on the other hand, you are desktop publishing and constantly using various Word for Windows tools, it might help to work in Page Layout view and to have certain tools easily accessible at all times. For example, you can choose the Drawing toolbar to display the Microsoft Draw tools on-screen. You can customize the view of your document as you change tasks.

Figure 5.2 shows one type of view you can choose in Word—Master Document view.

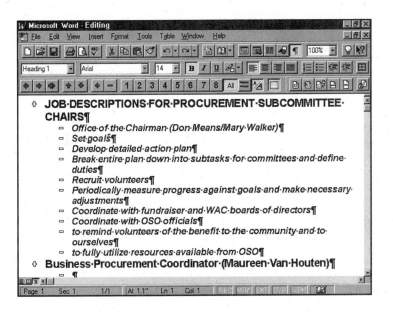

Fig. 5.2
Master Document view is used to assemble a long document from several shorter ones.

There are three ways that you can change the view:

■ Menu commands

■ Shortcut keys

■ View buttons that are found to the left of the horizontal scroll bar

If you are editing a master document and you use either the shortcut keys or the view buttons to select Outline view, Word for Windows automatically places the document in Master Document view.

To change the view using menu commands, follow these steps:

1. Choose View. Notice that the currently selected view is marked with a bullet.

2. Choose the view you want: Normal, Outline, Page Layout, Master Document, or Full Screen.

To change the view, you can use the following shortcut keys or view buttons located on the horizontal scroll bar:

Shortcut Key	Button	View
Alt+Ctrl+N		Normal view
Alt+Ctrl+P		Page Layout view
Alt+Ctrl+O		Outline view

Editing in Normal View

Use Normal view, shown in figure 5.3, for most of your typing and editing. In this view, which is the Word for Windows default view, you see character and paragraph formatting as they print. Line and page breaks, tab stops, and alignments are accurate. The area outside the text body—the area containing headers, footers, footnotes, page numbers, margin spacing, and so on—does not appear. You also cannot see the exact placement of such features as snaking columns, positioned paragraphs, or text wrapping around fixed paragraphs or objects.

Fig. 5.3
Normal view is used for basic typing and editing.

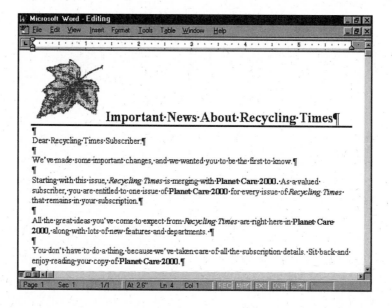

To display Normal view, choose View, Normal, or press Alt+Ctrl+N. The selected option appears with a bullet to the left of the option.

Editing in Full Screen View

Use Full Screen view when you want to maximize the typing area. Full Screen view is comparable to Normal view in its display of character and paragraph formatting, line and page breaks, tab stops, and alignments. However, the title bar, menu bar, all toolbars, the scroll bars, and the status bar are all removed from the screen in Full Screen view. The ruler remains. A special toolbar containing only the Full button appears at the bottom of the screen to indicate that Full Screen view is currently displayed. Figure 5.4 shows a document in Full Screen view with the Full Screen toolbar displayed.

◀ See "Displaying or Hiding Toolbars," p. 55

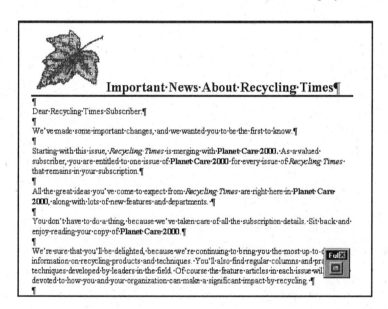

Fig. 5.4
You can use Full Screen view to maximize typing space.

To display Full Screen view, choose <u>V</u>iew, F<u>u</u>ll Screen. To return to the previous view, click the Full button or press Esc.

When you exit Full Screen view, you return to the previous view. For example, suppose that you are typing in Page Layout view and switch to Full Screen view. When you click the Full button or press Esc, you return to Page Layout view.

You can move the Full Screen toolbar to a new location on-screen. To move the Full Screen toolbar in Full Screen view, position the mouse pointer in the title bar of the Full Screen toolbar, then drag it to a new location. After you position the Full Screen toolbar where you want it, release the mouse button.

To close the Full Screen toolbar, place a mark in the check box. To redisplay the Full Screen toolbar, press Alt+V and choose View, Toolbars while you are in Full Screen view. Finally, select the Full Screen toolbar check box and choose OK.

If you don't want the Full Screen toolbar to appear as a floating window over your document, double-click its title bar. The button immediately moves to the top of the screen and becomes a full-screen width toolbar.

Editing in Page Layout View

In Page Layout view, your document shows each page as it will appear when printed. You can scroll outside the body copy area of the page to see such items as headers, footers, footnotes, page numbers, and margin spacing. Snaking columns and text that wraps around fixed-position objects appear as they will print. Although you can see exactly how the page will print, you still can type and make formatting changes.

 To change to Page Layout view, choose View, Page Layout, or press Alt+Ctrl+P.

► See "Setting Margins," p. 400

Figure 5.5 shows a document in Page Layout view. Notice the vertical ruler along the left side of the screen. You can use it to change the top and bottom margins of the document.

Fig. 5.5
Page Layout view shows how your page will appear in print.

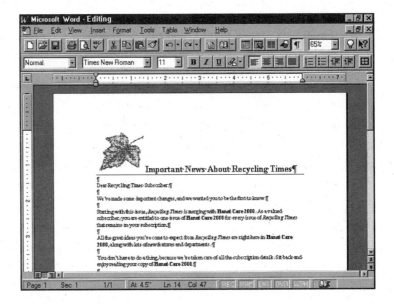

Zooming In or Out

You can choose <u>V</u>iew, <u>Z</u>oom to further hone your screen view.

To see more of your document, follow these steps:

1. Choose <u>V</u>iew, <u>Z</u>oom.

2. When the Zoom dialog box shown in figure 5.6 appears, select the desired magnification.

   The lower the magnification, the more you will see of your document on-screen.

3. Click OK.

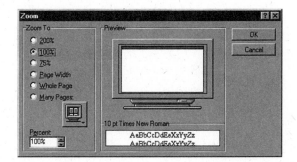

Fig. 5.6
The Zoom dialog box allows you to zoom in or out of your document.

Everyday Word Processing

To change the screen magnification from the toolbar, you have two options:

- Click the Zoom button's down arrow (this is the button beside the Per-cent box near the right side of the toolbar). Then select the preset percentage or document size.

- Select the Zoom button's edit box, type a new percentage between 10 percent and 200 percent, and then press Enter.

Naturally, you can zoom in for a closer look by selecting <u>2</u>00% magnification. This could be useful if you work with small font sizes or if you need to precisely align objects while doing desktop publishing. If none of the preset magnification options (<u>2</u>00%, <u>1</u>00%, and <u>7</u>5%) meets your needs, you can enter your desired magnification in the P<u>e</u>rcent box. You can select within the range of 10 percent to 200 percent.

If you are working with your document in Page Layout view, you can use the Zoom feature to see the entire page at the same time, or to view several pages at once.

To see the entire page at once, follow these steps:

1. Choose View, Page Layout if you are not already in Page Layout view.

2. Choose View, Zoom.

3. Select Whole Page.

4. Choose OK.

One screen is equal to one printed page. Figure 5.7 shows a page zoomed to Whole Page in Page Layout view. Whole Page view is available only in Page Layout view.

Fig. 5.7
An entire page is displayed with the Whole Page zoom option.

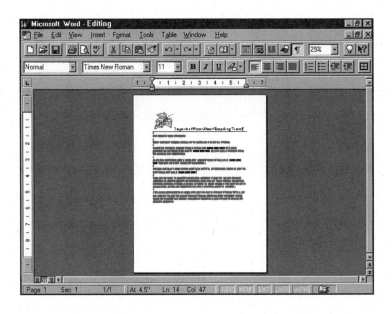

Tip
You can also change the number of displayed pages by increasing or decreasing the value in the Percent box in the Zoom dialog box.

Use Many Pages in Page Layout view to see and edit the layout of a group of pages.

To see more than one page at a time, follow these steps:

1. Choose View, Page Layout, if you are not already in Page Layout view.

2. Choose View, Zoom.

3. Select the Many Pages option.

4. Click the monitor button. A grid appears (see fig. 5.8).

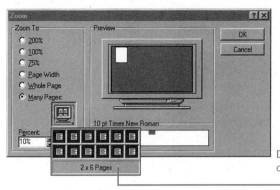

Fig. 5.8
The Many Pages zoom option allows you to see the layout of several pages.

Drag your pointer to the number of pages you want to see at a time

5. Drag across the grid to indicate how many pages you want displayed.

6. Click OK.

Editing in Outline View

In Outline view, your document shows the levels of outline structure. The Outline bar appears at the top of the screen, enabling you to promote and demote outline topic levels (see fig. 5.9).

▶ See "Promoting and Demoting Headings," p. 577

To change to Outline view, choose View, Outline, or press Alt+Ctrl+O.

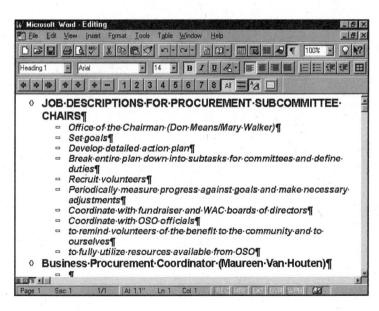

Fig. 5.9
Outline view shows topic levels of an outline or entire document.

The horizontal scroll bar at the bottom of the screen includes three buttons for changing the view. You can choose the first to switch to Normal view, the second to switch to Page Layout view, and the third to switch to Outline view.

Modifying the Screen Display

By choosing Tools, Options, you can further modify the display to fit your preferences. You can, for example, request that tab and paragraph marks be displayed as special characters, margins be displayed as dotted lines, or horizontal and vertical scroll bars be displayed. The Options dialog box presents each option on an index tab that is pulled to the front when you click its name or index tab. The View tab contains options that change the appearance of the screen.

To change your screen's appearance, follow these steps:

1. Choose Tools, Options. The Options dialog box appears, as shown in figure 5.10.

2. Select the View tab.

3. Select the appropriate options (see table 5.1).

4. Click OK.

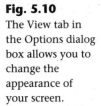

Fig. 5.10

The View tab in the Options dialog box allows you to change the appearance of your screen.

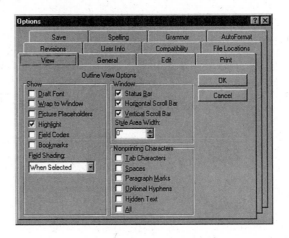

Table 5.1   View Options in the Options Dialog Box

Option	Function
Show Group	
Draft Font	Displays the document without formatting or graphics, to speed up editing
Wrap to Window	Displays the document with line breaks to fit the current window width
Picture Placeholders	Displays placeholders instead of the full pictures or graphics on-screen to speed up editing
Highlight	Displays highlighted text
Field Codes	Displays field code type and switches (if there are any in the field braces)
Bookmarks	Displays a thick I-beam symbol in the position of each bookmark
Field Shading	Shades fields never, always, or when selected
Window Group	
Status Bar	Displays the status bar
Horizontal Scroll Bar	Displays the horizontal scroll bar
Vertical Scroll Bar	Displays vertical scroll bar
Style Area Width	Controls the width for the area by the left margin where the style name is displayed. (If the width is too narrow, the name is cut off.)
Nonprinting Characters Group	
Tab Characters	Displays tabs as right arrows
Spaces	Displays spaces as dots
Paragraph Marks	Displays paragraph marks as ¶
Optional Hyphens	Displays optional hyphens as _
Hidden Text	Varies, depending on the particular type of hidden text
All	Displays all marks, including text boundaries

Figures 5.11 and 5.12 show two screens of the same document in Page Layout view. Each screen has different options selected in the View tab of the Options screen. The screen displays were modified by choosing Tools, Options.

Fig. 5.11
A screen displaying scroll bars but no status bars.

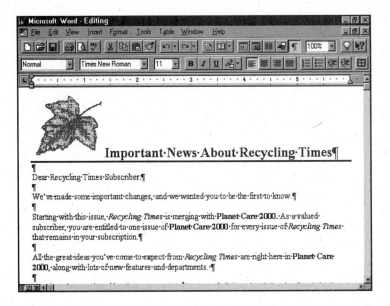

 To quickly show all special formatting marks, click the ¶ button on the Standard toolbar or press Shift+Ctrl+* (Show All). To remove the marks, click the ¶ button again or press Shift+Ctrl+* again.

Fig. 5.12
A screen with the scroll bars and status bars hidden.

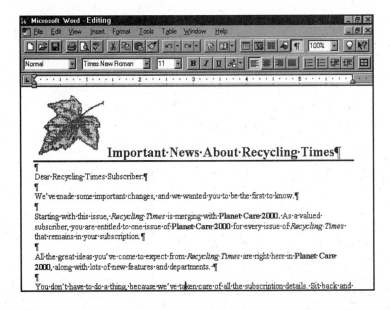

Moving in the Document

If you're familiar with word processing, you will learn to move efficiently through a Word for Windows document in no time at all. But don't stop trying to learn more, because Word for Windows provides a number of unique methods to cut your visual search time to the absolute minimum.

Moving and Scrolling with the Mouse

To relocate the insertion point by using the mouse, scroll so that you can see the location you want, and then click the I-beam pointer at the character location where you want the insertion point.

Using your mouse pointer in the horizontal and vertical scroll bars enables you to scroll the document easily so that a new area is displayed. Figure 5.13 shows the parts of the scroll bars, which include the scroll box and page view buttons. The scroll box shows the screen's location relative to the entire document's length and width. Page Layout view displays page buttons at the bottom of the vertical scroll bar, which you can click to turn a page. The horizontal scroll bar includes three buttons for changing the view.

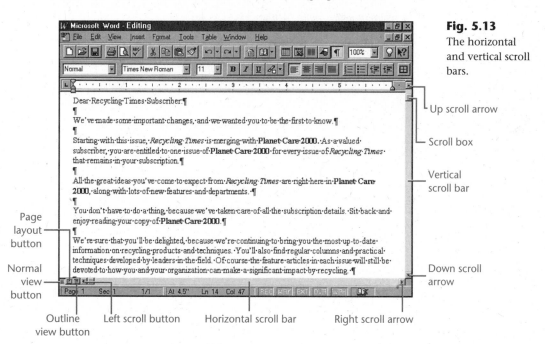

Fig. 5.13
The horizontal and vertical scroll bars.

If you use a mouse, display the horizontal and vertical scroll bars so that you can scroll with the mouse. As you drag the scroll box down the vertical scroll bar, the page number will show to the side of the scroll bar. If you use the keyboard, turn off the horizontal and vertical scroll bars to have more room on the typing screen.

Table 5.2 lists the scrolling methods you can use with the mouse and the scroll bars.

Table 5.2 Scrolling Methods for the Mouse and Scroll Bars	
To Move	**Click**
One line	Up or down scroll arrow
One screen up or down	Gray area above or below the scroll box in the vertical scroll bar
One page	Page buttons (in Page Layout view)
Large vertical moves	Drag vertical scroll box to a new location.
Horizontally in small increments	Right or left scroll arrow
Horizontally in relative increments	Drag horizontal scroll box to a new location in the horizontal scroll bar.
Into left margin	Left scroll arrow while holding Shift (Normal view); left scroll arrow (Page Layout view)

Don't forget to click the I-beam at the new typing location after the text you want to edit scrolls into sight. If you scroll to a new location and leave the insertion point at the old location, your typing or editing appears at the old location.

Moving and Scrolling with the Keyboard

The arrow keys (↑, ↓, ←, and →) and cursor-movement keys (Page Up, Page Down, Home, and End) move the insertion point as you would expect. Combine these keys with the Ctrl key, however, and they become powerful editing allies. Table 5.3 shows cursor movements you can make with the keyboard.

Table 5.3 Moving and Scrolling with the Keyboard

To Move	Press
One character left	← key
One character right	→ key
One line up	↑ key
One line down	↓ key
One word to the left	Ctrl+←
One word to the right	Ctrl+→
To the end of a line	End
To the beginning of a line	Home
One paragraph up	Ctrl+↑
One paragraph down	Ctrl+↓
Up one window	Page Up key
Down one window	Page Down key
To bottom of window	Ctrl+Page Down
To top of window	Ctrl+Page Up
To end of document	Ctrl+End
To beginning of document	Ctrl+Home

Going to a Specific Page

When you need to move to a specific page number, choose Edit, Go To. This command works with page numbers only when the document has been paginated. (You can also use Go To to move to specific sections, lines, bookmarks, annotations, footnotes, endnotes, fields, tables, graphics, equations, or objects. Creating bookmarks is covered later in this chapter. You can read about going to other locations in your document in the section, "Moving the Insertion Point a Relative Distance.")

To move to a specific page, follow these steps:

1. Choose <u>E</u>dit, <u>G</u>o To, or press F5. The Go To dialog box, shown in figure 5.14, appears. (Your dialog box may appear with another option selected.)

2. Click Page in the Go to <u>W</u>hat box, if it is not already selected.

3. Type a page number in the <u>E</u>nter Page Number text box.

4. Choose Go <u>T</u>o.

Fig. 5.14
The Go To dialog box allows you to move to a specific page in your document.

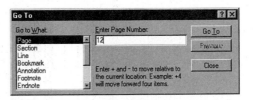

Going to a Bookmark

Bookmarks are locations in a document or sections of a document to which you assign a name. If you are familiar with Microsoft Excel or Lotus 1-2-3, bookmarks are similar to range names.

To go to a bookmark, follow these steps:

1. Choose <u>E</u>dit, <u>G</u>o To, or press F5. The Go To dialog box shown in figure 5.14 appears.

2. Select Bookmark in the Go to <u>W</u>hat box. The edit box to the right of the Go to <u>W</u>hat box becomes <u>E</u>nter Bookmark Name.

3. Type the name of the bookmark or click the down arrow to the right of the <u>E</u>nter Bookmark Name box to see a list of bookmarks and select one of the bookmarks.

4. Click Go <u>T</u>o.

Refer to the section, "Creating Bookmarks," later in this chapter to find out how to create bookmarks.

Moving the Insertion Point a Relative Distance

You can move a specified distance relative to the insertion point's current location by choosing Edit, Go To. The move can be in increments of pages, lines, sections, footnotes, annotations, fields, tables, graphics, equations, or objects. You even can move to a location that is a certain percentage of the way through the total document. The Next and Previous options move the insertion point to the next or previous item you select.

To move a relative distance, follow these steps:

1. Choose Edit, Go To, or press F5 to display the Go To dialog box.

2. Choose one of the options listed in Go to What box.

3. Enter the number or other identifier you want to go to. You can also click the Next or Previous button. (These buttons appear when appropriate.) Or, as a third option, you can enter a percentage that represents the distance you would like to move through the document.

4. Choose Go To.

5. Click Close or press Esc.

Sections, footnotes, annotations, tables, graphics, and equations are numbered from the beginning of the document. To move through these items, select the item in the Go To dialog box, then enter the number of the item you want to move to. You can use a plus sign (+) to indicate a relative number forward in the document or a minus sign (–) to indicate a relative number backward in the document. For example, 9 is the ninth footnote in the document, but +9 is the ninth footnote forward from the current position.

Table 5.4 shows how to move the insertion point to a particular location.

Table 5.4   Moving to a Relative Location

To Move Insertion Point	Type or Select
To page n	n
Forward n pages	$+n$
Backward n pages	$-n$
To section n	n

(continues)

Everyday Word Processing

Table 5.4 Continued

To Move Insertion Point	Type or Select
Forward *n* sections	+*n*
Backward *n* sections	-*n*
To line *n*	*n*
Forward *n* lines	+*n*
Backward *n* lines	-*n*
To bookmark	The name of the bookmark
To annotate	The reviewer's name, then choose Next or Previous
To footnote *n*	*n*
Forward *n* footnotes	+*n*
Backward *n* footnotes	-*n*
To a field	The field name
To table *n*	*n*
Forward *n* tables	+*n*
Backward *n* tables	-*n*
To graphic *n*	*n*
Forward *n* graphics	+*n*
Backward *n* graphics	-*n*
To equation *n*	*n*
Forward *n* equations	+*n*
Backward *n* equations	-*n*
To an object	The object name
n percent through document	*n*%

n *is the number of units (pages, lines, sections, footnotes, annotations, tables, graphics, equations) you want to move forward or backward from the current location.*

Combine move codes and their relative numbers to move to the exact location you want. When Page is selected in the Go To <u>W</u>hat list, the following code, for example, moves the insertion point to the 12th line on page 15 in the third section:

```
s3p15l12
```

Moving to Previous Locations

To return the insertion point to the last three locations where an action occurred, press Shift+F5. Each of the first three presses moves the insertion point to the immediately preceding place of action. Pressing a fourth time returns the insertion point to the starting location.

Pressing Shift+F5 after opening a document returns the insertion point to its location when you last saved the document.

Selecting Text

Word for Windows uses the principle common to all good Windows software—select, then do. Whether you want to delete a word, format a phrase, or move a sentence, you must select what you want to change before choosing the command. As with other commands and features, you can use the mouse or the keyboard to select text. Many shortcuts and tips also are available for selecting text quickly.

Selecting Text with the Mouse

Selecting text with the mouse is easy and convenient. You can select any amount of text from a single character to the entire document. You also can combine mouse and keyboard selection techniques. Use whichever method or combination is effective for you.

To select a small amount of text with the mouse, follow these steps:

1. Click and hold the mouse button at the beginning of the text you want to select.

2. Drag the pointer in any direction across the text you want to select.

If the pointer touches the edge of the window as you are dragging, the window scrolls in that direction if more text exists.

To select from the current insertion point to a distant location, follow these steps:

1. Click the I-beam at the beginning of the text to relocate the insertion point.

2. Hold down the Shift key or press F8 (Extend Selection).

   While you are in Extend Selection mode, EXT appears on the status bar at the bottom of the screen.

3. Scroll the screen so that the end of text you want selected shows.

4. Click the I-beam at the end of the text.

5. Release the Shift key if you held it down in step 2, or press Esc if you pressed F8 in step 2.

> **Note**
>
> As an alternative, position the insertion point where you want to start the selection, scroll until the end of the text is visible, and then hold down the Shift key while you click the I-beam where you want to end the selection.

To deselect text, click the mouse anywhere in the document window.

You can select specific units of text, such as words, sentences, lines, paragraphs, or the whole document, by using one of the techniques listed in table 5.5. Notice that clicking or dragging in the selection bar (as indicated in fig. 5.15), is a shortcut for selecting text. The *selection bar* is the blank vertical space on the left side of the Word for Windows document. Text never extends into this area.

Table 5.5 Selecting Blocks of Text with the Mouse

Text to Select	Mouse Action
A word	Double-click the word.
A sentence	Press Ctrl and click the sentence.
A line	Click in selection bar (blank margin to left of a line of text).

Text to Select	Mouse Action
Multiple lines	Click selection bar and drag up or down.
A paragraph	Double-click selection bar.
Document	Press Ctrl and click in selection bar.
Rectangular block	Click the top left of the rectangle you want of text, and then hold Alt while you drag to select a rectangular block of text.

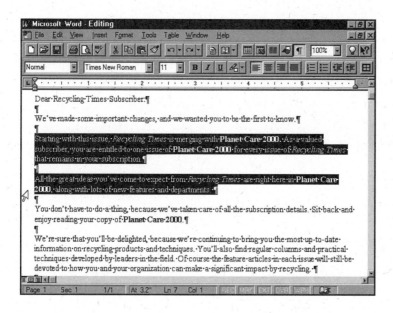

Fig. 5.15
Use the mouse to
select text in the
selection bar.

If you frequently select the same block of text or need to select text under macro control, use a bookmark. Refer to the section, "Creating Bookmarks," later in this chapter to find out how to create bookmarks.

▶ See "Prompting for Input," p. 1069

Selecting Text with the Keyboard

If you are a touch typist, you don't need to move your fingers from the keyboard to select text. Word for Windows enables you to select varying amounts of text quickly and conveniently.

The method most convenient for selecting text is to hold down the Shift key as you move the insertion point. Some of these key combinations are listed in table 5.6. You can select text by using Shift in combination with any move key.

Table 5.6 Selecting Text with the Shift Key	
To Select	**Press**
A word	Shift+Ctrl+← or → key
To the beginning of a line	Shift+Home
To the end of a line	Shift+End
One line at a time	Shift+↑ or ↓ key
To the beginning of a document	Shift+Ctrl+Home
To the end of a document	Shift+Ctrl+End

You can select large amounts of text or an amount relative to your current location by combining the F8 (Extend Selection) key with the F5 (Go To) key and a move code as described in the following procedure.

To select large amounts of text with the keyboard, follow these steps:

1. Move the insertion point to the beginning of the text you want to select.

2. Press F8 (Extend Selection).

3. Press F5 (Go To).

4. Select the item to which you want to move, and enter the number or other identifier that represents the relative location of the end of your selection, as described earlier in the section "Moving the Insertion Point a Relative Distance."

5. Choose Go To.

6. Press Esc to close the Go To dialog box.

To select the next 20 lines in your document, for example, press F8 (Extend Selection) and F5 (Go To). Select Line in the Go to What box and enter **+20**, and then choose Go To. Press Esc to exit Extend Selection mode.

Press Ctrl+5 to select the entire document. This shortcut works only with the 5 key on the numeric keypad. Num Lock can be on or off.

To select an entire table, place the insertion point inside the table and press Alt+5 on the numeric keypad. Num Lock must be off.

Another way of selecting text with the keyboard is to use the F8 (Extend Selection) key to select text the insertion point subsequently moves over.

To select from the insertion point to a distant location, follow these steps:

1. Move the insertion point to the beginning of the text you want to select.

2. Press F8 (Extend Selection).

3. Press one of the keys listed in table 5.7.

4. Press Esc to exit Extend Selection mode.

Table 5.7   Selecting Text in Extend Selection Mode

To Select	Press
Next or previous character	← or → key
A character	That character
The end of a line	End
The beginning of a line	Home
The top of the previous screen	Page Up
The bottom of the next screen	Page Down
The beginning of a document	Ctrl+Home
The end of a document	Ctrl+End

After you exit Extend Selection mode, you can press any arrow key to deselect the selected text.

You also can use Extend Selection mode to select specific units of text, such as a word, sentence, or paragraph.

To select specific units of text, move the cursor into the text, then press F8 (Extend Selection), as indicated in this chart:

To Select Current...	Press F8
Word	2 times
Sentence	3 times
Paragraph	4 times
Section	5 times
Document	6 times

► See "Understanding the Basics of Fields," p. 589

If the insertion point is in a field code when you press the F8 key, the field code and then the next larger block of text are selected. (Field codes are hidden codes used to automate Word for Windows processes. Reading Chapter 20, "Automating with Field Codes," will help you understand field codes.)

To select a unit of text smaller than the current selection, press Shift+F8 as many times as needed to decrease the selection.

Remember, press the Esc key, and then move the insertion point to turn off Extend Selection mode.

Deleting Text

Effective writing doesn't come easily, and good writers spend a great deal of time deleting text. Deleting is a simple operation in Word for Windows, but you should be aware of some nuances.

To delete text, first select it using any selection technique or shortcut, and then press the Delete or Backspace key. You can use one of the following key combinations to delete specific units of text:

To Delete	Press
Character to right of insertion point	Delete
Character to left of insertion point	Backspace
The next word	Ctrl+Delete
The preceding word	Ctrl+Backspace

To make editing quick and easy with the keyboard, use the F8 or Shift key combinations to select text; then press Delete or Backspace. To delete a sentence, for example, press F8 three times and then press Delete. Press Esc to turn off Extend mode.

> **Note**
>
> You can choose Edit, Replace to delete text formatted with a particular style. In the Replace dialog box, choose Format, Style. In the Find Style dialog box that appears, choose the style of the text you want to delete, and then choose OK. Leave the Find What and Replace With boxes empty. Click the Find Next button. If the text you find is text you want to delete, click Replace. If you don't want to delete the text, click Find Next again to proceed through the document to the next text with the style you specified.

> **Troubleshooting**
>
> *My text changes its formatting when I press the Delete or Backspace keys.*
>
> Word for Windows stores paragraph formatting in the paragraph mark at the end of each paragraph. If you delete the paragraph mark of a particular paragraph, it takes on the format of the following paragraph. Choose Edit, Undo immediately to reverse the deletion and restore the paragraph formatting.
>
> To repair the paragraph, reformat it or copy a paragraph mark from a similar paragraph and paste it at the end of the problem paragraph.

To avoid deleting a paragraph mark inadvertently, turn on paragraph marks by clicking the Paragraph Mark button near the right end of the Standard toolbar. You can also turn on nonprinting characters by choosing Tools, Options, selecting View tab, and marking the All check box in the Nonprinting Characters category.

Typing Over Text

One helpful feature in Word for Windows enables you to replace selected text with your typing. Before you can replace selected text with text you type or paste from the Clipboard, you may need to select a custom setting.

To set up Word for Windows to replace selected text with new typing, follow these steps:

1. Choose Tools, Options to bring up the Options dialog box.

2. Select the Edit tab.

3. Select <u>T</u>yping Replaces Selection.

4. Click OK. Anything you type or paste replaces whatever is selected.

If you accidentally type over selected text, you can undo your mistake by immediately choosing <u>E</u>dit, <u>U</u>ndo, clicking the Undo button, or pressing Ctrl+Z or Alt+Backspace.

> **Caution**
>
> If you're working in Overtype mode, typing replaces the selection and text following the selection. You cannot undo overtyping, so be very careful if you're working in this mode.

Tip
You can toggle Overtype mode on or off by pressing the Insert key or by selecting <u>O</u>vertype Mode in the Edit Settings section of the Options dialog box.

Hyphenating Words

Hyphenation joins words used in combination (for example, above-board) or splits long words so that they can break to the next line. Splitting long words with hyphens reduces the ragged appearance of your right margin or the amount of white space between words in justified text. Word for Windows has three types of hyphens: optional, regular, and nonbreaking.

Inserting Regular and Nonbreaking Hyphens

Use regular hyphens when you want to control where a hyphen is inserted or to join two words used in combination. A regular hyphen breaks the word, when necessary, so that it can wrap at the end of a line. Use a nonbreaking (or *hard*) hyphen to join words or acronyms that you do not want broken at the end of a line. Optional hyphens break words at the end of a line. Table 5.8 summarizes the three types of hyphens available in Word for Windows.

Table 5.8	Types of Hyphens		
Hyphen	**Keystroke**	**Appearance**	**Function**
Regular	Hyphen	-	For words that are always hyphenated and can be split at line breaks
Optional	Ctrl+Hyphen	¬	To split words at the end of a line. Not displayed unless the word appears at the end of the line

Hyphen	Keystroke	Appearance	Function
Nonbreaking	Ctrl+Shift+Hyphen	–	For words that are always hyphenated and you do not want to split at the end of the line

Inserting Optional Hyphens throughout a Document

Choosing Tools, Hyphenation automatically inserts optional hyphens throughout your document. It identifies the first word in each line and, if the word can be hyphenated, Word for Windows inserts an optional hyphen. The first part of the word then is moved to the end of the preceding line of text. Optional hyphens are printed in your document only if they are needed to break a word at the end of a line.

To see all optional hyphens, follow these steps:

1. Choose Tools, Options.

2. Select the View tab.

3. Select either the All or Optional Hyphens check boxes in the Nonprinting Characters group. Optional hyphens appear as a dash with a crook.

To hyphenate a document, follow these steps:

1. Select the text you want hyphenated, or move the insertion point to the top of the document. The Hyphenation command hyphenates text from the insertion point to the end of the document if no text is selected.

2. Choose Tools, Hyphenation. The Hyphenation dialog box appears (see fig. 5.16).

Tip
You normally don't see optional hyphens unless they are used to break a word.

Fig. 5.16
The Hyphenation dialog box options allow you to further customize your word document.

3. Select from among the options in the dialog box:

Option	Action
Automatically Hyphenate Document	Does not ask you to confirm each hyphenation
Hyphenate Words in CAPS	Hyphenates words in all caps
Hyphenation Zone	The space at the right margin within which a word can be hyphenated. To increase the number of hyphenated words and decrease right-margin raggedness, lower the number in the Hyphenation Zone box. Increase the number for less hyphenation with a more ragged right margin.
Limit Consecutive Hyphens To	Sets the maximum number of consecutive lines that can end with hyphens
Manual	Displays each word before hyphenating in the Hyphenate At box. Use the arrow keys to move the insertion point or click where you want the hyphen to appear. Choose Yes to add a hyphen, or No to skip the word. The next word is then displayed for hyphenation.

4. Choose OK.

5. When a dialog box appears telling you hyphenation is complete, click OK.

To remove optional hyphens, choose Edit, Replace. Type ^ - in the Find What text box. Delete any contents in the Replace With text box. Click Find Next to confirm each replacement, or click Replace All to remove all optional hyphens.

Undoing Edits

The Undo command reverses the most recent action (assuming that action can be reversed). You can undo most editing actions, such as deletions. Other actions that you can undo are Insert commands (except Insert, Page Numbers), Format commands (Style), and Tools commands (except Options).

You must choose Edit, Undo immediately after you make the mistake. If you continue working, you cannot undo your error by choosing Edit, Undo.

To undo the last action, choose Edit, Undo, or press the Undo keys—Ctrl+Z or Alt+Backspace.

You also can undo any of the last several actions from the Standard toolbar. The Undo and Redo buttons keep track of the editing functions you perform. You can choose to undo or redo actions in a series. For example, if you've just checked spelling, deleted a word, and pasted a sentence, choosing the Undo button can undo all three of those actions, the last two, or just the last one.

To undo or redo multiple actions from the toolbar, follow these steps:

1. Choose the Undo or Redo button.

2. Drag across to the number of previous actions you want to undo or redo.

3. Release the mouse button.

Inserting Frequently Used Material

Word for Windows AutoText feature is like word processing shorthand. It saves you time by storing selected text and graphics (and their formatting) that are used repeatedly. If you have a long company name that you frequently must type in documents, for example, you can abbreviate it as AutoText and insert it quickly into your document. AutoText also ensures that repetitive material is typed correctly and consistently. If you create templates for standardized documents, you should consider including AutoText entries in the templates for frequently used words, phrases, formats, or pictures. (A *template* provides a guide or pattern for creating specific types of documents.)

▶ See "Using Word's Predefined Templates," p. 178

AutoText is not limited to text. It can contain pictures and graphics of digitized signatures, graphic letterheads, logos, or symbols. If you frequently use a table with special formatting, you can make it an AutoText entry.

Creating an AutoText Entry

You can use the AutoText command to add text or graphics to an AutoText entry by choosing Edit, AutoText.

To add text or graphics to an AutoText entry, follow these steps:

1. Select the text, graphic, table, or combination of items from your document that you want to add to the AutoText entry.

2. Choose Edit, AutoText. The AutoText dialog box appears (see fig. 5.17). Notice that the selected text is shown in the Selection box.

Fig. 5.17

Use the AutoText dialog box to create an AutoText entry.

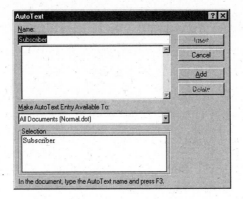

3. Type an abbreviated name for the text in the Name box. Use an abbreviation you can easily remember. To change an existing AutoText entry, select the name of the entry from the list and edit it.

4. Click the Add button.

AutoText entries belong to your current document and to a template. You can choose a template from the Make AutoText Entry Available To box. The AutoText entry will be attached to the template you select. If you choose the default—All Documents (NORMAL.DOT)—your AutoText entry will be available to all future documents you create using the NORMAL.DOT template. If you choose another template, the entry will be available to future documents you create using that particular template only.

When you exit Word for Windows after a session in which you created AutoText entries attached to the NORMAL.DOT template, a dialog box appears. It asks if you want to save changes that affect the global template, NORMAL.DOT. Choose Yes to keep your AutoText entries or No to discard them.

Inserting AutoText

Once you've created an AutoText entry, it's easy to use it in your document.

To insert an AutoText entry into your text, follow these steps:

1. Position the insertion point where you want the AutoText entry to appear.

2. Type the abbreviation you gave the AutoText entry.

3. Press F3, the AutoText key, or click the AutoText button in the Standard toolbar.

When you press F3, Word for Windows replaces the AutoText abbreviation with the AutoText. (The AutoText abbreviation you type in your document must be at the beginning of a line or preceded by a space. Otherwise, the AutoText abbreviation will not be replaced with the AutoText.)

If you cannot remember the AutoText abbreviation, you can access a list of AutoText entries in the AutoText dialog box.

To insert an AutoText entry from the Edit menu, follow these steps:

1. Position the insertion point where you want the AutoText entry to appear.

2. Choose Edit, AutoText.

3. In the AutoText name box, type the AutoText name or select it from the list.

4. Click the Insert button.

Deleting AutoText

You may want to delete an AutoText entry if you no longer use it.

To delete an AutoText entry, follow these steps:

1. Choose Edit, AutoText.

2. Type the name of the AutoText entry you want to delete in the Name box, or select the name from the list.

3. Click the Delete button.

Using the Spike

The *spike* is a special type of AutoText entry that enables you to remove selected items from different places in your document, collect them, and insert them into your document as a group. The term *spike* comes from the old office spikes that impaled bills and invoices until they could all be dealt with at once. Contents stored in the spike are inserted just as you would insert a regular AutoText entry. You also can empty the contents of the spike and make it available to store another collection of text and graphics.

To add text or graphics to the spike, follow these steps:

1. Select the text or graphics you want to add to the spike.

2. Press Ctrl+F3, the Spike key combination. Word for Windows cuts the selected text or graphic and adds it to the spike glossary entry.

3. Select additional items in the order you want them added to the spike and repeat step 2.

Tip
Note that spiked selections are cut from your document, not copied.

After you create a spike entry, you will see it listed as `Spike` in the AutoText dialog box list when you choose Edit, AutoTe<u>x</u>t.

To insert the spike's contents into your document, follow these steps:

1. Position the insertion point where you want the spike's contents to appear.

2. Press Shift+Ctrl+F3 (the Unspike key combination) to paste the spike and remove its contents from memory.

   You also can type **spike**, then press F3 (AutoText) to paste the spike and retain its contents so that you can paste them again.

   You also have a third option; choose <u>E</u>dit, AutoTe<u>x</u>t. Select Spike from the list and choose <u>I</u>nsert.

Printing AutoText Entries

▶ See "Using Templates as a Pattern for Documents," p. 178

If you do not use certain AutoText entries regularly, you will soon forget what the abbreviation in the AutoText list does. To see a more complete view of each AutoText entry, including its format, print a list of AutoText entries.

To print a list of AutoText entries, follow these steps:

1. Open a document based on the template containing the AutoText entries.

2. Choose <u>F</u>ile, <u>P</u>rint, and select AutoText Entries in the Print <u>w</u>hat list.

3. Click OK.

Correcting Spelling Errors as You Type

Almost every typist has at least one or two typing mistakes that are made frequently. The Word for Windows AutoCorrect feature recognizes common typing mistakes and automatically substitutes the correct spelling for you. You also can use AutoCorrect to automatically type long words from an abbreviation. You could use AutoCorrect to automatically type the phrase **not applicable**, for example, every time you type the abbreviation **na**.

The AutoCorrect feature can also correct accidental usage of the Caps Lock key, automatically capitalize the first word of every sentence, and automatically capitalize the names of days of the week.

> **Note**
>
> As you type, you may see words with a wavy red underline. These words do not appear in Word's spelling dictionary. You can right-click them to display a list of suggested corrections. To learn more about automatic spelling checking, see Chapter 7, "Using Editing and Proofing Tools."

Creating AutoCorrect Entries

You can create AutoCorrect entries in two ways:

- You can manually add entries using menu commands.

- You can add an AutoCorrect entry while you perform a spelling check.

Adding AutoCorrect Entries with Menu Commands

To add an AutoCorrect entry using the menu commands, follow these steps:

1. Choose <u>T</u>ools, <u>A</u>utoCorrect. Word for Windows displays the AutoCorrect dialog box.

2. In the <u>R</u>eplace text box, type the misspelling that you want to have corrected automatically.

3. In the <u>W</u>ith text box, type the correct spelling of the word or phrase (see fig. 5.18).

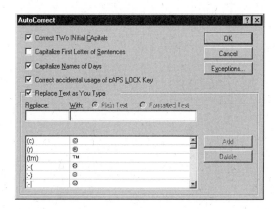

Fig. 5.18
Use the AutoCorrect dialog box to create new AutoCorrect entries and to set the AutoCorrect options.

4. Choose <u>A</u>dd to add the new entry to the list of AutoCorrect entries.

5. Click OK.

To have AutoCorrect automatically replace the misspelling or abbreviation with the correct spelling or complete phrase, make sure that the Replace <u>T</u>ext as You Type check box is marked.

Adding AutoCorrect Entries during a Spelling Check

You also can add AutoCorrect entries as you perform spelling checks on your document. To add an AutoCorrect entry during a spelling check, follow these steps:

▶ See "Checking Your Spelling," p. 211

1. Choose <u>T</u>ools, <u>S</u>pelling to start the spelling check, if you have not already done so.

2. Choose the AutoCo<u>r</u>rect button to add the misspelled word in the Not in Dictionary text box and the correct spelling in the Change <u>T</u>o text box to the list of AutoCorrect entries.

3. Continue the spelling check.

Using AutoCorrect

The AutoCorrect feature works automatically as you type, without any special actions on your part. AutoCorrect offers several options that you can change to suit your working style and preferences.

To change the AutoCorrect options, follow these steps:

1. Choose <u>T</u>ools, <u>A</u>utoCorrect. The AutoCorrect dialog box appears (refer to fig. 5.18).

2. Choose any combination of the available options. Each option is described in the following table:

Option	Result
Correct TWo INitial CApitals	Changes the second of two capital letters at the beginning of a word to lowercase
Capitalize First Letter of Sentences	Changes the first letter of a word beginning a sentence to uppercase
Capitalize Names of Days	Capitalizes the first letter of names of days of the week

Option	Result
Correct accidental usage of cAPS LOCK Key	Changes the case of text incorrectly typed using the Caps Lock key
Replace Text as You Type	Replaces misspelled words with correct spellings, based on the list of entries maintained by AutoCorrect

Deleting an AutoCorrect Entry

Occasionally, you may want to remove an AutoCorrect entry because you no longer use an abbreviation or because the AutoCorrect entry conflicts with a legitimately spelled word (it doesn't always make sense to have AutoCorrect replace misspellings such as *tow* for *two*, because *tow* is actually a correctly spelled word).

To delete an AutoCorrect entry, follow these steps:

1. Choose Tools, AutoCorrect to display the AutoCorrect dialog box.

2. Select the entry you want to delete in the list at the bottom of the dialog box.

3. Choose the Delete button.

4. Choose OK.

Marking Locations with Bookmarks

A *bookmark* in Word for Windows is a specific named item. The item can be a portion of the document—including text, graphics, or both—or it can simply be a specific location. Spreadsheet users will readily recognize the concept—bookmarks are similar to named ranges in a worksheet.

Use bookmarks to move quickly to a given point in a document, or to mark text or graphics for efficient moving, copying, indexing, or cross-referencing. Bookmarks also are vital when you create a macro that performs an operation on a specific portion of a document.

▶ See "Deciding How Your Macro Will Work," p. 1055

Bookmarks can be used in calculations, much as you use a range name in a spreadsheet. The bookmark represents the location of a number, rather than the number itself. The number can change, and the calculation will reflect the new result.

For example, to total an invoice, create a bookmark for each of the subtotals (job1, job2, job3, and so on). Position the insertion point where you want the total due to print. Choose Insert, Field; in the Field Codes box, type an expression using the bookmark names:

=job1+job2+job3

Choose OK. If the individual amounts change, position the cursor in the total due, press F9 to update the formula field, and the results will be updated.

Creating Bookmarks

When you create a bookmark, you assign a unique name to a location or item in the document.

To create a bookmark, follow these steps:

1. Position the insertion point at the location you want to name, or select the text or graphic you want named.

2. Choose Edit, Bookmark, or press Ctrl+Shift+F5. The Bookmark dialog box appears so that you can name a new bookmark, redefine an existing one, delete an existing one, or go to an existing bookmark (see fig. 5.19).

3. Type a new name for the bookmark in the Bookmark Name text box, or select from the list an existing name that you want to redefine.

4. Choose Add.

Fig. 5.19
The Bookmark dialog box allows you to add a name to a location in your document.

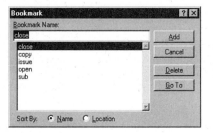

Bookmark names can contain up to 40 characters. A name must begin with a letter but can include numbers, letters, and underlines. Do not use spaces, punctuation marks, or other characters.

One way in which bookmarks can save you time is in selecting text or graphics that you frequently copy, move, or reformat. By naming the text or graphic with a bookmark, you can select the text or graphic no matter where you are in the document. Bookmarks are important when you construct macros in which a portion of text must always be found.

You can make bookmarks visible on-screen by choosing Tools, Options. Choose the View category by clicking the View tab. Choose Bookmarks. Open and closed brackets indicate the position of each bookmark that includes text. A thick I-beam marks the position of each bookmark that is a location only.

Editing, Copying, and Moving Bookmarked Text

The text you select and mark with a bookmark can be edited, copied, or moved. If you add text to any part of a bookmarked item, the following will result:

Add Text	Result
Between any two characters	Text is added to bookmarked text within bookmark brackets.
Immediately before opening bookmark bracket	Text is added to bookmarked text.
Immediately after closing bookmark bracket	Text is not added to bookmarked text.
To the end of a marked table, add row	Row is included with same bookmark.

You can copy a bookmarked item with the following results:

Copy Text	Result
That includes a bookmark to another document	Bookmark is inserted into the other document as well.
Entire item or a portion to same document	Bookmark stays with the first item.

You can delete bookmarked text with the following results:

Delete Text	Result
Part of a bookmarked item	The remainder stays with the bookmark.
Entire text and bookmark and paste elsewhere	Text and bookmark move to new location.

Moving to or Selecting a Bookmark

If you want to quickly go to and select items or a location named by a bookmark, choose Edit, Bookmark. Then select the bookmark name to which you want to move, and choose Go To. Bookmark names are listed alphabetically. To list bookmark names in the order they occur in the document, choose Sort By Location in the Bookmark dialog box.

You can also choose Edit, Go To, or press the F5 key, select the bookmark name from the Enter Bookmark Name box, and choose OK. (The Go To command is described earlier in more detail in "Moving in the Document.")

Deleting Bookmarks

You can remove bookmarks from a document. You might want to remove a bookmark if you no longer use it.

▶ See "Creating Cross-References," p. 920

▶ See "Using Bookmarks to Perform Calculations in Text," p. 678

To delete a bookmark, follow these steps:

1. Choose Edit, Bookmark.

2. Select the name of the bookmark you want to delete.

3. Click the Delete button.

4. Click the Close button. The bookmark is deleted and the previously marked text remains a part of the document.

You can undo a bookmark deletion by choosing Edit, Undo. You can remove a bookmark and its marked text by selecting all the text and pressing Backspace or Delete. If you delete only a portion of the marked text, the rest of the text along with the bookmark will remain.

Moving, Copying, and Linking Text or Graphics

With Word for Windows Move and Copy commands, you can reorganize your thoughts to make your writing flow smoothly and logically.

Word for Windows also has the powerful capability to link text or graphics within a document or to other documents. This feature enables you to link text or graphics in one location to another location in the same document. When you change the original, the linked copy changes simultaneously.

Word for Windows incorporates *OLE*, Object Linking and Embedding. This enables you to link documents and data, such as an Excel chart, into a Word for Windows document. When you want to update the Excel chart, you can double-click the chart to bring up Excel so that the chart can be edited.

▶ See "Linking Documents to a Part of a File," p. 996

Understanding the Clipboard

A section of text or a graphic being moved or copied is kept in a temporary area of memory known as the *Clipboard*. The Clipboard holds an item while it is being moved to a new location in the same or a different document. In fact, you can even move or copy text from Word for Windows to other Windows or DOS applications.

To see the contents of the Clipboard, follow these steps:

1. Click the Start button in the taskbar at the bottom of the screen.

2. Move the mouse pointer over the Programs command. The Programs group is displayed.

3. Move the mouse pointer over Accessories. The Accessories group is displayed.

4. Move the mouse pointer over Clipboard Viewer and click it or press Enter.

The Clipboard displays in its own window, as shown in figure 5.20. The Clipboard may be empty if you have not cut or copied something to it. Some commands clear the Clipboard after executing.

Tip

If the taskbar is currently hidden, move the pointer to the bottom of the screen and the taskbar will appear.

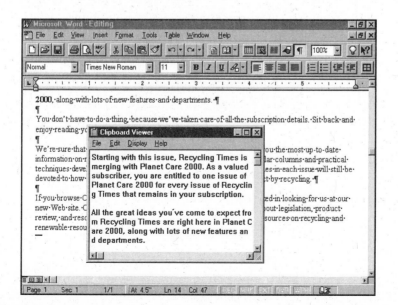

Fig. 5.20
The Clipboard window shows items that are held to be moved to a new location.

To close the Clipboard, press Alt+F4, or click the Clipboard's Close button.

Moving Text or Graphics

You probably are familiar with the concept of moving text or graphics. A portion of text or a graphic is "cut" from the original location and then "pasted" into a new location. The existing text at the new location moves to accommodate the new arrival. You can perform move operations from the menu command, the keyboard, or the Standard toolbar.

To move text or graphics, follow these steps:

1. Select the text or graphic you want to move.

2. Choose Edit, Cut, press Ctrl+X, or click the Cut button on the Standard toolbar.

   The selection is removed from the document and stored in the Clipboard.

3. Reposition the insertion point where you want the item to reappear.

4. Choose Edit, Paste, press Ctrl+V, or click the Paste button on the Standard toolbar. The selection is pasted into its new location.

If you need to accumulate and move multiple pieces of text to the same location, you will want to use the spike. The spike enables you to cut several pieces of text, move all of them to a new location, and paste them in the order they were cut. "Using the Spike," an earlier section in this chapter, describes how to use the Word for Windows AutoText feature to spike your selections.

Copying Text or Graphics

Copying text uses a process similar to moving text. The difference is that copying retains the original text and inserts a duplicate in the new location. You even can copy information from one document and paste the information into another document. You can choose the Copy command from the menu, the toolbar, or the keyboard.

To copy text or graphics to a new location, follow these steps:

1. Select the text or graphic you want copied.

2. Choose Edit, Copy, press Ctrl+C, or click the Copy button on the Standard toolbar.

   The selection is stored in the Clipboard.

3. If you want to paste into another document, open that document now. If it is already open, make it active by choosing it from the Window menu or by clicking any portion of that document if you can see it.

4. Reposition the insertion point where you want the copy to appear.

5. Choose Edit, Paste, press Ctrl+V, or click the Paste button on the Standard toolbar.

Shortcut keys for moving and copying text or graphics can save you time. Table 5.9 lists available shortcuts for moving and copying text or graphics quickly.

Tip
You can make repeated pastes of the same item until you cut or copy a new item to the Clipboard.

Table 5.9 Using Shortcut Keys to Move and Copy	
Keys	**Function**
Ctrl+X or Shift+Delete	Cuts the selected text or graphic to the Clipboard. This shortcut works the same as choosing Edit, Cut.
Ctrl+C or Ctrl+Insert	Copies the selected text or graphic to the Clipboard. This shortcut works the same as Edit, Copy. You can paste the copied material multiple times.
Ctrl+V or Shift+Insert	Pastes the Clipboard's contents at the cursor's location. This shortcut works the same as Edit, Paste.
Shift+F2	Copies the selected text or graphic one time without using the Clipboard. To use this shortcut, select what you want to copy and then press Shift+F2. The prompt Copy to where? appears in the status bar at the bottom of Word's window. Move the insertion point to the new location and press Enter.
Alt+Shift+↑	Cuts the selected paragraph and pastes it above the preceding one
Alt+Shift+↓	Cuts the selected paragraph and pastes it below the following one

Using the Mouse to Move and Copy Items

With Word for Windows, you can move, copy, and link items within a document by using only the mouse. This feature enables you to quickly move paragraphs or sentences, copy phrases, or drag pictures to new locations.

Word for Windows enables you to *frame* graphic objects or any amount of text, and then pick up the frame and place it somewhere else in the document. You can, for example, drag pictures to the center of a page and the text

▶ See "Framing Text, Pictures, and Other Objects," p. 728

will wrap around them, or you can drag a paragraph to the side, enclose it in borders, and use it as a "pull-quote."

To move text or a graphic to a new location using the mouse, follow these steps:

1. Select the text or graphic you want to move. (If you are dragging a picture to a new location, change to Page Layout view before dragging.)

2. Move the mouse pointer over the selected text or graphic. The mouse pointer changes from an I-beam into a pointer over selected text or into an arrow pointer over graphics.

3. Hold down the left mouse button and drag to where you want the text or graphic located.

   The text pointer becomes an arrow pointer combined with a small gray box. The text insertion point appears as a grayed vertical bar. The graphic will appear as a grayed outline as it is dragged to a new location.

4. Release the left mouse button to insert the selected text or graphic.

Tip

To move text or graphics quickly, select the text or graphic you want to move. Then scroll to the screen area where you want to move the text or graphic. Hold down the Ctrl key as you click the right mouse button at the target location.

You also can use the right mouse button to cut, copy, and paste. When you click the right mouse button, a context-sensitive menu appears at the position of the insertion point (see fig. 5.21).

Fig. 5.21
A quick cut, copy, and paste menu can be displayed by clicking the right mouse button.

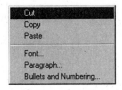

To move or copy text to a new location using the right mouse button, follow these steps:

1. Select the text or graphic you want to move or copy.

2. Place the pointer directly over the selected text and click the right mouse button to display the shortcut menu.

3. Choose Cut or Copy, or click the Cut or Copy button on the Standard toolbar.

After a selection has been copied to the Clipboard (using any method), you can use the right mouse button menu to paste it in other locations.

To paste text using the right mouse button, follow these steps:

1. Position the insertion point.

2. Click the right mouse button.

3. Choose <u>P</u>aste, or click the Paste button on the Standard toolbar.

Linking Text

A special technique exists for forging a link between the source and the destination when you copy text or an object between or within documents. The *source* is the original text or graphic that you select and copy; the *destination* is the location to which you copy the text or graphic. By linking the object as you copy it, you can automatically update the destination each time you make a change to the source. For example, a CPA might maintain a library of boilerplate paragraphs to borrow from when writing individual letters to clients advising them about tax matters. If tax laws change, the CPA can change the source (boilerplate) document and, by simply selecting a command or pressing a key, update the destination document to reflect the changes.

To copy and link text or an object, follow these steps:

1. Select and copy the text or object in the source document.

2. Position the insertion point where you want to link the text or object in the destination document.

3. Choose <u>E</u>dit, Paste <u>S</u>pecial. The Paste Special dialog box appears (see fig. 5.22).

4. Choose the Paste <u>L</u>ink option.

5. Select the type of object you want from the list in the <u>A</u>s box.

6. Select the Display as Icon check box if you want the linked selection to appear as an icon on-screen and in print. You can read the contents of an icon by double-clicking it.

7. Choose OK. Word for Windows inserts the linked object. This link is a field code that specifies the contents of the linked selection from the source document.

Fig. 5.22
The Paste Special dialog box allows you to place links in your document.

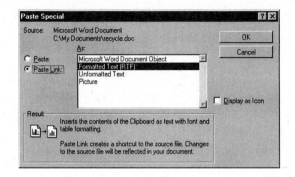

▶ See "Under-
standing the
Basics of
Fields," p. 589

The advantage of linking text is the ease of transferring changes between the original and the linked text. Linked text actually is created by inserting a hidden field code that links the original text to the location you indicate. An example of such a field code linking within the same document is as follows:

```
{ EMBED Word.Document.6 \s }
```

You can edit and format linked text just as you would normal text. When the linked text is updated, however, it changes to reflect the current status of the original text.

To update linked text to match any changes made to the original text, select the entire linked text, making sure to exceed at least one end of the linked text. You will see the linked text update to match the changes in the original.

You can unlink linked text from its original by selecting all of the linked text and pressing Shift+Ctrl+F9. This changes the link into normal text.

▶ See "Moving
and Position-
ing Frames,"
p. 738

▶ See "Linking
Documents and
Files," p. 993

To update the linked text or object (to reflect the changes made in the original), select the object to update and choose Edit, Links. In the Links dialog box, choose Update Now. To cancel the link, choose Cancel Link.

When you update a link, Word for Windows looks for the source document in the same location where it was when you created the link. If it's not there, the link cannot be updated unless you tell Word for Windows where to find the source document. To do that, change the source document's path in the field code that is entered when you link text or an object (to see and edit the path, press Shift+F9).

Troubleshooting
A message appeared on my screen, saying I don't have enough memory for a large Clipboard, and asked whether I want to discard the Clipboard. What should I do?
After you cut or copy information, it is stored on the Clipboard. Discarding the Clipboard clears its contents. In most cases, the Clipboard contains the information you last cut or copied. If you no longer need this material, discard the Clipboard. If you need the information, reduce memory use and recut or recopy the information.

▶ See "Managing System Memory," p. 1021

Working with Multiple Windows

You can have up to nine documents open at one time in Word for Windows. Each document occupies its own window. You can arrange these windows within Word for Windows just as you would place pieces of paper on a desk. By choosing <u>W</u>indow, <u>A</u>rrange All, you can arrange all open windows so that each has a portion of the screen. You can even open more than one window onto the same document when you need to work on widely separated parts of the same document. And as mentioned earlier in this chapter, you can even cut or copy from one document and paste into another.

Viewing Different Parts of the Same Document

If you are working with a long document, you may want to see more than one part of it at the same time. This can be useful when you need to compare or edit widely separated parts of the same document.

You can expand your view in two ways. The first method is to open a new window by choosing <u>W</u>indow, <u>N</u>ew Window. This technique creates a second window containing the same document. If you are displaying a single document with the document window maximized, the title bar will appear as `Microsoft Word—PAKINSTR.DOC`. If you display the same document in more than one window, each document's window will show the document name followed by the window number—for example, `PAKINSTR.DOC:1` and `PAKINSTR.DOC:2`. Figure 5.23 shows two windows displaying the same document.

To close a new window, choose the document control menu by pressing Alt+ - (hyphen) and select <u>C</u>lose. Or just press Ctrl+F4.

Fig. 5.23
View different
parts of a long
document by
displaying the
document in two
windows.

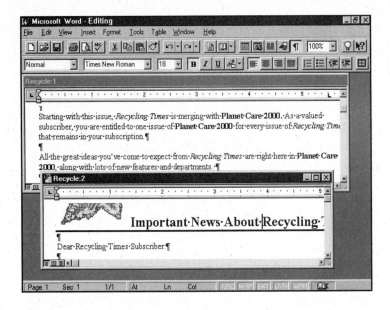

You also can split a window so that you can see two different areas of a document in the same window. This approach is helpful when you type lists. You
can split the document's window so that the upper part shows column headings and the lower part shows the list you are typing. As you scroll the list,
the headings stay in place.

To split a window with the keyboard, choose Window, Split. Then press the
↑ or ↓ key to position the horizontal gray line where you want the split, and
press Enter. To remove the split, choose Window, Remove Split.

To split the window with the mouse, look for the split box above the up arrow in the vertical scroll bar. Drag this split box down and release the mouse
button to position the split. To remove the split, drag the split box all the
way up or down, and then release the button.

Double-click the split bar to split the screen in half. Drag the split bar to reposition the split. Double-click the split bar when the window is split, and you
remove the split. (You must double-click the bar in the vertical scroll bar, not
the line separating the window panes.)

Cutting and Pasting between Documents

When you have several documents on-screen, you can move from one document window to the next in the stack by pressing Ctrl+F6 or by choosing Window and selecting the document you want active. Press Ctrl+Shift+F6 to move to the preceding document window. You also can use the mouse to move to a specific document window—just point and click.

Displaying two or more documents on-screen at one time can be useful. If you have two similar contracts to prepare, for example, you can choose Edit, Copy to copy paragraphs from one contract, press Ctrl+F6 to switch to the other contract, and then paste the paragraphs in the second contract by choosing Edit, Paste.

If you have many documents open, you may want to directly activate one. To do this, choose Window. At the bottom of the menu is a list of all open documents. Select the document you want active.

Working with Pages

Before you print your document, be sure that it's paginated correctly. You don't want a page to break right below a title, for example, and you may not want certain paragraphs separated on two pages. You can let Word for Windows manage page breaks for you, or you can control them yourself.

Repaginating a Document

By default, Word for Windows repaginates whenever you make a change in your document. Word for Windows calculates how much text fits into a page and inserts a soft page break, which appears as a dotted line in Normal view or as the end of a page in Page Layout view. This feature is called *background repagination*. You can have Word for Windows repaginate for you, or you can repaginate manually with a command.

To change background repagination, follow these steps:

1. Choose Tools, Options.

2. Select the General tab.

3. Select the Background Repagination check box to repaginate as you work and keep the page numbers in the status bar current.

4. Click OK.

Word for Windows operates faster with background repagination turned off. To update page breaks if you have background repagination turned off, change to Page Layout view or Print Preview; Word for Windows repaginates the document.

> **Note**
>
> Word for Windows repaginates automatically whenever you print, when you choose View, Page Layout or File, Print Preview, or when you compile or update an index or table of contents.

Inserting Manual Page Breaks

As you work on a document, Word for Windows breaks pages every time you fill a page with text or graphics. These breaks are automatic and known as *soft page breaks*. If background repagination is on, Word for Windows recalculates the amount of text on the page and adjusts soft page breaks as you work.

You can insert page breaks manually whenever you want to force a page break at a particular spot—at the beginning of a new section, for example. Page breaks you insert are called *hard page breaks*. A hard page break appears as a heavy dotted line with the words Page Break centered in the line. When you insert a hard page break, Word for Windows adjusts the soft page breaks that follow. Word for Windows cannot move hard page breaks; you must adjust them yourself.

To insert a hard page break using menu commands, follow these steps:

1. Place the insertion point where you want the page break to occur.

2. Choose Insert, Break.

3. Select the Page Break option.

4. Click OK.

To insert a hard page break from the keyboard, press Ctrl+Enter.

To delete a hard page break, choose one of two options:

- Move the insertion point onto the dotted line created by the page break, and press the Delete key.

- Place the insertion point just past the dotted line, and press Backspace.

If you find a page break difficult to delete, choose F_ormat, _Paragraph to format the paragraphs after the page break. If any of the Text _Flow options in the Pagination group are selected (_Page Break Before, Keep With Ne_xt, or _Keep Lines Together), they may be causing a page break before the paragraph. Try deselecting these options. ❖

Chapter 6

Using Templates and Wizards for Frequently Created Documents

Templates can save you work and increase the consistency of any documents you create frequently. A template acts as a guide or pattern for documents of a specific type, such as form letters, newsletters, letters of engagement, invoices, contracts, or proposals.

A *template* is a file that contains the parts of a document and features used for a specific type of document. Word for Windows templates can contain text, pictures, graphs, formatting, styles, macros, AutoText, buttons on the toolbar, field codes, custom menu commands, and shortcut keys. You can put text, formatting, and settings you use repeatedly for a specific task into a template.

When you open a new document, all the contents and features of the template are transferred to the new untitled document. The original template remains unaltered on disk.

Add-ins are supplemental programs that extend the functionality of Word. You can purchase add-ins from software vendors. Once installed, an add-in acts as if it is a part of Word, and may add a new menu command or toolbar, for example.

In this chapter, you learn how to use templates and wizards to quickly produce standardized versions of formal documents or any document that you produce frequently. In this chapter, you learn about the following:

- How to use and change the predefined templates provided with Word for Windows

■ How to create, use, and change new templates

■ How to use wizards

■ How to get more from Word with add-ins

Figures 6.1, 6.2, and 6.3 show some examples of templates in use.

Fig. 6.1
Everyday blank documents are based on the Normal template, which includes font selections and other formatting settings, but no text.

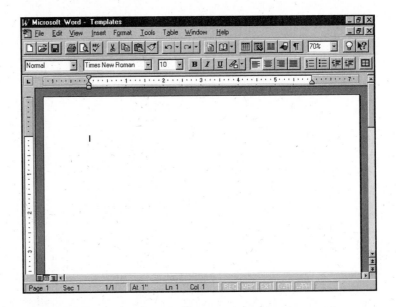

Fig. 6.2
You can base frequently used documents, such as forms, memos, and invoices, on a custom template.

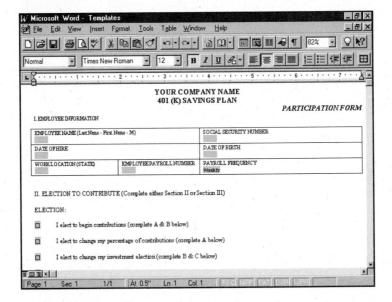

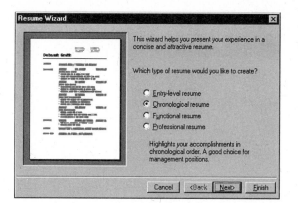

Fig. 6.3
Template wizards guide you through document creation for documents such as meeting agendas, résumés, brochures, and newsletters. Template wizards help you also with features such as tables.

You can use templates to simplify the creation of any frequently used document. Some of the types of documents for which you will find templates useful include:

- Invoices, employee records, or any standardized form
- Proposals and reports
- Newsletters and brochures
- Memos and fax sheets

Using templates in place of preprinted forms can significantly reduce your company's printing costs. Templates in reports ensure that all reports have the same format and layout. You can build into the template special commands or macros needed to produce a report, such as integrating Excel charts, so that they are readily available. When certain phrases and names are stored in AutoText, it makes it easier to keep the spelling and formatting the same across documents. All table and figure formatting, tables of contents, and indexes look the same from report to report because they are created and formatted with macros and styles attached to the template.

Many companies use templates to prepare interoffice memos and fax cover letters. The headings and document formatting are predefined and, therefore, are standardized. ASK or FILLIN fields prompt the operator for entries. The DATE and AUTHOR fields can be used to enter automatically the current date and name of the operator.

Word for Windows comes with several predesigned templates that you can use as a basis for your own business documents, including press releases, fax cover sheets, and reports. You can modify the Word for Windows templates to meet your needs, or you can create your own templates from scratch. In addition, Word provides wizards to automate customizing your documents. The wizard you select, such as Letter or Fax, displays a series of dialog boxes in which you make selections. Word uses your responses to design your document.

Working with Templates

Templates remove some of the tedium that comes with typing the same thing over and over. Rather than retyping a memo heading, for example, you can create or modify a template to include the repeated text. Many of the templates are automated and require only that you point, click, and type to fill out a form. Figure 6.4 shows an example of an easy-to-use memo template.

Fig. 6.4
This memo template provides on-screen instructions and requires only that you point, click, and type.

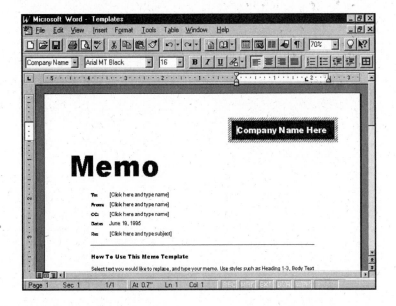

What You Need to Know about Templates

Word normally saves templates as files with the DOT file extension in the Template subfolder under the folder that contains Word. DOT files in this subfolder appear as choices in each category of the New dialog box. This makes templates readily accessible regardless of which folder you are working in.

Word normally looks to the TEMPLATE folder found underneath the MSOFFICE folder when it searches for the templates used in the New dialog box. The tabs that appear in the New dialog box are determined by the structure of the folder that contains the template files. Each tab corresponds to the name of a subfolder in the template folder. To change the folder Word uses for templates, choose Tools, Options, and select the File Locations tab. Double-click User Templates and select a new template folder.

All documents in Word for Windows are based on a template. Even the default new document is based on a template, NORMAL.DOT. The NORMAL.DOT file contains the formatting and default settings for the new document you open when you choose File, New.

Styles, macros, AutoText, and other items stored in the NORMAL.DOT template are available to all documents at all times. Because the information stored in NORMAL.DOT is available to all documents all the time, they are said to be available *globally*.

Templates can contain the following:

- Body text, headers, footers, footnotes, and graphics with formatting
- Page and paper layouts
- Styles
- AutoText entries
- Predefined or custom macros
- Custom menus and commands
- Tools
- Shortcut keys

When you create a document based on a template, the document opens to show the body text, graphics, and formatting contained in the template. All the styles, macros, tools, and so on that are in the template are available for use with the document.

After you create a document, you can attach the document to a different template so that you can use the features (but not the text or page formatting) found in that template. Later sections of this chapter show you how you can transfer features between templates so that a style or macro you create in one template can be transferred into another template.

Using Templates as a Pattern for Documents

Most people use only a few templates. The templates they use may include the NORMAL.DOT template for everyday work or one of a few custom templates for use in memos or reports. Many people use the NORMAL.DOT template to create the blank document with which they normally work. You should examine the predefined templates that come with Word, because you might find one appropriate to your particular task.

Using Word's Predefined Templates

Word for Windows comes with predefined templates you can use to create many typical business documents. Many of the templates contain custom features such as special tools, formatting styles, custom menus, macros, and AutoText for frequently used procedures. The template layouts fall into three categories: *contemporary*, *elegant*, and *professional*, and use similar design principles within each group. You can select a style that suits your needs and, using the templates from that group, be assured that all your documents will have a harmonious, professional appearance. Many of the templates include on-screen instructions that guide you step-by-step in creating some very sophisticated effects.

The predefined templates are organized on different tabs in the New dialog box and are described in table 6.1.

Table 6.1 Predefined Word Templates		
Category	**Template**	**Contents**
General	Blank Document	Default NORMAL.DOT document template
Letters & Faxes	Contemporary Fax	Point and click to fill in fax form.
	Contemporary Letter	Double-click the envelope icon to see detailed instructions on customizing the letter template.
	Elegant Fax	Point and click to fill in fax form.
	Elegant Letter	Double-click the envelope icon to see detailed instructions on customizing the letter template.
	Professional Fax	Point and click to fill in fax form.
	Professional Letter	Double-click the envelope icon to see detailed instructions on customizing the letter template.

Everyday Word Processing

Category	Template	Contents
Memos	Contemporary Memo	Point and click to fill in memo form.
	Elegant Memo	Point and click to fill in memo form.
	Professional Memo	Point and click to fill in memo form.
Reports	Contemporary Report	Includes instructions about how to use the Report template
	Elegant Report	Includes instructions about how to use the Report template
	Professional Report	Includes instructions about how to use the Report template
Other Documents	Contemporary Resume Elegant Resume Invoice	A protected form, ready for you to fill in. To change the labels, choose Tools, Unprotect Document.
	Professional Resume Purchase Order	A protected form, ready for you to fill in. To change the labels, choose Tools, Unprotect Document.
	Weekly Time sheet	A protected form, ready for you to fill in. To change the labels, choose Tools, Unprotect Document.
Publications	Brochure	Landscape orientation, including detailed instructions
	Contemporary Press Release	Contemporary format, includes hints for writing a professional press release
	Directory	Title page and three-column format, including detailed instructions
	Elegant Press Release	Elegant format, includes hints for writing a professional press release
	Manual	Sophisticated guide or handbook
	Newsletter	Newsletter in portrait orientation, three-columns, with hints for creating great newsletters
	Professional Press Release	Professional format, includes hints for writing a professional press release
	Thesis	Includes all required parts

Opening a New Document Based on a Template

◄ See "Opening a New Document," p. 83

Opening a new document is easy. To open a new document, follow these steps:

1. Choose File, New. The New dialog box opens to the General tab with the Blank Document icon selected (see fig. 6.5). This icon represents the NORMAL.DOT template.

Fig. 6.5
Most documents are based on the NORMAL.DOT template, which is shown as the Blank Document icon.

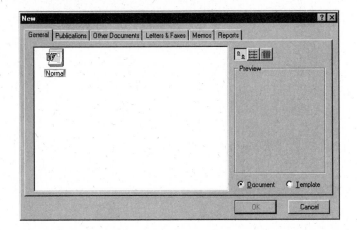

2. Select a tab, then click the name or icon of the template you want to use. The Preview box shows a sample document for which the template is designed.

3. Choose OK.

To open a new document based on NORMAL.DOT using a tool, click the New button in the Standard toolbar, or press Ctrl+N.

Opening a Template on Startup

You can make Word open a specific template when it starts. To do this, open the NORMAL.DOT template. With the NORMAL.DOT template active, you need to record a macro. Give the macro the name AutoExec. While the macro recorder is on, open a document based on the template you want. Save the NORMAL.DOT template. The next time you start Word, it automatically opens the document based on the template you specified.

If you want to load multiple templates on startup, so that the macros and styles in those templates are available, copy the dot file for each template into the STARTUP subfolder located in the WinWord folder. The STARTUP folder is the default folder used for startup files. If you do not have a STARTUP folder, choose Tools, Options and select the File Locations tab. Select the Startup folder in the File Types list, and then choose Modify to set a new folder as the startup folder.

> **Note**
>
> If you frequently use the same templates, you can save yourself time by creating a tool or menu command that opens a new document from each of these templates. Use the macro recorder to record a macro when you open a template. Assign this macro to a button on a toolbar or to a menu command.

Opening Word for Windows 6 Templates

Templates created for Word for Windows 6 can be opened and used in Word for Windows 95. When you close a document based on the old template, Word for Windows automatically saves the document in Word 95 format. If you edit and save the old template, it is saved in the Word for Windows 95 format. The file continues to be backward-compatible with Word 6, however.

Using Information from Another Template

If you are working on a document and decide you want to have access to all the features in another template, you can attach that template to the document. Attaching a new template does not change the existing document text, but it does change specified settings, such as macros, AutoText, menu commands, margins, shortcut key assignments, and buttons.

To attach another template to a document, follow these steps:

1. Open the document to which you want to attach a template.

2. Choose File, Templates. The Templates and Add-ins dialog box appears. Notice that the Document Template edit box displays the name of the template currently attached to the document (see fig. 6.6).

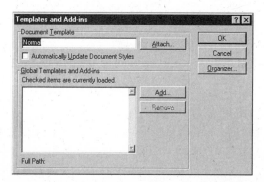

Fig. 6.6
Use features from other templates by attaching a different template containing those features to a document.

3. Click the Attach button to display the Attach Template dialog box (see fig. 6.7).

Fig. 6.7

Choose from the Attach Template dialog box the template to which you want to attach the document.

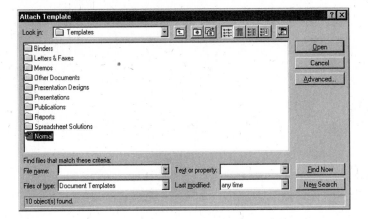

4. Double-click the folder that contains the template you want and select the template, or type the template name in the File name box.

5. Choose Open. The Attach Template dialog box closes and the template name you selected appears in the Document Template text box of the Templates and Add-ins dialog box.

6. Choose OK.

Transferring Template Contents Using the Organizer

As you work, you may find that you need a style, macro, toolbar, or AutoText that is stored in another template. Or you may develop a style, macro, toolbar, or AutoText in one document and want to use it with other documents. After you learn how to use the Organizer, you'll be able to transfer features between templates so that they are available wherever you need them.

To transfer a style, macro, toolbar, or AutoText from one template to another, follow these steps:

1. Open a document based on the template that you want to receive the feature.

2. Open the document based on the template from which you want to send the feature. If you want to transfer a style, open a document containing the style. If you want to transfer a macro, toolbar, or AutoText, open a document based on a template that contains the macro, toolbar, or AutoText.

3. Choose <u>F</u>ile, <u>T</u>emplates; then click the <u>O</u>rganizer button. The Organizer, shown in figure 6.8, appears.

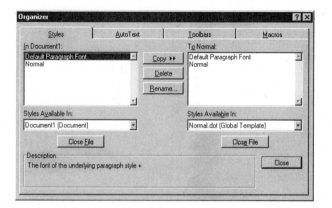

Fig. 6.8
Use the Organizer to transfer styles, macros, AutoText, or toolbars between templates and documents.

4. Select the tab for the type of feature you want to transfer.

5. Select from the lists on the left the document or template that contains the feature; then select the feature from the top-left list.

6. Select from the lists on the right the document or template that will receive the feature.

7. Click the <u>C</u>opy button.

8. Repeat steps 4–7 to transfer additional features, or choose Close to close the Organizer.

Transferring styles, macros, AutoText, or toolbars is described in more detail in the specific chapters that discuss those features.

◀ See "Creating an AutoText Entry," p. 151

▶ See "Customizing and Creating Toolbars," p. 1034

Storing Summary Information about a Document

Each Word document can have summary and other information attached. This information can remind you about the source or contents of a document, when the document was created, how much time you've put into creating it, and more. You can also search for key words, which can be very helpful if you forget a file's name or need a list of all files that have similar key words in the summary.

If you want to attach summary information to a document, choose <u>F</u>ile, Prop<u>e</u>rties, and complete the Properties dialog box. When you save the document you have opened, the property information is saved with the file. You can edit the property information for the active document by choosing <u>F</u>ile, Prop<u>e</u>rties.

The Properties dialog box includes the following tabs:

Tab	Description
General	Provides information about the file's location, size, and save dates
Summary	Provides space for you to note important information about the document itself, such as who wrote it, key words (for document searches), and comments
Statistics	Includes information like numbers of pages, lines, words, and so forth
Contents	Provides space for you to describe the document's contents
Custom	Provides space for you to customize the information you save with the document

---

Troubleshooting

The template on which my document was originally based is no longer available. What happened?

It may have been erased, renamed, or moved to a different folder. You cannot use the macros, AutoText, or toolbars that were assigned to that template. You do, however, still have the styles that were in that template.

You can attach another template to the document to gain the use of the other template's features by opening the document and choosing File, Templates. Follow the description in the section, "Using Information from Another Template," earlier in this chapter.

I can't find Word's predefined templates in the Template lists in the New dialog box.

If Word's predefined templates do not appear in the list, the templates may not have been installed when you installed Word for Windows. You can rerun the installation procedure and choose to install only the templates.

I created a custom template, but it doesn't appear in the New dialog box.

Templates use a DOT extension and are stored in the template folder. The folder to which Word normally looks for template files is C:\MSOFFICE\TEMPLATE. Choose Tools, Options, and select the File Locations tab. Confirm that User Templates shows the C:\MSOFFICE\TEMPLATES folder. If it does not, choose Modify and correct it. Click Close.

Modifying Templates

The templates that come with Word for Windows are designed to handle many daily business transactions; however, you might need to modify the template to fit your business formats more closely or to add AutoText and styles specific to your needs. For example, you might want to use the Memo1 template for creating interoffice memos, but the template might not include AutoText entries for words or phrases used in your department. You can modify Memo1 to include your own AutoText entries, change the format to fit your needs, and edit the boilerplate text.

You can modify templates to incorporate the specific text, graphics, styles, formatting, macros, and AutoText you need for your documents. This means you can modify templates to fit your needs, even if the template came with Word or was given to you by another Word user.

What You Need to Know about Changing a Template

After you make changes to a template, all new documents using that template include the modifications or edits you've made to the template. Documents created from the template before it was modified, however, have access to only some of the changes to the template. For example, styles, text, graphics, page formatting, or print formatting added to the template do not transfer to existing documents. Changes in a template that are available to documents that were created from the earlier template are:

- AutoText entries

- Macros

- Menus

- Shortcut keys

- Toolbar buttons

Caution

If you change a template and preserve the original name, the original template is replaced. To ensure that you will always have the original template available, consider either using a new name for the modified template or giving the original template a new name.

Changing a Template

If you have many changes to make to a template, it might be easier to use one of the methods described later in this chapter to create a new template from scratch or to use an existing document as the basis for the new template. When you have to make just a few modifications to a template, however, it is easier to modify the template with one of the following methods.

To change an existing template, follow these steps:

1. Choose File, Open, click the Open button, or press Ctrl+F12. The Open dialog box appears (see fig. 6.9).

Fig. 6.9
Select the template file you want to modify from the Open dialog box.

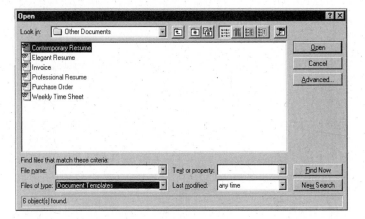

2. Double-click the TEMPLATES folder or the folder containing your template from the Look In box.

3. Select Document Templates (*.DOT) from the Files of Type list box.

4. Select the template you want to modify and choose Open.

5. Change the template by modifying text or graphics; changing formats; redefining styles or AutoText entries; or adding or changing macros, shortcut keys, or buttons.

6. Choose File, Save to save the template back to the same folder with the same name.

Setting Default Formats in the Normal Template

Word for Windows bases its default settings for a new document on a template stored in the file NORMAL.DOT. All documents you create by choosing File, New and pressing Enter are based on the Normal template. Settings, such as the style, font type and size, margins, and other formats, are stored in this file.

You can change default settings for new documents in two ways. In the more powerful method, you can set new defaults for styles, AutoText, page formatting, and so on by changing the setting in the NORMAL.DOT template. If you need to change only the default for a font, style, or page layout, you can change them while editing a document using the method described later in "Changing Template Features from within a Document."

If you want to change any of the default formatting or features controlled by a template, open the NORMAL.DOT template and change the appropriate format or settings. If you want to change the appearance of the normal body text, change the Normal style. Save the NORMAL.DOT template back to the same folder with the same name.

Making Template Features Available to All Documents

If you have macros, AutoText, buttons, or styles that you want to be available to all documents, put them in the NORMAL.DOT template. A conflict might occur if the active document is based on a template that has styles, macros, or AutoText that has the same names as those in the NORMAL.DOT template.

Whenever there is a conflict between styles, macros, or AutoText with the same name, the template that created the document takes priority over the NORMAL.DOT template. For example, if your report is based on the ELEGANTREPORT.DOT template that contains a style named List Bullet, and the NORMAL.DOT template also contains a style named List Bullet, your document will use the Bulleted List style found in ELEGANTREPORT.DOT.

Changing Template Features from within a Document

Default settings are format settings specified when a document opens—settings such as which font and font size are used when you first begin to type. You can change default settings in two ways: You can open and modify the template that creates a type of document, or you can change some formats within a document and transfer the changes back to the template so that the changes become new defaults.

The types of changes that can be transferred from a document back to its template are found in the Format, Font; Format, Style; and File, Page Setup menu choices.

To transfer a format change from the document back to the template, follow these steps:

1. Open a new or existing document based on the template you want to change.

2. Choose Format, Font; Format, Style; or File, Page Setup, depending on the type of default change you want made.

3. If you choose Format, Style, choose the Modify button.

4. Select the tab, if any, for the type of formatting you want changed, then select the formatting options you want to define as default settings on the template.

5. If you change the font or page setup, click the Default button. A dialog box appears asking you to confirm the update to the template.

   Or, if you change or add a style, select the Add to Template check box in the Modify Style dialog box.

6. Choose Yes or press Enter to update the document's template file with the selected default settings.

You may be able to save yourself some work when modifying a template by copying existing styles, macros, AutoText, or buttons, from another template. Use the Organizer to copy template items. The Organizer is described in each chapter that deals with a feature that can be transferred. It is covered lightly in "Using Information from Another Template" earlier in this chapter.

Creating a New Template

Although Word for Windows comes with many predesigned templates, you probably have many documents or forms that do not fit any of the templates. You can create a completely new template based on either an existing template or document.

Creating a New Template Based on an Existing Template

You can create a template in much the same way you create any document. If you have a template that already has most of the features that you want, you can save time by creating the new template based on the existing one.

To create a new template based on an existing template, follow these steps:

1. Choose File, New.

2. Click the Template button.

3. Choose the tab that contains the template on which you want to base the new template.

4. Select the template you want. Select the Normal template if you want to start with a blank template and the default settings.

5. Choose OK. Note that the title bar now displays Template rather than Document (see fig. 6.10).

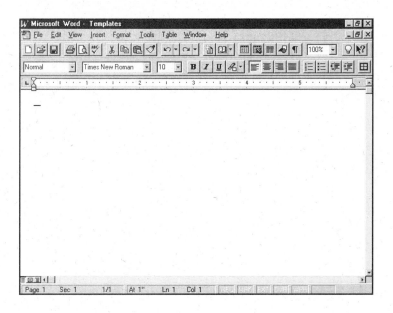

Fig. 6.10
The title bar indicates that you are creating a template. This one is based on the NORMAL.DOT template.

6. Lay out and format the template as you would a document. Include text that will not change between documents. The template can contain text and graphics you want to appear on all documents, formatting and styles, macros, AutoText entries, new commands, shortcut keys, and new toolbar buttons.

To save a template, follow these steps:

1. Choose File, Save As.

2. Select the folder in which you want to save the template. The one you select determines the tab on which the template displays when you choose File, New.

3. Enter a name for the template in the File name box. The extension DOT is assigned to templates.

4. Choose OK.

Creating a Template Based on an Existing Document

You already might have a document that contains most of the text, formatting, and settings you want to use in a template. Rather than re-create the document on a template, Word for Windows enables you to create a template based on the existing document.

To create a template based on an existing document, follow these steps:

1. Choose File, Open and open the document that you want to use as the basis for a template.

2. Modify this document by editing text and adding graphics, styles, macros, AutoText, or buttons that you want to include in the template.

3. Choose File, Save As.

4. Select Document Template from the Save as type pull-down list.

5. Select the folder in which you want to save the template. The one you select determines the tab on which the template displays when you choose File, New.

6. Type the template's file name in the File Name box (see fig. 6.11). You do not have to type the DOT extension. The template file automatically is saved to the folder that contains templates.

7. Choose OK.

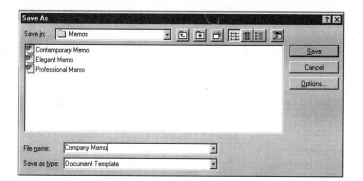

Fig. 6.11
If you create a particular document frequently, save it as a template.

Note

Templates are a key to creating forms that you use repeatedly. Word has the ability to create forms that include edit fields, drop-down lists, and check boxes. Because forms are used over and over, you will want to save forms as templates. Users can easily open the form template by choosing File, New. You don't have to worry about the form being accidentally changed, because the original template stays on disk and the user works with a copy of the form.

Using Wizards to Guide You

Word comes with some templates that guide you through the creation of a document. These special templates are called *wizards*. Wizards automate the process of creating a document to your specifications. For example, you can use an award wizard to create a customized award in portrait or landscape orientation, in your choice of presentation styles, including the name(s) you indicate. Another valuable wizard is the Newsletter Wizard. It creates multipage, multicolumn newsletters that include graphics, tables of contents, drop caps, and more.

In addition to creating a document with wizards, you can use them to create new templates that are based upon your choices. When a wizard template opens, it displays dialog boxes, messages, and graphics that tell you how to fill in a template or complete forms. Word comes with several wizards that are very helpful.

Creating Documents with Wizards

Tip

When you complete a document with a wizard and it looks like something you'll use frequently, you can save that document as a template.

Starting a wizard is like opening any other new document. Choose File, New, select the tab where the wizard you want is stored, and select the wizard template from the Template lists. Templates that contain wizards show the word `wizard` in their names.

Wizards That Come with Word

Wizards have you fill in information inside dialog boxes. They use your responses to fill in forms or prepare formatting. Some wizards are simple and prepare simple documents such as memos or fax cover letters (see fig. 6.12). Other wizards are more complex and create newsletters, brochures, or calendars. Table 6.2 lists the wizards supplied with Word for Windows. The tab on which the template is listed is included in parentheses.

Fig. 6.12

Use wizards to automate the creation of documents such as memos, newsletters, and calendars.

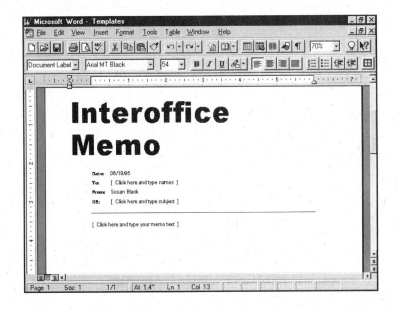

Table 6.2 Predefined Word Wizards		
Wizard	**Description**	**Category**
Agenda Wizard	Helps you create meeting agendas	Other Documents
Award Wizard	Helps you create customized award certificates	Other Documents
Calendar Wizard	Helps you create calendars for week, month, or year	Other Documents

Wizard	Description	Category
Fax Wizard	Helps you create customized fax cover sheets	Letters & Faxes
Letter Wizard	Helps you create prewritten or customized letters	Letters & Faxes
Memo Wizard	Helps you create customized memos	Memos
Newsletter Wizard	Helps you design and lay out a newsletter	Publications
Pleading Wizard	Helps you create a legal pleading paper	Other Documents
Resume Wizard	Helps you create a customized résumé	Other Documents
Table Wizard	Helps you create and format tables	Other Documents

Adding Power and Features with Add-Ins

Add-ins are a way of extending the capabilities of Word for Windows 95. An add-in program is not part of Word, but behaves as if it is a part of Word for Windows. An add-in program may add new menu choices to Word for Windows, or add new toolbars to Word. Like a template, the add-in program remains available until you exit Word. Add-in programs for various tasks are available from a variety of third-party vendors. For specific information about using a particular add-in, consult the documentation provided with the add-in program.

Add-in programs end with the file extension WLL. Follow the installation instructions provided with the add-in program for help in installing an add-in.

Loading Add-Ins

To load an add-in program, follow these steps:

1. Choose File, Templates. The Templates and Add-ins dialog box appears.

2. Click the Add button in the Global Templates and Add-ins section of the Templates and Add-ins dialog box. The Add Template dialog box appears.

3. Choose Word Add-ins in the Files of Type list box.

4. Select the add-in you want. If the add-in you want is not listed, change the folder or drive in the Look In box. (If you don't know the name of the add-in, consult the documentation provided with your add-in program.)

5. Choose OK.

Word for Windows loads the add-in program.

You also can load add-ins automatically, every time Word for Windows starts. To load an add-in program on startup, simply copy the add-in WLL file into the STARTUP subfolder located in the WinWord folder. The STARTUP folder is the default folder used for startup files. If you do not have a STARTUP folder, choose Tools, Options and select the File Locations tab (see fig. 6.13). Select the STARTUP folder in the File Types list, and then click the Modify button to set a new folder as the STARTUP folder.

Fig. 6.13
Modify the location of the STARTUP folder in the Tools, Options window.

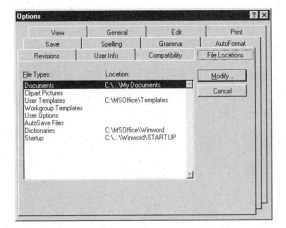

Removing Add-Ins

After an add-in is loaded, it remains available until you quit Word or explicitly remove the add-in. You might want to remove an add-in to make more system memory available.

To remove an add-in, follow these steps:

1. Choose File, Templates. The Templates and Add-ins dialog box appears.

2. Select the add-in you want to remove in the Global Templates and Add-ins list.

3. Click the Remove button. The add-in is unloaded.

4. Choose OK.

Chapter 7

Using Editing and Proofing Tools

By now, you're probably familiar with most of the basics of Word for Windows—how to create, edit, and save your documents. You can also use many tools to make entering text easier, ensure accuracy, and make sure that your document reads well.

With Word for Windows, you can use the Find and Replace feature to change text, formatting, special characters, and styles.

Before you print your document, check its spelling. Your eyes are trained to correct obvious spelling errors when you read them. However, you can still overlook a mistake when you proof a document. Use the spelling checker to catch mistakes that you missed and to correct spelling when you make an error. Use the Word for Windows grammar checker to correct faulty sentence construction and style. You can use the thesaurus to find just the right word or to define a term you're unsure about.

If you need to know how many words your document contains, use the Word Count feature to gather information about the number of words, lines, paragraphs, and more.

The following two figures show a document before (see fig. 7.1) and after (see fig. 7.2) Word checked its spelling and grammar. The user also used the thesaurus to improve some of the language.

Fig. 7.1
This rough draft of
a document has
not been revised
using Word for
Windows' editing
and proofing
tools.

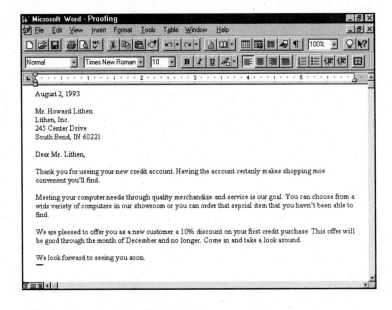

Fig. 7.2
You can polish
your writing with
the editing and
proofing tools.

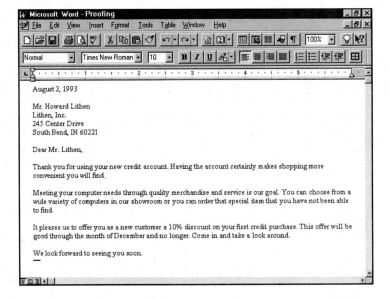

All the editing and proofing tools combine to help you hone the language of
your documents. Use them to do the following:

- Catch typos and spelling errors

- Make sure that your grammatical usage fits the type of document in
  question

■ Use the thesaurus to find the right replacement word. Then, choose Edit, Replace to exchange the new word for the original word.

In this chapter, you learn how to save time in your editing by using the following features:

■ The Find and Replace features for text items

■ Special formatting characters

■ Grammar and spell checkers

■ The thesaurus to find alternative terms

Using Find and Replace

Being able to find and replace text, formatting, styles, and special characters is an important time-saver. (This feature helps ensure that you catch every occurrence of whatever you need to find or replace.) The Edit, Find command finds and selects the text, formatting, style, or special character that you specify, enabling you to locate a certain phrase or a particular type of formatting easily. The Edit, Replace command enables you to find and replace text, formatting, and characters. You can replace items selectively or globally (changing your entire document all at once).

Finding Text

With the Word for Windows Find feature, you can quickly locate a specific word or phrase or a special formatting character in a document that is many pages long. The text can be as brief as a single letter or as long as a sentence containing up to 255 characters. You can also search for special characters, such as tabs, page breaks, line numbers, footnotes, or revision marks within your document. Alternatively, you might want to search for a particular format or style.

To find text (containing as many as 255 characters), empty spaces, or special characters, follow these steps:

1. Choose Edit, Find, or press Ctrl+F. The Find dialog box appears (see fig. 7.3).

Fig. 7.3

Use the Find dialog box to search through your document quickly.

2. In the Find What text box, type the text or special characters you want to search for. (For a list of special characters, see table 7.2 in the section "Finding and Replacing Special Characters.")

   The text scrolls to the right if you enter more text than what will fit in the box. You can enter as many as 255 characters.

3. Select one or more of the following options in the Find dialog box:

Option	Effect
Search	Determines the direction of the search. Down searches from the insertion point to the end of the document or selection. Up searches from the insertion point to the beginning of the document or selection. All searches the entire document or selection.
Match Case	Matches the text exactly as you have typed it—including capital letters. Word doesn't consider the use of small caps or all upper-case letters, but examines the case of the letters just as you originally typed them. Do not select this option if you want to find all occurrences of the text regardless of case.
Find Whole Words Only	Finds whole words only, not parts of words. Do not select this option if you want to find all occurrences of the text.
Use Pattern Matching	Uses special search operators and expressions with which to search. See the section "Finding and Replacing Special Characters" later in this chapter.
Sounds Like	Matches words that sound alike, but that are spelled differently, such as *seize* and *sees*.
Find All Word Forms	Finds all forms of a word, such as *entry* and *entries*.

Option	Effect
Format	Displays the Format options, including Font, Paragraph, Language, and Style. Depending on your selection, the dialog box displays the tab that contains the various types of formatting for each formatting option. (For more information on these options, refer to the section "Finding and Replacing Formats" later in this chapter.)
Special	Enables you to search for special codes in the text, such as paragraph marks and tab characters (see fig. 7.4). You can also type these codes. (See "Finding and Replacing Special Characters" later in this chapter.)
No Formatting	Removes any formatting codes displayed beneath the text box from a previous Find operation.

4. Click the Find Next button to begin the search, or click the Replace button to display the Replace dialog box.

Fig. 7.4
You can include special codes with search text.

Word for Windows finds the first occurrence of the text or special character and then moves to and selects that occurrence. The dialog box remains open so that you can immediately continue to search for other occurrences of the text or special character by choosing Find Next.

When you're finished with your search, close the Find dialog box by choosing Cancel or pressing Esc. For example, close the Find dialog box if you want to edit the found text.

After closing the Find dialog box, you can repeat the search by pressing Shift+F4. Alternatively, you can choose Edit, Find again and then choose Find Next.

If Word for Windows cannot find the text, the program displays a dialog box that indicates that Word has finished searching the document. Choose OK and try again.

Tip

You can also display the Find dialog box by pressing Ctrl+F.

If you're unsure of how to spell the word that you want to find, try using *special characters* in place of letters that you're not sure about. If you want to find *Smith*, for example, but aren't sure whether to spell it with an i or a y, search for **Sm^?th**. You can insert the question mark by typing **^?** (the caret character and the question mark) or by choosing Any Letter from the Special pop-up menu. Alternatively, you can search for part of a word, such as **Smi**.

Tip

Make sure that the Match Whole Word Only check box in the Find dialog box is not selected.

If you want to search for or replace text in only a portion of your document, select that portion. Then follow the general instructions for finding or replacing.

Replacing Text

Besides searching for text, formatting, or special characters, you also can replace them automatically. If you finish your document and realize that *Mr. Smith* really should have been *Ms. Smythe*, you can use a simple menu command to search for every occurrence of the incorrect spelling and replace it with the correct version. Or if your typist underlined every title in a long list of books and you decide that you want to italicize book titles, you can search for every occurrence of underlining and replace it with italic.

Replacing text works much the same way as finding text. The only major difference is that, in addition to the Find What text box, the Replace dialog box includes a Replace With text box in which you enter the text to replace the text that you find. The Replace dialog box enables you to confirm each replacement. Alternatively, you can replace all occurrences of the text with a single command.

To replace text, follow these steps:

1. Choose Edit, Replace or press Ctrl+H. The Replace dialog box appears (see fig. 7.5).

2. In the Find What text box, type the text that you want to replace.

3. In the Replace With text box, type the new text.

4. Select one or more of the options in the Replace dialog box:

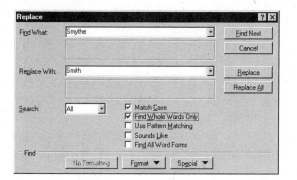

Fig. 7.5
Use the Replace dialog box to change one word or phrase to another throughout your document.

Option	Effect
Search	Determines the direction of the search. Down searches from the insertion point to the end of the document or selection. Up searches from the insertion point to the beginning of the document or selection. All searches the entire document or selection.
Match Case	Matches the text exactly as you have typed it—including capital letters. Word doesn't consider the use of small caps or all uppercase letters, but examines the case of the letters just as you originally typed them. Do not select this option if you want to find all occurrences of the text regardless of case.
Find Whole Words Only	Finds whole words only, not parts of words. Do not select this option if you want to find all occurrences of the text.
Use Pattern Matching	Uses special search operators and expressions with which to search. See the section "Finding and Replacing Special Characters" later in this chapter.
Sounds Like	Matches words that sound alike but are spelled differently, such as *seize* and *sees*.
Find All Word Forms	Finds all forms of a word, such as *entry* and *entries*.

(continues)

Option	Effect
Format	Displays Format options, including Font, Paragraph, Language, and Style. Depending on your selection, the dialog box displays the tab that contains the various types of formatting for each formatting option. (For more information on these options, see the section "Finding and Replacing Formats" later in this chapter.)
Special	Enables you to search for special codes in the text, such as paragraph marks and tab characters (refer to fig. 7.4). You also can type these codes. See "Finding and Replacing Special Characters" later in this chapter.
No Formatting	Removes any formatting codes displayed beneath the text box from a previous Find operation (unless you want these codes to affect the current search).

5. Click the Find Next or Replace All button.

   If you want to confirm each change, click Find Next. When Word finds an occurrence of the text, click the Replace button to change the text or the Find Next button again to continue the search without altering the selected occurrence.

   If you want to change all occurrences of the specified text without confirmation, click the Replace All button.

6. Choose Cancel to return to the document.

> **Note**
>
> If the dialog box is covering up the selected text, you can move this box by dragging its title bar. Alternatively, you can press Alt+space bar and then click Move. Then use the arrow keys to reposition the dialog box. Press Enter when you're finished moving the box.

If Word for Windows cannot find the text, you see a dialog box that indicates that Word has finished searching the document without finding the search item.

If you want to search for or replace text in only a portion of your document, select that portion. Then follow the general instructions for finding and replacing.

To cancel a Replace operation, press Esc or click the Cancel button.

> **Caution**
>
> Clicking the Replace All button saves time but can be risky. You need to be absolutely certain that you want to replace *every* occurrence of a word before you use this feature. You might want to start by confirming the first few replacements. When you are sure that you want to change all remaining occurrences of the text, choose Replace All. If you select Replace All and then realize that you made a mistake, immediately choose Edit, Undo Replace.

Unless you specify otherwise, Word for Windows applies the original formatting to the new replacement text. If you replace the boldface word *Roger* with the plain name *Ms. Smith*, for example, the replacement is a boldface *Ms. Smith*. To override this feature, specify formatting as part of your replacement (see this chapter's section "Finding and Replacing Formats").

You can undo a replacement by choosing Edit, Undo Replace. If you have confirmed each replacement, Edit, Undo Replace undoes only the last replacement (however, you can choose Edit, Undo Replace repeatedly to undo replacements sequentially, starting with the last replacement). If you choose the Replace All button and make all the replacements at once, Edit, Undo Replace undoes all the replacements.

You can use the Undo button on the Standard toolbar to undo all the replacements.

To undo all replacements using the Undo button, follow these steps:

1. Click the down arrow of the Undo button on the Standard toolbar. The box containing all the actions appears.

2. Drag to select all the Replace items listed on the Undo button's pull-down menu.

3. Release the mouse button. All the replacements revert to the original text.

After choosing Edit, Copy to copy text to the Clipboard, you can paste that text into the text boxes in the Find and Replace dialog boxes. This feature enables you to insert large amounts of text or text that uses noncontiguous formats. To use the contents of the Clipboard, position the insertion point in the Find What or Replace With text box. Then press Ctrl+V.

Finding and Replacing Formatting and Styles

Finding and replacing formatting is similar to finding and replacing text. Suppose that you have a document in which you have underlined many titles, and then you decide to italicize them instead. Or suppose that you have sprinkled an article with boldface phrases and decide to remove the boldface formatting. You can change the text, the formatting, or both the text and the formatting.

You can also find and replace paragraph formats, languages, and styles. For example, if your document has centered paragraphs, you can replace the centered formatting with right-aligned formatting. If you want to check the spelling in a French paragraph, you can assign a French language dictionary rather than an English (US) language dictionary. Or you can replace a style such as Heading 1 with another style, such as Heading 2.

Finding and Replacing Formats

You can find and replace text (or special characters), formatting, or both. For example, you can find text and replace it with different text, or you can find formatted text and replace it with differently formatted text. Or, you can find only formatting and replace it with different formatting.

To find or replace formatting, follow these steps:

1. Choose Edit, Find or Edit, Replace. The Find or the Replace dialog box appears.

2. Select the Find What box. Then type the formatted text that you want to locate, or leave the box empty to find only formatting.

3. Select the font, character, paragraph, language, or style formatting that you want to find or replace.

   To find a font or character formatting, choose the Format button and select Font from the menu that appears. The Find Font dialog box appears (see fig. 7.6). This dialog box looks the same as the Font dialog box that you use to format characters. Select the font or other options that you want to find. Then choose OK or press Enter.

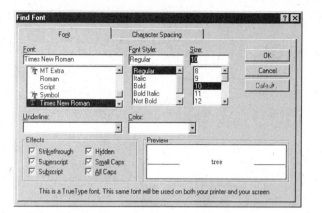

Fig. 7.6
You can include character formatting as a Find or Replace option in the Find Font dialog box.

To find paragraph formatting, choose the F<u>o</u>rmat button and select <u>P</u>aragraph from the menu that appears. The Find Paragraph dialog box appears. This dialog box resembles the Paragraph dialog box that you use to format paragraphs. Select the paragraph formatting options that you want to find. Then choose OK or press Enter.

To find language formatting (areas of the document to which you assign a dictionary for another language), choose the F<u>o</u>rmat button and select <u>L</u>anguage from the menu that appears. The Find Language dialog box displays (see fig. 7.7). Select the language assignment that you want to use in your <u>F</u>ind and R<u>e</u>place operations.

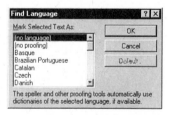

Fig. 7.7
Use the Find Language dialog box to search for or replace an area of text that has a foreign language dictionary assigned to it.

To find style formatting, click the F<u>o</u>rmat button and select <u>S</u>tyle from the menu that appears. The Find Style dialog box appears (see fig. 7.8). Select the style that you want to find or replace. Choose OK or press Enter.

Fig. 7.8

In the Find Style dialog box, choose the styles that you want to find or replace.

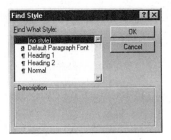

The font, paragraph, language, or style options that you select are listed beneath the Find What or Replace With text boxes.

To replace formatting, select the Replace With text box. Then type the replacement text, or leave the box empty to replace the contents of the Find What text box with formatting only.

To add formatting to the replacement text, choose the Format button. Select Font, Paragraph, Language, or Style. The Replace Font, Replace Paragraph, Replace Language, or Replace Style dialog box appears. Select the options that you want. Choose OK or press Enter.

The formatting options that you select are listed under the Replace With text box.

4. Choose Find Next to find the next occurrence of the specified text, formatting, or both.

   If you're replacing formatting, choose Find Next to find the next occurrence. Then choose Replace, or choose Replace All to find and replace all occurrences.

5. When the Find or Replace operation is complete, choose Cancel (or press Esc) to close the Find dialog box. Choose Close (or press Esc) to close the Replace dialog box.

Initially, check boxes are gray and text boxes are blank on the format dialog boxes. This indicates that these fields are not involved in the Find or Replace operation. Clicking a check box option once selects it—a check appears in the box. Clicking a second time clears (or deselects) the option. In this case, the option is still involved in the Find or Replace operation. However, you have specifically deselected that option, removing the format. Clicking a third time grays the option again so that it is no longer involved in the Find or Replace operation.

If you want to remove small caps from all occurrences of a certain word, for example, follow these steps:

1. Choose Edit, Replace and then type the word into the Find What text box.

2. Click the Format button. Then select Font.

3. Click the Small Caps option to select it. Choose OK to return to the Replace dialog box. Then type the same word into the Replace With box.

4. Choose the Format button and select Font. Click the Small Caps check box twice to deselect this option. If you leave this box grayed, the operation does not remove the formatting.

The formatting selections that you make for the Find What and the Replace With text boxes remain in effect until you change them. In other words, they are in effect the next time that you open the Find or Replace dialog box. To remove all formatting options, select Find What or Replace With, and then click the No Formatting button.

You can use the shortcut keys for formatting characters and paragraphs in the Find and Replace dialog boxes. To specify bold formatting, for example, press Ctrl+B. To specify a font, press Ctrl+Shift+F repeatedly until the font that you want is selected. See the reference card for a list of the shortcut keys.

The Find and Replace feature in Word for Windows is flexible, enabling you to replace text regardless of formatting, both text and formatting, or just formatting. You also can replace text with nothing (that is, delete specified text) or remove formatting. Table 7.1 outlines replacement options available when you use the Find and Replace commands.

Tip

As a safe practice, always confirm the first occurrence of your Replace operations before proceeding with a global replacement.

Table 7.1   Find and Replace Options

If You Replace	With	You Get
Text	Format	Old text and format, plus new format
Format or text and format	Format	Old text, new format
Text	Text and format	New text, old format, plus new format

(continues)

Table 7.1 Continued

If You Replace	With	You Get
Text	Nothing	Deleted text
Format or text and format	Nothing	Deleted text and formatting

Replacing Styles

A *style* is a combination of several formatting commands. You can have a style called Title, for example, that includes the formatting commands for Times New Roman font, 24-point size, centered, underlined, and bold. A style enables you to apply all these formats with a single command. You can use the Word for Windows Replace command to replace either a format with a style or one style with another. When you replace formatting or a style with a style, all paragraphs formatted by the replacement style take on its formatting.

▶ See "Creating Styles," p. 358

The procedure to replace a format with a style, or one style with another, is identical to that which you use for finding and replacing formats. When you click the Format button and select Style in the Replace dialog box, the Find Style or Replace Style dialog box displays all the defined styles (refer to fig. 7.8). When you select the style in the Find What Style or Replace With Style list, the formatting commands that compose the selected style appear below the list.

> **Note**
>
> Each time that you use the Find or Replace command, Word for Windows remembers the last words and formatting that you searched for or replaced. Click the No For-matting button in the dialog box when you need to clear formatting selections.

Finding and Replacing Special Characters

Finding and replacing text in your document is handy and easy. Sometimes, however, you want to search for and replace other items. You can find and replace many special characters, including a wild-card character (**?**), a tab mark, a paragraph mark, section marks, a blank space, and many more. If you open a text (or ASCII) file with carriage returns at the end of every line, for example, you can replace each of those paragraph marks with a space. Alter-natively, if you have a list that contains spaces rather than tabs, you can replace those spaces with tabs. Always be careful to confirm your changes at least once so that you don't inadvertently make an incorrect replacement.

You can find or replace special characters by using the Special button in the Find or Replace dialog box or by using the keyboard. Table 7.2 lists the codes that you can type from the keyboard.

Table 7.2	Codes for Special Characters
Code	**Special Character**
^p	Paragraph mark
^t	Tab character
^a	Annotation mark (Find only)
^?	Any character (Find only)
^#	Any digit (Find only)
^$	Any letter (Find only)
^^	Caret character
^n	Column break
^+	Em dash
^=	En dash
^e	Endnote mark (Find only)
^d	Field (Find only)
^f	Footnote mark (Find only)
^g	Graphic (Find only)
^l	Manual line break
^m	Manual page break
^~	Nonbreaking hyphen
^s	Nonbreaking space
^_	Optional hyphen
^b	Section break (Find only)

(continues)

Table 7.2 Continued	
Code	**Special Character**
^w	White space (any space—one space, multiple spaces, tab spaces—bordered by characters) (Find only)
^c	Clipboard contents (Replace only)
^&	Find What text (Replace only)
^0nnn	ANSI or ASCII characters (n is the character number) (Replace only)

To insert special codes by clicking the Special button, follow these steps:

1. Choose Edit, Find or Edit, Replace.

2. Select the Find What or Replace With text box.

3. Click the Special button.

4. Select the command that you want to find or replace.

To insert special codes from the keyboard, follow these steps:

1. Choose Edit, Find or Edit, Replace.

2. Type the appropriate code in either the Find What or the Replace With text box. Enter the caret character (^) by pressing Shift+6.

3. Click the No Formatting button if you do not want the formats to affect the action of the Find or Replace command.

 If you want to find or replace special characters, you should display nonprinting characters, such as paragraph marks and tab marks. To display nonprinting characters from the toolbar, click the Show/Hide ¶ button on the Standard toolbar.

To display nonprinting characters from the menu, follow these steps:

1. Choose Tools, Options.

2. Select the View tab.

3. Select the All check box in the Nonprinting Characters group.

4. Click OK.

Checking Your Spelling

After you enter your text and you're fairly sure that the words are correct, check your document's spelling.

The Word for Windows spelling checker quickly pinpoints words in your document that don't match those in its or the user's dictionary, or in your own custom dictionary. When you aren't sure about a word, you can ask Word for Windows to suggest alternative spellings. The program searches its dictionary for a match and offers you a list of other spellings. It can even suggest one as the most likely choice.

When automatic spell checking is turned on, Word for Windows underlines words it thinks are misspelled with a red wavy line, which makes it easy for you to spot when you proofread your document. An icon of an open book with a red X also appears at the bottom-right portion of the screen, indicating that spelling errors exist in your document.

> ### Note
>
> The Word for Windows spelling checker also searches for several other problems: double words (*the the*), oddly capitalized words (*mY*), words that should be capitalized (*california*), and words that should be all capitals (*ZIP*). You also can set additional options in the Spelling dialog box.

Spell checking begins at the beginning of your document and works through your document, checking its entire contents. You can check spelling in a smaller section of text by first selecting that area (it can be as little as a single word). Then you can check the spelling as usual.

A good spelling checker gives you the confidence of knowing that your work is accurate. However, be careful. No spelling checker can tell you when you have misused words, perhaps typing **for** when you mean *four*, or **thought** when the word should be *though*. A spelling checker is an important tool but cannot replace thorough proofreading.

Checking Your Document's Spelling Automatically

Word 95 automatically underlines misspelled words with a wavy red line. Spell checking and underlining occur as you type. Automatic spell checking only works when the feature is enabled. To turn on automatic spell checking, choose <u>T</u>ools, <u>O</u>ptions, select the Spelling tab, and then select the <u>A</u>utomatic Spell Checking check box. If you find that your system becomes unacceptably slow when using automatic spell checking, disable this option and use the command method of spell checking that is described in the next section.

To check spelling of words with a wavy underline, follow these steps:

1. Double-click the open book icon at the bottom of the screen to find the next underlined word in the document. You can also right-click an underlined word. A pop-up menu appears, showing a list of suggested words and additional options.

2. You have four choices in which you can correct the misspelled word:

   Correct the word if it is misspelled.

   Select a word from the list shown in the pop-up menu.

   Select Ignore All to ignore all occurrences of the word in your document.

   Select Add to add the word to the selected dictionary displayed in the Add Words To box in the Spelling dialog box.

3. Repeat this procedure for each word you want to check.

Checking Your Document's Spelling

To check spelling in your document using commands, follow these steps:

1. Select the word or section of your document that you want to check for spelling. If you select nothing, Word for Windows checks the entire document.

2. Choose Tools, Spelling, or click the Spelling button on the Standard toolbar. Alternatively, press F7.

   Word for Windows scrolls through your document, matching each word against the main dictionary. The program selects words that it does not recognize, and the Spelling dialog box appears. The unrecognized word is highlighted in the text and displayed in the Not In Dictionary box (see fig. 7.9). You can move the Spelling dialog box if it is hiding the selected word.

3. Correct the misspelled word in the Change To text box, or select the correct word from the Suggestions list.

Fig. 7.9
You can choose
Spelling to find
misspellings and
typos throughout
your document.

If the Always Suggest option is turned on in the Spelling Options, and
Word for Windows can suggest an alternative spelling, that suggestion
appears in the Change To text box. Other possible words appear in the
Suggestions list. If the Always Suggest option is turned off, the selected
word appears in the Change To text box. (For more information on
using Always Suggest, see the section "Setting Spelling Options" later in
this chapter.)

If the Always Suggest option is turned off, the Suggestions list is empty.
Choose the Suggest button to display a list of possible words, and then
select the correct word from the list.

4. If the correct spelling appears in the Change To box, click the Change
    button. The selected word changes to the spelling displayed in the
    Change To box. Choose Change All to change all occurrences of the
    misspelled word in your document.

    Alternatively, choose Ignore to leave the word as is. Choose Ignore All
    to ignore all future occurrences of the word in your document.

    If Word for Windows finds a word that it thinks is misspelled and you
    want to add that word to the dictionary, click the Add button. The
    program then adds the word to the selected dictionary displayed in the
    Add Words To box.

5. Word for Windows continues searching. Choose Cancel to discontinue
    the spell checking. You also can undo as many as five previous correc-
    tions by choosing the Undo Last command.

6. A dialog box appears when the spelling checker reaches the end of the
    document or the selection. If you are checking a word or a selected
    section, a dialog box asks whether you want to check the remainder of
    the document. Choose Yes or No.

If you start spell checking in the middle of the document, the spell checker completes checking of the document, then returns to the beginning and continues checking up to the point at which you began.

You can halt the spelling check to edit your document without closing the Spelling dialog box. Drag the Spelling dialog box away from the area that you want to edit. Then either click in the document or press Ctrl+Tab to activate the document window. After editing your document, choose the Start button in the Spelling dialog box to resume spell checking at the point at which you stopped. (If you're using a keyboard rather than a mouse, press Ctrl+Tab to reactivate the Spelling dialog box.)

You can use wild-card characters such as the asterisk (*****) or question mark (**?**) when searching for the spelling of a word. In the Change To text box of the Spelling dialog box, type the word, using as a wild card either ***** for multiple unknown characters or **?** for a single, unknown character. If you are not sure whether the correct spelling is *exercise* or *exercize*, for example, type **exerci?e** in the Change To text box. Then choose the Suggest button. Word for Windows displays the word's correct spelling.

You can undo all spelling changes made during a spell check in two ways. To undo all spelling changes from a menu command, choose Edit, Undo Spelling Change immediately after you complete the spell checking. To undo all spelling changes with the Undo button, follow these steps:

1. Click the Undo button on the Standard toolbar.

2. Drag down through all the Spelling edits.

3. Release the mouse button.

Finding Double Words

When the Word for Windows spelling checker finds double words, the Not In Dictionary box changes to the Repeated Word box, and the repeated word is displayed (see fig. 7.10).

To delete the repeated word, leave the Change To box blank and click the Delete button. Be sure to delete unwanted spaces.

Adding Words to a Dictionary

The spell-checking process enables you to add words to a custom dictionary. When Word for Windows selects an unrecognized word that you use often, choose the dictionary to which you want to add it. Thereafter, the spell checker will bypass the word.

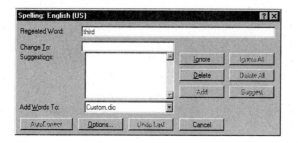

Fig. 7.10
Word indicates
double occurrences
during a spelling
check.

Everyday Word Processing

To add words to a custom dictionary, choose a dictionary from the Add
Words To list and then click the Add button.

> **Caution**
>
> Be careful not to accidentally add misspelled words to the dictionary. If you want to
> delete a misspelled word from a dictionary, use Windows WordPad to open the
> dictionary and delete the word. Dictionaries are located in the PROOF folder, found
> in the COMMON FILES folder within the PROGRAM FILES folder.

Setting Spelling Options

The Spelling dialog box includes the Options button. Choosing this button
enables you to use a non-English dictionary or to check spelling against a
custom dictionary that you create. (See the next section for information on
creating a custom dictionary.) The button also enables you to select automatic spell checking. The automatic spell checking feature underlines words
with a red wavy line that it cannot find in the dictionary. You can either
correct the underlined word immediately, or when you run the spell checker.

You can set options at any time by following these steps:

1. To set options before you check spelling, choose Tools, Options. Then
   select the Spelling tab.

   To set options while checking spelling, choose the Options button in
   the Spelling dialog box. The Spelling tab for adjusting spelling options
   appears (see fig. 7.11).

Fig. 7.11

In the Spelling tab
of the Options
dialog box, you
can customize a
spelling check.

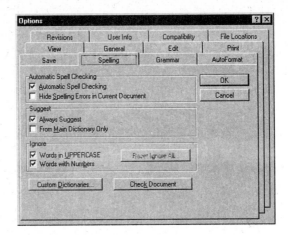

2. Under Automatic Spell Checking, select among the following options:

Option	Function
Automatic Spell Checking	Automatically identifies words not found in the dictionary by placing a red wavy line under each
Hide Spelling Errors in Current Document	Hides red wavy lines from beneath words not found in the dictionary

3. Under Ignore, select the class of words that you want Word for Windows to skip during every spell check. The following table lists these options:

Option	Function
Words in UPPERCASE	Ignores words in all uppercase letters
Words with Numbers	Ignores words that include numbers
Reset Ignore All	Removes all words that you have added to the Ignore All list during the current session. The next time that you spell check a document during the current Word session, Word does not ignore those words.

4. Choose the Custom Dictionaries button to open the Custom Dictionaries dialog box. Select from the Custom Dictionaries list the dictionaries that you want open (see fig. 7.12). As many as 10 custom dictionaries can be open during a spelling check. You might have many custom dictionaries available. However, Word for Windows checks spelling against only custom dictionaries that are open.

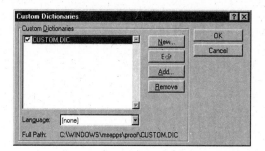

Fig. 7.12
You can select a custom dictionary in the Custom Dictionaries dialog box.

5. In the Suggest group, choose between the following options:

Option	Function
Always Suggest	Word will always suggest corrections. Deselect this option if you don't always want suggestions (and if you want the spelling checker to work faster).
From Main	Suggestions will come from the Main Dictionary Only dictionary only, not from any open custom dictionaries.

6. Choose OK.

Creating a Custom Dictionary

Each time that you run the spelling checker, it compares the words in your document with those in the dictionary. The Word for Windows standard dictionary contains thousands of commonly used words. However, this dictionary may not include certain words that you frequently use—for example, terms specific to your profession, your company's name, or the names of products that your firm sells. You can create custom dictionaries and specify that Word for Windows consult them each time that you check spelling. To learn how to open these dictionaries so that Word uses them when you check spelling, see the preceding section, "Setting Spelling Options." To learn how to add words to your custom dictionary, refer to the previous section, "Adding Words to a Dictionary."

To create a new custom dictionary, follow these steps:

1. Choose Tools, Options. Then select the Spelling tab.

2. Choose the New button in the Custom Dictionaries section. A dialog box prompts you for the name of the dictionary file.

3. In the File Name box, type a name for the new dictionary ending with the extension **DIC**. Your dictionary is stored in the C:\MSOFFICE\ WINWORD subfolder. You can select another folder in which Word is to store the dictionary.

4. Choose Save.

5. To close the Options dialog box, choose OK in the Spelling tab.

You can remove a word from a custom dictionary by selecting the dictionary in the Custom Dictionaries list and then clicking the Edit button. Choose OK to close the Options dialog box. The file lists all dictionary entries alphabetically. Delete the words that you no longer want. Then save the file in Text Only format (don't change the file's name or location).

The following table describes the options that you can choose from the Custom Dictionaries group:

Option	Function
Edit	Makes changes to the custom dictionary that you select. You must confirm that you want to open the dictionary as a Word document. Word warns you that it will stop automatic spell checking when you edit a dictionary. You must select the Automatic Spell Checking check box to enable Automatic Spell Checking. This check box is accessed by choosing Tools, Options, then selecting the Spelling tab.
Add	Adds a custom dictionary from another directory or disk.
Remove	Removes a dictionary from the Custom Dictionaries list. You must select the dictionary before you can remove it.
Language	Adds language formatting to a custom dictionary. Word will use that custom dictionary only when spell checking text formatted in that language. (See "Proofing in Other Languages" later in this chapter.) If you select (none), Word uses the dictionary to spell check text formatted in any language.

Troubleshooting

I tried to run the Spelling option and a dialog box appeared indicating that Word for Windows cannot locate that feature from the ⊥ools menu.

Many Word for Windows features, such as the spelling checker, are optional during the Word for Windows installation process. If a feature or command that you want to use is not installed, you can click Add/Remove Office Programs on the Office Shortcut Bar menu, and then select the options you want. For example, select Proofing Tools if you want to install the spelling checker. To complete the installation process, follow the instructions that appear.

Checking Your Grammar

While writing a document, you might be uncertain whether your sentence structure is grammatically correct. You might use the phrase *between you and I*, for example, when the grammatically correct version is *between you and me*. Use the Word for Windows grammar checker to spot grammatical errors and receive suggestions on how to correct them. The Grammar dialog box provides several choices for making changes (see fig. 7.13).

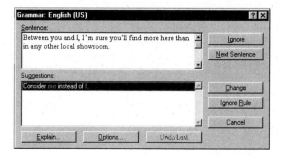

Fig. 7.13
Use the Grammar checker to flag possible errors in spelling and grammar.

If you do not select any text before using the grammar checker, Word for Windows checks the entire document, beginning at the insertion point. If you select text, Word checks only the selection. A selection must contain at least one sentence.

By default, Word for Windows checks spelling and grammar. If you want to check only grammar, turn off the Check ⊆pelling option in the Grammar tab of the Options dialog box. (To learn how to do this, see the upcoming section, "Selecting Grammar Rules.") If the Check ⊆pelling option is selected,

Word for Windows might display the Spelling dialog box before displaying the Grammar dialog box—it depends on whether Word locates a spelling or grammar error first.

To check a document's grammar, follow these steps:

1. Choose Tools, Grammar.

   The Grammar dialog box appears when Word for Windows finds a sentence with a possible grammatical error or questionable style (refer to fig. 7.13). The grammatically questionable words appear highlighted, and also appear in the Sentence box in the Grammar dialog box.

2. Select an option in the Grammar dialog box.

The Suggestions box explains why a selection is ungrammatical, and if possible, offers possible replacement text. You can update the sentence with a suggested correction by selecting it in the Suggestions box and then clicking the Change button. If the Change button is grayed, the Grammar checker cannot suggest a change. You can make a change directly in the document.

To leave the grammar checker temporarily to make a change in the document, follow these steps:

1. Choose the document window by clicking it or by pressing Ctrl+Tab.

2. Edit the sentence in the document.

3. Click the Start button that appears in the Grammar dialog box. The grammar check resumes at the insertion point.

You can also choose from these Grammar dialog box options:

Option	Function
Ignore	Ignores the questioned word or phrase.
Ignore Rule	Skips other similar occurrences that break the same grammar or style rule.
Next Sentence	Leaves the sentence unchanged and moves to the next sentence.
Explain	Provides more information about the error. A window appears describing the relevant grammar or style rule. After you read the information, press Esc or select the window's X button to clear the window and return to the Grammar dialog box.
Options	Selects different rules of grammar and style. The Grammar Options tab that appears enables you to select an option button for the rule group that you want to observe for the remainder of the check. (See "Selecting Grammar Rules" later in this chapter.)

After reaching the end of the document, the grammar checker continues checking from the beginning. When Word finishes checking the entire document, you see a message indicating that the grammar check is completed. Choose OK to return to your document.

If you select the Show Readability Statistics option, a dialog box displays the information about the document. (The section "Testing the Readability of a Document," later in this chapter, covers readability.) Choose OK to return to your document.

Selecting Grammar Rules

You can choose the rules of style and grammar that Word uses during grammar checks. Depending on your audience, your style, and the material, you might want to follow some rules and disregard others. Choose Tools, Options and select the Grammar tab. You can then choose among three predefined rule groups: Strictly (all rules), For Business Writing, or For Casual Writing. Table 7.3 describes these rule groups. You can also create as many as three custom rule groups or customize the three predefined rule groups by selecting or clearing grammar and style options.

Table 7.3 Grammar Checker's Rule Groups	
Rule Group	**Rules Applied**
Strictly (all rules)	All grammar and style rules
For Business Writing	Only those rules appropriate for written business communication
For Casual Writing	Only those rules appropriate for informal written communication (the fewest number of rules)
Custom 1, 2, 3	Rules that you apply

To customize a rule group, follow these steps:

1. Choose Tools, Options, and select the Grammar tab. If you have already started grammar checking, click the Options button in the Grammar dialog box. The Grammar tab appears (see fig. 7.14).

2. Select from the Use Grammar and Style Rules list the rule group that you want to change.

3. Click the Customize Settings button. The Customize Grammar Settings dialog box appears (see fig. 7.15).

Fig. 7.14
Use the Grammar tab in the Options dialog box to choose the grammatical rules and styles that you want to apply to your documents.

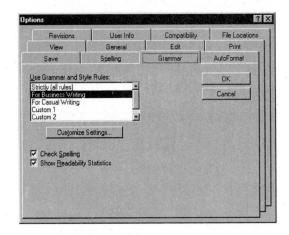

Fig. 7.15
You can customize the grammatical rules that Word for Windows uses to check your document.

4. If you base a custom rule group on an existing rule group, select the existing rule group from the Use Grammar and Style Rules list.

5. Choose Grammar, Style and then select in the rule check boxes the rules that you want Word for Windows to observe. Clear the check boxes for rules that you want Word to ignore.

6. From the pull-down lists in the Catch group, select how you want to control split infinitives, consecutive nouns, and prepositional phrases. Also, in the Sentences Containing More Words Than option, indicate the maximum number of words that you want in a sentence.

7. Choose OK to return to the Options dialog box.

8. Choose OK to return to the document or grammar checking.

Testing the Readability of a Document

Readability statistics measure how easy your writing is to read. Writing that is easier to read communicates more clearly. *The Wall Street Journal*, for example, writes at the eighth-grade level. Hemingway wrote at the sixth-grade level. Writing need not be boring when it's readable. To make his writing interesting, Hemingway used intriguing subject matter, active writing, colorful descriptions, and variable sentence lengths.

If you choose to display readability statistics, they appear at the end of grammar checking.

To display readability statistics after you use the Grammar command, follow these steps:

1. Choose Tools, Options.

2. Select the Grammar tab.

3. Select the Show Readability Statistics check box.

4. Click OK.

The Word for Windows readability statistics are based on the Flesch-Kincaid index. This index assigns a reading ease score and grade level based on the average number of words per sentence and syllables per 100 words.

Using the Thesaurus

When you're not sure of a word's meaning, or when you think you're using a certain term too often, take advantage of the Word for Windows thesaurus. It defines selected words and offers alternative terms (synonyms). For example, Word for Windows synonyms for the word *information* include *intelligence*, *data*, and *facts*.

The thesaurus looks up one word at a time. You can specify the word by selecting it. Otherwise, the thesaurus looks up the word that the insertion point indicates. If the insertion point is within a word, the thesaurus looks up that word. If the insertion point is outside a word, the thesaurus looks up the word preceding the insertion point.

To display a list of synonyms and definitions for a word in your document, follow these steps:

1. Select the word for which you want to locate a synonym.

2. Choose <u>T</u>ools, <u>T</u>hesaurus, or press Shift+F7. The Thesaurus dialog box appears (see fig. 7.16).

Fig. 7.16

In the Thesaurus dialog box, you can find a list of meanings for any word that you select.

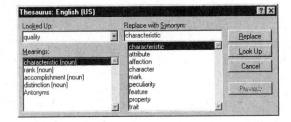

The Loo<u>k</u>ed Up text box displays the selected word. The Replace With <u>S</u>ynonym text box displays the first meaning, followed by a list of synonyms. The word's definition appears in the <u>M</u>eanings box.

3. You have several options at this point:

Action	Result
Choose a synonym in the Replace With <u>S</u>ynonym list.	The word moves into the Replace With <u>S</u>ynonym box.
Select a different meaning from the <u>M</u>eanings list.	A new list of synonyms appears in the Replace With <u>S</u>ynonym list. You can select a word from this list.
Select related words or antonyms in the <u>M</u>eanings list.	The Replace With list displays related words or antonyms.
Select the word from the <u>M</u>eanings or Replace with <u>S</u>ynonym list, or type a word and choose <u>L</u>ooked Up.	Meanings of the new words appear.
Select the word from the <u>M</u>eanings or <u>S</u>ynonym list, or type a word and choose <u>L</u>ook Up.	Meanings of the new words appear.
Choose <u>P</u>revious.	The word that the thesaurus previously looked up appears.

4. Choose the <u>R</u>eplace button to replace the selected word in the document with the word in the Replace with <u>S</u>ynonym, Replace with Ant<u></u>onym, or Replace with R<u>e</u>lated Word box, or click the Cancel button.

Proofing in Other Languages

If you're reading the English language edition of this book, most of your typing is probably in this language. However, your document might contain some text in Spanish, French, or another language. You can select that text, assign to it a language other than English, and all the Word for Windows proofing tools—the spell checker, hyphenation, thesaurus, and grammar checker—will use the other language dictionary that you specify to proof that text.

Before the Language command is available, you must purchase and install the appropriate language-proofing tools for the language that you want to use. If you want to check the spelling of French text, for example, you must install a French dictionary. Contact Microsoft Corporation or other vendors for information on the many language-proofing tools available.

To proof text in another language, follow these steps:

1. Select the text written in another language.

2. Choose Tools, Language to display the Language dialog box.

3. Select the language from the Mark Selected Text As list. To change the language for all the text that you proof, click the Default button.

   You can choose (no proofing) from the list if you want the proofing tools to skip the selected text. This feature is useful for technical material that contains terms not listed in any of the standard spelling dictionaries.

4. Click OK.

Counting Words

The Tools, Word Count command counts the number of pages, words, characters, paragraphs, and lines in a document (see fig. 7.17). You can choose to include footnotes and endnotes in the count.

To count words, lines, and more of the document on the screen, follow these steps:

1. Choose Tools, Word Count. The Word Count dialog box displays. Word performs the count and displays the results.

2. Select Include Footnotes and Endnotes if you want to include these items in the count. Word redoes the count and the new results appear.

3. Click the Close button.

Fig. 7.17
The Word
Count dialog box
provides statistics
about a document.

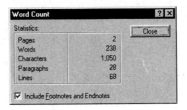

Chapter 8

Previewing and Printing a Document

Although printing with Word for Windows can be as simple as opening a document, choosing a print command, and starting the printing operation, Word for Windows 95 gives you many additional options. You can preview one or more pages in your document and change their margins while you're in the preview. You can print all or part of an open document. You can print a draft or a final version. You can print hidden text and field codes. You can also print multiple documents without opening them.

Often, your objective is not to print a document but to route it electronically to its destination. In this chapter, you learn how to do the following:

■ Print a document in Word

■ Fax a document in Word

■ Print documents to a file

■ Send files by electronic mail to someone in your workgroup

Selecting a Printer

Microsoft Windows is the common denominator that makes printing with Word for Windows 95 easy. Any printer that you install to use with Windows you also can use with Word for Windows 95.

Word for Windows 95 prints on whichever installed printer you currently have selected as the default printer. You can find out which printer is selected by choosing File, Print and looking at the top of the Print dialog box (see fig. 8.1).

Fig. 8.1
The Print dialog box offers a variety of options.

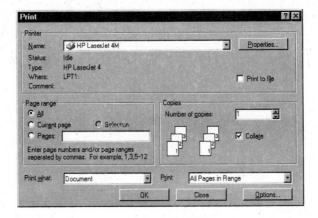

To select a printer, select the <u>N</u>ame drop-down list in the Print dialog box. If you use only one printer, select that printer the first time that you print a document with Word for Windows 95. After you print, your printer stays selected. If you switch between printers, you must select a printer each time that you change printers.

When you select a printer, Word lists the available printers in the <u>N</u>ame list of the Printer group (see fig. 8.2). This list includes all printers installed for use with Windows. If the printer that you want to use is not on the list, you must install it in Windows. To install a printer, see the following section, "Installing a Printer in Windows."

Fig. 8.2
Select the <u>N</u>ame drop-down list in the Print dialog box to view the installed printers.

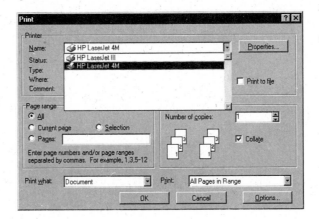

To select a printer, follow these steps:

1. Choose <u>F</u>ile, <u>P</u>rint. The Print dialog box appears.

2. Select a printer from the Name list in the Printer group.

3. Choose OK to print, or click the X in the top-right corner of the Print dialog box to close the dialog box and return to your document.

The next time that you choose File, Print, you see your selected printer listed at the top of the Print dialog box.

The Options button in the Print dialog box provides access to certain settings that affect the appearance of your printed document. You learn about these settings later in this chapter.

Setting Up Your Printer

Windows manages most details of setting up a printer. However, Windows leaves three tasks for you: selecting the printer that you want to use in Word for Windows 95, installing the printers that you want to use in Windows, and changing the printer setup for special printing needs.

Installing a Printer in Windows

Selecting a printer in Word for Windows 95 is simple—if the Print dialog box lists the printer. If your printer is not listed, Windows does not have that printer installed. You can install a printer in Windows from within Word for Windows 95.

To install a printer in Windows, follow these steps:

1. Click the Start button in the taskbar at the bottom of the screen.

2. Move the mouse pointer over the Settings command. The Settings group appears.

3. Move the mouse pointer over Printers. Then click it or press Enter.

4. Double-click the Add Printer icon from the Printers window. The first dialog box of the Add Printer Wizard appears.

5. Click the Next button to begin installation. Choose Local printer if your printer is attached to your computer, or choose Network Printer if the printer is attached to a network.

6. Click the Next button. You may have to wait several seconds while Word builds a driver information database.

7. From the Manufacturers list, select the printer's manufacturer.

Tip

If the taskbar is currently hidden, you can display it by moving the pointer to the bottom of the screen.

Everyday Word Processing

The list of available printers appears in the Printers list. The list of printer manufacturers and printer models appears, as shown in figure 8.3.

Fig. 8.3

Select your printer's manufacturer and model.

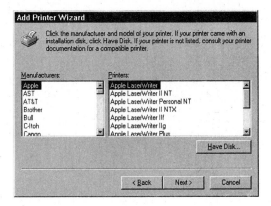

8. From the Printers list, select the printer that you want to install. Then choose the Next button.

   If the Printers list does not list your printer and you have a printer driver (a file with a DRV extension) from the printer manufacturer, choose the Have Disk button. If the list doesn't list your printer and you do not have a driver, you may be able to use the driver of a compatible printer model. Otherwise, you can select Generic as the manufacturer and Generic/Text Only as the printer, but this driver does not support special fonts or graphics.

   A dialog box prompts you to insert the disk issued by the printer manufacturer. The dialog box shows drive A as the default, but you can enter another drive letter.

9. Select the port to use with this printer from the Available ports list and then click the Next button (see fig. 8.4).

   If you want to configure the port settings, click the Configure Port button.

10. Type a name for this printer in the Printer Name dialog box, or keep the manufacturer's name. Select the Yes option button if you want this printer to be the default printer, or choose No. Then click the Next button. Figure 8.5 shows the Printer Name text box in the Add Printer Wizard.

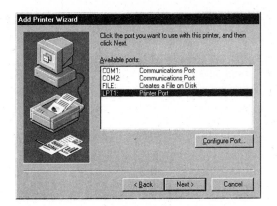

Everyday Word Processing

Fig. 8.4
Configure the port
that you want to
use with this
printer.

Fig. 8.5
Type a name to
identify this
printer.

11. A dialog box prompts you to print a test page after installing your printer. Choose Yes (recommended) or No.

12. Choose Finish. If the printer you chose is not supported by a driver that is already installed in Windows, Word prompts you to insert a particular Windows 95 disk where the selected driver is located. Insert the specified disk, or Windows 95 CD-ROM.

13. Choose OK. When the Copying Files dialog box appears, enter the drive and folder path that contains the new printer driver.

   If Windows does not find the driver on the disk, the dialog box reappears. Insert a different disk than the one requested and choose OK again.

   The printer driver may be on one of the other Windows installation disks.

   You return to the Printers window when the installation is complete.

14. Select the new printer's icon in the Printers window.

15. Choose File, Properties from the Printers window.

16. Select the appropriate tab in the Properties dialog box and select the settings that you use most frequently, such as printing in portrait (vertically) or landscape (horizontally), the resolution, paper source, printer memory, and font cartridges. The options vary depending on the printer you selected. Then choose OK.

17. Click the X in the top-right corner of the Printers window to close and complete the setup operation.

Using Special Print Setups

For the most part, after you install a printer in Windows, Word for Windows 95 completes the rest of the process of setting up the printer. Because Word for Windows 95 makes certain assumptions about such things as paper size and orientation (portrait or landscape), you usually do not have to select these options. In Chapter 13, "Formatting the Page Layout, Alignment, and Numbering," you learn how to change the default settings. Word does enable you to choose some printing options from the Print dialog box, however.

To set options when printing a document, follow these steps:

1. Choose File, Print. The Print dialog box appears.

2. Select a printer from the Name drop-down list.

3. Choose the Properties button in the Print dialog box. The Properties sheet opens. An example of a Properties sheet for the HP LaserJet 4 or HP LaserJet 4M on LPT1 is shown in figure 8.6.

4. Select the options that you want. (See the section "Controlling Printing Options" later in this chapter for details on the individual options.)

5. Choose OK.

6. In the Print dialog box, choose OK.

The actual Print Setup Options dialog box that you see varies depending on the printer that you select in step 2.

The Properties sheet controls options that are useful if your document contains sophisticated graphics or if you want to share the file on a network. These advanced features may be useful if you do desktop publishing with Word.

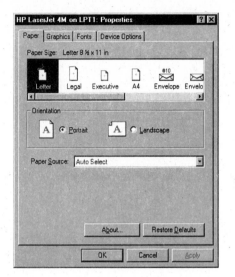

Fig. 8.6
The Print Proper-
ties sheet appears
for an HP LaserJet
printer.

Setting Up Printer Memory and Font Cartridges

If you use a laser printer, you may have to specify which font cartridge to use
and how much memory is in the printer. These settings affect the capabilities
of your printer, so you should not neglect to set them. You can change many
aspects of your printer setup, depending on what type of printer you have.

To set memory and select font cartridges for a laser printer, follow these steps:

1. Click the Start button in the taskbar at the bottom of the screen.

2. Move the mouse pointer over the Settings command. The Settings
   group appears.

3. Move the mouse pointer over the Printers command and click it or
   press Enter.

4. Select your printer's icon in the Printers window.

5. Choose File, Properties.

6. Select the Device Options tab. Choosing this tab opens a sheet like the
   one shown in figure 8.7.

7. Select Printer Memory, and select the amount of memory installed on
   your printer.

8. Select the Fonts page.

Fig. 8.7
The Device
Options sheet
appears for an HP
LaserJet printer.

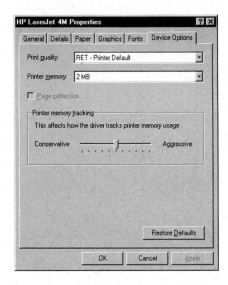

9. In the Cartridges list, select the one or two cartridges installed in your printer. Click once on a cartridge to select it, and click on it again to deselect it.

10. Choose OK to return to the Printers window.

> **Caution**
>
> Before you replace and select cartridges, remember to turn off your printer. Turn your printer back on only after you finish.

> **Note**
>
> You can change certain print options (document size and paper source, for example) in the Properties dialog box. Choose File, Print, Properties. You can change other options—such as print quality and print order (along with paper source)—by choosing Tools, Options and selecting the Print tab. The Page Setup dialog box settings override the defaults and affect only the current document. The Print tab settings change the global defaults.

Previewing Pages before Printing

Word for Windows 95 offers you two alternatives for viewing your document before you print. These alternatives are the Page Layout or Print Preview view.

In the Page Layout view, you can select text or graphics and enclose the selected item in a frame, and then drag the text or graphics to new locations. You can also drag page breaks to new locations.

The primary advantage of using the Print Preview view is the Preview screen's toolbar, which contains convenient buttons for zooming and displaying multiple pages.

Using Page Layout View

Different document views in Word for Windows 95 show different perspectives on your margins. In the Normal view, you don't see the margins, but you see the space between them, where your text appears. In the Page Layout view, you see the page as it will print, margins and all. Select this view if you want to see headers, footers, page numbers, footnotes, and anything else that appears within the margins.

At the left of the horizontal scroll bar are three buttons offering different views of documents. (If your horizontal scroll bar is not displayed, choose Tools, Options, select the View tab, and in the Window group, select Horizontal Scroll Bar.) The Standard toolbar includes a button that displays the Print Preview view. Table 8.1 summarizes the effects of the document view icons.

Table 8.1	Effects of Document View Icons	
Button	**Name**	**Effect**
≡	Normal	Displays document in Normal view
▣	Page Layout	Displays document in Page Layout view
≣	Outline	Displays document in Outline view
▤	Print Preview	Displays document in Print Preview view

To view the document in Page Layout view, follow these steps:

1. Open the document that you want to preview.

2. Choose View, Page Layout (if you haven't already selected the command). Alternatively, click the Page Layout button in the horizontal scroll bar.

3. If you want, adjust the magnification by choosing View, Zoom.

To return to Normal view, choose View, Normal or click the Normal button at the left of the horizontal scroll bar.

Using Print Preview

The other method of seeing how your document will print is to select Print Preview.

To see the entire document in print preview, you first must open the document that you want to preview. Then choose File, Print Preview or click the Print Preview button on the Standard toolbar. You then see a screen like that shown in figure 8.8.

Fig. 8.8
Display a screen representation of your printed document by using the Preview screen.

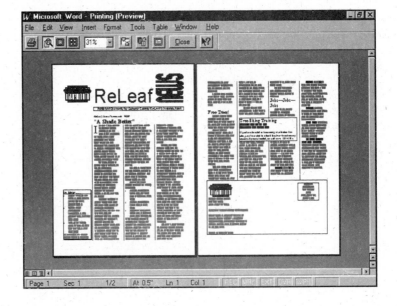

Across the top of the Preview screen is a toolbar with buttons that make it easier to work with your document in Print Preview. You can use the buttons on the toolbar to perform the actions listed in table 8.2.

Table 8.2	**Preview Screen Buttons**	
Button	**Name**	**Effect**
	Print	Prints the document using the printing options set in the Print dialog box
	Magnifier	Toggles the mouse pointer between a magnifying glass (for examining the document) and the normal mouse pointer (for editing the document)

Button	Name	Effect
	One Page	Displays document in single-page view
	Multiple Pages	Displays document in multiple-page view
26%	Zoom Control	Displays a list box of zoom magnification percentages and options
	View Ruler	Toggles the ruler display on and off
	Shrink to Fit	When the last page of the document contains very little text, tries to "shrink" the document to fit on one less page
	Full Screen	Toggles between full-screen display (which removes everything but the document and the toolbar) and normal display
Close	Close	Returns to your document
	Help	Provides context-sensitive help

In Print Preview, you also have access to the Normal, Page Layout, and Outline icons at the extreme left of the horizontal scroll bar (if the bar is displayed). Clicking any of these buttons closes the preview screen and displays the document in the view mode that you selected.

You can move around in the document in the Preview screen by using your keyboard's Page Up and Page Down keys and the scroll bars. When the rulers are displayed, you adjust margins in the same manner as in Page Layout view. You can also edit the document.

To edit a document in Print Preview, follow these steps:

1. Click the Magnifier button on the Standard toolbar. The mouse pointer changes to a magnifying lens.

2. Click the part of the document that you want to edit. Word displays the document at 100 percent magnification.

3. Click the Magnifier button again to restore the normal Word mouse pointer.

4. Edit the document, revising text and repositioning margins on the page as described in "Using Page Layout View" earlier in this chapter.

After you make your changes, you can reduce the document to the previous magnification by clicking the Magnifier button again and then clicking on the document with the magnifying glass icon.

Printing from Print Preview

You can print all or part of your document from the print preview screen. To do so, you can use the Standard toolbar's Print button or the Print dialog box.

 To print using the Standard toolbar, click the Print button to print the document using the current print settings. (The Print dialog box does not appear when you click this toolbar button.)

To print using the Print dialog box, follow these steps:

1. Choose File, Print.

2. Make the usual printing selections in the Print dialog box.

3. Choose OK.

Viewing One or Two Pages

You can view as many as 18 pages at once in 640×480 resolution—although you might not find it practical to display more than six or eight.

To view multiple pages, follow these steps:

 1. Click the Standard toolbar's Multiple Pages button.

2. Move the mouse pointer over the upper-left portion of the grid that appears below the Multiple Pages button.

3. Drag the mouse pointer down and to the right until the highlighted portion of the grid reflects the number of pages that you want to display. If you continue dragging, the grid expands to display additional pages to a maximum of three rows and six columns in 640×480 resolution.

4. Release the mouse button. The Preview screen now displays the arrangement of pages that the grid represented when you released the button.

 To change back to single-page view again, click the Standard toolbar's One Page button.

Canceling or Closing the Print Preview Screen

 To return to your editable document, click Close from the Standard toolbar.

Printing the Current Document

The simplest way to print is to open a document and choose File, Print. By default, Word prints one copy of all pages of the currently open document on the currently selected printer without printing hidden text.

To print one copy of a document, follow these steps:

1. Open the document that you want to print.

2. Choose File, Print or press Ctrl+Shift+F12. The Print dialog box appears.

3. Choose OK. The Print dialog box closes and a printer icon in the status bar displays the process of the print job.

To cancel printing while the Print icon is displayed, press Esc. When the Windows 95 printer icon appears in the taskbar, you can double-click it to open the Printer's folder. Select the document you want to cancel printing and then choose Document, Cancel Printing. If the Printer icon is no longer displayed in the Windows taskbar, Word may have already sent the print job to the printer.

You can bypass the Print dialog box and print your document quickly by clicking the Print button on the Standard toolbar. Word for Windows 95 prints your document using settings previously selected in the Print dialog box.

Printing Multiple Copies

With Word for Windows 95's Print dialog box, you can print more than one copy of your document. In fact, you can print 32,767 copies of your document (but you may want to plan a trip to Hawaii while all those copies print). By default, Word for Windows 95 collates the copies—a handy feature for long documents.

To print multiple copies of your document, follow these steps:

1. Open the document that you want to print.

2. Choose File, Print or press Ctrl+Shift+F12. The Print dialog box appears (see fig. 8.9).

3. Select the Number of Copies box in the Print dialog box and enter the number of copies that you want to print. (Alternatively, use the

increment/decrement arrows to increase or decrease the specified number of copies.)

4. Choose OK.

Fig. 8.9

You can print multiple copies of your document.

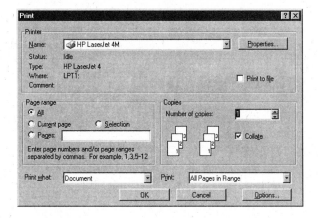

If print time is important, you can deselect the Collate option in the bottom-right corner of the dialog box. This step enables Word for Windows 95 to run multiple documents through the printer faster. You pay for choosing this option later, however, when you have to collate all the copies by hand.

Printing Part of a Document

Word for Windows 95 provides two ways to print part of a document. You can select the portion of your document that you want to print and then choose File, Print. You can also print the current page, selected text, or a specific range of pages.

Printing a selected area is useful when you want to print a section of a larger document but don't know on which page or pages the section is located.

To print a selected area of text, follow these steps:

1. Select the text to print.

2. Choose File, Print or press Ctrl+Shift+F12.

3. Choose the Selection option in the Page range area of the dialog box.

4. Choose OK.

If you know exactly which pages you want to print, you can print a range of pages. Suppose that you make changes to the first three pages of a long document. In that case, you might want to print from pages 1–3.

To print a specific range of pages, follow these steps:

1. Choose File, Print or press Ctrl+Shift+F12.

2. In the Pages box of the Page Range area, enter the range of pages that you want to print. (For instance, to print pages 1 through 3, enter **1–3**.)

3. Choose OK.

In the Pages box, you can specify multiple page ranges (such as **1–7,8–13, 14–20**) or multiple discontinuous pages (**1,2,8,13**). You can combine ranges with individual page numbers, as shown in figure 8.10.

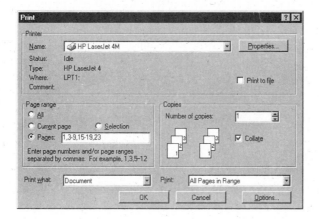

Fig. 8.10
Enter groups of page ranges and selected pages in the Pages box of the Print dialog box.

You can also print pages in a certain section. To print the second section in your document, type **s2** in the Pages box. If you want to print from page 7 in the second section to page 10 in the third section, type **p7s2–p10s3** in the Pages box.

In a long document, it's sometimes helpful to simply print the page on which you're working. To do so, follow these steps:

1. Position the insertion point on the page that you want to print.

2. Choose File, Print or press Ctrl+Shift+F12.

3. Choose Current Page.

4. Choose OK.

Everyday Word Processing

If you want to print on both sides of the paper and don't have a duplex printer, you should print the odd-numbered pages in one print run and the even-numbered pages in another. To print only the odd- or even-numbered pages, follow these steps:

1. Choose File, Print or press Ctrl+Shift+F12.

2. In the Print box, select the Odd Pages or Even Pages option.

3. Choose OK.

Printing Different Types of Document Information

Word documents contain associated information such as summary information, field codes, and data for forms. You can print this information with the document or separately. The first method that this section presents describes how to print the ancillary hidden information with the document. The second method describes how to print the hidden information separately.

Word for Windows 95 enables you to include the following hidden attributes as part of your printed document:

- Summary information

- Field codes

- Annotations

- Hidden text

- Drawing objects

To print hidden information with your document, follow these steps:

1. Choose Tools, Options, then select the Print tab if it is not already displayed (see fig. 8.11).

2. In the Include with Document Print options, select the options that you want to print (see table 8.3). If you choose Annotations, for example, Word prints a list of the annotations associated with your document. (You can use this option to display a list of the annotations that a reviewer has made to your document.)

3. Choose OK.

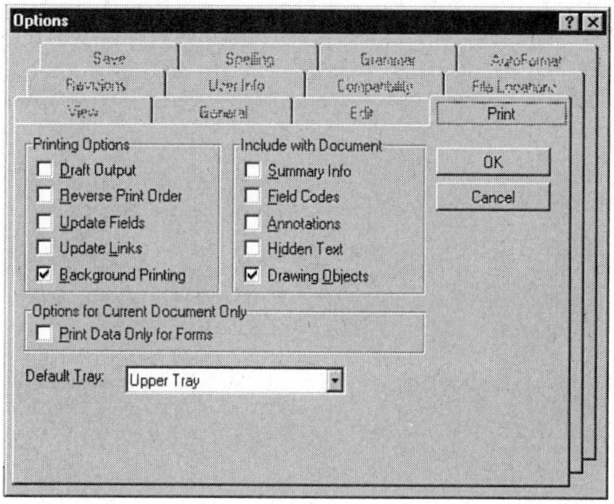

Fig. 8.11
Choose Tools, Options, and display the Print tab to specify a variety of printing options, including printing "nondisplaying" information when you print the document.

Table 8.3   Include with Document Print Options

Option	Effect
Summary Info	Prints a summary of information about the document— including author, subject, print date, and number of pages, words, and characters—on separate pages at the end of the document
Field Codes	Prints field codes rather than their results
Annotations	Prints at the end of the document a list of annotations that reviewers have attached to your document, with page number headings indicating where each annotation occurs
Hidden Text	Prints any hidden text, such as table of contents entries, where text appears in document
Drawing Objects	Prints drawing objects that you created in Word

Alternatively, you can print hidden information separately from the document itself, although you can select only one of the following items at a time:

- Summary Info
- Annotations
- Styles
- AutoText entries
- Key assignments

To print only a document's hidden information without printing the document, follow these steps:

1. Choose File, Print.

2. Select Print What to open the drop-down list.

3. Select one of the options from the list.

4. Choose OK.

Controlling Printing Options

Word for Windows 95 offers you many printing options. You can print the pages in reverse order or save time by printing a draft copy (on some printers). You can print text that usually is hidden, separately or as part of your document. You can update fields as you print, or you can print on paper from a specified bin if your printer has more than one paper source.

To set printing options, follow these steps:

1. Choose Tools, Options and select the Print tab.

2. Select the desired options.

3. Choose OK.

The following sections describe the available printing options.

Printing a Draft

Sometimes you need a quick, plain printed copy of your document. Perhaps someone else must edit the copy, or you want to take the copy home from work to review. For a quick, unadorned print, choose a draft copy. A draft prints quickly, without formatting. Word underlines enhanced characters instead of boldfacing or italicizing them, and prints graphics as empty boxes. (The exact result of a draft print depends on your printer. For example, a Hewlett-Packard LaserJet prints formatted text but no graphics in draft mode, but a PostScript printer does not support draft mode.)

If you select draft printing as your default, all printing is in draft mode until you deselect that option. Alternatively, on some printers, you can print in draft mode only once without changing the default (this option is not available for laser printers).

To select draft as your default print-quality mode, follow these steps:

1. Choose Tools, Options. Select the Print tab.

2. In the Print tab of the Options dialog box, select the Draft Output check box.

3. Choose OK.

To print a draft copy of a document one time using a dot-matrix printer, follow these steps:

1. Choose File, Print.

2. In the Print dialog box, choose Options. The Options dialog box appears with the Print tab opened.

3. In the Printing Options area, select Draft Output.

4. Choose OK.

5. In the Print dialog box, choose OK.

Printing Pages in Reverse Order

Some printers have a collator that produces printed pages stacked in the correct order. Other printers stack pages with the last page on top. If your printer stacks with the last page on top, you might want to select the Reverse Print Order option to stack your pages in the correct order.

To print in reverse order, select the Reverse Print Order check box in the Print tab of the Options dialog box. Then choose OK.

Updating Fields

Word for Windows 95 files can include field codes that instruct Word to insert special information into the document. A date field, for example, inserts the current date when Word prints the document. But some fields cannot be updated during the printing process. To update those fields when you print, you must choose a special option. In most cases, you want this option turned on.

To update fields when you print, select the Update Fields check box in the Print tab of the Options dialog box. Choose OK.

▶ See "Viewing and Printing Field Codes," p. 594

Updating Links

◄ See "Moving, Copying, and Linking Text or Graphics," p. 160

The Update Links option updates any linked information in the document before printing. To update links before you print, select the Update Links check box in the Print tab of the Options dialog box. Then choose OK.

Background Printing

The Background Printing option enables you to continue working in Word while you print a document. To print in the background while performing other operations in Word, select the Background Printing check box in the Print tab of the Options dialog box. Then choose OK.

Printing Form Input Data Only

► See "Printing a Form," p. 666

If you have entered data into fields on a form, printing only the input data might make it easier to compare the data in Word to the source document. To print the input data only, select the Print Data Only for Forms check box in the Print tab of the Options dialog box. Then choose OK.

Selecting the Paper Source

If you always want to print from a particular bin on your printer, you can change the default paper source. To do so, follow these steps:

1. Choose Tools, Options.

2. In the Print tab of the Options dialog box, choose Default Tray to open the drop-down list (see fig. 8.12).

Fig. 8.12

You can change the paper source with the Default Tray option in the Print tab.

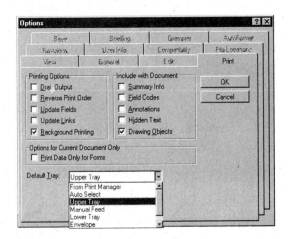

3. Select the paper source by selecting the option that you want from the Default Tray list box.

You also can set the paper source for your document by choosing File, Page Setup, selecting the Paper Source tab, and selecting the First Page and Other Pages options.

▶ See "Selecting the Paper Source," p. 433

In most single-bin laser printers, you can slide your letterhead into the manual tray as far as the letterhead goes and leave your bond paper in the paper bin. After you choose OK from the Print dialog box, the printer first pulls in the letterhead and then pulls in the bond for following sheets. As a result, on printers such as the HP LaserJet Series II, III, 4, or 5 you do not need to go through a series of steps. Just print.

Printing Multiple Unopened Documents

Occasionally, you might want to print an unopened document or several documents simultaneously. File, Print in the Windows Explorer enables you to open and print several documents at once.

To print one (or more) unopened documents, follow these steps:

1. Right-click the Start menu and choose Explore to open the Explorer. If you prefer to use My Computer, open a window into My Computer.

2. Select the files you want to print. Click the first file, then hold down the Shift key and click the last file to select contiguous files. Or click the first file, then Ctrl+click on other files to select non-contiguous files.

3. Move the pointer over a selected file and right-click to display the Send To shortcut menu.

4. Select the printer or fax you want to send the files to.

◀ See "Printing Files," p. 113

If you've assembled several Word documents into a master document, you can print the entire master document. You learn about master documents and related printing options in Chapter 32, "Assembling Large Documents."

Sending Documents Electronically

Traditionally, a printed document is the ultimate realization of what you create in word processing, and the printed hard copy is delivered physically. Increasingly, however, documents are routed electronically. Word can print a document to a file or route it to someone else in your organization or directly to a fax machine.

Printing to a File

Someday you might need to print a document to a file rather than to a printer. One way this method can be useful is to print a document set up for a PostScript printer to a file. You can then take the resulting encapsulated PostScript (EPS) file to a printer (or service bureau) to be printed on a Linotronic typesetting machine for high-quality documents.

Another use for printing to a file is to create a file that you can use on a computer that has a printer but no copy of Word. If you create the file for that printer, you can use the DOS COPY command to copy the Word file to the LPT1 printer port. The file prints even though Word is not running.

To print to a file, follow these steps:

1. Choose File, Print.

2. Select the Print to File option and then choose OK. The Print to File dialog box appears.

3. In the File Name box, type the full path name of the file to contain the document. Then choose OK.

You see the disk light come on as information sent to the printer is stored in a file with the name that you entered in the last step.

When you want to resume printing to your printer, deselect the Print to File option in the Print dialog box.

> **Note**
>
> You can create a text file easily in Word 7 for Windows 95. Just choose File, Save As; then select the Save as Type pull-down list and select one of the text file format files that Word for Windows 95 creates. In most cases, you should choose the Text Only (*.TXT) format.

Part II

Formatting Documents

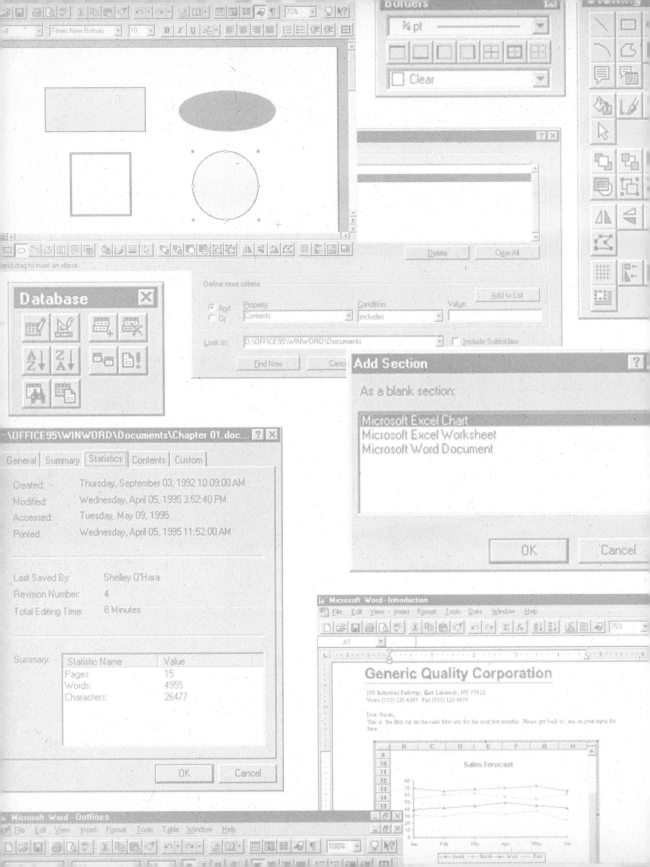

Chapter 9

Formatting Characters and Changing Fonts

Characters—individual letters, numbers, punctuation marks, and symbols—are the smallest unit of text you can format in a Word document. You can apply formatting styles such as bold, italic, or a different font to one character or to an entire document. You can also combine character formatting options; for example, you can make a word bold and italicized. You also can use as many different types of character formatting in a document as you want. Your document's title, for example, can be in a different font or larger size, subheadings can be boldfaced, and paragraphs of text can be plain text with some italic text for occasional emphasis.

In this chapter, you learn how to:

- Format characters

- Change fonts

- Copy formatting

- Format special characters

- Insert symbols and special fonts

- Use fonts correctly

What Is Character Formatting?

Character formatting options include fonts, sizes, boldface, italic, strikethrough, hidden text, colors, superscript and subscript, uppercase and lowercase, small caps, underlines, and character spacing.

Word for Windows also has many special characters to include in your document. You can create a list using bullets or decorative dingbats, for example, or you can include a copyright or trademark symbol. This chapter covers all the character formatting options.

Figure 9.1 shows some examples of the character formatting options available in Word for Windows 95.

Fig. 9.1
There are many formatting options you can apply to characters in Word for Windows.

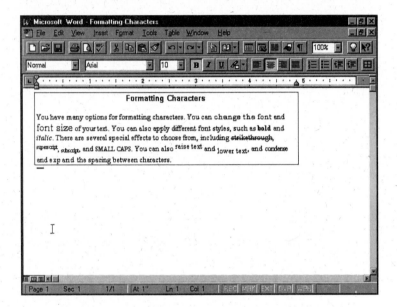

You can use character formatting to accomplish the following tasks:

- Add emphasis to text—you can boldface or enlarge important items.

- Hide notes to yourself or other readers—you can use hidden text to include notes that do not print.

- Add visual interest to text—you can change fonts to visually differentiate body text from headings.

Viewing Formatted Characters

The way characters appear on-screen depends on several factors. One factor is the selected document view. In Normal view—the default view—you see accurate character formatting (boldface appears **bold**, for example), unless you have selected the Draft Font option by choosing Tools, Options. In Page Layout view, you see the entire page exactly as it will look in print, including character formatting. Select the view you want from the View menu.

To see character formatting in Normal view, follow these steps:

1. Choose <u>V</u>iew, <u>N</u>ormal.

2. Choose <u>T</u>ools, <u>O</u>ptions.

3. Select the View tab.

4. Deselect the <u>D</u>raft Font check box (if it is selected).

5. Choose OK.

Another factor controlling how text appears on-screen is the printer you have selected. If your printer doesn't support a font or size you use to format your text, Word for Windows may substitute the closest possible font and size.

Understanding Screen Fonts and Printer Fonts

Finally, the issue of *screen fonts* (which control the screen appearance of fonts) versus *printer fonts* (fonts the printer uses) can affect the appearance of on-screen text. If you have printer fonts for which no corresponding screen fonts are available, fonts may look blocklike on-screen (the fonts are scaled up or down from the nearest font or size), even though they print just fine.

To resolve the discrepancy between screen fonts and printer fonts, you can use TrueType fonts with Word for Windows while operating under Windows versions 3.1 or later. *TrueType* is a type of built-in font-generation software that generates screen and printer fonts so that what you see on-screen is almost the same as what you print, whether you have a laser printer or a dot-matrix printer.

If you format text with fonts your printer cannot print, you may end up with a screen that doesn't match the printed output. You can make the following change to ensure that line and page breaks appear on-screen just as they appear in print.

To make sure your document looks the same on-screen as it does in print, follow these steps:

1. Choose <u>V</u>iew, <u>N</u>ormal.

2. Choose <u>T</u>ools, <u>O</u>ptions, and select the View tab.

3. Deselect the <u>D</u>raft Font check box (if it is selected).

4. Choose OK.

II

Formatting Documents

Tip
The Font list in
the Formatting
toolbar shows a
printer icon to the
left of each font
available from
your printer and
TT for TrueType
fonts. For best
results, always use
one of these fonts.

Troubleshooting

The character formatting I've added doesn't show up on-screen.

Some fonts, such as Courier, cannot accept some formatting. Another reason may be that the display options may be set to increase typing and scrolling speed rather than to display character formatting. Make sure that Normal view is set with Draft Font turned off in the View tab of Tools, Options (instructions for this setting appear earlier in this section). Also make sure that the printer you have selected can print the format you have applied. Choose File, Print, and then choose the Printer button to display the Print Setup dialog box. The printer you have selected is highlighted in the Printers list box.

I don't see the formatting codes on-screen.

Unlike some word processors, Word for Windows does not display formatting codes on-screen. Instead, you see the results of the formatting on-screen. The text appears as it will look in print. You can determine which formatting options have been applied by selecting the text and choosing Format, Font. The dialog box indicates those options that currently are active.

Formatting Characters

Word for Windows offers no shortage of techniques for applying character formatting. If you have a mouse, you can format using tools and lists on the Standard and Formatting toolbars. If you prefer the keyboard, you can access formatting commands from the menu. You also can take advantage of many helpful mouse and keyboard shortcuts.

Whether you choose to format text before or after you type it, you must remember that most character formatting commands *toggle* on and off—you turn them on the same way that you turn them off. If you select and boldface a word and then want to remove the boldface, select the word a second time and choose the Bold command again. Toggling applies when you use buttons on the toolbars or keyboard shortcuts to apply or remove formatting. Formatting with the menu commands varies slightly.

Selecting Characters to Format

◀ See "Selecting Text," p. 141

You can format characters as you type or after you finish typing. To format characters as you type, choose the formatting command, type the text, and then choose the formatting command a second time to turn off the command. To format characters after you finish typing, you must remember this rule: select, then do. Select the text to format, and then choose the formatting command.

Formatting with Menu Commands

Using a menu command is probably the most basic technique for formatting characters. Using the menu has three primary advantages: the Font dialog box displays all the character formatting commands at once; you can apply several types of character formatting simultaneously with the Font dialog box; and you can preview the results of the formatting choices you make in the Font dialog box.

To access the Font dialog box, choose Format, Font or press Ctrl+D. The Font dialog box displays two tabs: Font and Character Spacing (see figs. 9.2 and 9.3).

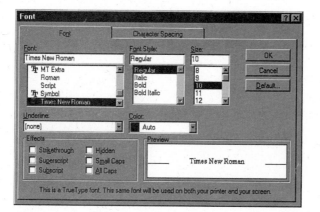

Fig. 9.2

Use the Font options to change fonts, character font styles, and effects.

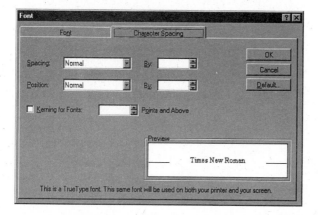

Fig. 9.3

Use the Character Spacing tab to control the spacing between characters.

The options of each tab are described in tables 9.1 and 9.2. (Options marked with asterisks are detailed later in this chapter.)

Table 9.1   Font Tab Options

Group	Option	Description
Font*	Selection varies depending on printer	A typeface style. Common fonts include Times New Roman, Arial, and Courier.
Font Style	Regular	The basic font with no enhancements. Used for most typing.
	Italic	Oblique, or slanted, text: *Italic*. Often used for book or magazine names, or for emphasis. Can be combined with bold.
	Bold	Heavy text: **Bold**. Often used for document titles or subheadings.
	Bold Italic	Bold and italic formatting combined.
Size*	8, 10, 12, and so on	Character size in points. An inch consists of 72 points (a typesetting measurement).
Underline*	None	Normal text. Used to remove underlining.
	Single	Single underline. The space between words is underlined.
	Words only	Single underline. The space between words is not underlined.
	Double	Double underline. The space between words is underlined.
	Dotted	Dotted underline. The space between the words is dotted underline.
Color*	Auto, Black, Red, Yellow, and so on	Changes the color of text on-screen if you have a color monitor, prints in color if you have a color printer.
Effects	Strikethrough	Text crossed with a line: ~~Strikethrough~~. Often used when making revisions.
	Superscript*	Text raised above the baseline.
	Subscript*	Text lowered below the baseline.
	Hidden*	Text that doesn't appear or print unless you want it to. Often used for private notes or comments.
	Small Caps	Short uppercase letters: SMALL CAPS. Used for emphasis or for graphic effect.
	All Caps	All uppercase letters: ALL CAPS. Used for emphasis or for graphic effect. Harder to read than format combining uppercase and lowercase.

Group	Option	Description
Default*	N/A	Applies selected formatting to the template attached to the document as well as to the current document. All future documents based on this template will use the selections in the Font dialog box as the default font.
Preview	N/A	Shows a sample of text formatted with selected options.

Table 9.2   Character Spacing Options

Group	Option	Description
Spacing*	Normal	Default spacing for the selected font.
	Expanded	Space between characters expanded to 3 points.
	Condensed	Space between characters condensed to 1.75 points.
By:*	1 pt (default), or enter your own amount	Number of points by which text is expanded or condensed. Measured in increments of tenths of a point.
Position*	Normal	Text is printed on the base line.
	Raised	Text is raised above the baseline by the increment you indicate in the By box.
	Lowered	Text is lowered below the baseline by the increment you indicate in the By box.
By:	3 pt (default), or enter your own amount	Number of points by which text is raised or lowered.
Default	N/A	Applies selected formatting to template attached to the document as well as to the current document. All future documents based on this template will use the selections in the Font dialog box as the default font.
Preview	N/A	Shows a sample of text formatted with selected options.

To format characters using a menu command, follow these steps:

1. Select the text to format, or position the insertion point where you want formatting to begin.

2. Choose Format, Font. The Font dialog box appears (refer to figs. 9.2 and 9.3).

3. Select the Font tab or the Character Spacing tab.

4. Select the formatting option or options you want.

5. Choose OK.

The Font dialog box tabs show formatting for the currently selected characters. If the selected text is bold, for example, the Bold option is selected in the Font Style box on the Font tab. If, however, the selection includes various formatting options, no items in the list boxes will be selected and the check boxes will be checked and shaded, indicating that the selection includes mixed formats.

Because any formatting options you select apply to all the selected text, you can use the Font dialog box to turn on or off formatting for large areas of text, even if the text includes a variety of formatting.

Troubleshooting

Characters appear OK on-screen, but they don't print as shown.

Use TrueType fonts in your documents. A selection of TrueType fonts come with Windows. In the Font list of the Font tab, TrueType fonts are preceded by a TT. TrueType fonts are designed to appear the same on-screen as they do in print. You are likely to have used a font on-screen that your printer cannot exactly reproduce. TrueType takes care of this problem. See "Using TrueType Fonts" later in this chapter for more information.

Formatting with Keyboard Shortcuts

You can use the keyboard to format characters in two ways. The first way is to press Alt+O, F to display the Font dialog box; you can use this dialog box to select character formatting options (as described in the preceding section). The second way to format characters with the keyboard is to use a shortcut key.

To format characters using shortcut keys, follow these steps:

1. Select the text to format, or position the insertion point where you want formatting to begin.

2. Press the appropriate key combination, described in the following table:

Format	Shortcut
Bold	Ctrl+B
Italic	Ctrl+I
Single underline	Ctrl+U
Word underline	Ctrl+Shift+W
Double underline	Ctrl+Shift+D
SMALL CAPS	Ctrl+Shift+K
ALL CAPS	Ctrl+Shift+A
Hidden text	Ctrl+Shift+H
Superscript	Ctrl+Shift+= (equal sign)
Subscript	Ctrl+= (equal sign)
Copy formatting	Ctrl+Shift+C
Paste formatting	Ctrl+Shift+V
Remove formatting	Ctrl+space bar
Change case of letters	Shift+F3
Font	Ctrl+Shift+F. This command activates the Font box in the Formatting toolbar. Type a new font name or use the arrow keys to highlight the desired font; press Enter to select it.
Symbol font	Ctrl+Shift+Q
Point size	Ctrl+Shift+P. This command activates the Point Size box in the Formatting toolbar. Type a new size or use the arrow keys to highlight the desired point size; press Enter to select it.
Next larger point size	Ctrl+Shift+> available for selected font
Next smaller point size	Ctrl+Shift+< available for selected font
Up one point size	Ctrl+]
Down one point size	Ctrl+[

II

Formatting Documents

See the following sections for more information about the preceding commands.

Troubleshooting

Character formatting appeared to be correct the last time the document was opened, but now the character formatting has changed. In some cases, formatting is missing.

The currently selected printer may not be the printer that was selected during the document's original formatting. If the current printer is not capable of reproducing the fonts, sizes, or styles that you originally formatted, Windows shows you the best that the current printer can do. Correct this problem by reselecting a printer that is capable of printing the formats. Choose File, Print, choose the Printer button, and then select a new printer from the Name drop-down list.

Formatting with the Formatting Toolbar

The Formatting toolbar is a handy tool for quick character formatting (see fig. 9.4). You can change the style, font, or size of text, and format characters with bold, italic, or single underline. Paragraph formatting options also are included on the Formatting toolbar. For more details about paragraph formatting, refer to Chapter 10, "Formatting Lines and Paragraphs."

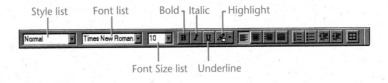

Fig. 9.4

You can select character formatting commands from the Formatting toolbar.

The following information provides general instructions for formatting with the Formatting toolbar; later in this section you will find more detailed instructions for using styles, bold, italic, and underline. Techniques for using the Formatting toolbar to format fonts and sizes are described in the sections "Changing Font Type" and "Changing Font Size" later in this chapter.

The Formatting toolbar first must be displayed before using it. To display the Formatting toolbar, choose View, Toolbars and specify the toolbars you want to display on-screen.

To format characters using the Formatting toolbar, follow these steps:

1. Select the text to be formatted, or position the insertion point where you want formatting to begin.

2. You can choose from one of several options: select a style from the Style list, select a font from the Font list, select a size from the Point Size list, or select the Bold, Italic, Underline, or Highlight button.

You can make as many of these selections as you want. For example, you can change the font and point size for the selected text and add boldfacing.

No matter how you apply formatting to text—whether you use a menu command, a shortcut, or the Formatting toolbar—the Formatting toolbar displays the formatting for that text when it is selected.

Notice that the Formatting toolbar also includes paragraph alignment options.

▶ See "Aligning Paragraphs," p. 297

Selecting Styles with the Formatting Toolbar

A *style* is a set of "memorized" formatting commands. Although styles apply to entire paragraphs, they often contain character formatting. Word for Windows uses the normal style to apply default formatting, but you can change the style easily.

To change the style with the mouse, follow these steps:

1. Position the insertion point inside the paragraph you want to format with a style.

2. Select a style from the Styles list box.

To change the style with a shortcut key, follow these steps:

1. Position the insertion point inside the paragraph you want to format with a style.

2. Press Ctrl+Shift+S to select the Styles list box.

3. Press the down-arrow key to drop down the list, and then press the up-arrow or down-arrow key to select the style you want.

4. Press Enter.

Even if the Formatting toolbar isn't displayed, you can apply a style by pressing Ctrl+Shift+S. The Style dialog box appears. You can select a style and then click the Apply button or press Enter. For details about creating and using styles, see Chapter 11, "Using Styles for Repetitive Formats."

▶ See "Creating Styles," p. 358

II

Formatting Documents

Selecting Bold, Italic, Underline, or Highlight with the Formatting Toolbar

When selected, the three-dimensional buttons on the Formatting toolbar are bright and appear pressed; when not selected, the buttons appear raised. If your selection includes mixed formatting, for example (if part of the selection is bold and the rest is not), the button will be raised. Selecting a button—raised or depressed—applies (or removes) formatting to all selected text.

To apply bold, italic, or underline with the Formatting toolbar, follow these steps:

1. Select the text to be formatted, or position the insertion point where you want the formatting to begin before you enter the text.

2. Click the Bold, Italic, or Underline button to apply the formatting you want to use.

Highlighting gives you the ability to drag a highlighting marker across on-screen text. You even have the ability to choose different colors of highlighter. In the same way that you might use a real highlighter, you can use Word's highlighter to emphasize certain text. You may also want to use its different colors as a way of quickly identifying edits or comments inserted by different people.

To apply highlight with the Formatting toolbar, follow these steps:

1. Click the Highlight button so the button appears depressed. The pointer changes to a highlighting pen.

2. Drag the pointer across the text you want to highlight.

Click the Highlight button a second time, or press Esc to turn off any highlighting.

To change the color used for highlighting, click the down arrow on the right side of the Highlight button and drag the mouse pointer down and to the right through the displayed palette until all of the colors are displayed, position the mouse pointer over the desired color, then release the left mouse button. The Highlight color appears in the small window of the Highlight button.

Remember that these buttons toggle on and off. If you select a boldfaced word and click the Bold button, the bold formatting is removed from the selected word. If you select both a bold word and a normal word that *precedes* it and click the Bold button, both words are formatted as bold. If you select both a bold word and a normal word that follows it and click the Bold button, however, both words are formatted as normal.

Troubleshooting

There are characters in the document that were highlighted, but the highlighting color does not display.

Make sure the Show Highlighting option is turned on. Choose Tools, Options; then select the View tab. Select the Highlight check box; then choose OK.

▶ See "Aligning Paragraphs," p. 297

▶ See "Creating Styles," p. 358

Changing Fonts

A *font* is a typeface style; all letters, punctuation, and other text characters of a given font have the same appearance. Three basic types of fonts exist: *serif*, with strokes at the ends of letters; *sans serif*, with no strokes; and *specialty*, such as symbols and script fonts.

Common fonts include Times New Roman, a serif font; Helvetica, a sans serif font; and Zapf Chancery, a script font. These and other fonts are shown in figure 9.5.

```
Times New Roman
Arial
Helvetica
Palatino
Bookman
ZapfChancery
Script
Symbol: αβχδψγλ
```

Fig. 9.5
The selection of fonts available to you depends on your printer.

The printer (or printers) you installed and selected determine what fonts are available for your use. An HP LaserJet, for example, may include CG Times, Univers, Courier, and LinePrinter. A PostScript printer usually includes Times New Roman, Palatino, Bookman, New Century Schoolbook (serif fonts), Helvetica, Avant Garde (sans serif fonts), Zapf Chancery (a script font), and Zapf Dingbats (a symbol font). The selected printer determines which fonts you see listed in the Font list box. (The Font list also includes built-in Windows fonts such as the symbol fonts, Symbol and Fences.)

You can add more fonts to your printer. You can buy software fonts (which tend to print slowly) and download them to a printer, or buy font cartridges to insert into your laser printer.

Because Word for Windows and other Windows programs use printer and screen fonts, you can select screen fonts in your document that your printer cannot print. If you do, what you see on-screen isn't necessarily what you get when you print. The ability to select fonts that your printer doesn't support is handy when you want to create a document that will be printed on another printer or used by a service bureau for producing a linotype. In this case, you can select fonts that you know are supported by the other printer or service bureau, and you can see on-screen how your document will look, even though you can't obtain an accurate printout on your own printer.

To make sure that your screen displays what you will actually get when you print, follow these steps:

1. In Normal view, choose Tools, Options.

2. Select the View tab.

3. Deselect the Draft Font check box.

4. Choose OK.

Even with the preceding procedure, lines of text may extend into the right margin, or text in a table may appear cut off at the right border of a cell. In spite of its on-screen appearance, however, text will print accurately.

Changing Font Type

You can change fonts with a menu command or from the Formatting toolbar. You can use either the mouse or the keyboard to make the change. This section includes instructions for all these methods.

Tip
You can choose Edit, Replace (or press Ctrl+H) to search for and replace fonts (without changing the text).

To change the font with the mouse from the menu, follow these steps:

1. Select the text whose font you want to change, or position the insertion point where you want the new font to begin before you begin typing.

2. Choose Format, Font, press Ctrl+D, or click the right mouse button and select Font from the shortcut menu.

3. Select the Font tab.

4. Select the font you want from the Font list or type its name.

5. Click OK.

To change the font using the Formatting toolbar, follow these steps:

1. Select the text whose font you want to change, or position the insertion point where you want the new font to begin when you begin typing.

2. Click the down-arrow to the right of the Font list box, or press Ctrl+Shift+F and press the ↓ key to display the list of fonts.

3. Select a font from the Font list box. Press Enter if you are using the keyboard.

◄ See "Finding and Replacing Formatting and Styles," p. 204

Changing Font Size

Font sizes are measured in *points*, the traditional typesetting measuring unit. An inch consists of 72 points; thus, an inch-high letter is 72 points, and a half-inch-high letter is 36 points. Text in a book may be 10 to 12 points.

Like fonts, your printer determines what font sizes you can use. PostScript printers and HP LaserJet 4 and 5 printers include scalable fonts. You can print scalable fonts from sizes as small as a barely readable 4 points to as tall as a page.

Screen fonts (fonts created without TrueType) that are included in Windows rather than in the printer don't come in all sizes, even if your printer has scalable fonts. If you change text to an odd size such as 17 points, the text looks blocklike on-screen, because Word substitutes the next closest font size for the missing screen font.

You can change font sizes in three ways: with the menu command, the Formatting toolbar, or shortcuts.

To change the font size using the menu command, follow these steps:

1. Select the text you want to resize, or position the insertion point where you want the new font size to begin when you start typing.

2. Choose Format, Font, press Ctrl+D, or click the right mouse button and select Font from the shortcut menu.

3. Select the Font tab.

4. Select the Size list.

5. Select the point size you want or type in the point size.

6. Choose OK.

Tip

If the Formatting toolbar isn't displayed, you can change the font by pressing Ctrl+Shift+F to display the Font dialog box; then select a font or type in the font name and press Enter.

II

Formatting Documents

The Formatting toolbar provides a quick way to change font size without using a menu command. (The Formatting toolbar must be displayed before you can use it.)

Tip

Even if the Formatting Toolbar isn't displayed, you can change point size by pressing Ctrl+Shift+P to display the Font dialog box; select or type a font size and press Enter.

To change font size with the Formatting toolbar, follow these steps:

1. Select the text you want to resize, or position the insertion point where you want the new size to begin when you start typing.

2. Select a size from the Font Size list box by clicking the down arrow next to the font size, or press Shift+Ctrl+P and type a size or use the down-arrow key to select a size; then press Enter.

Another shortcut is available for increasing or decreasing point size to the next size listed in the Font Size list on the Formatting toolbar or in the Font dialog box. If sizes 9, 10, and 12 are listed, for example, you can increase 10-point text to 12 points, and you can decrease 10-point text to 9 points.

To use keyboard shortcuts to change point size, follow these steps:

1. Select the text you want to resize before you enter text, or position the insertion point where you want the new size to begin.

2. Press Ctrl+Shift+> to increase the point size, or press Ctrl+Shift+< to decrease the point size.

> **Note**
>
> You can replace a font size in your document just as you can replace text. If all of your headlines in a report are 14 points and you want to change them to 12 points, for example, you can choose Edit, Replace to make the global change quickly (see Chapter 7, "Using Editing and Proofing Tools").

Changing the Default Character Formatting

Word for Windows uses the Normal style (contained in the Normal template) to control the default character and paragraph formatting choices for all documents. The Normal style's default type font, Times New Roman, has a default size of 10 points. If you always work with some other character formatting settings, you can apply those settings to the Normal style. Your new defaults take effect for the current document and for all future documents (but not for existing documents).

To change default character formatting, follow these steps:

1. Choose Format, Font.

2. Select the new defaults you want to use from either the Font or Character Spacing tabs.

3. Choose the Default button.

4. Click Yes to indicate that you want to change the Normal template.

Because you requested a change to the Normal template, when you exit Word for Windows, you see a message box asking whether you want to save changes to Word for Windows. Choose Yes.

◀ See "Changing a Template," p. 185

▶ See "Using Styles versus Direct Formatting," p. 336

Copying Formatting

If you do much repetitive character formatting, you can save some time by repeating or copying formatting between characters. You can use one of two different methods: the Edit, Repeat command or the Format Painter button.

You can choose Edit, Repeat to copy formatting immediately after you have formatted characters. The command repeats the *one* most recent edit. If you use the Font dialog box to apply several formatting choices at once, the Repeat command repeats all those choices because you made them as a single edit. But if you choose Repeat after making several formatting choices from the keyboard or with the Formatting toolbar, the command repeats only the most recent choice.

To repeat character formatting with Edit, Repeat immediately after formatting characters, follow these steps:

1. Select the new text to format.

2. Press F4, or choose Edit, Repeat.

To use this technique, you must perform it immediately after performing the edit that you want to repeat.

The Standard toolbar includes a button for copying character formatting. To copy character formatting with the Format Painter button, follow these steps:

1. Select the text whose format you want to copy.

2. Click the Format Painter button on the Standard toolbar. The mouse pointer changes to a paintbrush with an I-beam.

3. Select the text you want to change and release the mouse button. The selected text automatically takes on the new formatting when you release the mouse button.

You can copy the formatting to more than one location by double-clicking the Format Painter button in step 1, selecting the first block of text to which you want to copy the formatting, and releasing the mouse button. Then select each additional block of text to which you want to copy the formatting, and release the mouse button. When you have finished copying the formatting, click the Format Painter button again or press Esc.

If you find that the formatting you copied or added is not to your liking, you can remove all character formatting. The remaining formatting is part of the style to which the text is attached.

▶ See "Using Paragraph Formatting Techniques," p. 291

To remove all character formatting, follow these steps:

1. Select the text whose character formatting you want to remove.

2. Press Ctrl+space bar.

Applying Special Character Formatting Options

Many formatting options are simple and straightforward: a font is a specific character set design; size is measured in points; boldfaced text is heavier than normal text. Other options, however, aren't quite so obvious, and to use them, you may need to specify some criteria that further controls the option. For example, you can specify how high you want superscript text to appear in relation to the text baseline.

All the character formatting options described in this section toggle on and off. To remove superscripting, for example, you must select the Superscripted text, choose Format, Font to access the Font dialog box, and choose Superscript again.

Hiding Text

At times, you may want to include in your document *hidden text*—text that disappears until you choose a command to display it. When displayed, hidden text has a dotted underline (see fig. 9.6). Hiding text doesn't affect the text formatting.

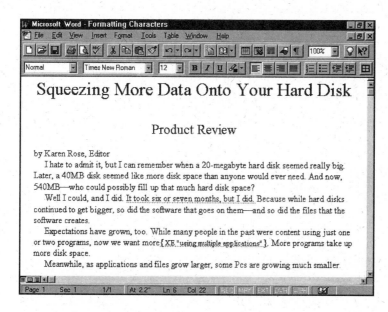

Fig. 9.6
Hidden text has a dotted underline on-screen; when printed, it has no underline.

You can format any text—such as notes to yourself—as hidden text. Word for Windows also uses hidden text to format table-of-contents entries, index entries (as shown in fig. 9.6), and annotations.

To hide text with the menu command, follow these steps:

1. Select the text you want to hide, or position the insertion point where you want hidden text to begin.

2. Choose Format, Font.

3. Select the Font tab.

4. Select the Hidden check box.

5. Click OK.

To hide text with the keyboard shortcut, follow these steps:

1. Select the text you want to hide, or position the insertion point where you want hidden text to begin.

2. Press Ctrl+Shift+H.

You can toggle hidden text on and off with the keyboard shortcut, as long as the text is selected. You also can display all hidden text on-screen in Normal, Outline, Page Layout, or Master Document views. If you intend to print hidden text, display it before you decide on final page breaks. Otherwise, page numbering and page breaks may be inaccurate.

To display hidden text, follow these steps:

1. Choose Tools, Options.

2. Select the View tab.

3. Select the Hidden Text check box (see fig. 9.7).

4. Choose OK.

Fig. 9.7
Select the Hidden
Text option to
display hidden
text on-screen.

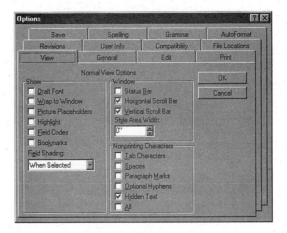

If you have not indicated that you want hidden text displayed on the Tools Options View tab, you can toggle the display of hidden text on and off with the Show/Hide ¶ button on the Standard toolbar.

To display the Standard toolbar, choose View, Toolbars, select Standard, and press Enter.

To hide and display hidden text with the Show/Hide ¶ button, click the Show/Hide ¶ button on the Standard toolbar.

You can also see hidden text by choosing File, Print Preview if you choose to print hidden text.

To print hidden text all the time, whether or not the text is displayed, follow these steps:

1. Choose Tools, Options.

2. Select the Print tab (see fig. 9.8).

3. Select the Hidden Text check box.

4. Choose OK.

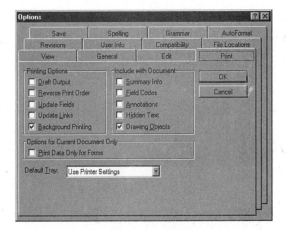

Fig. 9.8
Select the Hidden Text option on the Tools Options Print tab to print hidden text.

To include hidden text only when you print the current document, follow these steps:

1. Choose File, Print.

2. Click the Options button. The Tools Options Print tab appears.

3. Select the Hidden Text check box.

4. Choose OK.

Note

You can format any character as hidden text, even a page break or paragraph mark, but doing so affects the page numbering in a table of contents. For an accurate page count, remove the hidden formatting by choosing Edit, Find to locate the hidden character and remove the hidden formatting. For details about finding and replacing formatting, refer to Chapter 7, "Using Editing and Proofing Tools."

II

Formatting Documents

Highlighting Text

The Highlight feature makes it easy to highlight sections of text in up to 15 different colors, if you have a color monitor. This allows you, for example, to highlight the key points in a memo to the office staff. You also can create a color code for a documentation project: red for text that must not be changed, yellow for text that needs to be checked for accuracy, and green for text that needs further development.

To make sure that Word displays highlighted text with its highlighted color, follow these steps:

1. Choose Tools, Options.

2. Select the View tab.

3. Select the Highlight check box (see fig. 9.9).

4. Choose OK.

Fig. 9.9
Select the
Highlight option
on the Tools
Options View tab
to display
highlighted text.

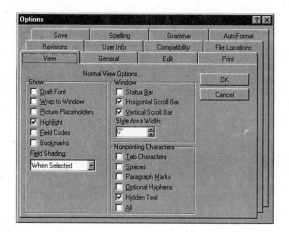

To actually highlight text, follow these steps:

1. Click the Highlight palette button that appears on the Formatting toolbar (refer to fig. 9.4). The pointer changes into a highlighting pen.

2. Drag across the text you want to highlight.

Click the Highlight button a second time or press Esc to turn off highlighting.

To change the highlighting color, follow these steps:

1. Click the down arrow to the right side of the Highlight button.

2. Drag the mouse pointer down and to the right through the displayed palette until all of the colors are displayed, position the mouse pointer over the desired color, then release the left mouse button. The Highlight color appears in the small window of the Highlight button.

To remove highlighting from text, select the highlighted text and click the Highlight button.

Changing Character Colors

If you have a color monitor, you can make good use of the 16 different colors available for text in Word for Windows. On an office task list, for example, you can format each person's duties in a different color so that every employee can easily see who must do which job. You also can format different levels of priority as different colors: for example, red items must be done right away; blue can wait. If you have a color printer, you can print text in color.

To color text, follow these steps:

1. Select the text to color, or position the insertion point where you want the new color to begin.

2. Choose Format, Font.

3. Select the Font tab.

4. Select a color from the Color drop-down list.

5. Choose OK.

Auto color, also listed in the Color list, is the color you select for Window Text in the Colors section of the Control Panel. Auto color is usually black.

Making Superscript and Subscript Text

Sometimes you may need to use subscripts and superscripts. You may use these features in scientific notations (for example, H_2O) or in references such as trademark or copyright symbols (for example, Microsoft™).

In calculating where superscripts and subscripts appear in relation to normal text, Word for Windows begins with the text baseline. You use the same procedure to add and remove both superscripts and subscripts.

To add or remove superscripts and subscripts, follow these steps:

1. Select the text you want to raise or lower, or position the insertion point where you want raised or lowered text to begin.

2. Choose Format, Font.

3. Select the Font tab.

4. In the Effects group, select Superscript to raise text, or select Subscript to lower text. A ✓ indicates that the feature is active.

5. Choose OK.

By default, Word for Windows raises superscript three points above the baseline and lowers subscript three points below the baseline. You can change the vertical position of superscript, subscript, or any text or graphic in the Font dialog box on the Character Spacing tab.

To change the vertical position of text, follow these steps:

1. Select the text you want to raise or lower.

2. Choose Format, Font.

3. Select the Character Spacing tab.

4. Choose Raised or Lowered from the Position box.

5. In the By box, accept three points as the default distance to raise or lower text, click the up- or down-arrows to change the distance, or type a new amount.

6. Choose OK.

Tip

To superscript text by three points, select the text and press Shift+Ctrl+= (equal sign). To subscript text by three points, select the text and press Ctrl+= (equal sign).

Underlining Text

Word for Windows offers four types of underlines: *single*, which underlines words and the space between words; *words only*, which underlines words but not the space between words; *double*, which double-underlines words and the space between words; and *dotted*, which underlines with dots the words and the space between words.

To add underlining from the menu command, follow these steps:

1. Select the text you want to underline, or position the insertion point where you want underlining to begin.

2. Choose Format, Font.

3. Select the Font tab.

4. In the Underline drop-down list box, select Single, Words Only, Double, or Dotted.

5. Choose OK.

To remove underlining with the menu command, follow these steps:

1. Select the underlined text.

2. Choose Format, Font.

3. Select the Font tab.

4. Select None from the Underline drop-down list box.

5. Choose OK.

To add or remove underlining with shortcut keys, follow these steps:

1. Select the text you want to underline or the text from which you want to remove underlining. Or position the insertion point where you want underlining to begin when you start typing.

2. Press one of the following shortcut keys:

Shortcut	Result
Ctrl+U	Single underline
Ctrl+Shift+W	Single underline words only
Ctrl+Shift+D	Double underline

To use the Formatting toolbar to add or remove underlining, follow these steps:

1. Select the text you want to underline or the text from which you want to remove underlining. Or position the insertion point where you want underlining to begin when you start typing.

2. Click the Underline button on the Formatting toolbar.

Tip

To place an underline below a superscript only, select the superscript—not the surrounding text—before issuing the Underline command. Subscripted text is always underlined just below the subscripted characters.

II

Formatting Documents

Adjusting Character Spacing

The normal spacing between letters in a word is right for most situations. Occasionally, however, you must fit more text on a line. Condensing the line can make the text fit. Sometimes, such as in large headlines, you also must condense the space between two individual letters to improve the headline's appearance. This process is known as *kerning*. The change in spacing is determined by the font design and the particular pair of letters being kerned.

In other instances, you may want to increase the space between letters to fill out a line or to create a special effect. Expanding makes text wider. For examples of condensed and expanded text, see figure 9.10.

Fig. 9.10
Use condensed and expanded text to change the spacing between characters.

This text is condensed by 1 point

This text is expanded by 3 points.

Letter pairs that might need kerning: AV   Ty   Pd
                           After kerning: AV   Ty   Pd

By default, Word for Windows expands and condenses the spacing between characters by three points. You can change the distance in increments of 0.1 of a point. You need this level of precision for kerning.

In the Font dialog box's Character Spacing tab, watch the Spacing Preview box to see how your text looks after condensing or expanding.

To condense or expand the space between characters, follow these steps:

1. Select the text you want to condense or expand, or position the insertion point where you want condensed or expanded text to begin when you start typing.

2. Choose Format, Font.

3. Select the Character Spacing tab.

4. In the Spacing drop-down list box, select Expanded or Condensed.

5. In the By box, accept the default, click the up or down arrows to increase or decrease the amount, or type a new amount.

6. Choose OK.

To return expanded or condensed text to normal, follow these steps:

1. Select the text you want to return to normal, or position the insertion point where you want normal text to begin.

2. Choose Format, Font.

3. Select the Character Spacing tab.

4. In the Spacing drop-down list box, select Normal.

5. Choose OK.

> **Note**
>
> If you select the Kerning for Fonts option in the Character Spacing tab of the Font dialog box, Word automatically adjusts the kerning for TrueType or Adobe Type Manager fonts. You can specify the point size at and above which you want automatic kerning to be applied in the Points and Above box.

Switching Uppercase and Lowercase

You can use a Word for Windows shortcut to change letters from uppercase to lowercase, or vice versa (the result depends on the case of selected text).

To change the letter case from the menu command, follow these steps:

1. Select the text whose case you want to change, or position the insertion point in or to the left of the word whose case you want to change.

2. Choose Format, Change Case. The Change Case box appears (see fig. 9.11).

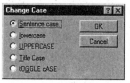

Fig. 9.11
Choose Format, Change Case to alter letter case quickly.

3. Select a case-change option from the following:

Option	Result
Sentence case	First character of the sentence to uppercase, all other characters to lowercase
lowercase	All lowercase
UPPERCASE	All uppercase

(continues)

Option	Result
Title Case	First character of each word to uppercase, all other characters to lowercase
tOGGLE cASE	Switches uppercase to lowercase and lowercase to uppercase

4. Choose OK.

To change the letter case from the keyboard, follow these steps:

1. Select the text whose case you want to change, or position the insertion point in or to the left of the word whose case you want to change.

2. Press Shift+F3 to change the case. You can toggle among three options: all uppercase, all lowercase, or first character uppercase. Continue to press Shift+F3 until the case appears as you want it.

Note

The terms *uppercase* and *lowercase* come from the days when type was set by hand from individual letters molded from lead. The capital letters were stored in the upper case above where the typesetters assembled their text, and noncapital letters were stored in the lower case.

Starting Paragraphs with a Drop Cap

You can add visual interest to a paragraph by starting it with a *drop cap*, a large capital letter or first word that is set into a paragraph. The top of the drop cap or word aligns with the top of the first line of the paragraph. Succeeding lines are indented to allow space for the dropped text. Drop caps usually mark the beginnings of key sections or major parts of a document.

If you select a different font for the drop cap, choose one that blends with the rest of the paragraph. Sans serif initial letters should be used with sans serif paragraphs; serif drop caps go well with paragraphs in serif fonts. Alternatively, you may combine an elegant script or cursive drop cap with a paragraph in a serif font. Figures 9.12 and 9.13 illustrate some uses of drop caps.

Fig. 9.12
A drop cap can use
the same font as
the body text.

Fig. 9.13
A drop cap can use
a decorative font
to enhance text.

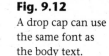

II

Formatting Documents

When you select a drop cap format, Word for Windows places the selected text in a frame. The rest of the paragraph wraps beside the frame. For information about frames, see Chapter 24, "Framing and Moving Text and Graphics."

> **Note**
>
> To increase horizontal spacing between the drop cap and the body text, select the drop cap. A frame will show around the drop cap when it is selected. Next choose Format, Frame. In the Frame dialog box that appears, increase the Horizontal Distance from Text to approximately 0.1". You may want to experiment with this distance. Choose OK.

To create large dropped capital letters, follow these steps:

1. Select the first letter, word, or segment of the paragraph you want to format as a dropped cap.

2. Choose Format, Drop Cap. The Drop Cap dialog box appears (see fig. 9.14).

Fig. 9.14

You can design drop caps by choosing Format, Drop Cap.

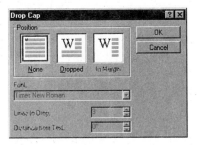

3. Select Dropped or In Margin in the Position group to place the drop cap as follows:

Option	Result
Dropped	Dropped flush with the left margin, inside the main text area
In Margin	Dropped in the left margin

4. Select a font from the Font box.

5. In the Lines to Drop text box, type or select the number of lines you want the capital to drop into the paragraph. The default is 3.

6. In the Distance from Text text box, type or select the distance you want between the drop cap and the paragraph text.

7. Choose OK.

If you are in Normal view, Word for Windows asks whether you want to switch to Page Layout view to see the dropped cap as it will appear in print.

Click the Yes button to switch to Page Layout view.

To remove dropped capital letters, follow these steps:

▶ See "Framing Text, Pictures, and Other Objects," p. 728

1. Select the first letter, word, or segment of the paragraph from which you want to remove the drop cap.

2. Choose Format, Drop Cap.

3. Select the None option from the Position group.

4. Choose OK.

The drop cap text is inserted into a frame and can be resized and repositioned.

Inserting Special Characters and Symbols

You can include many special characters in your document. Symbol fonts such as Symbol and Zapf Dingbats, for example, contain *dingbats* (decorative characters such as bullets, stars, and flowers) and scientific symbols. You can use foreign language characters such as umlauts (¨) and tildes (~), or ANSI characters such as bullets and *em dashes* (—), wide hyphens used in punctuation. You can also use invisible characters such as discretionary hyphens (which appear only when needed) and nonbreaking spaces (which prevent two words from separating at the end of a line).

Two techniques give you access to special characters. You can use the Symbol dialog box, which shows a keyboard of special characters to choose from, or you can use a series of special keystrokes.

Using the Symbol Dialog Box

The Symbol dialog box, shown in figure 9.15, gives you access to symbol fonts and ANSI characters. A symbol font, Symbol, is included with Word. Other symbol fonts may be built into your printer; for example, most PostScript printers include Zapf Dingbats. ANSI characters are the regular character set that you see on your keyboard, plus another hundred or so characters that include a copyright symbol, registered trademark symbol, and many foreign language symbols.

II

Formatting Documents

Fig. 9.15

You can insert symbols from the Symbol dialog box.

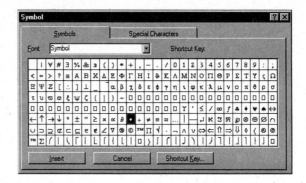

To insert symbols from the Symbol dialog box, follow these steps:

1. Position the insertion point where you want the symbol to appear.

2. Choose Insert, Symbol. The Symbol dialog box appears.

3. From the Font list box, select the font for which you want to see symbols. (Select Normal Text to see ANSI characters.)

4. Click a symbol to select it and/or to see it enlarged, or press Tab until the highlighted symbol in the box is selected (surrounded by a dotted outline), and then press the arrow keys keys to move the selection to the symbol you want.

5. Click the Insert button.

6. Insert more characters by repeating steps 3–5.

7. Choose the Close button.

Be sure to scan through all the interesting and useful symbols available in the Symbol and the Normal Text fonts.

Inserted symbols are actually field codes embedded in your document. This arrangement prevents you from accidentally selecting your symbol and changing it to a different font. Changing a symbol's font can change the symbol into a letter; for example, if you format text as Zapf Dingbats to include square bullets in your document, and then change the bullets to Times Roman, the bullet turns into *n*.

To delete an inserted symbol, you can position the insertion point to the right of the symbol and press Backspace. You can also follow these steps:

1. Select the symbol you want to delete.

2. Press the Delete key.

Customizing the Symbol Dialog Box

You may insert certain symbols, such as the copyright or trademark symbols, frequently in your work. You can customize the Symbol dialog box by adding shortcut keys. You then can use the shortcut keys to insert symbols directly from the keyboard.

To add shortcut keys to the Symbol dialog box, follow these steps:

1. Choose Insert, Symbol.

2. Click the symbol for which you want to add a shortcut key.

3. Click the Shortcut Key button. The Customize dialog box, shown in figure 9.16, appears. The symbol you have selected is displayed in the Symbol box.

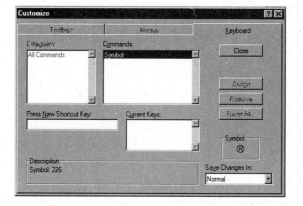

Fig. 9.16
You can add shortcut keys to symbols in the Customize dialog box.

4. Press the shortcut key combination you want to assign to the symbol. The shortcut you choose appears in the Press New Shortcut Key box. You can choose from any of the following key combinations:

Key Combination	Comments
Ctrl+ any letter or single digit	Most are previously assigned by Word
Ctrl+Shift+ any letter or single digit	Many are previously assigned by Word
Alt+ any letter or single digit	Most are not assigned
Alt+Shift+ any letter or single digit	Most are not assigned

5. Click the Assign button.

6. Click the Close button.

7. Repeat steps 2–6 for any additional symbols you want to assign a shortcut key.

8. Click the Close button.

Inserting Special Characters from the Keyboard

You can insert special characters from the keyboard in two ways: by using shortcut keys you assign in the Symbol dialog box (see the preceding section), or by using the ANSI character numbers. You must know the ANSI character numbers for the corresponding character or symbol you want.

To insert ANSI characters from the keyboard, follow these steps:

1. Position the insertion point where you want the symbol to appear.

2. Press Num Lock on the numeric keypad (so that numbers appear when you type).

◄ See "Hyphenating Words," p. 148

3. Hold down the Alt key and on the numeric keypad, type **0** (zero) followed by the ANSI code for the symbol you want. To type the fraction 1/4, for example, press Alt+**0188** on the numeric keypad.

If you have a symbol font such as Zapf Dingbats, or if you want to use a special character from the Symbol font, you can type and format the corresponding character with the Zapf Dingbats or Symbol font. To type a solid square (■), for example, you can type and format the letter n as Zapf Dingbats.

Using TrueType Fonts

You can use TrueType fonts with Word for Windows. A type of built-in font-generation software, *TrueType* generates screen and printer fonts so that what you see on-screen is almost exactly the same as what prints, whether you have a laser or dot-matrix printer.

When you choose Format, Font and select the Font tab, the fonts available with your printer appear in the Font list with printer icons next to them. TrueType fonts are listed with a TT icon next to them (see fig. 9.17). After you select a new font from the Font list, read the description of the font below the Preview box. The information in this box describes the type of font you have selected and how it affects printing.

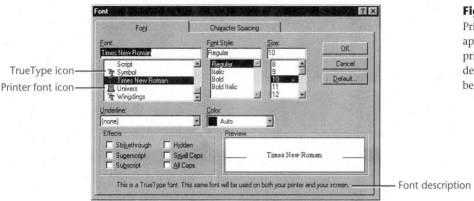

Fig. 9.17
Printer fonts
appear with a
printer icon and a
description of their
behavior.

TrueType icon
Printer font icon

Font description

You also can use screen fonts that don't match any font in your printer. Because the printer has no matching font, however, Windows selects a similar type and size of font when you print. In some cases, the printer font may be similar to the screen font; in others, it may be very different. Screen fonts that don't match a printer font appear in the Font list without an icon.

TrueType fonts give you a wide range of sizes and styles, and you can purchase additional typefaces designed for TrueType. The disadvantage of using TrueType fonts is that the generation time needed to create the screen fonts and download the characters slows system performance slightly. This slowing is only noticeable, however, on older systems. ❖

II

Formatting Documents

Chapter 10

Formatting Lines and Paragraphs

In writing, a paragraph is a series of sentences linked together to convey a single thought or idea, or to describe a single image. In Word for Windows 95, the definition of a paragraph is less lyrical: a *paragraph* is any amount of text—or no text at all—that ends when you press Enter. A paragraph may be the title of a story, an item in a list, a blank line between other paragraphs, or a series of sentences linked together to convey a single thought or idea.

The paragraph mark that ends a paragraph is normally hidden from view, but it stores all the paragraph formatting for the paragraph that it ends. Paragraph formatting includes such things as centering or aligning, shading and bordering, hanging indents, and more. When you delete the paragraph mark at the end of a paragraph, the paragraph takes on the paragraph formatting of the next paragraph mark in the document.

Whatever its contents, a paragraph, once selected, can be formatted in a variety of ways. The Word for Windows paragraph formatting options cover a wide range of features that enable you to communicate your thoughts visually, as well as through your choice of words.

Paragraph formatting is useful in many ways, including the following:

- Centering headings
- Creating hanging indents for numbered and bulleted lists
- Aligning columns of text using the Tab command

In this chapter, you learn how to format paragraphs and lines. Some of the most important procedures you learn are the following:

- Techniques for formatting paragraphs
- Displaying paragraph marks
- Aligning paragraphs
- Setting tabs and indents
- Numbering lines
- Adjusting line and paragraph spacing
- Adding shading and borders to paragraphs

Understanding Paragraph Formats

In Word for Windows, a paragraph is also a formatting unit. Just as you format individual characters with character formatting options such as bold and italic, you can format paragraphs with paragraph, tab, and border formatting options, such as the following:

- *Alignment.* Line up the text of a paragraph to the left, center, right, or both margins.
- *Indents.* Indent the left edge, right edge, or first line of a paragraph.
- *Tabs.* Create columns of text that line up perfectly and can be adjusted easily.
- *Spacing.* Add spaces between lines and paragraphs.
- *Lines, borders, and shading.* Add graphic interest to paragraphs with lines next to paragraphs, borders surrounding paragraphs, and shading to fill a border.

New paragraphs formed when you press Enter carry over the formatting from the previous paragraph. After you format a paragraph, you can continue that format into subsequent paragraphs simply by pressing Enter (see figs. 10.1 and 10.2).

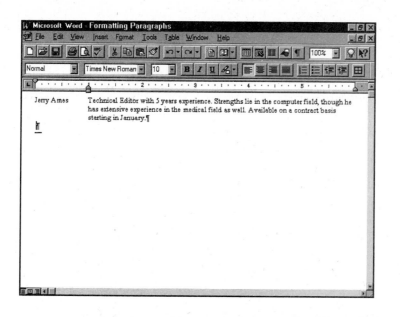

Fig. 10.1
The formatting is specified in the first paragraph of this document.

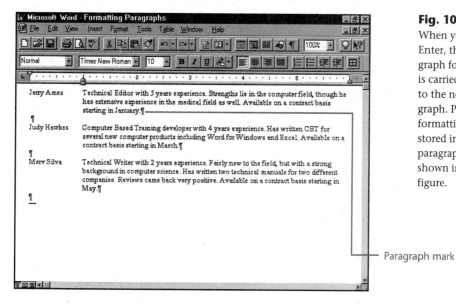

Fig. 10.2
When you press Enter, the paragraph formatting is carried forward to the new paragraph. Paragraph formatting is stored in the paragraph marks, shown in this figure.

Paragraph mark

II

Formatting Documents

Paragraph formatting affects the entire paragraph and is stored in the paragraph mark that ends each paragraph. If you delete one of these paragraph marks, the text preceding the mark becomes part of the following paragraph. If the paragraph mark you delete contains paragraph formatting, that formatting is also lost. The new paragraph formed of two merged paragraphs takes on the formatting of the second of the two paragraphs, as shown in figures 10.3 and 10.4.

Fig. 10.3

Display paragraph marks to avoid accidentally including them with selected text.

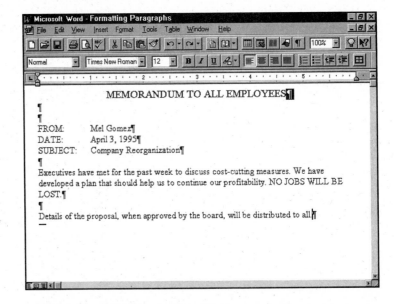

Fig. 10.4

If you delete paragraph marks, a paragraph takes on the paragraph formatting of the following paragraph.

Heading loses format of deleted paragraph mark and gains format of the follwing paragraph mark

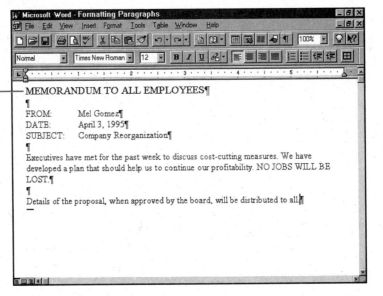

Displaying Paragraph Marks

When paragraph marks are hidden, you don't see them at the end of a paragraph. You can display paragraph marks, however (refer to fig. 10.4). If you expect to do much text editing, you should display paragraph marks to avoid accidentally deleting one of them and thereby losing your paragraph formatting.

To display paragraph marks from the menu, follow these steps:

1. Choose Tools, Options.

2. Select the View tab.

3. Choose Paragraph Marks under Nonprinting Characters.

To display paragraph marks from the keyboard, press Ctrl+Shift+8.

To display paragraph marks from the Standard toolbar, click the Show/Hide ¶ button on the Standard toolbar.

> **Note**
>
> If you turn on paragraph marks by choosing Tools, Options, then selecting the Paragraph Marks check box, you can turn on and off the display of tabs and spaces only by clicking the Show/Hide ¶ button. Paragraph marks remain on.

Using Paragraph Formatting Techniques

Every new document you create based on the default Normal template is controlled by the Normal style. The Normal style formats paragraphs as left-aligned and single-spaced, with left-aligned tab stops every half inch. If you usually choose different paragraph formatting selections, change the Normal style to reflect your preferences.

▶ See "Applying Paragraph Styles," p. 355

You can format a paragraph at two times: before you begin typing and after you finish typing. To format after typing, you must select the paragraph or paragraphs you want to format. If you are formatting only one paragraph instead of selecting the entire paragraph, you can position the insertion point anywhere inside the paragraph before making your formatting selections. Paragraph formatting commands apply to the entire paragraph.

◀ See "Selecting Text," p. 141

Word for Windows offers several alternative techniques for formatting paragraphs:

- Choose Format, Paragraph to select many formatting options at once and to get the widest possible range of paragraph formatting options.

- Select the Formatting toolbar to access paragraph formatting commands individually.

- Use the ruler to set tabs and indents quickly.

With keyboard shortcuts, you can format as you type. Figures 10.5 and 10.6 show examples of selecting and formatting text from the Formatting toolbar.

Fig. 10.5
Select the paragraphs you want to format.

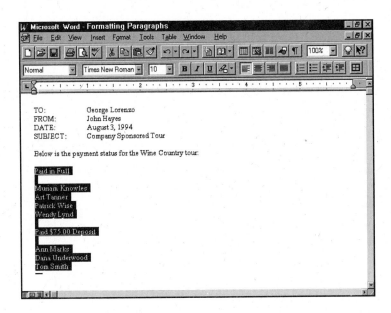

Formatting Paragraphs with Menu Commands

Tip
You also can access the Paragraph dialog box by clicking the right mouse button and choosing Paragraph from the shortcut menu.

The Paragraph dialog box offers the greatest number of options for formatting paragraphs and shows a sample of how the formatting you choose affects your paragraph in the Preview box (see fig. 10.7). You can choose the Indents and Spacing tab to change indentation, spacing, and alignment; or you can choose the Text Flow tab to change pagination and suppress line numbers and hyphenation. Because the Paragraph dialog box provides quick access to the Tabs dialog box, you also can do quite a bit of formatting at once by choosing Format, Paragraph. See Chapter 13, "Formatting the Page Layout, Alignment, and Numbering," for more details on pagination.

Align Center——— ———Align Right
Align Left——┐ ┌—Justify

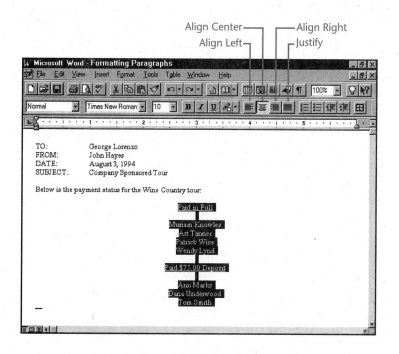

Fig. 10.6
Click the button for the formatting you want. The Align Center button is selected in this example.

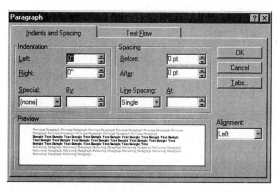

Fig. 10.7
Use the Paragraph dialog box to change the formatting of the selected text or the paragraph that contains the insertion point.

Specific instructions on using the Paragraph dialog box for setting indentation, spacing, and pagination options appear throughout this chapter.

Formatting Paragraphs with Shortcut Keys

You can choose from several shortcut keys for quick formatting changes, which you can make directly from the keyboard. To use a shortcut key for formatting, first select the paragraph or paragraphs you want to change or place the insertion point in the paragraph you want to change, then choose one of the following commands:

II

Formatting Documents

To Do This	Press
Left-align text	Ctrl+L
Center-align text	Ctrl+E
Right-align text	Ctrl+R
Justify text	Ctrl+J
Indent from left margin	Ctrl+M
Create a hanging indent out one tab stop	Ctrl+T
Reduce a hanging indent by one tab stop	Ctrl+Shift+T
Single-space text	Ctrl+1
Change to 1.5 line spacing	Ctrl+5
Double-space text	Ctrl+2
Add/remove 12 points of space before a paragraph (toggle)	Ctrl+0 (zero)
Remove paragraph formatting that isn't part of the paragraph's assigned style	Ctrl+Q
Restore default formatting (from the Normal style)	Ctrl+Shift+N

Tip

Displaying toolbars is optional but useful if you do a lot of formatting. To increase the typing space on-screen, remove the toolbar by placing the mouse pointer between buttons or list boxes, clicking the right mouse button, then clicking the name of the toolbar in the shortcut menu.

Formatting Paragraphs with the Formatting Toolbar

Word's Formatting toolbar, shown in figure 10.8, provides a quick way to choose certain paragraph formatting options using the mouse. Default paragraph formatting buttons on the Formatting toolbar include buttons for creating numbered lists and bulleted lists, indenting and unin-denting, and controlling a paragraph's alignment. You also can access a special toolbar for creating lines and borders in your document.

To use the Formatting toolbar for alignment, follow these steps:

1. Select the paragraph or paragraphs you want to align, or place the insertion point in the paragraph you want to align.

2. Choose the appropriate alignment button: Left, Center, Right, or Justify (both margins aligned).

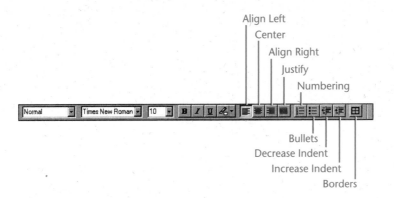

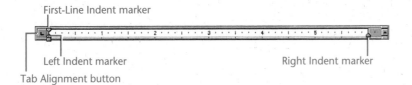

Align Left
Center
Align Right
Justify
Numbering

Bullets
Decrease Indent
Increase Indent
Borders

Fig. 10.8
You can change the format of selected paragraphs from the Formatting toolbar.

Note

You can add any button to the toolbar to either fill in blank spaces on the toolbar or replace existing buttons.

► See "Assigning a Command or Macro to a Toolbar Button," p. 1040

◄ See "Controlling Your Document's Appearance On-Screen," p. 123

Formatting Paragraphs with the Ruler

The *ruler*, shown in figure 10.9, is useful for quickly setting paragraph indentations and tabs with a click of the mouse. By default, tabs are left-aligned; if you want a different tab style, you must select that style and then position the tab on the ruler.

First-Line Indent marker

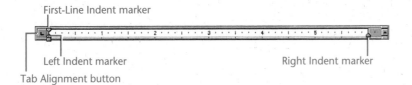

Left Indent marker
Tab Alignment button

Right Indent marker

Fig. 10.9
The ruler provides quick access to some formatting options.

Displaying the ruler, like the toolbar, is also optional. To display or remove the ruler, choose <u>V</u>iew, <u>R</u>uler. The Ruler command has a check mark to its left when displayed. Choose the command again to remove the ruler.

The sections "Setting Tabs" and "Setting Indents," later in this chapter, discuss using ruler options.

Duplicating Formats

The easiest way to duplicate paragraph formatting is to carry the formatting forward as you type. As you arrive at the end of the current paragraph and press Enter, the current paragraph ends and a new one begins—using the

Tip
Displaying the ruler can speed up formatting if you have a mouse; however, removing the ruler gives you more room on-screen.

II

Formatting Documents

same formatting as the preceding paragraph. If, however, you use the mouse or arrow keys to move out of the current paragraph, you move into a different paragraph, which may have different formatting.

Another way to duplicate formatting is to choose Edit, Repeat, or press F4. Remember that the Repeat command duplicates only your one most recent action. The command works best when you format with the Paragraph, Tabs, or Borders dialog box, making multiple formatting choices at once.

To duplicate paragraph formatting using a mouse, follow these steps:

1. Select the text containing the formatting you want to duplicate.

2. Click the Format Painter button in the Standard toolbar. The pointer changes to a combination insertion point and paintbrush.

Tip

To use the Format Painter repeatedly, double-click it, apply formatting to several selections of text, and click the Format Painter button again

3. Drag across the text you want formatted.

When you release the mouse button, the text over which you dragged changes to the copied format.

To duplicate paragraph formatting from the keyboard, follow these steps:

1. Select the paragraph whose format you want to copy.

2. Press Ctrl+Shift+C.

3. Select the paragraph(s) whose format you want to change.

4. Press Ctrl+Shift+V.

Tip

To avoid deleting a paragraph mark, turn on paragraph marks by clicking the paragraph mark button at the right end of the Standard toolbar.

Probably the most powerful way to duplicate paragraph formatting is to use styles. A *style* is a set of formatting commands that you can apply all at once and can change globally later. Styles are easy to use and create—especially when you use the "styles by example" technique. Styles are explained in detail in Chapter 11, "Using Styles for Repetitive Formats."

If you deleted a paragraph mark and you need to reapply the previous formatting, reformat it or copy a paragraph mark from a paragraph that has the formatting you want to apply and paste it at the end of the problem paragraph.

Troubleshooting

I set up formatting in a paragraph and then moved to the next paragraph, but the formatting didn't carry over.

You must press the Enter key at the end of the paragraph whose formatting you want to carry over to a new paragraph. If there is already a paragraph mark following the formatted paragraph and you use the mouse or arrow keys to move into this paragraph, the new paragraph will not necessarily have the same formatting as the previous paragraph.

Aligning Paragraphs

Paragraph alignment refers to how the left and right edges of a paragraph line up (see fig. 10.10). *Left-aligned* paragraphs line up on the left edge but are ragged on the right (the Word for Windows default). Left-aligned text is commonly used in informal letters or in the body text in a book, such as this book. *Right-aligned* paragraphs line up on the right edge but are ragged on the left. Right-aligned text can be used in headers and footers in a document—for example, page numbering—or when you are creating a list and want the items in the right column to line up along the right margin. *Centered* paragraphs are ragged on both edges, centered between the margins. Centered paragraphs are most often used for headings. *Justified* paragraphs are aligned on both edges and are often used in formal business letters and in text that appears in columns, as in a newsletter.

Paragraphs are aligned to the margins if no indentations are set for them. If paragraphs are indented, they align to the indentation.

You can set paragraph alignment while you're typing or editing your document. If you set alignment as you type, the alignment carries forward when you press Enter (as do all paragraph formatting selections). If you set alignment later, your setting applies only to the selected paragraph or paragraphs.

II

Formatting Documents

Fig. 10.10

You can choose from four styles of alignment: left, centered, right, and justified.

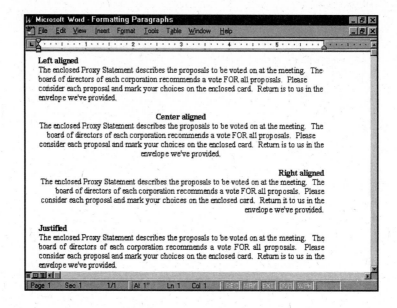

Aligning with Menu Commands

Tip

To justify the last line of a paragraph, end the line with a soft return, Shift+Enter, rather than Enter.

You can choose Format, Paragraph to set alignment with a mouse or your keyboard.

To set alignment using the menu command, follow these steps:

1. Select the paragraph or paragraphs to align, or position the insertion point where you want the new alignment to begin.

2. Choose Format, Paragraph. The Paragraph dialog box appears.

3. Select the Alignment option from the Indents and Spacing tab.

4. Select Left, Centered, Right, or Justified from the Alignment drop-down list, as shown in figure 10.11.

5. Click OK.

> **Note**
>
> You can choose formatting commands from the shortcut menu. Select the text you want to format, click the right mouse button, and choose Paragraph. The Paragraph dialog box appears.

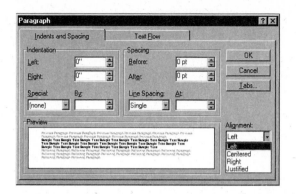

Fig. 10.11
You can choose paragraph alignment from the Alignment drop-down list box in the Paragraph dialog box.

Aligning with the Formatting Toolbar

If you have a mouse, a quicker way to set alignment is to display the Formatting toolbar and click the appropriate alignment button. If the Formatting toolbar isn't displayed, choose View, Toolbars, and specify the toolbar(s) you want to display.

◀ See "Using the Toolbars," p. 53

To align paragraphs with the Formatting toolbar, follow these steps:

1. Select the paragraph or paragraphs to align, or position the insertion point where you want the new alignment to begin.

2. Click the Align Left, Center, Align Right, or Justify Alignment button.

Aligning with Keyboard Shortcuts

One of the quickest ways to align selected paragraphs is to use keyboard shortcuts. With this technique, you also can save screen space by not displaying the Formatting toolbar.

To align paragraphs using keyboard shortcuts, follow these steps:

1. Select the paragraph or paragraphs to align, or position the insertion point where you want the new alignment to begin.

2. Press the appropriate Ctrl+key combination:

Paragraph Alignment	Shortcut
Left	Ctrl+L
Centered	Ctrl+E
Right	Ctrl+R
Justified	Ctrl+J

II

Formatting Documents

Troubleshooting

When I insert a page break immediately after a justified paragraph, Word justifies the words in the last line of the paragraph, resulting in very wide spacing between the words.

This problem occurs because the insertion point is located at the end of the justified paragraph when you insert the page break. Be sure to press Enter at the end of the paragraph before you insert the page break.

Setting Tabs

Tip

When you work with a table or list made up of tabs, displaying the tab characters in your document is helpful. The tab characters appear as right-pointing arrows.

Working with tabs is a two-part process. First, you must set the tab stops, or you must plan to use the Word for Windows default left-aligned tab stops at every 0.5". Setting the tab stops includes selecting the type of tab—left, centered, right, decimal, or bar—and specifying where the tab stops must appear. The second step in using tabs is to press the Tab key as you type your document to move the insertion point forward to the next tab stop. You also have three leader style options including dotted, dashed, or solid.

A wonderful advantage to working with tabs is that after the tabs are in your document, you can move or change the tab stops, and the selected text moves or realigns with the stops.

You can set tabs in one of two ways. You can use the Tabs dialog box, which gives you precise control over where each tab is to appear and enables you to customize tabs by adding tab leaders. Alternatively, you can use the ruler to select a tab style and then to set the tab's position using the mouse.

 To display the tab characters from the Standard toolbar, click the Show/Hide ¶ button at the right end of the Standard toolbar. To display the tab characters using menu commands, follow these steps:

1. Choose Tools, Options.

2. Select the View tab.

3. Select the Tab Characters option from the Nonprinting Characters group.

You must understand that, like all paragraph formatting options, tabs belong to paragraphs. If you set tab stops as you type text and then press Enter, the tab settings are carried forward to the next paragraph. If you add tabs later, however, they apply only to the paragraph or paragraphs selected when you set the tab stops.

Figure 10.12 shows how each of the different tab styles affects the text to which they're applied; figure 10.13 shows the three different tab leader styles.

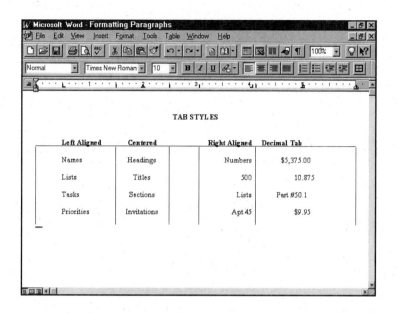

Fig. 10.12
You can select from five tab styles: left, centered, right, decimal, or bar. This example includes bar tabs set between and around the other tab styles.

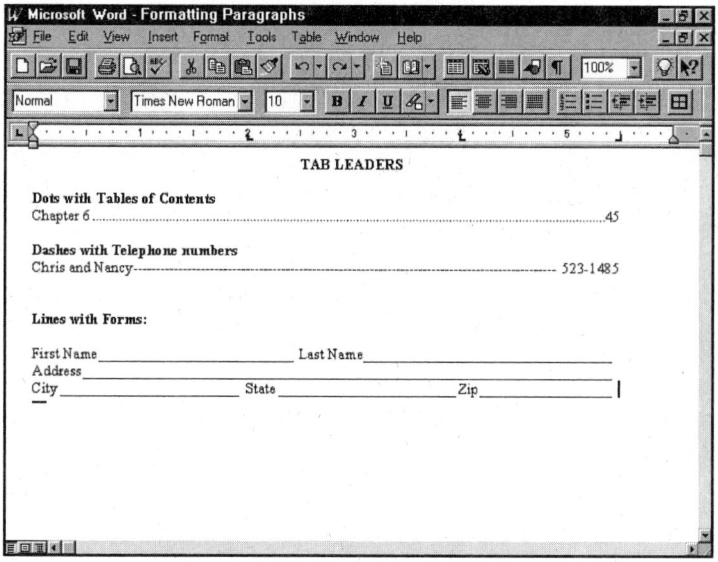

Fig. 10.13
Use any of the three leader styles to "lead" the eye to tabbed text.

▶ See "Creating Tables," p. 506

▶ See "Formatting a Table," p. 535

Although tabs are useful for lists, menus, tables of contents, and anything requiring tab leaders, a table sometimes works better for lists. A table contains *cells* formed by rows and columns, and it is the best choice when you have many columns or when the text in each cell varies in length.

Using the Tabs Dialog Box

Using the Tabs dialog box to set tabs has several advantages. You can set each tab's position precisely by typing in decimal numbers, and you can add dotted, dashed, or underlined tab leaders. (A *tab leader* "leads" up to tabbed text on the left side; refer to fig. 10.13.) With a mouse or a keyboard, you can quickly clear existing tabs and change the default tab settings for the rest of your document. You can even reformat existing tabs.

To set tabs using the menu command, follow these steps:

1. Select the paragraph or paragraphs for which you want to set tabs, or position the insertion point where you want the tab settings to begin.

2. Choose Format, Tabs. The Tabs dialog box appears, as shown in figure 10.14.

Fig. 10.14

You can set tabs at precise locations and include leaders from the Tabs dialog box.

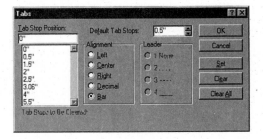

3. Using decimal numbers, type the position of the tab stop you want to set in the Tab Stop Position box.

4. From the Alignment group, select the tab style you want: Left, Center, Right, Decimal, or Bar.

5. In the Leader group, select the tab leader style you want (if any): 1 for no leader, 2 for a dotted leader, 3 for a dashed leader, or 4 for an underlined leader.

6. Click the Set button to set the tab stop.

7. Repeat steps 3 through 6 to set additional tab stops.

8. Click OK.

The Tab Stop Position list box displays your tab stops after you set them.

You can reformat existing tab stops by following the same general procedure for setting tabs.

To reformat existing tab stops, follow these steps:

1. Select the tab to reformat in the Tab Stop Position list box.

2. Select the new formatting options for the selected tab stop in the Alignment and Leader groups.

3. Click the Set button.

You can access the Tabs dialog box through the Paragraph dialog box. Choose Format, Paragraph or click the right mouse button and choose Paragraph in the shortcut menu; then click the Tabs button. Alternatively, you can double-click any tab set on the ruler to display the Tabs dialog box.

Clearing Tabs

After you set tabs, you can *clear* (remove) them individually or as a group. The following technique works whether you set the tabs through the Tabs dialog box or use the ruler (see "Using the Ruler to Set Tabs," later in this chapter).

To clear tab stops with the menu command, follow these steps:

1. Select the paragraph or paragraphs from which you want to clear tabs, or position the insertion point where you want to begin working with the new tab settings.

2. Choose Format, Tabs.

3. Click the Clear All button to clear all the tabs.

   You can also select the tab from the Tab Stop Position list box and click the Clear button to clear one tab. Repeat this process to clear additional tab stops.

4. Click OK.

As you clear tab stops with the Clear button in step 3, the tab stops are listed in the Tab Stops to Be Cleared area at the bottom of the Tabs dialog box.

Formatting Documents

Resetting the Default Tab Stops

If you do not set custom tabs, Word has preset tabs every 0.5". When you set a custom tab, all preset tabs to the left of the custom tab are cleared. You can use the Tabs dialog box to change the default tab stop interval if you routinely use the preset tabs and do not like the default tab setting. Any custom tab stops you may have set for existing paragraphs are not affected.

To change the default tab stops, follow these steps:

1. Choose Format, Tabs.

2. In the Default Tab Stops spin box, type in a new default tab interval or click the up or down arrow to change the number in the box.

3. Click OK.

Using the Ruler to Set Tabs

Tip
To display the ruler, choose View, Ruler.

◀ See "Controlling Your Document's Appearance On-Screen," p. 123

If you have a mouse, you can use the ruler to set, move, and remove left, center, right, or decimal tabs quickly. (Bar tabs are not available from the ruler.) This task involves two steps: selecting the tab style by clicking the Tab Alignment button on the ruler, and then setting the tabs where you want them on the ruler.

The ruler displays Word's default tab stops (set every 0.5", unless you change the interval) as tiny vertical lines along the bottom of the ruler. When you set your own tab stops, all default tab stops to the left are removed from the ruler (see fig. 10.15).

Fig. 10.15
This ruler shows the symbols for the various kinds of tabs.

Left tab   Bar tab   Center tab   Right tab   Decimal tab

To set tabs using the ruler, follow these steps:

1. Select the paragraph or paragraphs for which you want to set tabs, or position the insertion point where you want the new tab settings to begin.

2. Click the Tab Alignment button at the far left of the ruler until the symbol for the tab style you want to use is selected: Left, Centered, Right, or Decimal. (Refer to figure 10.12 to see how each Tab Alignment style looks on-screen.)

3. Position the pointer just below the tick mark on the ruler where you want the tab stop to appear. Click the left mouse button to place the tab stop on the ruler.

Repeat steps 2 and 3 to add various kinds of tab stops to the ruler, or just step 3 to add more tab stops of the same style.

The tab stop appears as a marker in the same style as the tab style you selected from the ruler. If you don't get the tab marker in just the right place on the ruler, position the mouse pointer on the marker, hold down the left mouse button to select the marker, and drag the tab marker to the correct position.

To use the ruler to change a tab stop's alignment or to add a leader, double-click the tab stop to display the Tabs dialog box. Select the tab stop you want to change in the Tab Stop Position list box and make whatever changes you want and click OK.

To use the mouse to quickly remove a tab from the ruler, follow these steps:

1. Drag the tab off the ruler onto the document.

2. Release the mouse button.

Setting Default Tabs

Default tabs are set every 0.5". If you find that you are changing them frequently, you can change the default tab settings in NORMAL.DOT, the template on which most documents are based. You first need to retrieve NORMAL.DOT, then change the tabs, and finally save the template.

◄ See "Setting Default Formats in the Normal Template," p. 187

To retrieve NORMAL.DOT, follow these steps:

1. Choose File, Open.

2. Open the MSOFFICE folder.

3. Open the TEMPLATES folder.

4. Click the down arrow of Files of type and choose Document Templates (*.DOT).

5. Choose NORMAL.

6. Click Open.

II

Formatting Documents

To change the default tabs, follow these steps:

1. Choose Format, Tabs.

2. Change the setting in the Default Tab Stops spin box to the interval you prefer.

3. Click OK.

To save and exit NORMAL.DOT, follow these steps:

1. Choose File, Close. You are asked whether you want to save the changes.

2. Click Yes to save the changes you have made.

The next time you create a document using NORMAL.DOT, the default tab settings will match the changes you've made to the template.

Troubleshooting

When I tried to adjust the column in a table created with tabs by dragging the tab stop on the ruler, only one row in the table changed.

Tab settings are a paragraph characteristic and are stored in the paragraph mark at the end of a paragraph. To adjust the columns in a table, you must select all of the rows (paragraphs) in the table and then drag the tab stops on the ruler.

When I select the rows in a table created with tabs, some of the tab stops are grayed on the ruler.

When you select a group of paragraphs that don't all have exactly the same tab settings, the tab stops that are not common to all of the paragraphs will appear in gray. You can drag a tab stop to a new setting, and it will then be applied to all of the paragraphs in the selection. This is a good way to synchronize the tab stops in a group of paragraphs if you accidentally change a tab setting in just one of the paragraphs.

Setting Indents

A document's margins are determined by selections made in the File Page Setup dialog box. Margins apply to the entire document or to sections within the document. But individual paragraphs or groups of paragraphs can be indented from those margins and therefore appear to have their own margin settings.

Although only two side margins (left and right) are available, you can indent a paragraph in many ways, as shown in figure 10.16. You can indent from the left, right, or both margins. You can indent just the first line of a paragraph, a technique that often substitutes for pressing Tab at the beginning of each new paragraph. You can create a *hanging indent*, which "hangs" the first line of a paragraph to the left of the rest of the paragraph; hanging indents often are used for bulleted or numbered lists. You also can create *nested indents*—indentations within indentations.

Several techniques exist for creating indents. You can use the Paragraph dialog box and enter the amount of indent for the selected paragraph or paragraphs. You can use the ruler, dragging indent icons left and right. You can use a button on the toolbar to indent or unindent paragraphs quickly or to create lists with a hanging indent. You also can use keyboard shortcuts.

Whichever technique you use, indenting is stored in the paragraph mark and is carried forward when you press Enter at the end of a paragraph. Alternatively, you can return to a paragraph later and format the text with an indent.

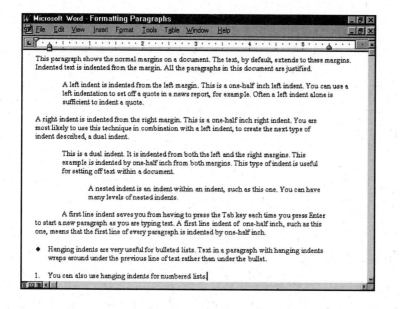

Fig. 10.16
You can use various levels of indenting to achieve various effects.

▶ See "Creating Bulleted Lists," p. 549

▶ See "Creating Numbered Lists," p. 555

Note

Note that numbered and bulleted lists are a special type of indented list.

Using the Paragraph Command to Set Indents

You can use the Paragraph dialog box to precisely set any type of indent. The Indentation list in the Paragraph dialog box lists three options: Left, Right, and Special, as shown in figure 10.17.

Fig. 10.17
Use the Indents and Spacing tab to change paragraph indentation.

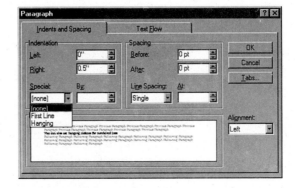

The indentation options give the following results:

Option	Result
Left	Indents selected paragraph or paragraphs from the left margin. If the number is positive, the paragraph is indented inside the left margin; if the number is negative, the paragraph is indented outside the left margin (sometimes termed *outdenting*).
Right	Indents selected paragraph or paragraphs from the right margin. If the number is positive, the paragraph is indented inside the right margin; if the number is negative, the paragraph is indented outside the right margin.
Special	Indents the first line or lines of selected paragraph or paragraphs from left indent (or margin, if no indent is made). Click the down arrow to select either First Line or Hanging. First Line indents inside the left indent. Hanging Indent indents outside the left indent. The default indent is 0.5". Change the indent by typing a new number or by using the up or down arrow to change the number.

To set indentations using the Paragraph dialog box, follow these steps:

1. Select the paragraph or paragraphs to indent, or position the insertion point where you want the new indentation to begin.

2. Choose F<u>o</u>rmat, <u>P</u>aragraph. The Paragraph dialog box opens.

3. Select the <u>I</u>ndents and Spacing tab.

4. Type or select a value in the <u>L</u>eft or <u>R</u>ight Indentation spin box. You also can select First Line or Hanging from the <u>S</u>pecial drop-down list box and type or select a value in the B<u>y</u> spin box. Or, you can preview the effects of the choices you make in the Preview box.

5. Click OK.

You can create indents in measurements other than decimal inches. To create a 6-point indent, for example, type **6 pt** in either indentation box. (An inch consists of 72 points.) To create an indent of 2 centimeters, type **2 cm**; to create an indent of 1 pica, type **1 pi** (six picas per inch; 12 points per pica).

Creating a Hanging Indent

A hanging indent is used for items such as bulleted and numbered lists, glossary items, and bibliographic entries (see fig. 10.18).

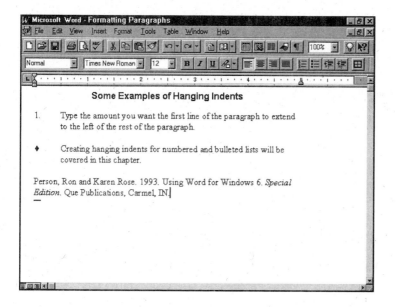

Fig. 10.18
Hanging indents can be used for creating bulleted and numbered lists and bibliographic entries.

To create a hanging indent, follow these steps:

1. Choose F<u>o</u>rmat, <u>P</u>aragraph.

2. Select the <u>S</u>pecial drop-down list box by clicking its down arrow.

3. Choose Hanging.

4. In the <u>B</u>y spin box type the amount you want the first line of the paragraph to extend to the left of the rest of the paragraph.

5. Click OK.

To use a hanging indent, type a number or bullet at the left margin, press Tab to advance to the left indent, and then begin typing the text of the paragraph. When text reaches the end of the line, the paragraph wraps around to the left indent, not the left margin. This technique is useful for numbered and bulleted lists. (You can create hanging indents for numbered and bulleted lists automatically with the toolbar or the Bullets and Numbering dialog box.) See Chapter 18, "Creating Bulleted or Numbered Lists," for further information.

> **Note**
>
> Symbol fonts such as Symbol and Zapf Dingbats are full of interesting characters you can use as bullets in a list.

◀ See "Inserting Special Characters and Symbols," p. 281

Using the Ruler or Formatting Toolbar to Set Indents

With the ruler, you easily can create indents of any kind. With the Formatting toolbar, you can indent a selected paragraph to the next available tab stop.

The ruler contains triangular markers, called *indent markers*, at the left and right margins. You can drag them left and right on the ruler to set indents. The top triangle at the left margin represents the first-line indent. The bottom triangle represents the left indent. Both the top and bottom triangles move independently. You use the square below the bottom triangle to move both the first-line and left paragraph indents at once. The triangle at the right margin represents the paragraph's right indent. Figure 10.19 shows the indent markers on the ruler.

Fig. 10.19
Use the indent markers to set left and right indentations.

First-line indent marker

Left Indent marker

First-line and left indent marker

Right indent marker

Left and right indents are measured from the left and right margins, respectively. First-line indents are measured relative to the left indent. In figures 10.20, 10.21, and 10.22, you can see that the position of the indent markers reflects the indentation settings for the selected paragraph.

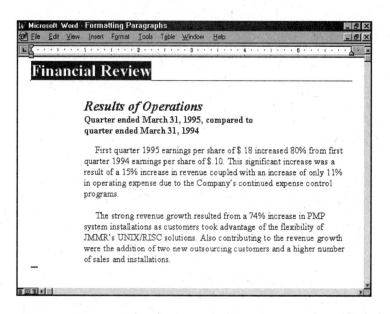

Fig. 10.20
The First-Line, Left, and Right Indent markers are set even with the left and right margins.

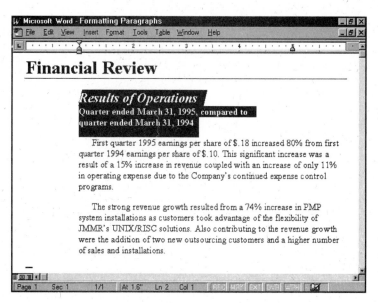

Fig. 10.21
The First-Line and Left Indent markers are set at 1.0", and the Right Indent marker has been moved to 6".

Fig. 10.22

The First-Line
Indent marker is
set in .25" from
the Left Indent
marker to create
a first-line
indentation.

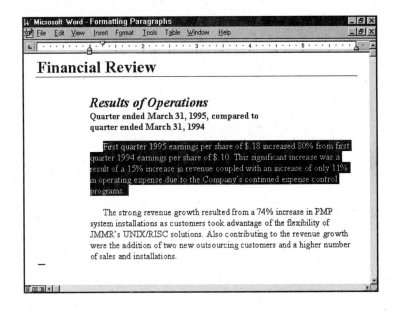

To set indentations with the ruler, follow these steps:

1. Select the paragraph or paragraphs to indent, or position the insertion point where you want the new indentation to begin.

Tip

To set indents with
the ruler, display
the ruler by choos-
ing View, Ruler.

2. To set a left indent, drag the square below the left indent marker to the ruler position where you want the indentation. (Notice that the top triangle moves also.)

   To set a right indent, drag the right indent marker to the position where you want the indentation.

   To set a first-line indent, drag the first-line indent marker to the position where you want the first-line indentation.

   To set a hanging indent with the first line at the left margin, drag the left indent marker to a new position on the ruler.

> **Note**
>
> While in Normal view, when you drag the left or first-line indent to the left of the left margin, the ruler automatically scrolls to the left. If you want to scroll on the ruler into the left margin without moving the indent markers, however, hold down the Shift key while you click the left scroll arrow in the horizontal scroll bar.

The Formatting toolbar includes two buttons for indenting a selected paragraph to the next tab stop: the Increase Indent and Decrease Indent buttons. Increase Indent is used to indent to the next tab stop. Decrease Indent is used to decrease the indent to the previous tab stop. You use these buttons to create left indents only—not first-line or hanging indents—and to indent to tab stops already set in the current paragraph(s). To use this technique, be sure the Formatting toolbar is displayed by choosing View, Toolbars.

To indent or unindent paragraphs using the Formatting toolbar, follow these steps:

1. Select the paragraph or paragraphs to indent, or position the insertion point where you want the new indentation to begin.

2. To indent the paragraph, click the Increase Indent button.

   To unindent the paragraph, click the Decrease Indent button.

You can click the Increase Indent button as many times as you want to continue moving the left indentation to the right. The Increase Indent button, therefore, is an easy way to create nested paragraphs, which are like indents within indents (refer to fig. 10.16).

Using Keyboard Shortcuts to Set Indents

If you're a touch typist, you might appreciate being able to create indents by using keyboard shortcuts. Just as when you use the Formatting toolbar to create indents, keyboard shortcuts rely on existing tab settings to determine the position of indents. If you haven't changed Word for Windows default tab stops, for example—and therefore they still are set every 0.5"—using the shortcut keys to create a hanging indent leaves the first line of the paragraph at the margin but moves the left edge for the remaining lines of the paragraph to one-half inch.

To set indents by using keyboard shortcuts, follow these steps:

1. Select the paragraph or paragraphs to indent, or position the insertion point where you want the new indentation to begin.

2. Use one of the following keyboard shortcuts to indent your text:

Shortcut	Indentation Type
Ctrl+M	Moves the left indent to the next tab stop
Ctrl+Shift+M	Moves the left indent to the preceding tab stop (but not beyond the left margin)

(continues)

II

Formatting Documents

Shortcut	Indentation Type
Ctrl+T	Creates a hanging indent
Ctrl+Shift+T	Removes an existing hanging indent

> **Note**
>
> Just as you use shortcuts to format a paragraph, you can use a shortcut to remove formatting. Select a paragraph and press Ctrl+space bar to remove all character formatting and return a paragraph to only the formatting specified by the paragraph's style.

Setting Default Indents

One of the most commonly used letter-writing styles is modified-block style, with indented paragraphs. If you find that you are frequently changing indentations to indent paragraphs, for example, you can change the default indentation settings in NORMAL.DOT, the template on which most documents are based. You first need to retrieve NORMAL.DOT, then change the indentation, and finally save the template.

Refer to "Setting Default Tabs" earlier in this chapter for information about changing default indentation settings in NORMAL.DOT.

Numbering Lines

Line numbers are useful in preparing manuscripts or legal documents, for reference, or if you simply need to know how many lines of text are on a page, in a poem, or in a document. You can choose the starting number for line numbering, the distance between numbers and text, the interval at which line numbers appear, and whether line numbering restarts with every new page or section or continues throughout your section. You can suppress line numbering for a specific paragraph or paragraphs.

Adding Line Numbers

You can add line numbers to sections of a document or to the entire document if it isn't formatted into sections. For information about formatting a document in sections, see Chapter 13, "Formatting the Page Layout, Alignment, and Numbering."

To number lines, follow these steps:

1. Position the insertion point inside the section in which you want line numbers, or anywhere in the document to number a document that hasn't been split into sections. To number an entire document that has been divided into sections, select the entire document.

2. Choose File, Page Setup. The Page Setup dialog box appears.

3. Select the Layout tab.

4. Click Line Numbers.

5. Select the Add Line Numbering option (see fig. 10.23). Change the following default line numbering settings if you want:

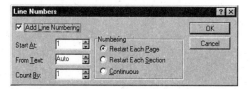

Fig. 10.23
Choose line numbering options from the Line Numbers dialog box.

Option	Description	Then Type
Start At	Starting line number	A new starting number in the box, or click the up or down arrow to increase or decrease the starting number. (By default, line numbering begins with 1.)
From Text	Distance between line numbers and text	A distance in the box or click the up or down arrow to increase or decrease the distance by tenths of an inch. (The Auto option places numbers .25" to the left of single-column text or .13" to the left of newspaper-style columns.) If the margin or the space between columns is too small, line numbers do not print.
Count By	Interval between printed line numbers (all lines are numbered but only those numbers specified here print)	An interval in a box, or click the up or down arrow to increase or decrease the interval.

6. Select an option from the Numbering group to establish when line numbers restart at the first number (but only those numbers specified here print):

Option	Restart Point
Restart Each Page	Beginning of each new page
Restart Each Section	Beginning of each new section
Continuous	None; number lines continuously through document

7. Choose OK twice.

◀ See "Control-ling Your Document's Appearance On-Screen," p. 123

You cannot see line numbering in Normal view. To see line numbers, choose View, Page Layout, or File, Print Preview. You also can print your document.

> **Note**
>
> You can change the formatting of line numbers by redefining the Line Number style. Refer to Chapter 11, "Using Styles for Repetitive Formats," for information about redefining styles.

Removing or Suppressing Line Numbers

You can remove line numbers entirely. Also, you have the chance to suppress line numbers by selecting the Suppress Line Numbers option in the Paragraph dialog box. This option clears line numbering from selected paragraphs or the paragraph containing the insertion point. (This option doesn't suppress line numbers applied in creating a numbered list, described in Chapter 18, "Creating Bulleted or Numbered Lists.")

To remove line numbers, follow these steps:

1. Position the insertion point in the section from which you want to remove line numbers, or select the entire document if it's formatted into more than one section.

2. Choose File, Page Setup.

3. Select the Layout tab.

4. Click the Line Numbers button.

5. Choose Add <u>L</u>ine Numbering to remove the check mark.

6. Click OK or press Enter twice to return to the document.

To suppress line numbers, follow these steps:

1. Select the paragraphs for which you want to suppress line numbering.

2. Choose F<u>o</u>rmat, <u>P</u>aragraph.

3. Select the Text <u>F</u>low tab.

4. Click the <u>S</u>uppress Line Numbers option.

5. Click OK.

▶ See "Changing the Page Layout within a Document," p. 1086

▶ See "Creating Numbered Lists," p. 555

Adjusting Line and Paragraph Spacing

Like all word processing and typesetting programs, Word for Windows spaces lines of text far enough apart so that lines don't crash into each other. If something large is on the line, such as a graphic or an oversized character or word, Word for Windows leaves extra space.

You're not limited to using Word's automatic spacing, however. You can add extra space between lines and paragraphs.

> **Note**
>
> Using styles is an excellent way to ensure that adjustments made to line and paragraph spacing are consistent throughout your document. If your document's format includes subheadings preceded by extra space, for example, create a style for your subheadings that includes the extra space, and apply the style to each subheading. For details about using styles, see Chapter 11, "Using Styles for Repetitive Formatting."

Adjusting Paragraph Spacing

You can adjust paragraph spacing by adding extra lines before or after the selected paragraphs. After you press Enter, Word for Windows skips the specified amount of space before starting the next paragraph. This technique is useful when your document's format requires extra spacing between paragraphs, before new sections, or around graphics. Adding extra spacing before or after paragraphs is like pressing Enter a second time each time you finish typing a paragraph (see fig. 10.24).

Fig. 10.24

Use paragraph spacing to add extra spacing around headings and paragraphs.

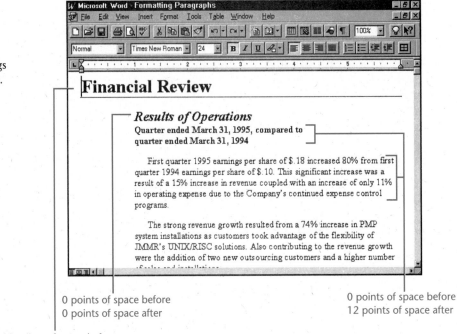

0 points of space before
0 points of space after

0 points of space before
12 points of space after

10 points of space before
14 points of space after

The Preview section of the Paragraph dialog box shows the effect of your selected spacing.

To adjust paragraph spacing, follow these steps:

1. Select the paragraph or paragraphs to add spacing before or after, or position the insertion point where you want the new spacing to begin.

2. Choose Format, Paragraph.

3. Select the Indents and Spacing tab.

4. To add line spacing before the selected paragraph or paragraphs, type a number in the Spacing Before text box or click the up or down arrow to increase or decrease the spacing amount in increments of half a line (see fig. 10.25).

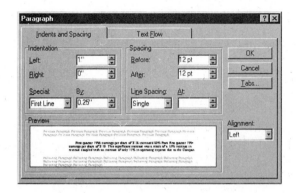

Fig. 10.25
Use the Paragraph Indents and Spacing tab to set paragraph spacing options.

5. To add line spacing after the selected paragraph or paragraphs, type a number in the Spacing After text box or click the up or down arrow to increase or decrease the spacing amount in increments of half a line.

You can use measurements other than decimal inches to specify spacing. To add six-point spacing, for example, type **6 pt** in the Before or After box. To add spacing of two centimeters, type **2 cm**, and to add spacing of one pica, type **1 pi**.

6. Click OK.

Adjusting Line Spacing

Typesetters and desktop publishers call the spacing between lines in a document *leading* (pronounced "ledding"). Typesetters have great control over precisely how much space appears between lines. They know that long lines need more spacing so that the eye doesn't lose its place in moving from the right margin back to the left. They know that font styles with small letters require less spacing between lines than fonts with big letters.

Word for Windows gives you a typesetter's control over spacing between lines in your document. The feature begins with automatic spacing and enables you to increase spacing, reduce spacing, permit extra spacing for a large character or superscript on the line.

Spacing is measured by lines. Normal text has single spacing of one line, but if you request spacing of .5, you get half-line spacing. Lines formatted this way are *condensed*. If you request spacing of 1.5, the paragraph has an extra half line of space between lines of text (see fig. 10.26).

Fig. 10.26
The line spacing is set at 1.5 to put more space between the lines of the selected text.

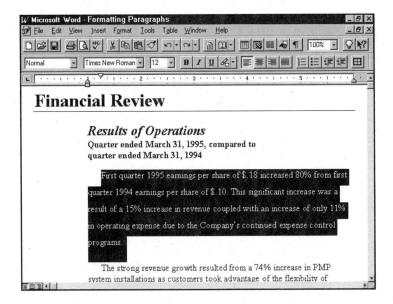

You can be very specific about line spacing. If your page design requires 10-point type with 12 points of leading, for example, type **12 pt** in the At box on the Indents and Spacing tab in the Paragraph dialog box. Word automatically changes the Line Spacing setting to Multiple and inserts a comparable number in inches.

> **Note**
>
> You can include line spacing with styles so that when you press Enter to end a paragraph, the exact spacing is inserted automatically for each style of text you type, whether it's a heading that requires 14 points of space before the next line of text or body text that requires only 12 points of space between lines.

▶ See "Applying, Copying, and Removing Styles," p. 354

To adjust spacing between lines using the menu commands, follow these steps:

1. Select the paragraph(s) to space, or position the insertion point where you want the new spacing to begin.

2. Choose Format, Paragraph to open the Paragraph dialog box.

3. Select the Indents and Spacing tab.

4. Choose one of the following options in the Line Spacing drop-down list box:

Option	Description
Single	Single-line spacing. Line height automatically adjusts to accommodate the size of the font and any graphics or formulas that have been inserted into a line.
1.5 Lines	Line-and-a-half spacing. Puts an extra half line between lines.
Double	Double-spacing. Puts an extra full line between lines.
At Least	At least the amount of spacing you specify in the At spin box. Word adds extra spacing, if necessary, for tall characters, big graphics, or super/subscript.
Exactly	The exact amount of spacing you specify in the At spin box. All lines are exactly the same height, regardless of the size of the characters in the line. Word doesn't add extra spacing for anything. Some text may be cut off if enough space isn't available. Increase the amount of spacing if characters are cut off.
Multiple	Multiples of single-line spacing, such as triple (3), quadruple (4)

5. If you want to specify your own line spacing, type the spacing amount in the At spin box (with decimal numbers, such as **1.25** for an extra quarter-line of space between lines) or click the up or down arrow to increase or decrease the amount.

You can choose a spacing amount in the At spin box without first choosing from the Line Spacing list box. Word for Windows assumes that you want at least this spacing and provides extra spacing if needed for large characters, superscript, and so on.

6. Click OK.

If you want to return to single-line spacing, select the paragraph or paragraphs, choose Format, Paragraph, and then choose Single in the Line Spacing drop-down list box of the Indents and Spacing tab.

II

Formatting Documents

You can change line spacing to single, 1.5, or double from the keyboard. You can also add or remove 12 points of space before a paragraph.

To adjust spacing between lines from the keyboard, follow these steps:

1. Select the paragraph or paragraphs, or place the insertion point in the paragraph in which you want to change the spacing.

2. Press one of the following key combinations:

Press	To Do This
Ctrl+1	Single-space text
Ctrl+5	1.5 line space text
Ctrl+2	Double-space text
Ctrl+0 (zero)	Add or remove 12 points of space before a paragraph

Inserting a Line Break

▶ See "Changing Styles," p. 368

When you type a paragraph formatted by a style that is automatically followed by a different style and then press Enter, the next paragraph is formatted with the next style. Sometimes, however, you may not be ready to change to the next style. If you have a two-line subheading, for example, you may want to press Enter after the first line and still be in the subheading style, rather than switch to the next style. In this case, you want to insert a line break, or *soft return,* rather than a new paragraph. To end a line without inserting a paragraph mark, press Shift+Enter.

Pressing Shift+Enter breaks a line without breaking the paragraph. After you finish typing your two-line subheading, press Enter in the usual way to end the paragraph and begin the following paragraph with the next style.

 If you click the Show/Hide ¶ button to display paragraph marks, you see that the line end marks at the ends of lines where you pressed Shift+Enter look like left-facing arrows rather than paragraph marks (see fig. 10.27).

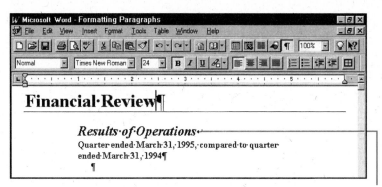

Fig. 10.27
Press Shift+Enter
to create a new
line without
creating a new
paragraph. Line
end marks display
as left-facing
arrows rather than
paragraph marks.

Shading and Bordering Paragraphs

For a finishing touch, you can add paragraph borders and shading to your
document. A *border* may be a box surrounding a paragraph (or paragraphs) on
all sides or a line that sets a paragraph off on one or more sides. A border can
include *shading*, which fills a paragraph with a pattern. Boxes and lines can
be solid black and shading can be gray, or, if you have a color monitor, they
can be more colorful than a rainbow.

Borders are particularly useful in setting special paragraphs apart from the
rest of your text for emphasis (see fig. 10.28) or for wonderful graphic effects.
If you use Word for desktop publishing, you may find boxes, lines, and
shading to be helpful. For examples of text enhancement, see Chapter 38,
"Desktop Publishing."

> **Note**
>
> Creating colored lines, boxes, and shading is easy if you have a color monitor. If you
> have a color printer, you also can print colored lines, boxes, and shading. Service
> bureaus in many cities offer color printing for a per-page fee. If you want to print
> your document with colored lines, boxes, and shading, use your own printer to proof
> the pages and then take a floppy disk containing your file to the service bureau to
> have the final pages printed in color. Before you go to the service bureau, check to
> see if they have Word for Windows. You may need to reformat your document
> slightly for their printer.

II

Formatting Documents

Fig. 10.28
Borders, lines, and shading can set paragraphs apart.

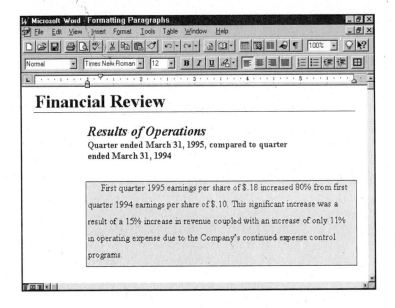

Tip
To change the color of the text inside a border, choose Format, Font. See Chapter 9, "Formatting Characters and Changing Fonts," for more information.

Borders, like all forms of paragraph formatting, belong to the paragraphs to which they are applied. They are carried forward when you press Enter at the end of a paragraph. Thus, if a group of paragraphs is formatted with a box around them and you press Enter at the end of the last paragraph, your new paragraph falls within the box. To create a new paragraph outside the border, move the insertion point outside the border before you press Enter. If you're at the end of the document and have nowhere to go outside of the border, create a new paragraph and remove the border.

Troubleshooting

The text changes its formatting when you press the Delete or Backspace key.

Word stores paragraph formatting in the paragraph mark at the end of each paragraph. If you delete the paragraph mark of a particular paragraph, it takes on the format of the following paragraph. Choose Edit, Undo immediately to reverse the deletion and restore the paragraph formatting.

Note

Sometimes the screen display inaccurately shows text extending beyond borders or shading. This situation results from screen fonts and screen resolutions that differ from the printer's fonts and resolution. Your printed text formats within the border or shading.

Enclosing Paragraphs in Boxes and Lines

A box fully surrounds a paragraph or selected group of paragraphs. Two types of preset boxes are available: box and shadow. A line appears on one or more sides of a paragraph or selected paragraphs, or may appear between selected paragraphs. You have 11 line styles to choose from and can use any line style to create a line, a box, or a shadowed box.

You use the Paragraph Borders and Shading dialog box to create boxes, lines, and shadows. Choose Format, Borders and Shading to access the dialog box. In the dialog box, you can choose either the Borders tab or Shading tab. The Borders tab shown in figure 10.29 offers the following choices:

Borders Option	Effect
None	No box. Use this option to remove an existing box. (This option is used often with the Shading options to create a shaded box with no border.)
Box	A box with identical lines on all four sides
Shadow	A box with a drop shadow on the bottom-right corner
Border	A line on one or more sides of the selected paragraph(s). Dotted lines at the corners and sides of the sample indicate where the lines appear; when they are selected, arrows point to these dotted lines. The sample displays each border as added (see fig. 10.30).
From Text	The distance between the line or box and the text, measured in points. Because 72 points make up an inch, select 9 points for a .125" distance or 18 points for a .25" distance.
Line None	No line. Use this option to remove individual lines.
Style	A line or box in the selected line style. Options listed show exact point size and a sample display.
Color	A line or box in the selected color. Sixteen colors and gray shades are available. If you select the Auto option, the default color for text is used. This is usually black, but can be changed in the Windows Control Panel.

II

Formatting Documents

Fig. 10.29
The Borders tab in the Paragraph Borders and Shading dialog box offers options for adding lines to any and all sides of a paragraph.

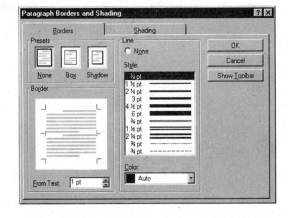

Fig. 10.30
The sample box in the Borders tab shows you which line is currently selected and gives you a preview of the lines you have inserted.

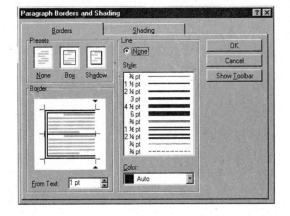

You also can use the Borders toolbar to add borders and shading to selected paragraphs (see fig. 10.31). Display the Borders toolbar by choosing View, Toolbars, or by clicking the Borders button on the Formatting toolbar.

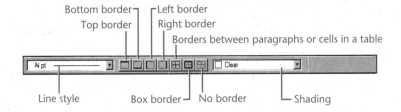

Fig. 10.31
You can add borders and shading from the Borders toolbar.

To create a box or line from the menu command, follow these steps:

1. Select the paragraph or paragraphs for which you want to create a box or line.

   If you create a box for more than one paragraph, the box encloses the paragraphs as a group, with no borders between them.

To Add a Box or Line to	Select
A paragraph, including paragraphs inside a table cell or frame	The paragraph
A table cell marker	The entire cell, including the end-of-cell
A frame	The frame

   ▶ See "Inserting Text or Graphics in a Blank Frame," p. 733

2. Choose Format, Borders and Shading. The Paragraph Borders and Shading dialog box appears.

3. Select the Borders tab.

4. To create a box, choose either Box or Shadow from the Preset group.

   To create a line using the mouse or the keyboard, do one of the following:

   With the mouse, click the side of the paragraph where you want the line in the Border group. Triangles are used to indicate when a line is selected. If a style has already been selected from the Style group, a line with that style will be inserted. You can continue inserting using this approach. If the None option is selected, you can select multiple lines by holding the Shift key while you click the sides you want to add lines to. Then select a line from the Style group to insert lines at all the selected locations. A line with the currently selected style will be inserted. If multiple paragraphs are selected, you can create a line between them by clicking the horizontal line between paragraphs in the Border box.

   With the keyboard, choose Border, then press any cursor-movement key to scroll through various line combinations. Triangles are used to indicate which line or lines are selected. Press the space bar to insert a line with the style that is currently selected in the Style list. If the None option is selected, select the Style box and use the arrow keys to select a style to apply to the select line or lines.

II

Formatting Documents

Choosing the line style before you create borders ensures that borders take on the appearance of the selected line style. (If None is selected as the line style, borders have no line.)

5. To set the spacing between a box and the text, specify a distance in the From Text text box.

6. To apply color to all your boxes and lines, choose a color from the Color list.

7. Click OK.

To create a box or line from the Borders toolbar, follow these steps:

1. Display the Borders toolbar by clicking the Borders button on the Formatting toolbar or by choosing View, Toolbars and specifying the Borders toolbar.

Tip

If you create a box for more than one paragraph, the box encloses the paragraphs as a group with no borders between them.

2. Select the paragraph or paragraphs for which you want to create a box or line.

To Add a Box or Line To	Select
A paragraph, including paragraphs inside a table cell or frame	The paragraph
A table cell	The entire cell, including the end-of-cell marker
A frame	The frame

3. Select the Line style list box by clicking the down arrow and choosing a line style.

4. Choose the border you want to add by clicking one of the following buttons:

Choose This Button	To Do This
	Add a border along the top
	Add a border along the bottom
	Add a border along the left edge

Choose This Button	To Do This
	Add a border along the right edge
	Add inside borders
	Add a box border
	Remove all borders

5. Choose shading or a pattern from the Shading list box, if you want shading or a pattern added.

The width of a paragraph border (box or line) is determined by the paragraph indent. (If no indent exists, width is determined by the page margins.) If you want a paragraph's border (or line) to be narrower than the margins, indent the paragraph (see figs. 10.32 and 10.33).

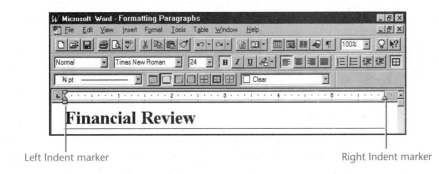

Left Indent marker   Right Indent marker

Fig. 10.32
With indents set to the left and right margins, borders extend the full width of the page.

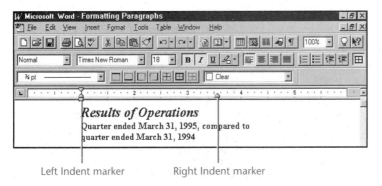

Left Indent marker   Right Indent marker

Fig. 10.33
To create a shorter border, move in the Left and Right Indent markers.

II

Formatting Documents

If you select and box several paragraphs that have different indents, each paragraph appears in its own separate box (instead of all appearing together in one box). To make paragraphs with different indents appear within a single box, you must create a table and put each paragraph in a row by itself and then select the table and format the outside border of the table (see Chapter 16, "Creating and Editing Tables").

When paragraphs extend exactly to the margins of your page (as they always do if you don't indent the paragraphs), borders extend slightly outside the margins. If you want borders to fall within or exactly on the margins, you must indent the paragraph. To make borders fall on the margins, indent the paragraph by the width of the border.

For example, if the border is the double 1.5-point line, the line width totals 4.5 points including the space between the double lines, indent the paragraph by 4.5 points. Type **4.5 pt** in the Left and Right indentation boxes in the Paragraph dialog box.

Note

If you format groups of paragraphs to have lines between them, those lines apply to blank spaces between paragraphs if you create those blank spaces by pressing Enter an extra time. To avoid extra lines between paragraphs, use the Spacing After option in the Paragraph dialog box to add blank space between paragraphs. (See "Adjusting Line and Paragraph Spacing" earlier in this chapter.)

You can remove borders all at once or line by line. Changing the line style of existing borders is essentially the same process.

To remove or change a box or line from the menu command, follow these steps:

1. Select the paragraph or paragraphs for which you want to remove or change boxes or lines.

2. Choose Format, Borders and Shading.

3. Select the Borders tab.

4. Select the None option in the Presets group to remove all borders.

   You can also select None in the Line group and then select the lines you want to remove.

5. Select the line you want to change and choose a different option from the Style box in the Line group.

   You also can select a different line color from the Color list box.

6. Select Box or Shadow to change the Preset border style.

7. Click OK.

To remove or change a line or box from the Borders toolbar, follow these steps:

1. Select the paragraph or paragraphs for which you want to remove or change boxes or lines.

2. Click the Borders button on the Formatting toolbar to display the Borders toolbar.

3. Click the No Border button to remove all borders.

4. Choose a new line style.

5. Click the button(s) for the box(es) or border(s) you want to add.

Shading Paragraphs

Paragraphs can be shaded as well as bordered. Shading comes in various percentages of black or the selected color, and in patterns (see fig. 10.34). Percentages of black appear as grays of various intensities. For each shade or pattern, you can select a foreground or background color. *Shades* create a blended effect: a foreground of yellow and a background of blue creates the effect of green.

Tip

Before you concoct patterns that you hope to use behind text, be sure to test whether the text is readable with that pattern behind it.

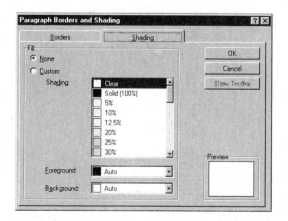

Fig. 10.34
The Shading tab from the Paragraph Borders and Shading dialog box offers options for adding varying degrees of shading and/or color to a paragraph.

But in *patterns*, the effect is more dramatic: in a Lt Grid pattern, for example, the yellow foreground forms a light grid pattern over a blue background. With some experimentation, you can create eye-catching results that can add visual impact to documents used for presentations or overhead transparencies. Colors are converted to shades of gray or patterns on a black-and-white printer.

You can use shading with borders so that a paragraph is surrounded by a line and filled with shading, or you can use shading alone so that no border goes around the shaded paragraph. Watch the Preview box on the Shading tab to see the effect of the patterns and colors you select. To add shading, choose the Shading tab in the Paragraph Borders and Shading dialog box. You have the following options:

Shading Option	Effect
None	No shading in selected paragraph(s)
Custom	Shading in the selected custom shading. Options are shown in Shading.
Shading	Shading in the selected custom darkness or pattern. Options include increasing degrees of shading and various patterns. Clear applies the selected background color; Solid applies the selected foreground color.
Foreground	A foreground color for the selected shading pattern. Auto selects the best color, usually black. You can select from 16 colors, including black and white.
Background	A background color for the selected shading pattern. Auto selects the best color, usually white. Select from 16 colors, including black and white.

To shade paragraphs with the menu command, follow these steps:

1. Select the paragraph or paragraphs you want to shade:

To Shade	Select
A paragraph, including paragraphs inside a table cell or frame	The paragraph
A table cell	The entire cell, including the end-of-cell marker
A frame	The frame

2. Choose F_ormat, _Borders and Shading.

3. Select the _Shading tab.

4. Select the Sha_ding pattern you want. Options include Clear (uses the background color), Solid (uses the foreground color), percentages, and striped and checkered patterns such as Dk Horizontal (for dark horizontal stripes) and Lt Grid (for a grid made of light cross-hatching).

5. Select a color from the _Foreground list to color a percentage pattern or a pattern foreground.

6. Select a color from the B_ackground list to color a percentage pattern or a pattern background.

7. Click OK.

To shade paragraphs using the Borders toolbar, follow these steps:

1. Select the paragraph or paragraphs you want to shade:

To Shade	Select
A paragraph, including paragraphs inside a table cell or frame	The paragraph
A table cell	The entire cell, including the end-of-cell marker
A frame	The frame

2. Click the Borders button on the Formatting toolbar to display the Borders toolbar.

3. Choose the shading or pattern you want from the Shading box.

To remove shading using the menu command, follow these steps:

1. Select the paragraph or paragraphs from which you want to remove shading.

2. Choose F_ormat, _Borders and Shading.

3. Click the _Shading tab.

Tip

If you want borders around your selected paragraph, select the _Borders tab and choose border options.

Tip

Percentage patterns consist of foreground and background colors. The result appears in the Preview box. For best results in creating colors, however, look first for the color you want in the _Foreground list.

II

Formatting Documents

4. Choose <u>N</u>one from the Fill group.

5. Click OK.

To remove shading with the Borders toolbar, follow these steps:

1. Select the paragraph or paragraphs from which you want to remove shading.

 2. Click the Borders button on the Formatting toolbar to display the Borders toolbar.

3. Choose the Clear setting from the Shading box.

Chapter 11

Using Styles for Repetitive Formats

What gives your document style? For the most part, *style* is the appearance of your document: the arrangement of text on pages, the shape of the paragraphs, the characteristics of the letters, the use of lines and borders to give your document emphasis. All these elements of style are formatting choices you make while working with Word for Windows 95.

Style involves more than just appearance, however. Style is also readability and consistency. When your document's style is appropriate to its content and is consistent from one section to the next, the reader's job of gleaning information from your text becomes much easier.

Word for Windows offers you tools designed to make the task of developing and maintaining your document's style much easier. Appropriately, these tools are called *styles*. In Word for Windows, a style is a set of formatting instructions you save with a name in order to use them again and again. All text formatted with the same style has exactly the same formatting. If you make a formatting change to a style, all the text formatted with that style will reformat to match the new formatting.

In this chapter, you learn to do the following:

- Redefine the built-in styles that determine your normal typing fonts, style, and size

- Decide which method is best for formatting your document

- Apply and remove styles

- Modify AutoFormat so that its results are closer to your preferences

Using Styles versus Direct Formatting

You can create and apply two types of styles: character styles and paragraph styles. *Character styles* include any of the options available from the Font dialog box, such as bold, italic, and small caps. Character styles store only character formatting, and apply to selected text or to the word containing the insertion point. *Paragraph styles* include character and paragraph formatting, tab settings, paragraph positioning, borders and shading, and language used for spell checking. Paragraph styles can store both character and paragraph formatting, and apply to selected paragraphs or the paragraph containing the insertion point.

You can type a plain business letter and then apply a set of styles automatically with the AutoFormat command on the Format menu to give it a professional appearance. Word applies styles to common text elements, such as bulleted and numbered lists and headings. In addition, Word makes small improvements, such as changing straight quotation marks (" ") to curved typesetting quotation marks, often called "curly quotes" (" "). You can review and undo the changes Word has made and make further changes of your own.

You can also choose from among many available style groups to change the document format automatically to the style you want. The Style Gallery command displays your document in other styles and lets you select from among them the one you like most.

See figures 11.1 and 11.2 for an example of how automatic formatting can quickly change your document's appearance with styles.

Fig. 11.1

You can choose between different families of styles. This letter uses the Contemporary Letter template.

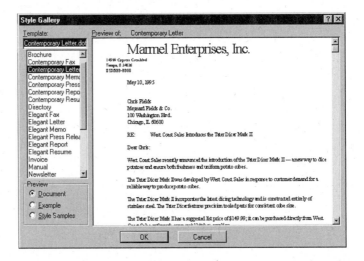

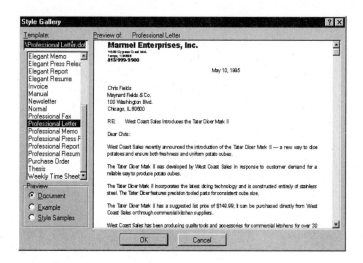

Fig. 11.2
This is the same letter, previewed with the Professional Letter template.

Instead of directly formatting each word, phrase, paragraph, or page individually, using styles offers several benefits:

- *You save time.* You can format one word or paragraph the way you like it and copy that formatting to other words or paragraphs. The AutoFormat command applies styles automatically, quickly formatting a simple document into a professional-looking presentation.

- *You preserve consistency.* By using styles to format your document, you can be sure that each selected item or paragraph looks the same as others of its type.

- *You reduce the effort required to change your document's appearance.* By changing a style, you also change all the selected text or paragraphs associated with that style.

Choosing a Formatting Method

You're always using at least one style when you work with Word for Windows. The *Normal style*, built into Word for Windows, gives your document its default formatting choices. If you have the Formatting toolbar displayed when you start a new document, you can see the Normal style in the Style box, already selected (see fig. 11.3). The Normal style's formatting selections are basic: it includes a font and font size (12-point MS Serif, 10-point Times New Roman, or a different font, depending on your printer), left alignment, and single-line spacing. Word also makes other styles available for items like page numbers, headers, and footers. You learn how to change the Normal style in the section "Redefining Standard Styles" later in this chapter.

Fig. 11.3
The Normal style is displayed in the Formatting toolbar when you start a new document.

The list of styles from which you can select depends on the *template* you select when you create a document. The default template is Normal. In addition to the Normal style, the template contains styles for indenting, tables of contents, titles, headings, lists, envelopes, and many more. You can use the styles built into a template as they come, you can modify them, or you can create your own styles.

◀ See "Using Templates as a Pattern for Documents," p. 178

Except for the Normal template, which is designed for general use, each template's styles have been designed to suit one particular application, such as a brochure, a fax cover sheet, or a resume. The Normal style in one template may be 10-point Times New Roman, while in another template it may be 12-point Century Schoolbook. Changing the template may change the formatting of the style. Word provides a Style Gallery in which you can preview the effects of changing a template and its resultant changes to the styles you use. The Style Gallery is covered later in this chapter, in the section "Using the Style Gallery."

You can apply and change styles in three ways. Each method has advantages and disadvantages, as described in the following paragraphs.

■ *Method 1.* The fastest formatting method is formatting automatically with Format, AutoFormat.

Advantage: The formatting is done automatically without having to select styles.

Disadvantage: You have less control over the selection of styles, although you can manually override any style selections.

■ *Method 2.* The method that allows you the greatest control over the format of the text is manually formatting by creating, selecting, and/or modifying those styles available in the template on which your document is based.

Advantages: You can make your document appear any way you choose by creating and selecting suitable styles.

Styles you create can be based on existing styles and/or followed by other styles. For example, you can follow a heading style with a body text style, automatically incorporating consistent spacing and other formatting.

Disadvantage: You have to create and/or select a style for each element of your document.

■ *Method 3.*   The third formatting method is selecting a new template with Format, Style Gallery.

Advantage: You can preview your document as it will appear based on each of many other templates, and then select and apply that template. For example, you can choose from three different letter styles.

Disadvantage: You have less control over the selection of styles, although you can manually override any style selections.

The following sections describe in detail each method of formatting.

Formatting a Document Automatically

Imagine that you quickly dash off an important business letter, paying no special attention to the letter's formatting. Then with a click of the mouse, the letter suddenly takes the shape of the formal business letter you had in mind. The Format, AutoFormat command gives you that power.

When you choose Format, AutoFormat, Word goes through your document paragraph by paragraph, applying appropriate styles. If you've included a list of items, each preceded with an asterisk, for example, Word reformats the list, replacing asterisks with bullets and adding the bulleted list style. If you've only formatted some of the text, AutoFormat completes the job. AutoFormat ensures that the formatting is consistent throughout the document and also improves the appearance. The styles Word applies come from the template that is currently attached to the document. See figures 11.4 and 11.5 for an example of a document that has been formatted with AutoFormat.

Fig. 11.4

You can type letters, documents, and memos without worrying about formatting.

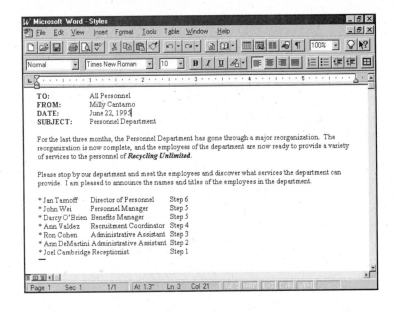

Fig. 11.5

The AutoFormat command uses its rules to apply formats, such as bullets, to your documents.

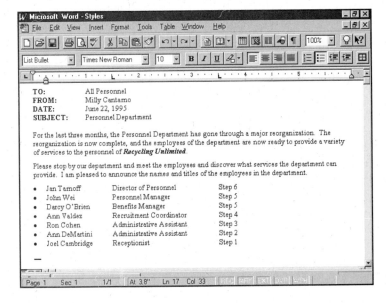

After the text has been formatted with AutoFormat, you can polish the document's appearance by manually applying styles or formatting to any elements of the document. You can also choose a new template from the Style Gallery to change the overall design of the document. Each of these topics is covered later in this chapter, in the sections "Using the Style Gallery," and "Applying, Copying, and Removing Styles."

Applying Styles with AutoFormat

AutoFormat analyzes the document in the active window and applies a style to each paragraph that is currently formatted with either the Normal or Body Text style. The styles AutoFormat applies are designed to format common writing elements such as quotations, bulleted lists, headings, and more. AutoFormat applies styles and makes corrections as described in the following list:

- Uses its formatting rules to find and format such items as headings, body text, lists, superscript and subscript, addresses, and letter closings

- Removes extra paragraph marks

- Replaces straight quotation marks (") and apostrophes (') with typesetting quotation marks (" ") and apostrophes (')

- Replaces "(c)," "(R)," and "(TM)" with copyright ©, registered trademark ®, and trademark ™ symbols

- Replaces asterisks, hyphens, or other characters used to list items with a bullet character (■)

- Replaces horizontal spaces inserted with the Tab key or the space bar with indents

To format text automatically with the menu command, follow these steps:

1. Select the text you want to format. If you want to format the entire document, position the insertion point anywhere in the document.

2. Choose Format, AutoFormat. The AutoFormat dialog box appears (see fig. 11.6).

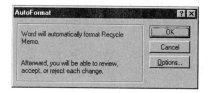

Fig. 11.6
You can automatically format a document by choosing Format, AutoFormat.

You can determine which changes AutoFormat makes by clicking the Options button in the AutoFormat dialog box or by changing the settings in the AutoFormat tab of the Options dialog box. See the section "Setting AutoFormat Options," later in this chapter, for more information.

3. Choose OK to begin formatting. Word reviews the text and selects styles from the current template.

4. When AutoFormat is finished, the AutoFormat dialog box is displayed again, and you have four choices (see fig. 11.7):

Choose Accept to accept all the changes.

Choose Reject All to reject all the changes.

Choose Review Changes to examine changes one by one, accepting or rejecting individual changes. See "Reviewing Format Changes" in this section for more information.

Choose Style Gallery to apply styles from another template. See "Using the Style Gallery" later in this chapter for more information.

Fig. 11.7
When AutoFormat is complete, you can choose to accept or reject all changes, to review the changes, or to change templates in the Style Gallery.

If you don't like the result of the autoformatting, you can undo the formatting changes you've made.

To undo all changes after accepting them, click the down-arrow button next to the Undo button on the Standard toolbar and undo AutoFormat Begin.

You can also run AutoFormat by clicking the AutoFormat button on the Standard toolbar (the toolbar must be displayed) or from a keyboard shortcut.

To format text automatically from the Standard toolbar, follow these steps:

1. Position the insertion point in the document you want to format or select the text you want to format.

2. Click the AutoFormat button on the Standard toolbar. Text is automatically formatted, using styles from the currently attached template and the options that are selected on the AutoFormat tab in the Options dialog box. (For more information, see the later section "Setting AutoFormat Options.") The Review option isn't available when you choose AutoFormat from the Standard toolbar.

To format text automatically with a keyboard shortcut, position the insertion point in the document you want to format or select the text you want to format and press Ctrl+K. Text is automatically formatted using styles from the currently attached template and the options that are selected in the Options dialog box. The Review option isn't available when you start AutoFormat from the keyboard shortcut.

> **Caution**
>
> If you use the AutoFormat button or the keyboard shortcut, Word doesn't prompt you to review the changes it makes—you simply see them on-screen. If you don't like what you see, click the Undo button.

Tip
You can automatically format tables with AutoFormat on the Table menu. See Chapter 16, "Creating and Editing Tables," for information.

Reviewing Format Changes

After a document has been automatically formatted, you may want to review the changes and possibly make some alterations. You can click the Review Changes button in the AutoFormat dialog box to review the changes one by one (refer to fig. 11.7). As you review each change, you can accept or reject it. You can also scroll through the document and select specific changes for review.

Word indicates changes to text and formatting with temporary revision marks and color (on color monitors). With paragraph marks displayed, Word highlights the extra paragraph marks it deleted and also those to which a style was applied.

To display paragraph marks, click the Show/Hide ¶ button on the Standard toolbar.

You can also review the document with the revision marks hidden. To hide revision marks, choose the Hide Marks button in the Review AutoFormat Changes dialog box.

Table 11.1 describes Word's revision marks.

Table 11.1 AutoFormat Revision Marks	
Visual Change	**Meaning**
Blue paragraph mark (¶) (Shown lighter on a monochrome monitor.)	Applied a style to that paragraph

(continues)

Table 11.1 Continued	
Visual Change	**Meaning**
Red paragraph mark (¶) (Shown lighter on a monochrome monitor.)	Deleted that paragraph mark
Strikethrough character (-) (indicated in red)	Deleted text or spaces
Underline (_) (indicated in blue)	Added the underlined characters
Vertical bar in the left margin	Changed the text or formatting in that line of text

To review changes made by AutoFormat, follow these steps:

1. After Word completes the AutoFormat, choose the Review <u>C</u>hanges button. The Review AutoFormat Changes dialog box appears (see fig. 11.8).

Fig. 11.8

Use options in the Review AutoFormat Changes dialog box to reject or accept the changes made by AutoFormat.

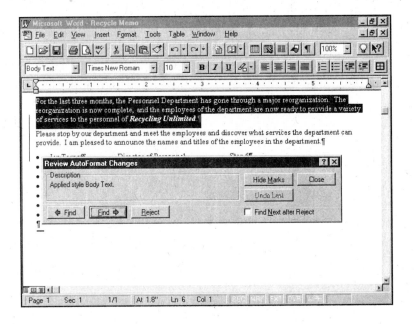

2. Choose from among the following options to target the change(s) you want to review:

   To see text under the dialog box, drag the box by its title bar to a new location.

To see the entire document, use the vertical scroll bar to scroll through the document.

To see changes one by one, use the Find buttons.

To see the effect of another style, select the text and then select another style from the Style box on the Formatting toolbar.

3. Choose from among the following options to alter the selected change:

To undo the displayed change, choose <u>R</u>eject.

To undo the last rejected change, choose <u>U</u>ndo Last.

To view the document with all remaining changes and revision marks turned off, choose Hide <u>M</u>arks.

To undo the displayed changes and automatically move to the next change, select the Find <u>N</u>ext after Reject check box.

4. Click the Close button to accept all remaining changes. The AutoFormat dialog box is displayed again.

5. Choose <u>A</u>ccept to accept all changes.

Or, you can choose <u>R</u>eject All to reject all changes.

You can even choose <u>S</u>tyle Gallery to select a different AutoFormat style.

Setting AutoFormat Options

You can change the rules that Word follows each time it performs an AutoFormat. You can choose whether to apply styles to headings and lists, for example.

To change the AutoFormat formatting rules, follow these steps:

1. Choose <u>T</u>ools, <u>O</u>ptions and select the AutoFormat tab (see fig. 11.9).

2. Select one of the following options in the Show Options For group:

Choose <u>A</u>utoFormat to display options that Word uses when you choose F<u>o</u>rmat, <u>A</u>utoFormat.

Or, choose AutoFormat As You <u>T</u>ype to display options that Word uses to format tables, lists, headings, and bulleted items as you type.

Tip

AutoFormat can format a document with styles you've designed if you redefine the built-in styles. See "Getting the Most from AutoFormat" and "Creating Styles" later in this chapter.

Fig. 11.9
Specify the settings you want in order to control the changes Word makes during an AutoFormat.

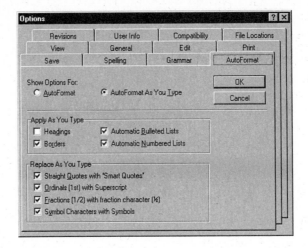

3. Select from the Apply As You Type group the document parts to which you want Word to apply styles (selected options are marked with ✓).

4. Select from the Replace As You Type group the characters or symbols you want Word to replace as you type (selected options are marked with ✓).

5. Click OK.

Getting the Most from AutoFormat

Any formatting you have applied using commands on the Format menu helps Word determine which styles to apply during AutoFormat. For example, styles previously applied can be preserved or changed, depending on the settings in the Options dialog box on the AutoFormat tab (see the preceding section). In addition, the following tips will help you maximize the results you get from the AutoFormat command.

- ■ *Use a larger font for level 1 headings than you use for subordinate level headings.* Higher heading style levels are applied to larger point sizes.

- ■ *Clear all the check boxes on the AutoFormat tab, choose OK, and then do an AutoFormat.* Extra hard returns will be removed from files, such as those you've converted from another file format.

- ■ *Type (**c**), (**R**), or (**TM**).* Word converts this text to the appropriate ©, ®, or ™ symbol.

◄ See "Checking Your Grammar," p. 219

- ■ *Redefine built-in styles.* Word assigns styles, such as heading styles, formatted as you want them.

Using the Style Gallery

Each document you create is based on a template. When you create a new document, the styles that are part of the template you select are copied into that document. Each template contains a set of standard styles, most of which are available with all Word's templates. Styles in one template may differ from those in another. For example, Heading 1 in the Normal template uses Arial 14-point, whereas in the Professional Fax template, Heading 1 is Arial MT Black 11-point. You can use Format, Style Gallery to preview and then change the appearance of a document by switching the style definitions to those of another template.

You can choose from the following types of document templates: brochure, directory, fax cover sheet, letter, manual, manuscript, memo, presentation, press release, report, resume, newsletter, invoice, purchase order, weekly time sheet, and thesis. Many of Word's templates fit into one of three families:

◄ See "Using Word's Pre-defined Templates," p. 178

- Contemporary

- Professional

- Elegant

Unlike Word 6, where each template name was followed by a number to indicate the family into which it fit, the new long file names feature of Windows 95 lets Microsoft eliminate the use of this coding system. A template name in Word 95 is preceded by its family name; for example, the fax template in the Contemporary style family is named CONTEMPORARY FAX.DOT.

To preview and change styles in the Style Gallery, follow these steps:

1. Display in the active window the document whose styles you want to change.

2. Choose Format, Style Gallery. The Style Gallery dialog box appears (see fig. 11.10).

3. Select one of the following in the Preview group:

   Select Document to see the active document formatted with the styles from the template you select.

   Select Example to see sample text formatted with the styles from the template you select.

   Select Style Samples to see a list of styles available in the selected template, including text samples of each style.

Fig. 11.10

Use the Style Gallery to preview your document with styles from other templates.

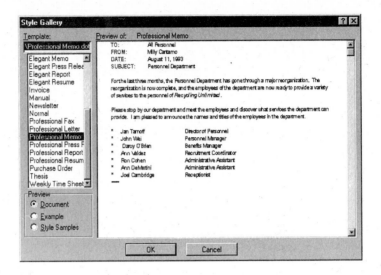

4. Select the Template you want to preview. Continue to preview other templates by selecting them.

◄ See "Creating Documents with Wizards," p. 192

5. Choose OK to accept the new template. Word copies the styles from the template you selected to the active document.

Or, choose Cancel to return to your document with its original template intact.

You can even change the folder name in the Template box to display a list of templates located in a different folder.

◄ See "Modifying Templates," p. 185

When you change the styles in the Style Gallery, you are copying the style formatting from the new template into the active document. You aren't replacing the template; you're replacing the style definitions in the current document only. For example, the original Body Text style of Times New Roman 10-point may be replaced by Times New Roman 12-point. In addition, any styles that exist in the new template and not in the one attached to the document are added to the document. Any styles that are unique to the document aren't affected by the change.

Using Word for Windows Standard Styles

Word for Windows includes a great number of *standard*, or *built-in* styles. You already are familiar with the Normal style, which Word for Windows uses to apply default formatting to all new documents based on the default Normal template. Other standard styles include those that provide formatting for outline headings, headers, footers, page numbers, line numbers, index entries, table of contents entries, annotations, and footnotes.

What You Need to Know about Standard Styles

In a new document, you see the styles Default Paragraph Font, Heading 1, Heading 2, Heading 3, and Normal listed in the Formatting toolbar's Style list box. Word applies these styles automatically when you use the AutoFormat feature, and you can apply these styles to selected paragraphs yourself. You are likely to apply some standard styles automatically by creating headers, footers, index entries, and so on. After you use these styles in your document, their names appear in the Formatting toolbar's Style list box.

Many standard styles do more than just format text. When you use the automatic heading styles (Heading 1 through Heading 9), for example, you later can collect these headings into a table of contents. Or, if you insert table of contents entries (formatted with the styles TOC 1 through TOC 9), you later can collect these entries as a table of contents. Similarly, if you insert index or footnote entries into your document, Word for Windows collects them where you have specified they are to appear in your document.

▶ See "Formatting an Index Using Styles," p. 871

▶ See "Creating a Table of Contents Using Any Style," p. 882

▶ See "Formatting Cross-References," p. 923

▶ See "Formatting Captions," p. 931

To apply standard styles from the menu command, follow these steps:

1. Position the insertion point where you want the new style to begin or select the text or paragraph(s) you want formatted in the new style. (To format a single paragraph, you can position the insertion point anywhere in the paragraph.)

2. Choose Format, Style. The Style dialog box opens (see fig. 11.11).

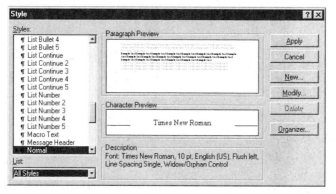

Fig. 11.11
Select any of the standard styles from the Style dialog box.

3. Choose All Styles in the List drop-down list. All styles are displayed in the Styles list.

   4. Select a style from the <u>S</u>tyles list and choose the <u>A</u>pply button.

To apply standard styles from the Formatting toolbar, follow these steps:

   1. Position the insertion point where you want the new style to begin or
      select the text or paragraph(s) you want formatted in the new style. (To
      format a single paragraph, you can position the insertion point any-
      where in the paragraph.)

   2. Click the down arrow next to the Style box in the Formatting toolbar.

   3. Click the style you want to apply.

Table 11.2 describes some of the Word for Windows standard styles.

Table 11.2 Word for Windows Standard Styles			
Standard Style or Style Family	**Style Type**	**Default Formatting**	**How Applied**
Normal (used by default to format all new text)	Paragraph	10- or 12-point serif font (varies with printer), left-aligned, single-line spacing, widow/orphan control	Applied to all text automatically in document that is based on the Normal template
Normal Indent (indents paragraphs)	Paragraph	Normal + 1/2-inch left indent	Manually
Heading 1 through Heading 9 (formats outline headings)	Paragraph	Formatting ranges from large and bold (Heading 1) to small and italic	Outline view
Annotation Reference (creates hidden annotation references)	Character	Normal + 8-point font	<u>I</u>nsert, <u>A</u>nnotation
Annotation Text (formats annotation text)	Paragraph	Normal	Typing annotation text in the annotation pane
Caption (formats figure captions)	Paragraph	Normal + bold	<u>I</u>nsert, Cap<u>t</u>ion
Footer (formats footers)	Paragraph	Normal + 3-inch centered tab, 6-inch right tab	<u>V</u>iew, <u>H</u>eader and Footer
Footnote Reference (formats footnote references)	Character	Default Paragraph Font	<u>I</u>nsert, Foot<u>n</u>ote

Standard Style or Style Family	Style Type	Default Formatting	How Applied
Endnote Reference (formats endnote references)	Character	Default Paragraph Font	Insert, Footnote
Footnote text (formats footnote text)	Paragraph	Normal	Typing footnote text
Endnote text (formats endnote text)	Paragraph	Normal	Typing endnote text
Header (formats headers)	Paragraph	Normal + 3-inch centered tab, 6-inch right tab	View, Header and Footer
Index 1 through Index 9 (formats index entries)	Paragraph	Varies with selection of index formats	Insert, Index and Tables, Index tab
Index Heading (formats optional heading separators in index)	Paragraph	Varies with selection of index formats	Insert, Index and Tables, Index tab
Line Number (formats line numbers)	Character	Normal	File, Page Setup, Layout tab, Line Numbers
Page Number	Character	Normal	Insert, Page Numbers
TOC 1 through TOC 9 (formats table of contents entries)	Paragraph	Varies with selection of Table of Contents formats	Insert, Index and Tables, Table of Contents tab
List	Paragraph	Normal+Indent, Hanging 0.25"	Manually
List Bullet	Paragraph	Normal+Indent, Hanging 0.25", Bullet	Manually
List Continue	Paragraph	Normal+Indent, Left 0.25", Space after 6 pt.	Manually
List Number	Paragraph	Normal+Indent, Hanging 0.25", Auto Numbering	Manually

II

Formatting Documents

Notice that the formatting for many standard styles is based on the Normal style. In other words, many styles include all the formatting contained in the Normal style plus additional formatting choices. The header and footer styles, for example, are Normal style plus tab settings.

> **Note**
>
> If you change the Normal style, any other style based on the Normal style also changes. If you change the Normal style to double spacing, for example, headers, footers, index entries, and all other styles based on Normal also will include double spacing.

Redefining Standard Styles

Tip
You can redefine a standard style except the Default Paragraph Font, but you cannot delete a standard style.

Standard styles come with predefined formatting, but you can easily redefine them. Suppose that you want to use the standard heading styles (Heading 1 through Heading 9) to format your document because you can use Outline view to apply these styles and because you want to collect the headings later as a table of contents. Unfortunately, you don't like the default formatting choices Word for Windows has made for the heading styles. Redefine the styles, using either the styles-by-example techniques, or by using Format, Style, both described later in this chapter.

Displaying Styles with the Style Area

If you're working with styles extensively, you can display the style area on your screen to list each paragraph's style name in the left margin (see fig. 11.12).

Fig. 11.12
Use the Style Area to display the names of the styles currently in use.

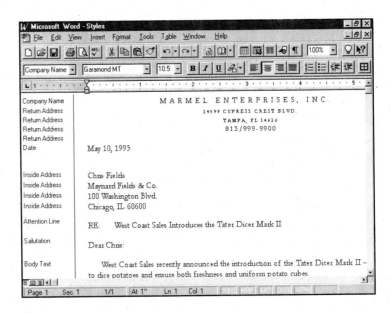

Using the Style area, you can see at a glance which style is applied to each paragraph. If you have a mouse, you also can use the style area to quickly access the Styles dialog box.

To apply and redefine styles quickly, double-click the style name in the Style area to display the Styles dialog box. From there, you can apply, create, or redefine a style.

The width of the style area varies. When you first display the Style area, you set its width. After it's displayed, however, you can vary its width by using a mouse to drag the line separating the Style area from the text to the left or right. You can close the style area entirely by dragging the arrow all the way to the left edge of the screen, or by resetting the Style area width to zero.

To display or remove the Style area, follow these steps:

1. In Normal view, choose Tools, Options.

2. Select the View tab. The View dialog box lists all the view settings you can modify.

3. Type the style area width you want in decimal inches in the Style Area Width box.

   Or, click the up or down arrows at the right end of the Style Area Width spin box to increase or decrease the style area width by tenths of an inch.

   Or, type **0** (zero) to remove the style area from the screen.

4. Choose OK.

Overriding Styles with Manual Formatting

Although you can do most of your formatting with styles, at times you will need to override the formatting in a style you have already applied. You may want to do something simple, like making one word in a paragraph bold, or maybe something more substantial, like italicizing a whole paragraph. You can modify the formatting in a paragraph without changing the style.

Be aware, however, of the effect your formatting will have on the paragraph if you later reapply the style. Reapplying the style may cancel some of the manual formatting changes you have made. Manual formatting works with styles as follows:

- If the reapplied style contains formatting choices in the same category as those you have applied manually, the style's choices override the manual formatting. If you have manually applied double line spacing, but the style specifies single line spacing, for example, then the double line spacing is canceled when you apply the style.

Tip
By single-clicking the style name in the Style area, you quickly can select an entire paragraph.

Tip
If you frequently display the Style area, record a simple macro that turns on the style area. (You can even edit your macro so that it toggles the Style area on and off.) Chapter 37, "Recording and Editing Macros," explains how to create macros.

II

Formatting Documents

■ If the reapplied style contains formatting choices unrelated to the formatting you have applied manually, the style won't affect manual formatting. If you add a border to a paragraph and then reapply a style that doesn't specify borders, for example, the border will remain.

■ Some character formatting choices toggle on and off—you select bold to turn it on and select it again to turn it off. If you apply a style containing bold to a paragraph with one or two words that are bold, for example, then all of the paragraph will be bold except the one or two words that you manually formatted as bold (the style toggles them off). On the other hand, if you make a whole paragraph bold, then reapply a style that contains bold, Word for Windows leaves the paragraph bold rather than toggling off the bold.

▶ See "Creating Tables of Contents," p. 879

▶ See "Creating a Table of Authorities," p. 892

▶ See "Creating an Outline," p. 575

■ If you want to remove all manually applied character formatting from a word formatted with a style, move the insertion point into the word that was manually formatted, then press Ctrl+space bar.

■ If you want to remove all manually applied paragraph formatting from a paragraph formatted with a style, press Ctrl+Q.

Applying, Copying, and Removing Styles

The power of styles becomes apparent when you use them to apply consistent formatting to paragraph after paragraph in your document. You can apply styles to text as you type or to selected text by choosing a style from a menu command, from the Formatting toolbar, or with a keyboard shortcut. You will mostly use the Formatting toolbar.

To display the Formatting toolbar, follow these steps:

1. Choose View, Toolbars.

2. Select Formatting from the Toolbars list. A ✓ appears in the check box to indicate that it is selected.

3. Choose OK.

> **Note**
>
> The Style box in the Formatting toolbar shows the style at the position of the insertion point or of the selected text. If the text selection includes text formatted with more than one style, the Style box is blank.

Resolving Conflicts between Paragraph and Character Style

Remember that paragraph styles can include both paragraph-level formatting commands and character-level formatting. Character styles include only character-level formatting commands. Any paragraph style you apply to text formats the entire paragraph (or the group of selected paragraphs). If a paragraph style includes character formatting, it too is applied to the entire paragraph. If you apply a character style, such as bold, to text in a paragraph, and then apply a paragraph style that includes bold, the text you boldfaced with the character style appears normal, rather than bold, because the paragraph style toggles off bold.

Applying Paragraph Styles

To apply a paragraph style to a single paragraph, the insertion point must first be positioned anywhere in that paragraph. You can apply a paragraph style to a group of paragraphs by first selecting those paragraphs, or at least part of each paragraph (see fig. 11.13).

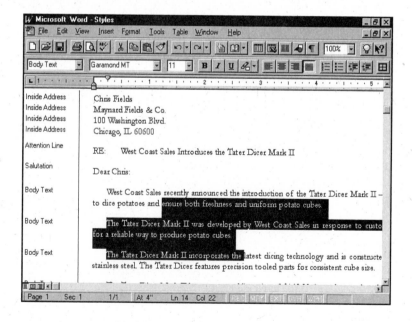

Fig. 11.13

All of these paragraphs will change with a new style selection because at least part of each paragraph has been selected.

Applying Character Styles

To apply a character style, you must first select the text to which you want to apply the character style. The formatting of the new style will be added to those formats already in effect on the selected text. For example, a character style that adds bold and italic doesn't change the font or point size or other formatting applied by the paragraph style in use.

To apply a style from the menu command, follow these steps:

1. Position the insertion point inside the paragraph, or select text in the paragraph(s) you want to format with a style.

2. Choose Format, Style. The Style dialog box appears.

3. Click the down arrow to the right of the List box and select one of the following options:

   Select the Styles in Use option to list standard styles and those you've created or modified for the current document.

   Select the All Styles option to list all styles available in the document.

   Select the User-Defined Styles option to list non-standard styles that you have created for the document.

4. Select the style you want from the Styles list box. Paragraph styles are listed in bold text; character styles are listed in normal text. The Paragraph Preview and Character Preview boxes provide a sample of how the style appears.

5. Choose Apply.

To apply a style from the Formatting toolbar, follow these steps:

1. Position the insertion point inside the paragraph, or select text in the paragraph(s) you want to format with a style.

2. Click the down arrow at the right side of the Style box in the Formatting toolbar to display a list of available styles. Paragraph styles are preceded by the ¶ symbol; character styles are preceded by the a symbol.

3. Select the style you want to apply to the paragraph(s) or selected text (scroll the list if necessary).

To apply a style from the keyboard, follow these steps:

1. Position the insertion point inside the paragraph, or select text in the paragraph(s) you want to format with a style.

2. Press any of the following key combinations:

Press This	To Apply This Style
Ctrl+Alt+1	Heading 1
Ctrl+Alt+2	Heading 2
Ctrl+Alt+3	Heading 3
Ctrl+Shift+L	List Bullet (bulleted list style)
Ctrl+Shift+N	Normal
Ctrl+Shift+S	Activates the Style box; choose the style you want from the list

Tip
The styles listed in the Style box are only a partial list of what's available. To see the entire list, hold down the Shift key while you click the down arrow next to the Style box.

When you press Ctrl+Shift+S, Word selects the currently displayed style in the Style box in the Formatting toolbar. To select another, either type a different name in the Style box, or use the arrow keys to highlight another style and then press Enter. If you type the name of a style that doesn't exist, you will create a style based on the example of the selected paragraph or paragraphs, rather than applying a style.

You can assign shortcut keys to other styles, as well. See "Creating Style Shortcut Keys" later in this chapter.

Copying Styles

You can apply the same style several times consecutively. Apply the style the first time, then select the additional text you want to format with that style, and press Ctrl+Y. Continue the procedure to apply the style in other locations. This method works for both paragraph styles and character styles.

You also can use the Format Painter button on the Standard toolbar to copy character styles to paragraphs or selected text one or several times.

To copy character styles with the Format Painter button, follow these steps:

1. Select the text or paragraph mark (¶) that has the formatting you want to copy.

2. Click the Format Painter button on the Standard toolbar.

3. Select the text you want to format with the character style. The new character style is applied to the selected text.

II

Formatting Documents

To copy character styles multiple times with the Format Painter button, repeat the steps above but double-click in step 2. To turn off the copy process, click the Format Painter button again.

Removing Character Styles

You can remove a character style and reapply the default character formatting, which will match the character formats defined for the selected paragraph style.

To remove a character style, place the insertion point in the word or select the text formatted with the character style you want to remove, and press Ctrl+space bar.

Creating Styles

The process of using styles of your own involves two steps. First you create the style, specifying formatting choices like paragraph indentations, line spacing, font, and font size. Then you apply that style—along with all your formatting choices—to other characters or paragraphs in your document.

You can create paragraph styles in two ways: by example (using the Formatting toolbar or a keyboard shortcut) or by menu command. Creating a style by example is so easy that even a beginner can do it. Using a menu command gives you more options, including creating character styles, and isn't difficult when you understand the concept of styles. (See "Creating a Style with a Menu Command" later in this chapter.)

> **Note**
>
> Styles are saved with the document or template in which you create them. You can share styles with other documents, however. (Refer to the section "Sharing Styles among Documents" later in this chapter.)

Naming the New Style

A new style name must be unique. If you try to create a new style with an existing name, you apply the existing style to your paragraph instead of creating a new style. If that happens, choose Edit, Undo and try again. Be aware that Word for Windows includes quite a few built-in styles (like Normal and Heading 1 through Heading 9); don't create new styles using the names of these built-in styles. For a list of built-in styles, refer to the section "Using Word for Windows Standard Styles" earlier in this chapter.

As you're naming your style, remember these rules:

- A style name can contain as many as 253 characters. Try, however, to use simple, memorable style names.

- The name can contain spaces, commas, and aliases. An *alias* is an optional, shorter name (see "Giving a Style a New Name or Alias" later in this chapter).

- Style names are case-sensitive—you can use uppercase and lowercase letters.

- Illegal characters include the following: \ (backslash), { or } (braces), and ; (semicolon).

Choose a style name that makes sense to you so that you will remember it later and so that you can use it consistently in other documents. If you frequently use small caps in your documents, for example, create a style called Small Caps and use it to quickly format text.

Creating a Style by Example

To create a style by example, you format a paragraph the way you want it, and then create a style based on the formatting contained in that paragraph. As you format your first paragraph (the one you will use as an example to create a style), remember that although paragraph styles are paragraph-level formatting commands, they also can contain character formatting. The character-level formatting is defined by the font, size, and other character formats of the first character of the selected text. If your example paragraph contains left and right indents and a border, those formatting choices will also be part of your style.

You can create a style by example by using the Formatting toolbar or by using a keyboard shortcut.

To create a style by example using the Formatting toolbar, follow these steps:

1. Choose <u>V</u>iew, <u>T</u>oolbars and select the Formatting toolbar (if it isn't already displayed).

2. Format your example paragraph. You can include character or paragraph formatting, borders and shading, frames and positioning, tabs, and a language for spell checking.

3. With the insertion point still in your example paragraph, select the entire name of the existing style in the Formatting toolbar's Style box (see fig. 11.14).

Fig. 11.14

Select the current style name in the Formatting toolbar's Style box.

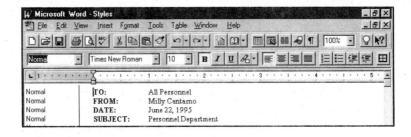

4. Type the name of the style you want to create (see fig. 11.15).

Fig. 11.15

Type the new style name to create a style by example.

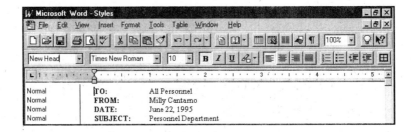

5. Press Enter to create the style.

After you create your style, look in the Formatting toolbar's Style box. You see your new style name displayed, indicating that its formatting choices control the appearance of your example paragraph.

To create a style by example using the keyboard, follow these steps:

1. Format your example paragraph and position the insertion point in it.

2. Press Ctrl+Shift+S. Word for Windows selects the current style name in the Style box.

3. Type the name of the style you want to create.

4. Press Enter to create the style.

Look at the Style box in the Formatting toolbar to see that your new style is now selected for your example paragraph.

You also can use a menu command to create a style by example. You might do this, for example, if you want to use a formatted paragraph as the basis for a style, but you also want to add additional formatting choices to the style.

To create a style by example using the menu command, follow these steps:

1. Format the paragraph you want to use as an example for your style, and leave the insertion point inside the paragraph.

2. Choose Format, Style and click the New button. (See the next section for details on using this dialog box.)

3. In the Name box, type the name of your new style. Notice that the Description box changes to show the selected paragraph's formatting.

4. Choose Format and make additional formatting choices, if necessary.

5. Choose OK to return to the Style dialog box.

6. Choose Close.

Creating a Style with a Menu Command

If you want to create styles before you use them, rather than creating them by example, use Format, Style. Using this command, you name a style, define its formatting characteristics, and select options such as whether to base the style on another style, whether to follow it with another style, and whether to add the style to the current template. You can also import and export styles to and from other documents and templates.

◄ See "Creating a New Template," p. 188

Using a menu command, you can create both types of styles: paragraph and character. When you create a style by using the menu command, you have the option to apply the style to the currently selected paragraph or simply to add it to the list of styles you created for your document (or for your template).

All new styles you create are based on the style of the currently selected paragraph. In the next section, you learn how you can base your new style on any other style.

Tip

If you plan to use your styles over and over in the same type of document, as in a monthly newsletter, create them in a new template.

To create a style from the menu command, follow these steps:

1. Choose Format, Style. The Style dialog box appears.

    Notice that the preview boxes display both the paragraph and character formatting of the currently selected paragraph. The Description box indicates the precise characteristics of the formatting.

2. Click the New button. The New Style dialog box appears (see fig. 11.16).

II

Formatting Documents

Fig. 11.16

You can create
styles in the New
Style dialog box.

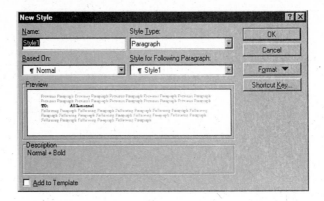

3. In the Name box, type the name of your new style. Use a unique, brief, and easy-to-recall name. Refer to "Naming the New Style," earlier in this chapter, for style naming rules.

   Now only the style name of the currently selected paragraph's style appears in the Description box.

4. In the Style Type box, select Character to create a character style, or Paragraph to create a paragraph style.

5. Click the Format button to pull down the list of format options and select the one you want (if you want to include bold formatting as part of your style, for example, select Font to display the Font dialog box, then select the Bold option from the Font Style group):

Select This	To Select These Formatting Options
Font	Font, style (bold, italic, underline), size, color, super/subscript, and character spacing
Paragraph	Paragraph alignment, spacing, indentation, and line spacing (not available for character styles)
Tabs	Tab stop position, alignment, and leaders, or clear tabs (not available for character styles)
Border	Border location, style, color, and paragraph shading (not available for character styles)
Language	The language that the spell checker, thesaurus, and grammar checker should use for the current paragraph
Frame	Text wrapping, frame size or position, or remove frame (not available for character styles)
Numbering	Bulleted and Numbered paragraphs in various styles (not available for character styles)

Repeat this step to include as much formatting as you want.

6. Choose OK. To create additional styles, repeat steps 2 through 5 before closing the dialog box.

7. To apply your new style to the currently selected paragraph, choose Apply.

Or, to exit the Style dialog box without applying the style to any paragraph, choose Close.

Caution

When you type the name of your new style in step 2, be sure that it is a unique name. If you type the name of an existing style and then make formatting choices, you will redefine the existing style. Any text formatted with the existing style then takes on this redefined formatting.

As part of the process of creating a style, you can assign shortcut keys to make the style easy to apply. See the later section "Creating Style Shortcut Keys."

Creating a Style Based on an Existing Style

You may need a group of styles that are similar to each other but have slight variations. For example, you may need a Table Body style for the contents of a table, and you also may need a Table Heading style and a Table Last Row style. Using the following technique, you can create a "family" of styles based on one foundation style.

To base one style on another style, follow these steps:

1. Choose Format, Style.

2. Choose New.

3. Choose Name and type the name of your new style.

4. Specify the name of the style on which you want to base your style in the Based On box. To display a list of styles, click the down arrow to the right of the Based On box.

When you select a style name, you see the name of the style plus any formatting attributes from the selected paragraph in the Description box. Your new style automatically is based on that existing style, unless you specify a different style.

> **Tip**
> If you want to print a list of a document's styles (along with a description of each style), choose File, Print, select Styles in the Print What box, and then choose OK.

> ◄ See "Creating a New Template," p. 188

II

Formatting Documents

5. Choose any of the Format button options to add formatting options to your style.

6. Choose OK to return to the Style dialog box.

7. Choose Close.

   Or, choose Apply if you want to apply your new style to the currently selected paragraph.

Creating Style Shortcut Keys

A fast way to apply a style is with a shortcut key, which you can assign as part of the process of creating or redefining a style. The shortcut keys usually include pressing the Alt key plus a letter that you designate. You could assign the shortcut Alt+S, for example, to a style called Sub. You can use other key combinations if you want, but they may conflict with shortcut keys pre-assigned to Word for Windows built-in macros. (Word for Windows uses the built-in macro Ctrl+Shift+S, for example, to enable you to create or apply a style quickly, so you wouldn't want to assign Ctrl+Shift+S to your style Sub.) To learn more about built-in macros, refer to Chapter 37, "Recording and Editing Macros."

To create shortcut keys for styles, follow these steps:

1. Choose Format, Style.

2. From the Styles list, highlight the style for which you want to create shortcut keys.

3. Click the Modify button.

4. Click the Shortcut Key button. The Customize dialog box opens and displays the Keyboard tab (see fig. 11.17).

5. Type a shortcut key combination in the Press New Shortcut Key box. You can use the letters A through Z, the numbers 0 through 9, Insert, and Delete, combined with Ctrl, Alt, and Shift.

   If the shortcut key combination you selected is already in use by another style or macro, Word displays the message Currently Assigned To and the command or macro to which the shortcut key is assigned. If the shortcut key isn't assigned, the Currently Assigned To message line displays [unassigned].

6. Click the Assign button.

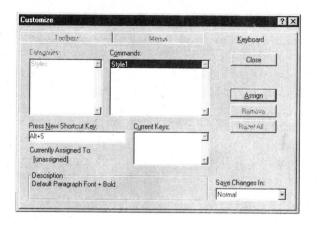

Fig. 11.17

You can assign shortcut keys to styles with the Customize Keyboard dialog box.

7. Click the Close button to return to the Modify Style dialog box.

8. Choose OK to return to the Style dialog box.

9. Choose Close.

To remove a shortcut key, follow these steps:

1. Choose Format, Style.

2. From the Styles list, highlight the style for which you want to remove the shortcut key.

3. Click the Modify button.

4. Click the Shortcut Key button.

5. Select the shortcut key you want to remove in the Current Keys box.

6. Click the Remove button.

7. Click Close to return to the Modify Style dialog box.

8. Choose OK to return to the Style dialog box.

9. Choose Close.

To apply a style with a shortcut key you have assigned, follow these steps:

1. Select the paragraph (or paragraphs) to which you want to apply the style.

2. Hold down the Ctrl, Alt, or Shift keys while you type the shortcut letter, number, function key, Insert, or Delete key. (If your shortcut is Alt+C, for example, hold down Alt while you press C.)

II

Formatting Documents

Following One Style with the Next Style

Tip

You can add styles to a menu or toolbar. See Chapter 36, "Customizing the Toolbar, Menus, and Shortcut Keys."

One of the most useful style options is the ability to follow one style with another. Suppose that you're editing a complex document with many subheadings, all formatted with styles. Text formatted with the Normal style follows each subheading. You would save time and effort if you didn't have to apply the Normal style each time you finished typing a subheading. If the style Subhead is followed by the Normal style, for example, when you finish typing a subhead and press Enter, the Normal style is applied automatically to the next paragraph. You can see this process in action by watching the Style box in the Formatting toolbar.

By default, Word for Windows follows each style with that same style so that when you press Enter, the style carries forward. In many cases, that's what you want. When you finish typing a paragraph formatted with the Normal style, you want the next paragraph also to be formatted with the Normal style.

To follow one style with another style, follow these steps:

1. Choose Format, Style.

2. Click the New button to create a new style. The New Style dialog box appears.

   Or, highlight an existing style from the list and click Modify. The Modify Style dialog box appears.

3. Select from the Style for Following Paragraph drop-down list box the style that you want to follow the current style. To display a list of styles, click the down arrow to the right of the Style for Following Paragraph box.

   If you select no style, your style will be followed by itself.

4. Choose OK to return to the Style dialog box.

5. Choose Close.

Sharing Styles among Documents

Every document you create includes styles—even if it's only the Normal style and Word for Windows' other standard styles. Each document's group of styles is provided by its template—either the Normal template, one of the other templates provided with Word, or a custom template you create.

In its simplest sense, using a template is the basic way you can share styles among documents. You create a template that contains certain styles you need, and then base your documents on that template. You may, for example, have a template called Letters that contains styles for formatting letters to be printed on your company's letterhead. If you regularly produce several different types of documents, you may create a template for each of them.

At some point, however, you may want to use the styles from one document or template in a different document or template. You can do that by copying styles from one document or template to another.

A likely scenario for sharing styles is the big, multidocument publication that undergoes design revisions as the project progresses. In the beginning of the project, you create a template containing styles for formatting each document. Because all documents are based on the same template, they contain identical formatting, which preserves consistency. Later, the publications committee issues major design changes. One way to change your documents is to open each one and revise its styles. But an easier way to make the changes is to revise the styles in the template instead, and then copy the template's revised styles into each document. The template's revised styles replace the document's identically named styles, and any text associated with those styles changes to reflect the revisions.

You can copy styles to or from any document or template. If you copy an identically named style, it replaces the one in the document or template you're copying to (you will be asked to confirm the replacement); new styles are added to the document or template to which you're copying.

To copy styles from a document or template, follow these steps:

1. Choose Format, Style.

2. Click the Organizer button. The Organizer dialog box appears.

   The In box on the left displays a list of the styles in the currently open document or template. The To box on the right displays a list of the styles of the NORMAL.DOT template.

3. Select Close File (below the appropriate list) to close the current document style list or the Normal template style list. When you close either the current document or the Normal template, the Close File button changes to an Open File button and you can open a different document or template.

4. Select Open File (below the appropriate list) to open a different document or template to copy its styles. The Open dialog box appears; select the document you want to use. If you want to select a template, open the Files of Type in the Open dialog box to choose Document Templates (*.DOT). If necessary, change folders or drives. Templates are stored in either the Letters folder or the Macros folder by default. When you find the document or template you want to open, choose the Open button to return to the Organizer dialog box.

5. Select the styles you want to copy from the In or To lists. The Copy button arrows change direction to indicate the direction from which the styles will be copied.

   You can select a contiguous group of styles by clicking the first one you want to copy, then holding down Shift while you click the last one you want to copy. To select noncontiguous styles, hold down Ctrl while you click each one.

6. Choose Copy.

7. Choose Close.

Tip
You can avoid copying the style along with the paragraph into the new document by *not* including the paragraph mark with the text you're copying.

Another way to merge a *single* style into a document is to copy into your document a paragraph formatted with a different style from another document. Be careful, though. Copying styles into your document this way doesn't override existing styles, as does copying styles through the Organizer dialog box. If you copy a paragraph formatted with a style called First Item, for example, and your existing document also contains a style called First Item, the new paragraph will take on the formatting of the existing First Item style.

Other commands for inserting text into a document, such as AutoText, Paste, and Paste Special, also can bring in new styles. You can copy in as many as 50 paragraphs that contain unique style names—if you copy in more than 50, Word for Windows merges in the document's entire style sheet.

Changing Styles

You can change any style, including standard styles. This capability makes it easy to adapt to the changing tasks you have to do. For example, instead of having to remember your company's new format for closing signatures, you can redefine a style you have created for closings. All you need to do is continue working like you did before; the new style definition takes care of the changes.

There are many ways to change a style. To name just a few, you can redefine the style to incorporate new or different characteristics, or you can delete or rename the style. To make assigning styles easier, provide an alias for a style. The following sections discuss these and other techniques for changing styles.

Deleting a Style

At some point, you may decide you no longer need a style. You can delete it, and all text associated with the deleted style will revert to the Normal style. You cannot delete built-in styles.

To delete a style, follow these steps:

1. Choose Format, Style.

2. Select the style you want to delete from the Styles list.

   If you have selected a paragraph containing the style you want to delete, the style already will be selected in the Styles list box.

3. Click the Delete button. You see a message asking whether you want to delete the style.

4. Choose Yes.

You also can delete several styles at once. Choose the Organizer button in the Style dialog box. Select the styles you want to delete and click the Delete button.

Note

You can choose Edit, Replace to delete text that has been formatted with a particular style. In the Find box, choose the name of the style whose text you want to delete from the Format, Style list. Leave the Replace box empty. Click the Find Next button. If the text you find is text you want to delete, click the Replace button. If you don't want to delete the text, proceed through the document with the Find Next button to the next item. Choose Close when you are finished deleting text.

Tip

You can select a group of contiguous files by clicking the first one, and then holding down Shift while you click the last one. To select noncontiguous files, hold down Ctrl while you click each one.

Giving a Style a New Name or Alias

You can rename a style, which doesn't affect the associated text but changes the style name throughout your document. You can choose to rename a style for two purposes: to give it a new name or to add an optional name, or alias. An *alias* is a shorter name or abbreviation that you can type quickly in the Style box in the Formatting toolbar. For example, if you're using the Heading

1 style frequently and applying it from the keyboard, you can give the style an alias of h1. Then to apply the Heading 1 style you press Ctrl+Shift+S, type **h1** (rather than the full name), and press Enter.

Standard styles cannot be renamed, but you can add an alias to them. Also, you cannot use a standard style name as an alias for another style.

To rename a style or add an alias, follow these steps:

1. Choose Format, Style.

2. Click the Modify button. The Modify Style dialog box appears.

3. Type the new name in the Name text box. To include an alias, type a comma after the new name and then type the alias.

   Or, to add an alias, type a comma after the current style name, and then type the alias.

4. Choose OK to return to the Style dialog box.

5. Choose Close.

Redefining a Style

When you *redefine* a style, all the text formatted with that style updates to reflect the changes you have made. Suppose that you finish a 35-page report with many subheadings formatted with a style called Subhead that includes 18-point, bold, Helvetica, centered text. Now your company's publications committee decides subheadings should be smaller and underlined. Just redefine the style Subhead to reflect the new formatting, and all the subheadings in your text will change.

It is as easy to modify a style by example as it is to create a style by example. To redefine a style by example, follow these steps:

1. Choose View, Toolbars and select the Formatting toolbar if it isn't currently displayed.

2. Reformat the paragraph you will use as an example for the redefined style.

3. Select the paragraph (or some portion of the paragraph).

4. In the Formatting toolbar, select the current style name, or just position the insertion point to its right.

   Or, press Ctrl+Shift+S and select or type the name of the style you want to redefine.

5. Press Enter. The Reapply Style dialog box appears (see fig. 11.18). You have the following options:

   Choose R̲edefine the Style Using the Selection As an Example? to change the formatting of the current style to match the formatting of the selected text.

   Choose Reapply the Formatting of the Selection to the S̲tyle? to reapply the formatting of the style to the selected text.

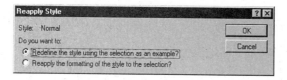

Fig. 11.18
The Reapply Style dialog box appears when you redefine a style by example.

6. Choose OK or press Enter to redefine the style.

The F̲ormat, S̲tyle command gives you the greatest flexibility for changing a style. You can make a change and add that change to the template on which you based the document. That way, each time you use the template in the future, the particular style will reflect the change.

To redefine a style using the menu command, follow these steps:

1. Choose F̲ormat, S̲tyle.

2. From the S̲tyles list, select the style you want to redefine. If the style isn't included in the list, select a different option from the L̲ist drop-down list.

3. Click the M̲odify button. The Modify Style dialog box appears (see fig. 11.19).

Select this check box to add your changes to the document template

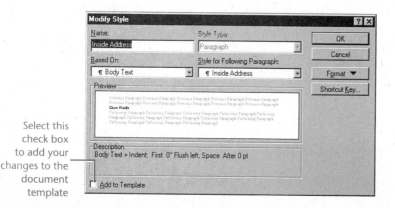

Fig. 11.19
You can change a style's formatting in the Modify Style dialog box.

II

Formatting Documents

4. Click the Format button and select any formatting options you want to add to your style. Remove any other options as needed.

5. Select the Add to Template check box to make the change in the document's template, as well as in the document.

6. Choose OK to return to the Style dialog box.

    Repeat steps 2 through 6 if you want to redefine additional styles.

7. Choose Close.

Changing the Normal Style

Each time you begin a new document based on the Normal template, Word uses the Normal style to determine the font, font size, line spacing, and other formats. If you find that you are always changing the font, point size, or some other aspect of the Normal style, you can change its default format settings.

Changing the formats defined for the Normal style in your document affects only the current document. Add the style to the template to apply the change to future documents. Existing documents are not changed unless you specifically have Word update their styles. See "Updating Styles" later in this chapter.

Remember that any change you make to the Normal style will be reflected in all styles that are based on that style, which includes most styles.

To change the default settings for the Normal style with the menu command, follow these steps:

1. Choose File, New and open the Normal template or the template that you use for new documents.

    The Style box on the Formatting toolbar should show `Normal`. In a new document, the first paragraph will automatically use the Normal style.

2. Choose Format, Style and choose Modify. The Normal style should be selected in the Name box. If it isn't, type **Normal**.

3. Make the changes you want to the style using the Format options.

4. When you return to the Modify Style dialog box, select the Add to Template check box.

5. Choose OK to return to the Style dialog box.

6. Choose Close.

To change the default settings for the Normal style by example, follow these steps:

1. Choose File, Open and select a document that is based on the Normal template or the template that you use for new documents.

2. Select text or position the insertion point in a paragraph that is formatted with the Normal style.

3. Select commands on the Format menu from the Formatting toolbar, or with shortcut keys to make formatting changes you want applied to most documents. For example, you might want to choose a different font in a different point size with a first line indent of .5".

4. Click the Style box in the Formatting toolbar and press Enter.

5. Word asks whether you want to redefine the style using the selection as an example. Choose OK.

6. Choose Format, Style. The Style dialog box opens with the Normal style selected in the Styles list. Select Normal if it isn't selected.

7. Click Modify, select the Add to Template check box, and choose OK.

8. Choose Close.

Updating Styles

If you create a group of documents, each based on the same template, you'll want to make sure that any change to a style is reflected in each of the documents. For example, if you're writing a book with each chapter in a separate file, you want any changes to headers, footers, and headings to be copied to each of the document files. When you select the Automatically Update Document Styles command, Word copies the attached template's styles to the document each time you open it. The Update feature follows these rules:

■ A style in the template that has the same name as a style in the document overrides the document style. The formatting from the template's style replaces the formatting from the document's style.

■ Styles not found in the document are copied from the template to the document.

■ Styles found in the document, but not in the template, are left unchanged.

Make sure that you use identically named styles in each of the documents. Otherwise, Word will not properly update the styles.

◄ See "Adding Power and Features with Add-Ins," p. 193

To update a document's styles each time you open it, follow these steps:

1. Place the insertion point anywhere in the file whose styles you want to update automatically.

2. Choose File, Templates. The Templates and Add-ins dialog box appears (see fig. 11.20). The template attached to the current document is named in the Document Template box.

Fig. 11.20

Select Automatically Update Document Styles, and each time you open the document its styles will be updated from the attached template.

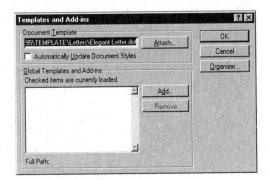

3. Select the Automatically Update Document Styles check box.

4. Choose OK.

Changing the Base of a Style

Unless you specify otherwise, a new style is based on the style of the currently selected paragraph. Often, that's the Normal style. You have the option, however, to base any style on any other style. When you do, any changes you make to the base style carry through to all styles based on that style. If you change Normal, those changes are reflected in any style based on the Normal style.

This often can be to your advantage. Suppose that you work in a legal office and you regularly type certain court documents that must always be double-spaced, in a certain font and size, and have specific margins. To help automate this task, you can create a template with the correct margins, and then modify the template's Normal style to include the correct font and size and double-spacing. You then can create additional styles based on that redefined Normal style, and they too will use the specified font and size and be double-spaced.

Keep in mind that Word for Windows standard styles are based on the Normal style, and if you alter the Normal style, your alterations will apply to all the standard styles as well.

If you don't want to alter your Normal style, you can create a base style in your document and use it as the basis for additional styles. By changing that base style, you can make extensive changes throughout a document.

To base one style on another style, follow these steps:

1. Choose Format, Style.

2. Select from the Styles list a style whose base style you want to change.

3. Click the Modify button. The Modify Style dialog box appears.

4. Specify the name of the style on which you want to base your style in the Based On box. To display a list of styles, click the down arrow to the right of the Based On box.

   If you want the selected style to remain unaffected by changes to any other style, select (no style) from the top of the list in the Based On box.

   When you select a style name, you see the name of the style plus any formatting attributes from the selected paragraph in the Description box. Your new style automatically is based on that existing style, unless you specify a different style.

5. Select any of the Format button options to add additional formatting options to your style.

6. Choose OK to return to the Style dialog box.

7. Choose Close.

   Or, choose Apply if you want to apply your new style to the currently selected paragraph.

Troubleshooting

I attached the wrong template to my document and updated the styles. Now, all the styles in my document look wrong. What can I do?

Repeat the process using the correct template or the original template. Attach either the original template or the correct template to your document and again update styles. The styles in your document should return to their original appearance or to the appearance of the styles in the correct template.

Checking Formats

Formatting can be applied from a style or manually from the Format menu or other commands. You can quickly determine how formatting was applied to any text with the Help button on the Standard toolbar.

To determine how formatting was added, follow these steps:

1. Click the Help button on the Standard toolbar.

2. Click the text you want to check. A formatting box appears, showing paragraph and font formatting (see fig. 11.21). You can continue to click other locations to see the formatting of other text.

3. Press Esc to turn off the Help feature.

Fig. 11.21
Use the Help button on the Standard toolbar to quickly check the formatting of any text.

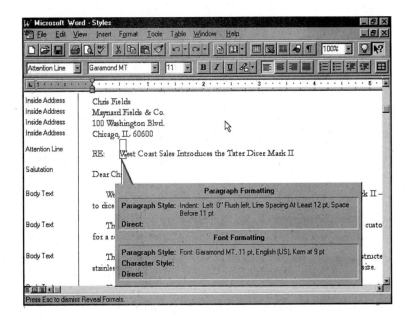

Chapter 12

Working with Columns

Sometimes what you have to say isn't best said in line after line of margin-to-margin text. Often you can help keep your reader interested and make your prose look a little more inviting by dividing the text into columns. Research has shown that text of newspaper column width is much faster to read. Columns not only make information more attractive, but also more readable.

In Word for Windows 95, you can create two types of columns: *snaking columns* of text you see in newspapers, magazines, and newsletters; and *parallel columns* of text and numbers you see in lists and tables. Tables (which consist of columns and rows of text, numbers, or dates) work well for parallel columns or for data that you want to keep aligned. This chapter discusses snaking columns (sometimes called *newspaper columns*), in which the text wraps continuously from the bottom of one column to the top of the next column. To learn more about the desktop publishing capabilities of Word for Windows, refer to Chapter 38, "Desktop Publishing."

You learn procedures in this chapter that make it easy to create documents such as newspapers, newsletters, and brochures. In this chapter, you learn how to do the following:

- Calculate the number and length of columns you need

- Understand how sections separate parts of a document with different layout

- Create even and uneven width columns

- Type and edit within columns

- Insert a vertical line between columns

- See the columns on-screen as they will print

- Change column layouts after they are created

Creating a Newsletter the Easy Way

If you've been using Word 6, you know about wizards. If you read Chapter 6, "Using Templates and Wizards for Frequently Created Documents," you know about wizards. In Word 95, you'll find a new wizard, the Newsletter Wizard, which makes creating a truly professional-looking newsletter a breeze (see fig. 12.1).

Fig. 12.1
Use the Newsletter Wizard to easily create a newsletter designed to your specifications.

To select the Newsletter Wizard, follow these steps:

1. Choose File, New. You'll see the General tab of the New dialog box.

2. Click the Publications tab. Word displays the available templates and wizards that relate to producing publications (see fig. 12.2).

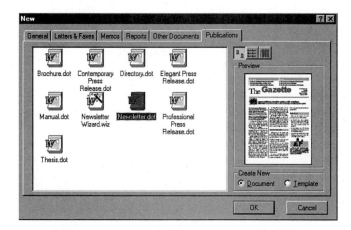

Fig. 12.2
In the New dialog box, you see templates and wizards available for several different categories of documents.

II

Formatting Documents

3. Click the Newsletter Wizard and choose OK. Word displays the first dialog box of the Newsletter Wizard (see fig. 12.3).

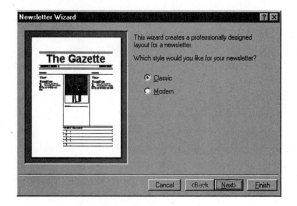

Fig. 12.3
In the first dialog box of the Newsletter Wizard, choose the style of newsletter you want to create.

To design your newsletter with the Newsletter Wizard, follow these steps:

1. Choose the style of newsletter you want to create—Classic or Modern. As you click each of the option buttons, the Preview box changes to show you examples.

◀ See "Using Wizards to Guide You in Creating Documents," p. 192

2. Click the <u>N</u>ext button. In the second Newsletter Wizard dialog box, choose the number of columns you want for your newsletter: <u>O</u>ne, <u>T</u>wo, Th<u>r</u>ee, or Fo<u>u</u>r. If you click each option button, you'll see the changes in the layout.

3. Click the <u>N</u>ext button. In the third Newsletter Wizard dialog box, type the name of your newsletter. You can edit the name later.

4. Click the <u>N</u>ext button. In the fourth Newsletter Wizard dialog box, type the number of pages you want for your newsletter. Again, you can change this later.

5. Click the <u>N</u>ext button. In the fifth Newsletter Wizard dialog box, select the options you want to include in your newsletter: <u>T</u>able of Contents, Fancy First <u>L</u>etters, <u>D</u>ate, and <u>V</u>olume and Issue.

6. Click the <u>N</u>ext button.

7. Click the <u>F</u>inish button. Word displays a skeleton newsletter like the one shown in figure 12.4, displayed in Print Preview mode.

Fig. 12.4
The Newsletter Wizard produces a skeleton document like this one, into which you type your information.

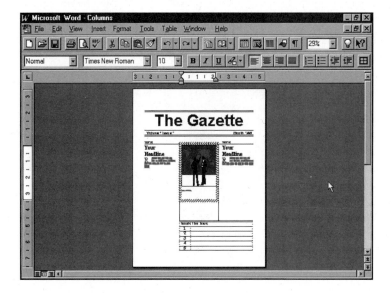

Creating Columns

If you need to work with columns and you're *not* creating a newsletter, Word's column features help you in your task. You can create columns of equal or unequal width. You can include different numbers or styles of columns in different sections of your document. Newsletters, for example, often have two or more sections. The first section contains a large one-column banner, and the remaining text is divided into multiple columns. You also can include a vertical line between columns.

You can include up to 14 columns in portrait orientation or 18 columns in landscape orientation. You can also include different numbers or styles of columns in different parts of your document, as long as you divide your document into sections.

> **Caution**
>
> From a readability standpoint, including too many columns on the page can make your document difficult to read. As a rule of thumb, try to include no more than three columns on a portrait-oriented sheet of paper, or five columns on a landscape-oriented sheet of paper.

Word for Windows gives you two methods of creating columns: choosing Format, Columns, or clicking the Columns button on the Standard toolbar. In Normal view, you see columns in their correct width, but not side by side; only in Page Layout or Print Preview views do you see columns side by side.

Calculating the Number and Length of Columns

Word determines how many columns you can have on a page based on three factors: page width, margin widths, and size and spacing of your columns. On a wide landscape-oriented page, for example, you have more room for columns than on a narrower portrait-oriented page. Similarly, if your margins are narrow, there's more room for text on the page, and thus you can have more columns. If columns are narrow, you can fit more of them on a page than if they are wide.

In Word, columns must be at least half an inch (0.5") wide. If you try to fit too many on a page, Word displays a message reading `Column widths cannot be less than 0.5"`. You might see this message if you change your margins, for example, making them wider so that there is less room on the page for columns. If you see the message, change either your page layout or the number, width, or spacing of your columns.

Columns are the length of the current section or of the current page if there are no sections.

Understanding Sections

▶ See "Changing the Page Layout within a Document," p. 1086

A new document based on the default Normal template is a single section with a one-column format, as shown in figure 12.5. *Sections* are divisions within a document that can be formatted independently of one another. If you want different numbers or styles of columns in different parts of your document, you must divide it into sections. Figure 12.6 shows a document divided into two sections. The upper section shows the title as a single column, whereas the lower section shows the body copy in three columns. Figure 12.7 shows a document with three sections; one column for the title, two columns for the upper text, and three columns for the lower text.

Fig. 12.5

This document has only a single section so that when you format in columns, the entire document changes.

Declaration of Independence

When in the Course of human events, it becomes necessary for one people to dissolve the political bands which have connected them with another, and to assume among the powers of the earth, the separate and equal station to which the Laws of Nature and of Nature's God entitle them, a decent respect to the opinions of mankind requires that they should declare the causes which impel them to separation.

We hold these truths to be self-evident, that all men are created equal, that they are endowed by their Creator with certain Unalienable Rights,that among these are life, Liberty and the pursuit of Happiness. That to secure these rights, governments are instituted among Men, deriving their just powers from the consent of the governed,

That whenever any form of Government becomes destructive of these ends, it is the right of the People to alter or to abolish it and to institute a new Government, laying its foundation on such principles and organizing its power in such form, as to them shall seem most likely to affect their Safety and Happiness. Prudence, indeed, will dictate that Governments long established should not be changed for light and transient

causes; and accordingly all experience has shown, that mankind is more disposed to suffer, which evils are sufferable, than to right themselves by abolishing the forms to which they are accustomed. But when a long train of abuses and usurpations, pursuing invariably the same Object evinces a design to reduce them under absolute Despotism, it is their right, it is their duty, to throw off such Government, and to provide new Guards for their future security.

Such has been the patient sufferance of these colonies; and such is now the necessity which constrains them to alter their former Systems of Government. The history of the present King of Great Britain is a history of repeated injuries and usurpations, all having in direct object the establishment of an absolute Tyranny over these States. To prove this, let Facts be submitted to a candid world.

He has refused his Assent to Laws, the most wholesome and necessary for the public good.

He has forbidden his Governors to pass Laws of immediate and pressing importance, unless suspended in their operation until his assent should be obtained; and when so suspended, he has utterly neglected to attend to them. He has refused to pass other Laws for the

accommodation of large districts of people unless those people would relinquish the right of Representation in the Legislature, a right inestimable to them and formidable to tyrants only.

He has called together legislative bodies at places unusual, uncomfortable, and distant from the depository of their public Records, for the sole purpose of fatiguing them into compliance with his measures.

He has dissolved Representative Houses repeatedly, for the opposing with manly firmness his invasions on the rights of the people.

He has refused for a long time, after such dissolutions, to cause others to be elected; whereby the Legislative powers, incapable of annihilation, have returned to the people at large for their exercises; the state remaining in the mean time exposed to all the dangers of invasion from without, and confusions within.

He has endeavored to prevent the population of these states, for that purpose obstructing the Laws of Naturalization of Foreigners, from gaining permission to pass, other than to encourage their migrations hither, and raised the conditions of new Appropriations of lands.

Declaration of Independence

When in the Course of human events, it becomes necessary for one people to dissolve the political bands which have connected them with another, and to assume among the powers of the earth, the separate and equal station to which the Laws of Nature and of Nature's God entitle them, a decent respect to the opinions of mankind requires that they should declare the causes which impel them to separation.

We hold these truths to be self-evident, that all men are created equal, that they are endowed by their Creator with certain Unalienable Rights,that among these are life, Liberty and the pursuit of Happiness. That to secure these rights, governments are instituted among Men, deriving their just powers from the consent of the governed,

That whenever any form of Government becomes destructive of these ends, it is the right of the People to alter or to abolish it and to institute a new Government, laying its foundation on such principles and organizing its power in such form, as to them shall seem most likely to affect their Safety and Happiness. Prudence, indeed, will dictate that Governments long established should not be changed for light and transient causes; and accordingly all

experience has shown, that mankind is more disposed to suffer, which evils are sufferable, than to right themselves by abolishing the forms to which they are accustomed. But when a long train of abuses and usurpations, pursuing invariably the same Object evinces a design to reduce them under absolute Despotism, it is their right, it is their duty, to throw off such Government, and to provide new Guards for their future security.

Such has been the patient sufferance of these colonies; and such is now the necessity which constrains them to alter their former Systems of Government. The history of the present King of Great Britain is a history of repeated injuries and usurpations, all having in direct object the establishment of an absolute Tyranny over these States. To prove this, let Facts be submitted to a candid world.

He has refused his Assent to Laws, the most wholesome and necessary for the public good.

He has forbidden his Governors to pass Laws of immediate and pressing importance, unless suspended in their operation until his assent should be obtained; and when so suspended, he has utterly neglected to attend to

them. He has refused to pass other Laws for the accommodation of large districts of people unless those people would relinquish the right of Representation in the Legislature, a right inestimable to them and formidable to tyrants only.

He has called together legislative bodies at places unusual, uncomfortable, and distant from the depository of their public Records, for the sole purpose of fatiguing them into compliance with his measures.

He has dissolved Representative Houses repeatedly, for the opposing with manly firmness his invasions on the rights of the people.

He has refused for a long time, after such dissolutions, to cause others to be elected; whereby the Legislative powers, incapable of annihilation, have returned to the people at large for their exercises; the state remaining in the mean time exposed to all the dangers of invasion from without, and confusions within.

He has endeavored to prevent the population of these states, for that purpose obstructing the Laws of Naturalization of Foreigners, from gaining permission to pass, other than to encourage their migrations

Fig. 12.6
This document has two sections—the title, formatted in one column, and body copy formatted in three.

With columns, there are three ways you can insert section breaks:

- Choose Insert, Break to display the Break dialog box (see fig. 12.8).

- Choose Format, Columns to create columns and specify that columns apply not to the whole document, but to "this point forward" in your document; Word adds a section break before the insertion point.

- Select the text that you want to appear in different columns before you create or change the columns; a section break is added before and after the selected text (or just after the selected text if it falls at the beginning of a document).

Fig. 12.7
This document
has three sections,
each formatted in
a different number
of columns.

Declaration of Independence

When in the Course of human events, it becomes necessary for one people to dissolve the political bands which have connected them with another, and to assume among the powers of the earth, the separate and equal station to which the Laws of Nature and of Nature's God entitle them, a decent respect to the opinions of mankind requires that they should declare the causes which impel them to separation.

We hold these truths to be self-evident, that all men are created equal, that they are endowed by their Creator with certain Unalienable Rights,that among these are life, Liberty and the pursuit of Happiness. That to secure these rights, governments are instituted among Men, deriving their just powers from the consent of the governed,

That whenever any form of Government becomes destructive of these ends, it is the right of the People to alter or to abolish it and to institute a new Government, laying its foundation on such principles and organizing its power in such form, as to them shall seem most likely to affect their Safety and Happiness. Prudence, indeed, will dictate that Governments long established should not be changed for light and transient causes; and accordingly all experience has shown, that mankind is more disposed to suffer, which evils are sufferable, than to right themselves by abolishing the forms to which they are accustomed. But when a long train of abuses and usurpations, pursuing invariably the same Object evinces a design to reduce them under absolute Despotism, it is their right, it is their duty, to throw off such Government, and to provide new Guards for their future security.

Such has been the patient sufferance of these colonies; and such is now the necessity which constrains them to alter their former Systems of Government. The history of the present King of Great Britain is a history of repeated injuries and usurpations, all having in direct object the establishment of an absolute Tyranny over these States. To prove this, let Facts be submitted to a candid world.

He has refused his Assent to Laws, the most wholesome and necessary for the public good.

He has forbidden his Governors to pass Laws of immediate and pressing importance, unless suspended in their operation until his assent should be obtained; and

when so suspended, he has utterly neglected to attend to them. He has refused to pass other Laws for the accommodation of large districts of people unless those people would relinquish the right of Representation in the Legislature, a right inestimable to them and formidable to tyrants only.

He has called together legislative bodies at places unusual, uncomfortable, and distant from the depository of their public Records, for the sole purpose of fatiguing them into compliance with his measures.

He has dissolved Representative Houses repeatedly, for the opposing with manly firmness his

invasions on the rights of the people.
He has refused for a long time, after such dissolutions, to cause others to be elected; whereby the Legislative powers, incapable of annihilation, have returned to the people at large for their exercises; the state remaining in the mean time exposed to all the dangers of invasion from without, and confusions within.

He has endeavored to prevent the population of these states, for that purpose obstructing the Laws of Naturalization of Foreigners, from gaining permission to pass, other than to encourage their migrations hither, and raised the conditions of new Appropriations of lands.

Fig. 12.8
You can insert
section breaks
using the Insert,
Break command.

Using the Break dialog box, you can specify that sections run continuously so that you can have a different number of columns on the same page, or you can specify that each section start on a new page or on the next even-numbered or odd-numbered page.

In Normal view, section breaks appear in your document as a double dotted line containing the words `End of Section`.

Formatting Columns

When formatting your document into columns, remember the following tips:

- If you want to format the entire document into columns and your document has only one section, position the insertion point anywhere in your document.

- If you want to format only one section into columns and you've already divided your document into sections, position the insertion point inside the section you want formatted into columns. (Columns apply to multiple sections if multiple sections are selected.)

- If you want columns to start at a certain point in your document and you haven't divided your document into sections, position the insertion point where you want columns to start. You can apply columns from that point forward. Word for Windows inserts a section break at the insertion point.

- If you want to format selected text into columns and you haven't divided your document into sections, select the text that you want in columns. Word inserts a section break before and after the selected text.

Creating Columns of Equal Width

The width of the columns in your document depends on the number of columns you choose, your margins, and the amount of space you set between columns. For example, if you have one-inch left and right margins on a standard 8 1/2-inch paper width, and you divide your text into three columns with one-quarter inch between them, you get three two-inch-wide columns.

Remember that only in Page Layout view (or Print Preview) will you see your columns side by side.

Tip
All column formatting is stored in the section break mark at the end of a section. If you delete this mark, that section takes on the column formatting and section formatting of the section after it.

Tip
If you don't like the number of columns you've created or don't like their widths, choose Edit, Undo Columns to return to your original number of columns.

II

Formatting Documents

To create equal-width columns with the menu or with the Columns button, follow these steps:

1. Specify which part of your document you want divided into columns (see "Formatting Columns" earlier in this chapter).

2. If the toolbar is not displayed, choose View, Toolbars. Select the Standard toolbar and click OK. Click the Columns button to display the column drop-down box. Drag right to select the number of columns you want (up to six). Figure 12.9 shows the Columns button drop-down box with three columns selected.

Fig. 12.9

The quickest way to format your document with columns is to use the Columns button on the Standard toolbar.

You also can choose Format, Columns. The Columns dialog box appears (see fig. 12.10).

3. In the Presets group, select One, Two, or Three columns. You also can select Number of Columns, and type or select the number of columns you want. If you want columns to start at the insertion point, click the Apply To drop-down list arrow and select This Point Forward from the list. Choose OK.

Fig. 12.10

Use presets to quickly format your text into columns, or select the number of columns you want.

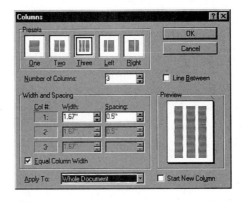

Creating Columns of Unequal Width

Although you can easily format your document with columns by clicking the Columns button, you can use more options when you use the Columns dialog box. You can define your own columns, or you can choose preset columns. *Preset columns* include a wide and a narrow column (the wide column is twice as wide as the narrow column). Preset columns make a good starting point for defining your own columns. Using them ensures that your columns are a consistent width.

When you create columns by choosing Format, Columns, you can specify whether columns apply to the whole document, the current section(s), the insertion point forward, or the selected text (if text is selected). (See "Formatting Columns," earlier in this chapter.)

By choosing Format, Column, you also can specify how wide you want your columns and how much space you want between them.

To create columns of unequal width, follow these steps:

1. Select the text you want to format into multiple columns, or position the insertion point inside the section you want to format or at the point where you want a new number of columns to begin.

2. Choose Format, Columns. The Columns dialog box appears.

3. Optionally, from the Presets group, select Left if you want a narrow column on the left, or Right if you want a narrow column on the right.

4. Select Number of Columns, and type or select the number of columns you want. Look at the Preview box to see how your columns will appear (see fig. 12.11).

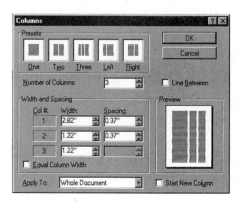

Fig. 12.11
To create columns of unequal width, use presets or define your own columns.

II

Formatting Documents

5. Deselect the Equal Column Width option if it is selected.

6. If you want to define the width or spacing for individual columns, place the insertion point in the Width or Spacing box for the column you want to change. The dialog box has space for only three column numbers; click or press the down arrow to display additional column numbers.

7. Type or select the width you want for the selected column.

   You can also type or select the spacing you want to the right of the selected column (there is no space to the right of the rightmost column).

8. Select from the Apply To drop-down list the amount of text you want to format. The options shown in the Apply To list change depending on whether text is selected or whether your document contains multiple sections. Usually Word correctly guesses where you want to apply your columns, based on the location of the insertion point:

   Selected Sections appears only when multiple sections are selected. It formats the sections you selected with columns.

   Selected Text appears only when text is selected. This option formats the text you selected with columns. It also puts a section break before and after the selection.

   This Point Forward appears only when no text is selected. This option formats with columns from the insertion point forward. It puts a section break at the location of the insertion point.

   This Section appears only when the insertion point is inside one of multiple sections. This option formats with columns the section containing the insertion point.

   Whole Document formats the entire document with columns.

9. Choose OK.

Typing and Editing Text in Columns

Typing, editing, and formatting text in columns follows all the same rules and takes advantage of the same shortcuts for typing, selecting, and editing any other text. The following two tips will help you as you move around in and select columnar text:

■ To move from one column to the top of the next column on the currect page using the keyboard, press Alt+↓. To move to the top of the previous column, press Alt+↑.

■ The selection bar that normally appears at the left margin of a page now appears at the left margin of each column in Page Layout view. When you move the mouse pointer into this area, it turns into an arrow you can use to select lines and paragraphs within a column.

◀ See "Selecting Text," p. 141

Troubleshooting

My text seems narrower than the columns.

This condition may appear if the text is indented. Use the ruler or choose Format, Paragraph to eliminate or change the indentation settings for selected text. Also check the margin settings within each column.

Adding a Line between Columns

Adding a vertical line between columns can add interest to your page. Lines are the length of the longest column in the section. You can see lines in the Page Layout view or in Print Preview.

To add lines between columns, follow these steps:

1. Click in the section containing columns where you want vertical lines.

2. Choose Format, Columns.

3. In the Columns dialog box, select the Line Between option.

4. Choose OK.

To remove lines between columns, deselect the Line Between option in the Columns dialog box. You can also add vertical lines on your page by choosing Format, Borders and Shading. If you do and you also add lines between columns, you may see two lines between columns. For columns, the Line Between option is a better choice than Format, Borders and Shading because it creates lines of uniform length in the section, even if one column of text is shorter than the others.

Viewing Columns

Word for Windows enables you to view a document in several ways. Views include Normal, Outline, Page Layout, Master Document, and Print Preview. Depending on which view you are in, columns appear differently on-screen.

◀ See "Viewing Documents and File Information," p. 106

Tip
You can switch between Normal, Page Layout, and Outline views using the three icons that appear at the left edge of the horizontal scroll bar.

Normal view is faster for text entry but does not display columns side by side as they will appear when printed. The text appears in the same width as the column, but in one continuous column. Page Layout view displays columns side by side, with vertical lines between columns if you've selected that option. Section and column breaks appear only when you've displayed paragraph marks. Print Preview gives an overview of the page as it will appear when printed. In all three views, you can change column width using the ruler, and you can display the Column dialog box to edit columns.

In both the Outline view and the Master Document view, columns appear similar to the way you see them in Normal view—the same width as the column, but in one continuous column.

When you are editing a document, you may need to view a particular section up close. At other times, you may need an overview of the entire page. The Word for Windows 2.0 toolbar includes three buttons that enable you to magnify or reduce the size of the display:

- *Zoom One Page buttons.* Shows you a miniature view of the whole page in Page Layout view.

- *Zoom 100% button.* Shows you a full-size page in Normal view.

- *Zoom Page Width button.* Shows you the full width of the page in whichever view you're currently working.

The Standard toolbar has a drop-down list with the same commands, along with several percentages at which you can view your page. You can also select magnification by choosing <u>V</u>iew, <u>Z</u>oom.

Changing Columns

◄ See "Controlling Your Document's Appearance On-Screen," p. 123

► See "Changing the Page Layout Within a Document," p. 1086

Once you format your document with columns, you can change the columns in many ways:

- You can change the number of columns, or switch between equal- and unequal-width columns.

- You can change the width of columns or the spacing between them.

- You can force text to move to the top of the next column, and you can force a column to start on a new page.

- You can balance columns on a page so that they are as close to the same length as possible.

You can make some changes to columns using the ruler; for example, you can change their width or the spacing between them. Other changes you make using the Columns dialog box.

Before you change columns, make sure you select the text you want to change, and be sure in the Columns dialog box to apply the changes where you want them (use the Apply To list). Follow these rules for selecting text and applying the changes:

- If you want to change columns for the entire document and your document has only one section, position the insertion point anywhere in your document. In the Apply To list of the Columns dialog box, choose Whole Document.

- If you want to change columns in only one section and you've already divided your document into sections, position the insertion point inside the section you want to change. In the Apply To list of the Columns dialog box, choose This Section.

- If you want columns to start at a certain point in your document and you haven't divided your document into sections, position the insertion point where you want columns to start. In the Apply To list of the Columns dialog box, choose This Point Forward.

- If you want to change columns in only part of your document and you haven't divided your document into sections, select the text that you want in columns. In the Apply To list of the Columns dialog box, choose Selected Text.

- If you want to change columns in multiple existing sections, select the sections. In the Apply To list of the Columns dialog box, choose Selected Sections.

Tip
You can quickly display the Columns dialog box by double-clicking the gray area between columns on the horizontal ruler.

Most of the time, Word understands where you want to apply changes by where you've positioned the insertion point, and you don't need to make a selection in the Apply To list.

Because you can format text in columns in the same way you can format text that is not in columns, you may create some unexpected results. If your column is too narrow, for example, you may find yourself with a vertical strip of text that isn't very readable. Try widening the column, lessening the space between the columns, reducing the number of columns, or reducing the size of the text.

II

Formatting Documents

Changing the Number of Columns

You can change the number of columns using either the ruler or the Columns dialog box. You can also change between equal- and unequal-width columns. If you want to change from equal-width to unequal-width columns, you must use the Columns dialog box, but you can change from unequal-width to equal-width columns using the ruler.

To change the number of equal-width columns, or to change from unequal-width to equal-width columns, follow these steps:

1. Position the insertion point or select the text where you want changes to apply.

2. On the Standard toolbar, click the Columns button and select the number of columns you want from the drop-down box (drag right in the box to display up to seven columns).

   You also can choose Format, Columns to display the Columns dialog box. From the Presets group, select One, Two, or Three. Or select Number of Columns, and type or select the number of columns you want. If you are changing from unequal-width to equal-width columns, select the Equal Column Width check box. Choose OK.

To change the number of unequal-width columns, or to change from equal-width to unequal-width columns, follow these steps:

1. Position the insertion point or select the text where you want changes to apply.

2. Choose Format, Columns to display the Columns dialog box. If you want two preset columns of unequal width, select Left or Right from the Presets group. Or, select Number of Columns, and type or select the number of columns you want.

3. If you're changing from equal-width to unequal-width columns, deselect the Equal Column Width option.

4. Choose OK.

Changing the Width of Columns and the Spacing between Columns

When you first create columns, Word determines their width based on your margins and the number of columns you want. You can change the width of all or some columns.

You can also change the spacing between columns. By default, columns have a half inch (0.5") of spacing between them, but you may want to decrease or increase this distance. You may want to decrease the distance if you have many columns, because the greater number of columns you have, the narrower they are, and the less space you need between them. You may want to increase the distance with fewer columns, as you might in a three-column brochure printed sideways on the page, for example.

You can change the width of columns or the space between columns in two ways: using the ruler or using the Columns dialog box. Using the ruler, you drag column margin markers to change the width and spacing at the same time.

If your columns are currently equal-width and you want to change them to unequal-width, you must use the Columns dialog box.

To change the width of columns or the space between columns using the ruler, follow these steps:

1. Make sure the ruler is displayed; if it is not, choose <u>V</u>iew, <u>R</u>uler.

2. Position the insertion point inside the section containing the columns you want to change.

3. The gray areas in the horizontal ruler indicate the spaces between columns. Move the mouse pointer over one of these gray areas until the pointer turns into a two-headed arrow as shown in figure 12.12. Choose any gray area if your columns are all the same width; choose the gray area above the space you want to change if your columns are different widths. When columns are different widths, the gray area contains a grid-like icon, as shown in figure 12.13.

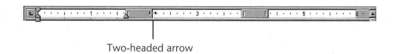

Two-headed arrow

4. Hold down the mouse button and drag the edge of the gray area away from the center to widen the space between columns, or drag it toward the center to lessen the space between columns. If columns are different widths, you can drag either side of the gray area to change the spacing in either direction.

Fig. 12.12
Using the ruler, you can change the width of columns and the spacing between them. If your columns are the same width, changing one changes them all.

Grid-like icon

Fig. 12.13
When columns are of unequal widths, or if they were created using the Columns button, the gray area of the ruler contains a grid-like icon.

> **Note**
>
> When dragging the unequal columns marker, remember that it functions two ways, depending upon how you drag it:
>
> - Drag the edge of the marker to change the widths of unequal columns.
>
> - Drag the grid-like icon to change the space between unequal columns.

Tip
If columns are all the same width, changing the spacing for one changes the spacing for them all. If columns are different widths, changing the spacing for one affects only that column.

Tip
If your columns are all the same width, you can change the width of column 1 only; all the rest use the same measurements.

To change the width or columns or the space between columns using the Columns dialog box, or to change columns of equal width into columns of unequal width, follow these steps:

1. Position the insertion point inside the section containing the columns you want to change.

2. Choose F<u>o</u>rmat, <u>C</u>olumns.

3. If you are changing equal-width columns to unequal-width columns, deselect the <u>E</u>qual Column Width option.

4. In the Width and Spacing group, place the insertion point in the W<u>i</u>dth box of the column you want to change and type or select the width you want for your column or columns.

5. In the Width and Spacing group, place the insertion point in the <u>S</u>pacing box of the column you want to change and type or select the spacing you want between your columns.

6. Choose OK.

Removing Columns

If your document is formatted into columns, you can remove them easily using either the Columns button or the Columns dialog box.

To remove columns, follow these steps:

1. Position the insertion point or select text where you want to remove columns.

2. Use the Columns button to select one column.

   You also can choose Format, Columns. From the Presets group, select One. Choose OK.

Starting a New Column

When Word for Windows creates columns, it automatically breaks the columns to fit on the page. Sometimes the column may break inappropriately. On a three-column page, for example, column 2 may end with a heading that should be at the top of column 3. By inserting a column break directly before the heading, you shift the heading to the top of the next column, keeping the heading and its following text together.

If you want a column to start on a new page, you can insert a page break. To insert a column break, press Ctrl+Shift+Enter or follow these steps:

1. Position the insertion point at the beginning of the line where you want the new column to start.

2. Choose Insert, Break. The Break dialog box appears (see fig. 12.14).

Fig. 12.14
Inserting a column break causes text to move to the top of the next column.

3. Select the Column Break option.

4. Choose OK.

To insert a page break, press Ctrl+Enter or repeat the steps above, choosing Page Break in step 3.

Balancing Column Lengths

On pages where the text in columns continues to the next page, Word for Windows automatically balances (lines up) the last line of text at the bottom of each column. But when columnar text runs out on a page, you may be left with two full-length columns and a third column that's only partially filled. You can balance column lengths so that the bottom of all the columns are within one line of each other. Figures 12.15 and 12.16 show unbalanced and balanced columns.

To balance the length of multiple columns, follow these steps:

1. Position the insertion point at the end of the text in the last column of the section you want to balance.

2. Choose Insert, Break.

3. Select the Continuous option in the Section Breaks group.

4. Choose OK.

▶ See "Changing the Page Layout within a Document," p. 1086

Troubleshooting

I have several columns and I want to change their width and spacing, but in the Columns dialog box I can select only column 1.

Your columns are currently of Equal width. Deselect the Equal Column Width option if you want to make them different widths.

Product lists, date schedules, and the dialog for plays all appear to use columns, but it's impossible to keep related items lined up across the columns. Adding or editing in one column changes the position of items in following columns.

Use Word's table feature to create scripts for plays, procedural steps, duty rosters, product catalogs, and so on. Tables are grids of rows and columns. Information within a cell in a table will stay adjacent or parallel to other information in the same row, even when you add lines in the cell. Cells can contain entire paragraphs, math calculations, field codes, and even pictures. Tables are described in detail in Chapter 16, "Creating and Editing Tables."

ReLeaf Plants and Trees Throughout the State

Lorem ipsum dolor sit amet, consectetuer adipiscing elit, sed diam nonummy nibh euismod tincidunt ut laoreet dolore magna aliquam erat volutpat. Ut wisi enim ad minim veniam, quis nostrud exerci tation ullamcorper suscipit lobortis nisl ut aliquip ex ea commodo consequat. Duis autem vel eum iriure dolor in hendrerit in vulputate velit esse molestie consequat, vel illum dolore eu feugiat nulla facilisis at vero eros et accumsan et iusto odio dignissim qui blandit praesent luptatum zzril delenit augue duis dolore te feugait nulla facilisi.

Lorem ipsum dolor sit amet, consectetuer adipiscing elit, sed diam nonummy nibh euismod tincidunt ut laoreet dolore magna aliquam erat volutpat.

Lorem ipsum dolor sit amet, consectetuer adipiscing elit, sed diam nonummy nibh euismod tincidunt ut laoreet dolore magna aliquam erat volutpat. Duis autem vel eum iriure dolor in hendrerit in vulputate velit esse molestie consequat, vel illum dolore eu feugiat nulla facilisis at vero eros et accumsan et iusto odio dignissim qui blandit praesent luptatum zzril delenit augue duis dolore te feugait nulla facilisi.

Lorem ipsum dolor sit amet, consectetuer adipiscing elit, sed diam nonummy nibh euismod tincidunt ut laoreet dolore magna aliquam erat

volutpat. Ut wisi enim ad minim veniam, quis nostrud exerci tation ullamcorper suscipit lobortis nisl ut aliquip ex ea commodo consequat.

Lorem ipsum dolor sit amet, consectetuer adipiscing elit, sed diam nonummy nibh euismod tincidunt ut laoreet dolore magna aliquam erat volutpat. Duis autem vel eum iriure dolor in hendrerit in vulputate velit esse molestie consequat, vel illum dolore eu feugiat nulla facilisis at vero eros et accumsan et iusto odio dignissim qui blandit praesent luptatum zzril delenit augue duis dolore te feugait nulla facilisi.

Lorem ipsum dolor sit amet, consectetuer adipiscing elit, sed diam nonummy nibh euismod tincidunt ut laoreet dolore magna aliquam erat volutpat. Ut wisi enim ad minim veniam, quis nostrud exerci tation ullamcorper suscipit lobortis nisl ut aliquip ex ea commodo consequat. Duis autem vel eum iriure dolor in hendrerit in vulputate velit esse molestie consequat, vel illum dolore eu feugiat nulla facilisis at vero eros et accumsan et iusto odio dignissim qui blandit praesent luptatum zzril delenit augue duis dolore te feugait nulla facilisi.

Lorem ipsum dolor sit amet, consectetuer adipiscing elit, sed diam nonummy nibh euismod tincidunt ut laoreet dolore magna aliquam erat

volutpat. Ut wisi enim ad minim veniam, quis nostrud exerci tation ullamcorper suscipit lobortis nisl ut aliquip ex ea commodo consequat.

Lorem ipsum dolor sit amet, consectetuer adipiscing elit, sed diam nonummy nibh euismod tincidunt ut laoreet dolore magna aliquam erat volutpat. Duis autem vel eum iriure dolor in hendrerit in vulputate velit esse molestie consequat, vel illum dolore eu feugiat nulla facilisis at vero eros et accumsan et iusto odio dignissim qui blandit praesent luptatum zzril delenit augue duis dolore te feugait nulla facilisi.

Fig. 12.15
These columns have not been balanced.

Fig. 12.16
You can balance columns by adding a section break at the end of your document.

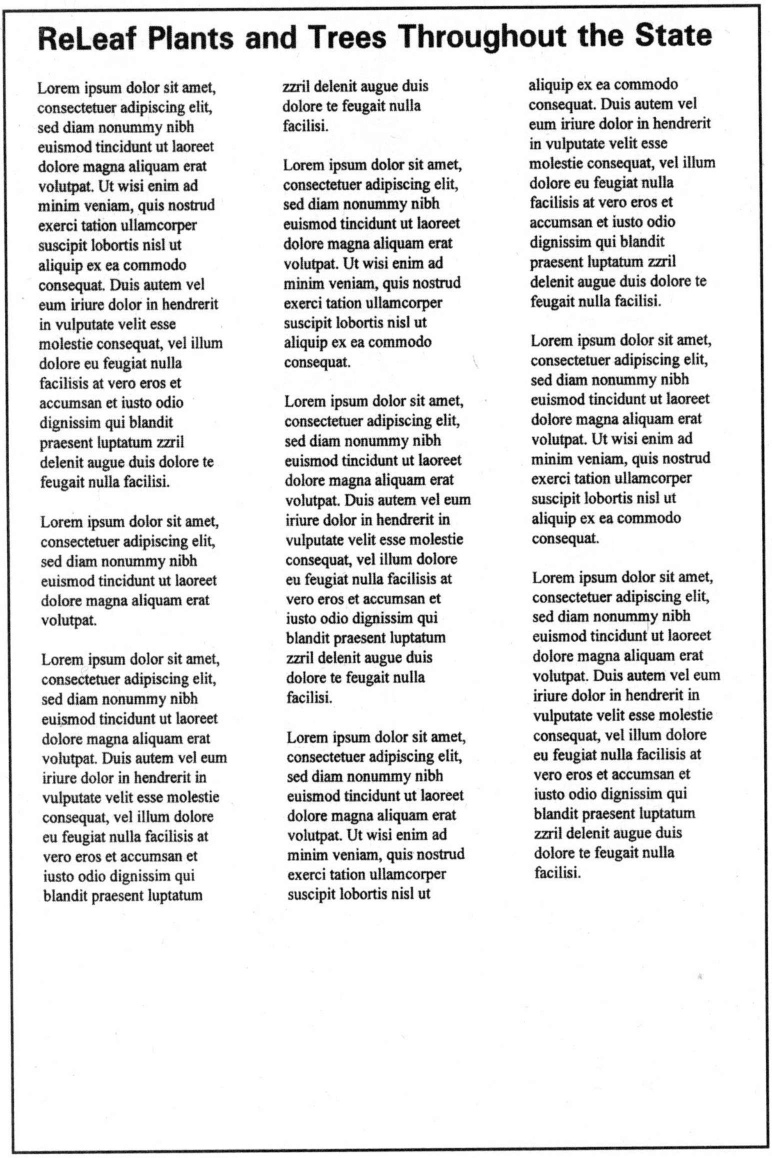

ReLeaf Plants and Trees Throughout the State

Lorem ipsum dolor sit amet, consectetuer adipiscing elit, sed diam nonummy nibh euismod tincidunt ut laoreet dolore magna aliquam erat volutpat. Ut wisi enim ad minim veniam, quis nostrud exerci tation ullamcorper suscipit lobortis nisl ut aliquip ex ea commodo consequat. Duis autem vel eum iriure dolor in hendrerit in vulputate velit esse molestie consequat, vel illum dolore eu feugiat nulla facilisis at vero eros et accumsan et iusto odio dignissim qui blandit praesent luptatum zzril delenit augue duis dolore te feugait nulla facilisi.

Lorem ipsum dolor sit amet, consectetuer adipiscing elit, sed diam nonummy nibh euismod tincidunt ut laoreet dolore magna aliquam erat volutpat.

Lorem ipsum dolor sit amet, consectetuer adipiscing elit, sed diam nonummy nibh euismod tincidunt ut laoreet dolore magna aliquam erat volutpat. Duis autem vel eum iriure dolor in hendrerit in vulputate velit esse molestie consequat, vel illum dolore eu feugiat nulla facilisis at vero eros et accumsan et iusto odio dignissim qui blandit praesent luptatum

zzril delenit augue duis dolore te feugait nulla facilisi.

Lorem ipsum dolor sit amet, consectetuer adipiscing elit, sed diam nonummy nibh euismod tincidunt ut laoreet dolore magna aliquam erat volutpat. Ut wisi enim ad minim veniam, quis nostrud exerci tation ullamcorper suscipit lobortis nisl ut aliquip ex ea commodo consequat.

Lorem ipsum dolor sit amet, consectetuer adipiscing elit, sed diam nonummy nibh euismod tincidunt ut laoreet dolore magna aliquam erat volutpat. Duis autem vel eum iriure dolor in hendrerit in vulputate velit esse molestie consequat, vel illum dolore eu feugiat nulla facilisis at vero eros et accumsan et iusto odio dignissim qui blandit praesent luptatum zzril delenit augue duis dolore te feugait nulla facilisi.

Lorem ipsum dolor sit amet, consectetuer adipiscing elit, sed diam nonummy nibh euismod tincidunt ut laoreet dolore magna aliquam erat volutpat. Ut wisi enim ad minim veniam, quis nostrud exerci tation ullamcorper suscipit lobortis nisl ut

aliquip ex ea commodo consequat. Duis autem vel eum iriure dolor in hendrerit in vulputate velit esse molestie consequat, vel illum dolore eu feugiat nulla facilisis at vero eros et accumsan et iusto odio dignissim qui blandit praesent luptatum zzril delenit augue duis dolore te feugait nulla facilisi.

Lorem ipsum dolor sit amet, consectetuer adipiscing elit, sed diam nonummy nibh euismod tincidunt ut laoreet dolore magna aliquam erat volutpat. Ut wisi enim ad minim veniam, quis nostrud exerci tation ullamcorper suscipit lobortis nisl ut aliquip ex ea commodo consequat.

Lorem ipsum dolor sit amet, consectetuer adipiscing elit, sed diam nonummy nibh euismod tincidunt ut laoreet dolore magna aliquam erat volutpat. Duis autem vel eum iriure dolor in hendrerit in vulputate velit esse molestie consequat, vel illum dolore eu feugiat nulla facilisis at vero eros et accumsan et iusto odio dignissim qui blandit praesent luptatum zzril delenit augue duis dolore te feugait nulla facilisi.

Chapter 13

Formatting the Page Layout, Alignment, and Numbering

Of the four levels of formatting—page, section, paragraph, and character—page layout is the broadest. Page layout often encompasses formatting choices that affect the entire document—for most documents, page layout choices such as margins and page size do apply to the whole document. In a change from tradition, however, Word for Windows 95 also enables you to apply page-level formatting to portions of the document known as *sections*.

Page layout options include margins, vertical alignment on the page, page and paragraph breaks, section breaks, page numbers, headers and footers, paper size and orientation, and the paper source. By default, many page setup options, such as margins, headers and footers, and page numbers, apply to the entire document. Alternatively, you can apply these options to a designated section of text or from the position of the insertion point forward in your document.

You can include an envelope and a letter in a single document, for example, by specifying different margins, paper size, paper orientation, and paper source for the first page of the document—the envelope—than you specify for the remaining pages—the letter. Or you can create different headers and footers for different parts of a long document. Being able to divide your document into sections and specify where page layout options apply gives you great flexibility in designing your document.

In this chapter, you learn to do the following:

- Set new margins for different documents

- Adjust the page orientation

- Create headers and footers

- Insert page numbers

Setting Margins

Margins are the borders on all four sides of a page within which the text of your document is confined. Margins aren't necessarily blank, however; they may contain headers, footers, page numbers, footnotes, or even text and graphics.

Word for Windows' default margins are 1 inch at the top and bottom and 1.25 inches on the left and right. You can change the margins for the entire document or for parts of the document, if you divide the document into sections (see fig. 13.1). If you use different margin settings regularly, you can modify the Normal template so that they become the new defaults.

◀ See "Setting Default Formats in the Normal Template," p. 187

Different views in Word for Windows show different perspectives on your margins. In Normal view, you don't see the margins, but you see the space between them where your text appears. In Page Layout view, you see the page as it will print, margins and all. Select that view if you want to see headers, footers, page numbers, footnotes, and anything else that appears within the margins.

To select a view, choose View, Normal or View, Page Layout; you can also click the appropriate icon at the left edge of the horizontal scroll bar.

You can change the margins in your document in two ways. First, you can make selections from the Page Setup dialog box. When you set margins this way, you control margin settings precisely. A second technique for setting margins is to use the ruler. Using this technique, you can see how margin settings affect the appearance of your page.

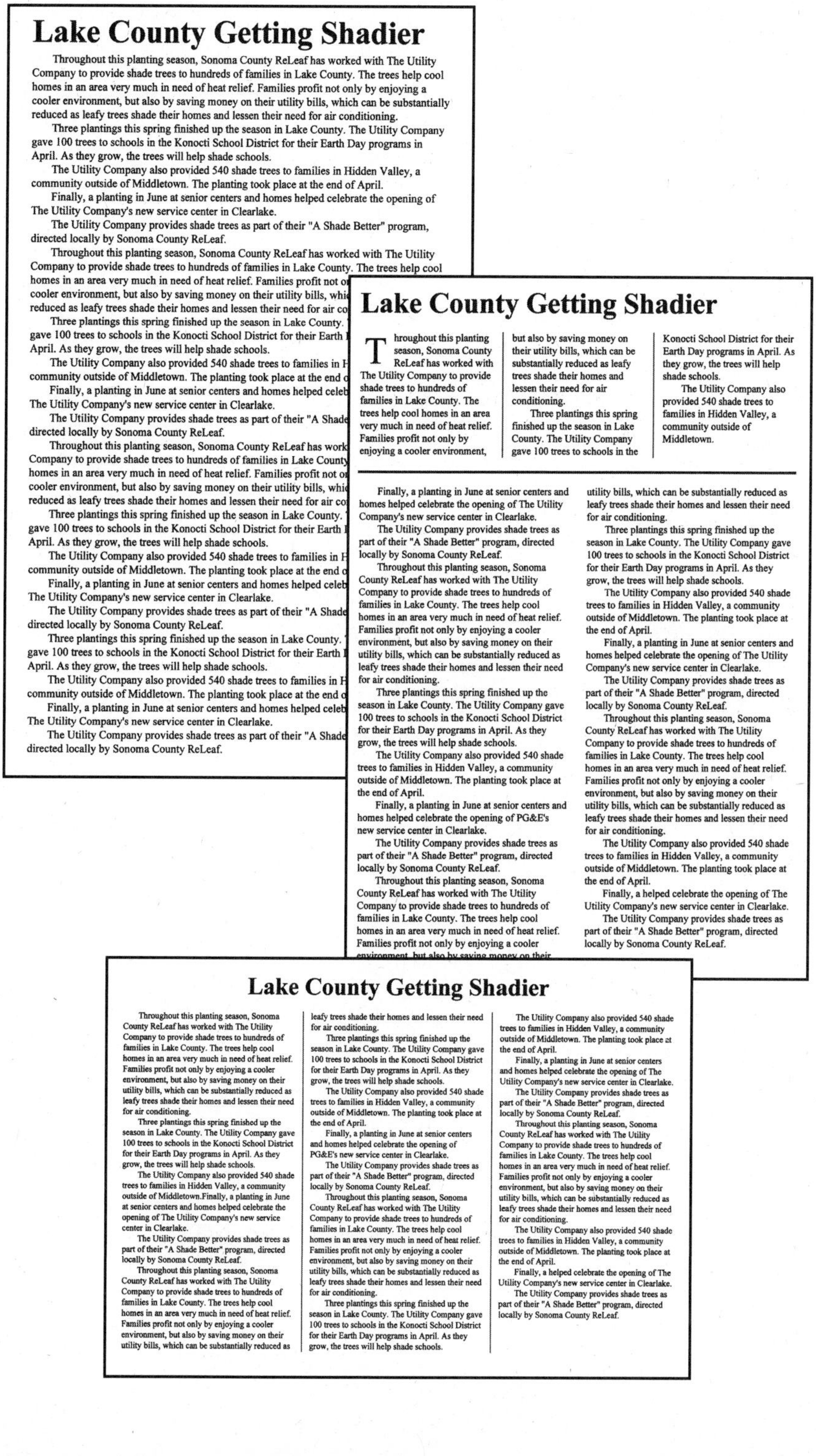

Fig. 13.1
You can set margins however you want.

Lake County Getting Shadier

Throughout this planting season, Sonoma County ReLeaf has worked with The Utility Company to provide shade trees to hundreds of families in Lake County. The trees help cool homes in an area very much in need of heat relief. Families profit not only by enjoying a cooler environment, but also by saving money on their utility bills, which can be substantially reduced as leafy trees shade their homes and lessen their need for air conditioning.

Three plantings this spring finished up the season in Lake County. The Utility Company gave 100 trees to schools in the Konocti School District for their Earth Day programs in April. As they grow, the trees will help shade schools.

The Utility Company also provided 540 shade trees to families in Hidden Valley, a community outside of Middletown. The planting took place at the end of April.

Finally, a planting in June at senior centers and homes helped celebrate the opening of The Utility Company's new service center in Clearlake.

The Utility Company provides shade trees as part of their "A Shade Better" program, directed locally by Sonoma County ReLeaf.

Throughout this planting season, Sonoma County ReLeaf has worked with The Utility Company to provide shade trees to hundreds of families in Lake County. The trees help cool homes in an area very much in need of heat relief. Families profit not only by enjoying a cooler environment, but also by saving money on their utility bills, which can be substantially reduced as leafy trees shade their homes and lessen their need for air conditioning.

Three plantings this spring finished up the season in Lake County. The Utility Company gave 100 trees to schools in the Konocti School District for their Earth Day programs in April. As they grow, the trees will help shade schools.

The Utility Company also provided 540 shade trees to families in Hidden Valley, a community outside of Middletown. The planting took place at the end of April.

Finally, a planting in June at senior centers and homes helped celebrate the opening of The Utility Company's new service center in Clearlake.

The Utility Company provides shade trees as part of their "A Shade Better" program, directed locally by Sonoma County ReLeaf.

Throughout this planting season, Sonoma County ReLeaf has worked with The Utility Company to provide shade trees to hundreds of families in Lake County. The trees help cool homes in an area very much in need of heat relief. Families profit not only by enjoying a cooler environment, but also by saving money on their utility bills, which can be substantially reduced as leafy trees shade their homes and lessen their need for air conditioning.

Three plantings this spring finished up the season in Lake County. The Utility Company gave 100 trees to schools in the Konocti School District for their Earth Day programs in April. As they grow, the trees will help shade schools.

The Utility Company also provided 540 shade trees to families in Hidden Valley, a community outside of Middletown. The planting took place at the end of April.

Finally, a planting in June at senior centers and homes helped celebrate the opening of The Utility Company's new service center in Clearlake.

The Utility Company provides shade trees as part of their "A Shade Better" program, directed locally by Sonoma County ReLeaf.

Lake County Getting Shadier

Throughout this planting season, Sonoma County ReLeaf has worked with The Utility Company to provide shade trees to hundreds of families in Lake County. The trees help cool homes in an area very much in need of heat relief. Families profit not only by enjoying a cooler environment, but also by saving money on their utility bills, which can be substantially reduced as leafy trees shade their homes and lessen their need for air conditioning.

Three plantings this spring finished up the season in Lake County. The Utility Company gave 100 trees to schools in the Konocti School District for their Earth Day programs in April. As they grow, the trees will help shade schools.

The Utility Company also provided 540 shade trees to families in Hidden Valley, a community outside of Middletown.

Finally, a planting in June at senior centers and homes helped celebrate the opening of The Utility Company's new service center in Clearlake.

The Utility Company provides shade trees as part of their "A Shade Better" program, directed locally by Sonoma County ReLeaf.

Throughout this planting season, Sonoma County ReLeaf has worked with The Utility Company to provide shade trees to hundreds of families in Lake County. The trees help cool homes in an area very much in need of heat relief. Families profit not only by enjoying a cooler environment, but also by saving money on their utility bills, which can be substantially reduced as leafy trees shade their homes and lessen their need for air conditioning.

Three plantings this spring finished up the season in Lake County. The Utility Company gave 100 trees to schools in the Konocti School District for their Earth Day programs in April. As they grow, the trees will help shade schools.

The Utility Company also provided 540 shade trees to families in Hidden Valley, a community outside of Middletown. The planting took place at the end of April.

Finally, a planting in June at senior centers and homes helped celebrate the opening of PG&E's new service center in Clearlake.

The Utility Company provides shade trees as part of their "A Shade Better" program, directed locally by Sonoma County ReLeaf.

Throughout this planting season, Sonoma County ReLeaf has worked with The Utility Company to provide shade trees to hundreds of families in Lake County. The trees help cool homes in an area very much in need of heat relief. Families profit not only by enjoying a cooler environment, but also by saving money on their utility bills, which can be substantially reduced as leafy trees shade their homes and lessen their need for air conditioning.

Three plantings this spring finished up the season in Lake County. The Utility Company gave 100 trees to schools in the Konocti School District for their Earth Day programs in April. As they grow, the trees will help shade schools.

The Utility Company also provided 540 shade trees to families in Hidden Valley, a community outside of Middletown. The planting took place at the end of April.

Finally, a planting in June at senior centers and homes helped celebrate the opening of The Utility Company's new service center in Clearlake.

The Utility Company provides shade trees as part of their "A Shade Better" program, directed locally by Sonoma County ReLeaf.

Throughout this planting season, Sonoma County ReLeaf has worked with The Utility Company to provide shade trees to hundreds of families in Lake County. The trees help cool homes in an area very much in need of heat relief. Families profit not only by enjoying a cooler environment, but also by saving money on their utility bills, which can be substantially reduced as leafy trees shade their homes and lessen their need for air conditioning.

Three plantings this spring finished up the season in Lake County. The Utility Company gave 100 trees to schools in the Konocti School District for their Earth Day programs in April. As they grow, the trees will help shade schools.

The Utility Company also provided 540 shade trees to families in Hidden Valley, a community outside of Middletown. The planting took place at the end of April.

Finally, a helped celebrate the opening of The Utility Company's new service center in Clearlake.

The Utility Company provides shade trees as part of their "A Shade Better" program, directed locally by Sonoma County ReLeaf.

Lake County Getting Shadier

Throughout this planting season, Sonoma County ReLeaf has worked with The Utility Company to provide shade trees to hundreds of families in Lake County. The trees help cool homes in an area very much in need of heat relief. Families profit not only by enjoying a cooler environment, but also by saving money on their utility bills, which can be substantially reduced as leafy trees shade their homes and lessen their need for air conditioning.

Three plantings this spring finished up the season in Lake County. The Utility Company gave 100 trees to schools in the Konocti School District for their Earth Day programs in April. As they grow, the trees will help shade schools.

The Utility Company also provided 540 shade trees to families in Hidden Valley, a community outside of Middletown. The planting took place at the end of April.

Finally, a planting in June at senior centers and homes helped celebrate the opening of PG&E's new service center in Clearlake.

The Utility Company provides shade trees as part of their "A Shade Better" program, directed locally by Sonoma County ReLeaf.

Throughout this planting season, Sonoma County ReLeaf has worked with The Utility Company to provide shade trees to hundreds of families in Lake County. The trees help cool homes in an area very much in need of heat relief. Families profit not only by enjoying a cooler environment, but also by saving money on their utility bills, which can be substantially reduced as leafy trees shade their homes and lessen their need for air conditioning.

Three plantings this spring finished up the season in Lake County. The Utility Company gave 100 trees to schools in the Konocti School District for their Earth Day programs in April. As they grow, the trees will help shade schools.

The Utility Company also provided 540 shade trees to families in Hidden Valley, a community outside of Middletown. The planting took place at the end of April.

Finally, a planting in June at senior centers and homes helped celebrate the opening of The Utility Company's new service center in Clearlake.

The Utility Company provides shade trees as part of their "A Shade Better" program, directed locally by Sonoma County ReLeaf.

Throughout this planting season, Sonoma County ReLeaf has worked with The Utility Company to provide shade trees to hundreds of families in Lake County. The trees help cool homes in an area very much in need of heat relief. Families profit not only by enjoying a cooler environment, but also by saving money on their utility bills, which can be substantially reduced as leafy trees shade their homes and lessen their need for air conditioning.

The Utility Company also provided 540 shade trees to families in Hidden Valley, a community outside of Middletown. The planting took place at the end of April.

Finally, a planting in June at senior centers and homes helped celebrate the opening of The Utility Company's new service center in Clearlake.

The Utility Company provides shade trees as part of their "A Shade Better" program, directed locally by Sonoma County ReLeaf.

Setting Margins with a Precise Measurement

Using the Page Setup command to set margins gives you the greatest number of options. You can set the margins to precise measurements, establish facing pages and gutters for binding (discussed later in this chapter), set varying margins for different sections of your document, and apply your margin settings to the Normal template so that they become the new default settings.

To apply margin settings to your entire document, you can locate the insertion point anywhere in the document when you set your margins. If you want to apply margins to only one part of your document, however, you must do one of three things:

- To apply margins to a selected portion of your text, select that text before you set the margins. If you apply margins to selected text, Word for Windows inserts section breaks before and after the selected text.

- To apply margins to existing sections, first place the insertion point in the section, or select those sections whose margins you want to change.

- To apply margins from a specific point forward in your document, position the insertion point where you want the new margins to start and then specify that the margins apply to the text from This Point Forward. If you apply margins from the insertion point forward, Word for Windows inserts a section break at the insertion point.

Setting different margins for different parts of your document is covered in a later section in this chapter, "Working with Sections in Your Document."

To set measured margins, follow these steps:

1. Position the insertion point inside the section for which you want to set margins. (The margins apply to the entire document unless the document has multiple sections.) Or select the text for which you want to set margins.

2. Choose File, Page Setup. In the Page Setup dialog box, select the Margins tab (see fig. 13.2).

3. Choose your margin settings. Your options include Top, Bottom, Left, Right, and Gutter. Gutter controls extra spacing on pages for binding (see the section "Creating Facing Pages and Gutters"). For each setting, type the amount of the margin or use the spinner (or press the up- or down-arrow key) to increase or decrease the margin setting by tenths of an inch.

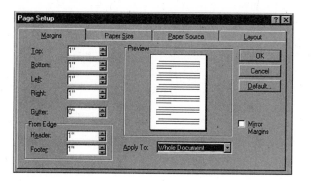

Fig. 13.2
Set precisely
measured margins
using the Page
Setup dialog box.

4. Choose OK.

> **Note**
>
> As you select your margin settings, notice that the Preview box in the Page Setup dialog box shows you how your page or pages will look.

Margins usually are measured in decimal inches, unless you change your default measurement system by using Tools, Options (General tab). You can create margins in a different measurement system by typing amounts such as **36 pt** for 36 points (72 points equal one inch), **3 cm** for 3 centimeters, or **9 pi** for 9 picas (6 picas equal an inch). If you use the inch measurement system, the next time you open the Page Layout dialog box you see that your measurements have been converted back to the equivalent in inches.

Setting Different Margins for Different Parts of Your Document

To vary the margin settings in different parts of your document, you must divide the document into sections. You can create sections with unique margins in several ways. You can insert section breaks manually and then format the text between the breaks, or after a break, with different margin settings. Alternatively, you can choose File, Page Setup to apply margins to only the selected text or from the insertion point forward in your document. When necessary, Word inserts section breaks.

▶ See "Customizing Commonly Used Features," p. 1018

The Apply To list in the Page Setup dialog box, which determines where margins are applied, changes depending on two factors:

■ Whether your document is divided into sections

■ Whether you've selected text before choosing File, Page Setup

Word tries to apply your margin settings logically; for example, if your document is divided into sections and the insertion point is inside one of those sections when you set the margins, then in the Apply To list Word proposes applying those margin settings to This Section. You can select a different option in the list, however.

You learn more about creating sections later in this chapter in the section "Working with Sections in Your Document."

To set different margins for specific parts of your document, follow these steps:

1. Position the insertion point inside the section or sections for which you want to set margins.

   You can also select the text for which you want to set margins.

   Or, you can position the insertion point where you want new margins to begin in your document.

2. Choose File, Page Setup, and in the Page Setup dialog box, select the Margins tab.

3. Type or select Top, Bottom, Left, and Right margin amounts.

4. From the Apply To list, select the section to which you want to apply margins (choices on the list vary depending on the amount of text currently selected):

Option	Applies Margins To	When
This Section	Current section (No section break is inserted)	Insertion point is located within a section
Selected Sections	Multiple sections (No section breaks are inserted)	At least part of more than one section is selected
This Point Forward	Insertion point (Inserts new-page section break at insertion point)	Insertion point is where you want new margin to start
Selected Text	Selected text (Inserts new-page section breaks at beginning and end of text)	Text is selected

Option	Applies Margins To	When
Whole Document	Entire document (No section breaks inserted)	Insertion point is anywhere

   5. Choose OK.

Creating Facing Pages and Gutters

Facing pages in a document are the left and right pages of a double-sided document, as in a book or magazine. You can set up your document for facing pages by selecting the Mirror Margins check box in the Page Setup dialog box (see fig. 13.3). When you do, you no longer have left and right margins; instead, you have inside and outside margins. Facing pages are ideal when you plan to print your document on both sides of the paper and want wider margins on the inside than on the outside edges.

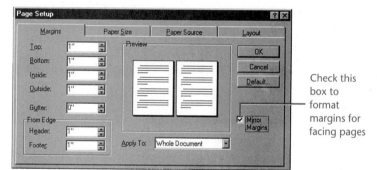

Check this box to format margins for facing pages

Fig. 13.3
When you select Mirror Margins, you create facing pages with inside and outside margins, rather than left and right margins.

With facing pages, you can have different headers and footers on each page and can position page numbers on opposite sides of the facing pages. In a newsletter footer, for example, you may want to position page numbers below the outside margins and the date below the inside margins.

Like margins, facing pages apply to sections. You can insert section breaks before you select facing pages, or you can create sections as part of the process. (For details, see "Setting Different Margins for Different Parts of Your Document" earlier in this chapter.)

To create facing pages, follow these steps:

   1. Position the insertion point or select the text where you want facing pages.

Formatting Documents

2. Choose File, Page Setup and select the Margins tab.

3. Select the Mirror Margins check box.

4. Choose OK.

Adding Extra Margin Space in Gutters

Whether you're working with normal pages that have left and right margins or facing pages that have inside and outside (mirror) margins, you can add a *gutter* to leave extra space for binding. A gutter on normal pages adds space at the left edge of the page; a gutter on facing pages adds space at the inside edges of each page. To leave an extra half-inch for binding, for example, include a gutter of 0.5". A gutter doesn't change your document's margins, but it does reduce the printing area.

Like margins, gutters apply to sections. You can insert section breaks before you select gutters, or you can create sections as part of the process. (For details, see "Setting Different Margins for Different Parts of Your Document" earlier in this chapter.)

To set a gutter, follow these steps:

1. Position the insertion point, or select the text where you want a gutter.

2. Choose File, Page Setup and select the Margins tab.

3. Select Gutter and type or select the amount by which you want to increase the left margin (if you have left and right margins) or the inside margin (if you select Mirror Margins so that you have inside and outside margins). The Preview box shows a shaded area where the gutter appears (see fig. 13.4).

4. Choose OK.

Fig. 13.4

Gutters appear as a shaded area in the Preview box.

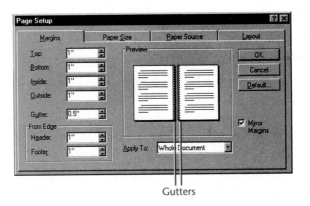

Gutters

Setting Margins Visually

A quick way to set margins for your document or for a section in your document is to click the ruler.

You must display a ruler to set margins with a mouse. In Page Layout or Print Preview view, Word has two rulers:

- A horizontal ruler, which appears at the top of your document and can be used to set left and right (or inside and outside) margins

- A vertical ruler, which appears at the left side of your document and can be used to set top and bottom margins (see fig. 13.5)

On each ruler is a gray area and a white area. The gray area indicates the margins; the white area indicates the space between the margins. The line where the gray and the white areas connect is the *margin boundary*. You can drag the margin boundaries on either ruler to change the margins for the currently selected section or sections. To make the left margin smaller, for example, you can drag the left margin boundary toward the left edge of the page.

Tip

Only the horizontal ruler is available in Normal view.

II

Formatting Documents

Margin boundaries   Horizontal ruler

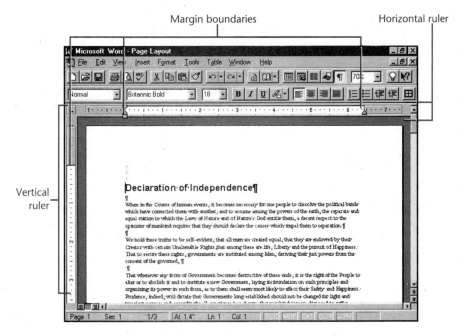

Vertical ruler

Fig. 13.5

You can set left and right (or inside and outside) margins with the horizontal ruler, and you can set top and bottom margins with the vertical ruler.

The ruler doesn't insert any section breaks into your document; it sets the margins for the entire document or for the section containing the insertion point. If you want to use the ruler to create margins for multiple sections in your document, insert section breaks before you begin. Then you can select the sections and use the ruler to change their margins.

Tip

Choose File, Page Setup if you want to change margins in the Outline or Master Document view.

◄ See "Setting
Indents,"
p. 306

If you want to change the margins for just one or a few paragraphs, use indents instead of the ruler. Use the ruler to change margins only when you want to change margins for the entire document or for a large section.

To change margins with a ruler, follow these steps:

1. If the ruler is not displayed, choose <u>V</u>iew, <u>R</u>uler. Switch to Page Layout view by clicking the appropriate icon at the left edge of the horizontal scroll bar or by choosing <u>V</u>iew, <u>P</u>age Layout. If you don't see the vertical ruler in Page Layout view, choose <u>T</u>ools, <u>O</u>ptions, then select the View tab, and in the Window group select the Vertical R<u>u</u>ler option.

> **Note**
>
> In Print Preview view, click the Ruler button to display rulers.

2. Position the mouse pointer between the indent markers of the margin boundary that you want to change. When the arrow turns into a two-headed arrow, you can drag the boundary (see fig. 13.6).

Fig. 13.6
When you see a two-headed arrow, you are ready to drag the margin boundary. (A one-headed arrow drags indents rather than margin boundaries.)

Two-headed arrow

> **Caution**
>
> You must see the two-headed arrow so that you can drag the margin boundaries on the ruler. If you see the one-headed mouse arrow, you're pointing to something other than the margin boundary—probably an indent marker. At the left margin boundary, for example, if you haven't set indents for your document, the indent markers are right on top of the margin boundary. If you move the mouse arrow so that it is between the indent markers, it turns into the two-headed margin boundary arrow.

Tip
You can hold down the Alt key as you drag a margin boundary to see margin measurements in the ruler.

3. Drag the margin boundary toward the edge of the page to make the margin smaller or toward the center of the page to make the margin wider. A dotted line on your document shows you where the new margin will appear (see fig. 13.7).

   If you change your mind about dragging a margin, you can cancel your change by pressing Esc before you release the mouse button, by choosing Edit, Underline Formatting, or by clicking the Undo button after you release the mouse button.

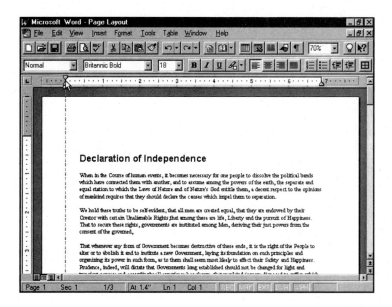

Fig. 13.7
You can drag margin boundaries to make your margins narrower or wider.

> **Note**
>
> If your document has facing pages (mirror margins), display multiple pages in Print Preview view so that you can see the effect of any change you make to the inside margins. If you change the inside margin on one page, all pages in the section reflect that change.

Aligning Text Vertically

Text is normally aligned to the top margin in your document. But you may want to align it differently—in the center of the page or justified on the page (see fig. 13.8). When you justify text, the paragraphs (not the lines within paragraphs) on the page are spread evenly between the top and bottom margins.

Text alignment applies to sections (you learn more about sections in "Working with Sections in Your Document," later in this chapter). If you haven't divided your document into sections, it applies to the entire document. If text fills each page, changing its vertical alignment does not make much difference; reserve this technique for pages that are not full or for sections that are less than a page in length.

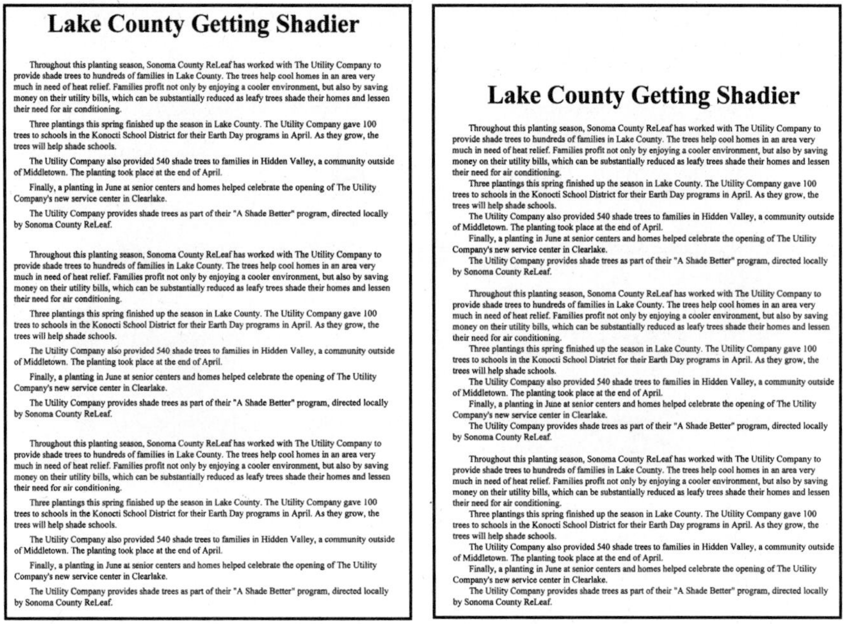

Fig. 13.8

You can align text in the center of the page or justified, both of which appear like normal top alignment when you have a full page of text.

To vertically align text on the page, follow these steps:

1. Position the insertion point inside the section where you want to align text.

2. Choose File, Page Setup. The Page Setup dialog box appears.

3. Select the Layout tab.

4. In the Vertical Alignment list, select Center to center text on the page.

   You can also select Justified to spread paragraphs between the top and bottom margins.

   Or, you can select Top to align text to the top margin.

5. Choose OK.

Controlling Where Paragraphs and Pages Break

As you type your document, Word automatically breaks text at the bottom margin of each page. Text continues on the next page, unless you specify otherwise. Word determines how much text appears on a page based on many factors, including margins, type size, paragraph specifications, and the size of footnotes. Displaying hidden text and field codes also can affect page breaks—hide them to see accurately how your pages will break.

You have many ways to control how text breaks on a page. You can specify that paragraphs stay together, for example, or with other paragraphs. You can also specify at which line a page will break.

Controlling Paragraph Breaks

By default, paragraphs break at the bottom margin of a page and continue at the top margin of the next page. Many times you want to prevent paragraphs from breaking arbitrarily at the bottom of the page. You may want to keep a heading paragraph together with the paragraph that follows it, for example. Or you may want certain paragraphs not to break at all. You may want to avoid *widows* and *orphans*, single lines of text that appear at the top or bottom of the page.

Regardless of how you format paragraphs to control paragraph breaks, hard page breaks that you insert manually take precedence. If you format a paragraph to stay together on a page but insert a hard page break inside the paragraph, for example, the paragraph always breaks at the line containing the hard page break. You must remove the hard page break if you want the paragraph to stay together (see the next section).

To control paragraph breaks, follow these steps:

1. Position the insertion point inside the paragraph you want to affect.

2. Choose Format, Paragraph. The Paragraph dialog box appears (see fig. 13.9).

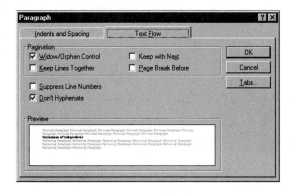

Fig. 13.9
In the Paragraph dialog box, you can control how paragraphs break— or don't break—at the bottom of a page.

3. Select the Text Flow tab.

4. Select the following options you want from the Pagination group:

Select This Option	To Get This Result
Widow/Orphan Control	Prevents single lines in selected paragraphs from appearing alone at the top or bottom of a page.
Keep Lines Together	Prevents a page break inside a selected paragraph. Moves the paragraph to next page if there's not room on current page for all of it.
Keep with Next	Ensures that the selected paragraph always appears on the same page as the next paragraph. Moves the paragraph to the next page if there's not room on the current page for it and the next paragraph.
Page Break Before	Starts the selected paragraph at the top of the next page. Inserts a page break before selected paragraph.

5. Choose OK.

A nonprinting square selection handle appears in the left margin next to any paragraph for which you've selected a pagination option. If text breaks on the page in a way you don't like, look for these squares to see whether the page break is caused by a pagination option. If it is, you can remove it by following the preceding steps and deselecting the offending pagination option.

Inserting Page Breaks

Word inserts soft page breaks at the end of every page and adjusts them as necessary when you edit, add, or remove text. If you want to force a page to break at a particular place in your document, you can insert a hard page break. Word always starts text following a hard page break at the top of the next page.

In Normal view, a soft page break appears as a dotted line; in Page Layout or Print Preview view, you see the page as it will print. In Outline view, you don't see soft page breaks. Hard page breaks appear in the Normal and Outline views as a dotted line containing the words `Page Break`; they appear this way in the Page Layout and Master Document views when you display nonprinting characters.

Note

Hard page breaks take priority over paragraph pagination options.

After you insert a hard page break, you can delete it, move it, copy it, or paste it.

You can insert a hard page break by using a command or a keyboard shortcut. You also can insert a page break by inserting a section break that begins on the next page, or on the next odd- or even-numbered page; see "Working with Sections in Your Document" later in this chapter. To insert a hard page break, follow these steps:

1. Position the insertion point at the beginning of the text that you want to start on a new page.

2. Choose Insert, Break. The Break dialog box appears (see fig. 13.10).

Fig. 13.10
In the Break dialog box, you can insert a hard page break by selecting the Page Break option.

3. Select Page Break.

4. Choose OK.

Tip
To insert a hard page break using a keyboard shortcut, press Ctrl+Enter

Working with Sections in Your Document

In early word processing programs, many formatting choices—margins, columns, headers and footers, line numbers, page numbers, and footnotes—applied to the entire document. Word for Windows, however, offers a way to divide your document into *sections*, each of which you can format differently. Each section is like a document within a document.

Sections are especially important in creating two types of documents: those with chapters, and those that fall into the desktop publishing category. Sections are useful for chapters because you can force a section to start on a right-facing page (as most chapters do) and change headers, footers, page numbers, line numbering, and so on for each chapter. Sections also are indispensable for desktop publishing, where you often need to vary the number of columns on a single page.

Dividing a Document into Sections

◀ See "Creating Columns," p. 380

◀ See "Changing Columns," p. 390

By default, a document contains only a single section. Section breaks divide your document into sections. The breaks appear as double-dotted lines containing the words End of Section in Normal view. You'll see section breaks in Page Layout view if all nonprinting characters are displayed (see fig. 13.11). (You can display nonprinting characters by choosing Tools, Options, selecting the View tab, and then selecting All.) The dotted lines do not print.

Fig. 13.11

Section breaks appear as a double-dotted line in Normal view and in Page Layout view when all nonprinting characters are displayed.

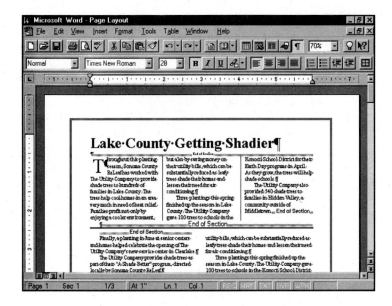

▶ See "Hints on Creating the Desktop Publishing Examples in This Chapter," p. 1111

▶ See "Laying Out the Page," p. 1083

A *section break* marks the point in your document where new formatting begins. In a newsletter, for example, a section break often follows the title, so that a multiple-column format can begin. The text following the section break, along with its new formatting, can begin in your document immediately, on the next page, or on the next even-numbered or odd-numbered page. You determine where the new section formatting begins when you insert the section break.

To insert a section break, follow these steps:

1. Position the insertion point where you want the section break.

2. Choose Insert, Break. The Break dialog box appears (refer to fig. 13.10).

3. Select from the following Section Breaks options:

Option	Section Starts
Next Page	Top of the next page in document
Continuous	Insertion point (causing no apparent break in the document)
Even Page	Next even-numbered page in the document (generally a left-facing page)
Odd Page	Next odd-numbered page in the document (generally a right-facing page)

4. Choose OK.

Use the Next Page section break when you want the new section to begin on the next page. Use the Continuous section break when you want the new section to begin at the insertion point; for example, when you create a newsletter that has different-width columns on the same page (such as a full-width title followed by a three-column story). Another use for the Continuous section break is to balance columns on a page: insert a Continuous section break at the end of a document that is divided into columns but that doesn't fill the last column of the last page.

Use the Odd Page section break for chapters when you want them to start always on a right-facing page (assuming page numbering in your document starts with page 1 on a right-facing page).

Use the Even Page section break to start a section on the next even-numbered page; on facing page layouts with mirror margins, even-numbered pages usually are on the left side of the layout.

Word for Windows inserts section breaks for you on some occasions. When you format a document for columns and specify that the columns take effect from This Point Forward, Word inserts a continuous section break at the insertion point. When you select text and format it for columns, Word inserts continuous section breaks both before and after the selected text. The same rule holds true when you make many page setup selections.

◀ See "Creating Columns," p. 380

Removing Section Breaks

In the same way that paragraph marks store paragraph formatting, section break marks store section formatting. Although you can remove a section break easily, remember that when you do, you also remove all section formatting for the section that precedes the deleted break. The preceding section merges with the following section and takes on its formatting characteristics.

If you accidentally delete a section break marker, immediately choose Edit, Undo to retrieve the marker.

To remove a section break, position the insertion point on the section break and press the Delete key. As alternatives, you can position the insertion point just after the section break marker and press Backspace; you can select the section break and click the Cut button or choose Edit, Cut.

To remove all the section breaks in your document, follow these steps:

1. Choose Edit, Replace.

2. Select Find What, and in the Special list, choose Section Break.

3. Make sure that the Replace With box contains no text, and choose Replace All.

4. Choose Close.

Copying Section Formatting

The section break stores section formatting. You can duplicate (or apply) section formatting quickly by selecting, copying, and then pasting the section break elsewhere. After you paste the section break, the preceding text takes on the formatting of the copied section break.

Another way to duplicate section formatting is to copy and store a section break as AutoText. That way, the break becomes available in all new documents and can be applied quickly and easily.

◀ See "Creating a New Template," p. 188

◀ See "Changing a Template," p. 186

A final way to duplicate section formatting is to include the formatting in a template—even the Normal template. Remember that by default, a new document includes only one section. That section carries certain default formatting characteristics: one column, a half-inch space between columns (if columns are selected), and no line numbers. If you always format sections differently, modify the Normal template or create a new template that includes your own custom section formatting selections.

Changing the Section Break Type

If you insert a continuous section break and want to change it to a new page section break, you must delete the existing section break and insert a new one. If you want to make this change without removing the previous section's formatting, insert the new section break after the old one and then delete the old page break.

Finding Section Breaks

If you want to find section breaks, choose Edit, Find. Next, select Special, and then select Section Break. Choose Find Next to find the next section break. You can find section breaks this way even if they are not displayed.

You can choose Edit, Replace to find a section break and replace it with some-thing else, but you cannot replace something with a section break. Use this technique if you want to remove all the section breaks in your document: simply replace section breaks with nothing.

◀ See "Using Find and Replace," p. 197

Creating Headers and Footers

Headers and footers contain information repeated at the top or bottom of the pages of a document. The simplest header or footer may contain only a chap-ter title and page number. More elaborate headers or footers may contain a company logo (or other graphic), the author's name, the time and date the file was saved or printed, and any other information that may be needed.

You can format headers and footers like any other part of the document, but you usually position them within a page's top and bottom margins, although Word for Windows enables you to position them anywhere on the page.

Word for Windows also gives you the option of having a different header or footer on the first page of a document or section. You also can have different headers and footers on even and odd pages. This feature is useful for chapter headers in books and manuscripts. Each section of a document—a chapter, for example—can have its own headers and footers.

When you create and edit headers and footers, Word switches you to Page Layout view and displays headers and footers at the top or bottom of the page, just as they appear when you print your document.

Adding Headers and Footers

When you add headers and footers, Word switches to Page Layout view, acti-vates a pane where you can create your header, displays a special Header and Footer toolbar, and dims the text of your document so that you can't edit it (see fig. 13.12).

You create your header or footer inside the pane, and you can edit and for-mat it the same way you do any text. After you finish creating the header or footer, close the Header and Footer toolbar. You can move the Header and Footer toolbar by dragging it to a different position on the page.

Fig. 13.12
You create headers
and footers in a
special pane.

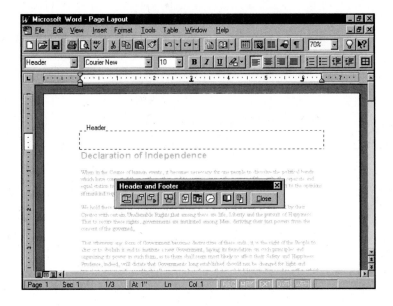

You can include text or graphics, or both, in a header or footer. If you want, you can insert page numbers, date and time, fields, symbols, cross-references, files, frames, pictures, objects, or a database. Or you can draw a picture using buttons on the Drawing toolbar.

Buttons on the toolbar aid you in creating your header or footer (see fig. 13.13). If the status bar is visible at the bottom of your screen, you can display a message explaining each button by pausing the mouse pointer over the button.

Fig. 13.13
Create a header or
footer using the
buttons in the
Header and Footer
toolbar.

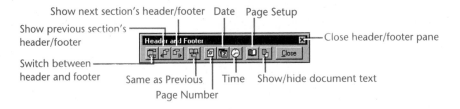

In Page Layout view, your document appears grayed when you're creating or editing headers or footers; headers and footers appear grayed when you're working on your document. To see both your document and its headers and footers, choose File, Print Preview.

To add a header or footer to your document, follow these steps:

1. Choose View, Header and Footer.

2. Type and format the text of your header. Click the Page Number, Date, and/or Time buttons to quickly add those elements to your header.

3. Click the Switch Between button to display the footer, and type and format just as you did the header (see step 2). Alternatively, use the scroll bars or press Page Up or Page Down to scroll to the footer.

4. Choose Close or double-click your document to close the header or footer pane and return to your document.

Another way to include an automatic date or time in a header or footer is to insert a date or time field by choosing Insert, Field. Using this command, you can select among different formatting options for your date or time.

If your header or footer is larger than your margin, Word adjusts the margins of your document to make room. If you don't want Word to adjust your margins, make your header or footer smaller or move it closer to the edge of the page (see "Positioning Headers and Footers," later in this chapter). If you want text to overlap a header or footer (as you might if the header or footer is a graphic that is to appear behind text), type a minus sign (–) in front of your margin measurement. If your header is four inches high, for example, and you want a top margin of one inch, and you want the text to overlap the header, type **–1"** as your top margin. You can use this technique to create a "watermark" that appears behind the text on every page of your document.

▶ See "Formatting Date-Time Results," p. 610

Varying Headers and Footers within a Single Document

Each section in a document can have unique headers and footers. This setup is helpful if you format each chapter in a book as a separate section. Or you can create different headers and footers on odd and even pages. You also can have a different header or footer on the first page of a document. If your document has facing pages and mirror margins, for example, you might want a right-aligned header on odd-numbered pages (which appear on the right side of a facing-page layout) and a left-aligned header on even-numbered pages (which appear on the left). In a newsletter, you might want no header on the first page.

Changing Headers and Footers for Specific Sections

When you first create headers and footers, Word applies them to all the sections in your document. That way, all the headers and footers in your document are the same. Similarly, if you divide into sections a document with existing headers or footers, the headers and footers are the same in all sections.

If you want a different header or footer in a section, you must go to that section and unlink the existing header or footer; then you must create the new header or footer. The new header or footer applies to the current section and to all following sections. Later, if you decide you want your new header or footer to be the same as the previous header or footer, you can relink it.

Tip
As a shortcut, activate a header or footer by double-clicking it in Page Layout view.

If you want different headers and footers in different sections of your document, you first must divide your document into sections. To learn how, see "Working with Sections in Your Document" earlier in this chapter. To change the header or footer in one section of your document, follow these steps:

1. Position the insertion point inside the section where you want to change the header or footer.

2. Choose View, Header and Footer. Word selects the header for the section in which you're located. If you want to change the footer for that section, click the Switch Between Header and Footer button instead.

3. To unlink the header or footer, click the Same as Previous button. The Same as Previous line disappears from the top right of the header or footer editing pane.

4. Create the new header or footer.

5. Choose the Close button or double-click your document to close the Header and Footer toolbar.

You also can click the Show Next button to change the header or footer in the following section.

The new header or footer applies to the current section and to all following sections.

As an alternative to steps 1 and 2, you can choose View, Header and Footer from within any section to activate headers and footers. Then click the Switch Between Header and Footer button to jump between headers and footers, or click the Show Next or Show Previous buttons to activate headers or footers in a different section.

To relink a different header or footer to the previous header or footer, follow
these steps:

1. Position the insertion point inside the section containing the header or
   footer you want to relink.

2. Choose <u>V</u>iew, <u>H</u>eader and Footer. Word selects the header for the section in which you're located. If you want to change the footer for that
   section, click the Switch Between Header and Footer button.

3. To relink the header or footer, click the Same as Previous button. Word
   displays a message box asking whether you want to delete the header/
   footer and connect to the header/footer in the previous section.

4. Choose <u>Y</u>es.

5. Choose <u>C</u>lose, or double-click your document to close the Header and
   Footer toolbar.

By relinking the header or footer to the previous header or footer, you change
not only the current header or footer, but also those in all the following
sections.

> **Caution**
>
> If you change one header or footer without unlinking it, all the headers and footers in
> all the sections change.

To make headers and footers different in all the sections, follow these steps:

1. Position the insertion point in the first section.

2. Choose <u>V</u>iew, <u>H</u>eader and Footer. Word selects the header for the first
   section. If you want to change the footer, click the Switch Between
   Header and Footer button.

3. Create the header or footer you want for the first section.

4. Click the Show Next button to move to the header or footer for the
   second section.

5. Click the Same as Previous button.

6. Create the header or footer you want for the second section.

7. Continue clicking the Show Next button to move to the header or
   footer for the next section, clicking the Same as Previous button to

unlink that section from the previous section, and creating the new header or footer you want.

8. After you create headers and footers for all the sections, choose <u>C</u>lose.

Creating Special First-Page and Odd/Even Page Headers and Footers

Many documents have a different header or footer on the first page—or have no header or footer on the first page. In Word, first-page headers and footers apply to sections, not to the whole document. That way, you can have a different header or footer at the beginning of each section in a document that is divided into sections.

Sometimes you want different headers and footers for the odd- and even-numbered pages in your document. In a document with facing pages (mirror margins), odd-numbered pages appear on the right side and even-numbered pages appear on the left side. You might want left-aligned headers on even-numbered pages and right-aligned headers on odd-numbered pages so that headers always appear on the outside edges of your document.

To specify special headers and footers for first pages or odd and even pages in your document, follow these steps:

1. Choose <u>V</u>iew, <u>H</u>eader and Footer.

2. Click the Show Previous or Show Next button to locate the section in which you want a different first-page header or footer.

3. Click the Page Setup button (or choose <u>F</u>ile, Page Set<u>u</u>p) to display the Page Setup dialog box.

4. Select the Layout tab.

5. In the Headers and Footers group, select Different <u>F</u>irst Page to create specific first page headers or footers, and then choose OK. The header or footer editing pane for the section you're in is titled First Page Header or First Page Footer.

Or, in the Headers and Footers group, select Different <u>O</u>dd and Even and choose OK. The header or footer editing box for the section you're in is titled Even Page Header, Even Page Footer, Odd Page Header, or Odd Page Footer.

6. If you want no header or footer, leave the header or footer editing area blank. If you want a different header or footer on the first page or odd/even pages of the section, create it now.

7. Choose Close or double-click your document.

To remove first-page headers and footers from a section or document, follow these steps:

1. Position the insertion point anywhere inside a document containing only one section.

You can also position the insertion point inside the section for which you want to remove first-page headers and footers.

2. Choose File, Page Setup.

3. Select the Layout tab.

4. Deselect the Different First Page option in the Headers and Footers group.

5. Choose OK.

Positioning Headers and Footers

By default, headers and footers appear one-half inch from the top or bottom edge of the document page. You can change that distance in the Header and Footer view.

To determine a header's or footer's distance from the edge of the paper, follow these steps:

1. Choose View, Header and Footer.

2. Click the Show Previous or Show Next button to locate the section containing the header or footer you want to affect.

3. Click the Page Setup button (or choose File, Page Setup) to display the Page Setup dialog box.

4. Select the Margins tab.

5. In the From Edge group, select Header and type or select the distance that you want your header from the top edge of the page.

Or, select Footer and type or select the distance that you want your footer from the bottom edge of the page.

6. Choose OK to close the Page Setup dialog box.

7. Choose Close or double-click your document to return to it.

Tip
Remember that most printers have a quarter-inch nonprinting edge on all sides.

As an alternative, you can position the insertion point inside the section containing the header or footer you want to affect, then choose File, Page Setup, select the Margins tab, set the distances you want, and choose OK.

Formatting Headers and Footers

Anything you can do to or in regular text, you can do to a header or footer. You can change the font, reduce or enlarge the size of the text, insert graphics, draw pictures, include a table, add a line or box, or add shading. You also can add tabs, change the alignment or indents, or change line or paragraph spacing. Use any of Word's formatting techniques to make headers and footers look distinct from the text in your document.

◄ See "Formatting Characters," p. 254

◄ See "Changing Fonts," p. 263

◄ See "Shading and Bordering Paragraphs," p. 323

You can use most of the commands in the Insert, Format, Tools, and Table menus to format headers and footers. You can use the ruler to set tabs and indents.

Editing Headers and Footers

In Normal view, you can't see headers or footers. In Page Layout view, you can see headers and footers, but they appear dimmed. In any view, you must activate a header or footer to edit it. You can activate a header or footer using the same command you used to create it, or in Page Layout view, you can double-click a header or footer to activate it. After it is activated, you edit the header or footer using the same commands you used to create it.

If your document contains only one section, the headers and footers are the same throughout your document, and you can edit headers and footers with the insertion point anywhere within the document. If your document contains multiple sections with different headers and footers, you must locate the header or footer you want to edit. You can do that two ways:

■ Activate headers and footers and then use the Show Previous and Show Next buttons on the Header and Footer toolbar to move between sections.

■ First locate the header or footer you want to edit and then activate it.

To edit headers and footers, follow these steps:

1. Choose View, Header and Footer. Word activates the header for the section containing the insertion point. Or, in Page Layout view, double-click the header or footer you want to edit.

2. To edit a footer rather than a header, click the Switch Between Header and Footer button or press Page Down to scroll to the bottom of the page.

3. To locate a header or footer in a different section of your document, click the Show Previous or the Show Next button.

4. After you locate the header or footer you want to edit, make the changes you want.

5. Choose <u>C</u>lose or double-click the document.

You can delete a header or footer by activating it, selecting all the text or objects contained in the header or footer, pressing Delete, and then choosing <u>C</u>lose.

Hiding the Text Layer

Normally, the text layer appears dimmed while you're working on headers and footers. If you want to hide it altogether, you can click a special button on the Header and Footer toolbar. Text is only hidden while you're working on the header or footer.

To hide or display the text layer, follow these steps:

1. Activate headers and footers by choosing <u>V</u>iew, <u>H</u>eader and Footer or by double-clicking an existing header or footer in Page Layout view.

2. Click the Show/Hide Document Text button. The text (grayed already), disappears from your screen. Click the button a second time to display the text.

3. Choose <u>C</u>lose or double-click your document to return to it.

Working with Page Numbers

Long documents are easier to read and reference when the pages are numbered. In Word for Windows, you can insert a page number quickly, and Word formats it as a header or footer for you. That way, you can use all the techniques for working with headers and footers to work with page numbers. See "Creating Headers and Footers" earlier in this chapter.

Inserting Page Numbers

Page numbers can appear at the top or bottom of the page and can be aligned to the center or either side of the page. When you insert a page number, Word for Windows includes a PAGE field and frames the page number. That way, you can move the number anywhere within the header or footer.

Another way to include page numbers is to insert them as part of creating a header or footer by clicking the Page Numbers button on the Header and Footer toolbar. This technique is the best if you want to include text with your page number.

▶ See "Inserting Field Codes," p. 597

To insert page numbers, follow these steps:

1. Choose Insert, Page Numbers. The Page Numbers dialog box appears (see fig. 13.14).

Fig. 13.14
Using the Page Numbers dialog box, you can include page numbers at the top or bottom of the page, in any alignment. You can choose whether to show them on the first page of your document.

2. In the Position drop-down list, select Bottom of Page (Footer) to position your page number at the bottom of the page as a footer, or choose Top of Page (Header) to position your page number at the top of the page as a header.

3. In the Alignment drop-down list, select Left, Center, Right, Inside, or Outside to line up your page number to the center or one side of the page.

4. Select Show Number of First Page if you want a page number to appear on the first page of your document. Deselect this option to prevent the page number from appearing on the first page.

5. Choose OK.

▶ See "Moving a Frame with a Mouse," p. 739

To reposition page numbers, choose Insert, Page Numbers and choose a different option from the Alignment list. Alternatively, in Page Layout view, double-click the page number to activate the Header or Footer editing pane. Select the page number and drag it to a new position (or select the frame and reposition it by choosing Format, Frame and making selections from the Frame dialog box). Then choose Close.

Removing Page Numbers

Because page numbers appear within headers or footers, to remove them you must activate the header or footer, select the page number, and delete it.

To remove page numbers, follow these steps:

1. In Page Layout view, double-click the page number.

   You can also choose <u>V</u>iew, <u>H</u>eader and Footer and click the Switch Between Header and Footer, Show Next, or Show Previous button to locate the page number.

2. Select the page number.

3. Press Delete.

4. Choose <u>C</u>lose or double-click your document.

Formatting Page Numbers

You can format your page numbers in a variety of ways. They can appear as numbers, uppercase or lowercase letters, or uppercase or lowercase roman numerals.

You can include chapter numbers if your document's chapter numbers are formatted with Word for Windows' default heading styles (Heading 1 through Heading 9) and if you've numbered the headings by choosing <u>Fo</u>rmat, <u>H</u>eading Numbering and making a selection from the Heading Numbering dialog box. If you include chapter numbers, you can separate them from the page numbers with a hyphen, a period, a colon, or a — (a wide hyphen).

You can format page numbers at the same time that you insert them, or you can format them later. To format page numbers, follow these steps:

▶ See "Creating Numbered Headings," p. 566

1. If you're creating new page numbers, choose <u>I</u>nsert, Page N<u>u</u>mbers. Make selections from the <u>P</u>osition and <u>A</u>lignment drop-down lists.

   If you want to format existing page numbers for a single section, you can also position the insertion point inside that section and choose <u>I</u>nsert, Page N<u>u</u>mbers.

2. Click the <u>F</u>ormat button. The Page Number Format dialog box appears (see fig. 13.15).

3. In the Number <u>F</u>ormat drop-down list, select the style you want your numbers to be.

4. Select Include Chapter <u>N</u>umber if you want to include a chapter number before your page number. In the Chapter Starts with Style drop-down list, choose the style (Heading 1 through Heading 9) that you use for chapter numbers in your document.

Fig. 13.15
You can format your page numbers as you create them or after you've already created them.

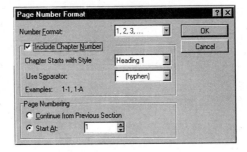

5. If you want a separator between the chapter number and page number, make a selection from the Use Separator drop-down list.

6. Choose OK.

Numbering Different Sections in a Document

Even if your document contains more than a single section, page numbering applies by default to your entire document, and numbers are continuous throughout the document. You can start page numbering at the number you specify in any section, however. You may want page numbering to restart at "1" for each section, for example.

To create page numbering by section, follow these steps:

1. If necessary, divide your document into sections by inserting section breaks.

2. Position the insertion point inside the section for which you want unique page numbering.

3. Unlink the header or footer from previous headers or footers (see the section "Varying Headers and Footers within a Single Document," earlier in this chapter).

4. Choose Insert, Page Numbers, and then choose Format.

5. In the Page Numbering group, select Start At and type or select the starting page number for the current section.

6. Choose OK to return to the Page Numbers dialog box; choose OK again to return to your document.

▶ See "Creating Numbered Headings," p. 566

If headers and footers containing page numbers are unlinked from previous sections but you want page numbering to be continuous from section to section, repeat the steps above, choosing Continue from the Previous Section in the Page Numbering Group. Finally, choose OK.

Repaginating in the Background

By default, Word for Windows automatically calculates page breaks as you work on your document. In the Normal, Outline, or Master Document view, you can turn off background pagination, but in Page Layout or Print Preview views, you cannot. You may see a slight performance improvement if you turn off background repagination.

To turn off background repagination, follow these steps:

1. Choose View, and then choose either Normal, Outline, or Master Document.

2. Choose Tools, Options, and select the General Tab.

3. Deselect the Background Repagination option.

4. Choose OK.

Inserting a Date and Time

In Word for Windows, there are several ways to insert the date and time automatically. You can use a command to insert the current date and time as frozen—that is, the date and time do not change—or you can insert them as a field that you can update to reflect the current date and time. You can choose among many different date and time formats. Or you can include a date and time field in a header or footer. These fields also update to reflect the current date or time.

To insert a date or time, follow these steps:

1. Position the insertion point where you want the date or time to appear. You can insert the date or time in your document or in a header or footer.

2. Choose Insert, Date and Time. The Date and Time dialog box appears (see fig. 13.16).

3. Choose the date and time format you want from the Available Formats list.

4. If you want the date and time to update to reflect the current date and time, select Update Automatically (Insert as Field).

5. Choose OK.

Tip
Word for Windows always repaginates when you print your document, switch to Page Layout or Print Preview view, or compile an index or table of contents.

Tip
Click the appropriate button on the horizontal scroll bar to switch to Normal or Outline view.

▶ See "Understanding the Basics of Fields," p. 589

▶ See "Inserting Field Codes," p. 597

Tip
To update a date or time field, select the field and press the F9 key. Date and time fields automatically update whenever you open or print a document if you set your options accordingly.

II

Formatting Documents

Fig. 13.16
Choose Insert,
Date and Time to
insert a date or
time.

Inserting Line Numbers

If a document is used for reference, it is helpful to readers if the lines are numbered. You can number lines in text that a class shares or in legal briefs, for example.

You can number some or all of the lines in a document. If your document contains no section breaks, line numbers apply to the entire document. If your document contains sections, line numbers apply to the currently selected section. If you select text before you assign line numbers, Word for Windows places page section breaks before and after the selected text, isolating it on a page (or pages) by itself. If you want to apply line numbers to an entire document that contains multiple sections, select the entire document before you apply the line numbers.

Word for Windows offers many options for controlling how line numbers appear. Numbers can start at 1 or some other number, and they can appear on each line or on only some lines. They can be continuous, or they can restart at each section or page. You can control the distance between text and the line numbers. You also can suppress line numbers for selected paragraphs.

Line numbers appear in the left margin of your page or to the left of text in columns.

To add and format line numbers, follow these steps:

1. Position the insertion point inside the section containing lines you want to number. (Position the insertion point anywhere inside a document that is not divided into sections.)

   You can also select the text whose lines you want to number.

   Or, you can select the entire document if it is divided into sections and you want line numbering for all the sections.

2. Choose File, Page Setup. The Page Setup dialog box appears.

3. Select the Layout tab.

4. Choose Line Numbers. The Line Numbers dialog box appears (see fig. 13.17).

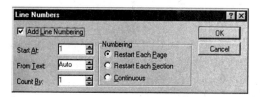

Fig. 13.17
Using the Line Numbers dialog box, you can number the lines of your text for easy reference.

5. Select Add Line Numbering.

6. Make changes to any of the following:

   Select Start At and type or select the starting line number.

   Select From Text and type the distance between the line numbers and text. (Be sure your margins are wide enough to accommodate this distance.)

   Select Count By and type or select the increment by which you want lines to be numbered. Select 3, for example, if you want every third line numbered.

7. In the Numbering group, select any of the following:

   Select Restart Each Page for numbering to start over on each page.

   Select Restart Each Section to start over in each section.

   Select Continuous if you want line numbers continuous throughout the document.

8. Choose OK. Choose OK again to close the Page Setup dialog box and return to your document.

To remove line numbers, follow these steps:

1. Follow steps 1-4 above.

2. Deselect the Add Line Numbering option.

3. Choose OK. Choose OK again to close the Page Setup dialog box.

II

Formatting Documents

To suppress line numbers, follow these steps:

1. Select the paragraphs where you don't want line numbers to appear.

2. Choose F̲ormat, P̲aragraph. The Paragraph dialog box appears.

3. Select the Text F̲low tab.

4. Select S̲uppress Line Numbers.

5. Choose OK.

Determining Paper Size and Orientation

You can change the paper size or orientation for your entire document or for part of your document. You may select a different paper size to create something smaller than usual, such as an invitation. You can select landscape (horizontal) orientation rather than the usual portrait (vertical) orientation to create a brochure or envelope.

Word for Windows offers several predefined paper sizes, including letter and legal. If none of these sizes suits your needs, you can select a custom size instead and enter your own measurements.

Tip

When you're changing paper size and orientation, you can insert a new-page section break to isolate the new section on a separate sheet of paper.

Paper size and orientation settings apply to the current section, just like margin settings. If you haven't divided your document into sections, your settings apply to the whole document, unless you choose to apply them to the currently selected text or from the insertion point forward in your document. If you apply settings to selected text, Word for Windows inserts a new-page section break before and after the selection. If you apply settings to the insertion point forward, Word for Windows inserts a new-page section break at the insertion point's current position.

To set paper size and orientation, follow these steps:

1. Select the text or section where you want to set paper size and orientation.

2. Choose F̲ile, Page Set̲up; in the Page Setup dialog box, select the Paper S̲ize tab (see fig. 13.18).

3. From the Pape̲r Size list, select a predefined paper size.

   In the W̲idth and H̲eight boxes, you can also type or select the width and height of your custom paper size.

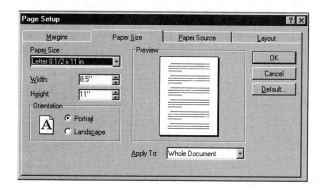

Fig. 13.18
You can select a preset or custom paper size, and you can choose the paper orientation—Portrait (vertical) or Landscape (horizontal).

4. For a vertical page, select Portrait from the Orientation group.

   Or, for a horizontal page, select Landscape from the Orientation group.

5. From the Apply To list, select the section to which you want to apply paper size and orientation settings. (For more information about the Apply To list, see "Setting Different Margins for Different Parts of Your Document" earlier in this chapter.)

6. Choose OK.

Note that if you create custom-size paper, the paper measurements you type are usually in inches, unless you change the default measurement system by choosing Tools, Options and then selecting the General tab. You can override the default inches by typing your measurement using text that describes a different measurement system. To set a paper width of 36 picas, for example, type **36 pi**; to set a paper height of 24 centimeters, type **24 cm**.

Selecting the Paper Source

In Word for Windows, you not only can alter margins, paper size, and paper orientation for your document or for a section of your document, but you also can specify where your printer finds the paper.

Many printers have different options for storing paper. Most laser printers, for example, have a default paper tray and a manual feed. You can specify that one section of your document be printed from the manual feed, whereas the rest of the document be printed from paper in the default paper tray. Some printers have two paper trays; you can specify that one section, such as the first page of a letter, be printed on letterhead in the first tray, whereas the remaining pages be printed on plain paper from the second tray.

As you can do with all page setup options, you can insert section breaks before you select paper source, or Word for Windows can insert section breaks for you.

To select a paper source for your document, follow these steps:

1. Position the insertion point inside the section for which you want to set the paper source. (The change applies to the entire document unless the document has multiple sections.)

   You can also select the section for which you want to set the paper source.

   Or, position the insertion point where you want the new paper source to begin in your document.

2. Choose File, Page Setup. In the Page Setup dialog box, select the Paper Source tab (see fig. 13.19).

Fig. 13.19
Using the Page Setup dialog box, you can print different sections of your document on paper from different sources.

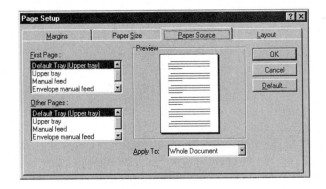

3. From the First Page list, select the paper source for the first page of your document.

4. From the Other Pages list, select the paper source for the remaining pages of your document.

5. From the Apply To drop-down list, select the section to which you want to apply paper source settings (the list displays different options, depending on how much text is selected in the document):

Option	Applies Margins To	When
This Section	Current section (No section break is inserted)	Insertion point is located within a section

Option	Applies Margins To	When
Selected Sections	Multiple sections (No section breaks are inserted)	At least part of more than one section is selected
This Point Forward	Insertion point (Inserts new-page section break at insertion point)	Insertion point is where you want new margin to start
Selected Text	Selected text (Inserts new-page section breaks at the beginning and end of text)	Text is selected
Whole Document	Entire document (No break inserted)	Insertion point is anywhere

6. Choose OK.

When you print a document with various paper sizes, orientations, or sources, your printer may pause at the end of each page and wait for you to indicate that it should continue. In some cases, you may need only to access the Print Manager and click Resume. In other cases, you may need to press a button on the printer. Newer laser printers work well with varying paper sizes and orientations, but if you experience difficulties, check your printer manual.

If you want to apply your paper source selections to the Normal template so that they become the default settings, choose the Default button before you choose OK.

Changing Page Setup Defaults

All new documents are based on a template, and unless you choose a different template, Word for Windows bases new documents on the Normal template, which contains default page setup choices. Because these default choices may not be exactly what you want, Word for Windows gives you the chance to change them—by applying your own page setup options to the Normal template and, thus, use your own page setup choices as defaults. You can change the default margins, for example, if you always print on paper that requires different margin settings than those supplied by the Normal template. You can change the paper size if you normally use paper different from standard letter size.

II

Formatting Documents

Tip
Be sure that you have installed the correct printer driver for your printer in Windows so that Word for Windows knows which paper trays your printer has available. Refer to your Windows book or printer manual for details.

◀ See "Setting Default Formats in the Normal Template," p. 187

You can change defaults for any option in the Page Setup dialog box. Then each new document you create based on the Normal template has your new defaults. (Your current document—or the text or section you've selected—also uses your new settings.)

To change the default page setup settings, follow these steps:

1. Choose File, Page Setup.

2. On each tab in the Page Setup dialog box, make the page setup selections you want.

3. Click the Default button on any of the tabs. A dialog box asks you to confirm that all new documents based on the Normal template are affected by the change.

4. Choose OK.

Part III

Creating Envelopes and Mailings

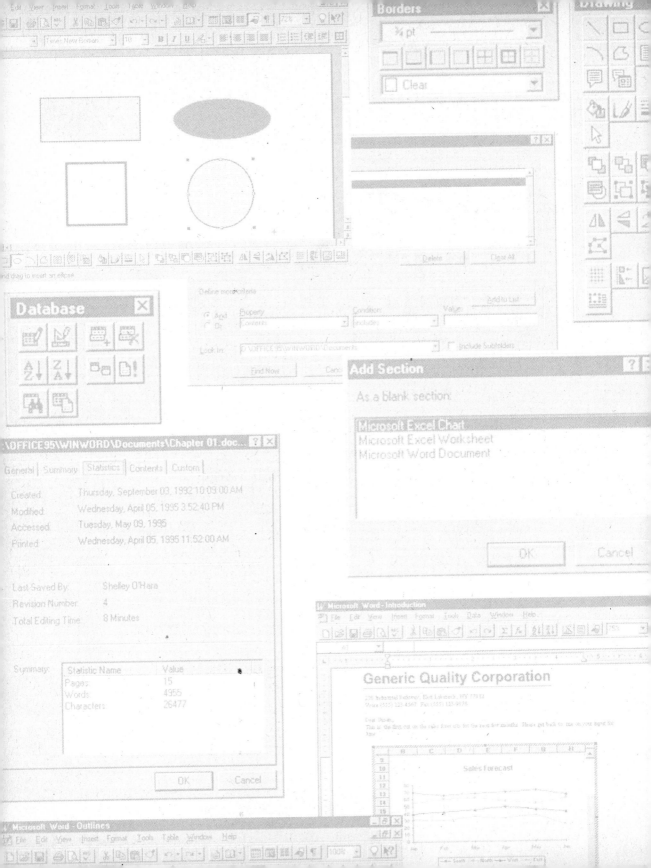

Chapter 14

Creating and Managing Data for Mail Merge

Word for Windows 95 does more than just publish text. Think of it as a report writer or publisher of database information as well. Word has the capability to retrieve, store, and manipulate rows of information such as names and addresses, billing information, invoice data, product catalog information, and so on. Some of the tasks that are commonly relegated to database report applications can be accomplished with Word, and Word can give you a more free-form, publishing-oriented result. For example, you can use data stored or linked into Word to create:

- *Form letters* using name and address information. Other information can be merged into the form letters such as amounts owed, product information, or notes.

- *Envelopes* to go with the form letters. Envelopes can be printed in sorted ZIP code order and include POSTNET and FIM bar codes to save you money.

- *Mailing labels* that even include logos, graphics, POSTNET, and FIM bar codes.

- *Product catalogs* that include graphics and a more professionally published appearance than what is normally produced from a database report.

- *Sales report data* in a more free-form layout. Word can publish data using features such as newspaper columns and integrated graphics that are not available in worksheets such as Excel or from database report writers.

In this chapter, you learn to do the following:

■ Create a new data document in Word

■ Retrieve an existing data file into Word or link a Word document to data located in an external database

■ Manage data through updating, sorting, finding, editing, and deleting

Understanding the Different Methods of Storing Data

There are three sources of data Word can use for a mail merge: a Word document, an external file, and shared office data.

A Word document can consist of a table containing rows and columns of information, as shown in figure 14.1. You can also use a tab or comma delimited Word document as your data source. Tab or comma delimited files can be created automatically from tables. For example, select the table you want to convert, choose Table, Convert Table to Text, select Tabs or Commas in the Convert Table To Text dialog box, then choose OK.

Fig. 14.1

A data source can be as simple as a table in Word containing rows and columns of information.

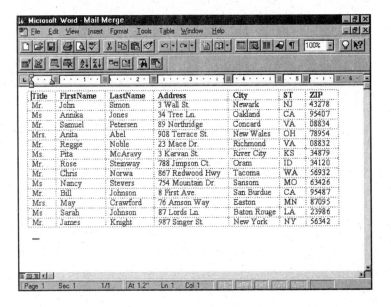

Title	FirstName	LastName	Address	City	ST	ZIP
Mr.	John	Simon	3 Wall St.	Newark	NJ	43278
Ms	Annika	Jones	34 Tree Ln.	Oakland	CA	95407
Mr.	Samuel	Petersen	89 Northridge	Concard	VA	08834
Mrs.	Anita	Abel	908 Terrace St.	New Wales	OH	78954
Mr.	Reggie	Noble	23 Mace Dr.	Richmond	VA	08832
Ms.	Pita	McAravy	3 Karvan St.	River City	KS	34879
Mr.	Rose	Steinway	788 Jimpson Ct.	Oram	ID	34120
Mr.	Chris	Norwa	867 Redwood Hwy	Tacoma	WA	56932
Ms	Nancy	Stevers	754 Mountain Dr.	Sansom	MO	63426
Mr.	Bill	Johnson	8 First Ave.	San Burdue	CA	95487
Mrs.	May	Crawford	76 Arnson Way	Easton	MN	87095
Ms	Sarah	Johnson	87 Lords Ln.	Baton Rouge	LA	23986
Mr.	James	Knight	987 Singer St.	New York	NY	56342

An external file can be a file imported from another application, or a database file that was created using Microsoft Access, Microsoft Excel, dBASE, Paradox, and so on. You can also use data from single-tier, file-based applications for applications where you have installed the appropriate ODBC driver. For more information about database files, see the upcoming section, "Inserting a Database from a File."

Shared office data refers to address books created in the Personal Address Book that is part of Word or in the address books available in other Microsoft applications such as Schedule+, the Postoffice Address List, and lists for Microsoft Network.

Managing Names and Addresses with Address Books

Managing a list of names and addresses is a simple task if you use an address book application such as the one in Schedule+ Personal Address Book that comes with Microsoft Office. After you have entered names and addresses, you can perform a number of tasks on the information. For example, you can edit, insert, delete, search, and sort the information.

Word 95 allows you to specify the address book in Schedule+ as the data source for a mail merge. Because many companies and individuals use Schedule+ to manage personal schedules, meeting rooms, and resources, it makes sense to use Schedule+ as your address book for names and contacts used by everyone in your workgroup. Names and contact information for your personal use can be stored in the Personal Address Book, described in the following section, "Using Addresses from the Personal Address Book."

Using Addresses from the Personal Address Book

Word comes with a built-in address book that is quickly accessible form the Standard toolbar. The address book stores information used to contact the person. The information can be telephone, fax, mailing addresses, network addresses, and so forth.

You can use the mailing address information from the Address Book to insert the name and address of a single person, or you can use it for mail merge when you need to address many documents.

III

Creating
Envelopes & Mailings

To enter data into Word's Address Book, follow these steps:

1. Click the Address button on the Standard toolbar to display the Select Name dialog box, shown in figure 14.2.

Fig. 14.2
Keep personal contact information in Word's Address Book. You can insert addresses or mail merge information stored in the Address Book.

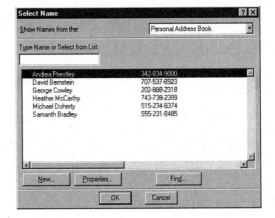

2. Click the New button to display the New Entry dialog box, shown in figure 14.3.

Fig. 14.3
You can choose the type of address information you want stored.

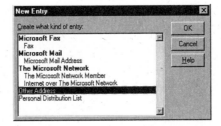

3. Select the way in which you prefer to send most messages to this person, then choose OK.

   In this example, the Other Address item is chosen to display the New Other Address Properties dialog box, shown in figure 14.4.

4. Type e-mail information in the New-Address tab. If you are not part of an e-mail system, you may need to enter fake information before switching to other tabs.

Click the Business, Phone Numbers, or Notes tab to enter other information about this person. Figure 14.5 shows the Business tab. Figure 14.6 shows the Phone Numbers tab.

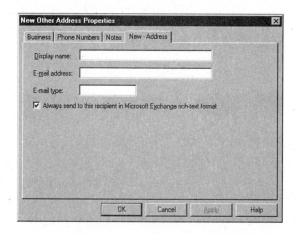

Fig. 14.4
The New Other Address Properties dialog box accepts information for the Address Book.

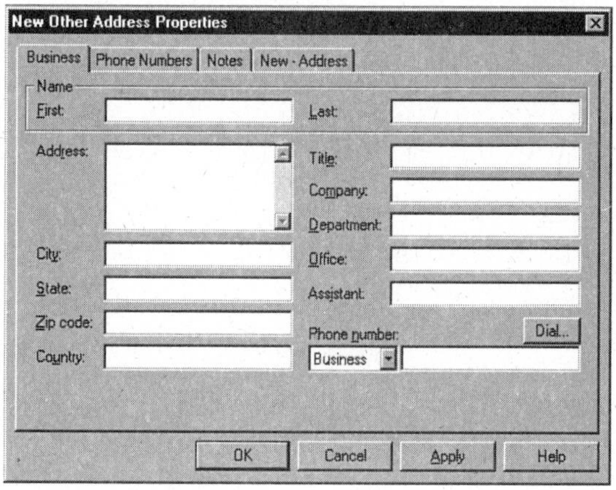

Fig. 14.5
The Business tab accepts address information you will need for mail merge documents.

5. Choose OK.

The information you have entered in your personal address book will be available to you when you want to paste a single name and address, or when you want to create multiple documents using mail merge.

Fig. 14.6
The Phone
Numbers tab
accepts alternate
phone numbers
for the person.

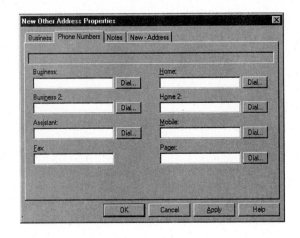

Tip
If the taskbar is
currently hidden,
move the pointer
to the bottom of
the screen and the
taskbar will ap-
pear, or press
Ctrl+Esc.

Using Addresses from Microsoft Schedule+

Microsoft Schedule+ is a useful scheduling program that you can use for your personal schedules and contact management, or that you can share in your workgroup. It even includes tips and a wizard on how to be more productive.

To enter information into the Schedule+ Address Book, follow these steps:

1. Click the Start button in the taskbar, then click Programs, Microsoft Word, and finally Schedule+.

2. If you are prompted, type your User Name and logon password in the Schedule+ Logon dialog box, and then choose OK. Schedule+ appears.

3. Click the Contacts tab to view the list of contacts to make changes or add new contacts. Figure 14.7 shows an example of a new Schedule+ address book.

4. In the edit boxes on the right side, type information you want stored in the Schedule+ Address Book.

The contact information you enter in the Schedule+ Address Book will be accessible in Word.

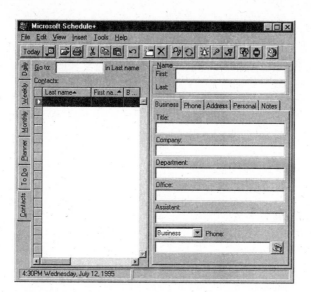

Fig. 14.7
Use the Microsoft
Schedule+ Address
Book to maintain
a list of your
contacts.

Creating Your Own Data Sources

The Mail Merge Helper allows you the flexibility to create your own data sources from a wide range of applications. You can create a data source from a Word document, spreadsheet application, database file, or some other external application. The obvious benefit to you is that you can create your data source in a familiar application and then use the data to create multiple documents in Word.

Managing Data

Word dialog boxes and the Mail Merge Helper refer to the object containing data as the *data source*. The data source can be on the same computer as Word and created in a personal computer such as a Word document, an Excel worksheet, or a dBASE file. The data source can also reside in another computer to which Word is linked via a network. The other computer can contain a large database application, such as Oracle or SQL Server. Word can retrieve just the part of the database it needs from these larger databases.

Information stored in the data source is normally laid out in a table format of rows and columns. Each row of information is known as a *record*. If the data source contains the names and addresses of clients, a record contains each individual's name, address, and specific client information. In this case, one record of information is like a card in a card file. Each row in a data source ends with a paragraph mark.

III

Creating
Envelopes & Mailings

Information is arranged within records by columns. These columns are known as *fields*. Each field, or column, contains one specific type of information. For example, the name and address data source might need one field for state and another for ZIP code. A *delimiter* separates each field of data. Delimiters that Word understands are commas, tabs, or separate cells in a table. If a record contains more than 31 fields, then Word cannot use a table; it uses tabs or commas instead. Word also recognizes paragraph marks and other characters as delimiters.

Data sources need a row of titles at the top that are known as *field names*. The field names should describe the contents of that field in the data source. You refer to these field names when you are searching for or limiting the data used from the data source. Field names are also used to indicate where information goes when it is taken from the data source and placed into the merge document such as a form letter or label.

Tip
You can also just capitalize the first letter of each word and not use any spaces (for example, **FieldName**).

Field names have specific requirements. They must be no longer than 40 characters, start with a letter, and cannot contain a space. Rather than use a space in a field name, you may want to use an underscore character.

A Look at the Database Toolbar

Word includes a toolbar specifically designed to help you manage tables, databases, and data sources. The Database toolbar automatically displays when you open a document that has been specified as a data source for mail merge. You can also open the Database toolbar by selecting View, Toolbars, selecting Database from the Toolbars list, and then choosing OK. Here's what the Database toolbar looks like:

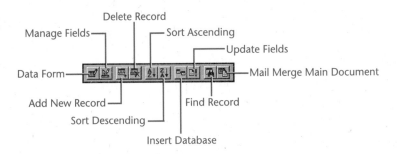

The different buttons in the Database toolbar are as follows:

Icon	Name	Description
	Data Form	Displays the Data Form, which makes adding, editing, and finding information easier in the database
	Manage Fields	Makes it easy to add, remove, or rename fields (columns) in a database
	Add New Record	Adds a new record at the current insertion point in a table or database
	Delete Record	Removes a record at the current insertion point in a table or database
	Sort Ascending	Sorts the table or database in ascending order on the current field
	Sort Descending	Sorts the table or database in descending order on the current field
	Insert Database	Displays the Database dialog box so that you can insert a file containing a database
	Update Fields	Updates fields and links in the document. Updates databases linked to files
	Find Record	Displays the Find in Field dialog box to help you search a database
	Mail Merge Main Document	Opens the main document attached to the current data source

Inserting a Database from a File

Small lists can be managed in a word processor; however, if you have lists or databases larger than a few hundred records, you will want to use a database application such as Microsoft Access in which to store, edit, and retrieve your data. Word makes it easy to store data in many different types of databases and then bring that data into a Word document so that it can be used as a data source for mail merge.

For Word to import or access a database file, it must have the appropriate file converters or Open Database Connectivity (ODBC) drivers installed. Installing converters and drivers can be done after Word has been initially installed. To install converters and drivers, rerun the Office or Word Setup program.

III

Creating
Envelopes & Mailings

Database files that Word can convert and insert include the following:

Microsoft Word	Microsoft Access
Microsoft Excel	dBASE
Paradox	Microsoft FoxPro
Word for Mac 3.x, 4.x, and 5.x	Word for MS-DOS 3.0–6.0
WordPerfect 5.x for MS-DOS or Windows	Lotus 1-2-3 2.x and 3.x

When you insert a database, you can choose to insert the data or insert a field code, which creates a link to the database file. Inserted data acts just as though it was typed in the document. Inserting a field code enables you to quickly update the database, because it has a link to the file on disk. If the data in the file changes, you can easily update the list.

To insert a database that is in a file on disk, follow these steps:

1. Position the insertion point in the document where you want the database.

2. Choose Insert, Database to display the Database dialog box, shown in figure 14.8.

Fig. 14.8
Use the Database dialog box to insert all or part of a database that is in a file from Word or another application.

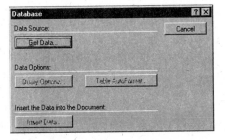

3. Click the Get Data button to display the Open Data Source dialog box, shown in figure 14.9.

4. Select or type the name of the file in the File Name drop-down list. Choose Open.

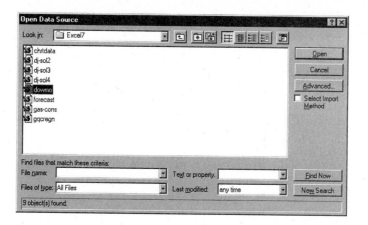

Fig. 14.9
From the Open Data Source dialog box, you can open the file containing your merge data.

If it is possible to select part of the data source, such as a range on a spreadsheet, a dialog box like the one in figure 14.10 appears. In this example, the Excel spreadsheet named DOWMO contains a named range, Database. Select the range or query that defines the data you want, then choose OK to return to the Insert Database dialog box.

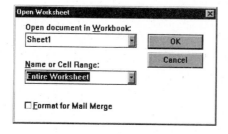

Fig. 14.10
You can insert a portion of some database files in the Open Worksheet dialog box.

5. Click the Query Options button from the Database dialog box if you want the data you insert to meet certain criteria.

6. Select Table AutoFormat if you want to be guided through custom formatting of the table.

7. Click the Insert Data button to display the Insert Data dialog box, shown in figure 14.11.

8. If you want to limit the number of records inserted, select From and To and enter the starting and ending record numbers.

9. If you want to create a link from your database to the database file on disk, select the Insert Data as Field check box.

10. Choose OK.

▶ See "Selecting Specific Records to Merge," p. 493

III

Fig. 14.11

From the Insert Data dialog box, you can select the amount of data you want and whether the database should be linked to the file on disk.

If you did not select the Insert Data as Field check box, the data is inserted as if it were typed. If the check box was selected, a link is created between the document and the database file. This link is created with a field code. You can update this field code by highlighting it and pressing F9. You can unlink the field code so that the database becomes fixed text by selecting the table and pressing Shift+Ctrl+F9.

Creating Your Mail Merge Data

The data source you use in Word for Windows can come from an existing Word document, be created in Word, or be linked into Word from another application.

If the amount of data you need to store is not extensive and you do not need to share the information with other users, the easiest way for you to store and manage your data is in a Word document. You can create a data source in a Word document either manually or with the guidance of the Mail Merge Helper.

Creating a Data Source Manually

You can manually create a data source document by typing data into a document. The fields of data must be separated into the cells of a table, or separated by tabs or commas. The field names in the first row of the data source document must fit the rules for field names:

- Names must start with a letter.

- Names must not contain a space. Use an underscore if you need to separate words.

- Names must not be longer than 40 characters.

- Names must be unique. You cannot have two field names spelled the same.

You must save the document containing your data source to disk before you can use it. Try to save the document with a file name that will not change frequently. If the file name of the data source changes, you must reconnect the mail merge document to use the data source.

Figure 14.1 shows an example of a table that is used as a data source for a mail merge document. Each field (column) in the table contains a type of information and each record (row) contains a group of information about a client. The information in this document could also have been separated by commas or by tabs.

Figure 14.12 shows the same information written as a data source with the data separated by tabs. If you decide to use commas or tabs to separate data, use one or the other throughout the data source—do not mix them in the same document. End each record (row) with a paragraph mark if it is a comma or tab-delimited record. See the upcoming section "Managing Information in the Data Source."

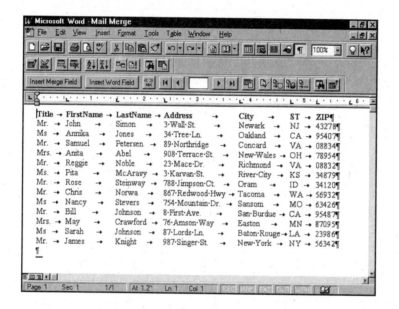

Fig. 14.12
You can manually create data source documents by typing data into tables or by typing each record in a row and separating the fields with commas or tabs.

After you have created your data source document, save it and remember its name and folder. When you run a mail merge, the Mail Merge Helper asks you to select the file name of the data source.

▶ See "Merging Mailing Lists and Documents," p. 470

If you create a comma-delimited data source and some of your data contains commas, Word may be confused as to the fields in which data belongs. To solve this problem, enclose any data that contains commas within quotation marks (" ") when you use commas to separate fields of data. The quotation marks around a piece of data tell Word that any comma within the quotation marks is part of the data.

III

Creating Envelopes & Mailings

Using the Mail Merge Helper to Create a New Data Source

If you want to be guided through the process of creating a data source document, use the Mail Merge Helper. The Mail Merge Helper is a series of dialog boxes that presents options for creating some of the most commonly used field names. After you have created the field names, the Mail Merge Helper gives you a chance to enter data into the new data source. A later section of this chapter, "Finding or Editing Records with the Data Form," describes how to add more records or find and edit existing records.

The following process helps you create a data source document with the Mail Merge Helper. The Mail Merge Helper assumes you are creating a form letter and the source document at the same time. Because most people create first one or the other and then return later to merge the two, the following steps show you how to create only the source document.

Tip

The blank document that opened would normally be used to create a new form letter, but you need it open only to appease the Mail Merge Helper while you create a new data source.

To create a new data source with the Mail Merge Helper, follow these steps:

1. Choose Tools, Mail Merge. The Mail Merge Helper dialog box appears.

2. Choose Create and then select Form Letters.

3. Click the New Main Document button. This opens a blank document and returns you to the Mail Merge Helper. The Get Data button is now available.

4. Click the Get Data button, then select Create Data Source from the list (see fig. 14.13). The Create Data Source dialog box appears, as shown in figure 14.14.

Fig. 14.13

Choosing Tools, Mail Merge displays the Mail Merge Helper. The Mail Merge Helper guides you through the process of creating data sources, creating main documents, and merging the data and document.

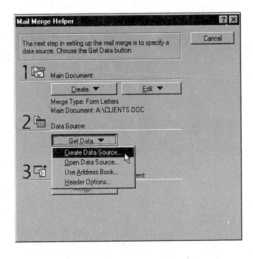

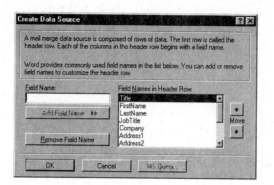

Fig. 14.14
The Create Data
Source dialog box
gives you the
opportunity to
accept, add, or
remove field
names for each
column in the
data source.

5. In the Create Data Source dialog box, add or remove field names for the columns in your data source. When the Create Data Source dialog box first appears, it shows in the Field Names in Header Row list the most frequently used field names for mail merge. Field names appear left to right across the first row of the data source in the order they are listed in the Field Names in Header Row list. Edit the field names in the list using the following steps:

   Add a new field name to the list by typing the name in the Field Name edit box and clicking Add Field Name. The name is added to the end of the list.

   Delete a field name from the list by selecting the name in the Field Names in Header Row list, and then click Remove Field Name.

   Move a field name up or down in the list by selecting the name and then clicking the up or down arrows.

Tip
Field names must
be 40 characters or
less and start with
a letter. Spaces are
not allowed.

6. Choose OK. The Save As dialog box appears.

7. Type a file name in the File Name edit box. Change to the folder in which you expect to keep the data source.

8. Choose OK to close the Save As dialog box. A dialog box appears warning you that the data source you created contains no data.

9. Click Edit Data Source to display the Data Form dialog box where you can add records to your new data source (see fig. 14.15).

10. Enter data in the Data Form. Press Tab or Enter to move to the next field of data. Click Add New to add another record. The Data Form is described in detail later in this chapter in "Finding or Editing Records with the Data Form."

III

Creating
Envelopes & Mailings

Fig. 14.15

Use the Data Form to add new data to your new data source. You can bring up the Data Form at any time to find or edit data in a data source.

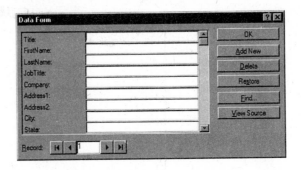

Tip

View more of a wide data source by choosing View, Zoom to fit more fields on-screen.

▶ See "Creating Tables," p. 506

11. When you are finished entering data and want to save the data source, click the View Source button. When the data source document appears, choose File, Save.

If you do not save the data source document, you will be given a chance to save it when you attempt to close the blank document you opened in step 3.

You can see the paragraph mark that ends a row of comma-delimited data if you click the Show/Hide ¶ button on the Standard toolbar.

Your data source document looks like a table if it has 31 or fewer field names. If it has more than 31 field names, data is separated by commas, and records end with a paragraph mark. The field names will be in the first row and data in following rows.

Working with an Existing Data Source

You can work with data sources that already exist, even if they aren't Word documents. The data may have come from a worksheet, database, or corporate mainframe.

You may want to work with an existing data source to edit its contents or to build new main document that contains merge fields. For example, if you want to create a new form letter using a data source you already have, follow this procedure:

1. Choose Tools, Mail Merge.

2. Click the Main Document Create button, then select the type of main document you want to create: Form Letters, Mailing Labels, Envelopes, or Catalog. From the dialog box that appears, choose either Active Window or New Main Document to attach the data source to the existing active document or to open a new document.

3. Click Get Data, and then choose Open Data Source from the pull-down list. The Open Data Source dialog box appears.

4. Change to the folder containing the data source, and then select or type the file name of the data source in the File Name box. Choose OK.

5. Click the Set Up Main Document or Edit Main Document button.

The data source is open but does not appear in a window. If you want to edit the data in the data source, refer to the section later in this chapter, "Finding or Editing Records with the Data Form."

You can use the data source documents you used in previous versions of Word for Windows with the Mail Merge Helper in Word for Windows 95. Make sure that Word has the converters installed to convert the old document into Word format. After you have resaved the document, you can treat it the same as any data source.

Using Data from Another Application

Word can use the data from other applications as a data source. Your main documents in Word can link to data in other applications such as Microsoft Access or Microsoft Excel. The document can read directly from databases such as Access, Paradox, FoxPro, or dBASE through the use of Open Database Connectivity (ODBC) drivers. You also can import and convert data from any files for which you have a converter.

Using the Mail Merge Helper with a Non-Word Data Source

To work with a non-Word data source, follow these steps:

1. Open a main document.

2. Choose Tools, Mail Merge.

3. Choose Main Document Create, and then select the type of main document you want to create: Form Letters, Mailing Labels, Envelopes, or Catalog. From the Help dialog box that appears, choose either Active Window or New Main Document to attach the data source to the existing active document or to open a new document.

4. Choose Get Data, and then select Open Data Source from the drop-down list.

5. Change to the folder containing the data source, and then select or type the file name of the data source in the File Name box. Choose OK.

Or, if you open an Excel worksheet, you are given an opportunity to specify a range name within the worksheet that describes the data you want to bring in. If you open an Access file, you can open an Access query file and only the data that satisfies that query will be brought in.

You can also choose MS Query to open Microsoft Query so you can connect to and query an external data source. Microsoft Query is a separate Microsoft application that comes with Microsoft Excel 5 or Microsoft Office. When you are finished in Microsoft Query, choose File, Return Data to Microsoft Word.

6. If the active document is not a main document that contains merge fields, Word displays a Mail Merge Helper dialog box. Click the Edit Main Document button.

Managing Information in the Data Source

You can manage the data in your data source just as though you had a small database program built into Word. You can find or edit records using the Data Form. You can also reorganize the columns in a data source or merge together two data source files.

Finding or Editing Records with the Data Form

The information in your data source is of little value unless it is accurate. Word includes features to help you keep your data source up-to-date.

To quickly find data when the data source is in the active document, follow these steps:

1. Click within a data source.

2. Click the Find Record button on the Database toolbar to display the Find in Field dialog box shown in figure 14.16.

Fig. 14.16
You can find records that contain information in the field name you select.

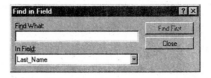

3. Select from the In Field list the field name of the column you want to search.

4. Type in the Find What box what you are searching for under the field name.

5. Click <u>F</u>ind First.

6. Examine the record found or click the <u>F</u>ind Next button to continue.

To find and edit information when a data source is in the active document, follow these steps:

1. Click within a data source.

   The database may have fields in table columns, tab-separated or comma-separated. A main document does not have to be opened or attached. It must have valid data source field names.

2. Click the Data Form button on the Database toolbar.

3. Begin at step 3 in the next procedure to find or edit data using the Data Form.

To find data within the data source when the main document is active, follow these steps:

1. Open a main document that uses your data source.

2. Click the Data Form button in the Database toolbar or choose <u>T</u>ools, Mail Me<u>r</u>ge, and then click the E<u>d</u>it button and select the data source. The Data Form dialog box appears.

3. Move to the first record in the data source if you want to begin the search from the first data record.

4. Click <u>F</u>ind.

5. Select from the In Fiel<u>d</u> list the field name of the column you want to search.

6. Type in the Fi<u>n</u>d What box what you are searching for under the field name.

7. Choose <u>F</u>ind First.

When the first record satisfying your request is found, the <u>F</u>ind First button changes to a <u>F</u>ind Next button. Select this button to find any further occurrences of what you are searching for. A message notifies you when you have reached the last record in the database.

When you find a record you want to edit, choose Close in the Find in Field dialog box and edit the record in the Data Form.

Tip
You can delete a record by displaying it in the Data Form and then clicking <u>D</u>elete.

If you delete or edit a record incorrectly, immediately choose Restore to return the record to its original condition. After you move to a new record when editing, you cannot restore previous edits.

Sorting a Data Source

Sorting a data source can be useful for a couple of reasons. If you are printing a large volume of mail merge envelopes or labels, you can get a discount on postage if ZIP codes are in sorted order. Another reason for sorting is if you need to create printed lists that will be searched manually.

To quickly sort a data source, follow these steps:

1. Click in the data source in the field (column) on which you want to sort.

2. Click the Ascending Sort or Descending Sort button on the Database toolbar.

If you have more complex sorts and your data is in a table, or can be converted to a table, choose Table, Sort.

Renaming, Inserting, or Removing Fields from a Data Source

When your information needs change, you will probably have to add or remove fields (columns) from your data source. For example, you might want to add a field that includes a customer's automatic reorder date, or you might want to delete an old, unnecessary field such as a Client Priority number.

To add or remove a field in a data source, follow these steps:

1. Save your current data source under a new name. Save this file as a backup in case you make mistakes and need to return to an original copy.

2. Open the data source document and display it in the active window.

3. Click the Manage Fields button in the Database toolbar to display the Manage Fields dialog box, shown in figure 14.17.

4. If you want to add, remove, or rename a field, follow these steps:

To add a field, type the new name in the Field Name edit box, then choose the Add button.

To remove a field name and its corresponding data, select the name from the Field Names in Header Row list, then click the Remove button. Choose Yes to confirm that you want to remove the field and data.

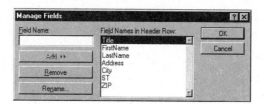

Fig. 14.17
Use the Manage Fields dialog box to add or remove new fields (columns) in the Data Source as your information needs change.

To rename a field, click the Re̲name button, then type your name in the N̲ew Field Name edit box that appears. Choose OK.

5. When you have finished making changes to your data source, choose OK.

Inserting or Removing Records from a Data Source

It seems that the amount of information demanded only seems to grow; however, sometimes you might need to delete a record from your data source. With Word, you can easily insert or delete records.

To insert a new blank record at the bottom of the data source, you can use the Data Form as described earlier in this chapter. Alternatively, you can follow these steps:

1. Open and activate the data source document.

2. Click the Add New Record button on the Database toolbar.

To delete a record from the data source, follow these steps:

1. Open and activate the data source document.

2. Click in the record (row) that you want to delete. Select down through many records if you want to delete multiple records.

3. Click the Delete Record button on the Database toolbar. You are not asked to confirm that you want to delete.

If you decide you have accidentally deleted the wrong record, immediately choose E̲dit, U̲ndo. You can undo only the last record you deleted.

Scrolling through the Data Form

You can browse through records in the data source using the buttons at the bottom of the Data Form. Clicking the left or right button moves the records one at a time. Clicking the left end or right end button (VCR end controls, |< and >|) moves to the beginning or end of the data record.

Tip

If records to be deleted have common data, sort the field containing that data so that you can delete multiple records at one time.

If you do not have a mouse, you can move to a specific record by pressing Alt+R and typing the numeric position of the record you want to see. When you press Enter, the insertion point moves out of the Record Number box and into the first field. ❖

Chapter 15

Mastering Envelopes, Mail Merge, and Form Letters

Successful businesses know that staying in touch with their clients and customers is crucial to the success of the business. Staying in touch with many people is difficult, however, unless you learn how to create personalized form letters and envelopes with Word for Windows.

One of the most frequent tasks people perform in business correspondence is entering the address block at the top of a letter. With Word's new Insert Address button, you can click a button to get a list of people you send letters to most frequently. Another click and you've pasted in their mailing address. Click a different part of the button and you go into Word's new Address Book. The Address Book gives you access to addresses, phone numbers, e-mail addresses, and other information about the people you deal with.

To make single letters easier to produce, Word for Windows has automated the process of printing an envelope. The envelope printing feature uses the address from a document to print an envelope, with or without a return address. The envelope can be printed separately or attached to the document with which it is associated. This feature is covered in the first section of this chapter.

Form letters broadcast information, yet add a personal touch to your work. You may produce only a few form letters each day, but they still can automate repetitive parts of your business and give you time to improve the creative end of your work. You also can generate invoices, appointment reminders, and so on. Creating form letters is challenging, but working through it will pay great dividends.

You can create two types of form letters with Word for Windows: those that are filled in manually and those that are filled in from computer-generated lists. In this chapter, you learn to create an automated form letter that prompts you for information the document needs in creating an invoice. You learn also how to fill in the blanks in a form letter by merging a mailing list with the main document. Finally, you learn Word for Windows' advanced techniques for document automation, including a form letter that combines manual fill-in with merging of information.

In this chapter, you learn to do the following:

- Use the Personal Address Book to insert an individual's name and address in a letter

- Print envelopes and include their bar code or FIM code

- Use the Mail Merge Helper to create a main document and a data source, and to control the merging of data into documents

- Perform mail merge with special documents such as letterhead, envelopes, and mailing labels

- Insert field codes that prompt you to enter a personal note in each mail merge document

Inserting a Name and Address from the Address Book

Word's Address Book makes it much easier to manage the names and addresses of people you write to frequently. After you enter the names, addresses, and e-mail information about people, you can retrieve them by clicking the Insert Address button in the Standard toolbar. You also can paste a person's address into your document by clicking their name.

◀ See "Managing Names and Addresses with Address Books," p. 441

If you have already entered names, addresses, and other information into an address book, you can look up or paste in a person's address by opening the Address Book and then double-clicking their name.

Before you can use the Address Book on a network or with the Address Book in Schedule+ you must gain access to the network and Schedule+. If your computer is on a network and you use Schedule+, then the first time you click the Insert Address button you will need to follow these steps:

1. Position the insertion point in the document where you want a person's address pasted.

2. Click the Insert Address button in the Standard toolbar to display the Group Enabling dialog shown in figure 15.1.

   Click <u>Y</u>es if you want to work with Schedule+ on a network. Click <u>N</u>o if you want to work without Schedule+. You can select the Don't Ask Me This Question Again check box if you do not want to see this dialog box again.

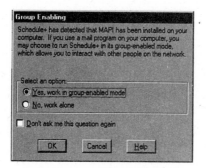

Fig. 15.1
You can use the Address Book in conjunction with Schedule+ on your network.

3. If you selected <u>Y</u>es, you will be prompted for your Microsoft Mail password. Enter the password, choose OK, and you will see the Select Name dialog box.

   Or, if you selected <u>N</u>o, you will be prompted for the logon name of the schedule you want to work with. Enter your user name if it is not already entered, and then choose OK. You will then be prompted for the Microsoft Exchange Profile you want to use. Select your profile and then choose OK. You will then be prompted for your Microsoft Mail password. After entering your Microsoft Mail password and choosing OK, the Select Name dialog box appears.

4. While the Select Name dialog box is open, use one of the procedures that follow to insert a name and address or edit information in an address book.

If you have already logged onto your network and have access to Schedule+, then you have quick access to the address books by just clicking the Insert Address button. To open one of the address books and insert an address, follow these steps:

III

Creating
Envelopes & Mailings

1. Position the insertion point in the document where you want a person's address pasted.

2. Click the Insert Address button in the Standard toolbar to display the Select Name dialog box shown in figure 15.2.

Fig. 15.2
The Select Name dialog box gives you access to different address books available in Windows.

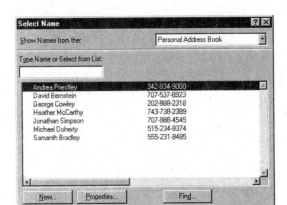

3. Select the <u>S</u>how Names drop-down list and select the address book containing the address you want inserted into your document.

   The address books available to you if you have installed Windows 95 and Office 95 include the following:

Address Book	Description
Schedule+ Contact List	A name, address, and information list stored in Schedule+ and shared with others on your network
Personal Address Book	A name, address, and information list used by you with Word. Information can be used for e-mail and fax through Microsoft Exchange
Postoffice Address List	A name, address, and e-mail address list used for sending e-mail messages from Word through your local network
Microsoft Network	A name, address, and e-mail address list used for sending e-mail messages from Word over Microsoft Network

4. Type the name you want into the <u>T</u>ype Name edit box or click the name in the list.

5. Choose OK to insert that person's name and address into your Word document.

If you have used the Address Book before, you will have a shortcut list available to you. Using this shortcut list is a very quick and convenient way of inserting names and addresses. To quickly insert a name and address you have used before, follow these steps:

1. Click the drop-down arrow to the right of the Insert Address button to display the list shown in figure 15.3.

Fig. 15.3
Use the drop-down list by the Insert Address button to quickly insert names and addresses.

2. Click the name whose name and address you want inserted.

Printing an Envelope

Word for Windows offers an easy and quick solution to a common word processing problem: printing envelopes. Word for Windows can print envelopes by themselves, attached to a document, or as part of a mass mailing.

To test the envelope feature, create a short letter like the one shown in figure 15.4.

To create an envelope, follow these steps:

1. Select the address in the letter.

   If the address is a contiguous block of three to five short lines near the beginning of the letter, you do not have to select it. Word for Windows automatically finds the address.

2. Choose Tools, Envelopes and Labels. Word displays the Envelopes and Labels dialog box (see fig. 15.5).

Fig. 15.4
This figure shows a sample business letter.

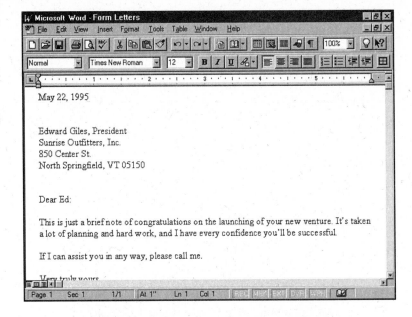

Fig. 15.5
Word will find the address in most letters and automatically display it in the Envelopes and Labels dialog box.

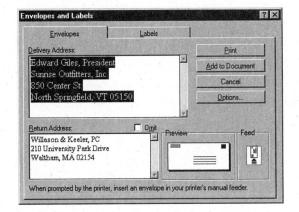

3. Select the Envelopes tab if it is not already active.

4. If necessary, edit the Delivery Address information. To insert line feeds (line breaks without a carriage return), press Shift+Enter.

5. If necessary, edit the Return Address information. If you do not want to print the return address (you may be working with preprinted envelopes, for example), select the Omit check box.

6. If you need to select an envelope size, click the Options button to display the Envelopes Options dialog box (see fig. 15.6); then select from the Envelope Size drop-down list.

> **Note**
>
> The Delivery Address and Return Address options enable you to customize the fonts and positions of the addresses. You learn about the postal mailing areas later in this section.

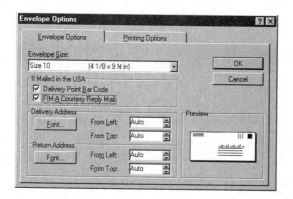

Fig. 15.6
Click the Options button in the Envelopes and Labels dialog box to display the Envelope Options dialog box.

7. When you're done with your selections, choose OK.

8. If necessary, load envelope(s) into your printer's feeder as indicated in the Feed area in the Envelopes and Labels dialog box.

9. Click the Print button to print an envelope immediately.

   You can also click the Add to Document button to add the envelope as a landscape-oriented section before the first page of your document (see fig. 15.7).

   When you click the Print button, most laser printers immediately print the envelope from the envelope bin. If you do not have an envelope feeder or envelope bin, insert the envelope—narrow side in—in the form-feed guides on top of the primary paper tray. The envelope prints first, followed by the document.

You can change the default Return Address information. Choose Tools, Options, and then select the User Info Category. In the Mailing Address text box, add or edit the return address. This becomes the default return address until you change it. Alternately, when you have the Envelopes and Labels dialog box open, you can directly edit the return address. When you click Print or Add to Document, you will be prompted to save the return address as the default.

To reposition the Delivery Address area, change to Page Layout view and move the mouse pointer to the striped border until a four-headed arrow appears. Then drag the entire box containing the Delivery Address to a new position (see fig. 15.8).

Fig. 15.7
The Add to Document button inserts a landscape envelope before the first page of your document.

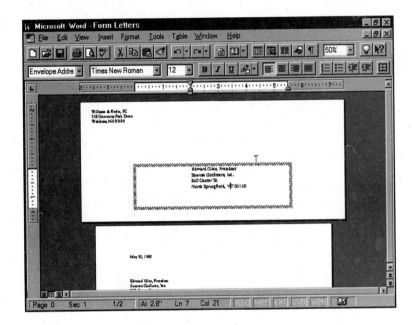

Fig. 15.8
You can drag the address area to a new position in the envelope section.

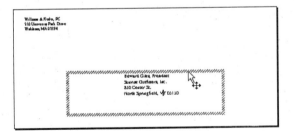

Troubleshooting

My address isn't printing properly on the envelopes.

If you have trouble printing an envelope with the envelope layout or with envelope and paper feeding, examine the printer driver. Choose File, Print, and look in the Name text box of the Print dialog box to see what printer driver is selected. Make sure you have the correct driver. Check with your printer manufacturer or Microsoft Corporation for a more current version of the Windows printer driver program if you continue to have problems. Use Windows' Control Panel to install the new driver.

Printing an Envelope with Bar Codes or FIM Codes

Word for Windows provides a way to print machine-readable codes on envelopes so that the U.S. Postal Service can process the envelopes by machine. These codes can be used as long as they are sent to addresses within the U.S., thus saving time and money.

You can print *POSTNET* codes (bar code equivalents of U.S. ZIP codes) and *facing identification marks*, or *FIMs* (vertical lines that indicate the address side of the envelope).

To print POSTNET bar codes and Facing Identification Marks on envelope(s) attached to the current document, follow these steps:

1. Choose <u>T</u>ools, <u>E</u>nvelopes and Labels.

2. In the Envelopes tab of the Envelopes and Labels dialog box, click the <u>O</u>ptions button. Word displays the Envelope Options dialog box (see fig. 15.9).

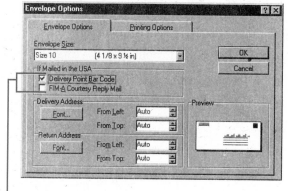

Checking these options adds bar codes and FIMs to your envelopes

Fig. 15.9
Set envelope printing options in the Envelope Options dialog box.

3. Select the Delivery Point <u>B</u>ar Code check box to print POSTNET bar codes.

4. Select the FIM-<u>A</u> Courtesy Reply Mail check box to print Facing Identification Marks.

5. Choose OK.

Customizing Envelopes with Text and Graphics

You can easily add a graphic—such as a company logo—to your envelopes, whether the graphic consists of formatted text or actual graphics.

To set up envelopes to print your logo, follow these steps:

1. Enter your logo text and/or graphics in a document.

2. Put the logo in a frame. The frame must first be selected in order for AutoText to work.

▶ See "Inserting Pictures in Frames and Text Boxes," p. 710

3. Choose <u>E</u>dit, AutoTe<u>x</u>t.

4. Type the name **EnvelopeExtra** in the <u>N</u>ame text box.

5. Click <u>A</u>dd.

Merging Mailing Lists and Documents

One of the most powerful and time-saving features available in any word processor is mail merge. *Mail merge* enables you to create multiple letters or envelopes by merging together a list of names and addresses with letters, envelopes, or address labels. Mail merge can also be used for such tasks as filling in administrative forms and creating invoices from accounting files. Whenever you keep a list or get a list from other programs and you need to put information into a Word for Windows document, you should consider using mail merge.

The time you save by using mail merge can be tremendous. Instead of typing or modifying tens or hundreds of documents, Word can make all the documents for you. All you need to do is keep your list (names, addresses, and so on) up-to-date and create a form letter in which the data will be inserted. In fact, you can even make each document pause during mail merge so that you can enter personalized information.

Understanding the Mail Merge Components: Data Sources and Main Documents

You need two documents to create form letters or mailing labels. One document, called the *data source*, contains a precisely laid-out set of data, such as names and addresses. The other document, the *main document*, acts as a form that receives the data. Most forms that receive data are form letters or multi-column tables for mailing labels.

Although most people would use the term *form letter* to describe a Word main document, a main document can take the form of a mailing list, catalog, mailing labels, or letters.

The main document is like a normal document except that it contains MERGEFIELD field codes that specify where merged data will appear. In a typical form letter, for example, the main document is a form letter that needs names and addresses inserted, and the data source is the list of names and addresses.

The data source document must be organized in a very specific way, or the merge process will generate errors. The first row of the data source must be one row of names. Below the row of names are rows of data. Each row of data is a *record*, and each piece of data in the row, such as a last name, is a *field*. The row of names in the first row of the documents is the *header record*. Each name in the first row is a *field name*. Each field can be referenced by the name for that field in the heading.

When you merge the documents, Word replaces the merge fields with the appropriate text from the data source. At merge time, you can choose to display the result as a new document on-screen or to print it directly to the current printer.

◀ See "Managing Mail Merge Data," p. 445

Understanding Word's Mail Merge Helper

Word for Windows Mail Merge Helper guides you through the three stages of creating a form letter, catalog, or other merged document:

- Creating or identifying the main document

- Creating or identifying the data source

- Merging the data source and main document

To start the Mail Merge Helper, follow these steps:

1. If you want to use an existing document as the main document, open that document. Otherwise, create a new document.

2. Choose Tools, Mail Merge.

The Mail Merge Helper dialog box lays out the three stages in creating a merged document (see fig. 15.10). Notice that the dialog box contains a lot of empty space; this space will fill up with useful information about the merge documents as you proceed.

The Mail Merge Helper is designed to be flexible; you can start setting up the merge at virtually any stage in the document-creation process. At appropriate points, Word requires you to make decisions or reminds you to go back and complete all necessary steps in creating a merged document.

III

Creating
Envelopes & Mailings

Fig. 15.10

The Mail Merge
Helper dialog box
is the central
dialog box from
which you
complete the three
stages of form-
letter production.

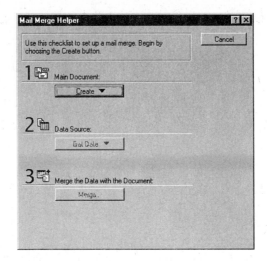

You'll see many dialog boxes resembling the one in figure 15.11. Although this box does not have a name, you might think of it as the "decision" dialog box.

Sometimes the decision box offers a choice between creating a new document or changing the type of the active document. Consider carefully before changing the document type; generally, you'll want to preserve the existing document in its current form.

Fig. 15.11

At different points
in the merge
process, Word asks
whether you want
to create a new,
blank document
or use an existing
one.

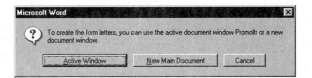

If you fail to complete a required portion of one of the three stages in the merge process, you'll see a dialog box like the one shown in figure 15.12. This type of dialog box essentially forces you to add detail to incomplete documents before going through with the merge. You see this dialog box only if the Mail Merge Helper detects that you have missed a step or incorrectly entered a response.

The following sections describe how to proceed through the three stages of creating mail merge documents. The Mail Merge Helper is used to centrally coordinate the mail merge documents and the final merging of main document and data source. When you click a button in the Mail Merge Helper, you are presented with a series of windows that guide you through the stage corresponding to the button.

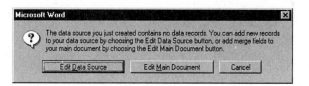

Fig. 15.12
Word's Mail Merge Helper forces you to create complete documents before it will let you begin merging.

Selecting the Main Document

You can use any existing document as a main document. Simply open that document before starting the Mail Merge Helper. If you need to create the main document, however, you have the following options:

1. Start Word and be sure you're in a new document.

2. Choose File, New.

3. Make sure that the Document button is selected.

4. Select the tab that contains the template you want to use.

5. Select the template you want to use.

6. Choose OK.

It's not necessary to enter any text in the document right now; you can come back to that later.

To create a main document for a form letter, follow these steps:

1. Choose Tools, Mail Merge.

2. Under the Main Document heading of the Mail Merge Helper dialog box, click the Create button.

3. Choose Form Letters. Word displays a decision dialog box asking what you want to use to create the form letter.

4. Click the Active Window button to use the active document as the main document. Click the New Main Document button to open a new document, which uses the Normal document template.

Word brings you back to the Mail Merge Helper dialog box, which now displays the type of merge and the name and path of the main document under the Main Document heading.

This process illustrates the Mail Merge Helper's flexibility; if you realize in step 4 that you don't want to use the active document, you don't have to start over again.

III

Creating
Envelopes & Mailings

Selecting a Data Source

Attaching the data source to the main document does three things:

- Shows Word the file name and path where the data will be located

- Attaches a mailmerge bar with merge tools to the top of the main document

- Enables Word for Windows to read the field names used in the data source

◀ See "Managing Data," p. 445

If you do not yet have a source for the data that will be merged, you should read Chapter 14 and create a data source before proceeding. An overview of creating a new data source is presented in the next section, "Creating a New Data Source."

Specifying an Address Book as the Data Source

If you have created a list of contacts in a Personal Address Book or in the Schedule+ Address Book, you already have a data source that you can use for a mail merge by following these steps:

1. Under the Data Source heading, click the Get Data button.

2. Choose Use Address Book. Word displays the Use Address Book dialog box, shown in figure 15.13.

Fig. 15.13
You can select one of the address books available to Word for use in mail merge.

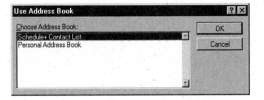

3. Select an address book from the Choose Address Book list and then choose OK.

What happens next depends on whether your main document was complete when you started the merge process. If you have not yet inserted any merge fields in your main document, Word displays the dialog box shown in figure 15.14.

To go directly to the main document to add the merge fields, choose Edit, Main Document. For instructions on inserting the merge fields in your main document, refer to "Editing the Main Document" in this chapter.

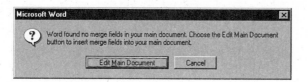

Fig. 15.14
After attaching
the data source,
the Mail Merge
Helper detects
that there are no
merge fields in
your main
document.

Specifying an Existing File as the Data Source

You can use a data source that you have already created for the mail merge.
In the Mail Merge Helper dialog box you can click the Get Data button to
give you access to different sources of data. If you want to use data that is in a
file or document, choose the Open Data Source item from the list.

To specify an existing file as a data source, follow these steps:

1. Under the Data Source heading, click the Get Data button.

2. Choose Open Data Source. Word displays the Open Data Source dialog
   box, shown in figure 15.15.

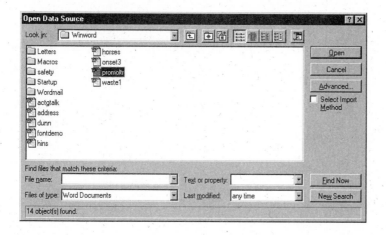

Fig. 15.15
Use the Open Data
Source dialog box
to access a data
source in Word or
many other
formats.

3. Select the data source from the File Name list. Word can read many
   different data source formats. Choose from the Files of Type list to see
   other formats. Choose OK after selecting the file.

   You can also choose the MS Query button if Microsoft Query is available on your computer. Use Microsoft Query to access specific data in a
   non-Word database.

III

Creating
Envelopes & Mailings

> **Note**
>
> Use Microsoft Query to retrieve data meeting specific criteria. The data may be on your computer, on a network, in an SQL Server, or on many types of mainframe databases. Microsoft Query is available as a separate application and comes with Microsoft Excel.

Word automatically converts non-Word files for which it has converters.

Creating a New Data Source

If you did not have a data source that contained your lists of names or database of information to be merged, you need to create one. You also can create a data source in a Word document while you are in the Mail Merge Helper.

◀ See "Managing Data," p. 445

◀ See "Creating Your Own Data Sources," p. 445

The Mail Merge Helper will guide you through the process of creating a data source in a Word document. It follows a set of rules that you can learn if you want to manually create a data source document. The *data source* is a grid of rows and columns. The first row in the data source must contain the field names. These label each column's contents. Only one row of field names can be at the top of the data source. Field names cannot contain blanks, because Word for Windows uses the names as bookmarks. Do not start a field name with a number (although a number can be included in the field name). If you need to use a two-part field name, use an underscore rather than a space. You may want to put words together and capitalize a word's leading letter, such as RegionManager. Each field name must be unique.

You can create a new data source within a Word document by using the Create Data Source command. Follow these steps:

1. Under the Data Source heading in the Mail Merge Helper, click the <u>G</u>et Data button.

> **Note**
>
> This button is available only if you attached a main document by clicking the Create button from the Main Document stage. If you want to create a data source and wait to create a main document, just attach a blank document as the main document.

2. Choose Create Data Source. Word displays the Create Data Source dialog box (see fig. 15.16).

   The Field Names in Header Row list box contains names traditionally
   used for fields in mailing lists. The names in the list box comprise a
   default list of field names.

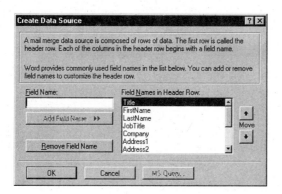

Fig. 15.16
The Create Data
Source dialog box
guides you
through creating a
data source. It
even presents the
most commonly
used headings for
mail merge data
sources.

3. Edit the list of names in the Field Names in Header Row list box, as
   described here:

   If you see any field names you won't use in your main document, select
   the name from the Field Names in Header Row box, and then choose
   the Remove Field Name button. Word removes the name from the list.

   To add a field name, type it in the Field Name box, and then choose
   Add Field Name.

   When you are satisfied with your list, choose OK.

   To change the sequence of names (reposition them), select a field name
   and then click the up or down arrow labeled Move. The top-to-bottom
   sequence you see in this list box determines the left-to-right sequence
   of the fields in the data source.

4. Word displays the Save As dialog box. In the File Name text box, enter a
   name for the data source document and choose Save.

5. Word displays a decision dialog box asking what you want to do next.
   To enter data in the data source, click the Edit Data Source button. To
   edit the Main document so that you can insert the merge fields to create a main document, click the Edit Main Document button.

III

If you click Edit Main Document, Word displays the main document as a normal Word document, with one exception—the Mail Merge toolbar is now displayed below the toolbar(s) and above the ruler (see fig. 15.17). With the main document on-screen, you can create a main document in which the data will be inserted.

Fig. 15.17

When you click the Edit Main Document button after using the Mail Merge Helper, Word displays the document and adds a Mail Merge toolbar.

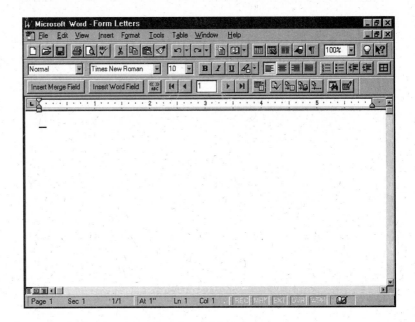

Merging Data into the Main Document

When you are satisfied with your main document, you can merge it with the data by choosing one of three merge buttons in the Mail Merge toolbar. Table 15.1 shows how these buttons work.

Table 15.1	Effects of Merge Buttons in the Mail Merge Toolbar
Button	**Effect**
	Creates the merged document and places it in a new Word document
	Creates the merged document and prints it on the currently selected printer
	Displays the Merge dialog box, which provides a wide range of options for record selection and other operations (see the next section for details)

Figure 15.18 shows the merged document. The Form Letters1 document contains the full text of the merged document, with each of the individually addressed letters contained in a section. This document contains no field codes; you can treat it as you would any typed document. Each section break (represented by a double dashed line) starts a new page, so printing the document produces individual letters. Naturally, if you want to make changes to individual letters, you can edit them in the usual manner.

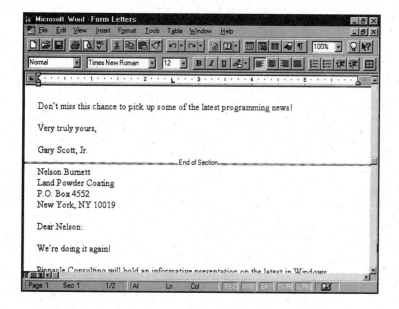

Fig. 15.18
Merging a form letter to a document can create a long document containing all the individual letters.

If you merge a large number of records, merge to the printer so that you do not exceed memory limits. You may want to merge a few records to a new document before printing. This enables you to see whether the merge is working correctly.

Merging Selected Records

Often you will not want to merge an entire data source into a letter. You may want to merge 20 letters at a time, or limit the merged data to specific ZIP codes or job titles. Or you may want to merge one or two letters as a test before running a large merge job.

To control the data that's merged into your main document, follow these steps:

1. Prepare your data source and save it.

2. Open your main document. When it opens, the Mail Merge toolbar also appears.

If Word cannot find the data source for the main document, it displays a dialog box that you can use to open the correct data source.

3. Choose <u>T</u>ools, Mail Me<u>r</u>ge to display the Mail Merge Helper, as shown in figure 15.19.

Fig. 15.19

A Mail Merge Helper that is ready to merge data shows both main document and data source types and locations.

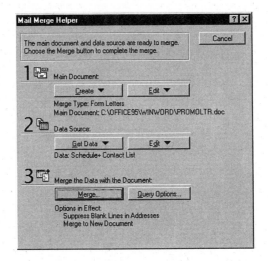

In figure 15.19, you can see that a properly completed Mail Merge Helper displays the type of main document and where it is located, as well as the data source for that main document and where the data source is located.

4. Click the <u>M</u>erge button to begin the merge process. The Merge dialog box shown in figure 15.20 appears.

Fig. 15.20

Select from the Merge dialog box how you want the merge to be performed.

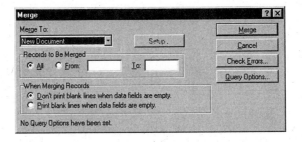

5. Select the Merge To list and select one of the following types of merges:

Merge To	**Effect**
Printer	Produces a printed result
New Document	Produces a new document containing all resulting merged documents

6. Select the number of records to be merged from the Records to Be Merged group:

Merged Records	**Effect**
All	Merges all records
From/To	Limits the range of data according to the record (row) numbers in the data source

7. Select from the When Merging Records group how blank lines will be handled:

   Don't print blank lines when data fields are empty.

   Print blank lines when data fields are empty.

8. Choose Merge.

Creating Mailing Labels

If you are sending many documents, mailing labels can save you lots of time. With Word for Windows, you can easily update your mailing lists and print labels on demand.

You can design a form that prints multiple labels on a page in much the same way you create a form letter. If you've designed main documents for mailing labels in a previous version of Word for Windows, you can continue to use those documents to print mailing labels. But if you need to create a new label form, it's quite easy in Word.

Creating a Mailing Label Main Document

The Labels tab of the Envelopes and Labels dialog box automates the process of creating mailing labels. For the example provided here, it is assumed that you have already created a form letter main document.

To create mailing labels for an existing form letter, follow these steps:

1. Choose Tools, Mail Merge. (You do not need to activate the main document for the form letter.)

2. Under the Main Document heading of the Mail Merge Helper dialog box, click the Create button.

3. Select Mailing Labels.

4. In the decision dialog box, click Active Window if it appears in the dialog box. Otherwise, click New Main Document.

5. Under the Data Source heading, click the Get Data button.

6. Select Open Data Source or Use Address Book.

7. Select the appropriate data source.

8. If Word displays a dialog box, click Set Up Main Document.

9. Word displays the Label Options dialog box. Select a label format. Label formats are explained in the following section.

Specifying Label Size and Type

Word now displays the Label Options dialog box (see fig. 15.21). You'll probably be able to select from this dialog box the label format you want; the dialog box contains specifications for dozens of commercial pre-printed label products.

Fig. 15.21
Select a label format from the Label Options dialog box.

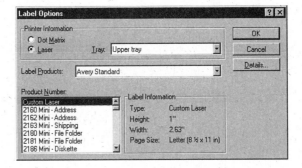

To specify the type and size of your mailing labels, follow these steps:

1. In the Label Options dialog box, select the appropriate label group from the Label Products drop-down list:

Label Products	Comments
Avery Standard	Avery U.S. products
Avery Pan European	Avery European products
Other	Products from other manufacturers

2. Select your type of label from the Product <u>N</u>umber drop-down list. If you are not using labels from any of the commercial products available in this dialog box, use the product number for the same size label. If none of the label formats produce the result you want, you will have to edit the label specifications, as explained in "Creating Custom Mailing Labels," later in this section.

3. If you're not sure which label type is correct, use the arrow keys to browse through the list so that you can view in the Label Information box the label and page dimensions for each type.

4. If you want to view more details about the selected label type, click the <u>D</u>etails button. Word displays a dialog box similar to the one in figure 15.22. Choose OK to return to the Label Options dialog box. To learn how to create a custom mailing label size, see "Creating Custom Mailing Labels," later in this section.

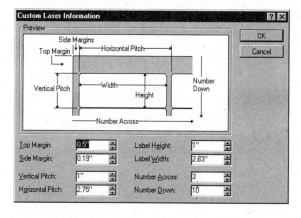

Fig. 15.22
In this dialog box, you can preview any available label type and set custom sizes.

III

Creating
Envelopes & Mailings

5. When you are satisfied with all your selections, choose OK.

6. Word displays the Create Labels dialog box (see fig. 15.23). Insert the appropriate merge fields in the Sam<u>p</u>le Label box and choose OK. Word then displays the Mail Merge Helper.

Fig. 15.23

Use the Create Labels dialog box to build a label by inserting merge field codes.

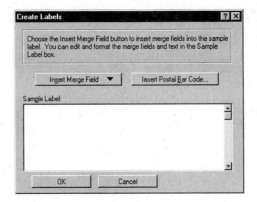

7. Click the <u>M</u>erge button to display the Merge dialog box.

8. Select the options you want and then proceed with error checking, query definition, and merging. When you are finished, click the <u>M</u>erge button.

Word creates a new document containing a table formatted for the type of labels you selected. You can merge the labels to a new document or print them in the usual manner.

Printing Labels for a Single Address

Naturally, not all your letters will be form letters. In the <u>L</u>abels tab of the Envelopes and Labels dialog box, you can print a single mailing label or several labels containing the same address.

To print one or more mailing labels for a single document, follow these steps:

1. Activate the main document for the form letter.

2. Choose <u>T</u>ools, <u>E</u>nvelopes and Labels.

3. In the Envelopes and Labels dialog box, select the <u>L</u>abels tab.

4. Examine the fields displayed in the Address box for accuracy. Or, if you want to print return address labels, select Use <u>R</u>eturn Address.

5. If you want to print a single address label, select Si<u>n</u>gle Label and specify the location of the label where you want to print. For single-wide, continuous-feed labels for dot-matrix printers, use the defaults (Ro<u>w</u> 1, <u>C</u>olumn 1). For labels on cut sheets for laser printers, you will usually have to specify the location of the next available blank label on the page, as shown in figure 15.24.

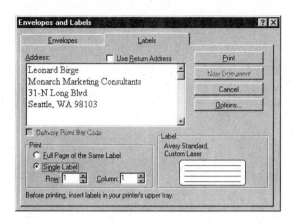

Fig. 15.24

In the Print area of the Envelopes and Labels dialog box, you can choose to print a single label. In this example, the address prints on the label in the first column of the first row of the label sheet.

6. If necessary, click the Options button and make changes in the Label Options dialog box. Then choose OK.

7. Make sure that the label paper is loaded in the printer; then click Print to print the labels.

Creating Custom Mailing Labels

You can design your own labels if you can't find the right size in the Label Options dialog box.

To change the label format to a nonstandard size when creating a mailing label document, follow these steps:

1. In the Label Options dialog box, select a label format similar to the format you want.

2. Click the Details button. Word displays the Label Preview dialog box.

   The Preview window contains a representation of the current label format. In the bottom portion of the dialog box, enter your custom label specifications. (The annotations in the Preview window illustrate the effects of the specifications.) Enter a new value for any of the measurements (or change the amount by clicking the attached arrow buttons), and watch the Preview window reflect the change.

   If you change the specifications in a way that makes it impossible to fit the specified number of labels on a page, Word displays a message.

3. When you are satisfied with all your selections, choose OK. Then click OK in the dialog box that appears to confirm that you want to override the existing custom label specifications.

III

Creating
Envelopes & Mailings

4. In the Label Options dialog box, Word updates the information in the Label Information box. Choose OK to accept the changes.

Word now displays the Create Labels dialog box, where you can proceed with label creation, merging, and printing.

Caution

Do not use labels with adhesive backing designed for copiers in laser printers. Laser printers operate at high temperatures, which can melt and separate labels, creating a mess in your printer. Suppliers such as Avery manufacture a complete line of labels of different sizes and shapes made especially for laser printers.

Suppressing Blank Lines in Addresses

Most business mailings include fields for information such as title, suite number, mail station, and so on. If some information is missing, however, blank lines can show up in your addresses or labels, producing an unfinished, unprofessional appearance. To ensure that blanks are skipped, after you choose the <u>M</u>erge button from the Mail Merge Helper the Merge dialog box appears. In this dialog box, make sure you select the <u>D</u>on't Print Blank Lines When Data Fields Are Empty option. Blank lines involving a MERGEFIELD are skipped if they end with a paragraph mark (¶). Lines ending with a line feed (Shift+Enter) are not skipped.

Modifying Your Mail Merge

Get in the habit of testing small mail merge runs before printing a large mail merge involving tens or hundreds of documents. In most cases you will find that you will want to make some modification of your main document, merge fields, or other information. This section contains tips on how to modify mail merge documents.

Checking for Errors

Browsing through the merged document is helpful in spotting problems with the merge, but when the data source contains a large number of records, you might want a higher level of assurance. You can check the entire data source for errors by clicking an error-checking button in the Mail Merge toolbar.

 When you click the Check for Errors button, Word for Windows reads your data source and checks for errors, such as field names that do not meet the rules for bookmarks. Word checks also to ensure that the number of field names and the number of fields in each record (or row) are the same. You are also warned if the data source cannot be found or if it contains blank records.

To check the main document and data source for errors, follow these steps:

1. Click the Check for Errors button in the Mail Merge toolbar. The Checking and Reporting Errors dialog box appears (see fig. 15.25).

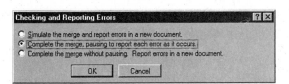

Fig. 15.25
Select the appropriate error-reporting option in the Checking and Reporting Errors dialog box.

Tip
Choose the Help button for more information specific to the

2. Select the error-reporting option you want. The first option simulates the merge, and the second and third complete it. The second option displays messages as errors occur, and the third option puts them in a new document. If you expect some errors, consider simulating the merge first.

3. Word next displays a dialog box. If you choose to report errors as they occur, the first dialog box displayed might contain an error message, like the one in figure 15.26. Choose OK to clear the dialog box (or boxes) and proceed accordingly.

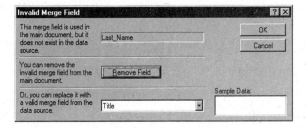

Fig. 15.26
This error message appears when Word cannot find a field name in the data source that corresponds to a merge field in the main document.

III

The Invalid Merge Field dialog box assists you in correcting the problem in the merge document. Click the Remove Field button to remove the offending field from the main document. If the field mismatch is the result of a typographical error in the main document, you can correct it by selecting the valid field name from the list box at the bottom of the dialog box. When you select a field name from this list, the corresponding value from the data source is displayed in the Sample Data box.

Creating
Envelopes & Mailings

The following guidelines can prevent errors that commonly cause problems:

- Field names must not have spaces. Use an underscore rather than a space.

- Field names must not start with a number but can have a number in them.

- Field names must be in one row at the top of the data source.

- Field names must be unique (no duplicates).

- Each field (column) of data must have a field name.

- The number of fields in each record must match the number of field names.

> **Note**
>
> If the records in the data source are not in a table and if commas, tabs, or cells are missing, the number of fields in a record may not match the number of fields in the heading.

Merging to Letterhead

The first page of a form letter is usually on letterhead paper and needs a different top margin from that of the following pages. To compensate for the difference in top margins in your normal documents and form letters, use a different header for the first page.

To create a first-page only header on the active document, follow these steps:

1. Choose View, Header and Footer.

2. Click the Page Setup button in the Header and Footer toolbar to display the Page Setup dialog box.

3. Select the Layout tab if it is not already selected.

4. Select the Different First Page check box.

5. Choose OK.

In the header-editing box that appears at the top of the document, enter the letterhead text. This header is for the first page; the following pages will begin body copy underneath the top margin set by the document format.

If your printer has double paper bins—like the HP LaserJet Series IIID, IIISi, and 4Si—you can pull letterhead paper from the letterhead bin. If your printer has only one bin, you can stack alternating letterhead and bond in the tray, or feed letterhead into the manual feed tray. If you push the letterhead far enough into the manual feed at the appropriate time, the LaserJet pulls from the manual feed before pulling from the bin.

Merging Envelopes

With the Mail Merge Helper, you can create mail-merge envelopes or a document that merges mail-merge envelopes and documents at the same time.

To create mail-merge envelopes, create a data source and main document. Attach the data source to the main document. Be sure that the top of the main document contains a three-to-five-line address composed of MERGEFIELD codes. If you are not mailing a main document, create a blank letter with the MERGEFIELD codes in an address block. The automatic envelope maker uses this document as a basis for its MERGEFIELD address information.

To set up a program for creating a mass-mailing envelope based on your main document, follow these steps:

1. Activate the main document.

2. Choose Tools, Mail Merge.

3. Under the Main Document heading of the Mail Merge Helper dialog box, click the Create button.

4. Select Envelopes.

5. Word displays a decision dialog box. The options offered depend on the condition of the active document when you began the procedure. Click Active Window if it appears in the dialog box. Otherwise, click New Main Document.

   Word displays the Mail Merge Helper dialog box (see fig. 15.27). The information under Main Document reflects the merge type (Envelopes) and new document name.

To finish creating the mass-mailing envelope, follow these steps:

1. Under Data Source, click the Get Data button.

2. Click Open Data Source.

Tip

The HP LaserJet accepts paper from the manual feed before pulling from the bin if the printer has the default menu settings.

Tip

If the Mail Merge toolbar is displayed, you can click the Mail Merge Helper dialog box button.

III

Creating
Envelopes & Mailings

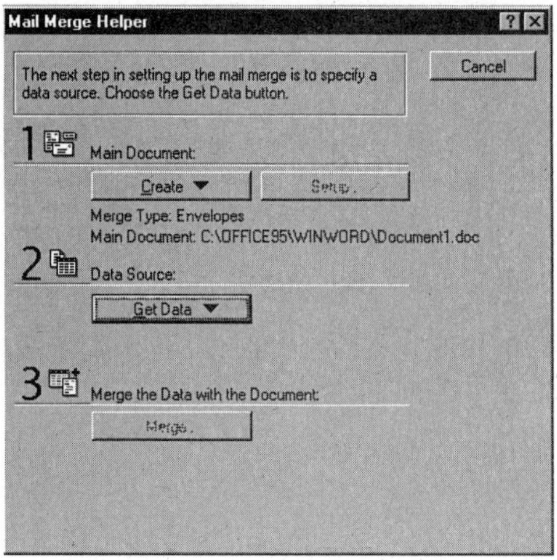

Fig. 15.27

The Mail Merge Helper dialog box changes to reflect the fact that you're creating a new main document.

3. Select the data source from the File Name list, and then choose Open. If necessary, browse through the folders in the usual manner. Word then displays the dialog box shown in figure 15.28.

   You can also click Use Address Book. Select Schedule+ Contact List, and then choose OK.

Fig. 15.28

Word displays this dialog box when it needs to set up your main document.

4. Click Set Up Main Document.

5. In the Envelope Options dialog box, change any settings in the Envelope Options and Printing Options tabs and then choose OK. Word displays the Envelope Address dialog box (see fig. 15.29).

6. Insert the merge fields for names and addresses, adding any necessary spaces and punctuation. You select these fields in the same way as when you created the form letter earlier in this chapter—by clicking the Insert Merge Field button and selecting the field names from the drop-down list.

   You can click the Insert Postal Bar Code button to print POSTNET codes on the envelopes. The Insert Postal Bar Code dialog box prompts you for the name of the field containing the postal code.

When you finish entering fields, choose OK. Word brings you back to the Mail Merge Helper dialog box.

Fig. 15.29
Use the Envelope Address dialog box to insert the field codes that will insert data into the address area of an envelope.

7. In the Mail Merge Helper, click <u>M</u>erge. Your document will look something like that shown in figure 15.30.

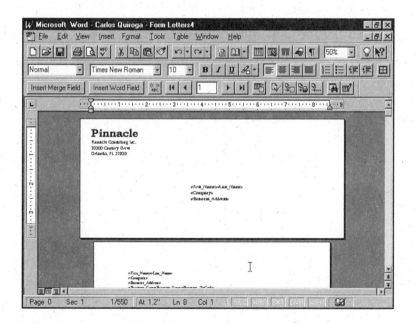

Fig. 15.30
You can create envelopes for mass mailings that use the merge fields you created for the related form letter document. The envelopes can also include graphics and logos.

8. Select the <u>M</u>erge To list and select one of the following types of merges:

Select the number of records to be merged from the Records to Be Merged group.

Select from the When Merging Records group how blank lines will be handled:

Don't print blank lines when data fields are empty.

Print blank lines when data fields are empty.

9. Choose Merge.

The envelope is now a new document—separate and distinct from the main document. You should save the envelope main document for later use.

You might ask why steps 5–7 were necessary; that is, why doesn't Word for Windows assume that you want to attach the envelope main document to the same data source that's attached to the form letter? Actually, it's because your envelope main document rarely changes—unless you change envelope sizes. By contrast, it's quite possible that you will generate a variety of form letters, which will be saved under different document names. By forcing you to create a "stand-alone" envelope, Word relieves you from having to go through the many steps just described for each envelope you create.

> **Note**
>
> Word for Windows no longer provides concurrent form letter and envelope printing.

Editing the Main Document

After the data source is attached to the main document, you can edit the document by using normal typing and formatting features. Whether you start with an existing document containing body copy or a new blank document, you must enter MERGEFIELD codes to tell Word where to insert specific data from the data source. Once the data source is attached, you can use the Insert Merge Field button in the Mail Merge toolbar to insert these codes.

To insert merge fields in the main document, follow these steps:

1. Move the insertion point to where you want the first merged data to appear.

Insert Merge Field

2. Click the Insert Merge Field button from the Mail Merge toolbar that appears under the formatting toolbar. This displays a list of the fields in your data source.

3. Select the field name from the Print Merge Fields list.

4. Choose OK or press Enter.

5. Move the insertion point to the next location where you want data inserted.

6. Continue inserting all the merge fields necessary for the form letter in this manner. Don't forget, however, to insert needed text—for example, spaces between merge fields for city, state, and ZIP code.

Tip

Make sure to leave a space before or after the merge field just as you would leave a space before or after a word you type.

To add ordinary word fields, such as Date, to main documents, you can choose Insert, Field. You can insert certain Word fields—such as Ask, Fill-in, and Next Record—by clicking the Insert Word Field button and selecting the field from the drop-down list. You learn how to do this later in the chapter.

You can delete unwanted fields from main documents in the same way you delete text in any other Word document.

You can get a sneak preview of the merged document by clicking the View Merged Data button in the Mail Merge toolbar. With View Merged Data off, your completed main document resembles the document at the top in figure 15.31. After you click the View Merged Data button, the document appears as shown at the bottom of that figure.

By default, the main document displays the data from the first record in the data source. You can use the VCR-type control icons in the Mail Merge toolbar to browse through the entire merged document. The controls move backward and forward through records in the data source in the same way VCR controls move through a video tape.

The top screen in figure 15.31 shows documents with the Field Codes option deselected (found in the View tab of the Options dialog box). When field codes are displayed, the document looks like that in figure 15.32.

Selecting Specific Records to Merge

Word for Windows enables you to select which records you want to merge. You can build *rules* that limit which data is merged. The rules form English statements specifying the data you want to merge. You can use this feature if you are doing a targeted mailing to a particular area (selected by ZIP code). For example, the statement Lastname is equal to Smith merges only those records in which the name *Smith* appears in the Lastname field.

To select specific records for merging, follow these steps:

1. Activate the main document.

2. Click the Merge dialog box button from the Mail Merge toolbar or choose Tools, Mail Merge. Click the Merge button to display the Merge dialog box (refer to fig. 15.20).

III

Creating
Envelopes & Mailings

Fig. 15.31

When the document displays the field names (top), click the View Merged Data button to display the data merged from the data source (bottom).

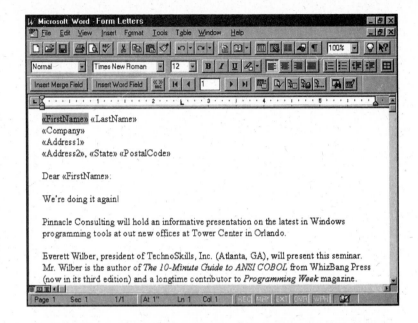

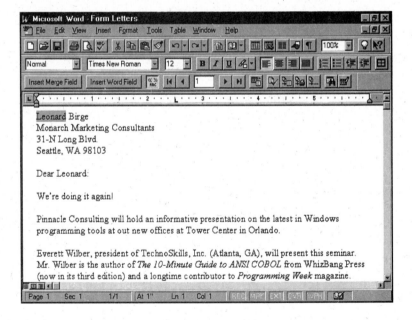

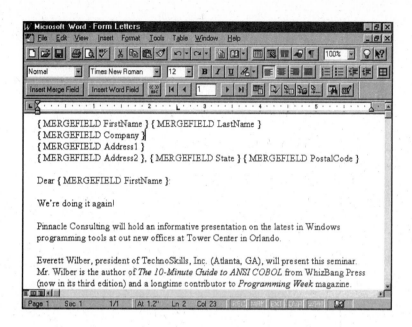

Fig. 15.32
When the Field
Codes option is
turned on, the
document shows
the MERGEFIELD
field codes.

3. From the Merge dialog box, click the Query Options button to display
   the Query Options list, shown in figure 15.33.

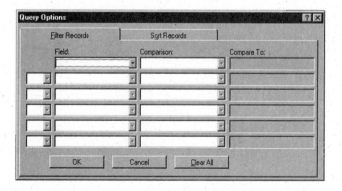

Fig. 15.33
The Query
Options dialog
box provides
control over
selection of
records.

4. Select from the Field drop-down list the first field you want to limit.

5. The phrase `Equal to` appears in the Comparison list. If you want something other than an exact match, select the type of comparison (such as
   `Less than` or `Greater than`) you want to make.

6. In the Compare To text box, type the numeric value or text you want
   compared to the field. Figure 15.34 shows an example that merges only
   those records in which the last name begins with a P or a letter following P in the alphabet.

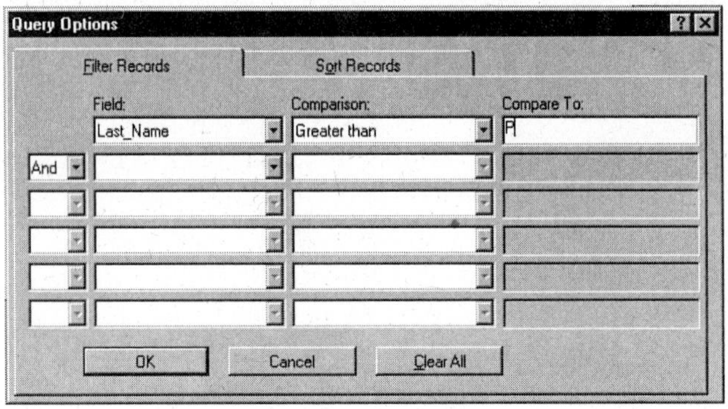

Fig. 15.34

To select an alphabetic or numeric range of records, enter the field name, comparison phrase, and comparison value. This rule merges records with last names beginning with P through Z.

7. After you make an entry in the Compare To box, the word And appears in the leftmost drop-down list in the next row. Select the And or Or option in this box to add another selection rule. If you want to merge only those records that meet both conditions, select And. To merge all records that meet either condition, select Or.

8. To add another rule, repeat steps 4–7.

9. To sort the resulting merged records on any of the selected fields, select the Sort Records tab (see fig. 15.35). You can sort by up to three key fields. Select (or enter) the name of the primary sort field in the Sort By drop-down list box. Enter secondary or tertiary keys, if used, in the Then By and Then By boxes, respectively. You can select the sort order with the option buttons to the right of the list boxes.

Fig. 15.35

Select the Sort Records tab to sort records in a merged document.

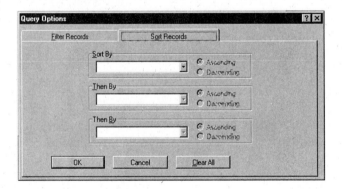

10. Complete the merge by choosing OK. When the merge is complete, click Cancel from the Mail Merge Helper.

If you make a mistake, you can revise any entry or selection at any time. To start over again, click the Clear All button in the Filter Records tab of the Query Options dialog box.

When you build rules, a complete English statement is built that specifies how data from the data source is selected for merging. Figure 15.36, for example, illustrates a rule that would be useful for mailing to a list of contributors. If the data source contains fields for amount pledged (Pledged) and amount contributed (Paid), this rule selects everyone who pledged $200 or more and paid less than $50.

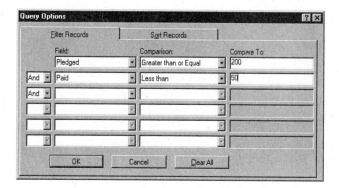

Fig. 15.36
A completed dialog box selects donors who have yet to fulfill their pledges.

Here are some tips for building rules:

- Text is compared in the same way as numbers. For example, B is less than C.

- Select ranges using And. A numeric range, for example, may be as follows:

```
ZIP is Greater than 95400
And
ZIP is Less than 95600
```

- A text range may be as follows:

```
State is Greater than or Equal to CA
And
State is Less than or Equal to NY
```

- Select individual names or numbers with Or. A numeric selection, for example, may be as follows:

```
ZIP is Equal to 95409
Or
ZIP is Equal to 95412
```

■ A text selection may be as follows:

```
Title is Equal to President
Or
Title is Equal to Manager
```

Changing the Data Source Your Main Document Is Attached To

Tip

To personally select which records to merge, create an extra field (column) with a field name such as **Selection** in your data document. In that column, enter **1** in the row of each record you want to merge. Use the Record Selection dialog box to specify that you want only records with 1 in the Selection field to merge.

You may have one form letter that you use with different mailing lists. In that case, you will want to attach your main document to other data sources. You can use the same procedure that you do for attaching the original data source.

To attach a main document to a different data source, follow these steps:

1. Choose Tools, Mail Merge.

2. Click the Get Data button.

3. If the data source is to be an existing file, click Open Data Source or Use Address Book.

   To create a new data source, choose Create Data Source or Use Address Book.

4. Select or create the data source file, as appropriate.

> **Caution**
>
> Quite often, field headers in the new data source do not match the field codes in the main document. It's a good idea to check for errors immediately after you attach a main document to a new data source.

Using One Main Document with Different Data Sources and Field Names

If you use a database program to maintain your mailing lists, you will appreciate this section. Your database program may generate data sources that do not have a *header record*, the top row that contains field names. Instead of opening what may be a huge data source and adding a top row of field names, you can attach a header file. This also enables you to use many data sources without having to change the MERGEFIELD in a main document. A *header file* contains a top row of field names, which are used with the data source. The header file can contain a single row of names or be an existing data source with the correct field names. The header file must have the same number of field names as there are fields in the data source.

To create a separate header file, follow these steps:

1. Be sure that the main document is the active document.

2. Choose Tools, Mail Merge.

3. Click the Get Data button.

4. Select Header Options. Word displays the Header Options dialog box.

5. Click Create. Word displays the Create Header Source dialog box (see fig. 15.37).

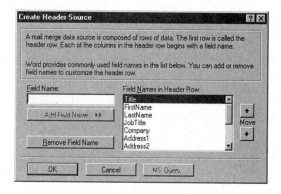

Fig. 15.37
The Create Header Source dialog box works much like the Create Data Source dialog box.

6. Edit the list of field names as you did earlier in the chapter when you created a data source. To remove the selected field name, click Remove Field Name. To add a field name, enter it in the Field Name box and click Add Field Name. When you are satisfied with your list, choose OK, The Save As dialog box appears.

7. Enter a file name for the header source in the File Name box in the Save Data Source dialog box; then choose OK.

Word displays the Mail Merge Helper dialog box, updated for the new header source. The header source you created is attached immediately to the active main document. You still must attach a data source to the main document. The data source itself should not contain a header record because Word for Windows will merge the row of names as it would a data record.

> **Note**
>
> To print with separate header and data sources, be sure that you attach the header and data sources in the Mail Merge Helper dialog box before you choose Merge.

III

Creating
Envelopes & Mailings

Putting Custom Entries in Mail Merge Documents

Having worked through all the basics of merging documents, you are now ready for a few of the most powerful features of Word for Windows. One of these features eliminates blank lines in mail-merge addresses and labels—a feature that gives you a more professional appearance. You also see how to use a main document with different data sources without having to re-create field names. The secret is to use a header file that shows the field names. Another important topic is how to make merge documents pause and ask you for a customized entry. Finally, this section describes some of the databases you can use to manage large or complex Word for Windows mailing lists.

Inserting Word Fields in a Main Document

You can insert certain Word fields from the Mail Merge toolbar. Suppose that you want Word to insert one of two different personalized messages in your form letter, depending on whether a condition was satisfied.

To insert an IF field in a main document, follow these steps:

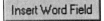

1. Click the Insert Word Field button to display a subset of Word fields.

2. Select If... Then... Else. Word displays the dialog box shown in figure 15.38. Enter your comparison criteria and the two conditional texts you want in the letter; then choose OK.

Fig. 15.38

Using the Insert Word Field button to insert an IF field displays a helpful dialog box.

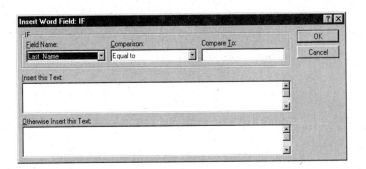

If you then display field codes in the document (by choosing Tools, Options and clicking Field Codes), the IF field will look something like the one in figure 15.39.

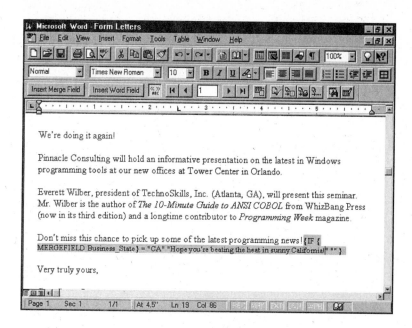

Fig. 15.39
The IF field shown
in this letter will
add a personal
touch to recipients
with a California
address.

Requesting User Input during a Mail Merge

Word for Windows can automate and personalize your written communication at the same time, but for truly personal form letters, you can put FILLIN
fields in form letters so that you can type custom phrases into each mail-
merge letter.

FILLIN is a Word field (as opposed to merge fields) that can automate document creation. You learn about fields in depth in Chapter 20, "Automating
with Field Codes." The following example illustrates how Word fields can be
useful in form letters.

Figure 15.40 shows a main document with a FILLIN field in the second paragraph of the body text. During the merge operation, this field displays a dialog
box that prompts the user to enter a personalized message to the recipient.
The \d switch and the text that follows tell Word for Windows to display Go
Blue against the Wildcats in the Silicon Bowl! as a default response.

III

Creating
Envelopes & Mailings

Fig. 15.40
Use the FILLIN field when you want to prompt the user to type information in merged letters.

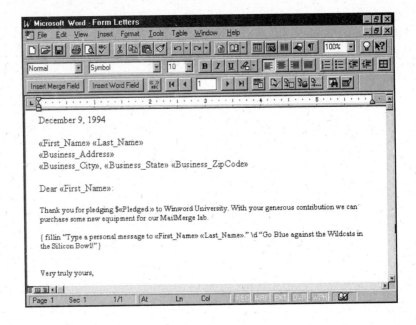

To enter the FILLIN field in your document, insert or type the following field code where you want the results to appear:

```
{fillin \d "Go Blue against the Wildcats in the Silicon Bowl!" }
```

Naturally, you can type the FILLIN field code in the document (remember to press Ctrl+F9 to create the field characters {}), or you can insert it by choosing Insert, Field.

▶ See "Understanding the Basics of Fields," p. 589

To personalize the letter, you need to know to whom you are sending it. To display in the fill-in dialog box the name of the person being addressed, type a prompt in quotes; then in the quotes, use the Insert Merge Field button to insert a MERGEFIELD of the person's name. The field should look like the following:

```
{fillin  "Type a personal message to
➥{mergefield Firstname}  {mergefield Lastname}"
➥\d  "Go Blue against the Wildcats in the Silicon Bowl!" }
```

Notice that the MERGEFIELD code is inside the quotes that enclose the prompt. ❖

Part IV

Mastering
Special Features

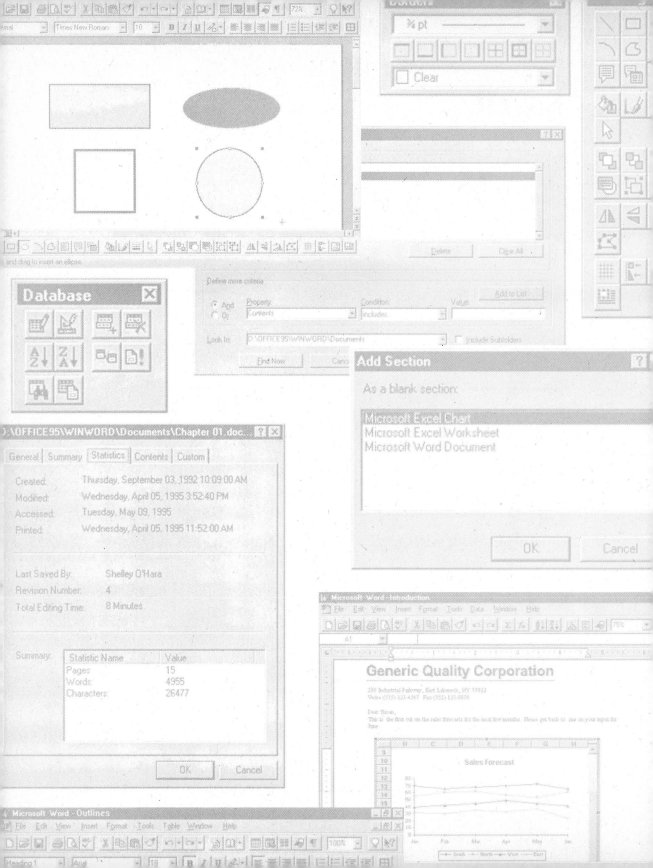

Chapter 16

Creating and Editing Tables

Word for Windows has a very powerful Tables feature that provides an excellent way of working with columns or tabular data and for simplifying many other tasks. You can use tables to show lists of data, personnel rosters, financial information, scripts, and procedural steps. Tables can even include pasted illustrations that explain steps in a list, display side-by-side text and graphics, or present sideheads beside text in a document.

In many cases, tables provide an easier and more flexible solution to problems that you might have solved in the past by using tabs. The commands available for working with tables simplify the job of arranging and formatting tables of information.

In this chapter, you learn how to:

- Create a table with the Table Wizard

- Use the Table menu options

- Type and move to cells in a table

- Move and copy cells

- Change column widths and row heights

- Add or delete cells, rows, or columns

Understanding Tables

If you have worked with a spreadsheet application such as Microsoft Excel or Lotus 1-2-3, you may find working with tables is similar to working with a spreadsheet. A *table* is simply a grid of columns and rows. The intersection of a column and a row is a rectangular or square box called a *cell*. Each cell is independent and can be sized or formatted. Figure 16.1 shows an example of a table of data that was created and formatted by using the table feature.

Fig. 16.1

Producing tables with a professional look is simple in Word for Windows.

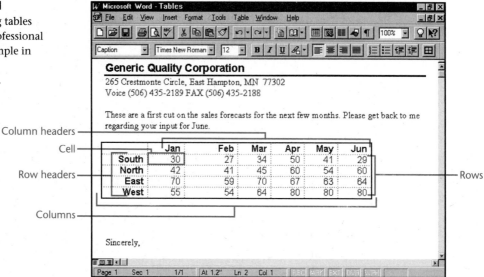

You can insert text, numbers, pictures, or formulas in a cell. If you enter text in a cell, the text wraps to the next line according to the width of the cell. If you adjust the width of the cell or column, the text adjusts to the new width. You can enter or edit text in any cell of the table. A table enables you to present text in columns and align paragraphs or graphics. Figure 16.2 shows text in a table.

Creating Tables

You can insert a table anywhere in a document. A table can span more than one page, and you can frame a table as well as resize and position it on the page. You can attach a caption to a table and designate headings for the table so that if the table splits between pages, Word automatically repeats the headings at the top of the table.

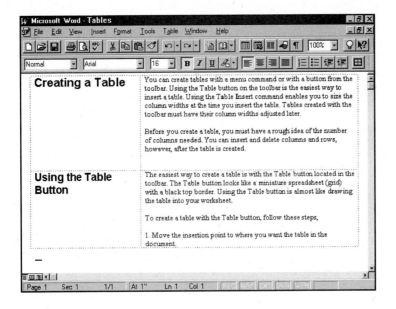

Fig. 16.2
You can use tables to create headings to the left of the body text in your documents.

You can create tables by choosing T**a**ble, **I**nsert Table from the pull-down menus, or you can click the Insert Table button on the Standard toolbar. Often, the Insert Table button is the easiest way to create a table because it takes fewer keystrokes. When you click the Insert Table button, Word sets the width of the columns automatically, so you might have to adjust the widths later. When you use the menu command, you can determine the width of the columns when you insert the table.

You can also use the Wi**z**ard command, which is available when you choose T**a**ble, **I**nsert Table to create a table. The Wi**z**ard command accesses the Table Wizard. The Table Wizard guides you step-by-step through the process of creating a table. After you create a table, you can use the Table Auto**F**ormat command to select from a collection of predefined table layouts, which can simplify the task of formatting your table.

If the information that you want to include in a table already appears in your document as text, you can convert the text to a table.

Creating a Table with the Table Wizard

The Table Wizard easily formats tables of any size. The Table Wizard guides you through the table-creation process by displaying a series of boxes that graphically present the most common choices made for preformatted tables. The Table Wizard also makes it easy to handle special situations, such as re-peating column headings at the top of pages when a table is longer than a

Tip
Before you create a table, it's helpful to have a general idea of the number of columns that you need. You can insert and delete columns and rows, however, after you create the table.

Tip
Drag tables to any location on a page by framing them as described in Chapter 24, "Framing and Moving Text and Graphics."

single page. The Table Wizard also formats the headings and table content, and finishes by going directly into AutoFormat, which guides you through the table-formatting process.

To create a table with the Table Wizard, follow these steps:

1. Position the insertion point where you want the top-left corner of the table.

2. Choose Table, Insert Table, and then click the Wizard button.

3. Select the table layout from the Table Wizard window shown in figure 16.3. Then click the Next button.

Fig. 16.3

In the first box of the Table Wizard, select the table layout you want.

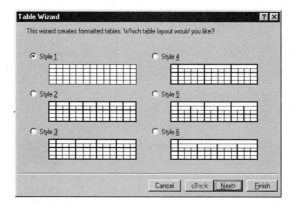

4. Select the type of column headings from the window shown in figure 16.4. Then click Next.

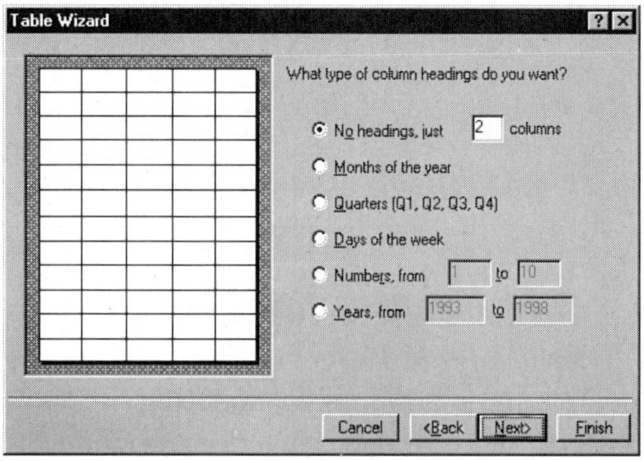

Fig. 16.4

In the second box of the Table Wizard, select the type of column headings you want.

5. Select the type of row headings from the window shown in figure 16.5. Then click <u>N</u>ext.

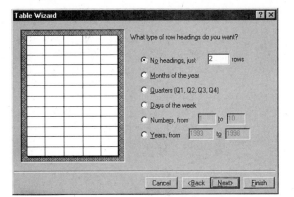

Fig. 16.5
In the third box of the Table Wizard, select the type of row headings you want.

6. Select the type of numeric or text alignment you want for the table contents, as shown in figure 16.6. Then click <u>N</u>ext.

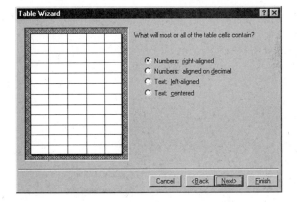

Fig. 16.6
In the fourth box of the Table Wizard, select the alignment for the table contents.

7. Select the table orientation as shown in figure 16.7. Then click <u>N</u>ext.

8. In the final Wizard window, select whether you want to see a Help window that will guide you as you create the table. Then click the <u>F</u>inish button.

9. Word displays the first window of Table AutoFormat. Click the Cancel button if you do not want to use AutoFormat to format the table.

Fig. 16.7
In the fifth box of the Table Wizard, select the table orientation.

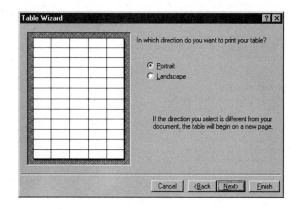

Table AutoFormat presents predesigned formats for tables. It makes formatting very easy.

▶ See "Formatting a Table with Table AutoFormat," p. 535

Using the Table, Insert Table Command

Choose Table, Insert Table if you want to specify the width of the columns in the table at the same time you insert the table.

To insert a table in a document, follow these steps:

1. Position the insertion point where you want the top-left corner of the table.

2. Choose Table, Insert Table. The Insert Table dialog box appears, as shown in figure 16.8.

Fig. 16.8
You can insert a table by using the Insert Table dialog box.

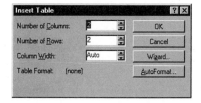

Tip
If you are unsure how many columns or rows you need, you easily can add rows and columns to the end of a table or in the middle of the table.

3. Select or type the number of columns that you want in the Number of Columns text box.

4. If you know how many rows you need, select or type the number of rows in the Number of Rows text box.

5. If you know how wide you want all columns, adjust the Column Width box.

You easily can change column widths if you are unsure of the column width or if you later want to adjust the table.

6. Click the Wizard button to be guided through the creation of a table.

7. Click the AutoFormat button to apply predefined formats to the table when Word creates it.

8. Click OK.

Word inserts the table in your worksheet. The table may be visible or invisible depending on whether you have turned on table gridlines (see "Displaying or Hiding Gridlines and End Marks" later in this chapter). The insertion point appears in the first cell.

Using the Insert Table Button

The easiest way to create a table is by using the Insert Table button on the Standard toolbar. Using the Insert Table button is almost like drawing the table into your worksheet.

To create a table using the Insert Table button, follow these steps:

1. Move the insertion point to where you want to insert the table in the document.

2. Click the Insert Table button on the Standard toolbar and drag the mouse pointer within the grid down, to the right, or down and to the right.

When you click the button, a grid of rows and columns that looks like a miniature table appears. As long as you continue to hold down the mouse button, you can move the pointer within the grid to select the size of the table that you want to insert. If you move the pointer beyond the right or lower borders, the grid expands. Figure 16.9 shows the Insert Table button expanded and a table size selected.

3. Release the mouse button when the selected grid is the size you want your table to be.

If you have already begun the selection process with the Insert Table button and then decide that you do not want to insert a table, continue to hold down the mouse button and drag the pointer until it is outside the grid and to the left; then release the button. You also can drag up until the pointer is over the button and then release the button.

Fig. 16.9
The Insert Table
button enables
you to draw your
table the size that
you want.

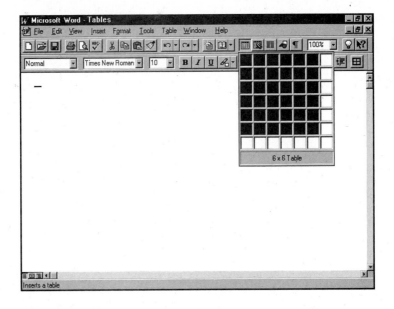

◀ See "Editing a
Document,"
p. 123

Note

You can store tables, like text, as an AutoText entry. If you use the same type of table repeatedly, you can save considerable time by storing the table as an AutoText entry, then typing the AutoText name in the document where you want it inserted.

To store a table as a glossary, select the entire table and choose Edit, AutoText. Type a name for the entry in the Name box and click OK. To later insert the table glossary, type the table glossary name and press F3.

Tip
You can add to any
toolbar a custom
button that toggles
gridlines on or off.
See Chapter 36,
"Customizing the
Toolbar, Menus,
and Shortcut Keys"
to learn about
custom buttons.

Displaying or Hiding Gridlines and End Marks

Table gridlines can show you the outline of your cells and table. Such outlines can make working in tables easier. The end-of-cell mark indicates where the contents of a cell end, and the end-of-row mark indicates the end of the row. Figure 16.10 shows a table in which the gridlines and end marks are turned off. Figure 16.11 shows the same table with the gridlines and end marks turned on. As you can see, these lines and marks make it easier to read a table. The gridlines do not print.

If you want gridlines on or off, choose Table, Gridlines. This command toggles gridlines on or off. A check mark appears to the left of the menu command if gridlines are turned on. To turn end marks on or off quickly, press Shift+Ctrl+8 or click the Show/Hide ¶ button on the Standard toolbar.

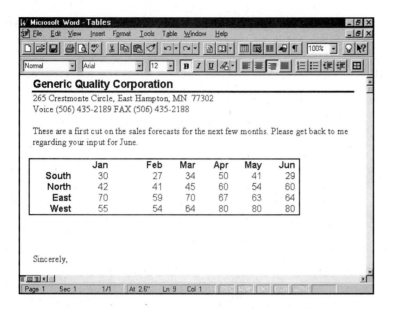

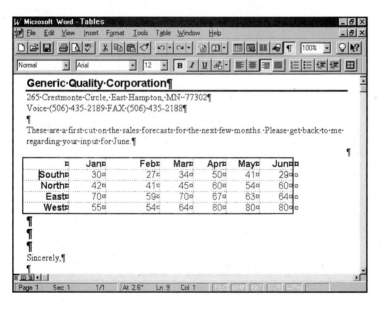

Fig. 16.10
In this table,
gridlines and end
marks are turned
off.

IV

Mastering Special Features

Fig. 16.11
This table is easier
to read and edit
because gridlines
are turned on.

Typing and Moving in a Table

When you create a new table, the insertion point flashes in the first cell—the
cell at the upper-left corner of the table. To insert text or numbers in the cell,
just start typing.

As you enter text into a cell, characters will automatically wrap to the next line in the cell as needed. In a Word for Windows table, the entire row of cells expands downward to accommodate the text. The same thing happens if you press Enter in a cell. The insertion point moves to the next line down, and the row becomes taller. Each cell acts like a miniature word processing page.

To move forward through the cells in the table, press Tab. Press Shift+Tab to move backward through the cells. When you press Tab to move to a cell, you select any text in the cell. To move with the mouse, click the cell at the point where you want the insertion point to appear.

If you reach the table's last (lower-right) cell and press Tab, you create a new row of cells at the end of the table and move the insertion point into the first cell of that row. To leave the table, you must press an arrow key or use the mouse to move the insertion point outside the table. Don't be concerned with the number of rows in a table. You add additional rows to the end of the table by pressing Tab when the insertion point is in the table's last cell.

Arrow keys also help you move around in a table. Table 16.1 summarizes these keyboard movements and includes several other handy shortcuts to help you move around in a table.

Table 16.1 Shortcut Keys Used to Move in a Table	
Key(s)	**Function**
Tab	Moves the insertion point right one cell; inserts a new row when pressed in the bottom-right cell
Shift+Tab	Moves the insertion point left one cell
Arrow key	Moves the insertion point character-by-character through a cell and into the next cell when the insertion point reaches the end of the current cell
Alt+Home	Moves the insertion point to the first cell in the row
Alt+End	Moves the insertion point to the last cell in the row
Alt+Page Up	Moves the insertion point to the top cell in the column
Alt+Page Down	Moves the insertion point to the bottom cell in the column

Using Indents and Tabs in a Cell

Just like regular text paragraphs, cells contain indents. You can format these indents using the same techniques that you use to format a paragraph. Use the ruler or choose Format, Paragraph.

To change the indent or first-line indent within a cell using Format, Paragraph, follow these steps:

1. Select the cell.

2. Choose Format, Paragraph.

3. Set indents in the Paragraph dialog box's Indentation group. Then choose OK.

To change the indent or first-line indent within a cell using the ruler, follow these steps:

◀ See "Setting Indents," p. 306

1. Select the cell.

2. Click the right mouse button in the selected cell and select Paragraph. If you select Paragraph in the right-click menu so that the paragraph box is displayed, you cannot move the indent markers.

3. Drag the indent and first-line indent markers to a new location.

Pressing Tab moves you from one cell to the next in a table. Pressing Shift+Tab moves you to the previous cell. You also can set tabs within a cell. Select the cells in which you want tabs, and set the tab stops in the usual way—using the ruler or Format, Tabs. To move the insertion point to the tab stop within the cell, however, press Ctrl+Tab rather than just Tab.

◀ See "Setting Tabs," p. 300

Attaching Captions to Tables

You can add a caption to a table to identify it, to enable you to cross-reference the table, or to create a list of tables in your document. When you insert a caption, Word uses the SEQ field code to number the table. If you insert a new table before or after an existing table, Word automatically updates the numbering for all the tables.

To attach a caption to a table, follow these steps:

1. Select the entire table by moving the insertion point anywhere in the table and choosing Table, Select Table or press Alt+Num5.

2. Display the Caption dialog box by choosing Insert, Caption (see fig. 16.12).

Fig. 16.12

You can attach a caption to a table in the Caption dialog box.

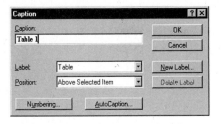

3. Select Table in the Label list if it isn't already selected.

4. Type text after the caption label in the Caption text box, if you want.

5. Select the position for the label in the Position list.

6. Choose OK.

► See "Adding Cross-References and Captions," p. 917

A caption for the table then appears at the position that you specified (see fig. 16.13). If Word displays the SEQ field code rather than the table number, choose Tools, Options, select the View tab, and clear the Field Codes option. Then choose OK.

Fig. 16.13

A caption is shown above the table.

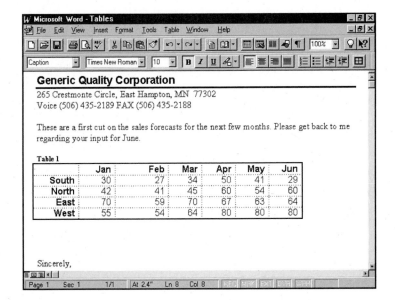

Editing Tables

After you create and fill your table, you probably will have to make changes to the table. You might need to move or copy cells, or insert new cells, rows, or columns to make room for additional text or graphics. Often you must adjust row heights and column widths. In the following sections, you learn how to perform all these tasks.

You can edit the contents within a cell using the same techniques that you use to edit text or graphics in a document. You can delete characters using the Backspace and Delete keys, and move around in the text using the mouse or the arrow keys. To edit the cells, rows, and columns in a table, you use different techniques, which the following sections describe.

By using the shortcut menus, you can quickly access many of the commands that you learn about in the following sections. To use the shortcut menus, point to a cell or selection that you have made in a table and click the right mouse button. A list of commands that you can use to edit or format the selection appears. Use the mouse to select the appropriate command.

Selecting and Editing Cells

Before you use the table editing commands, you must select the correct cells, rows, or columns for whatever changes you are making to the table. You have two ways to select the contents of a table:

- By character, for which you use Word for Windows' usual character-selection techniques

- By cell, for which Word for Windows offers special techniques

When you select the entire cell (or cells), the entire cell appears darkened (see fig. 16.14). Word for Windows enables you to select an entire row, an entire column, or the entire table easily.

	Jan	Feb	Mar	Apr	May	Jun
South	30	27	34	50	41	29
North	42	41	45	60	54	60
East	70	59	70	67	63	64
West	55	54	64	80	80	80

Fig. 16.14
A cell appears darkened when you select it.

Selecting by Menu

You can select rows, columns, or the entire table by using commands from the menu.

To select cells, rows, or columns, follow these steps:

1. Move the insertion point into the cell that contains the row or column you want to select. To select a table, you can select any cell in that table.

2. Choose T<u>a</u>ble. Then choose Select <u>R</u>ow, Select <u>C</u>olumn, or Select T<u>a</u>ble.

Selecting Cells with the Mouse

You also can use a mouse to select a cell's contents. Just drag across characters or double-click words in the usual way.

As you can do with the keyboard, you can use the mouse to extend the selection beyond the cell: as soon as the selection reaches the border of a cell, you begin selecting entire cells rather than characters. In addition, you can use special selection bars with the mouse. When you move the I-beam into a selection bar, the pointer changes to an arrow. You can use the mouse to select a cell, row, or column, depending on where you click the mouse pointer.

Table 16.2 summarizes the mouse selection techniques.

Table 16.2 Using the Mouse to Select in a Table	
Item to Select	**Mouse Action**
Characters	Drag across characters.
Cell	Click the cell selection area at the left inside edge of the cell.
Group of cells	Select the first cell or characters, then drag to the last cell or Shift+click the last cell.
Horizontal row	Click the selection area to the left of the table; drag down for multiple rows.
Vertical column	Click the top line of the column; drag to either side for multiple columns. (When positioned correctly, the pointer appears as a solid black down arrow.)
Table	Click the selection area to the left of the top row and drag down to select all rows or Shift+click to the left of the last row.

Troubleshooting

When I try to drag and drop cells I have selected, it doesn't work. The mouse pointer doesn't change to an arrow when I point to the selected cells.

When the drag-and-drop feature is turned off, the mouse pointer does not change to an arrow when you point to a selection, and you cannot drag the selection to a new location. To turn on drag-and-drop, choose <u>T</u>ools, <u>O</u>ptions, select the Edit tab, select the <u>D</u>rag and Drop Text Editing option, and then click OK.

Selecting Cells with the Keyboard

Word for Windows provides several other keyboard techniques for selecting cells and groups of cells. Table 16.3 lists these methods.

Table 16.3 Using Shortcut Keys to Select Cells	
Key(s)	**Selects**
Tab	The next cell
Shift+Tab	The previous cell
Shift+arrow key	Character-by-character in the current cell and then the entire adjacent cell
F8+up or down arrow	The current cell and the cell above or below (press Esc to end the selection)
F8+left or right arrow	Text in the current cell (character by character) and then all adjacent cells (press Esc to end the selection)
Alt+Num5 (on the numeric keypad)	An entire table

When you select with an arrow key, you first select each character in the cell. As soon as you go beyond the border of the cell, however, you begin selecting entire cells. If you change arrow directions, you select groups of adjacent cells. If you press Shift+right arrow or F8+right arrow to select three adjacent cells in a row and then press the down-arrow key once, for example, you extend the selection to include the entire contents of the three cells below the original three.

Moving and Copying Cells

Unless you do everything perfectly the first time, you might have to reorganize data in your tables. Word for Windows gives you all the flexibility of moving and copying in a table that you have with text.

Using the Mouse to Drag and Drop Cells, Rows, and Columns

The mouse shortcuts that work with text in body copy also work on cell contents, cells, or an entire table.

To move or copy the characters in a cell or one or more cells and their cellular structure, follow these steps:

1. Select the characters, cells, rows, or columns you want to move or copy.

2. Move the mouse pointer over the selected characters until it changes from an I-beam to an arrow pointed upward and to the left, as shown in figure 16.15. (The pointer might remain an arrow if you don't move it from the selected area.)

Fig. 16.15

Use the pointer to drag cells, rows, or columns.

	Jan	Feb	Mar	Apr	May	Jun
South	30	27	54	50	41	29
North	42	41	45	60	54	60
East	70	59	70	67	63	64
West	55	54	64	80	80	80

3. To move, hold down the left mouse button. To copy, hold down Ctrl and then the left mouse button. Notice the message in the status bar: Move to where? or Copy to where?

4. Position the grayed insertion point at the location where you want the moved or copied characters or cells to appear. Position the pointer over the top-left cell at the place where you want a range of cells to appear. The insertion point appears gray and displays a gray box at its bottom end.

5. Release the mouse button.

If you include the end-of-cell mark in your selection, the formatting for your selected cell or cells is moved or copied to the destination, along with the cell contents.

Using Cut, Copy, and Paste

Choosing Edit and then Cut, Copy, or Paste works much the same way in a table as with text outside a table. These commands enable you to move or copy cells within a table or copy a table to another location. You can cut and copy a single cell, multiple cells, or an entire table.

If you select only the text, number, or picture within a cell, you copy or cut only what you have selected, just as you do in a document's body copy. But if you select the entire cell or multiple cells, you copy the cell boundaries as well.

If you select an entire cell, the Copy command copies the entire cell to the Clipboard. The Cut command moves the entire contents of the cell to the Clipboard. The cell's boundaries remain in the table. When you paste cells from the Clipboard, the cell containing the insertion point receives the first cell on the Clipboard. The contents of the cells on the Clipboard replace the table's original cells, as shown in figures 16.16 and 16.17.

	Jan	Feb	Mar	Apr
South	30	27	34	50
North	42	41	45	60
East	70	59	70	67
West	55	54	64	80

Fig. 16.16
You can copy selected cells.

	Jan	Feb	Mar	Apr	Apr
South	30	27	34	50	50
North	42	41	45	60	60
East	70	59	70	67	67
West	55	54	64	80	80

Fig. 16.17
The same cells are pasted into a blank area.

When you copy cells, the Paste command becomes Paste Cells, and the command pastes the cells as cells in a table. If you copy an entire row or column, the command becomes Paste Row or Paste Column, respectively. When you paste cells into an area not formatted as a table, they arrive as a table. When you paste a group of cells into an existing table, the table expands, if necessary, to accommodate the new cells.

You also can paste text from outside a table into a single cell in a table. Just copy or cut the text, move the insertion point inside a cell, and choose Edit, Paste.

To move or copy cells, follow these steps:

1. Select the cells, rows, or columns that you want to move or copy.

2. To move the cells, choose Edit, Cut, press Ctrl+X, or click the Cut button on the Standard toolbar. Or, you can select Cut on the right-click menu.

   To copy the cells, choose Edit, Copy, press Ctrl+C, or click the Standard toolbar's Copy button.

3. Select an area in the table to which you're moving the cells that matches the shape and size of the area that you selected in step 1.

4. Choose Edit, Paste Cells, press Ctrl+V, or click the Paste button on the Standard toolbar.

Tip
Word warns you if the shape and size of the copied cells do not match the shape and size of the cells into which you're pasting.

Using the Outliner
The Word for Windows Outline view provides another option for reorganizing rows, columns, and cells. Switching to Outline view enables you to move an entire row of selected cells by dragging the selection to the location where you want the data to appear.

To move a row of cells using Outline view, follow these steps:

1. Choose <u>V</u>iew, <u>O</u>utline. A small box, called a *body text symbol*, appears to the left of each row (see fig. 16.18).

Fig. 16.18

To move a row, drag its body text symbol up or down.

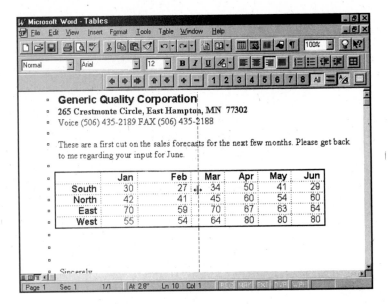

2. Select the row by clicking the body text symbol.

3. Select the up or down arrows in the outline bar or drag the body text symbol up or down to move the selected row to the desired location.

> **Note**
>
> A shortcut for moving table rows up or down is to select the entire row and then press Shift+Alt+up- or down-arrow. You do not have to be in Outline view for this shortcut to work, nor does the document need an outline.

Changing the Column Width

When Word for Windows first creates a table, the columns are sized equally to fill the area between the right and left margins. You can change column or cell widths in three ways:

- Drag the right cell border of the column in the table.

- Drag the column marker on the ruler.

- Choose T<u>a</u>ble, Cell Height and <u>W</u>idth.

Dragging Cell Borders or Using the Ruler

To change the width of a column with the mouse, position the pointer on the column's right border. The pointer changes to a vertical double bar when you position it properly. (The pointer changes even if the gridlines are turned off.) Figure 16.19 shows the shape of the pointer when it is positioned correctly to drag a cell border.

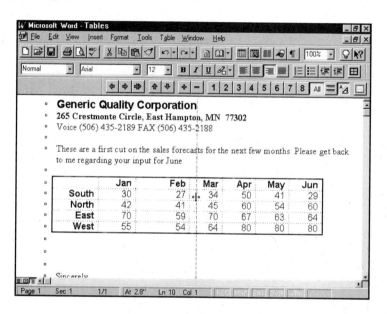

Fig. 16.19
Drag the border of a cell or selected column to change its width.

Drag this column marker to the desired column width and release the mouse button. If you have selected either the entire column or nothing in the column, the entire column adjusts to the new width. If you select cells within the column, only the selected cells adjust to the new width.

You can affect the other columns and the overall table width differently by pressing different keys as you drag the border. To see the width measurements of the columns displayed on the ruler, hold down the Alt key as you drag the border. Table 16.4 indicates the different ways that you can adjust the columns.

Table 16.4   Changing Column Widths with the Mouse

Action	Result
Drag the border without holding down any keys	Resizes all columns to the right in proportion to their original width

(continues)

Table 16.4 Continued	
Action	**Result**
Drag the border while holding down Shift	Changes only the width of the column to the left; does not change the table width
Drag the border while holding down Ctrl	Adjusts all columns to the right equally; does not change the table width
Drag the border while holding down Ctrl+Shift	Leaves columns to the right unchanged; adjusts the table proportionally
Double-click the border	Adjusts the column width to fit the widest content

You can also use the table markers on the ruler to change column widths. Dragging the table markers has the same result as dragging the column borders, as discussed in the preceding paragraphs. If the ruler is not turned on, choose <u>V</u>iew, <u>R</u>uler.

Using the Column Width Command

Tip

To change the width of an entire column rather than just a cell in a column, be sure to select the entire column first.

Choosing T<u>a</u>ble, Cell Height and <u>W</u>idth is useful when you want to change the width of multiple columns with a single command or if you want to define the width of columns by specific amounts. The command also enables you to change the distance between columns.

To change the column width by choosing T<u>a</u>ble, Cell Height and <u>W</u>idth, follow these steps:

1. Select the columns or cells whose width you want to change.

2. Choose T<u>a</u>ble, Cell Height and <u>W</u>idth and select the Column tab in the Cell Height and Width dialog box. The Column tab is displayed (see fig. 16.20).

Fig. 16.20

You can set the width of any number of columns at one time in the Cell Height and Width dialog box.

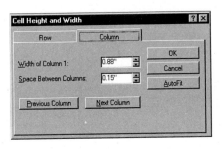

3. Select or type a number in the <u>W</u>idth of Column X text box, where X is the column number.

4. If you want to adjust other columns, click the <u>P</u>revious Column or <u>N</u>ext Column buttons to keep the dialog box open and move to the next column. The Width of Columns label changes to tell you which row you are formatting.

5. Choose OK.

Using the AutoFit Command

You can have Word for Windows automatically adjust the width of a column in a table to accommodate the width of the column's longest line of text. One advantage to using AutoFit to adjust the columns in a table is that you ensure the columns are as wide as (but no wider than) they have to be to accommodate the table's data. This feature helps you optimize the use of space on a page.

To AutoFit the column width, follow these steps:

1. Select the columns that you want to AutoFit.

   If you do not select the entire column, only the selected cells are AutoFit.

2. Choose T<u>a</u>ble, Cell Height and <u>W</u>idth, and select the Column tab in the Cell Height and Width dialog box.

3. Click the <u>A</u>utoFit button.

Word then automatically adjusts the column, closes the dialog box, and returns you to the document.

Changing Column Spacing

The Cell Height and Width dialog box also enables you to control the amount of space between columns. When you first create a table, the columns that you choose for the table are the same size and span the distance between page margins. Included in the column width is a default column-spacing setting of 0.15".

To change the spacing between columns, follow these steps:

1. Select the columns you want to adjust. Select a row if you want to adjust all columns in the table.

2. Choose T<u>a</u>ble, Cell Height and <u>W</u>idth and select the Column tab.

3. Select or type a number in the <u>S</u>pace Between Columns text box.

   The space that you set in this box is divided by the left and right margins within the cell—just as if the cell were a small page and you were entering the combined value for the left and right margins.

4. Click OK.

The column spacing affects the cell's usable column width. If a column width is 2 inches and the column spacing is set to 0.50 inch, for example, the column width available for text and graphics is 1.5 inches.

Changing Row Height and Position

When you first create a table, each row has the same height. However, the text and amount of paragraph spacing that you add changes the rows' height. The Cell Height and <u>W</u>idth dialog box enables you to specify how far Word indents a row from the left margin, the rows' height, and the rows' alignment between margins. You also use the vertical ruler to change the rows' height.

Changing Row Height

You can change the height of the rows in a table by using either the Cell Height and <u>W</u>idth dialog box or the vertical ruler. If you want to change several rows at the same time to the same height, using the menu command is easier.

To set row height using the Cell Height and Width dialog box, follow these steps:

1. Select the rows whose height you want to adjust.

2. Choose T<u>a</u>ble, Cell Height and <u>W</u>idth and select the Row tab in the Cell Height and Width dialog box. The Row tab appears (see fig. 16.21).

Fig. 16.21
You can control the height and indentation of rows in a table.

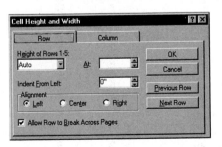

IV

3. Select a Height of Row option. The following are the available options:

Option	Result
Auto	Automatically adjusts row height to the size of the text or graphic
At Least	Sets the minimum row height; automatically adjusts the row if text or graphics exceed this minimum
Exactly	Sets a fixed row height; when printed or displayed on-screen, cuts off text or graphics that exceed the fixed height

4. If you choose At Least or Exactly in step 3, type or select the row height in points in the At box.

   You can also specify the height in lines (**li**) or inches (") by including the abbreviation after the numeric value in the At box.

5. Clear the Allow Row to Break Across Pages option to keep the selected row from splitting at a page break.

   When this option is selected, if the text or graphic in a cell in the row cannot fit on the current page, Word splits the row and continues it on the next page.

6. Click the Previous Row or Next Row buttons if you want to format other rows. The Height of Row label changes to tell you which row you are formatting.

7. Click OK.

To set row height with the vertical ruler, follow these steps:

1. If you are not in Page Layout view, choose View, Page Layout.

   Every row in a table has a corresponding horizontal marker in the vertical ruler (see fig. 16.22). You can adjust the height of a row by dragging its marker.

2. Drag the marker to set the height of the row that you want to change.

   If you drag the marker without pressing any keys, you set the row height to at least whatever the new measurement is. The row height automatically adjusts if the text or graphics exceed this minimum setting. If you hold down Ctrl as you drag the marker, you set the row height to exactly the new measurement. When displayed on-screen or printed, text or graphics that exceed the fixed height are cut off.

Fig. 16.22
You can use the
vertical ruler on
the left to set row
heights.

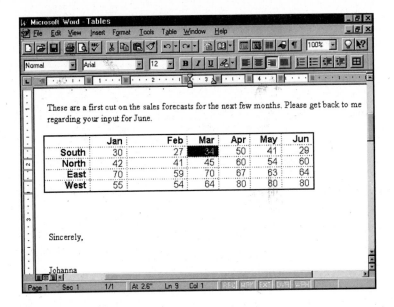

Changing Row Spacing

A little extra vertical spacing between rows can make your table easier to read. You can adjust the amount of space between rows by choosing Format, Paragraph.

To add space between rows, follow these steps:

1. Select the rows to which you want to add spacing.

2. Choose Format, Paragraph, and select the Indents and Spacing tab in the Paragraph dialog box.

3. Type or select a spacing in the Spacing Before or the Spacing After boxes. You can use lines (**li**) or point (**pt**) measurements by typing the number and space and then the abbreviation.

4. Click OK.

Aligning and Indenting Rows

With Word for Windows, you can control a table's position by changing the alignment of rows. You also can indent selected rows to align with other text in your document. Row alignment and indentation does not affect the alignment of text within the cells.

To align rows between page margins, follow these steps:

1. Select the rows that you want to align.

2. Choose Table, Cell Height and Width and select the Row tab in the Cell Height and Width dialog box. The Row tab appears (refer to fig. 16.21).

3. Select Left, Center, or Right alignment.

4. Click OK.

The Cell Height and Width dialog box also enables you to indent selected rows. When you indent a row, the entire row shifts right by the amount that you specify, just as though you were indenting a paragraph.

To indent a row, follow these steps:

1. Select the row or rows that you want to indent.

2. Choose Table, Cell Height and Width and select the Row tab in the Cell Height and Width dialog box.

3. Type or select in the Indent From Left box the number of inches of indentation that you want.

4. Click OK.

Adding or Deleting Cells, Rows, or Columns

Word for Windows enables you to change a table's structure by adding and deleting cells, rows, and columns. You can add or delete one or many cells, rows, or columns by using a single command. The Table menu changes its Insert and Delete commands depending on what you have selected.

If a cell is selected, the Table menu displays the Insert Cells and Delete Cells commands. If a column is selected, the Table menu displays the Insert Columns and Delete Columns commands. If a row is selected, the menu displays Insert Rows and Delete Rows.

Adding or Deleting Cells

You can add or delete individual cells if you don't want to add or delete entire rows or columns. Word for Windows shifts the other cells in the table to accommodate the added or deleted cells.

To add cells to or delete cells from an existing table, follow these steps:

1. Select the cells that you want to add or delete.

2. Choose T<u>a</u>ble, <u>I</u>nsert Cells, or T<u>a</u>ble, <u>D</u>elete Cells. The <u>I</u>nsert Cells or Delete Cells dialog box appears, depending on which command you chose (see figs. 16.23 and 16.24).

Fig. 16.23
The Insert Cells dialog box appears if you are inserting cells.

Fig. 16.24
The Delete Cells dialog box appears if you are deleting cells.

3. Choose the appropriate option button that corresponds to shifting the existing cells to the position that you want. You also have the option of inserting or deleting an entire column or row.

Choosing <u>I</u>nsert Cells inserts blank cells at the location of the selected cells and shifts the selected cells either down or right.

Choosing <u>D</u>elete Cells deletes the selected cells and shifts adjacent cells either up or left to fill the vacancy.

4. Choose OK.

If you want to delete cell contents without deleting the actual cell, select the cell contents that you want to delete and press Delete or Backspace.

Adding or Deleting Rows and Columns

You can insert and delete columns and rows from a table using the same commands that you use to insert or delete cells. You can add columns and rows to the end of the table or insert them within the table.

To insert a new row at the end of the table, move the insertion point to the last position in the last cell and press Tab.

To insert or delete rows in the middle of an existing table, follow these steps:

1. Select the row or rows where you want to insert or delete.

When you insert a row, Word shifts the selected row down and inserts a blank row (see fig. 16.25). When you delete a row, Word deletes the selected row and shifts up lower rows.

	Jan	Feb	Mar	Apr	May	Jun
South	30	27	34	50	41	29
North	42	41	45	60	54	60
East	70	59	70	67	63	64
West	55	54	64	80	80	80

Fig. 16.25
An inserted row shifts the selected row down.

IV

Mastering Special Features

2. Choose Table, Insert Rows, or Table, Delete Rows.

If you are inserting a row or rows, you can click the Insert Table button on the Standard toolbar instead of choosing Table, Insert Rows.

To insert or delete one or more columns within a table, follow these steps:

1. Select one or more columns where you want to insert or delete columns.

If you are inserting a column or columns, you can click the Insert Table button on the Standard toolbar instead of choosing Table, Insert Columns.

2. Choose Table and then Insert Columns or Delete Columns.

When you insert columns, the selected columns shift right to make room for the inserted blank columns. When you're deleting, Word removes the selected columns and shifts columns to the right leftward to fill the gap.

If you insert a column, the table looks like the one shown in figure 16.26. If you delete a column, the table looks like the one shown in figure 16.27.

	Jan	Feb	Mar	Apr		May	Jun
South	30	27	34	50		41	29
North	42	41	45	60		54	60
East	70	59	70	67		63	64
West	55	54	64	80		80	80

Fig. 16.26
Inserting a column shifts existing columns right.

	Jan	Feb	Mar	Apr	Jun
South	30	27	34	50	29
North	42	41	45	60	60
East	70	59	70	67	64
West	55	54	64	80	80

Fig. 16.27
Deleting a column shifts existing columns left to fill the gap.

Inserting a column as the last column requires a different procedure. To insert a column to the right of a table, follow these steps:

1. Position the insertion point at the end of a table row outside the table, which places it in front of an end-of-row mark.

If gridlines and end marks are not displayed on-screen, see "Displaying or Hiding Gridlines and End Marks" earlier in this chapter.

2. Choose Table, Select Column.

3. Choose Table, Insert Columns, or click the Insert Table button on the Standard toolbar.

To insert additional columns to the right of the table, choose Edit, Repeat, or press F4.

Note

If you want to insert multiple columns quickly at the right edge of the table, select from the existing table as many columns as you want to insert. (Dragging across with the right mouse button is a quick way to select these columns.) Choose Edit, Copy. Move the insertion point to the end of the first row of the table and choose Edit, Paste. To clear them, reselect these new columns and press Delete.

◄ See "Moving, Copying, and Linking Text or Graphics," p. 160

Troubleshooting

When I try to insert rows or columns in a table, the Insert Rows and Insert Columns commands do not appear in the Table menu.

If the Table menu doesn't display Insert or Delete commands for rows or columns, you have selected only cells. You must select the rows or columns with which you want to work so that Word for Windows knows which Insert or Delete command to add to the menu.

Chapter 17

Modifying Tables

Tables are one of the easiest yet most productive features in Word for Windows. They are a feature that everyone seems to find useful. After creating your tables, however, you might find that you want to do some formatting or creative manipulation with them. This chapter explains how.

In this chapter, you learn how to do the following:

- Merge and split cells
- Format tables
- Number rows and columns
- Split a table into two tables
- Convert a table to text, or text to a table

Merging and Splitting Cells and Creating Table Headings

Sometimes you want text or a figure to span the width of multiple cells. A *heading* is an example of text that you might want to stretch across several columns. Word for Windows enables you to merge multiple cells in a row into a single cell. Merging cells converts their contents to paragraphs within a single cell.

Merging Cells

You can merge cells only horizontally. Selecting cells in more than one row results in the selected cells in each row being merged horizontally.

To merge multiple cells in a row into a single cell, follow these steps:

1. Select the cells that you want to merge (see fig. 17.1).

Fig. 17.1

Select the cells
that you want to
merge in the table.

		Sales Forecast				
	Jan	Feb	Mar	Apr	May	Jun
South	30	27	34	50	41	29
North	42	41	45	60	54	60
East	70	59	70	67	63	64
West	55	54	64	80	80	80

2. Choose Table, Merge Cells.

The selected cells condense into a single cell (see fig. 17.2). You might have to reformat the contents so that the cell aligns correctly.

Fig. 17.2

Merge cells to put
text such as titles
into a single,
wider cell.

		Sales Forecast				
	Jan	Feb	Mar	Apr	May	Jun
South	30	27	34	50	41	29
North	42	41	45	60	54	60
East	70	59	70	67	63	64
West	55	54	64	80	80	80

Creating Table Headings

To create table headings, follow these steps:

1. Select the first row and any following rows that you want to use as table headings.

2. Choose Table, Headings.

Splitting Cells

After you have merged cells, you can return them to their original condition. The text in the merged cells is divided among the split cells by paragraph marks. The first paragraph is placed in the first cell, the second paragraph in the second cell, and so on.

To split merged cells, follow these steps:

1. Select a cell that was previously merged.

2. Choose Table, Split Cells.

Formatting a Table

You can format the text and cells in a table to produce attractive and professional-looking tables. You format text and paragraphs just as you do in the body text of your document. To make a table more attractive and more readable, you can add borders and shading around the entire table or to selected cells. You also can draw gridlines within the table. To enhance the appearance or make important data stand out, you can use colored borders or shaded or colored backgrounds. In addition, 26 different shades and patterns are available for black-and-white laser printers—an important feature when you want your document to make a good impression.

You can format the contents in the table's cells by using the same procedures that you use to format regular text. To change the font, font size, and font style, you can choose Format, Font. To adjust the spacing and indentation of cell contents, you can choose Format, Paragraph. Remember that you can use the shortcut menus to access these formatting commands. Click the right button after you select the cells, columns, or rows that you want to format, and then choose from the shortcut menu the formatting command that you want to use.

To add borders, shading, and color to a table, choose Format, Borders and Shading. You also can add a Borders toolbar to the screen to access the border and shading options with a mouse click.

Formatting a Table with Table AutoFormat

Formatting a table to achieve a professional appearance could take you longer than creating and filling the table—unless you use Table AutoFormat. This feature automatically applies predesigned collections of formatting to the table that you select. The formatting includes borders, shading, fonts, colors, and AutoFit column widths. If you are familiar with Excel's time-saving AutoFormat command, you are already familiar with this feature's usefulness.

To format a table using Table AutoFormat, follow these steps:

1. Move the insertion point inside the table.

2. Choose Table, Table AutoFormat to display the Table AutoFormat dialog box shown in figure 17.3.

◀ See "Using Paragraph Formatting Techniques," p. 291

◀ See "Shading and Bordering Paragraphs," p. 323

Tip

To add the Borders toolbar to your screen, click an existing toolbar with the right mouse button and choose Borders from the menu. Repeat these steps to remove the toolbar.

IV

Mastering Special Features

Fig. 17.3

Apply collections of predefined formats by using the Table AutoFormat dialog box.

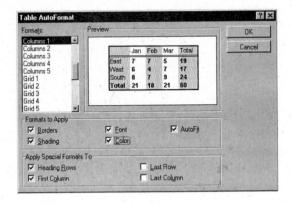

3. Select from the Formats list a predefined format. The Preview box displays an example of the format that you select.

4. If you do not want to lose existing formats in the table, deselect the appropriate type of format in the Formats to Apply group: Borders, Shading, Font, Color, and AutoFit. The Preview box changes as you select or deselect formats.

5. If you want to apply only selected portions of the AutoFormat to your table, select from the Apply Special Formats To group the parts of the table that you want to format: Heading Rows, First Column, Last Row, and Last Column.

6. Choose OK.

Selecting Border Formats

With Word for Windows, adding borders to a table is easy. You can add borders to individual cells, rows, and columns, or to the entire table. Figure 17.4 shows a table formatted with multiple border styles.

Fig. 17.4

You can format a table with multiple border styles.

	Jan	Feb	Mar	Apr	Jun	May
South	30	27	34	50	29	41
North	42	41	45	60	60	54
East	70	59	70	67	64	63
West	55	54	64	80	80	80

To add borders to all or selected parts of your table, follow these steps:

1. Select the entire table or the cells that you want to shade or border.

2. Choose F̲ormat, B̲orders and Shading, and select the B̲orders tab in the Table Borders and Shading dialog box. The B̲orders tab appears (see fig. 17.5).

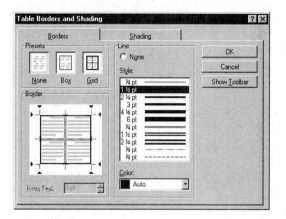

Fig. 17.5
Add borders to your table by using the Table Borders and Shading dialog box.

3. Select the line weight and style from the St̲yle list.

4. Select a line color from the C̲olor list.

5. Select one of the border patterns in the Presets group: N̲one, Bo̲x, or G̲rid.

6. Choose OK.

If you want to specify custom combinations of border types, weights, and colors, you can select which lines are affected by the St̲yle and C̲olor selections that you make in the Bo̲rder group.

To specify custom combinations, follow these steps:

1. Select the line type and weight from the St̲yle options as described in the preceding steps.

2. Select the line color from the C̲olor list.

3. Select from the samples in the Bo̲rder group the line or edge that you want to change. Figure 17.6 shows the arrowhead handles that point to the lines that the St̲yle and C̲olor selections change.

Fig. 17.6

You can select any combination of individual edges or the interior gridlines to which to add borders.

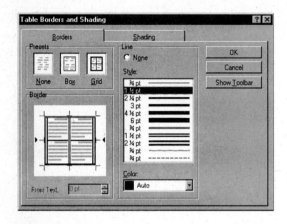

Using the mouse, click the line or outside border that you want to change. To change multiple lines or edges at one time, hold down Shift, and click the lines. After selecting the lines, click the line type shown in the Style box in the Line options.

Using the keyboard, press Alt+R to move the focus to the Border group. Press the up- or down-arrow keys to cycle through combinations of selected lines. Stop on the combination that you want and press the space bar to change them to the current Style and Color selections. You can alternate among the Style, Color, and Border options until you get the right combination.

4. Watch the sample in the Border group to see the result of your choices. To remove a selected border, select the None option in the Line group. If you do not like the sample's appearance, choose None from the Presets group and return to step 1.

5. Choose OK.

> **Note**
>
> The preceding steps show you how to add borders to an entire table or individual cells in a table. You also can add borders to the paragraphs in a cell.
>
> To add borders to paragraphs, click the Show/Hide ¶ button on the Standard toolbar to display paragraph marks, select the paragraph mark for the paragraph to which you want to add borders, and choose Format, Borders and Shading. You might have to insert a paragraph mark after the text by pressing Enter. When you apply borders to the paragraph, Word removes the extra line from this paragraph mark.

Selecting Shading and Colors

You can enhance a table or selected cells with *shading*. Shading draws attention to a particular section of a table. You also can use it to create reserved areas on office forms.

The selections that you make in the Table Borders and Shading dialog box affect the currently selected cells. If you place the insertion point in a single cell without selecting that cell, Word for Windows applies shading to the entire table.

To add shading to a table, follow these steps:

1. Choose Format, Borders and Shading, and select the Shading tab in the Table Borders and Shading dialog box. The Shading tab appears (see fig. 17.7).

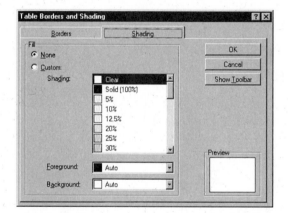

Fig. 17.7
You can add shading and color to a table by using the Shading options.

2. Select None to remove shading or Custom to apply shading.

3. If you choose Custom, select the pattern or percentage of shading from the Shading list. Many shades are available.

4. Select a foreground color from the Foreground list. Select Auto or Black if you are printing to a black-and-white printer.

5. Select a background color from the Background list. Select Auto or White if you are printing to a black-and-white printer.

6. Check the Preview box to see the pattern that you have created. If you like the pattern that you see, choose OK; otherwise, return to step 3 and make other selections.

> **Note**
>
> When you apply shading, Word shades the background of selected cells. You can control the type of shading by setting the shading percentage. If you want lighter shading, choose a lower shading percentage. A higher percentage applies darker shading.

Your printer's resolution controls shading patterns. The higher the resolution—measured in dots per inch (dpi)—the finer the shading. The resolution at which your printer prints graphics and shading is an option within the Properties dialog box. To access this dialog box, choose File, Print, click the Properties button, and then select the Graphics tab.

In the Table Borders and Shading dialog box, experiment with the Shading, Foreground, and Background options in the Shading tab to find the shading pattern that looks best.

Numbering Rows and Columns

Tip

If you frequently use the same collection of formats on a table, learn about styles in Chapter 11, "Using Styles for Repetitive Formats."

To add numbers to the cells and rows in a table, you can click the Numbering button on the Formatting toolbar or choose Format, Bullets and Numbering. You can add numbers to just the first column in the table, or you can add numbers across rows or down columns in as many cells in the table as you want.

Adding Numbers with the Numbering Button

The quickest way to add numbering to a table is to use the Numbering button on the Formatting toolbar. When you use this method, however, you are limited to the numbering style currently selected in the Bullets and Numbering dialog box.

To add numbers to a table using the Numbering button, follow these steps:

1. Select the cells, rows, or columns that you want to number. In most cases, you want a number in the first cell of each row, so select the first column.

2. Click the Numbering button on the Formatting toolbar. The Table Numbering dialog box appears.

IV

3. Select one of the following options:

Option	Action
Number Across Rows	Numbers across rows
Number Down Columns	Numbers down columns
Number Each Cell Only Once	Inserts one number in each cell

4. Choose OK.

Adding Numbering with the Menu

You can choose Format, Bullets and Numbering to add numbers to a table. When you use this method, you can select from a variety of numbering styles in the Bullets and Numbering dialog box.

To add numbers using the menu, follow these steps:

1. Select the cells, rows, or columns that you want to number.

2. Choose Format, Bullets and Numbering and select the Numbered tab in the Bullets and Numbering dialog box. The Numbered tab appears (see fig. 17.8).

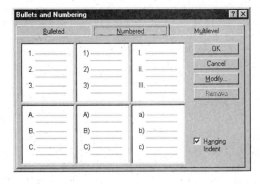

Fig. 17.8

You can select from several numbering styles in the Numbered tab of the Bullets and Numbering dialog box.

3. Select one of the numbering styles.

4. To modify the predefined style, click the Modify button and make selections in the Modify Numbered List dialog box to change the format of the numbering. Then choose OK.

▶ See "Creating Numbered Lists," p. 555

Splitting a Table

Occasionally you might want to insert a paragraph or heading between rows in a table. If you start a table at the top of a document and later decide that you need to insert some text before the table, you can do it easily.

To insert text above the table or between rows, follow these steps:

1. Position the insertion point in the row below where you want to insert the text. If you want to enter text above the table, position the insertion point in the first row of the table.

2. Choose Table, Split Table or press Ctrl+Shift+Enter. A paragraph mark formatted with the Normal style is inserted above the row.

Sorting Tables

Tables often are created to arrange data in columns and rows. You can sort a table that is a database of names and addresses first by the last name, for example, and then within that sort, by the first name. You can sort text, numbers, and dates in either ascending or descending order.

To sort a table, follow these steps:

1. Select the entire table to include all the rows in the sort or select only the rows that you want to sort.

2. Choose Table, Sort. The Sort dialog box appears (see fig. 17.9).

Fig. 17.9

You can sort a table by up to three columns in the Sort dialog box.

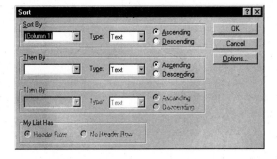

3. Select the first column that you want to sort by in the Sort By list.

4. Select either Text, Number, or Date from the Type list.

5. Select either the Ascending or Descending option.

6. Repeat steps 3 through 5 if you want to sort by additional columns in your table. Make your selections from the Then By boxes.

7. If your table has headings that you don't want to include in the search, select the Header Row option in the My List Has group.

8. To make the sort case-sensitive, click the Options button, select the Case Sensitive option, and choose OK.

9. Choose OK.

Edit, Undo reverses the Sort command if you use it immediately after you sort. You might want to save your document before sorting so that you can return to it if it is sorted incorrectly.

Converting a Table to Text

You can convert a table's cell contents to text separated by commas, tabs, or another single character, or you can convert each cell's contents into one or more paragraphs.

To convert a table to text, follow these steps:

1. Select the rows of the table that you want to convert to text, or select the entire table.

2. Choose Table, Convert Table to Text. The Convert Table to Text dialog box appears.

3. Select a Separate Text With option from the dialog box. You can separate each cell's contents by Paragraph Marks, Tabs, Commas, or Other (Other can be any single character).

4. Choose OK.

Converting Text to a Table

When you copy data from another application or convert a word processing file that does not have tables, your data might be in tabbed columns. To make the data easier to work with, convert the data to Word for Windows tables.

To convert text to a table, follow these steps:

1. Select the lines of text or paragraphs that you want to convert to a table.

2. Choose Table, Convert Text to Table, or click the Insert Table button on the Standard toolbar. The Convert Text to Table dialog box appears (see fig. 17.10).

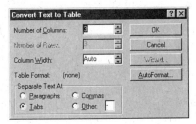

Fig. 17.10
Use the Convert Text to Table dialog box to separate text at the character that you specify.

Based on the selected text, Word for Windows proposes the number of columns and rows, the width of the columns, and the separator character to use to delineate columns from the text. You can change these settings to suit your own needs.

3. Type or select the number of columns in the Number of Columns box to specify a different number of columns.

4. Type or select the number of rows in the Number of Rows box to specify a different number of rows.

5. Type or select an exact column width in the Column Width box if you don't want to use the automatic settings.

6. Select a different separator character if the default character is incorrect.

Choose one of the following options from the dialog box's Separate Text At group:

Option	Result
Paragraphs	A paragraph separates information to be in a cell. Each paragraph becomes its own row.
Tabs	A tab character separates information in a cell. Word for Windows converts each paragraph and each line ending in a hard line break (created by pressing Shift+Enter) into a row. The number of columns is determined by greatest number of tab characters in the paragraphs or lines.

Option	Result
Commas	A comma separates information in a cell. Word for Windows converts each paragraph and each line ending in a hard line break (created by pressing Shift+Enter) into a row. The number of columns is determined by greatest number of commas in the paragraphs or lines.
Other	Some other character separates information in a cell. Word for Windows converts each paragraph and each line ending in a hard line break (created by pressing Shift+Enter) into a row. The number of columns is determined by the greatest number of specified characters in the paragraphs or lines.

7. Choose OK.

Calculating Math Results in a Table

You can perform calculations in a table just as you do in a spreadsheet. In a Word for Windows table, you can add, subtract, multiply, and divide numbers, and you also can perform several other types of calculations, such as averaging and finding minimum and maximum values.

To perform a calculation in a table, you must locate the insertion point in the cell where you want the calculation's result to appear. If text or numbers are already in that cell, you should delete them. When you choose Table, Formula to add a group of cells, Word assumes that you want to add the cells immediately above or to the left of the cell and inserts either ABOVE or LEFT in the parentheses of the SUM function in the Formula dialog box. If you want to perform other types of calculations, you must replace the SUM function with another function and specify the cells that you want to use in the calculation. You specify a cell by using the cell address, which consists of the row and column designation for that cell. The first cell in the upper-left corner of a table, for example, is designated as A1, where A is the column and 1 is the row. You can designate a range of cells by typing the addresses for the first and last cells in the range separated by a colon.

When you perform a calculation in a cell, a field code is inserted. The field includes the function name—for example, SUM—and the cells on which the calculation is being performed. To see the field code, choose Tools, Options and select the View tab. Select the Field Codes option and choose OK. Word for Windows displays the field code rather than the result.

Note

A shortcut for toggling between a field code and its result is to locate the insertion point within the code and press Shift+F9. If the numbers used in the calculation change, you can update the results of the calculation by selecting the cell in which the results appear and pressing F9, the Field Update key.

Chapter 18

Creating Bulleted or Numbered Lists

A bulleted or numbered list is a special type of list formatted with a *hanging indent*. (A hanging indent occurs when a paragraph's first line goes all the way to the left margin, but all other lines in the paragraph are indented. Chapter 10, "Formatting Lines and Paragraphs," describes hanging indents and other paragraph formatting.) Bulleted lists have a bullet at the left margin; numbered lists have a number and are numbered sequentially. Many writers use bulleted lists to distinguish a series of important items or points from the rest of the text in a document, such as a summary of product features in a sales letter, or a list of conclusions reached in a research project. Writers often use numbered lists for step-by-step instructions (as in this book), outlines, or other types of lists in which the specific order of the information is important.

In this chapter, you learn how to do the following:

- Create and customize bulleted, numbered, and multilevel lists

- Create and customize numbered or bulleted headings

- Remove bulleting and numbering from lists and headings

Word for Windows 95 provides flexible, easy-to-use methods for creating bulleted or numbered lists with a variety of standardized numbering or bullet formats. You can vary the size of the hanging indent or the space between the numbers or bullets and the following text. You can also create your own custom numbering formats for numbered lists, or you can select characters from any of your installed fonts to use as a bullet in a bulleted list. Word even provides an easy way to remove bullets or numbering.

You can type the text for the bulleted or numbered list and then apply to the text the list formatting (see fig. 18.1); alternatively, you can place the insertion point in a blank line, apply the bulleted or numbered list format to that line, and then type the list. Either way, after you select a bulleted or numbered list format, Word for Windows sets a 1/4-inch hanging indent and adds the bullets or numbers in front of each paragraph in the selected text, or adds them to each new paragraph that you type.

Fig. 18.1

An example of the types of numbered and bulleted lists that you can create.

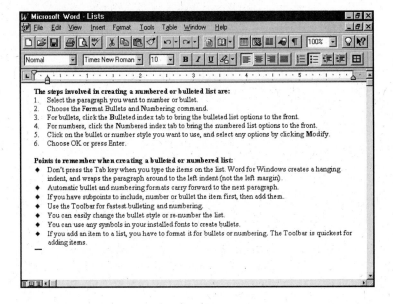

Like paragraph margin and indent formatting, the bulleted or numbered list format carries forward from paragraph to paragraph. Each time that you press Enter to begin a new paragraph, Word for Windows adds to the list a new bulleted or numbered paragraph. You can add another bulleted or numbered item anywhere in a list by placing the insertion point where you want to add the new item and then pressing Enter to begin a new paragraph. Word for Windows automatically adds a bullet or number sequentially to the beginning of the new paragraph and formats the paragraph with a hanging indent to match the other paragraphs in the bulleted or numbered list. You can also use the AutoFormat feature described in Chapter 11, "Using Styles for Repetitive Formats," to create numbered or bulleted lists automatically.

Creating Bulleted Lists

Word for Windows offers six standard bullet shapes: round (large or small), diamond (solid or hollow), arrow, and asterisk. If you want to use a heart, pointing hand, or some other symbol as your bullet, Word enables you to select the character for the bullet from any of your installed fonts.

◄ See "Formatting Characters and Changing Fonts," p. 251

You can create a bulleted list in three ways: with menu commands, with a toolbar shortcut, or by right-clicking and selecting Bullets and Numbering. As usual, you have many more options when you use menu commands.

Creating Bulleted Lists with Menu Commands

To create a bulleted list with menu commands, follow these steps:

1. Type the list at the left margin (without pressing Tab to indent the text) and then select it, or place the insertion point on a blank line.

2. Choose Format, Bullets and Numbering. The Bullets and Numbering dialog box appears (see fig. 18.2).

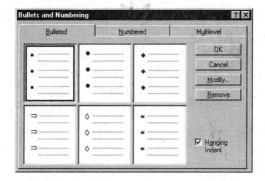

Fig. 18.2
Use the Bullets and Numbering dialog box to select the bullet and indent style options for a bulleted list.

3. Click the Bulleted tab to display the bulleted list options, if they are not already displayed.

4. Select the bulleted list format that you want from the predefined choices by clicking it with the mouse or using the arrow keys.

    Later in this chapter, "Customizing Bulleted Lists" describes how to use the Modify button to customize a bulleted list's formatting.

5. If you prefer a bulleted list with no hanging indent, select the Hanging Indent option in the Bullets and Numbering dialog box so that no mark appears in that check box. Word for Windows then sets no indent.

6. Choose OK. Word for Windows formats the current line or selected text as a bulleted list.

If you have not yet typed the bulleted list, type it now. Each time that you begin a new paragraph, Word for Windows formats the paragraph as part of the bulleted list. To end the bulleted list, see "Ending the Bulleted List" later in this chapter.

> **Note**
>
> You can open the Bullets and Numbering dialog box by placing the pointer over the selected text and then clicking the right mouse button. A context-sensitive menu appears to the right of the insertion point. Choose Bullets and Numbering to display the Bullets and Numbering dialog box.

If you want to replace an existing bulleted list with new bullets or change any of the bulleted list's other formatting properties, select the list and then follow the instructions in the section "Customizing Bulleted Lists" later in this chapter. If you want to replace bullets with numbers, select the list and see "Creating Numbered Lists," later in this chapter, for instructions on creating a numbered list. Word for Windows does not ask you to confirm that you want to replace bullets with numbers. If you inadvertently change a bulleted list to a numbered list, choose Edit, Undo Number Default.

To add bulleted items anywhere in a bulleted list, position the insertion point where you want to add the new bulleted item, and press Enter to add a new paragraph to the list. Word for Windows automatically formats the new paragraph as part of the bulleted list.

Creating Bulleted Lists with the Toolbar

 With the Formatting toolbar, you can easily set up a bulleted list by clicking the Bullets button (near the right side of the Formatting toolbar). When you create a bulleted list with the Bullets button, Word for Windows uses the bulleted list formatting options selected most recently in the Bullets and Numbering dialog box.

To create a bulleted list with the toolbar, follow these steps:

1. Choose <u>V</u>iew, <u>T</u>oolbars and select Formatting, if the Formatting toolbar is not already displayed.

2. Type the list at the left margin and select it, or place the text insertion point in a blank line.

3. Choose the Bullets button on the Formatting toolbar. Word for Windows formats the current line or selected text as a bulleted list.

If you have not yet typed the bulleted list, type it now. Word for Windows formats each new paragraph as part of the bulleted list. The next section explains how to end the bulleted list.

By default, Word for Windows uses a small, round bullet and a 1/4-inch hanging indent to format lists that you create with the Formatting toolbar's Bullets button. If you recently selected different options in the Bullets and Numbering dialog box, however, Word uses those selections instead.

Ending the Bulleted List

If you apply bulleted list formatting to a blank line and then type the list, Word for Windows continues formatting each new paragraph you type as part of the bulleted list, until you end the bulleted list.

To end a bulleted list, follow these steps:

1. Press Enter to add a bulleted, blank line to the end of the bulleted list.

2. Move the pointer over the blank line and click the right mouse button. Word for Windows moves the insertion point to that line and displays a context-sensitive menu to the right of the insertion point.

3. Choose Stop Numbering to end the bulleted list. Word for Windows removes the bullet and hanging indent from the blank line, ending the bulleted list.

Adding Subordinate Paragraphs to a Bulleted List

Sometimes you cannot adequately or gracefully discuss the topic of a bulleted list item within a single paragraph. Usually, if you require more than one paragraph to describe a single topic in a bulleted list, you want only the first paragraph for that topic to have a bullet. The remaining subordinate paragraphs for that topic do not need bullets, although they must have the same hanging indent as the list's bulleted paragraphs.

Whether you are changing an existing bulleted paragraph to a subordinate paragraph or typing the bulleted list as you go along, you can change a bulleted paragraph into a subordinate paragraph by using either a context-sensitive shortcut menu or the Formatting toolbar.

Adding a Subordinate Paragraph with the Menu

To change a bulleted list item to a subordinate paragraph, follow these steps:

1. Select the bulleted list items from which you want to remove the bullets.

2. Move the pointer over the selected text and click the right mouse button. Word for Windows moves the insertion point to that line and displays a context-sensitive menu to the right of the insertion point.

3. Choose Skip Numbering. Word removes the bullet from the selected paragraphs, but the hanging indent remains.

If you added a subordinate paragraph at the end of a bulleted list and you want to add another bulleted list item after the subordinate paragraph, choose the Bullets button from the Formatting toolbar to resume the bulleted list format.

Adding a Subordinate Paragraph with the Toolbar

To use the Formatting toolbar to change a bulleted list item to a subordinate paragraph in the list, follow these steps:

1. Select the bulleted list items from which you want to remove the bullets.

2. Choose the Bullets button from the Formatting toolbar. Word removes the bullet from the selected paragraphs, but the hanging indent remains.

Use the Bullets button to resume formatting the bulleted list on the next line.

Customizing Bulleted Lists

To customize an existing bulleted list or to make your own specifications for the formatting of a new bulleted list, choose the Modify button from the Bullets and Numbering dialog box. Modify enables you to choose a character from any of your installed fonts to use as a bullet, and to specify the bullet's point size and color. You can also specify the size of the hanging indent, how much space appears between the bullet character and the text in the bulleted item, and whether the bullet is right-, left-, or center-justified within the indent space.

The only way to customize a bulleted list format is to use menu commands; no toolbar shortcut exists. If your custom bulleted list format is the most recently applied format, however, the Bullets button applies your custom format.

To create a custom bulleted list format, follow these steps:

1. Select the bulleted list that you want to customize.

2. Choose F_ormat, Bullets and _Numbering. The Bullets and Numbering dialog box appears.

3. Choose the _Bulleted tab to display the bulleted list options, if that tab is not already up front.

4. Choose the _Modify button. The Modify Bulleted List dialog box appears (see fig. 18.3).

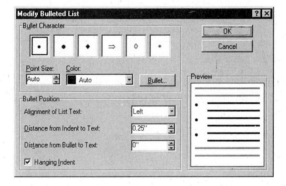

Fig. 18.3
The Modify Bulleted List dialog box enables you you to select custom bullet characters, colors, and point sizes for the bullet, and to choose the bullet character's alignment with the text.

5. In the B_ullet Character group, select the character that you want to use as a bullet by clicking it or by using the arrow keys.

   The section "Selecting a Custom Bullet Character" describes how to use the _Bullet button to select a custom bullet character.

6. Choose any of the following options:

Option	Function
P_oint Size	Type the point size that you want the bullet character to be, or type **Auto** to have Word for Windows automatically select the size of the bullet.
_Color	Choose the bullet's color. Select Auto to have Word for Windows automatically select the color.

(continues)

Option	Function
Alignment of List Text	Choose the bullet's alignment within the space used for the indent. Word for Windows offers you the choice of left-aligned, right-aligned, centered, or justified.
Distance from Indent to Text	Type or select a number to set the hanging indent's size.
Distance from Bullet to Text	Type or select a number to set the distance in the bulleted paragraph between the bullet and the text.
Hanging Indent	Select this check box to indent each line of the bulleted list.

7. Choose OK. The Modify Bulleted List dialog box closes and the Bullets and Numbering dialog box appears.

8. Choose OK. Word for Windows closes the Bullets and Numbering dialog box and applies the new bullet format to the bulleted list.

> **Caution**
>
> If you customize or reformat an existing bulleted list that contains subordinate (unbulleted) paragraphs, Word for Windows adds bullets to the subordinate paragraphs.

Selecting a Custom Bullet Character

Word for Windows enables you to select any character from any of your installed fonts to use as the bullet character in a bulleted list.

To select a custom bullet character, follow these steps:

1. Choose the Bullet button in the Modify Bulleted List dialog box. Word for Windows displays the Symbol dialog box (see fig. 18.4).

2. Select from the Symbols From list box the font that the Symbol dialog box displays. Select the bullet character that you want from the Symbol dialog box by clicking the character or by using the arrow keys.

3. Choose OK. Word closes the Symbol dialog box and displays your selected bullet character in the Bullet Character and Preview group of the Modify Bulleted List dialog box.

Tip
A modified bullet character is not applied to any new lists you create.

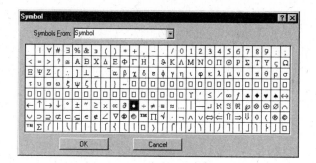

Fig. 18.4
The Symbol dialog box enables you to choose a bullet character from any installed font.

IV

Mastering Special Features

Creating Numbered Lists

Numbered lists are much like bulleted lists. The main difference is that a numbered list is numbered sequentially instead of bulleted. If you add a paragraph in the middle of a numbered list or rearrange the order of paragraphs in a numbered list, Word for Windows automatically renumbers all the paragraphs in the list so that they retain their sequential numbering.

Word for Windows 95 offers six standard numbering formats and enables you to customize them. Word also offers a special type of numbered list, called a multilevel numbered list. In a multilevel numbered list, you can number each successive indentation level in the list. Later in this chapter, "Creating Multilevel Lists" describes multilevel numbered lists.

You can create a numbered list in three ways: with menu commands, with a toolbar shortcut, or by right-clicking the menu. As usual, the menu commands offer you many more options.

◀ See "Formatting a Document Automatically," p. 339

Creating Numbered Lists with Menu Commands

To create a numbered list with menu commands, follow these steps:

1. Type your list and then select it (don't use the Tab key to indent the items on your list). Or, place the text insertion point on a blank line.

2. Choose Format, Bullets and Numbering. The Bullets and Numbering dialog box appears (refer to fig. 18.2).

3. Choose the Numbered tab to display the numbered list options if they are not already displayed (see fig. 18.5).

4. Select from the predefined choices the numbering style that you want. Your choices include Arabic numbers, Roman numerals, and letters, with either periods or parentheses to separate the numbers from the list text.

Fig. 18.5

Use the Bullets
and Numbering
dialog box to
select the num-
bered list format.

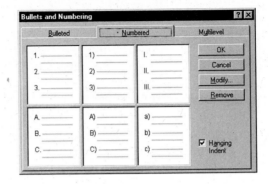

Later in this chapter, "Customizing Numbered Lists" describes how to
use the Modify button to customize a numbered list.

5. If you prefer a numbered list with no hanging indent, select the Hanging Indent option in the Bullets and Numbering dialog box so that no
mark appears in that check box. In that case, Word for Windows will
set no indent.

6. Choose OK. Word for Windows formats the selected text or line as a
numbered list.

If you have not yet typed the numbered list, type it now. Each time that you
begin a new paragraph, Word for Windows formats the paragraph as part of
the numbered list. "Ending the Numbered List" later in this chapter describes
how to end the numbered list.

Note

You can open the Bullets and Numbering dialog box by placing the pointer over the
selected text and clicking the right mouse button. A context-sensitive menu appears
to the right of the insertion point; choose Bullets and Numbering to display the
Bullets and Numbering dialog box.

If you want to replace an existing numbered list with new numbers or change
any of the other formatting properties of the numbered list, select the list and
then follow the instructions in "Customizing Numbered Lists," later in this
chapter. If you want to replace numbers with bullets, select the list and see
the previous section "Creating Bulleted Lists" for instructions on creating a
bulleted list. Word for Windows does not ask you to confirm whether you
want to replace numbers with bullets. If you inadvertently convert a numbered list to a bulleted list, choose Edit, Undo Number Default immediately
after the conversion.

To add numbered items anywhere in a numbered list, position the insertion point where you want to add the numbered item, and simply press Enter to add a new paragraph to the list. Word for Windows automatically formats the new paragraph as part of the numbered list and renumbers the list's paragraphs so that all the numbers remain sequential.

Creating Numbered Lists with the Toolbar

A quicker way to number a list is to use the Numbering button on the Formatting toolbar. The Numbering button appears near the right side of the Formatting toolbar. When you create a numbered list with the Numbering button, Word for Windows uses the numbered list formatting options selected most recently in the Bullets and Numbering dialog box. You can change the numbered list formatting options by choosing Format, Bullets and Numbering.

To create a numbered list with the toolbar, follow these steps:

1. Choose View, Toolbars and select Formatting. Word for Windows displays the Formatting toolbar, if it is not already displayed.

2. At the left margin, type the list and then select it, or place the text insertion point on a blank line.

3. Click the Numbering button on the Formatting toolbar. Word for Windows formats the current line or selected text as a numbered list.

If you have not yet typed the numbered list, type it now. Word for Windows formats each new paragraph as part of the numbered list. The next section, "Ending the Numbered List," explains how to end the numbered list.

By default, Word for Windows uses Arabic numbers and a 1/4-inch hanging indent to format lists with the Formatting toolbar's Numbering button. If you recently selected different options in the Bullets and Numbering dialog box, however, Word uses those selections instead.

Ending the Numbered List

As with bulleted lists, if you apply numbered list formatting to a blank line and then type the list, Word for Windows continues formatting each new paragraph that you type as part of the numbered list, until you end the numbered list.

To end a numbered list, follow these steps:

1. Press Enter to add a numbered, blank line to the end of the numbered list.

2. Move the pointer over the blank line and click the right mouse button. Word for Windows moves the insertion point to that line and displays a context-sensitive menu to the right of the insertion point.

3. Choose Stop Numbering to end the numbered list. Word removes the number and hanging indent from the blank line, ending the numbered list.

Adding Subordinate Paragraphs to a Numbered List

As with bulleted lists, sometimes the topic of a numbered list item requires more than one paragraph. And as with bulleted lists, you probably want to number only the first of several paragraphs for the same numbered list item.

You can change a numbered paragraph into a subordinate paragraph by using either a context-sensitive shortcut menu or the Formatting toolbar.

Adding a Subordinate Paragraph with the Menu

To use the shortcut menu to change a numbered list item to a subordinate paragraph, follow these steps:

1. Select the numbered list items from which you want to remove the numbers.

2. Move the pointer over the selected text and click the right mouse button. Word for Windows moves the insertion point to that line and displays a context-sensitive menu to the right of the insertion point.

3. Choose Skip Numbering. Word removes the number from the selected paragraphs, but the hanging indent remains.

If you add a subordinate paragraph at the end of a numbered list and then want to add another numbered list item after the subordinate paragraph, choose the Numbering button from the Formatting toolbar to resume the numbered list format.

Adding a Subordinate Paragraph with the Toolbar

To use the toolbar to change a numbered list item to a subordinate paragraph in the list, follow these steps:

1. Select the numbered list items from which you want to remove the numbers.

2. Choose the Numbering button from the Formatting toolbar. Word for Windows removes the number from the selected paragraphs, but the hanging indent remains.

Customizing Numbered Lists

To customize an existing numbered list or to make your own specifications for the number format, choose the Modify button from the Bullets and Numbering dialog box. Modify enables you to specify the text that comes before and after the number, to specify the numbering style, and to choose the font for the numbers. In addition, you can specify the size of the hanging indent, how much space appears between the bullet character and the text in the bulleted item, and whether the number is right-, left-, or center-justified within the indent space.

The only way to customize a numbered list format is with the menu commands; no toolbar shortcut exists for altering the format of a numbered list. If your custom numbered-list format is the most recently specified format, however, the Formatting toolbar's Numbering button applies your custom format.

To create a custom numbered-list format, follow these steps:

1. Select the numbered list whose format you want to customize.

2. Choose Format, Bullets and Numbering. The Bullets and Numbering dialog box appears (refer to fig. 18.2).

3. Click the Numbered tab to display the numbered list options, if they are not already displayed.

4. Choose the Modify button. The Modify Numbered List dialog box appears (see fig. 18.6).

5. Choose any combination of the following numbered list options:

Option	Function
Text Before	Type the characters, if any, that you want to insert before each number. If you want to enclose each number in parentheses, for example, type ((the opening parenthesis) in this text box.
Number	Select the numbering style that you want. Available choices include Arabic numerals, upper- and lowercase Roman numerals, upper- and lowercase alphabet letters, and word series (1st, One, and First). You can also choose no numbers at all.

(continues)

Option	Function
Text After	Type the characters, if any, that you want to insert after each number. If you want to enclose each number in parentheses, for example, type **)** (the closing parenthesis) in this text box.
Font	Displays a standard Font dialog box in which you can select a special font or font attributes (such as bold, italic, and underline) or set the point size for the numbers.
Start At	Type the starting number for your list. (If you're creating a series of lists, the starting number can be a number other than 1.)
Alignment of List Text	Select the alignment of the number within the space used for the indent. Word for Windows offers you the choice of left-aligned, right-aligned, centered, or justified.
Distance from Indent to Text	Type a number to set the size of the hanging indent.
Distance from Number to Text	Type a number to set the amount of space between the number and the text in the numbered paragraph.

Fig. 18.6

Use the Modify Numbered List dialog box to select the starting number of the list, the text before and after the number, and the number's alignment.

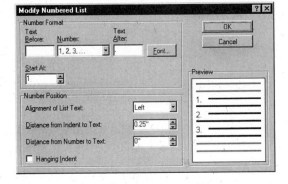

6. Choose OK in the Modify Numbered List dialog box.

7. Choose OK in the Bullets and Numbering dialog box.

Caution

If you customize or reformat an existing numbered list that contains subordinate (unnumbered) paragraphs, Word for Windows adds numbers to the subordinate paragraphs.

Creating Multilevel Lists

Multilevel lists are similar to numbered and bulleted lists but number or bullet each paragraph in the list according to its indentation level. In multilevel lists, you can mix numbered and bulleted paragraphs based on indentation level.

You can create multilevel lists with as many as eight levels. You might use a multilevel list format if you want your list to have numbered items that contain indented, bulleted subparagraphs. Many types of technical or legal documents require that you sequentially number each paragraph and indentation level. You can also use multilevel lists to create outlines of various types.

Don't confuse multilevel lists, however, with Outline view and outlining features described in Chapter 19, "Organizing Content with an Outline," or with the heading numbering discussed later in this chapter. In Outline view and heading numbering, only paragraphs that have one of the nine heading styles are numbered. In a multilevel list, only paragraphs that have a body text style (such as Normal) can be part of the list.

You can create a multilevel list only by using the menu commands; no toolbar shortcut exists. Although you can customize the numbering formats for the various indentation levels of a multilevel list, you cannot use more than one multilevel list format in the same document.

To create a multilevel list, follow these steps:

1. Type and select your list. Use paragraph indenting to indent text by choosing F<u>o</u>rmat, <u>P</u>aragraph; don't use the Tab key. Alternatively, place the text insertion point on a blank line.

2. Choose F<u>o</u>rmat, Bullets and <u>N</u>umbering. The Bullets and Numbering dialog box appears.

3. Click the M<u>u</u>ltilevel tab to display the multilevel list options, if the options are not already displayed (see fig. 18.7).

4. Select from the predefined choices the multilevel numbering style that you want. Your choices include combinations of numbered and lettered paragraphs, and technical and legal numbering styles.

   "Customizing Multilevel Lists" describes how to use the <u>M</u>odify button to customize a multilevel numbered list.

◀ See "Formatting a Document Automatically," p. 339

◀ See "Formatting Characters," p. 254

Fig. 18.7
Use the Bullets
and Numbering
dialog box to
select the multi-
level list format
that you want.

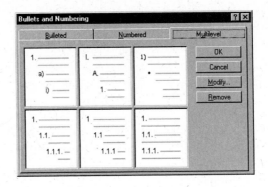

5. If you prefer a multilevel list with no hanging indent, select the Hanging Indent option in the Modify Bulleted List dialog box so that no
   check mark appears inside that check box.

6. Choose OK. Word for Windows formats the selected text or line as a
   multilevel list.

  If you have not yet typed the multilevel list, type it now. Each time that you
begin a new paragraph, Word for Windows formats the paragraph as part of
the multilevel list and applies the appropriate numbering for that level of
indentation. Use the Formatting toolbar's Increase Indent and Decrease Indent buttons (or the shortcuts Shift+Alt+right arrow and Shift+Alt+left arrow)
to set the indentation level of each paragraph in the list. Word for Windows
automatically adjusts the numbering to accommodate the paragraph's new
level of indentation.

Ending a multilevel list is the same as ending a regular numbered list: click
the right mouse button and choose Stop Numbering. For more detailed information, follow the instructions given in the previous section, "Ending the
Numbered List." You can also add unnumbered subordinate paragraphs to a
multilevel list the same way that you would for a numbered list.

Making Changes to a Multilevel List

If you want to replace an existing multilevel list with new numbers or change
any of the other formatting properties of the multilevel list, select the list and
follow the instructions in the next section, "Customizing Multilevel Lists." If
you want to replace a multilevel list with a numbered or bulleted list, select
the list and see the previous sections "Creating Bulleted Lists" or "Creating
Numbered Lists" for instructions on creating a bulleted or numbered list.

Word for Windows does not ask you to confirm whether you want to replace a multilevel list with a bulleted or numbered list format. If you inadvertently convert a multilevel list, choose Edit, Undo immediately after the conversion.

To add a new item to the multilevel list at any indentation level, position the insertion point where you want to add the item, and press Enter to add a new paragraph to the list. Finally, choose Format, Paragraph to indent the paragraph to the desired level. Word for Windows automatically formats the new paragraph as part of the multilevel list and renumbers the paragraphs in the list so that all the numbers remain sequential.

Customizing Multilevel Lists

Customizing a multilevel list format is similar to customizing a numbered or bulleted list. To customize a multilevel list format, you can only use the menu commands.

To create a custom multilevel list format, follow these steps:

1. Select the multilevel list for which you want to customize the format.

2. Choose Format, Bullets and Numbering. The Bullets and Numbering dialog box appears (refer to fig. 18.7).

3. Click the Multilevel tab to display the multilevel list options, if they are not already displayed.

4. Choose the Modify button. The Modify Multilevel List dialog box appears (see fig. 18.8).

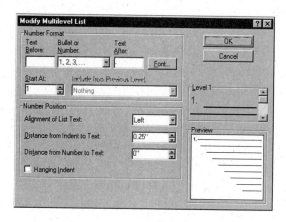

Fig. 18.8
Use the Modify Multilevel List dialog box to customize the numbering or bullet styles, alignment, and indentation levels of a multilevel list.

5. Use the Level list box to select the indentation level for which you want to adjust the formatting. You must customize each indentation level separately.

6. For each indentation level that you customize, set the following options in any combination:

Option	Function
Text Before	Type the characters, if any, that you want to precede each number or bullet at this indentation level.
Bullet or Number	Select the numbering or bullet style that you want. Available choices include a combination of the numbering choices available for numbered lists and the bullet choices available for bulleted lists, or no number or bullet at all.
Text After	Type the characters, if any, that you want to precede each number or bullet at this indentation level.
Font	Select any special font or font attributes (such as bold, italic, and underline) or set the point size for the numbers or bullets used at this indentation level.
Start At	Type the starting number for paragraphs at the selected level of indentation.
Include from Previous Level	Select whether the numbering of indented paragraphs includes nothing from the previous level, the number only, or the number and position from the preceding indented paragraphs. This control is not available if you have selected level 1 in the Level list box.
Alignment of List Text	Select the alignment of the number or bullet within the indent space.
Distance from Indent to Text	Type a number to set the size of the hanging indent.
Distance from Number to Text	Type a number to set the amount of space between the number and the text in the numbered paragraph.
Hanging Indent	Select this check box to indent each bulleted list item.

7. Choose OK in the Modify Multilevel List dialog box.

8. Choose OK in the Bullets and Numbering dialog box.

IV

Splitting a Numbered or Bulleted List

You might occasionally want to divide a long numbered or bulleted list into two or more smaller lists. To split a list, follow these steps:

1. Place the insertion point at the place where you want to divide the list.

2. Press Enter to create a blank line.

3. Remove the bullet or numbering from the blank line by placing the insertion point on the blank line, choosing Format, Bullets and Numbering, then clicking the Remove button.

   If you want to rejoin the lists, either delete any text or blank lines separating the lists, or cut and paste the lists one after the other with no space in-between.

If you split a numbered or multilevel list, Word for Windows renumbers the list so that both lists start with the starting number (specified in the Modify Numbered List dialog box) and are numbered sequentially.

Removing Bullets or Numbering

You can remove bullets or numbering from a list by using either a menu command or the Formatting toolbar's Numbering and Bullets buttons.

To remove bulleted, numbered, or multilevel list formatting by using a menu command, follow these steps:

1. Select the list from which you want to remove bullets or numbering.

2. Choose Format, Bullets and Numbering.

3. Choose the Remove button.

To remove list formatting by using the toolbar, do one of the following:

- To remove list formatting from a bulleted list, select the list and click the Bullets button on the Formatting toolbar.

- To remove list formatting from a numbered or multilevel list, select the list and click the Numbering button on the Formatting toolbar.

Creating Numbered Headings

▶ See "Number-
ing an Out-
line," p. 584

When you number headings, Word for Windows looks for different heading styles to determine how to number each heading paragraph. Paragraphs formatted with the heading 1 style, for example, are numbered with the first outline level (I., II., III.), paragraphs with the heading 2 style are numbered with the second level (A., B., C.), and so on. Word for Windows provides six predefined outline numbering formats for these different levels and enables you to establish your own custom numbering formats.

Only paragraphs with a heading style are numbered. You can apply heading styles by promoting or demoting the paragraphs in the outline view or by applying the appropriate heading styles. When you delete or rearrange numbered headings, Word for Windows automatically renumbers them. You can have only one heading numbering format in your document, although you can set the heading numbering so that numbering starts over at the beginning of each new document section. You can also choose to have headings appear with bullets rather than numbers.

To number headings, follow these steps:

1. Choose Format, Heading Numbering. The Heading Numbering dialog box appears (see fig. 18.9).

Fig. 18.9
Use the Heading Numbering dialog box to choose the numbering or bulleting style for headings.

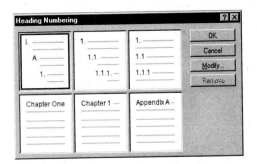

2. Select from the predefined choices the heading numbering style that you want.

   The next section, "Customizing Numbered Headings," describes how to use the Modify button to customize heading numbering.

3. Choose OK.

Word for Windows applies your selected numbering format to all paragraphs in your document with a heading style.

> **Note**
>
> You can open the Heading Numbering dialog box by placing the pointer over any paragraph with a heading style and clicking the right mouse button. The insertion point moves to that line, and a context-sensitive menu appears to the right of the cursor. Choose Heading Numbering to open the Heading Numbering dialog box.

Customizing Numbered Headings

To specify your own heading number format, use the Modify option from the Heading Numbering dialog box.

The only way to customize heading numbering is with the menu commands; no toolbar shortcut exists.

To create a custom heading number format, follow these steps:

1. Choose Format, Heading Numbering. The Heading Numbering dialog box appears (refer to fig. 18.9).

2. Choose the Modify button. The Modify Heading Numbering dialog box appears (see fig. 18.10).

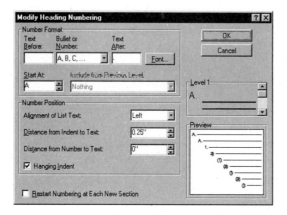

Fig. 18.10
By selecting options in the Modify Heading Numbering dialog box, you can vary the appearance of your heading number formats.

3. In the Level list box, select the heading level for which you want to adjust the formatting. You must customize each heading level separately.

4. Choose or set any of the following options, in any combination:

Option	Function
Text Before	Type the characters, if any, that you want to have appear before each number or bullet at this heading level.
Bullet or Number	Select the numbering or bullet style that you want. Available choices are a combination of the choices available for numbered lists and the choices available for bulleted lists, or you can choose to have no number or bullet at all.
Text After	Type the characters, if any, that you want to have appear after each number or bullet at this heading level (such as a closing parenthesis or a period).
Font	Select any special font or font attributes (such as bold, italic, and underline), or set the point size for the numbers or bullets used at this heading level.
Start At	Type the starting number for the selected heading level.
Include from Previous Level	Select whether the heading numbering includes nothing from the previous level, the number only, or the number and position from the preceding heading level. This control is not available if you have selected level 1 in the Level list box.
Alignment of List Text	Select the alignment of the number or bullet within the indent space.
Distance from Indent to Text	Type a number for the size of the hanging indent.
Distance from Number to Text	Type a number for the amount of space between the number or bullet and the text in the heading.
Hanging Indent	Select whether you want a hanging indent for this heading level. If you don't want a hanging indent, make sure that this check box does not include a check mark.
Restart Numbering	Select whether you want the heading numbering to start over at the beginning of each new document. If you don't want numbering to restart, make sure that this check box does not include a check mark.

5. Choose OK to close the Modify Heading Numbering dialog box.

6. Choose OK to close the Heading Numbering dialog box.

Removing Heading Numbers

You can remove heading numbering by placing the insertion point in any heading paragraph and choosing the Remove button in the Heading Numbering dialog box. You can also format the text to remove heading numbering. ❖

◄ See "Formatting Characters," p. 254

► See "Creating an Outline," p. 575

Chapter 19

Organizing Content with an Outline

Many writers feel comfortable organizing their thoughts and even their schedules with outlines. If you're in that group of organized people, you are going to enjoy working with the Word for Windows outlining feature. In Word for Windows, an *outline* is a special view of your document that consists of formatted headings and body text. Nine possible outline heading levels are available. Each heading level can have one level of body text. Assigning each heading level a different formatting style enables you and the reader to discern your document's organization quickly.

Having an outline for your document is useful in many ways. For example, an outline can help you organize your thoughts as you compose a new document. At a glance, you can quickly see an overview of your document that shows only the headings. Later, an outline can help you reorganize and edit your document. By "collapsing" parts of your document so that only the headings show, you can easily move an entire section—heading, subheadings, and any associated body text. But Word for Windows has some other not-so-obvious uses for outlines: you can easily number the parts of a document, change heading-level formatting (each heading level has its own specific style), and use headings to generate tables of contents and other lists.

This chapter helps you maintain your documents and manage changes made within a workgroup. You learn how to do the following:

- Create and work with an outline

- Reorganize your document easily by using an outline

- Use outline headings to create tables of contents

Viewing an Outline

To view an outline, choose <u>V</u>iew, <u>O</u>utline, or click the Outline view button at the left of the horizontal scroll bar (see fig. 19.1). Figure 19.1 shows the first page of a document in the Normal editing view, and figure 19.2 shows the same document in Outline view with headings displayed. Figure 19.3 shows the document in an Expanded Outline view, with text and subheadings displayed.

Fig. 19.1

A document in Normal view that does not show outline headings.

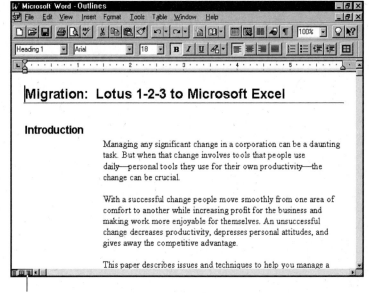

Outline view button

As you can see, the Outline view looks different than the Normal editing view in several ways. First, the *Outline toolbar* replaces the ruler. Second, Word for Windows indents the formatted headings and body text paragraphs to different levels. Third, a + or – icon appears to the left of each heading and paragraph. A plus sign (+) means that subordinate headings (those at a level lower than the heading being examined) or paragraphs of body text are associated with the heading. A minus sign (–) indicates that no headings or paragraphs are beneath the heading.

Outline
toolbar

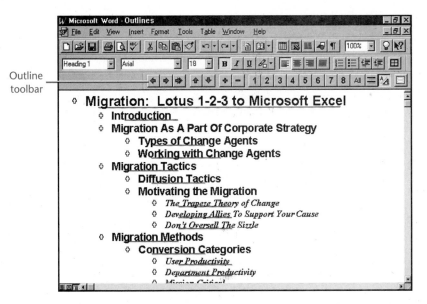

Fig. 19.2
The Outline view
showing an
overview of
contents
(headings only).

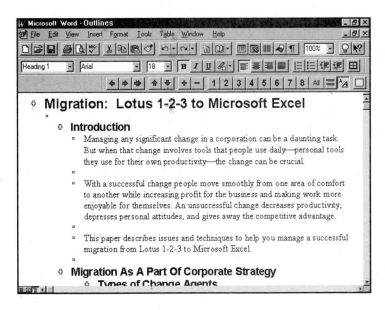

Fig. 19.3
The Outline view
showing detailed
contents by
expanding the
outline.

When you are in Outline view, you have the option of viewing headings at
different levels or of viewing the entire document, including all body text.
You also can choose to display headings at selected levels or to display headings and text. By viewing only the headings of a large document, you can see
an overview of your document. You can also see where you have missed or
misplaced topics.

The Outline toolbar includes buttons that you can use to assign heading levels to text, promote or demote headings, and hide or display headings. Table 19.1 summarizes the functions of the Outline toolbar's buttons.

Table 19.1   The Functions of the Outline Toolbar's Buttons

Icon	Button	Function
←	Promote	Promotes the heading (and its body text) by one level, and promotes body text to the heading level of the preceding heading
→	Demote	Demotes the heading by one level, and demotes body text to the heading level below the preceding heading
⇒	Demote to Body Text	Demotes the heading to body text
↑	Move Up	Moves the selected paragraphs before the first visible paragraph that precedes selected paragraphs
↓	Move Down	Moves the selected paragraphs after the first visible paragraph that follows selected paragraphs
✚	Expand	Expands the first heading level below the currently selected heading; repeated clicks expand through additional heading levels until the body expands
−	Collapse	Collapses body text into headings and then collapses lowest heading levels into higher heading levels
1	Show Heading 1	Displays all headings and text through the lowest level number that you click
2	Show Heading 2	
3	Show Heading 3	
4	Show Heading 4	
5	Show Heading 5	
6	Show Heading 6	

Icon	Button	Function
7	Show Heading 7	
8	Show Heading 8	
All	All	Displays all text if some is collapsed, and displays only headings if all text is already expanded
≡	Show First Line Only	Toggles between displaying all the body text or only the first line of each paragraph
ᴬ**A**	Show Formatting	Toggles between displaying the outline with or without full character formatting
▭	Master Document	Changes to master document view or back to simple outline view. If master document view is selected, the Master Document toolbar appears to the right of the Outline toolbar.

▶ See "Creating a New Master Document," p. 940

In the sections that follow, you learn how to use these buttons to create and reorganize your outline.

Creating an Outline

Creating an outline does two things: it organizes your work by heading, sub-heading, and body text, and applies formatting to each heading level. Styles define the formatting applied to each heading level. The style Heading 1 formats the first level of heading, Heading 2 formats the second level, and so on, through Heading 9. The Normal style formats body text. Word for Windows has predefined the Heading and Normal styles; however, you can redefine any of those styles by choosing Format, Style.

Word for Windows provides two ways to create an outline. The first method is to select the outline view and then use the Outline toolbar's buttons to assign heading levels to your text (while creating or after creating the document). This chapter describes this method. The second method is to work in the normal view (or draft or page layout view) of your document and assign to headings appropriate styles such as Heading 1 or Heading 2. To learn how to apply styles to text, see Chapter 11, "Using Styles for Repetitive Formats."

To create an outline in a new or existing document, follow these steps:

1. Choose View, Outline.

2. Type a heading or select the text that you want to convert to a heading. Select the heading by moving the insertion point anywhere within the heading's text, or by clicking to the left of the heading (but not clicking the + or – icon).

   If you're creating an outline from scratch (in a new file), Word for Windows applies the level 1 heading (Heading 1) as you begin typing.

3. Assign the appropriate heading level by clicking one of the following icons on the Outline toolbar by clicking the Outline toolbar's arrow buttons with the mouse, or by pressing one of the following shortcut keys:

Icon	Mouse Action	Shortcut Key	Result
⬅	Click the left-arrow button	Press Alt+Shift+←	Promotes the heading one level
➡	Click the right-arrow button	Press Alt+Shift+→	Demotes the heading one level
⏩	Click the double-arrow button		Demotes the heading to body text
⬆ ⬇	Click the up- or down-arrow	Press Alt+Shift+↑ or ↓	Move line up or down

4. Press Enter to end the heading (or body text) and start a new heading (or paragraph) at the same level.

Note

As you work in your document in normal or page layout view, you might reach text that should be a heading in the outline. You can stay in the normal or page layout view and create this heading. One way is to format the paragraph with a heading style. Another method is to move the insertion point into the heading text and press Alt+Shift+←. The paragraph containing the insertion point is formatted to the same heading level as the preceding outline heading in the document. Press Alt+Shift+← or Alt+Shift+→ to adjust the heading to the level that you want.

Formatting Your Outline

When you create an outline, you actually apply styles to the headings in your document. The styles determine your document's formatting. Unless you redefine Heading 1 for your document, for example, the style applies the Arial font in 14-point size, boldface, with extra space before and after the heading.

If you want to format your document's headings differently than the pre-defined heading styles, you must redefine the heading styles. If you want to format your outline's level 1 headings differently, for example, you must redefine the Heading 1 style. You can redefine styles by formatting an example or by choosing F̲ormat, S̲tyle, choosing the M̲odify button, and then redefining a style. When you redefine a style for a heading, the format change applies to all headings formatted with that style.

◀ See "Redefining Standard Styles," p. 352

Promoting and Demoting Headings

When you *promote* a heading, you raise its level in the outline. You can promote a Heading 3 to a Heading 2, for example, to make the indent smaller. *Demoting* does just the opposite. When you promote and demote headings, Word for Windows assigns the appropriate heading style for that level.

Using the Mouse to Promote or Demote Headings

You can use the mouse to promote or demote headings in two ways. One method uses the buttons in the Outline toolbar. Using this technique, you promote or demote only the selected heading. In the other method, you drag the heading's + or – icon left or right until the heading is at the level that you want; with this technique, you promote or demote the heading and all subordinate text.

If you want to use the mouse to promote or demote only the selected headings or text, follow these steps:

1. Choose V̲iew, O̲utline (if you haven't already).

2. Select the paragraphs to promote or demote.

3. To promote the heading, click the Promote button (the left-arrow button) on the Outline toolbar.

   To demote the heading, click the Demote button (the right-arrow button) on the Outline toolbar.

To convert the heading to body text, click the Demote to Body Text button (a double-arrow button) on the Outline toolbar.

Word for Windows treats headings independently, and thus does not promote or demote associated subheadings along with the headings. Body text, however, always remains associated with its heading. The preceding mouse method is useful for changing only the selected heading level while leaving subordinate text or levels alone.

To promote or demote a heading and have all subordinate headings and text change at once, follow these steps:

1. Choose View, Outline.

2. Move the mouse pointer over the + or – icon that appears to the left of the heading that you want to promote or demote (the pointer becomes a four-headed arrow). Click and hold down the mouse button.

3. Drag the icon to the left to promote the heading and its subordinate subheadings and body text, or drag the icon to the right to demote them. (Drag to the right edge of the outline to demote a heading to body text.)

As you drag a heading to a new level, the mouse pointer becomes a two-headed arrow, and a gray vertical line appears as you drag across each of the heading levels. When you have aligned the gray vertical line with the new heading level that you want—that is, you have aligned the line with other headings at the level that you want—release the mouse button.

Using Keyboard Shortcuts to Promote or Demote Headings

You can also use keyboard shortcuts to promote and demote individual headings (and body text). You need not be in outline view to use this method; any view works.

To use shortcut keys to promote or demote a heading or portion of body text, follow these steps:

1. Select the headings or body text to promote or demote.

2. To promote one level, press Alt+Shift+←.

   To demote one level, press Alt+Shift+→.

This method affects only the selected headings and text; Word for Windows does not promote or demote associated subheadings along with the selected headings.

Whichever method you use, when you return to the normal editing view and display the ruler, you see that Word has applied the appropriate heading styles to your outline headings. (You can return to normal editing view by choosing View, Normal; View, Page Layout; or click on the Normal View or Page Layout View icons on the horizontal scroll bar.)

Collapsing and Expanding an Outline

A *collapsed* outline shows the headings down to only a specific level. When you *expand* an outline to a specific level, you see all headings down to that level, as well as body text. You can collapse an outline all the way down so that only level 1 headings show, or you can expand the outline all the way so that all headings and body text show. You also can expand the outline to show all headings and only the first line of each paragraph of body text.

Collapsing and expanding your outline can help you to write and edit. By collapsing your outline, you can see an overview of your entire document and can move around quickly in the outline. To move to a particular section, just collapse to the level of the heading to which you want to move, select the heading, and then expand the outline. You can also use shortcuts to move entire headings and all their subordinate headings and text to new locations in the outline.

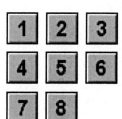

To collapse or expand the entire outline, use the numeric buttons on the Outline toolbar. Click the lowest level that you want to display in your outline. If you want to show levels 1, 2, and 3 but no lower levels, for example, click the Show Heading 3 button.

To display all levels, including body text, click the Outline toolbar's All button. To display all heading levels but no body text, first click the All button to display all levels and body text (if not already displayed), and click All again to collapse the body text, leaving only the headings for all levels displayed. Clicking one of the Show Heading number buttons on the Outline toolbar collapses or expands your entire outline uniformly. Figure 19.4 shows the outline presented in figure 19.2 with only two levels of headings displayed.

Fig. 19.4
Collapsing an
outline to display
only the higher
levels of headings.

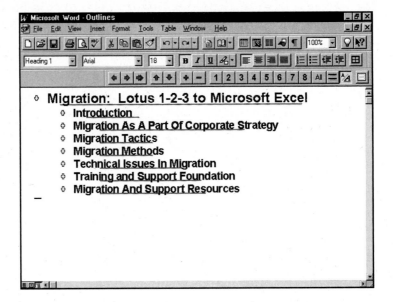

Using the Mouse to Collapse or Expand Headings

You can use the mouse and the Expand (+) and Collapse (–) buttons on the
Outline toolbar, as well as the + and – icons in the outline, to collapse or
expand headings selectively. Here are the methods that you use:

- Collapse headings and body text into the selected heading by clicking
  the Collapse (–) button on the Outline toolbar.

- Expand contents of selected headings by clicking the Expand (+) button
  on the Outline toolbar.

- Expand or contract a heading's contents by double-clicking the + icon
  to the left of the heading in outline view.

Using Keyboard Shortcuts to Collapse or Expand Headings

If you don't have a mouse or if you work faster using the keyboard, you can
collapse and expand your outline by using shortcut keys. Table 19.2 lists the
shortcut keys available. Before using a shortcut key, you must select the heading or text that you want to collapse or expand.

Table 19.2 Using Shortcut Keys to Collapse and Expand Headings	
Shortcut Key	**Description**
Alt+Shift+- (hyphen)	Collapses the selected heading's lowest level and collapses all body text below the heading. Repeated presses collapse additional levels.
Alt+Shift++ (+ sign)	Expands the selected heading's next lower level. Repeated presses expand additional levels and, after expanding all headings, the body text.

Fitting More of the Outline into the Window

One of the great benefits of using an outline view of your document is that you get an overview of your document's organization. As you work with an outline to organize a document, you might want to view more of the outline than usually fits into the display window. To enable you to do so, Word for Windows provides two methods that you can use separately or in combination.

If you expand all or some headings to display subordinate body text, you might find that parts of the outline are pushed out of the display window. To view more of the outline, you can display the first line of each body text paragraph only, instead of the entire paragraph. You can also display the outline view without the full character formatting for each heading style. Because the character formatting for many of the heading styles usually uses boldface text and fairly large point sizes, each heading takes up a lot of room on the screen. If you omit the character formatting, the headings take less space.

Displaying an outline without character formatting affects the display in outline view only; it does not make any permanent changes in the heading styles or their formatting. Figure 19.5 shows the same outline as in figure 19.2, but without the full character formatting. Notice that you can now see much more of the outline.

Fig. 19.5
By displaying the outline without character formatting in the headings, you can fit more of the outline in the window.

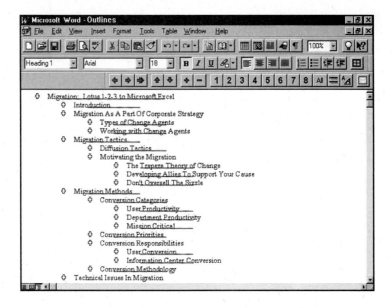

Using the Mouse to See More of the Outline

You can use the mouse and the Outline toolbar to fit more of the outline into the display window. Use either of the following methods:

■ To show only the first line of expanded body text paragraphs, click the Show First Line Only button on the Outline toolbar. If the body text paragraphs are already showing only the first line, clicking this button causes Word for Windows to display the entire paragraph.

■ To display the headings without full character formatting, click the Show Formatting button on the Outline toolbar. If the headings are already shown without character formatting, clicking this button causes Word to redisplay the formatting.

Using Keyboard Shortcuts to See More of the Outline

If you prefer to use the keyboard, you can fit more of the outline into the display window by using shortcut keys. Table 19.3 lists the shortcut keys available.

Table 19.3 Using Shortcut Keys to See More of the Outline	
Shortcut Key	**Description**
/ (the slash key on numeric keypad)	Shows or hides character formatting for headings
Alt+Shift+L	Shows only first line of each paragraph of expanded body text. Pressing this key combination a second time displays all text.

Reorganizing an Outline

Using Word for Windows selection techniques, you can select outline headings in any of the normal ways. The outline view, however, offers a shortcut for selecting that can be a real time-saver. When you select an outline heading by clicking its icon in the outline view, you select the heading and its subordinate headings and body text.

Even if you don't use an outline to organize your thoughts before you begin writing, you can use an outline later to reorganize your document quickly. After you click a heading's + or – icon, you can move all the subordinate headings and text as a unit. (If you select only the words in an expanded heading, you move only the heading.)

You can move selected headings (along with associated subheadings and body text) by using the mouse or the keyboard. To move a selected heading upward (toward the first page) or downward (toward the last page), use any of these methods:

- Press Alt+Shift+↑ or ↓.

- Drag the heading's icon up or down.

- Click the Move Up or Move Down button on the Outline toolbar.

By selecting multiple headings and paragraphs, you can move them as a unit. Hold down Shift as you click adjacent headings and paragraphs to select them together.

Numbering an Outline

If you need numbered outlines for legal documents, bids, or proposals, you can have Word for Windows add the numbers for you.

◀ See "Creating Numbered Lists," p. 555

To number your outline (from any view), choose Format, Heading Numbering. You can then select the type of numbering method. Figure 19.6 shows some of the numbering options available. Figure 19.7 shows an outline that uses the legal numbering style.

Fig. 19.6
Use the Heading Numbering option to renumber outlines.

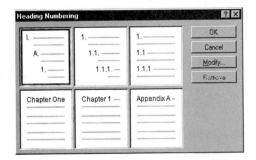

Fig. 19.7
Automatic numbering makes legal and proposal documents easy to construct.

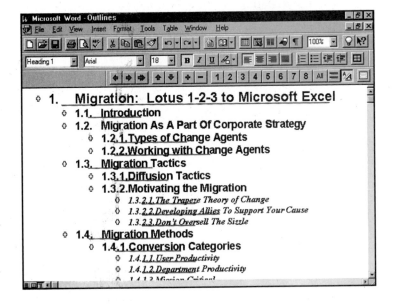

To apply heading numbering quickly, click with the right mouse button on any heading and select Heading Numbering from the shortcut menu that appears.

Using Outline Headings for a Table of Contents

If you need a table of contents, Word for Windows can build one from the outline. Word for Windows constructs tables of contents by accumulating outline headings and their page numbers.

To create a table of contents from outlining, choose Insert, Index and Tables. Chapter 29, "Creating Indexes and Tables of Contents," goes into detail on how to use the Index and Tables dialog box, shown in figure 19.8, which you can use to create a table of contents like that shown in figure 19.9.

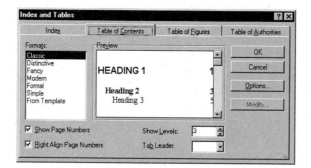

Fig. 19.8
In the Index and Tables dialog box, you can create a table of contents.

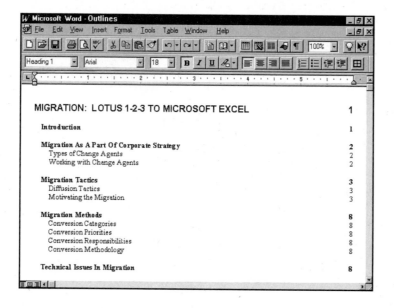

Fig. 19.9
The finished table of contents, consisting of outline headings and document page numbers.

To create a table of contents, follow these steps:

1. Position the insertion point where you want the table of contents to appear.

2. Choose Insert, Index and Tables.

3. Select the Table of Contents tab.

4. Select the options that you want.

5. Click OK.

Replacing Outline Headings

◀ See "Using Find
and Replace,"
p. 197

You format outline headings with styles—specifically, Word for Windows built-in styles Heading 1 through Heading 9. Because you can search for and replace styles in Word for Windows, you can globally change outline headings.

Using Custom Styles to Create an Outline

If you formatted a document with custom styles and want to convert the document to an outline, you can replace the custom styles with outline styles.

Suppose, for example, that you formatted your document with custom heading styles called *title*, *heading*, and *subheading*. Choose Edit, Replace. With the insertion point in the Find What text box, choose Format, select Style, and then select the style title. Then in the Replace With text box, choose Format, select Style, and select the style Heading 1. (Type no text in either text box.) In the Replace dialog box, choose Replace All to replace all title styles with Heading 1 styles. Do the same for all other headings and subheadings in your document. Then you can view your document as an outline.

Globally Replacing Outline Headings

In your document, you might want to promote or demote heading levels globally. For example, you might want to change all level 3 headings to level 4 headings. To do so, replace Heading 3 styles with Heading 4 styles (see the general instructions in the previous section, "Using Custom Styles to Create an Outline").

Removing Text from within an Outline

You can remove all text from within an outline if the text is formatted with a style. You might want to remove all the text from an outline, for example, so that you can save just the headers. To remove the text instead of replacing the style (or styles) that formats the text with another style, replace the style with nothing. To remove text in an outline formatted with Word for Windows default styles, for example, replace the style Normal with nothing. For details, see the general instructions in the previous section "Using Custom Styles to Create an Outline."

Printing an Outline

You can print your document as displayed in the outline view. To print the outline, choose <u>V</u>iew, <u>O</u>utline, display the levels of headings and body text that you want to print, and then choose <u>F</u>ile, <u>P</u>rint or press Ctrl+P. ❖

Chapter 20

Automating with Field Codes

Fields are a necessary, but often invisible, part of such features as a table of contents, an index, or a table of authorities. Fields also perform such simple tasks as inserting the date or displaying a data-entry box. They also display the text edit box, check box, and drop-down list used in forms. The value you gain from using fields comes from the repetitive work they can automate for you.

This chapter gives you an introduction to fields, and covers the following topics:

- How to view, insert, update, edit, and format the fields

- How to lock and unlock fields

- The more frequently used field codes and their functions

Understanding the Basics of Fields

Fields are hidden codes you type into a document or insert by using commands from the Insert menu. You normally see the results of fields, such as dates, page numbers, text linked to other documents, or mail-merge data. You can also see the field code for an individual field or for all fields in a document.

If you have used worksheet functions in Microsoft Excel or Lotus 1-2-3, you are familiar with the concept of fields. Fields are similar to functions. Most worksheet functions are mathematically and financially oriented; Word for Windows fields are oriented toward words, document processing, and mail-merge functions.

Figures 20.1 and 20.2 show two views of the same document. Figure 20.1 shows the field codes in the document; figure 20.2, a document after the fields it contains have been updated. As you can see, the field codes create an automated document that you can use repeatedly. Display field codes in the document by pressing Alt+F9 for the whole document or Shift+F9 for the selected area.

Fig. 20.1

Fields appear as codes in this document.

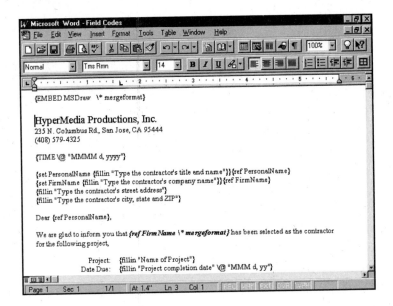

In Word for Windows, the only time most fields are updated to produce a new result is when you print, print merge, or select and then update the fields. You can update fields individually or throughout the entire document.

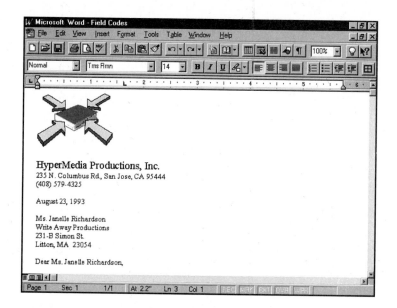

Fig. 20.2
When the field results are displayed, the document looks as though it was typed.

Many of the other features described in this book use fields, although you may not have been aware of them. In Chapter 13, "Formatting the Page Layout, Alignment, and Numbering" for example, the dates and page numbers in headers and footers are created with fields; in Chapter 29, "Creating Indexes and Tables of Contents," the indexes and tables of contents are created with fields. Fields are used in Chapter 15, "Mastering Envelopes, Mail Merge, and Form Letters" and Chapter 32, "Assembling Large Documents" to create mail-merge letters, build online forms, and assemble large documents.

More than 60 types of field codes are available. With these field codes, you can do the following:

- Build tables of contents, tables of authorities, and indexes

- Build mailing lists, labels, and form letters

- Prompt operators for information used repeatedly in a document

- Insert dates, times, or document summary information

- Link Word for Windows documents or data in other Windows applications with the current Word for Windows document

■ Update cross-referenced page numbers automatically

■ Calculate math results

■ Enable operators to jump between related words or contents

■ Start macros

Examining the Types of Fields

Tip

For a full list of field codes and descriptions, choose <u>H</u>elp, Microsoft Word Help Topics, select Reference Information, and then select Field Types and Switches.

Fields can change your documents in a number of ways. Three types of Word for Windows fields are available: result fields, action fields, and marker fields.

■ *Result fields* produce a result in your document by inserting information. This information may be from the computer or document, as in the {author} and {date} fields. Other fields, such as {fillin} display a dialog box that requests information from the operator and then inserts the information into the document.

■ *Action fields* do something to the document but don't insert visible text. The action is performed either when you update the field, as in the {ask} field, or when you click the field, as in the {gotobutton} and {macrobutton} fields. The {ask} field, for example, displays a dialog box and prompts you to enter information. But instead of displaying the information, Word for Windows stores it in a bookmark you designate.

■ *Marker fields* produce neither results nor actions. A marker field simply marks a location in the document so that you can find the location when you build such things as indexes and tables of contents. The index entry {xe} and table of contents entry {tc} fields are marker fields.

Understanding the Parts of Fields

Fields contain three parts: field characters, field type, and field instructions. A field that displays the current date in a format such as Sep 12, 96, may look like the following:

```
{date \@ "MMM d, yy"}
```

where the braces ({ and }) are field characters, date is the field type, and \@ "MMM d, yy" is the field instruction.

■ *Field characters* define the beginning and end of a field. Although they look like braces, { and }, you cannot type the field characters. You create them by choosing a menu command that creates a field.

■ *Field type* defines the type of action the field performs. The field type follows the first field character, {, and must be a field type (see "A Reference List of Field Codes" later in this chapter), an equal sign (=), or a bookmark name.

■ *Field instructions* define the type of action performed. You can customize the action of some fields by giving different instructions.

You need to understand the following terms also:

■ *Arguments* are numbers or text used to control a field's action or results. If an argument contains more than one word, the argument usually must be enclosed in quotation marks (" "). (Exceptions are described in each field's description.) You can use the {ask} field, for example, to prompt the operator for text to be assigned to the bookmark First_Name, as follows:

```
{ask First_Name "Enter the first name."}
```

Note that the text arguments must be enclosed in quotation marks. If a field result, such as a Fillin dialog box, shows only the first word of the text you typed, you have probably forgotten to enclose the rest of the argument in quotation marks. Word for Windows uses the first word of the argument but doesn't see the rest unless it is in quotation marks.

The following table briefly describes arguments and their functions:

Argument	Function
Bookmark	In a field, is the same as a bookmark you assign to text. It names a location or selection of text. Fields use bookmarks to take action on the text or object in the document having that bookmark name. Fields also can store information in a bookmark or use the page number or sequence value of a bookmark's location.
Identifier	Distinguishes between different parts of the same document. You may use the letter F as an identifier of figures, for example, and the letter P as an identifier of pictures.
Text	Includes words or graphics used by the field. If you are entering a text argument with more than one word, you need to enclose all the text argument in quotation marks.
Switch	Toggles field results on or off. Type switches with a backslash (\) are followed by the switch letter. Switches can be specific to a field or can be general and used by different fields. A field can contain as many as 10 field-specific switches and 10 general switches. Field-specific switches are described in "A Reference List of Field Codes," later in this chapter.

Field Code Shortcut Keys

Table 20.1 lists shortcut keys that can make your work with fields quicker and easier. These shortcut keys and their equivalent commands are described in the appropriate sections throughout this chapter.

Table 20.1 Field Shortcut Keys	
Key Combination	**Function**
F9	Updates fields in the selection
Shift+F9	Toggles the selected field codes between the code and result
Ctrl+F9	Inserts field characters, { }, to manual type field
Ctrl+Shift+F9	Unlink—Permanently replaces a field with its last result
Alt+Shift+F9	Equivalent to double-clicking selected {gotobutton} and {macrobutton} fields
F11	Go to next field
Shift+F11	Go to previous field
Ctrl+F11	Locks field to prevent updates; field remains
Ctrl+Shift+F11	Unlocks field to permit updates
Alt+Shift+D	Inserts {date} field
Alt+Shift+P	Inserts {page} field
Alt+Shift+T	Inserts {time} field

Viewing and Printing Field Codes

Fields appear in two ways: as a field code and as the field result. Field results display as though they were typed. You normally don't see the field codes when you work on a document, but if they return text, you see their results after the fields have been updated. If the fields have not been updated, you see the fields' previous results.

Some fields produce no visible result. Instead, they produce an action that affects other field codes. The fields that do not produce results include {ask}, {data}, {nextif}, {next}, {print}, {rd}, {set}, {skipif}, {ta}, {tc}, and {xe}.

Displaying Field Codes

You may need to see field codes on-screen so that you can review, delete, or edit them. You can display the field codes throughout the entire document or for an individual field.

To display field codes on-screen throughout the entire document, follow these steps:

1. Choose Tools, Options.

2. Select the View tab.

3. Select the Field Codes check box.

To display an individual field code, follow these steps:

1. Move the insertion point within the field code or its result.

2. Press Shift+F9.

   Or, click the right mouse button and choose Toggle Field Display from the shortcut menu.

These commands switch the display between showing field codes or the result. Your document probably will change its word wrap when you reveal or hide field codes. This change occurs because of the differences in length between the field codes and their results.

A few field codes do not display. The {xe} (index entry), {tc} (table of contents entry), and {rd} (referenced document) field codes are formatted automatically as hidden text.

To see codes that display as hidden text when you display field codes, follow these steps:

1. Choose Tools, Options.

2. Select the View tab, and then select the Hidden Text check box.

3. Choose OK.

Most fields do not update automatically to show you the most current result. You must update fields manually or by using a macro. When you load a document that contains fields, each field shows its previous result. This feature enables you to load a document, such as a contract or form letter, and update only the items you want changed.

Tip

Pressing Alt+F9 displays all field codes, and pressing Alt+F9 a second time redisplays field results.

Tip

A fast way to switch all the fields in a selected area between displaying field codes or their results is to select the area containing the fields and press Shift+F9. Press Shift+F9 again to redisplay field results.

Displaying Field Results as Shaded

Field results—whether they are text, dates, or numbers—appear on-screen just as though they were entered normally. If you are working on forms or documents and want to see which items are fields, you can shade the field results at certain times so that they stand out.

To shade field results, follow these steps:

1. Choose Tools, Options.

2. Select the View tab.

3. Select from the Field Shading drop-down list the time when you want field results shaded: Never, Always, or When Selected.

4. Click OK.

Printing Field Codes

You probably should keep a printed copy of your documents and macros. These copies are a help if you ever lose the file or if someone else takes over your operation.

To print a copy of the document so that you can see the field codes, follow these steps:

1. Choose File, Print.

2. Click the Options button from the Print dialog box.

3. Select the Field Codes check box under the Include with Document group.

4. Click OK to return to the Print dialog box, and then print your document.

Remember to deselect the Field Codes check box when you want to print just the document (without visible field codes).

Entering Field Codes

You can enter fields in a number of ways. Several commands enter field codes at the insertion point's position. Some of the commands that insert field codes include the following:

Edit, Paste Special, Paste Link   Insert, Caption

Insert, Page Numbers   Insert, Cross-Reference

Insert, Annotation   Insert, Index and Tables

Insert, Date and Time   Insert, File

Insert, Field   Insert, Picture

Insert, Form Field   Insert, Object

Another way to insert field codes into a document is to choose Insert, Field and then select the appropriate field codes from the Field dialog box. Or you can enter field codes directly into a document by pressing Ctrl+F9 to insert the field characters, { }, and then typing between the field characters.

Inserting Field Codes

To insert field codes by using Insert, Field, follow these steps:

1. Position the insertion point in the document at the location where you want the field result.

2. Choose Insert, Field.

   Figure 20.3 shows the Field dialog box, from which you can select field types and instructions.

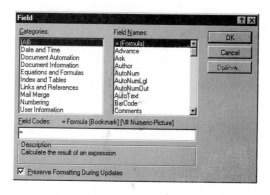

Fig. 20.3
The Field dialog box inserts fields and enables you to select appropriate switches to change format or actions.

3. Select the type of field you want from the Categories list, or select All.

4. Select a field type from the Field Names list.

5. Select a switch to modify the field by choosing the Options button, when it is not dimmed. Select switches or bookmarks as described in the following text; then choose OK in the Field Options dialog box.

6. Choose OK.

When you choose OK, some fields update immediately. When you insert the {fillin} field, for example, Word for Windows displays the Fillin dialog box that prompts you for an entry.

Inserting Field Code Switches or Bookmarks

Some field codes have mandatory or optional switches. Some codes also require a bookmark, a named location in the document. You can find out what a field code needs and what is mandatory in two ways: look for a short prompt in the Field dialog box, or select Help for a full explanation.

In the Field dialog box, shown in figure 20.3, look to the right of the Field Codes label in the lower third of the dialog box. You'll see a short prompt that shows what you can put in the field code that is selected in the list.

To insert switches or bookmarks into a field code, follow these steps:

1. Follow the steps in the preceding procedure, and select a field from the Field Names list.

2. Click the Options button. The Field Options dialog box appears (see fig. 20.4).

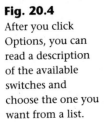

Fig. 20.4

After you click Options, you can read a description of the available switches and choose the one you want from a list.

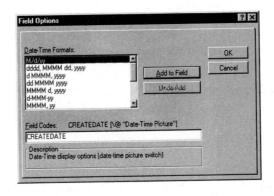

3. Select the Field Specific Switches tab.

4. Select a switch from the S<u>w</u>itches list, and check the switch Description at the bottom of the dialog box. Choose <u>A</u>dd to Field if you want to add the switch. Continue to add more switches, if necessary.

5. If the field code requires a bookmark, select the <u>B</u>ookmarks tab.

6. Select a bookmark from the <u>N</u>ame list, and click the <u>A</u>dd to Field button.

7. Choose OK in the Field Options dialog box.

8. Choose OK in the Field dialog box.

The field code you have built is then inserted into your document at the location of the insertion point.

Inserting Field Codes Manually

After you are familiar with the field code syntax, you can manually enter the field codes quickly. Because you are not prompted and do not have lists of correct switches, making mistakes is easier.

To enter a field code manually, follow these steps:

1. Position the insertion point in the document at the location where you want the field action or result.

2. Press Ctrl+F9. Even if fields are not displayed currently, Word for Windows shows the field characters you have just inserted. The insertion point appears between two field characters, { }.

3. Enter the field name followed by a space; then type the field instructions. If the field references a path name, be sure to type two backslashes instead of a single backslash to separate folders.

4. Update the field code by pressing F9.

An incorrect syntax in the field code causes a beep when you press F9 to see the results. Select the field and press Shift+F9 to see the field code and switches.

Another method of manually entering fields is to position the insertion point where you want the field, type the field type and instructions, select them, and then press Ctrl+F9. Word for Windows encloses the selection in field characters, { and }. This method works well when you need to nest fields inside other fields (see "Creating Complex Fields by Nesting" later in this chapter).

> **Note**
>
> Remember that although the field characters appear to be braces, they are not. Fields do not work if you type brace characters. You can create a matching set of field characters only by pressing Ctrl+F9 or using a command to insert the field characters and field code.

Moving between Fields

You can find fields in two ways: use a shortcut key to find the next field, or choose Edit, Find to find a specific field type.

To move to and select the next field after the insertion point, press F11 (Next Field). To move to and select the field preceding the insertion point, press Shift+F11 (Previous Field).

> **Note**
>
> The F11 and Shift+F11 shortcuts do not find the {xe} (index entry), {tc} (table of contents entry), or {rd} (referenced document) fields. You can find these fields by first displaying hidden text (by choosing Tools, Options), selecting the View tab, and then selecting the Hidden Text check box. After the codes are visible, you can choose Edit, Find.

Tip

If your keyboard does not have an F11 key, press Alt+F1. To move to the preceding field, press Alt+Shift+F1.

To find a specific field code, follow these steps:

1. Choose Tools, Options.

2. Select the View tab.

3. Select the Field Codes check box to display field codes. For some field codes, you may have to select the Hidden Text check box also (in this same tab). Then click the OK button.

4. Choose Edit, Find from the menu bar.

5. In the Find What text box, type the field type you want to find, such as **fillin**. Do not type the field characters.

6. Click the Find Next button.

7. If you want to edit the field, choose Cancel or press Esc.

8. Press Shift+F4 to find the next field of the same type. The insertion point moves to the next field of the type you requested.

Editing Fields

You can edit field codes or their results manually. This approach is useful for correcting the results of a field or for changing the information or switches in a field code after it has been created. By editing simple fields, you can change them into larger, nested fields containing multiple parts, which you then can use to accomplish complex tasks.

To edit a field code, follow these steps:

1. Choose Tools, Options.

2. Select the View tab.

3. Select the Field Codes check box. Then click the OK button.

4. Move the insertion point inside the field.

5. Edit the field as you edit text. Make sure that you preserve the correct syntax of the parts within the field. You cannot edit the field characters, { }.

To see the results of your editing, select the field and press F9 (Update Field).

Tip

You can edit fields while the Find dialog box is open. Simply click once in your document to refocus Word on the document. When you want to use the Find dialog box again, click Find Next.

Tip

You also can select the text that encloses the field, and press Shift+F9 to display the fields.

Troubleshooting

I edited the results of fields on-screen and then when I printed, the fields updated and what I edited is lost. How can I keep a field from updating when I print?

You can change the results of a field by editing the results on-screen as if you were editing normal text. If you edit the results, however, you do not want the field code to update when it prints. To make sure that the field code does not update, choose File, Print, click the Options button, and make sure that the Update Fields check box is not selected.

Note

Some fields, such as {include}, {dde}, and {ddeauto}, use DOS path names (folder names). When you type path names in fields, you must use double backslashes (\\) wherever the path name normally has a single backslash (\). Keep this fact in mind if you have to change the folder names used in a field. Always use a backslash before any quotation mark (") in a string that's enclosed in quotation marks. For example, the field

```
{fillin "Who wrote \"Brahms' Lullaby\""}
```

places quotation marks around the phrase Brahms' Lullaby when it appears in the prompt of a Fill-in dialog box.

Creating Complex Fields by Nesting

When you *nest* fields, you put one or more fields inside another field. This technique enables you to use the result of one field to change the actions of another. You can nest the {fillin} field inside the {set} field, for example, so that the typed entry in the {fillin} field can be stored by the {set} field in a bookmark. Then the text in the bookmark can be redisplayed at other locations with the {ref} field, as in the following example:

```
{set Name {fillin "Type the name"}}
```

This method is used in the letter shown in figures 20.1 and 20.2.

To nest a field inside another field, follow these steps:

1. Display the field codes, if they are not already displayed, by choosing Tools, Options, selecting the View tab, and selecting the Field Codes check box.

2. Insert the first field into the document, using the method you normally use.

Tip
Another quick way to update a field is to right-click the field and select Update Field

3. Position the insertion point inside the existing field at the point where you want the nested field.

4. Insert the nested field by following the Insert Field procedure for this code, or by pressing Ctrl+F9 and typing the field type and its instructions between the field code characters, { }.

5. Return to step 3 and insert additional field codes, if necessary.

6. Select the field and press F9 (Update Field) to check the results.

Deleting Fields

Delete a field by selecting it and pressing Delete. A quick way to select and delete fields is to press F11 (Next Field) until the appropriate field is selected, and then press Delete.

Tip
If you select fields manually by dragging across them, you need to drag across only the field character, { }, at either end of the field to select the entire field code

Formatting Field Results

You can format the results of field codes in two ways:

- Using the techniques you use to format any other text or graphics.

- Inserting formatting switches in a field code.

If you use the latter technique, the formatting switches take priority over manual formatting when the field code updates.

IV

Formatting the result of a field code is the same as formatting any item in a document. You select what you want to format and then choose a command. The next time the field code updates, however, it may lose the formatting you have applied. This situation can occur if the formatting you apply is different from the formatting contained in the switch in the field code.

Switches enable you to format the results of a field. When the field updates, the formatting specified by the switch applies itself again to the field code result. You can insert switches in a field code by selecting them from the Field Options dialog box, as described in "Inserting Field Code Switches or Bookmarks" earlier in this chapter. And you can add or change a switch by editing an existing field code.

You can format field results in the following three ways:

- * mergeformat.   Format the field results with multiple formats by inserting this switch in the field and then choosing Format, Font or Format, Paragraph.

- * charformat.   Format the field results with a single-character format by inserting this switch in the field and then formatting the first character of the field type.

- *General switches.*   These switches enable you to format such things as date, time, and numeric formats. Enter a general switch in the field code after the field type.

Table 20.2 lists the general switches. The * mergeformat and * charformat switches are described in the following sections, which also describe the switch types, numeric pictures, and date-time pictures used in the switches and explain how to use them in fields.

Table 20.2   General Switches for Formatting Fields

Switch	Syntax	Effect
*	{field-type * switchtype}	Formats the text result with case conversion, number conversion, or character formatting
\#	{field-type \# numericpicture}	Formats the numeric result to match a "picture" showing the pattern of numeric format
\@	{field-type \@ date-timepicture}	Formats the date or time result to match a "picture" showing the pattern of date-time format
\!	{field-type \!}	Locks a field's results

The following fields' results cannot be formatted with general switches:

{autonum}	{rd}
{import}	{eq}
{autonumlgl}	{tc}
{macrobutton}	{gotobutton}
{autonumout}	{xe}

Formatting Numbers, Dates, and Text Case

Tip

Always use a single space to separate the field instructions, such as formatting switches, from the field type, such as FILLIN.

In the following sections, the {fillin} field is used to illustrate how each * switch works. The {fillin} field displays a dialog box in which you can type sample text or numbers and see how the switch affects what you type.

To duplicate the examples, press Ctrl+F9, type **fillin**, press the space bar, and then type the switch type and switch. To update the field and see the results, select the field and press F9. Remember that you can switch quickly between viewing the field codes and their results by pressing Shift+F9.

Preserving Manual Formats

Two of the most valuable switches, * charformat and * mergeformat, enable you to retain formats you have applied to a field result. Without the use of these switches, your manual formatting of a field's result is removed when the field updates.

Switch Type	Effect
* charformat	Formats the field result the same as the format of the first character of the field type, the character after {. This format takes precedence over other formatting. Formatting the f in the {fillin} field as boldface, for example, produces a boldface field result.
* mergeformat	Preserves your manual formatting of a field's result. Character and paragraph formatting you apply to a field result are preserved after the field updates. The updated field results are reformatted on a word-by-word basis, using the original formatting as a template. If the updated results have more words than the originally formatted result, the extra words use the format of the first character after the opening field character, {. If the previous field result was not formatted, mergeformat acts like charformat.

The following example formats the first letter in the field name FILLIN with the character format you want to apply to the entire result:

```
{fillin "Type a sample result" \* charformat}
```

Formatting remains even after the field is updated.

The following example formats the results of the field with character or paragraph formatting:

```
{fillin "Type a sample result" \* MERGEFORMAT}
```

After the field updates, the * mergeformat field reapplies the formats you applied previously. Your formats are reapplied according to word-by-word locations. If the updated field contains words in a different order, the formatting may not coincide with the updated position of words.

Converting Uppercase and Lowercase Text

The following switches change the capitalization of the field's results:

Switch	Result
* Upper	Converts characters in the field results to all uppercase
* Lower	Converts characters in the field results to all lowercase
* FirstCap	Converts the first letter of the first word in the field result to a capital; converts other letters to lowercase
* Caps	Converts the first letter of each word in the field result to a capital; converts other letters to lowercase

The following example uses a capitalization switch:

```
{fillin "Type a sample result" \* Upper}
```

Formatting Numeric Results

The following switches change the way a numeric result appears:

Switch	Result
* Arabic	Uses Arabic cardinal numbers such as 1, 2, 3, and so on. If the field type is {page}, the switch overrides the page-number formatting set by the Edit Header/Footer dialog box.
* Ordinal	Converts a numeric field result to an ordinal Arabic number. When used with the {page} field, it produces page numbers such as 18th.
* Roman	Converts a numeric field result to Roman numerals, such as XV or xviii. Type the switch as *** Roman** for uppercase Roman numerals, or *** roman** for lowercase Roman numerals.
*Alphabetic	Converts a numeric field result to its alphabetical equivalent (changing the number 5 to the letter *e*, for example). Type the switch as *** Alphabetic** for uppercase letters, or *** alphabetic** for lowercase letters.

The following example uses a numeric switch:

```
{fillin "Type a number" \* Ordinal}
```

Formatting Numbers as Text

The following switches convert numeric results to a text equivalent. This process is useful for calculated numeric results that appear in documents—a check or invoice amount, for example. Use the capitalization switches described earlier in "Converting Uppercase and Lowercase Text" to change the capitalization of a number as text.

Switch	Result
* Cardtext	Converts a numeric field result to text, with the first letter in uppercase (changing the number 35 to `Thirty Five`, for example).
* Ordtext	Converts a numeric field result to ordinal text (changing the number 35 to `Thirty Fifth`, for example).
* Hex	Converts a numeric field result to a hexadecimal number.
* Dollartext	Converts a numeric field result to a text and fractional dollar amount. For example, 53.67 becomes `Fifty three and 67/100`.

The following example uses switches to format text:

```
{fillin "Type a number" \* Cardtext \* Upper}
```

Formatting with Custom Numeric Formats

You can format numeric field results so that they appear in the numeric format you want. You can, for example, define your own custom formats that round results to the desired precision, display only significant numbers, include text, or have different formats for positive, negative, and zero results.

To format numeric results, you create a numeric picture. The switch for a numeric picture is \#. A *numeric picture* is a pattern that follows the switch and is composed of symbols that define placeholders, commas, and signs.

To format numeric fields with character formatting, such as boldface and italic, format the numeric picture. Formatting the negative portion of a numeric picture in italic, for example, produces italic formatting of negative results.

The examples use a fill-in data-entry box that enables you to type any number or text into a data-entry box. To duplicate one of the examples, use Insert,

Field to display the Field dialog box. Select the FILLIN field, and then type the \# switch and the numeric picture following `fillin` in the Field Codes edit box. Leave a single space between the field name, the switch, and the numeric picture. The result should be similar to the following:

    {fillin \# $#,##0.00}

To update the field so that a dialog box asks for your entry, select the field and press F9. To toggle the display between field results and field codes, press Shift+F9.

You can use the following characters to generate numeric pictures:

0 # x . , – +

You also can specify formatting variations for positive, negative, and zero results and can include text, sequence names, and other symbols and characters in a numeric picture. The following sections describe how to use these characters in numeric pictures.

Positive, Negative, and Zero Formatting Variations

You can specify three numeric pictures that Word for Windows can use, depending on the sign of the field's result. The three numeric pictures must be separated by semicolons (;). If the field result is positive, Word for Windows uses the numeric picture to the left of the first semicolon. If the result is negative, Word for Windows uses the numeric picture between the two semicolons. And if the result is 0, Word for Windows uses the numeric picture to the right of the second semicolon.

The numeric picture does not have to be enclosed in quotation marks if it contains only numeric formatting. If the numeric picture contains text or space characters, you must enclose the entire numeric picture in quotation marks. For example, the numeric pictures in this field

    {fillin \# #,##0.00;(#,##0.00);0}

produce 4,350.78 when the field result is 4350.776; (4,350.78) when the result is -4350.776; and 0 when the result is 0.

> **Note**
>
> The right parenthesis,), accompanying a negative number can cause positive and negative numbers to misalign. If this problem occurs, align the numbers by using a decimal tab, or insert a space in the positive format to the right of the last zero.

The 0 Placeholder

Put a 0 in a numeric picture wherever you want a 0 to display when a number is missing. The field {fillin \# 0.00}, for example, produces the following results:

Number	Result
.646	0.65
250.4	250.40

Most currency formats use two zeros (00) to the right of the decimal.

The # Placeholder

The # character is a digit placeholder used when you do not want leading or trailing 0s (zeros) in results. The field {fillin \# #.00}, for example, produces the following results:

Number	Result
0.6	.60
250.4	250.40

The x Placeholder

The x character is a digit placeholder that *truncates*, or cuts off, numbers that extend beyond the x position. For example,

    {fillin \# #.#x}

produces .24 when the numeric result is .236.

The Decimal Point

Use the decimal point along with other numeric picture characters to specify the decimal location in a string of digits. Change the character used as the decimal separator by changing the Decimal Symbol on the Currency tab of the Regional Settings Properties dialog box. You can access this dialog box by opening the Start list, highlighting Settings, clicking the Control Panel, and then double-clicking the Regional Settings icon.

The Thousands Separator

Use the thousands separator (usually a comma) along with # or 0 numeric picture characters to specify the location of the thousands separator in a result. Change the character used as the thousands separator by changing the Digits Grouping Symbol on the Currency tab of the Regional Settings Properties dialog box. You can access this dialog box by opening the Start list, highlighting Settings, clicking the Control Panel, and then double-clicking the Regional Settings icon.

The Minus Sign (–)

Used in a numeric picture, this character (–) displays a minus sign if the result is negative and a blank space if the number is positive or 0.

The Plus Sign (+)

Used in a numeric picture, this character displays a plus sign (+) if the result is positive, a minus sign (–) if the result is negative, and a space if the result is 0.

Text

Use text formatting in a numeric picture to include measurements or messages along with the numeric result. Enclose text and the numeric picture in quotation marks (" "). The text displays in the field result in the same location as it appears in the numeric picture. For example, the numeric picture

```
{fillin \# "Amount owed is $#,##0.00"}
```

produces `Amount owed is $4,500.80` when the user types **4500.8** in the Fill-in dialog box.

If the text string contains a character that Word for Windows might interpret as an operator or as field information, enclose that character in apostrophes (' '). In the following example, the dashes on either side of the zero, `- 0 -`, normally do not display for the 0 result. But by enclosing the entire numeric picture in double quotation marks and the numeric picture for `- 0 -` in apostrophes, as in the following example, you can tell Word for Windows to display `- 0 -` for zero results:

```
{fillin \# "0.0;(0.0);'- 0 -'"}
```

If you use text in a numeric picture that includes positive, negative, and zero format variations, enclose the entire pattern in quotation marks, as in the following line:

```
{fillin \# "0.0;(0.0);Enter a non-zero number"}
```

If the text itself contains quotation marks, precede those quotation marks with a backslash (\), as follows:

```
{fillin "Who wrote \"Brahms' Lullaby\"?"}
```

Other Characters

When you use symbols and characters in the numeric picture, they appear in the result. This feature is useful when you need to format a numeric result to include dollar signs, percent symbols, and international currency. A simple example is the use of the dollar sign, as in

```
{fillin \# $#,##0;($#,##0)}
```

or the percent sign, as in

```
{fillin \# #0%}
```

Tip

ANSI characters and their codes are usually listed in the back of printer manuals.

To enter ANSI characters such as the cent, pound, Yen, and section symbols, turn on the numeric keypad (press Num Lock) and hold down the Alt key as you type the appropriate four-number ANSI code. The character appears when you release the Alt key. Do not leave a space between the character entered and the numeric picture.

Formatting Date-Time Results

You can format date and time field results so that they appear in standard or custom formats. To format date-time results, you create a date-time picture. The switch for a date-time picture is \@. A *date-time picture* is a pattern composed of characters that define date and time formats such as month, day, and hour. Word for Windows uses the pattern as a sample format. For example, the following field and pattern:

```
{DATE \@ "MMMM d, yyyy"}
```

displays the computer's current date in the format

```
December 24, 1995
```

To format date-time pictures with character formatting such as boldface and italic, format the first letter of each portion of the date-time picture. In the preceding example, you can format the first M in boldface and italic to make the entire month boldface and italic but leave the day and year as they were.

You can use the following characters to generate date-time pictures:

M d D y Y h H m am pm AM PM

You also can include text, sequence names, and other characters and symbols in a date-time picture. The following sections describe how to use these characters in date-time pictures.

The Month Placeholder

Uppercase M is the month placeholder (lowercase m designates minutes). The four formats are as follows:

M	1 through 12
MM	01 through 12
MMM	Jan through Dec
MMMM	January through December

The Day Placeholder

Uppercase or lowercase d is the day placeholder. The four formats are as follows:

d or D	1 through 31
dd or DD	01 through 31
ddd or DDD	Mon through Sun
dddd or DDDD	Monday through Sunday

The Year Placeholder

Uppercase or lowercase y is the year placeholder. The two formats are as follows:

yy or YY	00 through 99
yyyy or YYYY	1900 through 2040

The Hour Placeholder

Uppercase or lowercase h is the hour placeholder. Lowercase designates the 12-hour clock. Uppercase designates the international 24-hour clock. The four formats are as follows:

h	1 through 12
hh	01 through 12
H	1 through 24
HH	01 through 24

The Minute Placeholder

Lowercase m is the minute placeholder. (Uppercase M designates months.) The two formats are as follows:

m	0 through 59
mm	00 through 59

Morning and Afternoon Indicators

You use uppercase or lowercase AM and PM with h or hh 12-hour clock formats to designate morning or afternoon. You can select characters other than AM/am and PM/pm by using the Control Panel to change settings in the International icon. The four formats are as follows:

\@ h AM/PM	8AM and 6PM
\@ h am/pm	8am and 6pm
\@ h A/P	8A and 6P
\@ h a/p	8a and 6p

Text Characters

Use text formatting in date-time pictures to include measurements or messages with the results. Enclose text and the date-time picture in quotation marks (" "). If the text includes characters that Word for Windows can interpret as field information characters, such as a minus (-) or zero (0), enclose those characters in apostrophes (' '). The text displays in the field result in the same location it appears in the date-time picture. For example, the following field and date-time picture

```
{DATE \@ "Job complete at HH:mm"}
```

displays a result such as Job complete at 12:45.

Other Characters

You can use the colon (:), hyphen (-), and comma (,) in the date-time picture. These characters display in the result in the same position in which they are used in the date-time picture. The date-time picture \@ "HH:mm" displays 23:15, for example, and the date-time picture \@ "MMM d, yy" displays Jun 15, 92.

Updating, Unlinking, or Locking Fields

As you learned earlier in the chapter, many field codes update automatically. You can update some codes manually, however. In some cases, you don't want field codes to update; for example, you may have a letter that begins with an automatic date field. You do not want the date on a completed letter to change the next time you open the letter.

Another instance in which you want to control updating is when you have data from an application such as Microsoft Excel linked into your Word document. You probably do not want the link refreshed each time you update the document—you may not know at that time whether the data in the source Excel worksheet is correct. Using the methods described in the following sections, you can update the document without updating the Excel data, and then return later to update just the Excel data.

Updating Fields

Updating a field produces a new result or action from the field—perhaps a change in text, numbers, or graphics. Some fields may not produce a visible change but instead affect the results in other fields.

Different fields update at different times. Fields such as {date} update when the document opens or when updated by command. Fields such as {Next} take effect only during print merge. Fields such as {Fill-in} update when you select the field and press F9 (Update Field). Other fields may update during printing, print merge, or repagination.

To update a field manually, select the field and press F9 (Update Field). You can select the field by selecting the text around it, using one of the selection methods described in previous chapters, or by pressing F11 (Next Field) or Shift+F11 (Previous Field) to move to and select the field. If field codes are visible, you can select a specific field by dragging across one of the field characters.

Tip
You also can select a visible field code by moving the insertion point inside the field and pressing F8 (Extend Selection) until the field is selected.

If Word for Windows beeps when you attempt to update a field, the field is locked, there is a syntax error in the field code, or that field code does not update—as happens, for example, with the fields that generate equations on-screen.

If you want to update only part of a document, select only the portions of the document you want to update, and press F9. To update fields in a table, select the portion of the table you want to update (using any table-selection method), and then press F9.

Tip
You can select the entire document by pressing Ctrl+A. Or, press Ctrl and click the selection bar.

To update an entire document, select the entire document, either by pressing Ctrl and clicking the selection bar (the blank area to the left of the document), or by choosing Edit, Select All. Press F9 to update fields.

The following list shows fields unaffected by F9 (Update Field). Fields with an asterisk update automatically.

Field	Use
*{AutoNum}	Automatic numbers with Arabic (1, 2, 3 and so on) format
*{AutoNumLgl}	Automatic numbers with legal (1.1.1 and so on) format
*{AutoNumOut}	Automatic numbers with outline format
{Seq}	Math formulas
{gotobutton}	On-screen buttons that jump to a location when double-clicked
{macrobutton}	On-screen buttons that run a macro when double-clicked
{Print}	To send information to the printer

Undoing or Stopping Updates

Tip
The status bar displays the percentage of updates completed.

You can undo field updates if you choose Edit, Undo Update Fields (or press Alt+Backspace or Ctrl+Z) immediately after updating one or more fields. This capability gives you a chance to make changes throughout a document, see how they affect the document, and then remove the changes if necessary.

If you are updating a document and want to stop the updates, press Esc. This method is handy if you have selected the entire document and realize that you do not want to update all fields.

Locking Fields to Prevent Updates

When you want to prevent a field from changing, you can lock it. Locking fields is useful if you want to archive a file that will not change, to prevent accidental changes, or to prevent updating a link to a file that no longer exists. Word for Windows does not update a locked field. If you attempt to update a locked field, you hear a beep and see in the status bar a warning that an attempt was made to update a locked field.

To prevent a particular field from being updated while those around it are updated, lock the field. Select the field and then press Ctrl+F11 (Lock Field). To unlock the field, press Shift+Ctrl+F11 (Unlock Field).

Locking a field is different from unlinking a field with Shift+Ctrl+F9. Unlinked fields replace the field code with the results. You are unable to return to a usable field code.

Unlinking Fields

You may want to unlink fields and convert them to their fixed results. Unlinking and then converting fields freezes the result at its current value, removes the field code, and ensures that the result does not change if the fields are updated. You may want to unlink field codes that link pictures, charts, and text into your document before you pass the document to someone else. If you do not want to pass all the linked documents as well as your Word document, you should unlink the linked field codes before you give another user the document.

To unlink a field, select the field code and press Ctrl+Shift+F9 (Unlink Field).

Getting Help on Field Codes

Word for Windows has more than 60 field codes that enable you to automate many of the features in documents you work in repetitively. Although most field codes are not difficult to use, much information is required about switches, bookmarks, and so on.

To get general or specific help about field codes, open the Help menu system. Choose Help, Microsoft Word Help Topics, and then select Contents. Next, from the Customizing Microsoft Word section, select Fields. Select a topic and choose Display. If you need help about a specific field code, choose Help, Microsoft Word Help Topics, select Reference Information, and then select Field Types and Switches. You will see a list of fields (in alphabetical order). Select the one you need information about.

A Reference List of Field Codes

Exploring all the power and possibilities available with field codes is beyond the scope of this book. The following list shows some of the more frequently used field codes and their functions:

Function	Field Code
Date, Time, Summary Info	date, time, author, createdate
Index	xe, index

(continues)

Function	Field Code
Forms	`formtext, formcheckbox, formdropdown`
Linking, embedding	`embed, import, include, link, dde, and importing ddeauto`
Mathematical calculations	`eq`
Mail merge	`data, mergerec, mergefield, next, nextif, ref`
Numbering	`autonum, autonumlgl, autonumout`
Page numbering	`page, numpages`
Prompting	`ask, fillin`
Reference figures, objects, or locations	`pageref, ref, seq, xe`
Symbol	`symbol`
Table of Contents	`tc, toc`

In the following sections, the syntax of each field code shows whether the code contains field instructions, such as bookmarks, prompts, or switches. Remember that a *bookmark* is a name assigned to a selection or insertion point location. A bookmark also can be a name used to store information for future use by a field code. A *prompt* is a text message that appears on-screen when the field code updates. The prompt must be enclosed in quotation marks (" "). A *switch* alters the behavior or format of a field code in some manner. A field may use multiple switches. Included in some field code descriptions is an explanation of the specific switches used in that field code.

The syntax also shows the order in which you must enter information between field characters. Italicized words are information used by the field type. Optional information is enclosed in square brackets.

{ask}

Syntax:

```
{ask bookmark "prompt" [switches]}
```

Displays a dialog box that asks the user to enter text. Word for Windows assigns that text to the bookmark, which then can be used throughout the document to repeat the typed text. The following field code, for example, displays a dialog box asking the operator to enter the first name; Word for

Windows stores the typed information in the bookmark named `Firstname` so that it can be used by other fields in the document:

```
{ask Firstname "Enter the first name"}
```

If you type **Mary** in response to the dialog box, you can repeat Mary throughout the document by using the field code `{ref Firstname}`.

Switch	Result
\o	Requests a response to the dialog box only at the beginning of the first document during a print merge.
\d	Defines default text for the dialog box. If no default exists, the last entry is repeated. Use \d " " if you want nothing as the default.

Updates during printing merge. You cannot use `{ask}` fields in footnotes, headers, footers, annotations, or macros.

If you want a dialog box for data entry, which you can update by pressing the F9 key, see the `{fillin}` field code.

{author}

Syntax:

```
{author ["new_name"]}
```

Inserts or replaces the author's name as it appears in the document's File, Properties, Summary tab.

The new name can be up to 255 characters long.

Updates when you press F9 or when you print.

{autonum}

Syntax:

```
{autonum}
```

Displays an Arabic number (1, 2, 3, and so on)when inserted at the beginning of a paragraph or outline level. Numbers display in the document in sequence, and update as other `{autonum}` paragraphs are inserted or deleted. Choose Format, Bullets and Numbering to insert these fields more easily.

{autonumlgl}

Syntax:

```
{autonumlgl}
```

Displays a number, using legal numbering (1.2.1) format, when inserted at the beginning of a paragraph formatted with a heading style. See also {autonum}.

{autonumout}
Syntax:

    {autonumout}

Displays a number, using outline number (I, A, 1, a, and so on) format, when inserted at the beginning of a paragraph formatted with a heading style. See also {autonum}.

{autotext}
Syntax:

    {autotext AutoTextEntry}

The AutoTextEntry is the name in Edit, AutoText under which text or an object is stored. As a result of updating this field, the latest definition is stored in AutoText.

{bookmark}
Syntax:

    {bookmark}

Bookmarks are names that refer to text or graphics. They appear not as {bookmark}, but as the actual bookmark name enclosed in braces, such as {Premise}. Different field codes use bookmarks in different ways. Some fields return or display the contents of the bookmark. Some fields return or display the number of the page on which the bookmark's contents are located. You load data into a bookmark by choosing Insert, Cross-Reference or by displaying an input box for operator entry using {ask} or {fillin} field control.

Bookmarks may be up to 40 characters in length and cannot include spaces. Use only letters, numbers, and underscore characters (_) in a bookmark. If you need to separate words, use an underline instead of a space.

If the bookmark FirmName contains the text Generic Quality Corporation, for example, the text appears in the document at every location of the field {ref FirmName}.

Updates when you press F9, when you choose File, Print Merge, or when you choose File, Print the first time (in a header or footer). See also {ref bookmark}.

{comments}

Syntax:

```
{comments ["new_comments"]}
```

Inserts or replaces comments from the File, Properties, Updates when you press F9 or when you print or print merge.

{createdate}

Syntax:

```
{createdate}
```

Inserts the date the document was created, as shown on the File, Properties, Summary tab. Formats according to the system's default format.

Updates when you press F9, when you choose File, Print Merge, or when you choose File, Print the first time (in a header or footer).

{database}

Syntax:

```
{database [switches]}
```

Used to insert data from an external database.

{date}

Syntax:

```
{date ["date_format_picture"]}
```

Inserts the current date or time.

Updates when you select this field and press F9 or print. Formats with the date-time picture-switches listed in "Formatting Date-Time Results," earlier in this chapter.

{edittime}

Syntax:

```
{edittime}
```

Inserts the number of minutes the document has been edited since its creation, as shown on the File, Properties, Statistics tab .

Updates when you press F9 or when you merge a mail document.

{embed}

Syntax:

```
{embed object}
```

▶ See "Embedding Data," p. 986

Embeds an object into a Word for Windows document. For example,

```
{embed ExcelChart \s  \* mergeformat}
```

embeds a Microsoft Excel chart into the document.

{=}

Syntax:

```
{= formula}
```

Displays the result of a mathematical calculation, such as

```
{ = Sales - Cost}
```

◀ See "Creating Bookmarks," p. 158

Expressions can use bookmarks to define the locations of numbers or can use row and column locations in document tables. Calculations on bookmarks can use common arithmetic operators, such as + (plus) and * (multiply). Calculations on row and column contents in a table use functions such as Average, Count, Sum, and Product.

▶ See "Performing Calculations in a Table," p. 680

Updates when you press F9 or print merged documents. If the expression is in the header or footer, it is updated when you print.

Following are examples of expression fields:

Field Code	Result
`{= Sales - Cost}`	Subtracts the value in Cost from the value in Sales
`{= if (Sales > 450,Sales*.1,Sales*.05)}`	Tests whether the value in Sales is greater than 450; if it is, the result is the Sales value multiplied by .1; if not, the result is the sales value multiplied by .05
`{= if (Sales > 450,Sales*.1,Sales*.05)*2}`	Multiplies the result of the if statement by two

> **Note**
>
> If you need to create a large mathematical expression, build it in pieces within the field characters. As you complete each *integral unit* (one that can calculate by itself), select the entire field and press F9 to see whether the result is correct. Select the completed expression, and press Ctrl+F9 to enclose that expression in another set of field characters. This method enables you to find errors in construction as you go, instead of trying to find problems in a large, completed expression.
>
> You can lose a bookmark used in calculations by carelessly deleting a character. If you delete a value as well as the spaces that enclosed the value, you may have deleted the bookmark. In this case the formula no longer works because the bookmark no longer exists. You can re-create the bookmark to restore the formula. If you are in doubt about whether a bookmark still exists, press Alt+B and select the bookmark. See whether the correct value is selected in the document. If the bookmark is a name in which data is stored, rather than a document location, you may not be able to go to the bookmark.

Use the following math operators with bookmarks only:

Operation	Operator
Add	+
Subtract	–
Multiply	*
Divide	/
Exponentiate	^
Less than	<
Less than or equal to	<=
Greater than	>
Greater than or equal to	>=
Parenthetical	( )
Absolute value	Abs
Integer	Int
Sign	Sign
Test for error	Define

(continues)

Operation	Operator
Modulus (remainder)	Mod
Round	Round
And	And
Or	Or
Not	Not

When you refer to a cell in a table, use the A1 format, in which rows are numbered, starting with 1 and going down. Columns are labeled with letters, beginning with A at the leftmost. If the expression is in the same table as the cells, only the A1 reference in brackets, [ ], is necessary.

▶ See "Performing Calculations in a Table," p. 680

You should use the functions and operators in the following table for any math calculations within a table. Functions can result in 1 for TRUE or 0 for FALSE.

Function	Name/Examples	Result
Abs	Absolute value `{= Abs -4}`	Operator Results in 4
And	Logical And `{= And (Sales>500,Cost<300}`	Operator Returns 1 if both arguments are true; 0 if either argument is false (maximum of two arguments).
Average	Averages arguments `{= Average (Budget[R1C1:R1C2])}`	Reduction function Averages the content of cells in row 1, column 1 and row 1, column 2 from the table named Budget.
Count	Counts arguments `{= Count (Budget[C1])}`	Reduction function Counts the number of numeric items in the cells of column 1 in the table Budget. Empty cells and text count as zero.

IV

Mastering Special Features

Function	Name/Examples	Result
Defined	Checks for errors `{Defined (Sales)}`	Operator Results in 1 if `Sales` bookmark exists and expression evaluates without error; otherwise, results in 0.
Int	Results in integer `{= Int (Sales)}`	Operator Deletes decimal fraction of an argument. To round numbers, use the Round operator.
Max	Returns largest argument `{= Max (Budget[R1C1:R2C2])}`	Reduction function Returns the maximum value in the table named `Budget` within the range R1C1 to R2C2.
Min	Returns smallest argument `{= Min (Budget[R1C1:R2C2])}`	Reduction function Returns the maximum value in the table named `Budget` within the range R1C1 to R2C2.
Mod	Returns remainder `{= Mod (500,23.6)}`	Operator Returns the *modulus* (in the example, the remainder of 500 divided by 23.6).
Not	Reverses logical value `{= Not (Test)}`	Operator Returns 1 if the `Test` is 0 or if condition in `Test` is false; returns 0 if the `Test` is not zero or if condition in `Test` is true.
Or	Logical Or `{=Or (Sales$mt500,Cost$lt300)}`	Operator Returns 1 if either condition is true; returns 0 if either condition is false.

(continues)

Function	Name/Examples	Result
Or	Product `{= Product (Budget[R1C1:R2C1],2)}`	Returns the product of values in the range R1C1 to R2C1 of the table `Budget` and the number 2.
Round	Rounds value to specified digits `{= Round (SalesTotal,2)}`	Operator Returns the value of `SalesTotal` rounded to two decimal places.
Sign	Tests for sign of arguments `{= Sign (Profit)}`	Operator Returns 1 if `Profit` is positive, 0 if `Profit` is zero, or −1 if `Profit` is negative.
Sum	Totals arguments `{= Sum(Budget[R1C1:R2C1])}`	Reduction function Returns the sum of values in the range R1C1 to R2C1 of the table `Budget`.

{filename}

Syntax:

```
{filename}
```

Displays the file name shown on the File, Properties, Summary tab.

Updates when you press F9, when you choose mail merge documents, or (in the header or footer) when you choose File, Print.

{fillin}

Syntax:

```
{fillin [""prompt"] switch}
```

Produces a dialog box, like the one shown in figure 20.5, that displays a generic data-entry box. You can type a response in the dialog box. The result appears at the field location or can be used by other fields in which `{fillin}` is nested. Enclose the prompt and default text in quotation marks.

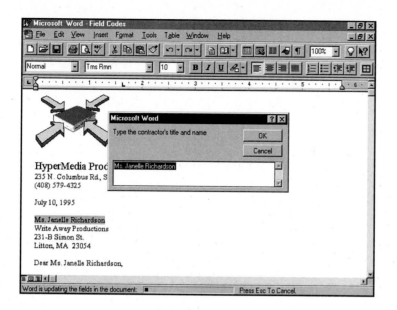

Fig. 20.5
Fillin fields display
a data-entry dialog
box in which a
message prompts
the user to type a
correct entry.

Updates when you press F9 or when you mail merge. Updates once in header
or footer when you choose File, Print.

Switch	Result
\d	Default text follows the switch. The default text appears in the dialog box and is used if no entry is made. Enclose the default text in quotation marks. Use **\d** "" if you do not want any text to appear in the dialog box.

In the following example, MegaCorp appears as default text:

```
{fillin "Type your company." \d "MegaCorp" \* mergeformat}
```

{gotobutton}

Syntax:

```
{gotobutton destination button_text}
```

Produces a button in the document at the field's location. Double-clicking
this button (or selecting the field by pressing F11 and then pressing
Alt+Shift+F9) moves the insertion point to the destination. Use any destination you would when you're using F5 (Go To). destination can be any location where Edit, Go To will accept.

Create a button to surround the `button_text` by putting the field into a single-celled table or into a paragraph, and then formatting it to have a border. The `button_text` appears in the button. Do not enclose `button_text` in quotation marks.

{if}

Syntax:

```
{if expr1 oper expr2 if_true_text if_false_text}
```

Use this field when you want Word for Windows to change a field action or result that depends on some value or text in the document. The {if} field uses the operator `oper` to compare the value of `expr1` to `exper2`.

`expr1` and `expr2` can be bookmarks of selected text, bookmarks assigned to store text, or R1C1 cell addresses from a table. `oper` is a mathematical operator separated from the `expr1` and `expr2` arguments by spaces. The following operators can be used:

=	equal
>	greater than
>=	greater than or equal to
<	less than
<=	less than or equal to
<>	not equal to

`if_true_text` is a result that produces text when the `expr1 oper expr2` statement is true. `if_false_text` is the result when the statement is false. If the statement is text, enclose it in quotation marks. Consider the following example:

```
{if daysdue >= 30 "As a reminder, your account is more than thirty
days overdue." "Thank you for your business."}
```

If the `daysdue` bookmark contains 12 when the field is updated, the field results in `Thank you for your business`. If the `daysdue` bookmark contains 45 when the field is updated, the field results in `As a reminder, your account is more than thirty days overdue`.

Updates when you press F9 or when you mail merge. In a header or footer, updates when you choose File, Print. See also {nextif} and {skipif}.

{includepicture}

Syntax:

```
{includepicture filename [\c converter]}
```

Inserts the contents of the filename into your document. Use **\c converter** to specify a converter file if the included file must be translated before being imported. You insert the {includepicture} field by choosing Insert, Picture.

Switch	Result
\c	Specifies the converter file to be used for files Word for Windows does not convert automatically. The appropriate converter file must have been installed in Word.

{includetext}

Syntax:

```
{includetext filename [bookmark] [\c converter]}
```

Inserts the contents of the filename at the location bookmark. Use **\c converter** to specify a converter file if the included file must be translated before being imported. See Chapter 32, "Assembling Large Documents," for more information.

Switch	Result
\c	Specifies the converter file to be used for files Word for Windows does not convert automatically. The appropriate converter file must have been installed in Word.

{index}

Syntax:

```
{index [switches]}
```

Accumulates all the text and page numbers from the {xe} (index entry) fields or from outline headings, and then builds an index. Insert this field by choosing Insert, Index and Tables. See also {xe}.

You use switches to specify the range of the indexes, the separator characters, the entry's page number formatting, and more as follows:

Switch	Result
\b	Specifies the amount of text indexed
\c	Creates multicolumn indexes
\d	Specifies the separator character between a sequence number and a page number
\e	Specifies the separator character between the index entry and page number
\f	Creates indexes using xe fields of a specified type
\g	Specifies the page range separator
\h	Specifies heading letter formats used to separate alphabetical groups
\l	Specifies the page number separator
\p	Specifies the alphabetical range of the index
\r	Puts sublevel indexes on the same level
\s	Includes the sequence number with page number

{info}

Syntax:

```
{[info] type ["new_value"]}
```

Results in information from the File, Properties, Summary tab, according to the type you use. Available types include the following:

author	numpages
comments	numwords
createdate	printdate
edittime	revnum
filename	savedate
keywords	subject
lastsavedby	template
numchars	title

Updates when you press F9, when you print merge, or (in the header or footer), when you choose File, Print.

{keywords}

Syntax:

```
{keywords ["new_key_words"]}
```

Inserts or replaces the key words from the File, Properties, Summary tab.

Updates when you press F9, when you print merge, or (in the header or footer), when you choose File, Print.

{lastsavedby}

Syntax:

```
{lastsavedby}
```

Inserts the name of the last person to save the document, shown in the File, Properties, Statistics tab.

Updates when you press F9, when you print merge, or (in the header or footer), when you choose File, Print.

{link}

Syntax:

```
{link class_name file_name [place_reference] [switches]}
```

Links the contents of a file into the Word for Windows document. The link is created by choosing Edit, Paste Special with the Paste Link option. This field updates when you press F9.

If the linked file cannot be updated, the results remain unchanged.

Use the following switches to modify the link:

Switch	Result
\a	Updates link when source data change
\b	Inserts a Windows bitmap
\d	Does not store graphic data with file (smaller file size)
\p	Inserts linked data as a picture
\r	Inserts linked data as an RTF file (with converted formatting)
\t	Inserts linked data as text

{macrobutton}

Syntax:

```
{macrobutton macroname instruction_text}
```

Displays the instruction_text. The macro specified by macroname runs when you double-click instruction_text or select it and press Alt+Shift+F9. Create a button to surround the text by putting the field into a single-celled table or into a paragraph, and then formatting it to have a border. The instruction_text must fit on one line. Do not enclose instruction_text in quotation marks.

{mergefield}

Syntax:

```
{mergefield merge_name}
```

Inserted when you choose Tools, Mail Merge. Defines the field of data used at this location from the source file during a merge.

If you need to change the field name specified in a merge field, edit the field name only.

{mergerec}

Syntax:

```
{mergerec}
```

Inserts the number of the current print-merge record.

{mergeseq}

Syntax:

```
{mergeseq}
```

Inserts the number of the current print-merge sequence.

{next}

Syntax:

```
{next}
```

No result appears, but the field instructs Word for Windows to use the next record in the data file. {next} is used in mailing label templates, for example, to increment the mailing list from one record (label) to the next.

{nextif}

Syntax:

```
{nextif expr1 oper expr2}
```

No result appears. {nextif} acts like a combination of the {if} and {next} fields. You can use {nextif} to specify a condition that data file records must satisfy before you use them for mail merge or form letters.

{numchars}

Syntax:

```
{numchars}
```

Inserts the number of characters in the document, as shown on the File, Properties, Summary tab.

Updates when you press F9 or when you print merge. In a header or footer, updates when you choose File, Print.

{numpages}

Syntax:

```
{numpages}
```

Inserts the number of pages the document contained when it was last printed or updated. The number comes from the File, Properties, Summary tab. See also {page}.

Updates when you press F9 or when you print merge. In a header or footer, updates when you choose File, Print.

{numwords}

Syntax:

```
{numwords}
```

Inserts the number of words in the document, as shown in the File, Properties, Summary tab.

Updates when you press F9 or when you print merge. In a header or footer, updates when you choose File, Print.

{page}

Syntax:

```
{page [page_format_picture] [switch]}
```

Inserts the page number for the page on which the field code is located. Use numeric picture or format switches to format the number.

Updates when you press F9 or when you print merge. In a header or footer, updates when you choose File, Print.

{pageref}
Syntax:

```
{pageref bookmark \* format switch}
```

Results in the page number on which bookmark is located. This field produces a cross-reference page number that updates itself.

Updates when you select it and press F9, or when you choose File, Print.

{print}
Syntax:

```
{print ""printer_instructions"}
```

Sends the printer_instructions text string directly to the printer, without translation. You use this field to send printer control codes to a printer or to send PostScript programs to a PostScript printer.

{printdate}
Syntax:

```
{printdate [\@ Date_time-picture] [switch]}
```

Inserts the date on which the document was last printed, shown on the File, Properties, Statistics tab. The default date format comes from the Date tab of the Regional Properties dialog box that you access through the Control Panel. For other date formats, use a date-time picture, as described in "Formatting Date-Time Results," earlier in this chapter.

{quote}
Syntax:

```
{quote ""literal_text""}
```

Inserts the literal_text in the document. Updates when you select the field and press F9, or when you print merge.

{rd}

Syntax:

```
{rd filename}
```

No result appears. {rd} helps you create a table of contents or index for large documents that cross multiple files.

{ref}

Syntax:

```
{[ref] bookmark [switches]}
```

Results in the contents of the bookmark, which specifies a selection of text. The formatting of the bookmark displays as in the original. You can use a bookmark within field characters, such as {datedue}, and produce the same result as {ref datedue}. You must use the {ref bookmark} form, however, to avoid using bookmark names that conflict with field types. If a bookmark's name conflicts with that of a field type—{ask}, for example—use {ref ask} whenever you want to refer to the bookmark.

Updates when you press F9 or when you print merge. In the header or footer, updates when you choose File, Print.

{revnum}

Syntax:

```
{revnum}
```

Inserts the number of times the document has been revised, as shown in the File, Properties, Summary tab. This number changes when the document is saved.

Updates when you select the field and press F9, or when you print merge. In the header or footer, updates when you choose File, Print.

{savedate}

Syntax:

```
{savedate}
```

Inserts the date the document was last saved, as shown on the File, Properties, Summary tab. To change formats, use a date-time picture, as described in "Formatting Date-Time Results," earlier in this chapter.

Updates when you select the field and press F9, or when you print merge. In the header or footer, updates when you choose File, Print.

{section}
Syntax:

```
{section}
```

Inserts the current section's number.

Updates when you select the field and press F9, or when you print merge. In the header or footer, updates when you choose File, Print.

{seq}
Syntax:

```
{seq seq_id [bookmark] [switches]}
```

Inserts a number to create a numbered sequence of items. Use this field for numbering figures, illustrations, tables, and so on. seq_id specifies the name of the sequence, such as Figure. bookmark specifies a cross-reference to the sequence number of a bookmarked item. If you insert the following field wherever you need a figure number,

```
{ref chap}.{seq figure_num}
```

the field produces an automatically numbered sequence of chapter number, period, and figure number—5.12. You must define the bookmark chap at the beginning of the document, and it must contain the number of the chapter. figure_num tracks only a specific sequence of items.

Updates the entire sequence when you select the entire document and press F9. Unlink (fix as values) the figure numbers by selecting them and pressing Shift+Ctrl+F9.

Switch	Result
\c	Inserts the sequence number of the nearest preceding item in a numbered sequence.
\n	Inserts the next sequence number. If no switch is used, Word for Windows defaults to \n.
\r	Resets the sequence number as specified. The following field restarts the sequence numbering to 1 when it reaches 10, for example: {seq figurenum \r 10}.

{set}

Syntax:

```
{set bookmark ""text""}
```

No result appears. Use this field to store text (data) in a bookmark. You then can use the bookmark in multiple locations to repeat that text. See also {ref}.

You cannot use {set} in annotations, footnotes, headers, or footers.

Updates when you select the field and press F9, or when you print merge.

{skipif}

Syntax:

```
{skipif expr1 oper expr2}
```

No result displays. You use this command in print merge to skip merges to meet specified conditions.

Updates when you print merge.

{styleref}

Syntax:

```
{styleref "style_id" [switch]}
```

Displays the text of the nearest paragraph containing the specified style, style_id. This field is useful for accumulating headings and topics that contain a specific style; for example, to create a dictionary-like heading.

{subject}

Syntax:

```
{subject ["new_subject"]}
```

Inserts or replaces the subject in the File, Properties, Statistics tab.

Updates when you select the field and press F9, or when you print merge.

{symbol}

Syntax:

```
{symbol character [switches]}
```

Inserts a symbol character. Inserted by choosing Insert, Symbol.

Switch	Result
\f	Font set used, {symbol 169 \f "courier new bold"}
\s	Font size used, {symbol 169 \f Helv \s 12}

{tc}

Syntax:

```
{tc ""text"" [switch] [table_id]}
```

No result displays. {tc} marks the page and associates a text entry for later use in building a table of contents. See also {toc}.

text is the text that should appear in the table of contents.

table_id is a single letter used to identify a distinct table. This letter should follow the \f switch, with one space between the switch and the table_id letter.

Switch	Result
\f	Defines this {tc} as belonging to the table indicated by the table_id. This switch enables you to accumulate tables of contents for different topics.
\l	Specifies the level number for the table entry. The default is 1.

{template}

Syntax:

```
{template [switches]}
```

Inserts the name of the document's template, as shown on the File, Properties, Summary tab.

Updates when you select the field and press F9, or when you print merge. In the header or footer, updates when you choose File, Print.

{time}

Syntax:

```
{time [time_format_picture]}
```

IV

Results in the time or date when the field was updated. Reformat by using a `time_format_picture`, as described in "Formatting Date-Time Results," earlier in this chapter.

Updates when you select the field and press F9, or when you choose File, Print.

{title}

Syntax:

```
{title ["new_title"]}
```

Inserts or replaces the document title, shown in the File, Properties, Summary tab.

Updates when you select the field and press F9, or when you print merge. In the header or footer, updates when you choose File, Print.

{toc}

Syntax:

```
{toc [switches]}
```

Shows a table of contents built by accumulating the text and page numbers of `{tc}` fields throughout the document.

Switch	Result
\a	Builds a table of figures with no labels or numbers.
\b	Builds a table of contents for the area of the document defined by the bookmark, as in `{toc \b firstpart}`.
\c	Use **SEQ** as a table identifier.
\d	Defines a sequence separator number.
\f	Builds a table of contents from `{tc}` fields with specific table identifiers. The following field builds a table of contents from only those fields with the table identifier graphs: `{toc \f graphs}`.
\l	Controls the entry levels used in the table of contents.
\o	Builds a table of contents from the outline headings. The following field builds a table of contents from the outline by using heading levels 1, 2, and 3: `{toc \o 1-3}`.
\p	Defines the separator between a table entry and its page number.
\s	Uses a sequence type to identify the sequence used in the table of contents.

{xe}

Syntax:

```
{xe "index_text" [switch]}
```

▶ See "Creating
Indexes,"
p. 863

No result appears. Specifies the text and associated page number used to generate an index. You generate the index by choosing the Insert Index and Tables command.

Switch	Result
\b	Toggles the page numbers for boldface.
\f	Specifies the type. Indexes can be built on this specific type of XE.
\i	Toggles the page numbers for italic.
\r	Specifies a range of pages to be indexed.
\t	Specifies the use of text in place of page numbers.

Chapter 21

Building Forms and Fill-In Dialog Boxes

In the past, one office task that word processors were not able to do well was fill in forms. Typewriters were always needed to fill in a form. Storage rooms and filing cabinets took up space just to keep months' worth of inventory of forms that, in some cases, were so seldom used they were obsolete before they ever left the shelf.

Word's new forms features are a big step in the direction of being able to do away with preprinted forms. By using Word's desktop publishing features, many companies are now designing forms that they save as *templates* and print on demand. The cost savings over printing large volumes of forms can be huge.

Word now includes—in addition to its capability to produce a high-quality form on demand—features that make the task of filling in forms easy to do. By using Word's form fields, you can put edit boxes, check boxes, and pull-down lists directly into your documents. The use of {fill in} and {ask} fields enables a document to pop up dialog boxes that ask for input.

In this chapter, you learn to do the following:

- Create a template in which you can put edit boxes, check boxes, or pull-down lists

- Lock the template to prevent users from changing unauthorized parts of a document

- Specify lists of data that show up in pull-down lists, or format the data that a user types in a data entry box

■ Use a {fill in} field to display a dialog box

■ Ask once for an item of data, yet use it several times throughout the document

■ Create a simple macro that controls these dialog boxes as soon as the dialog box opens

Form Basics

A *form* is a special kind of protected document that includes fields where people can type information. Any document that includes form fields is a form. A *form field* is a location on-screen where you can do one of three things: enter text, toggle a check box on or off, or select from a drop-down list.

Tables provide the structure for many forms, because a table's cells are an ideal framework for a form's labels and information fields. You can type labels in some cells, and insert form fields in others. Tables also make adding shading and borders to forms an easy job. You can place a dark border around a selected group of cells in a table, for example, while including no border at all around other cells. With the gridlines turned off, a table doesn't have to look like a table at all, and thus makes the ideal framework for a form.

A form can be based on any type of document. A real estate contract, for example, may include several pages of descriptive paragraphs containing form fields in which you insert information. The text in the paragraphs doesn't change—you insert information in the form fields only.

You can include three types of form fields in a form: text, check box, and drop-down. You can customize each of these field types in many ways. You can format a text field, for example, to accept only dates and to print dates such as January 1, 1995, as 1/1/95, or in another format. Figures 21.1, 21.2, and 21.3 show examples of three forms that can be created using Word.

You can use forms in a variety of ways to save time, effort, and money. You can create your own commonly used business forms such as sales invoices, order sheets, personnel records, calendars, and boilerplate contracts. You can print a copy of your blank form and have it reproduced in quantity, using color if you want. Then print only the information contained in your form onto your preprinted forms—the information will be positioned correctly.

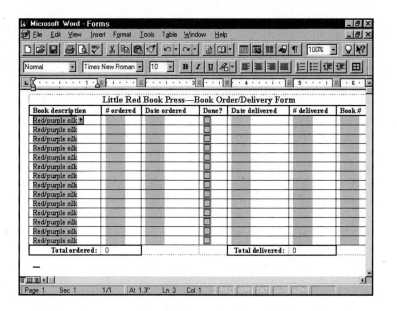

Fig. 21.1
An example of an order/delivery form.

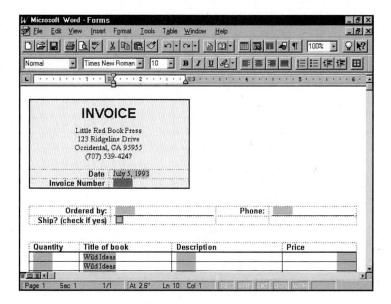

Fig. 21.2
An example of an invoice form.

Fig. 21.3

Another example
of a form.

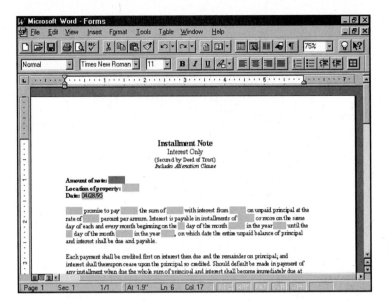

You also can automate forms that don't need to be printed at all. Distribute
form templates, rather than paper forms, to people in your company. You
can make forms easy to use by including helpful on-screen messages and
automatic macros.

You can include calculations in forms—adding up the prices of items in a
sales invoice form, for example, to show a total invoice amount. And you can
add form fields to documents other than forms. When the fields are shaded,
people can easily see where they should insert necessary information.

The most useful forms are based on templates, which can be used over and
over again. When someone fills in such a form, he or she fills in a copy—the
original does not change. (You can, of course, create a form as a document
instead of a template if you plan to use the form only once.) When someone
creates a new document based on your form template, they can type information only in the fields you designated when you created and protected the
form.

Caution

Unless you add password protection, someone using the form can unprotect it and
make changes not only to the fields but also to other parts of the form. Later in this
chapter, you learn how to provide maximum protection for form templates.

You can create forms by using two important tools:

- Insert, For<u>m</u> Field, which you use to insert and customize form fields

- The Forms toolbar, which contains tools for building and customizing forms (see fig. 21.4).

Fig. 21.4
The Forms toolbar includes tools to help you build and customize forms.

You can display the Forms toolbar by choosing <u>I</u>nsert, For<u>m</u> Field and choosing <u>S</u>how Toolbar, or by choosing <u>V</u>iew, <u>T</u>oolbars and selecting Forms from the <u>T</u>oolbars list. Alternatively, you can click with the right mouse button on the Standard toolbar, and select Forms from the drop-down list of toolbars that appears.

Building Forms

Building a simple form is a three-part process. First, you create a new template and build the *form structure*—the framework for the form—and add labels, formatting, shading and borders, and anything else that won't change when users fill in the form. Next, you insert form fields where you want to type information when you fill in the form. Finally, you protect and save the form.

Creating and Saving the Form Structure

Another way you might create a form is by using frames. By framing a table or selected text, you can position it anywhere you want on the page (see fig. 21.5). In this way, you can separate the portion of a document that contains fields in which you must insert information from other parts of the document where the text may not change.

> **Note**
>
> Before you begin designing a form on your computer, sketching it out on paper may be helpful, particularly if you're using a table as the structure for the form. By sketching out the form, you'll know how many rows and columns you need in your table, and you'll know where to type labels and where to insert form fields. Even if you change the form as you go, it's easier to start with a plan.

Fig. 21.5

By framing
selected text that
includes form
fields, you can
create a form like
this.

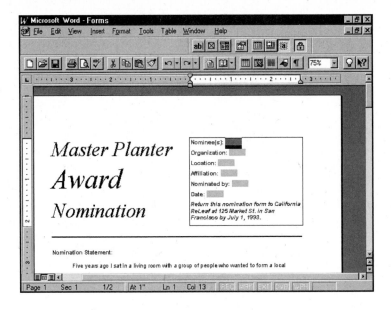

To create and save the form structure as a template, follow these steps:

1. Choose File, New. The New dialog box appears.

2. Select from the Template list the template you want to use as the basis for your form. In most cases, you can use the Normal template.

3. Select Template from the New group.

4. Choose OK.

5. Establish the form structure in one of these ways:

   Insert a table by choosing Table, Insert Table, or by clicking the Table button on the Standard toolbar. Type labels and any other text that will not change in the form. Format the table with lines, borders, and shading.

   Create a form based on paragraphs by inserting form fields where you need them as you type the text of your document. Read the next section, "Adding Form Fields," to learn how to insert form fields.

   At the top of your document, insert the table or type the text that will contain form fields. Select, frame, and position this portion of your document. Then type the remainder of the form, which includes text that will not change when you fill in the form.

6. Choose File, Save As to save the template. Type the template's name in the Save As box, then choose OK. Leave your template open so that you can add the form fields.

Templates normally are saved in the TEMPLATE folder under the folder containing Word. If Microsoft Office is installed then templates are stored in the MSOFFICE\TEMPLATE folder.

Adding Form Fields

After you've established the structure for your form—whether it's a table, a framed block of text, or a paragraph—you can add the form fields. Form fields enable the user to enter data. As mentioned earlier, the three types of form fields are text, check box, and drop-down. You can add form fields to your template by using a menu command or by clicking buttons on the Forms toolbar.

To add form fields to your document using a menu command, follow these steps:

1. Position the insertion point where you want the form field to appear.

2. Choose Insert, Form Field. The Form Field dialog box appears (see fig. 21.6).

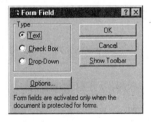

3. Select Text, Check Box, or Drop-Down from the Type group.

4. Choose OK. The form field appears in your document (see fig. 21.7).

Tip
If you create a new form as a document, you can still save it as a template. Save it again by choosing File, Save As. Select Document Template (*.DOT) in the Save As Type drop-down list.

Fig. 21.6
The Form Field dialog box allows you to choose the type of field.

Fig. 21.7
A form field
appears in your
document.

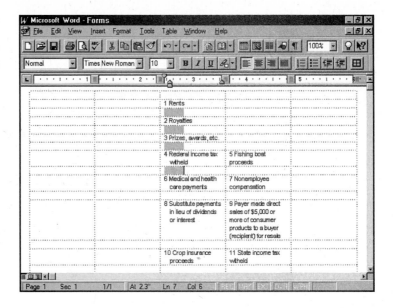

◀ See "Using the
Toolbars," p. 53

To add form fields to your document by using the Forms toolbar, follow these
steps:

1. Display the Forms toolbar by choosing Insert, Form Field and clicking
the Show Toolbar button. The Forms toolbar appears (see fig. 21.8).

Fig. 21.8
You can use the
Forms toolbar to
simplify form
creation.

Alternatively, use another technique to display the Forms toolbar.

2. Position the insertion point where you want a form field.

3. Click one of the form field tools displayed at the left side of the Forms
toolbar:

To insert a text field, click the Text button.

To insert a check box, click the Check Box button.

To insert a drop-down list, click the Drop-Down button. (Note that a
drop-down list is empty until you customize it by adding items to the
list; see the later section "Customizing Drop-Down Form Fields.")

A form field appears in your document.

4. Repeat steps 2 and 3 to add form fields to your document.

Notice that the Forms toolbar contains a Shading Options button. If you select this tool, form fields appear as shaded rectangles on your screen (see fig. 21.9). If you don't select this tool, text fields appear with no shading or border, check box fields appear with a square outline, and drop-down fields appear with a rectangular outline (see fig. 21.10).

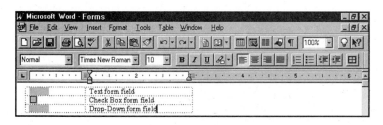

Fig. 21.9
Form fields appear shaded when you click the Shading Options button on the Forms toolbar.

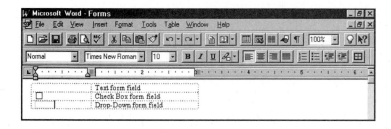

Fig. 21.10
If you don't click the Shading Options button, text form fields don't appear at all, and check box and drop-down form fields are outlined.

The preceding steps insert text boxes, check boxes, or lists, but you cannot use these form fields until you protect the document or template, as described in the next section.

> **Note**
>
> Refer to the "Customizing Form Fields" section later in the chapter to learn how to customize each form field you add to your document. For example, you can customize a text field so that the current date automatically appears; you can customize a drop-down field to add items to the drop-down list.

Tip
If you're creating a form that contains many of the same form fields, save time by copying one or more existing form fields and pasting them into a new location.

Tip
Even if you don't want form fields shaded in your final online form, use shading while you create your form to make the fields easy to see and edit.

Protecting and Saving the Form

Until you protect a document containing form fields, you can edit any part of it, text or form fields. After the document is protected, you can fill in a form field, but you can't edit the document.

A protected form is different from an unprotected form in several ways. For example, a protected document appears in Page Layout view, and you cannot edit the document—you can only insert a response into a form field. You can't select the entire document, and you can't use most commands, including formatting commands. Tables and frames are fixed, and fields with formulas display results, rather than the formulas.

You can easily unprotect a document when you want to edit it—unless someone has protected it with a password. To learn how to use password protection, refer to the upcoming section "Protecting and Unprotecting a Form with a Password." To learn how to protect only part of a form, see the later section "Protecting Part of a Form."

Tip

When you give someone an online form to use, be sure to give that person the template. Tell the person to copy the template into the TEMPLATES subfolder under the MSOFFICE folder.

As long as you designate your new document as a template, Word automatically saves it as a template (using the extension DOT) and proposes saving it in the TEMPLATE subfolder, where it *must* remain for Word to find it when you create a new document. To use your form as a template that appears when you choose File, New, don't change the folder or file extension. (You can, however, specify that all templates be stored in a different subfolder by choosing Tools, Options, selecting the File Locations tab, and modifying the User Templates.)

To protect and save your form, follow these steps:

1. Choose Tools, Protect Document. The Protect Document dialog box appears (see fig. 21.11).

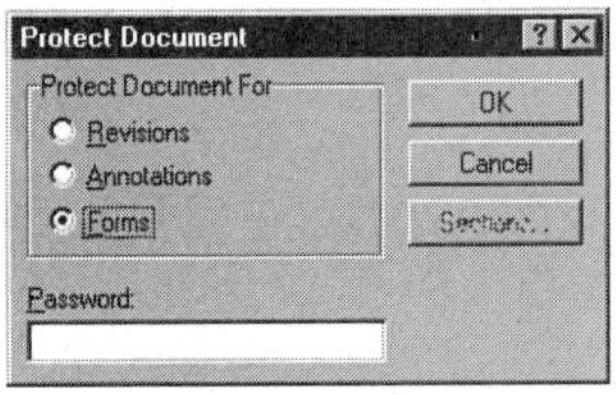

Fig. 21.11

After you protect a document, you can't edit it.

Tip

Someone may have changed the names of your MSOFFICE folder and TEMPLATES subfolder; accept these changed names if they appear as the defaults.

2. Select Forms, and choose OK.

3. Choose File, Save As (see fig. 21.12). Type a name in the File Name text box, and make sure that Document Template is selected in the Save as Type list, and that the TEMPLATES subfolder in the MSOFFICE folder is selected in the folders list. The TEMPLATES folder is located under the WINWORD folder if you do not have Office 95.

4. Choose OK to save the file as a template.

Mastering Special Features

IV

Fig. 21.12
Be sure to save
your form as a
template.

To unprotect your form, choose Tools, Unprotect Document.

If your form is protected with a password, you must enter the password in order to unprotect the form. See the upcoming section "Protecting and Unprotecting a Form with a Password."

To protect or unprotect your form using the Forms toolbar, click the Protect Form button on the Forms toolbar. When the button appears pressed, the form is protected; when the button appears raised, the form is unprotected.

Word has two ways of saving forms. You can save the complete form, including fields, labels, and the information you enter in the form. Or you can save just the information you entered in a form, so that you can use this data with another program. See the section "Saving an On-Screen Form" later in this chapter, for details on the second method.

Using an On-Screen Form

The great advantage to forms is that you *can't* edit them—instead, you open a blank copy of the form (thus preserving the original), and then move from field to field, filling in information as necessary.

The three types of form fields (text, check box, and drop-down) not only look different; you use a distinct approach with each type (see fig. 21.13).

◀ See "Using Templates as a Pattern for Documents," p. 178

◀ See "Creating Tables," p. 506

Fig. 21.13

Click the arrow or press Alt+down arrow to display the items in a drop-down list.

Clicking this arrow displays the items in a drop-down list

Select or clear a check box by pressing the space bar

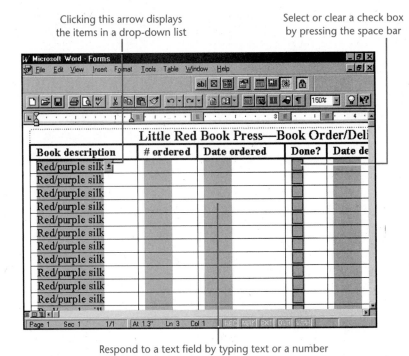

Respond to a text field by typing text or a number

You can customize your form in several ways. For example, you can customize a text field to hold only dates and to format the date you enter in a certain way. Any type of field may have a help message attached so that when you enter the field or press F1, instructions for using the field appear in the status bar. In some fields, a particular response may cause some action in another part of the form; for example, a positive response to a check box field may activate another field later in the form. Be alert to what happens onscreen as you fill in your form.

To open a form, follow these steps:

1. Choose File, New. The New dialog box appears (see fig. 21.14).

2. From the Template list, select the name of your form.

3. Choose OK. An unnamed copy of the form appears on-screen, with the first field in the form highlighted.

◀ See "Creating and Saving Documents," p. 75

If your form isn't based on a template, you can still use it by opening it as a regular file. Choose File, Open, locate and select your form, and choose OK. Save it with a new name to preserve the original.

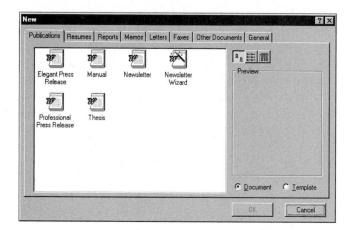

Fig. 21.14
Open a form by choosing File, New.

Filling In an On-Screen Form

When you open a new, protected form, the first field is selected (highlighted).

To fill in the fields in a form, follow these steps:

1. Respond to the selected field as appropriate.

   In a text field, type the requested text or number.

   Check boxes toggle on and off. Press the space bar once to place a mark in an empty check box; press the space bar a second time to remove a mark from the box. (Check boxes may contain a mark by default; if so, press the space bar once to remove the mark, and press the space bar a second time to replace the mark.)

   In a drop-down field, click the arrow to display a list of selections, then click the item you want to select. Or, with the keyboard, press Alt+down arrow to display the list, and press the down- or up-arrow keys to select an item from the list.

2. Press Tab or Enter to accept your entry. One of two things happens:

   If your entry is acceptable, Word selects the next field.

   If your entry is unacceptable, Word displays an error message and returns you to the current field so that you can make a correct entry. You might get an error message, for example, when you type text in a text field that's formatted to hold a number.

3. Continue filling in fields until you complete the form.

Tip
Except while a drop-down list is displayed, you can use the up- and down-arrow keys to move between fields in a form.

Tip
Watch the status bar for messages that may help you fill each field in a form. You can also try pressing F1 to get help for a particular field when that field is selected.

If you make a mistake and want to return to a previous field, hold down the Shift key while you press the Tab or Enter key until you reach that field. To move to the next field without making an entry, just press Tab or Enter. You can also move between fields by pressing the up- or down-arrow keys, and you can move to the beginning or end of your form by pressing Ctrl+Home or Ctrl+End.

To edit an entry in a field you've already left, use the mouse or arrow keys to position the insertion point next to the text you want to edit; press Backspace to delete characters, or type the characters you want to insert.

If you want to insert a Tab character in a field, without moving to the next field, hold down the Ctrl key as you press Tab.

Always watch the way Word interprets your response to a field. For example, if a text field is formatted to include numbers formatted with no decimal places, and you respond by spelling out a number (four, for example), Word interprets your response as 0 (zero) because it's expecting numbers, not letters. Return to the field and type the correct response.

If the form isn't protected, the first field isn't highlighted when you open the form, and you can't move between fields by pressing Tab or Enter. To fill in an unprotected form, use Word's normal techniques for moving the insertion point from field to field. Or better yet, protect the form by choosing Tools, Protect Document, and selecting the Forms option.

Saving an On-Screen Form

◄ See "Using Templates as a Pattern for Documents," p. 178

Because most on-screen forms are based on templates, they do not have names when you open them. You must save and name the forms. (If a form is not based on a template, use the following steps to save your form with a unique name. In this way, you preserve the original for future use.)

◄ See "Typing and Moving in a Table," p. 513

To save a form, follow these steps:

1. Choose File, Save As. The Save As dialog box appears.

2. Type a name in the File Name box, and select the folder for the form from the list of folders. You can save the form to a different drive by selecting a drive from the Save In list.

3. Choose OK.

Troubleshooting

I opened a new form and the first field isn't selected.

The form isn't protected. To fill it in, protect it by choosing Tools, Protect Document. (It may be a good idea to open the form template and protect it, so that the next time you open the form, it's protected.)

Customizing Form Fields

There are many ways you can customize form fields to make your forms more informative, more automated, and easier to use. Automatic date and time fields, for example, insert the current date or time into your form. Default entries suggest a likely response to a field. Help messages give users hints on how to fill in a particular field. Controls prevent certain types of errors. Formulas calculate results in a field. Macros run when users enter or exit a particular field. Controls prevent certain types of errors.

You can also apply most types of formatting to form fields. For example, you can make a form field boldface so that the response stands out. Or you can apply a border to a form field to add boxes in a form that isn't based on a table.

You can customize form fields while you're creating your form, by customizing fields as you insert them, or after you've created your form, by editing selected fields. To edit form fields after you've inserted them, the document must be unprotected.

To customize form fields as you insert them, follow these steps:

1. Choose Insert, Form Field. The Form Field dialog box appears (see fig. 21.15).

2. From the Type group (Text, Check Box, or Drop-Down), select the type of form field you want to insert and customize.

3. Click the Options button. A dialog box containing options for customizing the type of form field you've selected appears (see fig. 21.16).

Fig. 21.15

Choose Insert, Form Field to customize form fields as you insert them.

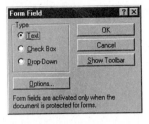

Fig. 21.16

If you select Text from the form field Type group and then click the Options button, the Text Form Field Options dialog box appears.

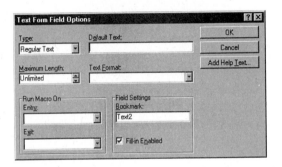

To customize an existing form field, follow these steps:

1. Unprotect your document, if it's protected, by choosing Tools, Unprotect Document or by clicking the Protect Form button on the Forms toolbar.

Tip

If you use a form field repeatedly in a form, duplicate it by placing it in AutoText.

2. Double-click the form field you want to customize, displaying the Form Field Options dialog box.

Or, select the form field you want to customize by clicking it, positioning the insertion point above or below it, and pressing the up- or down-arrow key, or by positioning the insertion point next to it and holding down the Shift key as you press the right- or left-arrow key. Then do one of the following:

Click the Options button on the Forms toolbar.

Or, click the form field you want to customize with the right mouse button to display the shortcut menu. Select Form Field Options.

◀ See "Creating an AutoText Entry," p. 151

3. Select the options you want, and choose OK.

◀ See "A Reference List of Field Codes," p. 616

Customizing Text Form Fields

Text fields are probably the most customizable of the three form field types. You can customize them by type (regular, number, date, or calculation, for example), by default text, by the size of the field, by the maximum number of characters in the response, or by the format of the response. As with all form field types, you can also customize text fields by adding macros (see the later section "Adding Macros to a Form"), by adding Help text (see the section "Adding Help to a Form"), by renaming the bookmark (see "Naming and Finding Fields in a Form"), or by disabling the field for entry (see "Disabling Form Fields").

Tip

Specifying a field size is particularly important when you are using preprinted forms.

To specify the restrictions on a text form field, follow these steps:

1. Open the Text Form Field Options dialog box (see fig. 21.17).

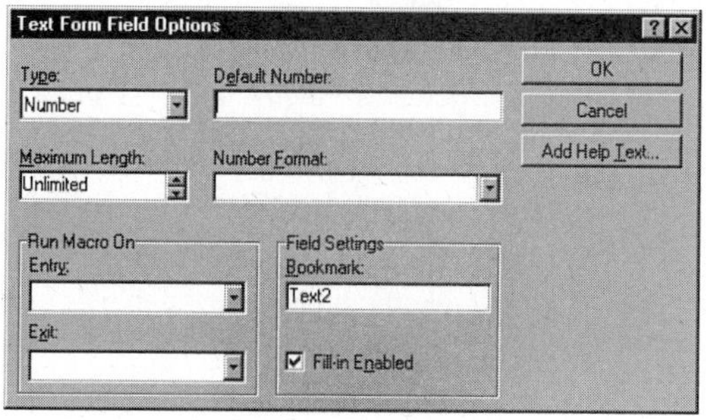

Fig. 21.17

Text form fields have numerous customizing options.

2. Select from the following types of options (see the upcoming tables for details about the Type and Format options):

Option	Description
Type (see table 21.1)	Select from six types of text entries: Regular Text, Number, Date, Current Date, Current Time, and Calculation.
Default Text	Type the text that you want to appear as the default entry in this field. Users can change the entry.
Maximum Length	Type or select "Unlimited" or the number of characters or numbers you want the field to accept (up to 255).
Text Format	Select from various types of text, numeric, and date formats, depending on what you've selected in the Type option (see table 21.2).

3. Choose OK.

You will often use two or more of these options together. For example, if you select Number as the Type, then you might choose 0.00 as the Format so that a numeric response appears in two decimal places.

IV

Mastering Special Features

Table 21.1 Type Options for Text Form Field Options Dialog Box

Select This Option	When Users Should Respond by Typing
Regular Text	Text. Word formats the text according to your selection in the Text Format list.
Number	A number. Word formats the number according to your selection in the Number Format list, and displays an error message if user types text.
Date	A date. Word formats the date according to your selection in the Date Format list. Word displays an error message (A valid date is required) if user types text or a number not recognizable as a date, and returns user to the current field for an appropriate response. (Almost any response resembling a date will work, however.)
Current Date	No user response allowed. Word enters the current date (and updates the date when the document is opened*).
Current Time	No user response allowed. Word enters the current time (and updates the time when the document is opened*).
Calculation	Enter a formula when inserting or editing this field; no user response allowed. Word applies your formula, and prints the result of the calculation in this field. For example, you can insert a simple SUM formula to add up the numbers in a column if your form is based on a table. (Word updates the result when the document is opened.*)

◀ See "Creating and Editing Tables," p. 505

◀ See "Automating with Field Codes," p. 589

You can specify that Word update the date, time, or a formula when you print your form by choosing Tools, Options, selecting the Print tab and then selecting Update Fields from Printing Options. Or you can use an exit macro to update the fields.

Table 21.2 Text Format Options for Text Form Field Options

Type Option	Text Format Option	What Entry Looks Like
Regular Text	Uppercase	ALL CAPITAL LETTERS
	Lowercase	all lowercase letters
	First Capital	First letter of first word is capitalized
	Title Case	First Letter Of Each Word Is Capitalized
Number	0	123456
	0.00	123456.00
	#,##0	123,456
	#,##0.00	123,456.00
	$#,##0.00;($#,##0.00)	$123,456.00
	0%	10%
	0.00%	10.00%

Type Option	Text Format Option	What Entry Looks Like
Date	M/d/yy	1/1/95
	dddd, MMMM dd, yyyy	Sunday, 3 January, 1995
	d MMMM, yyyy	3 January, 1995
	MMMM d, yyyy	January 3, 1995
	d-MMM-yy	3-Jan-95
	MMMM, yy	Jan, 95
	MM/dd/yy h:mm AM/PM	01/03/95 2:15 PM
	MM/dd/yy h:mm:ss AM/PM	01/03/95 2:15:58 PM
	h:mm AM/PM	2:15 PM
	h:mm:ss AM/PM	2:15:58 PM
	H:mm	2:15
	H:mm:ss	2:15:58
Current Date	same as Date	same as Date
Current Time	h:mm AM/PM	3:30 PM
	h:mm:ss AM/PM	3:30:00 PM
	H:mm	15:30
	H:mm:ss	15:30:00
Calculation	same as Number	same as Number

Customizing Check Box Form Fields

You can customize check box fields, which require the user to make a simple "yes or no" response, by determining size and by choosing whether they will be checked or unchecked by default. As with all form field types, you can also customize check box fields by adding macros (see the later section "Adding Macros to a Form"), by adding Help text (see the "Adding Help to a Form" section), by renaming the bookmark (see "Naming and Finding Fields in a Form"), or by disabling the field for entry (see "Disabling Form Fields").

To customize a check box field, follow these steps:

 1. Open the Check Box Form Field Options dialog box (see fig. 21.18).

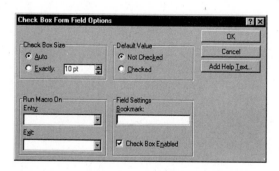

Fig. 21.18
You can make a check box exactly the size you want, and you can specify whether it's checked or unchecked by default.

2. Determine the check box size by selecting the appropriate option:

   Select <u>A</u>uto to make the check box the same size as the text around it.

   Select <u>E</u>xactly to make the check box a specific size. Click the up or down arrow or press the up- or down-arrow key to increase or decrease the box size. Or type the size you want; for example, type 12 pt for a 12-point box, .25" for a quarter-inch box, 1 pi for a 1-pica box, or 1 cm for a 1-centimeter box. (When you next open the dialog box, the measurement is converted to an equivalent value in points.)

3. Determine the Default Value by selecting one of the following options:

   If you select Not Chec<u>k</u>ed, the check box will be empty by default (a negative response). The user must press the space bar to check the box.

   If you select <u>C</u>hecked, the check box will have a mark in it by default (a positive response). The user must press the space bar to deselect the box.

4. Choose OK.

Customizing Drop-Down Form Fields

A drop-down list gives users a list of up to 25 items to choose from. It helps ensure that the user's response to a field is valid, because the list contains only valid responses. It also helps users to fill in the form, because they don't have to guess what kind of response the field requires.

You will most likely customize a drop-down form field as you insert it, because there's nothing in the list until you add items. You may want to add items to the list later, or remove some items, or rearrange the items, however. You can do this by editing the drop-down field.

To add items to the list in a drop-down field, follow these steps:

1. Open the Drop-Down Form Field Options dialog box (see fig. 21.19).

2. In the <u>D</u>rop-Down Item box, type the item you want to add to the list.

3. Click the <u>A</u>dd button.

4. Repeat steps 2 and 3 to add more items to the list.

5. Choose OK.

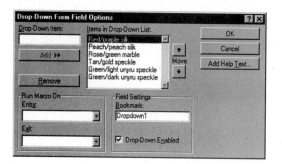

IV

Mastering Special Features

Fig. 21.19
You can add items to a drop-down list, remove items from it, or rearrange the items in the list.

To remove items from a drop-down list field, follow these steps:

1. Select the drop-down field and open the Drop-Down Form Field Options dialog box.

2. Select the item you want to remove from the Items in the drop-down List list.

3. Click the Remove button.

4. Repeat steps 2 and 3 to remove more items.

5. Choose OK.

To rearrange items in a drop-down list field, follow these steps:

1. Select the drop-down field and open the Drop-Down Form Field Options dialog box.

2. Select the item you want to move in the Items in Drop-Down List list.

3. Move the item up by clicking the Move up arrow, or move it down by clicking the Move down arrow. (With the keyboard, press the up or down arrow to select the item you want to move, press Tab to select the Move up or Move down arrow, and then press the space bar to move the selected item up or down.)

4. Repeat steps 2 and 3 to move more items.

5. Choose OK.

Formatting Form Fields

Users can't format entries in a protected form when they're filling in the form. But when you're creating a form, you can apply font and paragraph formatting, as well as many other formatting options, to fields. Responses will then appear in that formatting.

You must insert a form field before you can format it. Remember, the document must be unprotected.

To format a form field, first select the form field you want to format. Then use one of the following methods to apply formatting:

- Choose the formatting command you want to use, and select the formatting options you want to apply.

- Click a formatting option on a toolbar.

- Press formatting shortcut keys.

- Click the selected field with the right mouse button to display the shortcut menu, and select Font, Paragraph, or Bullets and Numbering. Then select the formatting options you want to apply.

Disabling Form Fields

In most forms, you want users to respond to each field. But sometimes you'll want to disable a field, so that users cannot respond. You may want to include a default entry in disabled fields.

To disable a form field, follow these steps:

1. Unprotect the document, if necessary.

2. Select the field you want to disable, and display the Form Field Options dialog box.

3. Clear the appropriate option: Fill-in Enabled (for text fields), Check Box Enabled (for check box fields), or Drop-Down Enabled (for drop-down fields).

4. Choose OK.

Naming and Finding Fields in a Form

◀ See "Editing a Document," p. 123

Each form field you insert in a document has a name: its *bookmark*. You can use this bookmark to help you find a field quickly. By default, Word numbers the fields you insert, calling them Text1, Check7, Dropdown13, and so forth. You can name a form field whatever you want (subject to bookmark naming rules, however).

To name a form field, follow these steps:

1. Unprotect the document, if necessary.

2. Select the field and display the Form Field Options dialog box.

3. In the Field Settings group, select the Bookmark text box and type the name.

4. Choose OK.

To find a named form field, follow these steps:

1. Unprotect the document.

2. Choose Edit, Bookmark.

3. Type the name you want to find in the Bookmark Name box, or select it from the list.

4. Click the Go To button. Word displays the field, but doesn't close the dialog box. Go to another field, or choose Close to close the dialog box.

Adding Help to a Form

By adding help messages, you can make it much easier for users to respond correctly to a field in your form. When the field is selected in your form, help messages can appear in the status bar at the bottom of the screen, or as a message box displayed when the user presses the F1 key.

You can type your own text for a help message, or use an existing AutoText entry. For example, you may have an AutoText entry that reads `Press F1 for Help`, which you include as a status bar help message in each field for which you've included F1 help (see fig. 21.20).

Tip

The document must be protected for your help message to appear; if it isn't protected, pressing F1 displays Word Help.

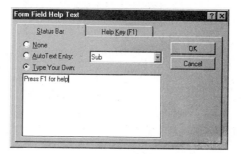

Fig. 21.20
Help can appear in the status bar if you use the Status Bar tab.

To add help to a form field, follow these steps:

1. Display the Form Field Options dialog box for the field to which you want to add help.

2. Click the Add Help Text button.

3. Select the Status Bar tab to add a line of help in the status bar, or select the Help Key (F1) tab to add help that appears as a message box when the user presses F1 (see fig. 21.21).

Fig. 21.21
Help can appear as a message box when you press F1 if you use the Help Key (F1) tab.

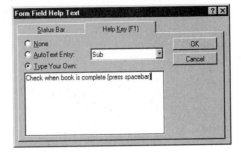

4. To add your own help message, select the Type Your Own option and type your message (up to 255 characters).

   Or, to use the text of an AutoText entry as help, select the AutoText Entry option, and select the AutoText entry you want to use from the list.

5. Choose OK.

6. Choose OK again to close the Form Field Options dialog box and return to your document.

Tip
If you add F1 help to a field, also include a status bar message reading `Press F1 for help` so that users know where to find help.

▶ See "Recording and Editing Macros," p. 1053

If you're including status line help messages, be aware that even if your form is protected, users can turn off the status line. Also be aware that users have no way of knowing whether F1 help is attached to a field (though a message in the status line can help, if the status line is displayed). If your form is based on a template, try including a message (to alert users to the presence of F1 help) in an AutoNew macro that runs when users create a new form.

> **Note**
>
> Help users fill in your form, or give them some instructions about what to do with the form when they're finished with it, by including a helpful message as part of an AutoNew macro that runs when users open the form. (AutoNew macros are attached to templates, and run when you create a new document based on the template. This idea works best for forms that are based on a template.)

Adding Macros to a Form

Macros can automate your forms in many ways. They can activate or deactivate fields, depending on the user's response to an earlier field. They can update fields that contain calculations. They can cause Word to skip over unneeded fields.

◀ See "Calculating Math Results in a Table," p. 545

To use a macro in a form, you must create the macro before you apply it to a particular field in the form. Macros run at one of two times: when the user enters the field or when the user leaves the field.

When you record or write macros for your form, be aware that macros use bookmarks to locate particular fields, and make sure that your form contains no duplicate bookmark names. You can find out the automatic bookmark name of any field, or give the field a new bookmark name, by selecting the field, displaying the Form Field Options dialog box, and then looking at the Bookmark text box (for details, see the "Naming and Finding Fields in a Form" section, earlier in this chapter).

To make your macros useful, attach them to the template your form is based on. You can do this most easily as you create the macro, or you can attach a macro to your template by choosing File, Templates, clicking the Organizer button, and then selecting the Macros tab.

> **Note**
>
> For more information on macros, refer to Chapter 37, "Recording and Editing Macros."

Before you can apply macros to a field, the document must be unprotected. And remember, before you can apply a macro to a form field, you must create the macro.

To apply a macro to a form field, follow these steps:

1. Select the field to which you want to apply a macro, and display the Form Field Options dialog box.

2. If you want the macro to run when the user moves the insertion point into the field, select the Entry option in the Run Macro On group, and select the macro you want from the list.

Or, if you want the macro to run when the user moves the insertion point out of the field, select the Exit option in the Run Macro On group, and select the macro you want from the list.

3. Choose OK.

If no macros appear in either the Entry or Exit list, no macros are available for your form's template. You must either create a macro, or attach it to your template.

Protecting and Unprotecting a Form with a Password

If you don't want users to change your form, protect it with a password. In this way, anyone who attempts to unprotect the form must supply the password (including you—don't forget your password).

To password-protect a document, follow these steps:

1. Choose Tools, Protect Document. The Protect Document dialog box appears (see fig. 21.22).

Fig. 21.22

Type your password in the Password box.

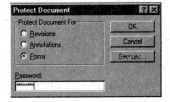

2. Select the Forms option.

3. Select the Password box, and type your password. Choose OK. The Confirm Password dialog box appears (see fig. 21.23).

Fig. 21.23

To confirm your password, you must retype it exactly as you typed it the first time.

4. In the Reenter Protection Password box, retype your password. Spelling, spacing, and capitalization must match exactly. Choose OK. (If you don't retype the password exactly as you originally typed it, you get an error message. Choose OK and try again.)

5. Choose OK to return to your document.

To unprotect a password-protected document, follow these steps:

1. Choose Tools, Unprotect Document, or click the Protect Form button on the Forms toolbar. If the document is password protected, the Unprotect Document dialog box appears (see fig. 21.24).

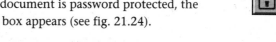

Fig. 21.24
To unprotect a password-protected document, you must enter the password exactly as you typed it originally.

2. Type the password exactly as you originally typed it in the Password box. Spelling, spacing, and capitalization must match exactly.

3. Choose OK. If you typed the password correctly, your document will be unprotected. If you typed the password incorrectly, Word displays a message that the password is incorrect, and you must choose OK to return to your document, which remains protected.

Protecting Part of a Form

If your form is divided into sections, you can protect parts of it, while leaving other parts unprotected. You can include password protection for the protected sections.

To protect or unprotect part of a form, follow these steps:

1. Choose Tools, Protect Document. The Protect Document dialog box appears.

2. Select the Forms option.

3. Click the Sections button to display the Section Protection dialog box (see fig. 21.25).

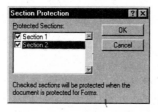

Fig. 21.25
You can protect part of a document if it's divided into sections.

IV

Mastering Special Features

4. In the Protected Sections list, select each section you want protected, so that it appears with a mark in the box. Clear each section you want unprotected.

5. Choose OK to return to the Protect Document dialog box. (If you want to protect the sections with a password, do so now. For details, see the earlier section "Protecting and Unprotecting a Form with a Password.")

6. Choose OK to return to the document.

Converting Existing Forms

The forms you want to create may already exist on paper or in another program's format. Sometimes the easiest way to convert a form is to simply retype it, but at other times you may want to use existing data.

You can use a scanner to help you retype an existing form. Scan the form as a picture, and insert it into a text box. When a picture is in a text box, you can move it to the layer behind the text in your document. In the text layer, you can trace over the scanned form to create your new form. When you're finished, select and delete the scanned form.

> **Note**
>
> For more information on using pictures, refer to Chapter 23, "Inserting Pictures in Your Document." And to find out more about tracing, see Chapter 25, "Drawing with Word's Drawing Tools."

Although you can't import form fields from a document created by another program into a Word document, you can import text. If a form exists in another program, import the text, format it as you need it, and add the form fields. You can change text to a table by selecting the text and choosing Table, Convert Text to Table. To learn about tables, see Chapter 16, "Creating and Editing Tables."

Printing a Form

There are three ways you might want to print a form. You might want to print it exactly as it appears on-screen, including the labels, any graphics, and the data in the fields. You might want to print the data onto preprinted forms only. Or you might want to print the labels and graphics only, to create a preprinted form.

Printing the Filled-In Form

To print the entire form, including everything that appears on your screen, use Word's usual printing commands. Use this method to print forms that you've already filled in.

To print the entire form, follow these steps:

1. Fill in the form, or open a filled-in form.

2. Choose File, Print.

3. Select the printing options you want from the Print dialog box, and choose OK.

To learn more about printing options, refer to Chapter 8, "Previewing and Printing a Document."

Printing Form Data Only

Print only data when you're using preprinted forms. Because you use the same form template to print the blank form as you use when you print only the data, the form data will line up correctly with the fields.

To print only data onto a preprinted form, follow these steps:

1. Insert the preprinted form into your printer.

2. Choose Tools, Options.

3. Select the Print tab (see fig. 21.26).

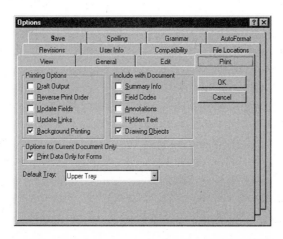

Fig. 21.26
Choose Tools,
Options to print
form data only.

   4. Select Print Data Only for Forms from the Options for Current Document Only group, and choose OK.

   5. Choose File, Print, select printing options, and choose OK.

Notice that this procedure ensures that each time you print this form, you will print data only. Repeat the procedure, deselecting the Print Data Only for Forms option in step 4, if you want to print the entire form.

Printing a Blank Form

To make your own preprinted form, print the form only, without the data.

To print a blank form, follow these steps:

   1. Choose File, New, select the form you want to print from the Template list, and choose OK.

   2. Without filling in the form, print it by choosing File, Print, selecting printing options, and choosing OK.

 Remember that fields in a form appear shaded if the Shading Options button is selected in the Forms toolbar. This shading does not appear when you print your forms. If you want shading to appear on a printed form, use Format, Borders and Shading to shade selected areas of your form.

◄ See "Printing the Current Document," p. 239

> **Troubleshooting**
>
> *When I print the form data, it doesn't line up with the form fields on the preprinted form.*
>
> Be sure you're using the same form to print your data as you used to create the preprinted form.

Saving Data Only

You may want to use the data you collect in your forms with another program, such as a database. To do that, save only the data, and import the data into the other program. Word saves a copy of the data as a Text Only document (with the extension TXT), creating a comma-delimited document containing only the responses in your fields.

Many applications can read the data stored in comma-delimited files. Microsoft Excel, for example, can open and automatically separate each piece of data into a worksheet cell if the file uses the file extension CSV (comma separated values).

To save data only from your form, follow these steps:

1. Choose Tools, Options.

2. Select the Save tab.

3. In the Save Options group, select the Save Data Only for Forms option.

4. Choose OK.

5. Choose File, Save As to save and name your data file.

Building Forms with Fill-In Dialog Boxes

With {fillin} fields, you can design a form letter so that you need to enter a data item (such as a name) only once—no matter how many times it appears in the letter. This feature is extremely useful for filling out invoices, contracts, proposals, or business forms in which the majority of the body copy remains unchanged. {fillin} fields are useful also when you need to insert personal phrases in mass mailings. Figure 21.27 shows a document you can create to demonstrate how {fillin} fields work.

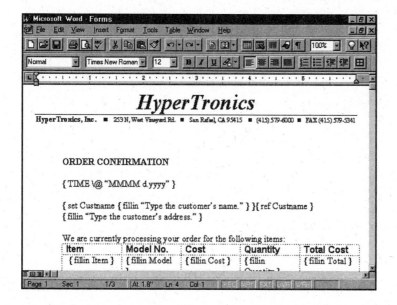

Fig. 21.27
Field codes can enter data or display dialog boxes that prompt users to enter data that can be used repeatedly through the document.

First you should create a new template for form letters.

To create a new template, follow these steps:

1. Choose File, New. The New dialog box appears (see fig. 21.28).

Fig. 21.28
By using a
template to
create a form, you
prevent users
from accidentally
changing the
original.

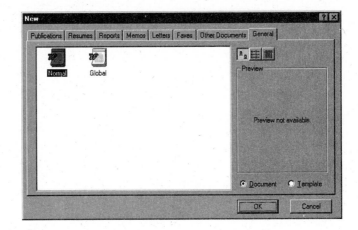

Fig. 21.28
By using a
template to
create a form, you
prevent users
from accidentally
changing the
original.

2. Select the Template option in the New box.

   Normal should already be selected in the Template list.

3. Select a different template on which to base the letter, if you prefer. You may have created a template, for example, that includes a letterhead or company logo.

4. Choose OK.

5. Modify the template to include any body text, graphics, tables, and so on that you want in the form letter. Format the template's page layout to account for letterhead, if necessary.

Keep the template open and on-screen so that you can add {fillin} fields as described in the next section.

Using {fillin} Fields

To set up your template to prompt the user to enter key information, use {fillin} fields. Figure 21.29 shows a dialog box prompt generated by a {fillin} field.

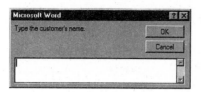

Fig. 21.29
The {fillin} field is an easy way to ask users to enter data in a dialog box. You don't need to create a macro to display the dialog box.

To insert the {fillin} field code in a document, move the insertion point to where you want the operator's input to appear. Choose Insert, Field. Make sure that [All] is selected in the categories list, then select Fill-in from the Insert Field Names list. In the Field Codes text box, move the insertion point past FILLIN, type the user prompt—enclosing it in quotation marks—and choose OK.

Alternatively, you can type the {fillin} field into the template. To do this, move the insertion point to where you want the results to appear, then press Ctrl+F9, the Insert Field key. Position the insertion point between the field characters, and type the following field type and instructions:

fillin "Type the customer address."

To display the dialog box requesting the customer's name, and to update the {fillin} field, follow these steps:

1. Select the field character at either end of the code to select the {fillin} field.

2. Press F9. The Fillin dialog box appears.

3. Type a customer address in the box. To start a new line in the box, press Enter. Choose OK to complete the box and insert your entry in the document.

The entry you typed appears in the document in the same location as the field code. Text following the inserted entry is pushed down or right, just as if you had manually typed text in the location. To switch between displaying fields and their results, press Alt+F9, or display the Options dialog box (by choosing Tools, Options) and click the Field Codes check box in the View tab.

Reusing Field Results

If you use field codes in form letters, you can request an input from the operator once, but have that information appear in multiple locations. To reuse an entry from one {fillin} box in other locations in a form letter, you must use the following three field codes:

Tip

Enclose prompts of more than one word in quotation marks (" "). If you don't enclose a phrase in quotation marks, Word uses only the first word.

Tip

To update {fillin} fields throughout an entire document, select the entire document, then press F9 (Update).

■ {set bookmark data} assigns data to a bookmark, which stores information so that it can be reused later. In the next example, because the data argument for {set} is a {fillin} field, the operator's entry in response to the [fillin] field is stored in the bookmark name Custname. If the data is explicit text that doesn't change, such as Montana, you must enclose it in quotation marks. Don't include a space in the bookmark name.

■ {fillin [prompt]} displays an input box in which the operator can enter data. The brackets ([]) indicate that the prompt is optional.

■ {ref bookmark} displays the contents of a bookmark at the field location. You enter this field to repeat a bookmark's contents in other locations within the document.

Figure 21.30 shows a field code that requests the customer's name and stores it in the Custname bookmark. The {fillin} field requests the name. The {set} field sets Custname equal to the {fillin} entry. The {ref} field displays the entry stored in Custname. You can use {ref} throughout the letter, following the {set} field, even though the data was entered only once.

Fig. 21.30

The combination of {fillin}, {set}, and {ref} field codes enables the user to fill in one dialog box and have the data used throughout a document.

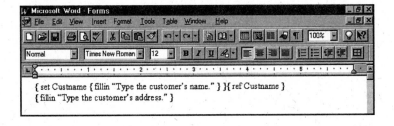

In figure 21.30, the {fillin} field data was entered into a dialog box. The {set} field code then stores the entry in the bookmark Custname. The data stored in Custname can be redisplayed anywhere in the document with {ref Custname}. The {ref} field code references the data stored in that bookmark. You can reuse {ref} as many times as you want in the document. Using the switches described in Chapter 20, "Automating with Field Codes," you can format the information that {ref} returns.

Tip

You can make up your own single words to use as bookmarks.

As you may recall, *nested* fields are one field code inside another field code. In the example, a {fillin} field is nested inside a {ref} field. The result of the {fillin} is used to supply one of the arguments required by the {ref} field. To build the nested field in figure 21.30 from the inside out, follow these steps:

1. Position the insertion point where you need to insert the entry.

2. Press Ctrl+F9, the Insert Field key.

3. Between the field characters, type **fillin**, a space, then a prompt to the operator (enclosed in quotation marks), such as **"Type the customer's name."**

4. Select the field you just typed. To select field characters and field contents, select a field character at one end or the other to select the entire field.

5. Press Ctrl+F9 to enclose the selection in field characters.

   This step *nests* the first field entirely inside another set of field characters. The insertion point moves to directly follow the first field character.

6. Directly after the first field character, type **set**, a space, and then the appropriate bookmark, such as **Custname**. Leave a space after the bookmark, but don't leave spaces in the name.

This new nested field requests a name and stores it in the bookmark, but the entry doesn't appear on-screen. To see the field's result, you must update the field.

To update both of these new fields and see the customer's name requested and displayed, follow these steps:

1. Select the entire line (or lines) containing both fields.

2. Press F9 (Update Fields). A dialog box appears, requesting the customer's name (refer to fig. 21.29).

3. Type the entry as requested.

4. Choose OK.

The {set} field stores in the bookmark the name you entered in the {fillin} field. The {ref bookmark} field displays the contents of a bookmark in the letter. You can enter a {ref bookmark} field in multiple locations in the document, wherever you need the name repeated. In figure 21.31, the Custname bookmark is repeated at the last line on the screen. The new contents of {ref bookmark} don't appear, however, until each {ref bookmark} field is updated.

Fig. 21.31

Reuse data by repeating the {ref bookmark} combination wherever you want the data displayed. {ref} only displays the new data when it is selected and updated.

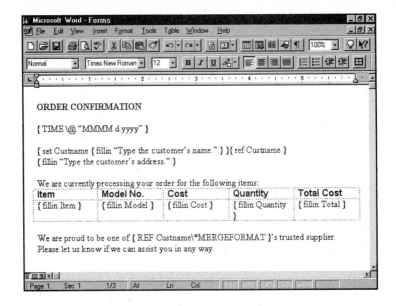

After you enter all the field codes, choose File, Save As, and choose OK to save the template.

These fields display data entered in the address block; they also request and display the type, model, and cost of the items the customer ordered. The switch * mergeformat, used in the {ref bookmark * mergeformat} field, ensures that the formatting you applied to the field name in the document doesn't change when the field is updated. The format of field results matches the format you apply to the letter r in ref.

The inclusion of the * mergeformat switch is controlled by the Preserve Formatting During Updates option in the Field dialog box. For more information, see Chapter 20, "Automating with Field Codes."

Saving and Naming the Template

This document must be saved as a template because you opened it as one. To save your template, choose File, Save As. In the File Name text box, type an eight-letter name to describe your form. Notice that you cannot change many of the text or list boxes. Choose OK. Word saves the template and adds the extension DOT. When you save a new template, give it a name that reflects the type of document it creates.

Updating Fields in a Form

To test the fields you entered, update them. This action will display new values, or enable you to enter new ones.

To enter data in the {fillin} fields and update the {ref} fields, follow these steps:

1. Choose File, New, and select a template containing {fillin} fields. Choose OK.

2. Move the insertion point to the top of the document, then press F11 to select the next field. (Press Shift+F11 to select the preceding field, or select the entire document by choosing Edit, Select All to update all fields.)

3. Press F9 to update the selected field or, if the entire document is selected, to update each field in turn, from the beginning to the end of the document.

4. Type the data requested, and choose OK.

If an error appears at a field's location, display the field codes in the document. Check for correct spelling and spacing. Use one space between field types, instructions, and switches.

Creating a Macro to Update Fields Automatically

Because this type of fill-in form is designed for repetitive use, you can have Word automatically prompt the user for the information as soon as the document is opened. You can do this with an automatic macro that updates all fields in the document when the document opens. With the fill-in template as the active document, follow these steps:

1. Choose Tools, Macro. The Macro dialog box appears (see fig. 21.32).

> **Tip**
> To preserve the previous entry, select Cancel; nothing is produced if no previous entry existed.

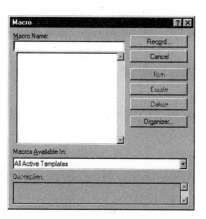

Fig. 21.32
You can record a macro that automatically updates field codes when a document or template opens.

2. Type **AutoNew** in the Macro Name box.

3. In the Macros Available In list, select the Documents Based on [template] option, where [template] is the name of the template. The macro will be available only to this template or to documents that originate from this template. (The option of where a macro is saved is described in Chapter 37, "Recording and Editing Macros.")

4. Click the Record button.

5. Enter a description, such as **Automatically updates all fields**, in the Description box.

6. Choose OK.

The Macro Record toolbar appears, and the REC indicator is highlighted in the status bar, indicating that the recorder is on. Follow these steps to record a process that updates all fields in the document:

1. Press Ctrl+5 (use the numeric keypad) to select the entire document.

2. Press F9. A prompt generated by the first {fillin} field appears.

3. Click the Cancel button for each {fillin} prompt.

4. Press Ctrl+Home to return the insertion point to the top of the document.

 5. Click the Stop button in the Macro Record toolbar.

Choose File, Save All to save the macro and close the template. To test the macro, follow these steps:

1. Choose File, New.

2. Select the template from the Use Template list.

3. Choose OK.

When you open the document, the AutoNew macro runs the update macro. Enter a response to each dialog box, or choose Cancel. If the macro doesn't run correctly, record it again. If you rerecord, using the same name (AutoNew), Word asks whether you want to replace the previous recording. Choose Yes. ❖

Chapter 22

Working with Math and Equations

Have you ever wanted to perform calculations on the numbers in a Word for Windows table you created, and have the results automatically updated if the figures in the table change, much as you would in a spreadsheet? Or perhaps you would like to perform a calculation on numbers scattered throughout a document, without searching for each number and then performing the math yourself. Word for Windows simplifies these tasks.

If you are a scientist or engineer, you might have wished for an easy way to enter equations and formulas in a polished document, instead of having to draw them by hand. Word for Windows simplifies all these tasks with its built-in Equation Editor. With the Equation Editor, you can insert mathematical symbols and operators, such as integrals and fractions. You can also control the size, placement, and formatting of the different elements in an equation.

In this chapter, you learn to do the following:

- Calculate totals or mathematical results by using data from the cells in a table, much like a worksheet

- Calculate results from numbers used in the text of a document

- Create an equation

- Format an equation

- Work with matrices

- View, edit, and print equations

Choosing Word's Math Functions or a Spreadsheet

Word 95 has its own basic math and table features. If you have both Word and a Windows worksheet, such as Microsoft Excel or Lotus 1-2-3, you should learn the advantages and disadvantages of both.

You may want to use Word's built-in math capabilities under the following conditions:

- When problems involve simple math, such as totals or averages

- When numbers are arranged in rows and columns in a table

- When numbers are distributed throughout a document, and the math result depends on those numbers

- When results do not need to be linked to or updated in other documents

You may want to do math in a worksheet and then paste, link, or embed the results into Word under these conditions:

- When problems involve complex math operations unavailable in Word

- When problems involve worksheet analysis, such as database analysis or trends forecasting

- When numbers are arranged in different cell locations throughout a table, rather than in simple rows and columns

- When one worksheet can be updated, with the result of that worksheet then updating multiple linked Word documents

Using Bookmarks to Perform Calculations in Text

► See "Transferring Data with Copy and Paste," p. 984

► "Linking Documents and Files," p. 993

To perform calculations on numbers scattered throughout a document, and to allow the results of a calculation to be updated if any of the numbers change, you need to use bookmark names and fields. Bookmarks are used to name a location. You must use two steps to perform math on numbers within a document:

IV

1. Mark the location of numbers in the text by assigning bookmark names to them.

2. Enter a field code that calculates the mathematical result.

To create the bookmarks that will contain numbers used in the calculations, follow these steps:

1. Create your document and type numbers where you want them. Save your document.

2. Choose Tools, Options, and select the View tab.

3. Select the Bookmarks check box, then choose OK.

4. Select in the document a number you want to use in a calculation.

5. Choose Edit, Bookmark to display the Bookmark dialog box.

6. Type a name in the Bookmark Name edit box. Use a descriptive name, such as **Profit**, **Expense**, or **Budget**, that starts with a letter and has no spaces.

7. Click the Add button. Square brackets surrounding the selected number indicate the bookmark.

8. Repeat the process, starting with step 4, until you have assigned a bookmark to each number used in calculations.

◀ See "Marking Locations with Bookmarks," p. 157

Note

Be careful when you delete or change a number entered at a bookmark location, because you may delete the bookmark. If you accidentally delete the bookmark, a math field that uses that bookmark will produce an error. To prevent yourself from deleting bookmarks, edit the numbers in bookmarks only while the screen is set so that you can see bookmark end symbols.

To insert the math function or formula that calculates by using the numbers you have just identified with bookmarks, follow these steps:

1. Position the insertion point where you want the calculation result to appear, and choose Insert, Field. Word for Windows displays the Field dialog box (see fig. 22.1).

Fig. 22.1

Enter a calculation formula in the Field dialog box.

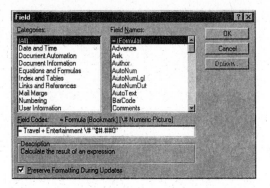

2. Select Equations and Formulas from the Categories list, and select = (Formula) from the Field Names list.

3. In the Field Codes text box, type the mathematical expression for calculating the desired result, using bookmark names and mathematical operators.

   Type a formula, using the bookmarks and math operators as you would expect to write a formula:

   =Revenue-Cost

   You can use any of the functions or mathematical operators listed under the entry for the {=} field in Chapter 20, "Automating with Field Codes."

4. Following the mathematical formula, add any formatting instructions.

5. Click OK.

◀ See "Editing Fields," p. 601

◀ See "Formatting Field Results," p. 602

The results of the calculation in the field are displayed, unless you have set Word for Windows to display field codes by choosing Tools, Options, in which case the field code and formula itself are displayed. To turn the field code display on or off, select the field (or the field's result) and press Shift+F9. To update the field, select the field and press F9.

Performing Calculations in a Table

To perform a calculation in a table, you use table references and special functions to create a field expression for calculating the desired result. *Functions* are built-in mathematical formulas that perform operations such as Sum and Average.

Specifying Table Cells in a Formula

As you enter a formula in a field in a table, you refer to individual cells or ranges of cells in the table by using column and row coordinates. The columns of a table are lettered A, B, C, and so on; the rows of a table are numbered 1, 2, 3, and so on, just as they are in a spreadsheet. To refer to an individual cell in a table, specify first the column letter, followed by the row number. To refer to the cell in the second column of the third row of a table, for example, you use the coordinates B3.

> **Note**
>
> Unlike the cell coordinates in Excel, the cell coordinates in Word for Windows are always absolute; you do not need to use the dollar sign ($) notation used by Excel.

You can specify ranges of cells in a table by using two cell coordinates separated by a colon (:). To specify the first three cells in column C of a table, for example, you use the coordinates C1:C3. You can specify an entire column or row by using a range without starting or ending cells. The coordinates B:B specify all the cells in the second column of a table, and the coordinates 2:2 specify all the cells in the second row of a table. This second form of cell coordinates is useful if you expect to add or remove rows or columns from a table in which you use all the cells in your calculation.

> **Note**
>
> Formulas in tables do not automatically update themselves to reflect inserted or deleted rows or columns, as they do in Microsoft Excel or Lotus 1-2-3. If you insert or delete a row or column, and your formula uses specific cell references, you must edit the formula to adjust it to include the new cells.

Entering a Formula in a Table

Many calculations that need to be made in a document are in the form of a table. To enter a formula in a table, follow these steps:

1. Position the insertion point in the cell where you want the result to appear.

2. Choose Table, Formula. The Formula dialog box appears (see fig. 22.2).

◀ See "Creating Tables," p. 506

◀ See "Editing Tables," p. 516

Fig. 22.2
Use the Formula
dialog box to enter
a formula in a
table.

Word for Windows analyzes the table and automatically enters in the
Formula text box an expression that seems most appropriate for the cell
containing the insertion point. If Word for Windows cannot determine
what formulas are appropriate, it leaves the Formula text box empty.

◀ See "A Refer-
ence List of
Field Codes,"
p. 616

3. Type any additions to the suggested expression in the Formula text box,
   or delete the suggested expression and type your own, using any combination of reduction functions, cell references, bookmarks, and mathematical operators.

4. If you are writing your own formula, select the Paste Function list box
   to see a list of available functions. As you select the function from the
   Paste Function list box, it is pasted in the Formula text box.

   To sum a column of numbers, for example, the formula expression
   might look like this:

       { =SUM(D2:D10) }

5. If you want your formula expression to include numbers referenced by
   bookmarks, you can select the bookmark names from the Paste Bookmark list box to paste them in the Formula text box.

6. To format the formula expression's results, select a format from the
   Number Format list box.

7. Choose OK.

The results of the calculation in the field are displayed, unless you have set
Word for Windows to display field codes by choosing Tools, Options, in
which case the field code and formula itself are displayed. To turn the field
code display on or off, select the field (or the field's result) and press Shift+F9.
To update the field, select the field and press F9.

Recalculating Formulas

Formula fields, whether you enter them in a table or elsewhere in your document, do not update automatically, as do some other types of fields. You must update formula fields manually using one of the following methods:

- Place the insertion point in the field (or its result) and press Alt+Shift+U or F9 to update the field.

- Move the pointer over the field (or its result) and click the right mouse button. Choose Update Field from the context-sensitive menu.

- To update all the fields in the document, select the entire document by choosing Edit, Select All. Then press F9 to update the fields.

What You Need to Know about Displaying Formulas and Equations

Word for Windows comes with an Equation Editor that enables you to easily create publishable equations in a document. You insert as an object an equation created with the Equation Editor in your document, just as you can insert pictures, graphs, and spreadsheet tables (see fig. 22.3). To edit the equation, you must reopen the Equation Editor; you cannot edit the equation from within Word for Windows. You can, however, position and resize an equation from within a Word for Windows document, as with any object.

The Pearson Product moment correlation coefficient can be used to measure the linear relationship between the set of independent values (x values) and dependent values (y values) in a scatter gram. The value of the coefficient ranges from –1.0 to 1.0 and is calculated using the following equation:

$$r = \frac{n\left(\sum xy\right) - \left(\sum x\right)\left(\sum y\right)}{\sqrt{\left[n\sum x^2 - \left(\sum x\right)^2\right]\left[n\sum y^2 - \left(\sum y\right)^2\right]}}$$

Fig. 22.3

You can insert an equation in a document by using the Equation Editor.

> **Note**
>
> If you did not choose to install the Equation Editor when you set up Word for Windows, it will not appear in the list of object types. You must run the setup program again to install the Equation Editor. You do not have to reinstall the entire program; just tell the setup program to install only the Equation Editor.

When you first open the Equation Editor, you are presented with a screen containing a single slot (see fig. 22.4). Slots demarcate the different components of an equation. If you are entering a fraction, for example, one slot is available for the numerator, and another slot is available for the denominator.

Fig. 22.4

The Equation Editor window has menu commands and palettes to help you build your equations.

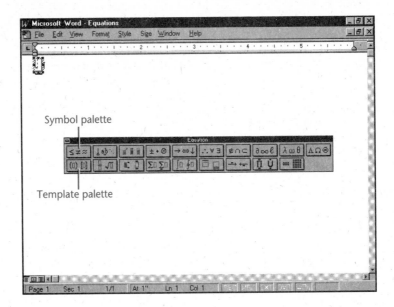

The Equation Editor has several tools that simplify the task of creating an equation. The toolbar consists of buttons that open the symbol and template palettes. To access these palettes, you simply click the button to open the palette you want. In the first row of the toolbar are several palettes for entering symbols, including math operators, Greek symbols, arrows, and so on. The template palettes, displayed in the second row of the toolbar, contain collections of ready-made templates that enable you to create the different components in an equation. For example, the second template from the left in the second row of buttons contains a collection of templates for entering fractions and roots (see fig. 22.5).

Fig. 22.5

The Equation Editor contains a template palette that has been opened.

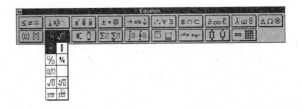

Building an Equation

The process of constructing an equation consists largely of using the template and symbol palettes and the keyboard to assemble the equation, piece by piece. Text and symbols are entered in slots, which are either separate from or part of a template. Text or symbols are entered in the slot that contains the insertion point. You can use the mouse, or the arrow and Tab keys, to move the insertion point from one slot to another.

The templates take care of most of the tasks that deal with positioning and spacing in equation building. Other commands are available to fine-tune spacing and alignment of the equation's components. Commands are available for controlling the font type and font size of the elements in an equation, as well.

Notice in figure 22.6 the slot near the end of the equation into which characters have yet to be inserted.

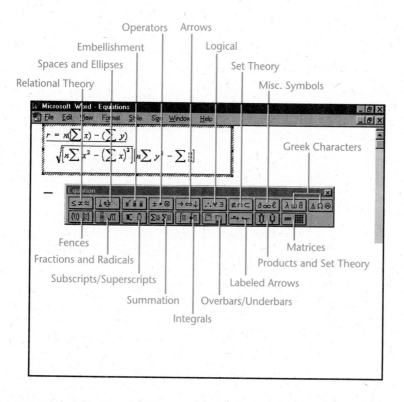

Fig. 22.6
The Equation Editor shows a partially completed equation.

Inserting an Equation

You can choose Insert, Object to open the Equation Editor and to create an equation at the current insertion-point position.

To insert an equation in a document, follow these steps:

1. Position the insertion point where you want to insert the equation you will create.

2. Choose Insert, Object, and select the Create New tab.

3. Select Microsoft Equation 2.0 from the Object Type list box, and choose OK. When you choose OK, the Equation Editor opens (refer to fig. 22.4).

4. Create the equation in the Equation Editor. (See the following sections for detailed instructions on creating an equation.)

5. Click outside the Equation box to return to the document. The Equation Editor is closed.

To return to the Equation Editor, double-click the equation you want to edit.

Typing in the Equation Editor

Typing in the Equation Editor is similar to typing in a Word for Windows document, although there are some important differences. Whenever you type in the Equation Editor, text is entered in the slot containing the insertion point. As with a Word for Windows document, you can use the Backspace and Delete keys to delete characters.

Unless you use the Text style from the Style menu, the space bar has no effect. The Equation Editor takes care of the spacing in an equation. When you type an equal sign, for example, the Equation Editor adds spacing before and after it. If you press the Enter key, a new line begins.

If you want to type regular text, choose the Text style from the Style menu. Then you can enter text as you normally would. Choose Math style from the Style menu to return to the Math style, the style you normally work with when creating an equation.

Selecting Items in an Equation

You might need to select an item in an equation—to change the point size or reposition the item, for example. To select characters in a slot, use the mouse to drag across characters. To select an entire equation, choose Edit, Select All.

To select *embedded* items (items not contained in a slot), such as *character embellishments* (carets, tildes, prime signs, and so on) or integral signs, press and hold down the Ctrl key. When the mouse pointer changes to a vertical arrow, point to the embedded item and click to select it.

Entering Nested Equation Templates

Complex equations involve templates nested within templates. The result is an equation involving many templates, each nested within the slot of a larger template. An example of nested templates is the square root nested within the denominator of the equation shown in figure 22.6.

To enter a template within an existing equation, follow these steps:

1. Place the insertion point where you want to insert the template.

2. Use the mouse to choose a template from one of the template palettes. The template is inserted immediately to the right of the insertion point.

   Or, you can use one of the shortcut keys listed in table 22.1 to insert the template.

3. Type text or enter symbols in each slot in the template. The insertion point must be positioned in the slot before you begin entering text or symbols.

Table 22.1 lists the shortcut keys for inserting templates. To use these shortcuts, press Ctrl+T and then press the shortcut key. You can insert the items marked with an asterisk by pressing just the Ctrl key and the shortcut key—you do not have to press T first.

Table 22.1 Shortcut Keys for Inserting Templates		
Template	**Description**	**Shortcut Key**
(⬚)	Parentheses	(or)
[⬚]	Brackets*	[or]
{⬚}	Braces*	{ or }
|⬚|	Absolute Value	|
⬚	Fraction*	F
⬚/⬚	Slash Fraction*	/
⬚	Superscript (high)*	H

(continues)

Table 22.1	Continued	
Template	**Description**	**Shortcut Key**
▓▪	Subscript (low)*	L
▓▪	Joint sub-/superscript*	J
√▥	Root*	R
∛▥	Nth Root	N
∑▥	Summation	S
∏▫	Product	P
∫▫	Integral*	I
▦▦▦	Matrix (353)	M
▫	Underscript (limit)	U

Entering Symbols

Many fields of mathematics, science, and medicine use symbols to represent concepts or physical structures. To insert a symbol in a slot, follow these steps:

1. Position the insertion point in the slot where you want to insert the symbol.

2. Select the symbol you want from one of the symbol templates.

Table 22.2 lists the shortcut keys for inserting symbols. To use these shortcuts, press Ctrl+S and then the shortcut key.

Table 22.2	Shortcut Keys for Inserting Symbols	
Symbol	**Description**	**Shortcut Key**
∞	Infinity	I
→	Arrow	A

Symbol	Description	Shortcut Key
∂	Derivative (partial)	D
$\leq$	Less than or equal to	<
$\geq$	Greater than or equal to	>
$\times$	Times	T
$\in$	Element of	E
$\notin$	Not an element of	Shift+E
$\subset$	Contained in	C
$\not\subset$	Not contained in	Shift+C

Adding Embellishments

The Equation Editor has several embellishments—such as prime signs, arrows, tildes, and dots—that you can add to characters or symbols.

To add an embellishment, follow these steps:

1. Position the insertion point to the right of the character you want to embellish.

2. Choose the embellishment icon from the embellishment palette (third button from the left in the top row of buttons).

    Or, you can use one of the shortcut keys listed in table 22.3 to add an embellishment.

Table 22.3 Shortcut Keys for Inserting Embellishments		
Icon	**Description**	**Shortcut Keys**
$\bar{}$	Overbar	Ctrl+Shift+-
$\tilde{}$	Tilde	Ctrl+~ (Ctrl+" on some keyboards)

(continues)

Table 22.3 Continued		
Icon	Description	Shortcut Keys
	Arrow (vector)	Ctrl+Alt+-
	Single prime	Ctrl+Alt+'
	Double prime	Ctrl+" (Ctrl+~ on some keyboards)
	Single dot	Ctrl+Alt+.

Formatting an Equation

After you create an equation, you can format it to appear exactly as you want. You can work on the spacing of the elements in the equation, adjust the positioning and alignment within the equation, and change the font and font size for any element.

Controlling Spacing

You can modify several spacing parameters by choosing Format, Spacing (line spacing, or row and column spacing in matrices are examples).

To modify the spacing setting used by the Equation Editor, follow these steps:

1. Choose Format, Spacing. A dialog box appears that displays a list of dimensions you can scroll through (see fig. 22.7).

Fig. 22.7
In the Spacing dialog box, you can control the spacing used by the Equation Editor.

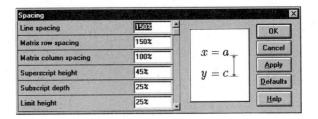

2. Select the text box next to the dimension you want to modify. Use the scroll bar to move through the list of dimensions.

3. Type a new measurement.

The default unit of measure is points. You can specify other units by typing the appropriate abbreviation from the following list:

Unit of Measure	Abbreviation
Inches	in
Centimeters	cm
Millimeters	mm
Points	pt
Picas	pi

4. Choose Apply or OK.

   Choosing Apply applies the modified dimension to the current equation and leaves the dialog box open, so that you can continue modifications. Choosing OK applies any modifications and closes the dialog box.

In practice, you probably should specify the spacing dimensions as a percentage of the point size given for Full Size type, which is set in the Size Define dialog box. The advantage to this approach is that if you change the type size, you don't have to redefine your spacing dimensions; spacing will always be proportional to the type size.

Although the Equation Editor manages the spacing between elements in an equation, you can insert spaces manually by using four spacing symbols. These symbols are located in the second symbol palette from the left in the top row. You can also access these symbols with shortcut keys. A list of the spacing symbols and shortcut keys is shown in table 22.4.

Table 22.4   Shortcut Keys for Inserting Spaces

Icon	Function	Shortcut Keys
a̶b̶	Zero space	Shift+space bar
a̱ḇ	One point space	Ctrl+Alt+space bar

(continues)

Icon	Function	Shortcut Keys
Table 22.4 Continued		
a b	Thin space	Ctrl+space bar
a b	Thick space (two thin spaces)	Ctrl+Shift+space bar

To delete a space, press the Delete or Backspace key, as you would with text.

Positioning and Aligning Equations

You can adjust the positioning of any selected item by using the Nudge commands. First select the item (refer to the "Selecting Items in an Equation" section, earlier in this chapter). Then use one of the following keystrokes to move the item, one pixel at a time:

Keystrokes	Function
Ctrl + ←	Moves item left one pixel
Ctrl + →	Moves item right one pixel
Ctrl + ↓	Moves item down one pixel
Ctrl + ↑	Moves item up one pixel

The Equation Editor enables you to align horizontally one or more lines of single or multiple equations, using either the Format menu or the alignment symbol. You can align lines to the left, center, or right; or you can align lines around equal signs, decimal points, or alignment symbols. To align a group of equations, simply choose one of the alignment commands from the Format menu. To align lines in an equation, position the insertion point within the lines; then choose one of the alignment commands.

To insert an alignment symbol, position the insertion point and choose from the Spaces palette (second button in the top row of buttons) the alignment symbol at the far left of the top row of symbols. The alignment symbols are used as a reference point around which one or more lines of single or multiple equations are aligned. They override the Format commands.

Selecting Fonts

Usually, when you work in the Equation Editor, you will use the Math style from the Style menu. When you use the Math style, the Equation Editor automatically recognizes standard functions and applies to them the Function style (typeface and character formatting, for example). The Variable style is applied otherwise. If the Equation Editor fails to recognize a function, you can select it and apply the Function style manually.

To define the font and character attributes for a style, follow these steps:

1. Choose Style, Define.

2. Select the style you want to define.

3. Select the font from the list of available fonts.

4. Select the Bold or Italic boxes if you want bold or italic.

5. Choose OK.

You use the Text style to type regular text. Selecting this style applies the Text style to the text you type, and enables you to use the space bar to enter spaces as normal. With the other styles, spacing is handled automatically by the Equation Editor.

Select the Other style when you want to select a font and character format that is not one of the standard styles. Selecting the Other style opens a dialog box in which you can choose a font and character format for characters that are selected or about to be entered.

Selecting Font Sizes

The Equation Editor provides not only several predefined font styles, but also certain predefined font sizes. The Full size is the choice you normally work with when you are building equations. You also have selections for subscripts, sub-subscripts, symbols, and subsymbols. You can use the Other size option for those cases in which you want to specify a size not defined by one of these standard sizes.

To apply a font size to an equation, follow these steps:

1. Select the characters whose point size you want to modify.

2. Choose the Size menu and select a size. If no defined size matches your needs, choose Size, Other and specify a size in the Other Size dialog box. Or, choose Size, Define to modify the default settings for each size in the Size menu.

To apply a size, select one from the Size menu; then type the characters you want the size applied to. Alternatively, you can select the characters after they have been typed, and then choose a size.

Working with Matrices

The Matrix template palette includes several vectors and matrices of pre-defined sizes. You can also select one of the template symbols in the bottom row of the palette to open the Matrix dialog box. In this box, you can specify the dimensions of the matrix or vector, and also control several other matrix characteristics.

To insert a matrix template, click the matrix template button (the last button on the right in the bottom row). Then click the palette you want. Selecting a template from the last row of icons opens the Matrix dialog box (see fig. 22.8). (Another way to display this dialog box is to choose Format, Matrix.) In the Matrix dialog box, you can specify the dimensions of the matrix and make several other selections, including alignment, column widths and row heights, and the type of partition lines you will use. To control the spacing between rows and columns, use the Spacing dialog box displayed when you choose Format, Spacing.

Fig. 22.8
You can specify the dimensions of a matrix in the Matrix dialog box.

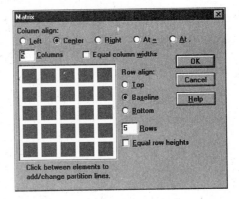

Press Tab to move from left to right through the matrix, one element at a time, or Shift+Tab to move right to left. You can also use the arrow keys to move from element to element in a matrix.

To format an existing matrix, select the entire matrix and then choose Format, Matrix. Make your selections from the dialog box, and choose OK.

> **Note**
>
> To create a determinant, you can nest a matrix within absolute value bars. Insert the absolute value bar template first, and with the insertion point inside the absolute value bars, insert a matrix template.

Viewing Equations

You can choose from three predefined magnifications of the equation in the Equation Editor window. Alternatively, you can choose View, Zoom to set a custom magnification for viewing your equation. To change the view, choose View. To display the equation at the actual size you want it to appear in the document and on the printed page, select 100%. Select 200% and 400% to display the equation at twice and four times the actual size, respectively. To set a custom magnification, choose View, Zoom, and select the Custom option in the Zoom dialog box. Next, enter the magnification you want in the Custom text box; then choose OK.

Editing an Equation

To edit an equation, you must return to the Equation Editor. To open the Equation Editor, follow these steps:

1. Double-click the equation you want to edit, or select it. Then choose Edit, Equation Object, Edit.

2. Make your editing changes.

3. Click outside the Equation Editor to return to your document.

◀ See "Setting Up Your Printer," p. 229

Printing Equations

> **Caution**
>
> If you see boxes on screen instead of equations, choose Tools, Options, then click the View tab. Clear the Picture Placeholders check box.

To print equations, you need to have one of three kinds of printers: a PostScript printer; a laser printer that lets you download fonts; or a dot-matrix or DeskJet printer, used with a font-scaling utility, such as TrueType or Adobe Type Manager. ❖

Part V

Publishing with Graphics

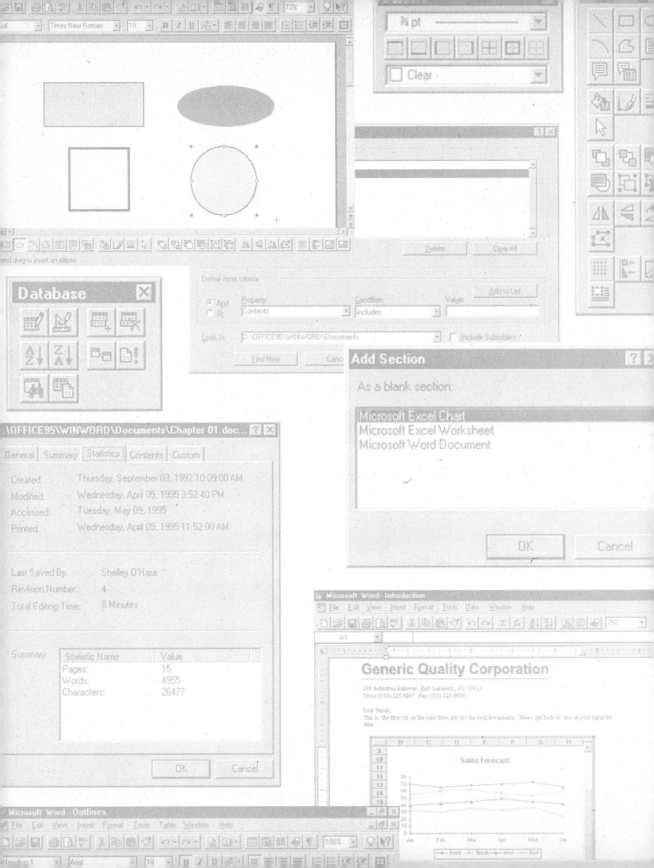

Chapter 23

Inserting Pictures in Your Document

With Word for Windows 95, you can illustrate your ideas by using pictures created with a graphics program. If a picture is worth a thousand words, think how much typing you can save! Even if your picture is worth somewhat less than a thousand words, illustrating your document with graphics can make your pages more appealing—which means that readers pay more attention to your words.

Pictures that you insert in your Word for Windows documents come from many sources. Some come from a stand-alone graphics program, which you can use to create illustrations ranging from the simple to the sophisticated. Some—including photographs—come from scanners that digitize artwork for use in a computer. Some pictures come from clip art packages that provide ready-to-use artwork. Office 95 includes many clip art images in the CLIPART subfolder.

All the pictures you insert come from a source outside Word for Windows (and can be used in many programs besides Word for Windows). That makes the pictures different from the graphics objects you create with Microsoft WordArt, Microsoft Graph, or the Drawing toolbar. (You can learn about each of these built-in programs in Chapter 25, "Drawing with Word's Drawing Tools," Chapter 26, "Creating Banners and Special Effects with WordArt," and Chapter 27, "Graphing Data"). Using one of the built-in graphics programs, you can create a graphic that exists only as a part of your Word for Windows document.

Stand-alone graphics programs often are more powerful than the simple built-in programs that come with Word for Windows. Thus, Word for Windows gives you the flexibility to include a range of graphics in your documents—from simple drawings that you create yourself without leaving Word for Windows, to sophisticated graphics that you can make with a powerful stand-alone graphics program.

In this chapter, you learn how to insert many different types of graphics and work with them in your document. You learn how to do the following:

- Insert previously created graphics into your document and copy graphics into your document.

- Edit, size, crop, and move graphics.

- Add lines and borders to graphics.

- Hide graphics so you can work faster with text.

Reviewing Compatible Formats

Word for Windows is compatible with many of the most frequently used graphics programs and scanner formats. You can import pictures created with any of the following programs or in any of the formats listed:

Program Format	File Extension
PC Paintbrush	PCX
Tagged Image Format	TIF
Windows Metafile	WMF
Encapsulated PostScript	EPS
Windows Paint	BMP
Windows Bitmap	BMP
Computer Graphics Metafile	CGM
HP Graphic Language	HGL, PLT
WordPerfect Graphics	WPG
Micrografx Designer	DRW
Micrografx Draw	DRW
Targa	TGA
AutoCAD Format 2-D	DXF

Program Format	File Extension
CorelDRAW!	CDR
Macintosh PICT	PCT
CompuServe GIF	GIF
Kodak PhotoCD	PCD
JPEG Filter	JPG

Your favorite graphics program might not be listed. Many programs easily export graphics (or even part of a graphic) from the native format to a commonly used format. If your program isn't listed, see whether it can save graphics in one of the formats in the preceding list so that you can use them in Word for Windows.

Installing the Import Filters

To import pictures into a document, Word for Windows uses special "import filters." One filter is required for each type of file you want to import. If you selected the Complete Setup option when you installed Word for Windows, all the graphics import filters were put into your system. If you selected a Custom installation, you might not have installed all the filters. To see which filters are installed (and consequently which types of graphics you are able to import), read the contents of the Files of Type list in the Insert Picture dialog box. This dialog box appears when you choose Insert, Picture.

Inserting and Copying Pictures into Your Document

You can insert a picture in the text of your document, or in a frame or table. When you work with the Drawing toolbar, you can insert a picture in a text box or picture container. Inserting a picture directly in your text is the simplest way to put an illustration in your document. Other techniques, however, offer advantages. Inserting a picture in a frame enables you to wrap text around the picture. Inserting a picture in one cell of a table enables you to position the picture adjacent to text in the next cell. Inserting a picture in a text box enables you to layer the picture above or below the text.

▶ See "Drawing with Word's Drawing Tools," p. 755

▶ See "Including Text or Another Picture in a Drawing," p. 789

Tip
You can automatically include a numbered caption with each picture you insert by choosing Insert, Caption, AutoCaption.

You can use one of three ways to insert a picture in your document:

- You can insert pictures by choosing Insert, Picture. This command asks you to locate the file and then inserts the picture from disk. If you use this method, you don't even need to own the program used to create the picture.

- You can open the program used to create the picture, and copy the picture into the Windows Clipboard. Then you can paste the picture into your Word for Windows document.

- You can insert picture objects by choosing Insert, Object to open a graphics program from within Word for Windows. You can use this command to insert a picture that you later can edit using the program that created it.

Inserting Pictures into Your Document

You can insert a picture in your document without ever opening the program used to create the picture. As with opening or saving a Word for Windows file, you must first locate the file before you insert a picture.

Word offers many tools for helping you find a file. You can find files that match a certain name, file type, or property, or that were modified recently.

You can insert a picture with or without a link to the graphics program used to create the picture. By linking to the graphics program, you might be able to reduce the size of your document (see the upcoming section, "Minimizing File Size through Linking").

To insert a picture, follow these steps:

1. Position the insertion point where you want to insert the picture.

2. Choose Insert, Picture. The Insert Picture dialog box appears (see fig. 23.1).

3. Locate your picture file. If it is not in the current drive or folder, select from the Look In list the drive or folder containing your file. Click the Up One Level button to show files or folders in the folder one level higher.

4. From the displayed list, select the picture file you want to insert.

   Click the List button to list file names only; the Details button to see file size and type; the Properties button to see file properties including title, author, revision number, and so forth.

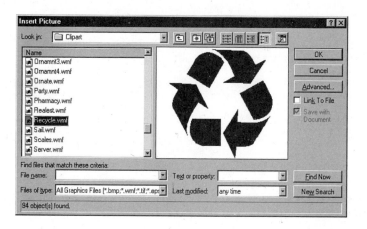

Fig. 23.1
Use the Insert
Picture dialog box
to locate a picture
you want to insert.
The Preview box
shows the selected
picture—an Office
95 clip art image.

5. To search for files that meet certain criteria, select among the following options, and then click <u>F</u>ind Now:

    To find a file with certain characters in its name, select File <u>N</u>ame and type the characters you want to find. You can type part of a name or the whole name.

    You can restrict the file list to a particular file type. In the Files of <u>T</u>ype list, simply select the file type you want to list.

    If you want to find files modified today, last week, last month, or any time, select Last <u>M</u>odified and choose from the list.

    Click Ne<u>w</u> Search to clear old search criteria before starting a new search (old criteria may restrict your search in ways you don't want).

6. If you want to see the picture before you insert it, select the file and click the Preview button. A miniature version of your picture appears.

7. Choose OK.

When you insert a picture in your Word for Windows document, it falls into place at the location of the insertion point. If you add or delete text preceding the picture, the picture moves with the edited text. Unless you frame and position the picture, it stays with the text. For details on framing a picture and positioning it independently of the text, refer to Chapter 24, "Framing and Moving Text and Graphics."

Performing Advanced Picture File Searches

If you're having a hard time locating the picture you want to insert, Word can help you find it. In the Insert Picture dialog box (refer to fig. 23.2),

Tip
Use <u>I</u>nsert, <u>P</u>icture when you want to insert pictures that you won't want to edit later.

V

Publishing with Graphics

Tip
To quickly insert a picture, position the insertion point where you want it, choose <u>I</u>nsert, <u>P</u>icture, and double-click the picture's file name.

◀ See "Managing Documents and Files," p. 105

choose <u>A</u>dvanced to display the Advanced Find dialog box. Select from the many options to find files matching naming criteria, properties such as the application name or the picture's author, or location.

> **Note**
>
> If you cannot insert a picture because it's in a format Word doesn't recognize, try opening the picture in Windows Paint or some other graphics program. Then save the picture in a format Word does recognize, such as BMP.

◀ See "Adjusting Paragraph Spacing," p. 317

> **Note**
>
> If you format a paragraph to have line spacing of an exact amount—one inch, for example—and you insert in that paragraph a picture two inches high, you won't see all of the picture. You can reformat the paragraph containing the picture for any line spacing other than Exactly, and the paragraph will adjust to fit the picture.

Minimizing File Size through Linking

◀ See "Moving, Copying, and Linking Text or Graphics," p. 160

When you insert a picture in your document, Word usually includes all the information in the picture file, as well as a representation of the picture. Each time you open your document, you see the picture. However, this method can make your Word for Windows file quite large: the file size is increased by the file size of the picture (which can be very large).

Tip

Word can't display pictures that are larger than 1M.

Another way to insert a picture is to link the picture to its picture file, but not store a copy of the picture in your Word for Windows file. In this way, each time you open your document, Word refers to the original file to draw a representation of the picture. This method has the advantage of minimizing your file size, as Word does not store a copy of the picture in your document.

Minimizing file size in this way is helpful if your graphics files are very large, or if you're using the same graphic file over and over in different documents (like a logo in your stationery). However, if the file is not available, Word cannot display or print the picture—when you open the Word file, a message box warns you that Word cannot open the graphics file. Use this method for minimizing file size only when you are sure Word will be able to locate the picture file.

To minimize file size through linking, follow these steps:

1. Position the insertion point where you want the picture to appear. Then choose <u>I</u>nsert, <u>P</u>icture and select the picture you want to insert.

2. In the Insert Picture dialog box, select the Link to File option (at the far right of the dialog box, under the Advanced command button). Then deselect, or clear, Save with Document.

3. Choose OK.

If you move the original picture file, you must update the link by selecting the picture and choosing Edit, Links and then Change Source. (You also can use this command to save the picture in the document.) For more information, refer to Chapter 34, "Using Word with Office Applications."

If you give someone a Word file containing a picture that is linked to the file, be sure to give that person a copy of the picture file as well. Have him use Edit, Links and then Change Source to identify the picture file's location on the hard disk.

Minimizing File Size through File Format

When you insert a picture that you created on another computer, such as a Macintosh, Word saves two versions of the picture: the version that works with Word (the "native" version), and the version that came from the Macintosh. This feature is handy if you ever need the Macintosh version again sometime, but it makes your file larger. You can conserve file size by saving only the native version of the picture.

To minimize file size through file format, follow these steps:

1. Choose Tools, Options.

2. Select the Save tab.

3. Select Save Native Picture Formats Only from the Save Options group.

4. Choose OK.

Another way to minimize file size is to save picture files in a format that creates smaller files, when that is an option. PCX, BMP, and WMF files are usually smaller than EPS or TIF files, for example. You can also minimize document file size by using black and white pictures, rather than color, especially if you'll print in black and white anyway.

Copying Pictures into Your Document

Sometimes the easiest way to get a picture you created with a graphics program into Word for Windows is to use the Clipboard to copy the picture. You can even link the picture to the original file when you paste it into Word; in

V

Publishing with Graphics

Tip
If you're illustrating your Word document with pictures drawn in Windows Paint, you can greatly minimize your Word file size by copying the picture from Paint into Word, rather than inserting a saved Paint picture.

▶ See "Embedding Data,"
p. 986

this way, you can update the picture if you later make changes to the original. To link a picture, the graphics program must support the older Dynamic Data Exchange (DDE) or the newer technology, Object Linking and Embedding (OLE). Some of the programs that support the older DDE technology are Lotus 1-2-3 for Windows, Microsoft Access 1.1, Microsoft Excel 4.0, and WordPerfect for Windows. Programs that support both DDE and the newer OLE 2.0 technology are Microsoft Excel 5.0 or Excel 95 and CorelDRAW! 5.0.

To copy a picture into your document, follow these steps:

1. Start your graphics or charting program. Then open the file containing the picture you want to copy into your Word for Windows document.

2. Select the picture or chart.

3. Choose Edit, Copy.

4. Switch to your Word for Windows document.

5. Position the insertion point where you want to insert the picture.

6. Choose Edit, Paste.

   Or, choose Edit, Paste Special to link the picture to the original file. Select Paste Link from the Paste Special dialog box. In the As list, select the format for your picture (formats vary depending on what type of picture you copied). Select the Display as Icon option if you want to display an icon, rather than the picture, in your text. (You can double-click the icon to display and edit the picture.)

7. Choose OK.

When you paste in a picture with a link, you get some choices. If you paste the picture as an *object*, you can edit it later. If you paste the picture as a *picture*, it might take up less space. To get an idea of the best way to paste in your picture, read the Result box at the bottom of the Paste Special dialog box as you select each of the different formats in the As list.

For more information about how to work with links, refer to Chapter 34, "Using Word with Office Applications."

Inserting Picture Objects in Your Document

▶ See "Creating a WordArt Object," p. 803

A *picture object* is a picture in your Word for Windows document that you can edit. You edit the picture by double-clicking it to display the program used to create the picture, if the program is available. All the data that creates a picture object is contained within the Word document—it is not linked to a file outside the document.

You can insert many types of picture objects in your document. If CorelDRAW! is installed on your computer and you put in the CorelDRAW! filter when you installed Word, you can insert a CorelDRAW! (or other Corel program) object. If Microsoft Excel 5.0 or Excel 95 is installed, you can embed an Excel chart as an object. You can insert an equation, graph, picture, or WordArt image as objects, and you can insert a Microsoft Word Picture object.

You can insert new or existing picture objects. If you insert new picture objects, Word displays the graphics program you've chosen, and you must draw the picture. For example, if you choose to insert a new CorelDRAW! picture object, Word starts CorelDRAW! and presents you with a blank drawing screen. You draw the picture, and then you choose a command to return to your Word document with the picture.

If you insert existing picture objects, the existing picture appears in your document. Whether you insert new or existing picture objects, you always can double-click one of these objects to display the program used to create the picture. Then you can edit the picture. Alternatively, you can use a command to edit the picture.

To insert a new picture object, follow these steps:

1. Position the insertion point where you want to insert the picture object.

2. Choose Insert, Object. The Object dialog box appears (see fig. 23.2).

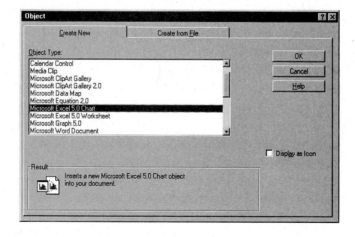

Fig. 23.2
When you insert a new picture object, Word displays the program you use to create it.

Tip
A good selection of clip art objects is contained in the Microsoft ClipArt Gallery. To insert these pictures, choose Insert, Object, Create New, and select Microsoft ClipArt Gallery.

3. Select the Create New tab.

4. From the Object Type list, select the type of picture object you want to insert. For example, to insert a Microsoft Word picture, select Microsoft Word Picture from the list.

   Select the Display as Icon check box if you want to display an icon rather than the picture. Icons can be used if a picture will take too much room in a document. The icon appears on-screen or when printed. You can double-click the icon to see its contents.

5. Choose OK. The program you use to create the picture starts.

   For example, if you chose Microsoft Word Picture, the screen shown in figure 23.3 appears. Notice the Drawing toolbar appears at the bottom of the screen.

6. Create the picture.

   In Microsoft Word Picture, you can click the Reset Picture Boundary button to shrink the picture's edges close to the picture.

7. Return to your Word document. The way that you do this varies from one program to another. In Microsoft Excel or WordArt, simply click the Word document somewhere outside the picture. In Microsoft Word Picture, click Close Picture. In other programs, choose File, Exit and Return to Document. Then answer Yes when a message box asks whether you want to update your document.

Fig. 23.3
You can insert or draw a picture in Microsoft Word Picture.

Tip
A quick way to insert a Microsoft Word Picture object is to display the Drawing toolbar and click the Create Picture tool.

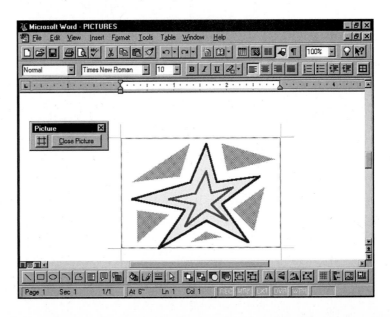

For more information on working with other applications, see Chapter 34, "Using Word with Office Applications."

To insert an existing picture object, follow these steps:

1. Position the insertion point where you want to insert the picture object.

2. Choose Insert, Object. The Object dialog box appears (see fig. 23.4).

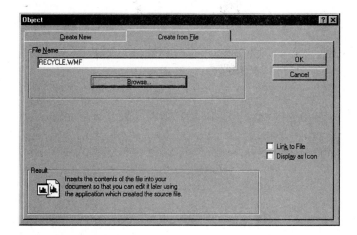

Fig. 23.4
You can insert an existing picture object and edit it later.

3. Select the Create from File tab.

4. In the File Name box, type the path and file name of the picture you want to insert. Locate the file, if necessary, by selecting Browse.

5. Select Link to File if you want the picture in your Word document to update when you change the original picture.

6. Select Display as Icon if you want to display an icon rather than the picture.

7. Choose OK.

Read the message in the Result box at the bottom of the Object dialog box to see the results that the currently selected options have produced in your document.

To learn more about the Browse dialog box, which is a standard Word dialog box, refer to Chapter 3, "Creating and Saving Documents."

Tip
Paint uses embedded objects, so updating the original file does not affect the embedded file. You must double-click the embedded object, and then manually edit it to update the Paintbrush object in the Word document.

Inserting Clip Art in Your Document

Tip

If you're copying pictures from Microsoft applications, display the Microsoft toolbar. This will help you quickly start Microsoft applications.

Word includes two good sources of clip art ready for you to use in your document. In the CLIPART subfolder in your MSOFFICE folder you'll find a collection of images that you can insert as pictures. Choose Insert, Picture to view and insert these pictures. (For details about inserting pictures, see the earlier section, "Inserting Pictures into Your Document.")

Another set of images includes graphic *objects* you can use in your document. Choose Insert, Object, Create New and then select Microsoft ClipArt Gallery to access these graphic objects. Figure 23.5 shows the Microsoft ClipArt Gallery. (For details about inserting objects, see the earlier section, "Inserting Picture Objects in Your Document.")

Fig. 23.5

The Microsoft ClipArt Gallery comes with Microsoft Office 95 and contains collections of graphic objects you can edit and insert in documents.

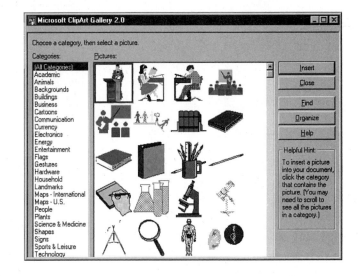

Tip

Use Insert, Object when you want to insert pictures that you can later edit.

Inserting Pictures in Frames and Text Boxes

▶ See "Framing Text, Pictures, and Other Objects," p. 728

▶ See "Wrapping Text around a Frame," p. 750

▶ See "Framing Objects Together," p. 733

By inserting a picture in a frame or framing a picture you've already inserted, you free the picture from being locked into a position relative to the text. You can move a framed picture anywhere on the page by simply dragging the picture. You can wrap text around a framed picture. You also can frame a picture together with text or another object—helpful when you want to keep objects grouped. Framed pictures are very useful with desktop publishing projects.

To frame a picture, follow these steps:

1. Choose Insert, Picture and select the picture you want to insert. Choose OK to insert the picture at the insertion point in your document. Make sure that the picture remains selected.

Or, if the picture you want framed is already inserted in your document, select the picture by clicking it.

2. To frame the selected picture, choose Insert, Frame.

   Or, click the Frame button on the Drawing toolbar. (Frame buttons are also included on the Word for Windows 2.0 and Forms toolbars.)

   If you insert a frame in Normal view, Word displays a dialog box suggesting you switch to Page Layout view. Respond by choosing Yes.

Alternatively, you can first create a frame and then insert the picture in the frame (simply reverse the preceding steps 1 and 2, drawing the frame with a crosshair). The frame reshapes itself to the shape of the picture, and the picture resizes itself to the width of the frame.

Inserting a picture in a text box offers some advantages. You can move a picture in a text box to the layer below the text in your document so that the picture appears to be behind the text. You can also use tools in the Drawing toolbar to quickly format a text box with fill and line colors and with styles. For more information on working with the Drawing toolbar, see Chapter 25, "Drawing with Word's Drawing Tools."

To insert a picture in a text box, follow these steps:

1. Display the Drawing toolbar by choosing View, Toolbars. Select Drawing from the Toolbars list.

2. Click the Text Box tool in the Drawing toolbar.

3. Move the crosshair into the document and drag the crosshair to draw a text box.

4. When you see the insertion point flashing at the upper-left corner of the text box, choose Insert, Picture. Select the picture you want to insert; then choose OK. The text box reshapes to the shape of the picture, and the picture resizes to the width of the text box.

Use the techniques described in the following section, "Working with Pictures," to resize or crop the text box to fit the picture, if necessary. Use the Fill Color, Line Color, and Line Style buttons on the Drawing toolbar to change the fill and edges of the text box.

V

Publishing with Graphics

Working with Pictures

After you insert a picture in your document, you can manipulate the picture in many ways. You can scale it to a smaller or larger size, proportionally or non-proportionally. You can size the picture to the exact dimensions you want. You can crop it, cutting away portions you don't want to use. You can add a border to the picture; and you can move, copy, or paste the picture. You can frame it or insert it in a text box, freeing the picture for positioning anywhere on the page. Finally, you can wrap text around the picture.

You can work with pictures in any view. (An exception is a picture in a text box, which appears only in the Page Layout view or the Print Preview screen.) The Page Layout view shows you exactly where the picture is positioned and how text wraps around it. Working with pictures in the Page Layout view can be slow, however, as even the fastest computers slow down when scrolling a graphic. The Normal view displays the picture at the left margin and scrolls a little more quickly than the Page Layout view. To save scrolling time, you can hide pictures.

Selecting Pictures

Before you change a picture, you must select it. When a picture is selected, it has square selection handles on all four corners and sides—eight in all. With a mouse, you can use the selection handles to size, crop, or scale the picture. Selected pictures appear differently if they're in a text box or framed (see fig. 23.6).

Fig. 23.6
A selected picture has eight selection handles (top). A text box containing a picture (middle) has a gray border and may have a colored fill or border. In Page Layout view, a selected framed picture (bottom) has a shaded border.

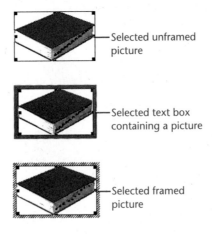

Selected unframed picture

Selected text box containing a picture

Selected framed picture

To select a picture with the mouse, follow these steps:

1. Display the picture on your screen.

2. Click the picture.

To select a picture with the keyboard, follow these steps:

1. Position the insertion point to one side of the picture.

2. Press Shift+← to select a picture to the left of the insertion point. Or, press Shift+→ to select a picture to the right.

Clicking an inserted picture selects it. Double-clicking a picture often has a very different effect: it will usually bring up a graphics program in which you can edit the picture. Windows' OLE technology makes this action possible.

> **Note**
>
> You can select inserted pictures, which exist as part of your text, by dragging across them or using other text-selection techniques. The pictures appear in reverse color when you do this. When you select a picture this way, you can format it with paragraph-formatting commands but not with picture-formatting commands. You can use this technique to align a picture that exists on a line by itself.

◀ See "Aligning Paragraphs," p. 297

V

Publishing with Graphics

Resizing and Cropping Pictures

After you insert a picture in your document, you can scale the picture to a smaller or larger size. You also can size it to the exact dimensions you want, or crop away parts of the picture you don't want to use. Resizing is useful when you need a picture to be a certain size in your document. Cropping helps when you want to zoom in on the most important part of the picture.

You can change the dimensions of a picture in three ways:

- Scale the picture larger or smaller by a percentage (proportionally or non-proportionally).

- Size the picture to an exact width and height.

- Crop away part of the picture.

You can make any of these changes with the mouse or keyboard commands.

Resizing and Cropping with the Mouse

Using the mouse to scale, size, or crop a picture is visual: it enables you to see how your changes look while you're making them. At the same time, you can monitor your picture's dimensions because a readout in the status bar tells you its exact size. (You can display the status bar by choosing <u>T</u>ools, <u>O</u>ptions and selecting Status <u>B</u>ar on the View tab.) If you use the mouse to change a picture, and you later want to see what its dimensions are, select the picture. Then choose F<u>o</u>rmat, Pictu<u>r</u>e. The entries in the Crop From, Scaling, and Size groups tell you the picture's current dimensions.

To change a picture, you select it and drag the small black selection handles that appear on the sides and corners of the picture. After you select the picture and move the mouse pointer over the selection handles, the pointer changes shape: it turns into a two-headed arrow if you're resizing the picture (left side of fig. 23.7) or a cropping tool if you're cropping the picture (right side of fig. 23.7).

Fig. 23.7

You can resize a picture by dragging its handles (left), or crop the picture by holding Shift as you drag the handles (right).

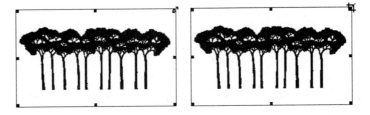

Each of the eight selection handles surrounding a selected picture has a specific purpose. The corner handles enable you to scale or crop from two sides. When you use a corner handle to resize a picture, the picture remains proportional. The side handles enable scaling and cropping from just one side. When you use a side handle to resize, the picture's proportions change. Whenever you drag a handle, the opposite handle stays anchored to its current position.

When you resize a picture by dragging a handle toward the center of the picture, you make the picture smaller. When you crop a picture by dragging toward the center, you cut away part of the picture. When you drag the handle away to resize a picture, you make the picture larger. If you're cropping, you add a blank border after you pass the picture's original edges. Figure 23.8 shows an original picture (on the left) that has been sized smaller (top-right example) and cropped (bottom-right example).

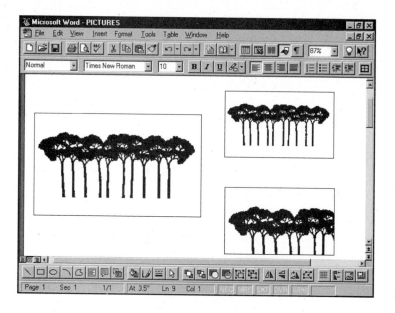

Fig. 23.8
The original picture (left) becomes smaller or larger when you resize it (top-right). Some of it is cut away when you crop it (bottom-right).

As you drag the handles to resize or crop the picture, you see a dotted-line box that represents the picture's new size and shape. When you release the mouse button, the picture snaps to fit inside the box.

To resize a picture with the mouse, follow these steps:

1. Select the picture.

2. Move the mouse pointer over a black selection handle until it turns into a two-headed arrow.

3. Drag a corner handle to scale the picture proportionally, or drag a side handle to scale a picture nonproportionally. The status bar reads Scaling and gives the picture's proportions. (Proportional changes keep the height and width proportions the same.)

4. Release the mouse button when the picture is the size you want.

To crop a picture, follow these steps:

1. Select the picture.

2. Press and hold down the Shift key.

3. Drag any black selection handle. Notice that the status bar reads Cropping and gives the picture's dimensions.

4. Release the mouse button when only the part of the picture you want to show is within the box boundary.

Resizing and Cropping with the Picture Dialog Box

You can use the Picture dialog box to scale, size, or crop a picture. The Picture dialog box includes boxes in which you must enter measurements. Each box has up and down arrows to its right; you can click the up arrow to increase the measurement, or click the down arrow to decrease it.

To scale, size, or crop a picture with the Picture dialog box, follow these steps:

1. Select the picture.

2. Choose Format, Picture. The Picture dialog box appears (see fig. 23.9).

Fig. 23.9

You can crop, scale, and size a picture to specific dimensions.

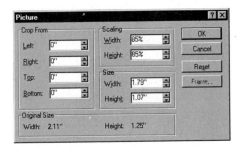

3. If you want to crop the picture, use the Crop From group. Enter the crop amount in the Left, Right, Top, or Bottom box (or click the up or down arrows to increase or decrease the crop amount).

   To crop one-half inch off the bottom of the picture, for example, type **.5** in the Bottom box. To crop one-quarter inch off the right side, type **.25** in the Right box.

4. If you want to scale your picture by a percentage, use the Scaling group. In the Width or Height box (or both), enter the percentage by which you want to scale the picture.

   To scale the picture to half its original size, for example, type **50** (for 50%) in the Width box, and **50** in the Height box. To double its size, type **200** (for 200%) in both boxes.

   Typing the identical scaling amount keeps the scaled picture proportional. If you type a different scale in the Width and Height boxes, the picture is distorted.

5. If you want to make your picture an exact size, use the Size group. Enter the dimensions for your picture in the Width and Height boxes.

   If you want your picture to be exactly three inches wide, for example, type **3** in the Width box; if you want the picture to be two inches high, enter **2** in the Height box.

6. Choose OK.

The percent you enter in the Scaling boxes is always a percent of the original size, not of the previous percent; therefore, it is easy to return to the original size.

Resetting the Picture to Its Original Dimensions

You easily can reset your picture to its original dimensions (even if you changed it with the mouse rather than the Picture dialog box). Follow these steps:

1. Select the picture.

2. Choose Format, Picture.

3. Choose the Reset button.

Adding Lines and Borders

Unless a border is part of your original composition, pictures arrive in your document with no lines around their edges. You easily can add lines or a box. Many line styles, widths, and colors are available. Pictures in text boxes are an exception to this rule—they are formatted with fill color, line color, and style selections that you make from the Drawing toolbar.

You can add lines and borders to a picture whether or not it is framed. When you select an unframed picture and choose Format, Borders and Shading, the Picture Borders dialog box appears. If your picture is framed, however, the Picture Borders and Shading dialog box appears.

The Picture Borders and Shading dialog box contains the Shading tab, which you can use only when a picture is framed. You can add shading to a frame, but the shading does not change the picture—it applies only to the frame around the picture. It is, therefore, of minimal use when you're working with pictures. On the Borders tab is the From Text option, which you can use only when text is framed. The From Text option sets the distance between the text and the border and does not apply to pictures. Refer to Chapter 24, "Framing and Moving Text and Graphics," to learn more about frames. Refer to Chapter 10, "Formatting Lines and Paragraphs," to learn about shading.

V

Publishing with Graphics

Tip

You quickly can display the Picture Borders and Shading dialog box by clicking a picture (or its border, if it's framed) with the right mouse button to display the shortcut menu, and then selecting the Borders and Shading command.

Adding Boxes around a Picture

A box is the same on all four sides of a picture, unless it is a shadowed box. This type of box adds a black drop shadow on both the right and bottom sides of the box.

To add a box around a picture, follow these steps:

1. Select the picture.

2. Choose Format, Borders and Shading. The Picture Borders and Shading dialog box appears (see fig. 23.10).

Fig. 23.10

You can add borders and lines of many styles and colors to your pictures.

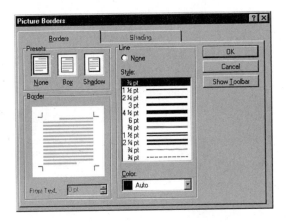

3. Select the Borders tab.

4. Select Box or Shadow from the Presets group (with a mouse, just click the appropriate icon). The Box option adds lines of the selected style and color to all four sides of the picture; the Shadow option adds a black drop shadow as well (see fig. 23.11).

5. From the Line group, select the line Style you want for the box.

6. From the Color list, select a color for the box.

7. Choose OK.

Adding Lines around a Picture

You can add lines to any or all sides of a selected picture. Use lines instead of a box when you want lines on only some sides of the picture. Use lines also when you want the sides of the picture to have different line styles.

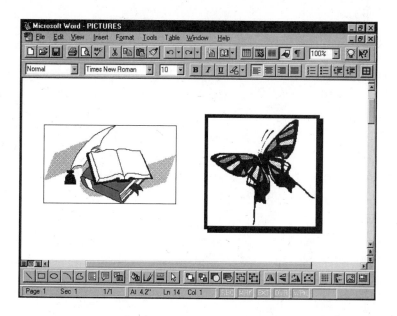

Fig. 23.11
Boxes and shadow
boxes add
definition to
pictures.

The easiest way to add lines to a picture is to select your line style and color and then click the sides of the sample picture where you want lines. The lines appear in the selected line style and color on each side where you clicked. If you want lines of different styles or colors on different sides, select the sides you want to alter, and then select the style and color you want for them. Any line style or color selection you make applies to a side while it is selected.

To add lines around a picture, follow these steps:

1. Select the picture.

2. Choose F_ormat, _Borders and Shading. Select the _Borders tab.

3. From the Line group, select the line St_yle you want for the selected lines or future lines.

4. From the _Color list, select the line color you want for the selected lines or future lines.

5. Select Bo_rder. Click the side of the sample picture where you want a line to appear. The side is selected: a line appears on that side in the selected style and color (see fig. 23.12). (Click the side a second time to remove the line.) Selected sides have black, triangular selection handles at each end. Press and hold down Shift to select multiple sides (or to deselect a selected side).

Tip

Select Bo_x from the Presets group to add lines quickly on all four sides in the selected line style and color. Then select and change the lines that you want to be different.

V

Publishing with Graphics

Fig. 23.12
Select the sides of
the picture where
you want lines to
appear. While the
sides are selected,
you can change
their line style and
color.

To use the keyboard, select Border and press any arrow key to cycle
through various combinations of lines.

6. Choose OK.

To remove a line or box from a picture, follow these steps:

1. Select the picture.

2. Choose Format, Borders and Shading. Select the Borders tab.

3. To remove either a box or all the lines, select None from the Presets
   group.

   Or, to remove a line, select Border and click the line you want to
   remove. Alternatively, select None in the Line group.

4. Choose OK.

Moving or Copying a Picture

▶ See "Framing
and Moving
Text and
Graphics,"
p. 727

▶ See "Moving
and Positioning
Frames," p. 738

▶ See "Wrapping
Text around a
Frame," p. 750

You can use either the mouse or keyboard commands to move or copy any
picture. But the way the picture behaves when you move or copy it depends
on what type of container holds the picture. If it is not in a container—that
is, if you simply inserted or copied the picture—it remains tightly linked to
the text. Moving the picture means relocating it in the text; you even see an
insertion point as you drag it to a new location. Moving or copying an inserted picture is the same as moving or copying text. If a picture is framed or
in a text box, however, and you're working in Page Layout view, you can drag
the picture freely around on the page, regardless of where text appears. For
more information on moving pictures in text boxes, refer to Chapter 25,
"Drawing with Word's Drawing Tools."

To move a picture, follow these steps:

1. Select the picture.

2. Choose <u>E</u>dit, Cu<u>t</u> (Ctrl+X or Shift+Delete). Move the insertion point to the place where you want to move the picture. Then choose <u>E</u>dit, <u>P</u>aste (Ctrl+V or Shift+Insert).

Or, drag the picture to its new location, as shown in figure 23.13.

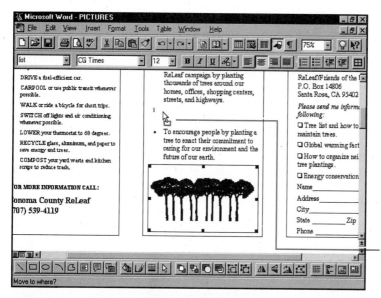

Fig. 23.13
The Move icon has a different appearance, depending on what type of picture you're moving.

Moving a framed picture displays a four-cornered arrow

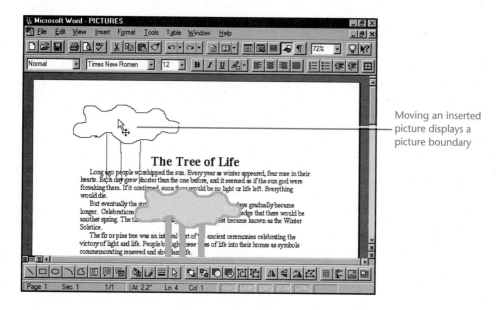

Moving an inserted picture displays a picture boundary

To copy a picture, follow these steps:

1. Select the picture.

2. Choose Edit, Copy (Ctrl+C or Ctrl+Insert). Move the insertion point where you want to copy the picture in your document. Then choose Edit, Paste (Ctrl+V or Shift+Insert).

   Or, press and hold down the Ctrl key while you drag the picture to its new location.

Displaying and Hiding Pictures

Pictures use up a lot of your computer's memory (and disk space). Thus, they can slow you down when you're working, especially if there are several pictures in your document. Hiding pictures is a good way to save time when you don't need to see them. You might display the pictures while you're inserting and formatting them. Then you can hide them while you work on the text in your document.

When hidden, pictures appear as placeholders—simple line borders in your document (see fig. 23.14). You can select and work with them just as though they were displayed.

Fig. 23.14

Hidden pictures appear as line borders (boxes) in your document.

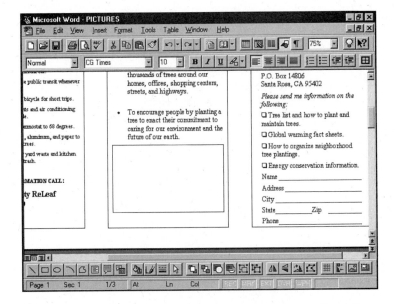

To hide pictures, follow these steps:

1. Choose <u>T</u>ools, <u>O</u>ptions and select the View tab.

2. In the Show group, select Picture Placehol<u>d</u>ers.

3. Choose OK.

To display pictures, follow these steps:

1. Choose <u>T</u>ools, <u>O</u>ptions and select the View tab.

2. In the Show group, deselect Picture Placehol<u>d</u>ers.

3. Choose OK.

Separate commands exist for hiding pictures and drawings you create with the Drawing toolbar.

To hide drawings you've made with the Drawing toolbar, choose <u>T</u>ools, <u>O</u>ptions and select the View tab. In the Show group, deselect Dra<u>w</u>ings.

Editing and Converting Pictures

To edit a picture using the program in which it was created, you must have on your computer the program used to create the picture, and the picture must have been inserted as an object. If not, when you attempt to edit the picture, Word places it in a Microsoft Word Picture window, where you can edit it. The editing capabilities of Microsoft Word Picture, however, may not give you all the capabilities of the program that originally created the picture.

▶ See "Embedding Data," p. 986

To edit picture objects, follow these steps:

1. Double-click the picture to edit.

   Or, select the picture and choose either <u>E</u>dit, <u>P</u>icture or <u>E</u>dit, Picture <u>O</u>bject. (The name of the command depends on the type of picture you've selected.)

   Either the program used to create the picture or Microsoft Word Picture appears on your screen.

2. Make your changes to the picture. In Microsoft Word Picture, you can replace the picture or enhance it by using tools on the Drawing toolbar.

3. Choose File, Update and then File, Exit in some programs, such as CorelDRAW!; in other programs, such as Excel, simply click your document.

   Or, choose the Close Picture button to close Microsoft Word Picture and return to your document.

Note that if you use Edit, Picture to edit a picture with Microsoft Word Picture, Word converts the picture to an object. The next time you select the same picture for editing, Edit, Picture Object appears instead.

Converting Picture Objects

You can convert a picture object from its original format to a different format. You might want to convert a picture created in CorelDRAW! to a picture that can be edited by Microsoft Word Picture. You might do this, for example, if you do not own CorelDRAW! but you want to use Microsoft Word Picture to add to the picture.

An alternative exists that preserves your picture in its original format. You simply specify that the picture be activated in a different format, but not converted.

To convert an inserted picture or picture object, follow these steps:

1. Select the picture you want to convert.

2. Choose Edit, Picture Object. (The name of the object varies, depending on the program used to create it.)

3. From the submenu, select Convert. The Convert dialog box appears; the current format of your picture is displayed as Current Type near the top of the dialog box (see fig. 23.15).

4. Select Convert To. Then select the format to which you want to convert your picture or picture object.

   Select Display as Icon if you want to display your converted picture as an icon.

5. Choose OK.

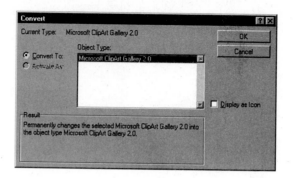

Fig. 23.15
You can convert pictures and picture objects into another format.

To activate a picture in a different format without converting, follow these steps:

1. Select the picture you want to activate in a different format.

2. Choose Edit, Picture Object.

3. From the submenu, select Convert.

4. Select Activate As. Then select the format in which you want to activate your picture or picture object.

5. Choose OK.

V

Publishing with Graphics

Chapter 24

Framing and Moving Text and Graphics

Word for Windows has many features that help make your pages look graphical—boxes, lines, columns, pictures, and much more. Frames, however, take your document a step beyond traditional word processing and into the world of page layout. Frames allow you to move objects freely on the page.

In Word for Windows, you can frame many types of objects, including text, tables, drawings, inserted pictures, WordArt logos, captions, charts, equations, and even blank space (in case you want to add noncomputer art to your document after you print it). You can frame objects singly or together. (For example, you can frame a picture with a caption.) You can add lines, borders, and shading to frames.

Using frames, you can accomplish the following:

- Position text, pictures, tables, or any object wherever you want it on the page

- Wrap text around text, pictures, tables, or any object

- Group text and other objects so that you can position them as a unit anywhere in your document and wrap text around them

- Leave a blank space—with or without a border—where you can paste in noncomputer graphics after you print your document

By positioning a framed object on the page, you free the object from its surrounding text. Frames are a critical tool in helping you use Word for Windows to design a pleasing, professional, and creative page layout.

In this chapter, you learn to do the following:

■ Frame pictures and other graphic objects

■ Insert text or graphics in a blank frame

■ Change the position of frames

Framing Text, Pictures, and Other Objects

To create a frame, select the object—or objects—that you want to frame and choose Insert, Frame or click a button. For quick framing, three of Word's toolbars—the Word for Windows 2.0, Forms, and Drawing toolbars—contain frame buttons. Several shortcut menus—the Picture, WordArt, Equation, and other object shortcut menus—contain framing commands. Alternatively, you can draw a frame and then insert text or a graphic inside it.

You can create a frame in any view. Page Layout and Print Preview are the only views, however, that accurately show where a frame is positioned in your document and how text wraps around the frame. If you create a frame in Normal view, Word for Windows displays a dialog box to suggest that you switch to Page Layout view.

Framing Text

Tip

You can choose Edit, Undo to remove a frame you've just inserted.

You can frame any amount of text—from one character to an entire page. You can frame text that's already in your document, or you can insert a blank frame and type text inside it (see the section "Inserting Text or Graphics in a Blank Frame" later in this chapter). When you first frame selected text, the frame is the same size as the text. If you change the size of the frame, the text wraps to accommodate the frame's new dimensions. Similarly, if you add text to a frame, the frame expands downward to accommodate the new text. If you frame only part of a paragraph, the framed text becomes a separate paragraph and moves outside the paragraph that contains it.

In Page Layout view, you can see your frame interact with the rest of the text on the page. You can see how frames appear in the Normal view in the section "Working in Different Views" later in this chapter.

To frame text, follow these steps:

1. Choose <u>V</u>iew, <u>P</u>age Layout or click the Page Layout View button to the left of the horizontal scroll bar.

2. Select the text you want to frame.

3. Choose <u>I</u>nsert, <u>F</u>rame or click the Insert Frame button on the Word for Windows 2.0, Drawing, or Forms toolbar. Selection handles and a shaded border appear around the edges of your framed text (see fig. 24.1).

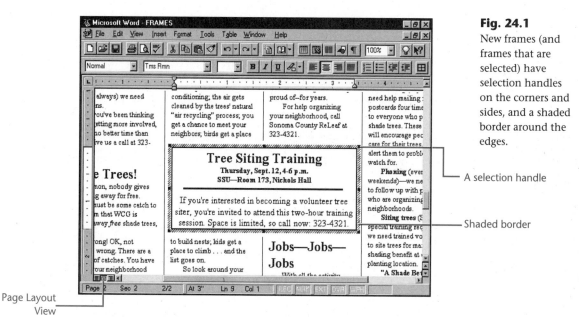

Fig. 24.1
New frames (and frames that are selected) have selection handles on the corners and sides, and a shaded border around the edges.

A selection handle

Shaded border

Page Layout View

Framed objects that are selected have eight selection handles on the corners and sides. Selection handles appear as small, black squares, which you can use to size your frame. (See the section "Sizing Frames" later in this chapter.)

If you are in the Normal view when you insert a frame, Word for Windows displays a dialog box suggesting that you switch to the Page Layout view. Choose <u>Y</u>es if you want to switch to Page Layout view.

Formatting Text within a Frame

When you frame text, it keeps the same text and paragraph formatting it had before you added the frame. You can change the formatting in any way you want by using Word's usual selection techniques and formatting commands. You can even use styles to format text within a frame, or include framing as part of a style. Sometimes framing text in a box makes the text look different enough that you *should* change its formatting. For example, big text in a small frame may look awkward; make the frame larger. Similarly, small text in a huge frame gets lost; make the text larger.

◄ See "Format-
ting Charac-
ters," p. 254

For variety, use text and paragraph formatting commands to change the appearance of text within a frame. Choose a different font, or add spacing between lines. Use bold or italic. Add borders or shading to framed text (see the section "Bordering and Shading Frames" later in this chapter). Align the text however you want inside the frame: no matter where the frame is positioned, the text remains aligned within the frame as you specify.

Watch out for indentations inside a frame; if you have a two-inch-wide frame, and the text inside the frame has one-inch left and right margin indents that you set before inserting the frame, you get a frame containing a vertical string of characters trying to fit within impossible specifications (see fig. 24.2). To fix this, reduce the indentations or widen the frame.

Fig. 24.2
When a frame contains paragraphs with indents that are too wide, select the text and reduce the indentations.

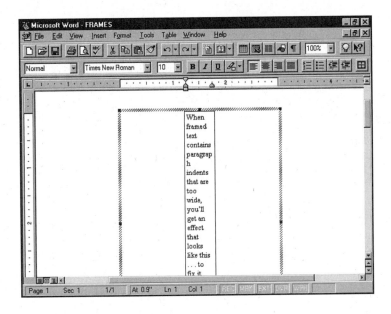

Framing Pictures and Other Graphic Objects

◄ See "Inserting
Pictures in
Frames and
Text Boxes,"
p. 710

If you frame an inserted, embedded, drawn, or copied picture or other graphic in your document (such as a Microsoft WordArt object or a piece of clip art), you can easily move the graphic wherever you want it in your document. You can frame a graphic that's already in your document, or you can insert a blank frame and then insert the graphic inside it (see the section "Inserting Text or Graphics in a Blank Frame" later in this chapter). When you frame an existing graphic, the frame is the size of the graphic; when you insert a graphic into a frame, the graphic conforms to the size of the frame. A selected unframed picture looks different from a selected framed picture (see fig. 24.3).

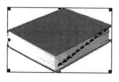

Selected picture

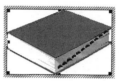

Selected framed picture

Fig. 24.3
A selected graphic has square handles on the corners and sides (left); once framed, a shaded border appears around the selected graphic (right).

To frame a picture or graphic, follow these steps:

1. Select the graphic by clicking it.

   You also can use the keyboard to position the insertion point next to the graphic, and then press Shift+arrow key to move the insertion point across the graphic. Just be sure you don't select the invisible end-of-paragraph marker, or you'll select not just the picture, but the entire paragraph containing the picture (the picture will appear reversed).

   A correctly selected figure has selection handles on all corners and sides, as shown on the left in figure 24.3.

2. Choose <u>I</u>nsert, <u>F</u>rame or click the Insert Frame button on the toolbar.

You can remove a frame from a graphic (see the upcoming section "Selecting and Removing Frames"). If you remove a frame, however, the graphic loses its position. To later reposition the graphic by choosing F<u>o</u>rmat, Fra<u>m</u>e, first frame the graphic.

Tip
If you want to position a graphic in the layer behind your text, insert it in a text box or picture container.

Framing Tables

A framed table can work as an illustration in a financial or business document, such as an annual report. Framing a table is like framing text: you select a row or the entire table and insert the frame. You cannot frame just a cell; if you select a cell and choose <u>I</u>nsert, <u>F</u>rame, you frame the entire row containing the selected cell. You also cannot frame a single column in a table; if you select a column and insert a frame, you frame the entire table.

To frame a row or a table, follow these steps:

1. Select the row you want to frame, or select the entire table.

◄ See "Formatting a Table," p. 535

V

Publishing with Graphics

To frame a row, select one cell or an entire row.

To frame a table, select one column or the entire table.

2. Choose <u>I</u>nsert, <u>F</u>rame, or click the Frame button on the toolbar.

Framing a table makes it a movable object on the page. In a report, for example, you may want to center a table containing pertinent data to give it prominence on the page. Or you may want the flexibility to move the table around to different locations on the page—to see what looks best. You can move a framed row to a different location on the page and make it a separate table.

Inserting a Blank Frame

Sometimes you want to insert a blank frame to leave a space for a photograph or artwork to be inserted during copying or offset printing. Or, you may want to insert a blank frame and then type text in it or insert a graphic into it. You can create a blank frame of any size.

To insert a blank frame, follow these steps:

1. Make sure that no text, table, or other object is selected.

2. Choose <u>I</u>nsert, <u>F</u>rame or click the Frame button on the toolbar. A crosshair appears on-screen, and a message in the status bar at the bottom of the screen reads Click and drag to insert a frame (see fig. 24.4).

Fig. 24.4

When you insert a blank frame, you draw it to size. Notice how the rulers in this example help ensure the frame is the same width as the column.

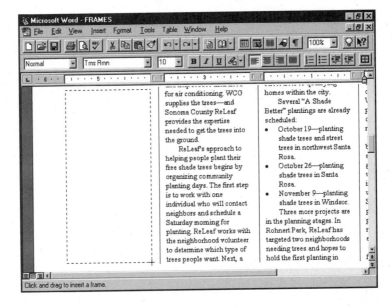

3. Click and hold the left mouse button where you want to start the frame, drag to where you want the frame to end, and release the button.

Like text, a blank frame is automatically formatted with a border. Use F̲ormat, B̲orders and Shading to change the frame's border (see "Bordering and Shading Frames" later in this chapter).

Inserting Text or Graphics in a Blank Frame

When you draw an empty frame, it appears with a flashing insertion point at the top-left corner. To include text in the frame, type the text. To include a graphic in the frame, choose I̲nsert, P̲icture or I̲nsert, O̲bject. Or copy a graphic from another application and paste it inside the frame.

◄ See "Inserting Pictures in Frames and Text Boxes," p. 710

Text wraps inside a frame just as it does in a Word document. When you type text in a frame, the frame stays the same width as you drew it, but gets taller as you continue typing. When you insert a graphic into a frame, the graphic becomes as wide as the frame, and the frame adjusts in height to the graphic.

You cannot draw a picture inside a frame to frame the picture. Instead, first draw the picture, and then select and frame it.

Framing Objects Together

To include multiple objects in a frame, simply select them all and choose I̲nsert, F̲rame or click the Frame button. The objects are framed as one, and you can move them as a unit on the page.

You can add text, a picture, or an object to an existing frame by positioning the insertion point inside the frame and typing the text, or by inserting the picture or object as usual. You can move the insertion point inside a frame with the keyboard (if the frame contains text or an object) by pressing the arrow keys. With the mouse, click the frame to select it, and then press the right- or down-arrow key to position the insertion point at the bottom right of the frame. Press Enter to add a new line inside the frame.

Including a Caption in a Frame

There are two ways to include a caption in a frame:

- Create the object and caption separately and frame them together.

- Frame the object and then add a caption.

You can use either technique with captions you type yourself or with Word's automatic captions.

► See "Creating Captions," p. 923

To frame an object and caption together, select them both and choose Insert, Frame or click the Frame button. To add a typed caption to a framed object, position the insertion point inside the frame and type the text (see the previous section "Framing Objects Together"). To add an automatic caption to a framed object, select the frame and choose Insert, Caption.

Working in Different Views

◄ See " Controlling Your Document's Appearance On-Screen," p. 123

In Page Layout view, you can see where framed objects are positioned and how the text wraps around them (see fig. 24.5). In any view besides Page Layout, a framed object or text appears at the left margin with one or more small black squares at the left margin (see fig. 24.6). You usually work with frames in Page Layout view.

Fig. 24.5
In Page Layout view, a framed object appears in place in your document.

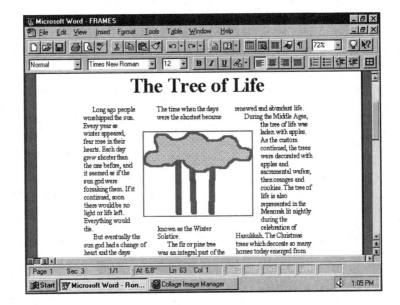

You can select a framed object in any view, and you can format it in any view by choosing Format, Frame (options include sizing the framed object, positioning it, and wrapping text around it). You can even insert a frame in Normal view, although Word for Windows advises you to switch to Page Layout view. In Normal and Outline views, you see the framed object aligned to the left margin, not positioned. Unlike Page Layout view, however, you cannot move the object by dragging it with the mouse.

Working in Normal view is faster—anything graphical takes longer to redraw on your computer screen in Word for Windows or any other program. If you're working very fast and you're on a deadline, do your layout in Page Layout view and switch to Normal view for typing.

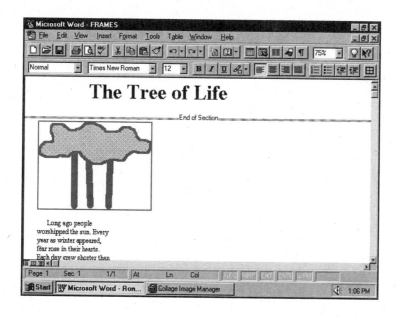

Fig. 24.6
In Normal view, a framed object appears with black squares in the left margin when paragraph marks are displayed.

To switch to Page Layout view, choose <u>V</u>iew, <u>P</u>age Layout or click the Page Layout View button to the left of the horizontal scroll bar.

Troubleshooting

When I frame multiple lines with paragraph end marks, the frame extends from margin to margin.

Size the frame using techniques described in the section "Sizing Frames" later in this chapter.

I tried to put a drop cap in my frame, but couldn't.

A drop cap is already framed, and you can't create a frame within another frame. You can drag an existing frame inside another existing frame, and you can select an existing frame along with unframed text and frame the two together. However, neither of these techniques will cause text in the larger frame to wrap around the smaller frame. Use some other technique to emphasize your text, such as a raised initial cap. See Chapter 38, "Desktop Publishing," for ideas.

Selecting and Removing Frames

In most Windows programs, as in many other programs, you must select an object before you can do something to it so that the program knows where to apply your actions. In Word for Windows, before you can move, border, size, position, or wrap text around a framed object, you first must select it.

Removing a frame is not the same as removing the framed text or object—the text or object remains, whereas the frame and its positioning go away. To remove a frame you must select the frame and choose a command—pressing the Delete key removes the frame and its contents.

Selecting a Framed Object

You can select a framed object using the mouse or the keyboard. Usually, the easiest way is to use the mouse. Again, make sure that you are in Page Layout view, because you cannot see frames in Normal view. (However, even in Normal view you can select framed text or objects and choose Format, Frame to format or remove the frame.)

If you move the mouse pointer across the selected frame, the arrow or insertion point changes. On top of the selection handles, the insertion point turns into a two-headed arrow (used to size the frame); on top of the border surrounding the frame, it turns into a four-headed arrow (used to move the frame). See the section "Moving and Positioning Frames" later in this chapter for details.

Note that when you see a shaded border around framed text or a framed object, the frame may not be selected. The shaded border, which appears only in Page Layout view, simply indicates that the text or object is framed and that the insertion point is inside the frame. Only when you see square selection handles on each corner and side of a shaded frame is the frame selected (see fig. 24.7).

Fig. 24.7
A graphic or text might be selected even if the frame is not (left); you see selection handles inside the shaded frame border when a frame is selected (right).

Picture selected

Frame selected

When you see only the frame's shaded border, as in the left side of figure 24.7, you can choose Format Frame to format the frame. If text is selected inside the frame, you can add borders or shading to the frame. However, if an object is selected inside the frame, as in the right side of figure 24.7, borders and shading apply to the object—not the frame.

To select a frame with a mouse, follow these steps:

1. Choose <u>V</u>iew, <u>P</u>age Layout if you are in any view besides Page Layout.

2. Click the framed text or object to display the shaded frame border, and if necessary, click the shaded border to select the frame. (When a frame contains text or only a single object, then selecting the text or object also selects the frame. When a frame contains multiple objects, or text and an object, selecting an object does not select the frame.)

   You can also position the mouse pointer over the edge of the framed object until it turns into a four-cornered arrow. Then click the mouse button to select the frame.

   Or, you can click the framed text or object to display the shaded frame border, and then choose F<u>o</u>rmat, Fra<u>me</u>. Make your selections and choose OK.

To select a frame with the keyboard, follow these steps:

1. Position the insertion point inside the frame.

2. Choose F<u>o</u>rmat, Fra<u>me</u>.

3. Make your frame formatting choices, and then choose OK.

Note that you can select a framed object by using Shift+an arrow key, but that if the object appears reversed, then it is the paragraph that is selected, not the frame. You cannot format the frame using this selection technique.

Removing Frames versus Deleting Frames

Removing a frame does not remove its contents; deleting a frame does delete its contents. You can remove a frame from a paragraph or a table, for example, and even though the frame is gone, the paragraph or the table is still there.

Removing a frame does remove frame formatting. If text is wrapped around the framed paragraph, it doesn't wrap after you remove the frame. If the framed table was positioned in the center of the page, it moves back to where it was before you inserted the frame.

Tip

If you want to remove a frame *and* the framed object, select the frame and press Delete.

V

Publishing with Graphics

To remove a frame, follow these steps:

1. Select the framed object, or select the blank frame.

For text, position the insertion point inside the framed text.

2. Choose Format, Frame.

3. Select Remove Frame.

A frame is a paragraph-level formatting command, and like a paragraph, the paragraph mark at the end of a frame stores the information defining the frame. If you delete the paragraph mark, you delete the frame (but not the paragraph). If the framed text has been moved from its original position, the text loses its position and moves back to where you inserted it. If two paragraphs are in a frame, and you delete the paragraph mark for the second paragraph, the second paragraph moves outside of the frame and the first stays in.

Moving and Positioning Frames

◀ See "Moving, Copying, and Linking Text or Graphics," p. 160

Tip

Use the View buttons on the Word for Windows 2.0 toolbar to help you position objects. The Zoom Page Width button shows the full width of a page and is helpful when you're moving a framed object.

A frame separates a block of text or an object from the text on a page so that you can move it independently. Word for Windows by default anchors a framed object to the paragraph where you created it, not to the page. (You can easily override this default; see "Anchoring a Frame," later in this chapter.) Every framed object also retains its connection to its roots—if you remove the frame, the object moves back to the beginning of the paragraph to which it's anchored.

You can move or position a framed object or text in two ways: you can select and drag it with the mouse, or you can select the text or object, choose Format, Frame, and specify its precise position on the page.

If a framed object or text is linked to another program, and you move part of it (for example, the caption) away from its original position, you break the link for the part of the text you moved. Similarly, if you designate a framed object as a bookmark, and you move part of the bookmark, then you remove the part you moved from the bookmark. If you frame and move the entire bookmark, however, Word for Windows remembers the bookmark and still finds it, even in its new position.

> **Note**
>
> Text boxes and picture containers, which you can create using the Drawing toolbar, are similar to frames. You can place text or graphics inside them, add borders (and even shading), and move them freely on the page. You even can place them in the layer behind your text. However, you cannot wrap text around them. Choose the container—frame, text box, or picture container—that works best for you.

◀ See "Marking Locations with Bookmarks," p. 157

▶ See "Framing Objects to Wrap Text around Them," p. 798

Moving a Frame with a Mouse

Using a mouse is probably the easiest way to move a framed object. It isn't as precise, however, as positioning the frame using the Frame dialog box (discussed in the following sections on positioning frames).

By default, framed objects move with their surrounding text. If you add or delete text near the framed object, causing the text to move up or down on the page (or even to the next page), the object stays with its related text. If you want a framed object linked to its position on the page, regardless of where the surrounding text moves, choose Format, Frame and deselect or clear Move with Text.

To move a framed object with the mouse, follow these steps:

Tip
If you don't like where you've moved a frame, choose Edit, Undo to return it to its original position.

V

Publishing with Graphics

1. In Page Layout view, select the framed object or text you want to move.

2. Move the mouse pointer over the frame until it turns into a four-headed arrow (see fig. 24.8).

Selected frame

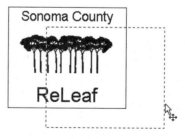

Frame being moved

Fig. 24.8
The easiest way to move a frame is to select it (left) and then drag it to its new position (right).

3. Hold down the left mouse button, drag the framed object to its new location, and release the mouse button. The frame appears as a dotted line as you move it.

You can use Word for Windows' automatic scrolling feature to move a framed object from one page to another. In any view, select the object you want to move, drag it to the top of the screen (if you want to move it to the preceding page) or to the bottom of the screen (if you want to move it to the next page). By "pushing" the object into the top or bottom of your screen, you cause the text to scroll. If you continue holding the mouse button, the pages continue to scroll, and the frame continues to move. Release the mouse button when you get to the page where you want to move your framed object. If the status bar is displayed, you can see what page you're on when you release the mouse button.

Moving and Copying Frames

You can move and copy frames by choosing Edit, Cut; Edit, Copy; or Edit, Paste; or by using the Cut, Copy, and Paste buttons on the Standard toolbar. To move a frame, select and cut it, position the insertion point where you want to move it, and paste it. To copy a frame, select and copy it, then position the insertion point where you want to copy it, and paste. You can also copy a frame by holding down the Ctrl key while you drag the frame with a mouse.

Frames have a shortcut menu for quick moving and copying. Click the frame with the right mouse button to display the shortcut menu, then select the command you want (see fig. 24.9). The contents of the shortcut menu vary depending on where you click and what the frame contains. For example, if you click a framed picture with the left mouse button to select it, then click the frame with the right mouse button to display the shortcut menu, the shortcut menu displays commands for both editing the picture and formatting the frame.

Fig. 24.9
Click the frame with the right mouse button to display the shortcut menu.

Positioning a Frame Horizontally

Positioning a frame with a command is different from dragging it with a mouse. Dragging is visual, but it's not precise. When you position a frame using a command, you specify exactly where it appears on the page.

When you position a frame horizontally, you define its exact position relative to the left, center, or right of the margin, column, or page. If you're working with facing pages, you can position the frame relative to the inside or outside of the margin, column, or page.

You can position a frame in any of the following ways:

- At the left margin, for example, to have the frame appear flush against the left text margin.

- At the outside edge of the page in a facing page layout to have the frame appear in the outside margin (if the frame is wider than the margin, then text wraps around it; if the margin is wider than the frame, then the frame is completely within the margin).

- At the center of the page in a two-column layout to have text in both columns wrap around the frame.

- To the left or right of a column, to place the frame flush with the text on either side of the column (see fig. 24.10).

Fig. 24.10
Positioned left relative to the page (top); positioned center relative to the margins (top right); positioned right relative to the page (bottom).

Alternatively, you can position a frame some specific distance relative to the margin, page, or column. For example, you may want a frame to appear one-quarter inch away from the left edge of the page, because most printers don't print to the edge of a sheet of paper. If you position a frame with a specific distance, the distance is measured from the left edge of the margin, page, or column. To position a frame some specific distance from the right edge, add the distance to the width of the frame and subtract it from the width of the page. For example, to position a one-inch frame one-quarter inch from the right edge of an 8 1/2-inch page, set its position at 7.25".

To position a frame horizontally, follow these steps:

1. In Page Layout view, select the framed object.

2. Choose Format, Frame or choose Format Frame from the shortcut menu. The Frame dialog box appears (see fig. 24.11).

Fig. 24.11

Use the Frame dialog box to position a frame horizontally or vertically.

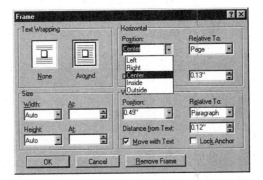

3. In the Horizontal Position box, select the horizontal position for your frame:

Type or Select	To Position the Frame
A measured distance	At a measured distance from the left of the margin, page, or column
Left	At the left side of the margin, page, or column
Right	At the right side of the margin, page, or column
Center	Centered between the left and right margins, page edges, or column edges
Inside	At the inside edge of the margin, page, or column
Outside	At the outside edge of the margin, page, or column

4. In the Relative To box, select the boundary you want your frame positioned relative to.

Select	To Position the Frame Relative To
Margin	The left or right margin
Page	The left or right edge of the page
Column	The left or right edge of the current column

5. In the Distance from Text box, type the amount of space you want between the frame and the text on the left and right sides of the frame, or click the up or down arrows to increase or decrease the distance.

6. Choose OK.

Positioning a Frame Vertically

Positioning a frame vertically anchors it somewhere between the top and bottom of the page. You can position the frame at the top, bottom, center, or some absolute distance relative to the margin, page, or paragraph.

You can center a frame between the top and bottom edge of the page, for example, or between the top and bottom margin. You can position the frame flush against the top or bottom margin. Or you can position the frame some specific distance from the top margin or edge of the page. Alternatively, you can position a frame at the top, bottom, or center of the paragraph to which the frame is anchored. Or you can position a frame some specific distance from a paragraph—a negative number places the frame before the paragraph, whereas a positive number places the frame after the paragraph (see fig. 24.12).

Unless you deselect the Move with Text option, a frame moves with the paragraph it's anchored to. If the paragraph moves to the next page, so does the frame—but it remains positioned in the same relative place. If you center a frame vertically between the top and bottom margins, for example, then add so much text before the frame that the paragraph it's anchored to moves to the top of the next page, the frame also moves to the next page, but it is still centered on the page.

Fig. 24.12

A frame can be centered vertically between the margins (top left); two-and-one-half inches relative to the top margin (top right); and relative to the bottom margin (bottom).

To position a frame vertically on the page, follow these steps:

1. In Page Layout view, select the frame.

2. Choose F<u>o</u>rmat, Fra<u>m</u>e or choose Format Frame from the shortcut menu. The Frame dialog box appears.

3. In the Vertical Position box, select or type the vertical position for your frame.

Type or Select	To Position the Frame
A distance in inches	At a measured distance from the top of the margin, page, or paragraph
Top	At the top margin, top of the page, or top edge of the paragraph
Bottom	At the bottom margin, bottom of the page, or bottom edge of the paragraph
Center	Centered between the top and bottom margins or page edges, or centered between the top and bottom of the paragraph

4. In the Relative To box, select the boundary you want the frame positioned relative to.

Select	To Position the Frame Relative To
Margin	The top or bottom margin
Page	The top or bottom edge of the page
Paragraph	The top or bottom of the current paragraph

5. In the Distance from Text box, type the amount of space you want between the frame and the text above or below the frame. Or click the up or down arrows to increase or decrease the distance.

6. If you don't want the frame to move with its surrounding text, deselect the Move with Text option so that no check mark appears in the option box.

   With this option unselected, the frame stays anchored to its spot on the page, no matter how the text moves. If you select this option, a frame moves with its surrounding text.

7. Choose OK.

Positioning a Frame in a Margin

Because you can move or position a frame independently of the text on the page, you can move it into the margin, or partially into the margin with text wrapping around it. You frame a picture, for example, and move it to the top left of the first page of a newsletter to give the masthead a graphic effect

V

Publishing with Graphics

(see fig. 24.13). Or you can use a style to format tips in a training document as italicized and positioned in the inside margins. Perhaps your document's style is to include headings in the left margin of each page. Positioning text in a margin can give it emphasis in your document; positioning a graphic in a margin can make your page more interesting. Be creative!

Fig. 24.13

You can frame text or graphics for positioning in margins.

One use for frames in margins is to create *sideheads*—subheadings that appear not above text, but outside of text in the margin. If you create sideheads, be sure to select the <u>M</u>ove with Text option in the Frame dialog box so that sideheads stay with the paragraphs they're attached to.

When you position a frame in a margin, remember your printer's limitations. Most laser printers cannot print within one-quarter of an inch from the paper's edges.

Anchoring a Frame

A frame is always anchored to a paragraph. Initially, it is anchored to the paragraph where you created it. As you move a frame, the anchor moves to the nearest paragraph. A frame always appears on the same page as the paragraph to which it's anchored.

You can move a frame's anchor to another paragraph without moving the frame itself. If you then lock the anchor, you can be sure the frame remains in the same position on the page, but also always prints on the same page as the paragraph. For example, you may position a frame at the center of a page and anchor it to a paragraph; if the paragraph moves to the next page, the frame does too, but it still prints in the center of the page. Similarly, if a frame is too big to fit on a page with the paragraph it's anchored to, both the frame and the paragraph move to the next page.

You can display anchors to move them.

To display anchors, follow these steps:

1. In Page Layout view, choose Tools, Options and select the View tab.

2. In the Show group, select Object Anchors. Anchors appear as anchor icons in the left margin.

To move an anchor, follow these steps:

1. Display the anchors in Page Layout view, and select the framed, anchored object.

2. Drag the anchor icon to a new paragraph.

To lock an anchor to a paragraph, follow these steps:

1. Make sure the frame is positioned inside the paragraph where you want it.

2. Choose Format, Frame.

3. Select Lock Anchor.

If you want a frame to stay on a specific page and not move with the paragraph it's anchored to, in the Frame dialog box deselect Move with Text and Lock Anchor in the Frame dialog box.

Sizing Frames

When you first insert a frame around text or an object, the frame is selected. Square black selection handles appear on each corner and side of a selected frame—eight in all—and a shaded border appears around the outside of the frame (only in Page Layout view). The frame is the same size as the text or object.

You can size a frame using the mouse or keyboard. Using a mouse, drag one of the handles to size the frame. With the keyboard, choose Format, Frame to size a frame. You can size a frame proportionally so that it becomes larger or smaller but keeps its shape, or nonproportionally so that it stretches into a new shape.

When you size a frame that contains only a graphic, you size the graphic. When you size a frame that contains only text, the text rewraps, but the frame remains large enough to hold the text. (If you make the frame too large for the text, the frame will include blank space at the end of the text.)

When you use a mouse to size a frame that contains multiple objects, you can make the frame larger or smaller than the objects it contains (making the frame smaller crops the frame's contents). You also can make a frame larger or smaller than the object or objects it contains by sizing it using Format, Frame rather than the mouse—use this technique when you want to make a frame larger than the single object it contains.

You can select a frame around a graphic object rather than the graphic itself only when the frame is larger than the graphic. The frame might be larger than the graphic if your graphic is framed together with text (such as a caption) or if you choose Format, Frame to specify for the frame an exact measurement that is larger than the graphic.

Sizing Frames with a Mouse

Using a mouse to size a frame is quick, and it gives you visual control over the frame's appearance (as well as its position). If only a single object is in the frame, the object adjusts to fit your frame's new size. If text or multiple objects are in the frame, you can size the frame so that it is smaller or larger than its contents.

When you size a framed picture with the mouse, you really are sizing the picture—the frame adjusts to fit. A picture remains proportional when you size it by dragging corner handles, but it changes proportions (distorting the picture) if you drag side handles. If you hold Shift while you size a picture—framed or not—you crop the picture (cut away part of it) rather than size it.

When you size framed text, you size the frame, not the text. You can keep a frame proportional when you size it with a mouse by holding Shift while you drag a corner handle.

To size a frame using a mouse, follow these steps:

1. In Page Layout view, select the frame so that the black selection handles appear on all four sides and corners, and the shaded frame border appears.

2. Move the mouse pointer over one of the selection handles so that it turns into a two-headed arrow. This arrow is the sizing arrow (see fig. 24.14).

Sizing arrow

Fig. 24.14
Use the two-
headed sizing
arrow to size the
frame.

3. Click and hold the left mouse button, then drag the sizing arrow to reshape the frame. A dotted-line box shows you the frame's new shape as you resize the frame. The sizing arrow becomes a crosshair.

   If you are sizing a framed picture, drag a corner handle to keep the picture proportional. If you are sizing framed text, hold Shift as you drag a corner handle to keep the frame proportional. Do not hold Shift as you drag the corner handle on a picture unless you want to crop the picture.

4. Release the mouse button when the frame is the size you want.

Caution

If you resize a frame containing text, you can make the frame smaller than the text, thus hiding some text. This happens because resizing the frame sets it to an exact size, rather than auto size. To fix this, choose Auto for the frame's Width or Height in the Frame dialog box.

Sizing Frames with the Keyboard

By choosing Format, Frame to size a frame, you can specify the frame's precise dimensions.

When you frame an existing object or text, the frame is automatically the same size as what it contains. (When you draw a frame, it has exact dimensions.) But by using a keyboard command, you can size a frame to have exact dimensions, or to have a minimum height (useful for text frames).

If you make a frame an exact size rather than the auto size, the frame is likely to be a different size than its contents. If the frame is larger than its contents, you insert a blank space below the contents. If the frame is smaller than the contents, you hide, or crop, part of the contents. The text or graphic itself does not change size. (If you want to change the size of a graphic, use the mouse technique described in the preceding section to drag the selection handles, or choose Format, Picture.)

Tip
You may want to size a frame larger than the object it contains, to add another object or more text inside the frame.

V

Publishing with Graphics

To size a frame with the keyboard command, follow these steps:

1. Select the framed text or object. The square, black selection handles and the shaded frame border appear.

2. Choose Format, Frame. The Frame dialog box appears.

3. Select Width and Height options in the Size group.

Select	To Size a Frame This Way
Auto	Sizes the frame so that it is the same size as the framed object
At Least (Height only)	Makes the frame at least as tall as you specify, but always tall enough to include the entire text or graphic
Exactly	Makes the frame exactly the size you specify

4. If you select Exactly for your Width, specify the exact width of your frame in the At box. Type the width, or click the up or down arrow to increase or decrease the width.

5. If you select At Least or Exactly for your Height, specify the minimum or exact height of your frame in the At box. Type the height, or click the up or down arrow to increase or decrease the width.

Wrapping Text around a Frame

If a frame is smaller than the page or column it's in, you may want to wrap text around it. By default, when you first insert a frame, the surrounding text wraps around the frame. If text does not wrap around a frame, then the text stops above and continues below the frame, with no text to either side of the frame.

Text wraps around a frame no matter how many columns of text are on a page (see fig. 24.15). For text to wrap, however, at least one inch of text must be on the left or right of the frame. You can specify how much distance there is between the frame and the text that wraps around it.

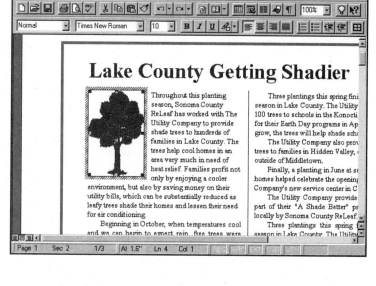

Fig. 24.15
By default, text
wraps around a
frame.

To wrap text around a framed object and specify the distance between the frame and text, follow these steps:

1. In Page Layout view, select the frame.

2. Choose F**o**rmat, Fra**m**e. The Frame dialog box appears.

3. In the Text Wrapping group (top left), select Aro**u**nd (see fig. 24.16).

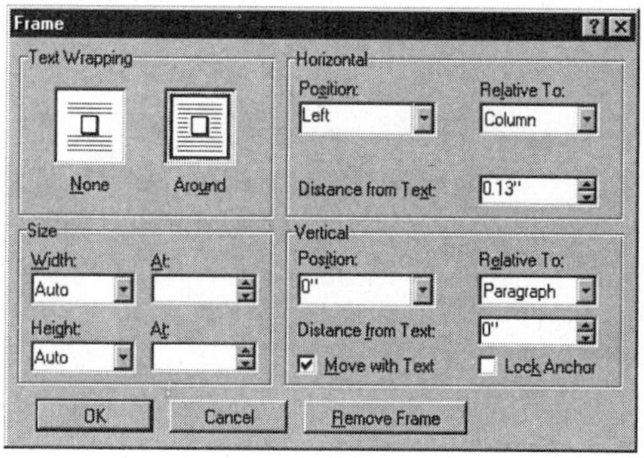

Fig. 24.16
Select Aro**u**nd to
have text wrap
around the frame.

4. From the Horizontal group (top right), select Distance from Te**x**t. Type, in decimal numbers, the distance you want between the frame and the text to its left and right; or click the up or down arrows to increase or decrease the distance.

5. From the Vertical group (bottom right) select Distance from Text. Type, in decimal numbers, the distance you want between the frame and the text above and below; or click the up or down arrows to increase or decrease the distance.

6. Choose OK.

Tip

If you specify a wide Distance from Text, you may create a space around the frame that is too narrow for text. You need at least an inch of space around a frame for text to wrap around it.

The Distance from Text options usually are measured in decimal inches. If you want to use some other measurement system, however, type the distance measurements followed by the appropriate abbreviation (pt for points, pi for picas, or cm for centimeters). You can change your measurement system by choosing Tools, Options and selecting the General tab. Then in the Measurement Units list, select inches, centimeters, points, or picas.

If later you don't want text to wrap around the frame, select the frame and choose Format, Frame. Select None from the Text Wrapping group. Deleting the frame also causes text to no longer wrap around the object.

Bordering and Shading Frames

◀ See "Shading and Bordering Paragraphs," p. 323

◀ See "Adding Lines and Borders," p. 717

Word automatically borders text that you frame, but not pictures. However, you can easily add borders and shading to frames.

When you add borders and shading to framed text, they apply to the frame, not the text. The appearance is the same as unframed text: borders appear around the outside edge or edges of the text and between paragraphs, as you specify, and shading appears behind the text. If you remove the frame, the borders and shading disappear.

Framed pictures can act a little differently, depending on what's inside the frame. If you border a single picture, the border applies to the picture, not the frame. However, if the frame is larger than the picture, then you can border the picture and frame separately. If the frame is larger than the graphic, you see both borders (see fig. 24.17).

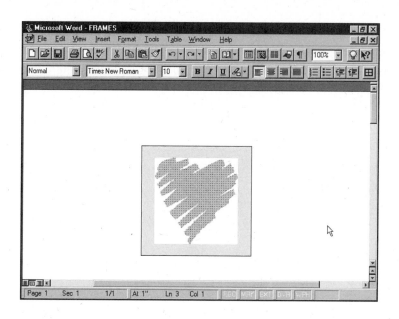

Fig. 24.17
This bordered and shaded frame is larger than the bordered picture inside it, creating a double border.

To create the effect shown in figure 24.18, select and center the picture inside its frame. Use paragraph alignment to center it horizontally, and blank lines above and below to center it vertically. Add a box around the picture, and add a box and shading to the frame.

To add borders or shading to frames, follow these steps:

1. In Page Layout view, select the frame you want to border or shade.

2. Choose Format, Borders and Shading. The Borders and Shading dialog box appears.

3. Select the Borders tab and select the borders you want around the edges of the frame. For a box, select Box or Shadow from the Presets group. Or select the sides you want bordered from the Border group. From the Line group, select a line Style and Color.

4. Select the Shading tab and select the shading you want within the frame. In the Custom group, select a Shading pattern, and from the Foreground and Background lists select the colors you want applied to the pattern.

5. Choose OK.

For quick bordering, display the Borders toolbar shown in figure 24.18. To display the toolbar, click the Borders button on the Formatting toolbar, or choose View, Toolbars and select Borders. To use the Borders toolbar, select the frame you want bordered. Choose a line style from the lines list, a border style from among the border buttons, and a pattern from the patterns list. For color, you must choose Format, Borders and Shading.

Fig. 24.18

The Borders toolbar lets you quickly border selected pictures, text, or frames.

You can quickly border a frame using a shortcut menu. Click a selected frame with the right mouse button, then select Borders and Shading. ❖

Chapter 25

Drawing with Word's Drawing Tools

Word 95 makes it easier than ever to include drawings in your documents. A drawing can be as simple as a circle, or as complex as a painting on a canvas. With the Drawing toolbar, you can create a drawing without leaving your document—you draw right on the page.

Although the Drawing toolbar includes simple tools for drawing, filling, and coloring lines and shapes, these simple tools are powerful enough that they may be all you ever need for illustrating your pages with graphics.

You will find the Drawing toolbar useful in some of the following ways:

- Illustrating concepts better explained with pictures than with words alone

- Making newsletters, brochures, and flyers more interesting with graphics

- Adding emphasis to important points in your document with shapes and colors

- Highlighting portions of imported pictures with callouts

- Nesting blocks of text within a document

What You Need to Know about Drawing

When you create a drawing by using buttons from the Drawing toolbar, you work directly on a page in your document in Page Layout view. The objects you create are location-independent—you can move them anywhere on the page (or even onto another page) by simply dragging them.

When you first draw objects, those objects appear on top of any text on the page. Your document, however, exists in three layers: the text layer, the layer above the text, and the layer below the text. You can move drawn objects, or the entire drawing, between these layers. Within your drawing, you can move objects in front of or behind each other.

Although you draw your lines and shapes one at a time, you can group them into a whole drawing. That way, you don't have to worry about keeping track of each piece of a drawing, and you can work with the drawing as a whole, moving or resizing it as a single piece. You can ungroup the pieces of your drawing whenever you want.

A drawing can include more than objects you draw with tools from the toolbar. You can insert a graphic you've created in a different program into a drawing, and you can include text in your drawing.

You can work on your document without displaying drawing objects. To hide drawing objects, choose Tools, Options and select the View tab; then in the Show group, clear the Drawings check box. To display the drawing objects, select the Drawings check box.

Displaying and Understanding the Drawing Toolbar

Tip
You must be in Page Layout view to draw.

To use Word's drawing tools, you must display the Drawing toolbar. Each button on the Drawing toolbar has a specific purpose: some tools draw lines or shapes; some tools allow you to add color or change the appearance of a line or shape; some tools help you position the objects you draw where you want them; some tools insert special objects on your page.

Displaying the Drawing Toolbar

The Drawing toolbar is one of many predefined toolbars available with Word for Windows (see fig. 25.1). Unlike other toolbars, it appears at the bottom of your screen (unless you moved it the last time you used it).

◀ See "Using the Toolbars," p. 53

You can display the Drawing toolbar by choosing <u>V</u>iew, <u>T</u>oolbars and selecting Drawing from the <u>T</u>oolbars list. Or, you can click the Drawing button on the Standard toolbar. Alternatively, you can click with the right mouse button on the gray area in any toolbar and select Drawing from the drop-down list of toolbars that appears, or you can click the Drawing button on the Standard toolbar.

Fig. 25.1
The Drawing toolbar gives you tools for drawing directly onto the page.

Understanding the Drawing Tools

Each button on the Drawing toolbar performs a specific function. Browse through the buttons and their descriptions in table 25.1 to get an idea of what you can do with the Drawing toolbar; then refer to later sections in this chapter to learn how to use each tool.

Table 25.1   Drawing Buttons

Drawing Button		Function
	Lines	Draws straight lines. Lines are vertical, horizontal, or at a 30-, 45-, or 60-degree angle if you hold Shift as you draw.
	Rectangle	Draws rectangles, or squares when you hold Shift as you draw.
	Ellipse	Draws ellipses or circles when you hold Shift as you draw.
	Arc	Draws an elliptical arc or a circular arc when you hold Shift as you draw.
	Freeform	Draws a curving freeform, straight line-segment polygon, or composite shape. Line segments are vertical, horizontal, or at a 30-, 45-, or 60-degree angle if you hold Shift as you draw.
	Text Box	Draws a text box into which you can type text or insert a picture created in another program.

(continues)

V

Publishing with Graphics

Table 25.1 Continued

Drawing Button	Function
Callout	Inserts a callout.
Format Callout	Formats a callout.
Fill Color	Fills a selected shape with color, or sets the default fill color if no shape is selected.
Line Color	Colors a selected line (or the line around a selected shape), or sets the default line color if no line is selected.
Line Style	Changes the style of a selected line (width, pattern, arrowheads), or sets the default line style if no line is selected.
Select Drawing Objects	Draws a selection box around objects in the drawing.
Bring to Front	Brings a selected drawing object in front of other drawing objects.
Send to Back	Sends a selected drawing object behind other drawing objects.
Bring in Front of Text	Brings selected drawing objects in front of the text layer.
Send Behind Text	Sends selected drawing objects behind the text layer.
Group	Groups together selected drawing objects.
Ungroup	Ungroups a selected group of drawing objects.
Flip Horizontal	Flips selected drawing object(s) left to right.
Flip Vertical	Flips selected drawing object(s) top to bottom.
Rotate Right	Rotates selected drawing object(s) 90 degrees to the right.
Reshape	Reshapes a freeform or polygon line by letting you drag points along the line.
Snap to Grid	Establishes an invisible drawing grid.

Drawing Button	Function
Align Drawing Objects	Aligns a selected object to the page or selected objects to each other.
Create Picture	Inserts a picture container (same as choosing Insert, Object, Microsoft Word Picture).
Insert Frame	Frames selected drawing object, or inserts empty frame.

> **Note**
>
> If you insert or draw invisible objects (such as empty picture frames, or shapes with no fill or line), or if you lose objects that become layered behind other objects, use the Select Drawing Objects tool to draw a section box around the area where you've lost the object. All objects inside the selection box will be selected, and you can see their square selection handles, even if they're invisible or behind another object.

Drawing and Changing Shapes and Lines

Drawing in Word is like working on paper: you create your image line by line and shape by shape. The objects you draw appear directly on the page where you're working. Unlike paper, however, you can move the objects you draw anywhere on the page—even underneath the text.

Basic Procedure for Drawing and Changing Objects

The general process for creating a drawing is to select the colors and line styles you want to use, click the drawing button to select the drawing tool you want to use, and use the drawing tool to draw an object on the page.

There are two ways to select colors and line styles:

- The easiest way is to display the Drawing toolbar and make selections from the color and line style palettes.

- Another way is to display the Drawing dialog box by choosing Format, Drawing Object.

Any time you select colors and line styles, these selections become your new "defaults." Even changing a selected object changes the color and line style defaults.

When you click a drawing button and then move the pointer onto the page, the arrow turns into a crosshair (it looks like a +, as shown on the lower right in fig. 25.2). You draw an object by holding down the left mouse button as you drag the crosshair. You can drag the crosshair in any direction to draw. When you release the mouse button, the object is completed. (The Freeform button works slightly differently; you must click once on the starting point or double-click anywhere to complete a freeform shape.)

Fig. 25.2

Drag the crosshair (left) to draw. A newly drawn object has selection handles on its sides and corners (right).

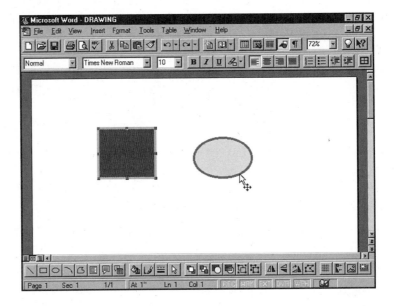

When you draw any object, it appears in the selected default fill color and line style. The object you draw appears in the layer above the text, and it appears on top of any other objects you've drawn.

Immediately after you draw your object, and before you do anything else, the object is selected (see the circle object in fig. 25.2). It appears with square selection handles at its edges. While the object is selected, you can change it. If a shape's fill color isn't quite right, for example, while the shape is selected, you can select a different fill color to change it. You can reshape a selected object by dragging its selection handles.

When you click the page to draw a new object, or when you click a different drawing button in the toolbar, the object is deselected. You can simply point to a drawn object and click the left mouse button to select it again.

After you draw a line or shape, the crosshair turns back into an insertion point for typing text, unless you double-clicked the Drawing button to select it. In that case, the crosshair remains so you can draw additional lines or shapes. The crosshair changes back to an I-beam when you click the page.

Tip

If you delete an object or objects and then realize you still want them, choose Edit, Undo before doing anything else.

Choosing Colors and Line Patterns Using the Drawing Toolbar

You can choose colors and line styles using the Drawing toolbar. If no object is selected when you choose colors and a line style, your choices become defaults. If objects are selected, the objects change *and* your choices become the new defaults.

To select line color, fill color, and line style, follow these steps:

1. Display the Drawing toolbar. (Choose View, Toolbars and select Drawing or use a shortcut; see the earlier section "Displaying the Drawing Toolbar.")

2. Click the Fill Color button to display the Fill Color palette (see fig. 25.3). Select the color you want to fill the shapes you draw (or the selected shape). Select None for an empty shape.

3. Click the Line Color button to display the Line Color palette (see fig. 25.3). Click the color you want for lines or to border shapes. Click None for an invisible line or no border.

4. Click the Line Style button to display the Line Style palette, shown on the right of figure 25.3. Click the line style you want—thin, thick, dashed, or arrowhead.

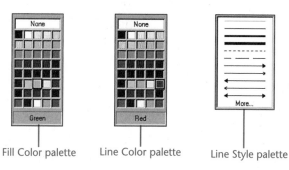

Fill Color palette   Line Color palette   Line Style palette

Fig. 25.3
Use Drawing toolbar palettes to quickly choose fill color (left), line color (center), or line style (right).

Choosing Colors and Line Patterns Using the Drawing Dialog Box

By using the Drawing dialog box, you can choose fill color and pattern, line color and style, and size and position all at once. This method is the quickest for making several choices at the same time.

> **Note**
>
> The Drawing dialog box has two names: if no object is selected when you display it, it is called Drawing Defaults; if an object is selected, it is called Drawing Object.

Remember that changing colors and line styles always changes the defaults, whether or not an object is selected when you make the changes.

To change colors and line styles with the Drawing dialog box, follow these steps:

1. Display the Drawing dialog box in one of these ways:

Choose Format, Drawing Object.

Double-click the shape you want to change (exception: do not use this technique for freeform lines or polygons—double-clicking them allows you to reshape them, not change their colors or line styles).

Click with the right mouse button on an object you want to change, and then select Format Drawing Object from the shortcut menu that appears, as shown in figure 25.4.

Fig. 25.4
Click with the right mouse button on a selected object to display the shortcut menu.

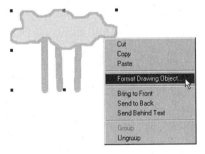

 Click the Line Styles button and select More from the menu. The Drawing dialog box appears.

2. Select the Fill or Line tab to make your selections. Figure 25.5 shows both tabs. See table 25.2 for details.

3. Choose OK.

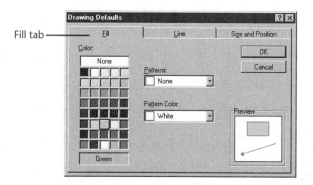

Fig. 25.5
You can change fill color and pattern in the Fill tab, and line color and style in the Line tab of the Drawing dialog box.

V

Publishing with Graphics

The Drawing dialog box contains a third tab, Size and Position, which is described later in this chapter in the section "Resizing a Line or Shape."

Table 25.2 explains the color and line style options in the Drawing dialog box.

Table 25.2 Options for the Fill, Line, and Size and Position Tabs

Selection	Application
Fill Tab **Options Apply to Shapes**	
Color	Click the object fill color you want
Patterns	Select from the list the percent fill or pattern you want. It fills closed shapes
Pattern Color	Select from the list the color you want your pattern to be
Preview	Look at the Preview box to see how your selections appear
Line Tab **Line Group** **Options Apply to Lines and the Borders around Shapes**	
None	Removes lines
Custom	Makes line Style, Color, and Weight options available
Style	Lists solid, dotted, and dashed line style options
Color	Lists colors and gray screens
Weight	Lists line weight (thickness) options; also includes text box for custom line weight. Weights measured in points (1 inch=72 points)
Arrowhead Group **Options Apply to Lines**	
Style	Lists line and arrow options (single arrowhead, double arrowhead, different arrowhead styles)
Width	Lists different arrowhead widths (applies to arrows only)
Length	Lists different arrowhead lengths (applies to arrows only)

Selection	Application
Other Options	
Shad<u>o</u>w	Adds black drop shadow to lines and shapes
<u>R</u>ound Corners	Rounds the corners of squares, rectangles, and polygons
Preview	Shows how your selections affect drawing objects
Size and Position Tab **Options Apply to Selected Drawing Objects** **Position Group**	
Hori<u>z</u>ontal	Selects distance from left edge of margin, page, or column
<u>V</u>ertical	Selects distance from top edge of margin, page, or paragraph
Lock <u>A</u>nchor	Anchors objects to the paragraph in which they were drawn
Size Group	
H<u>e</u>ight	Selects height of a drawing object
Wi<u>d</u>th	Selects width of a drawing object
Other Options	
In<u>t</u>ernal Margin	Selects distance between text and border in a text box or callout
<u>C</u>allout	Selects the Format Callout dialog box

Selecting Shapes, Lines, and Whole Drawings

When you first draw an object, it remains selected until you click the mouse button somewhere else on-screen. Selection handles appear at each corner or end (see fig. 25.6). You can change a selected object in many ways: you can change its color, its line, or its size; you can move it to another layer; you can rotate or flip it; you can frame or align it.

Fig. 25.6

When objects are selected, you can change them in many ways. The object on the left is selected; the selection pointer is shown near the object on the right.

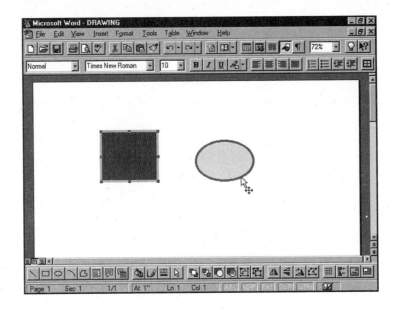

The "select and do" principle applies to drawing objects just as it does to text: you must select an object before you can do something to it. You can easily select one object, multiple objects, or your entire drawing.

Although you can select all objects using the techniques described in this section, there is a special button for selecting freeform or polygon shapes when you want to reshape them by changing the line segments that comprise them. See the later section, "Drawing and Reshaping Freeform Shapes and Polygons," for details.

To select one drawing object, follow these steps:

1. With no drawing button selected, move the insertion point over the object you want to select until it turns into a selection arrow with a four-headed arrow below it (refer to fig. 25.6).

2. Click the mouse button when the arrow is on the object.

To select several objects one by one, follow these steps:

1. Click the first object to select it.

2. Hold the Shift key.

3. Click the other objects you want to select. Release the Shift key when you're finished selecting objects.

To select several objects all at once, follow these steps:

1. Click the Select Drawing Objects button.

2. Move the pointer to the page somewhere outside all the objects you want to select.

3. Click and hold the left mouse button. The pointer turns into a crosshair. Drag to draw a selection square around all the objects you want to select. The selection square appears as a dotted line.

4. Release the mouse button. The selection square disappears, and all the objects inside the selection square are selected.

To deselect a single object from a group of selected objects, hold down the Shift key and click the object you want to deselect.

To deselect one or all objects, click somewhere outside the selected objects.

Troubleshooting

I made a change, but my object didn't change.

Your object was not selected. Select the object you want to change, then make the change.

I drew a selection box around objects, but not all of them were selected.

A selection box must completely enclose all objects you want to select. Make sure no part of any object you want to select is outside the selection box.

I clicked an object to select it, but I couldn't select it.

If an object such as a square or circle is unfilled, you must click its edge to select it. You can't select an unfilled object by clicking in its center.

Tip

If an object is hidden behind another object so that you can't see it or select it, select the top object and move it behind the hidden object by clicking the Send to Back button.

Drawing Lines

With the Line button, you can draw straight lines in your choice of colors, weights, and styles.

As with most drawing tools, you can hold down the Shift key as you draw to constrain the way the tool works. Holding down Shift as you draw a line ensures that the line appears vertical, horizontal, or at a 30-, 45-, or 60-degree angle. Be sure to use this feature when you want perfectly vertical or horizontal lines; if you don't, your line might print at a slight angle, even if it looks right on-screen.

You can use a different tool, the Freeform tool, to draw curved or jagged lines. In reality, a curved or jagged line is a polygon with no fill. You can learn more about the Freeform drawing tool in the later section "Drawing and Reshaping Freeform Shapes and Polygons."

To draw a straight line, follow these steps:

1. Click the Line button and move the mouse arrow to the page, where it turns into a crosshair for drawing. Double-click the Line button if you want to draw more than one line.

2. Click and hold down the left mouse button while you drag the crosshair in any direction to draw a line (see fig. 25.7).

Fig. 25.7
Hold down the left mouse button while you drag the crosshair to draw a line.

3. Release the mouse button to complete the line.

   If you want to draw a perfectly horizontal or vertical line, or a 30-, 45-, or 90-degree line, press the Shift key before you click the mouse button to draw, and hold it until after you release the mouse button to complete your drawing.

To draw a curved or jagged line, follow these steps:

1. Select None from the Fill Color palette. If you don't, you'll draw a filled polygon rather than a line.

2. Select the Freeform button.

3. To draw a curved line, click and hold down the mouse button as you draw your curved line, such as the one shown at the top of figure 25.8. Don't release the mouse button until you're finished; if you do, you'll draw a straight line segment.

   Or, to draw a jagged line, click the left mouse button where you want the line to start, and then click where you want each corner of the line (see the bottom line in fig. 25.8).

4. Double-click at the end of the line to complete it. Don't click the beginning point of the line; if you do, you'll connect the beginning and end points to create a closed polygon rather than a line.

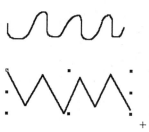

Fig. 25.8
Click the Freeform
button, with None
as the fill color, to
draw curved or
jagged lines.

Tip
Choose the Snap
to Grid button and
turn off the Snap
to Grid option to
have more control
when you draw
curved or jagged
lines.

Tip
You can press the
Esc key to cancel
a line or shape
before it's com-
pleted.

To change a line, select it. Drag its selection handles to resize it, or select a different color or line style. You can also use a special technique to reshape any freeform—even a curved or jagged line. See the later section, "Drawing and Reshaping Freeform Shapes and Polygons."

Drawing and Changing Arrows

An arrow is a special kind of line formatted to include arrowheads at either or both ends. You can include arrowheads on straight, curved, or jagged lines (see fig. 25.9), but not on arcs or other shapes.

You can change arrows after you draw them, remove an arrowhead from an arrow, or add an arrowhead to an existing line.

To draw a new arrow, follow these steps:

1. Click the Line Style button to display the line style palette.

2. Select the arrowhead style you want.

3. Click the Line button and draw a straight arrow, or click the Freeform button to draw a curved or jagged arrow. Drawing lines is described earlier in "Drawing Lines."

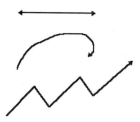

Fig. 25.9
Draw straight
arrows using the
Line button, or
curved or jagged
arrows using the
Freeform button.

If you want more arrowhead options than appear on the Line Style palette, display the Drawing dialog box. Select the Line tab, and in the Arrowhead group select Style, Width, and Length options.

To change an arrow or remove an arrowhead, follow these steps:

1. Select the arrow or line you want to change or the arrow from which you want to remove an arrowhead.

2. Click the Line Style button and select a different line or arrowhead style. To remove an arrowhead, select a line with no arrowhead.

You can also display the Drawing dialog box and select the Line tab. Select different Style, Width, and Length options in the Arrowhead group. To remove an arrowhead, select the line that shows no arrowheads (the top line in the list). Choose OK.

Tip
To remove an arrowhead from an arrow, select the arrow and display the Line Style palette. Select a line style with no arrow.

Drawing Rectangles or Squares, and Ellipses or Circles

With the rectangle and ellipse tools, you can draw rectangles, squares, ellipses (ovals), or circles. By default, the tools draw rectangles and ellipses; if you hold the Shift key as you draw, the tools draw perfect squares and perfect circles. The shapes you draw with these tools can be empty or filled, bordered or not, in color or in blacks and grays.

Like the Shift key, the Ctrl key is also a constraint key. Hold it to draw a rectangle or ellipse from the center outward. Hold down Ctrl and Shift to draw a square or circle from the center outward.

Squares and rectangles normally have 45-degree corners. However, you can select an option that rounds the corners of selected squares and rectangles.

To draw a rectangle or square, or an ellipse or circle, follow these steps:

1. Click the Rectangle or Ellipse button and move the mouse arrow to the page, where it turns into a crosshair for drawing. To draw more than one rectangle or square, or ellipse or circle, double-click the Rectangle or Ellipse button.

2. Click and hold down the left mouse button while you drag the crosshair in any direction to draw a rectangle, square, ellipse, or circle (see fig. 25.10).

3. Release the mouse button to complete the shape.

To draw a perfect square or circle, press the Shift key before you click the mouse button to draw, and hold it down until after you release the mouse button to complete your drawing. Hold down the Ctrl key as you draw to draw from the center outward.

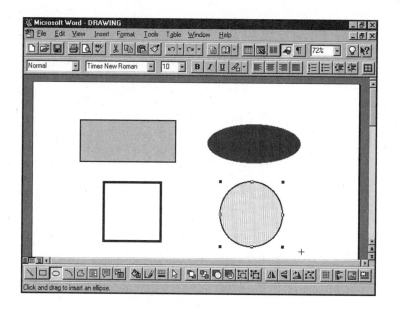

Fig. 25.10
You can draw empty or filled rectangles and ellipses, with or without borders. Hold down the Shift key for perfect squares and circles.

To draw a square or rectangle with rounded corners, follow these steps:

1. Select the square or rectangle whose corners you want rounded.

2. Choose Format, Drawing Object.

3. Select the Line tab.

4. Select Round Corners.

5. Click OK.

Select Round Corners as a default if you want all corners rounded.

Tip
A quick way to display the Drawing Object dialog box is to double-click the object you want to change.

> **Note**
>
> To fill a shape, including wedges and freeforms, with a "screen" or "percent screen" use a fill color and pattern. Double-click the shape you want to fill to select the shape and display the Drawing Object dialog box. Select the Fill tab. Select a color from the Color grid, and from the Patterns list, select 5%, 10%, or one of the other percents. In effect, you create a tint of the color you selected. If the screened shape goes behind text, use a light screen—no darker than 20%.

V

Publishing with Graphics

> **Note**
>
> To help you measure or align drawing objects, use Word's temporary "guidelines." Click and hold the mouse button on the ruler at the top of the screen to display a guideline; then drag the line left or right to measure an object or check the alignment of multiple objects. The guideline disappears when you release the mouse button.

To change a shape, select it. Drag its selection handles to resize it (see the later section "Resizing a Line or Shape"), or select a different fill color or line style for its border.

Troubleshooting

I drew a shape, but none appeared.

"None" is selected as both your fill color and line color. Select a color.

Using the Snap to Grid

The Snap to Grid tool constrains the movement of your crosshair as you draw. It acts like a magnetic grid of invisible intersecting lines that attract your crosshair and do not allow the crosshair to stray outside the grid. Use the drawing grid to help you draw straight lines, and to get the sides of objects you draw to appear in certain increments. For example, to draw squares with sides measured in one-quarter inch increments, set your drawing grid at .25".

The grid also works when you move objects, by aligning those objects to the grid. Use the grid to help you keep drawing objects lined up in relation to each other.

By default, the grid's starting point is at the top left corner of the page. You can change its origin, however. For example, you may want the grid to originate at the top left margin of the page rather than the top corner of the page.

To use the Snap to Grid tool, follow these steps:

1. Click the Snap to Grid button to display the Snap to Grid dialog box, which is shown in figure 25.11.

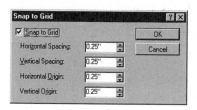

Fig. 25.11
You can turn on
the Snap to Grid
tool to help you
create shapes with
precise measure-
ments.

2. Select the Snap to Grid check box.

3. Select Horizontal Spacing, and type the side-to-side spacing increment
    you want for the grid. Or use the arrows or arrow keys to increase or
    decrease the increment.

4. Select Vertical Spacing, and type the top-to-bottom spacing increment
    you want for the grid. Or use the arrows or arrow keys to increase or
    decrease the increment.

5. Click OK.

To turn off the Snap to Grid tool, clear the Snap to Grid option.

To set the Snap to Grid tool's point of origin, display the Snap to Grid dialog
box and enter or select measurements, relative to the top left edge of the
page, in the Horizontal Origin and Vertical Origin boxes.

Tip
If the grid is off,
you can turn it on
temporarily by
holding down the
Alt key as you drag
the mouse to draw
or move an object.
Alternatively, if
the grid is on, you
can turn it off
temporarily by
holding Alt as you
drag.

Troubleshooting

I can't draw small shapes.

The increments in the snap to grid are too large. Turn off the snap to grid or
decrease its increments.

Drawing Arcs and Wedges

An arc is one quarter of an ellipse or circle (see fig. 25.12). If you don't select
a fill color or pattern, an arc is simply a line drawn in the selected line color
and style. Similarly, if you don't select a line color or style (but do select a
fill), an arc is a wedge without an outline.

Fig. 25.12
Use the Arc tool to draw arcs and wedges. An arc has no fill; a wedge is an arc with a fill color or pattern.

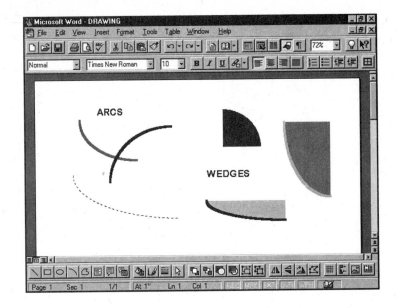

As with the other drawing tools, two constraint keys work when you draw arcs and wedges. Hold down Shift as you draw if you want your shape to be one quarter of a perfect circle. Hold down Ctrl as you draw if you want to draw your shape from the center.

To draw an arc or wedge, follow these steps:

1. Click the Arc button and move the mouse arrow to the page, where it turns into a crosshair for drawing. Double-click the arc button if you want to draw more than one arc or wedge.

2. Click and hold down the left mouse button while you drag the crosshair in any direction to draw an arc or wedge.

3. Release the mouse button to complete the shape.

   If you want your arc to be one quarter of a circle, press the Shift key before you click the mouse button to draw, and hold it until after you release the mouse button to complete your drawing. Hold down the Ctrl key as you draw to draw from the center outward.

To change an arc, select it. Drag its selection handles to resize it (for details, see the next section "Resizing a Line or Shape"), or select a different color or line style.

Resizing a Line or Shape

When a shape is selected, it has square selection handles at its corners and sides. When a line is selected, it has selection handles at each end. You can resize the object, making it smaller or larger, by dragging these handles. Alternatively, you can use the Drawing Object dialog box to set precise measurements for any object.

Keep these rules in mind as you resize a shape:

- If you drag a side handle, you resize only from that side.

- If you drag a corner handle, you can resize from two directions at once.

- If you hold down the Shift key as you drag a corner handle on a shape, the object retains its proportions (a square stays square, a circle stays round, and a freeform retains the same shape). Hold the Shift key as you resize a line to keep its angle.

- If you hold down Ctrl as you resize, you resize from the center outward.

To resize a line or shape, follow these steps:

1. Select the line or shape so that its selection handles appear.

2. Click and hold the mouse button on any selection handle, and drag the handle to resize the line or shape. When you release the mouse button, the shape assumes its new size (see fig. 25.13, left).

You can also display the Drawing Object dialog box (choose Format, Drawing Object) and select the Size and Position tab (fig. 25.13, right). In the Size group, type or select measurements for the object's Height and Width. Choose OK.

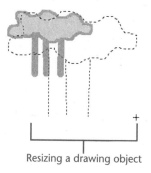

Resizing a drawing object

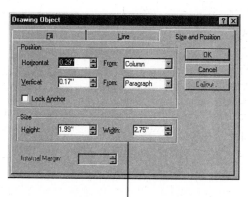

You can size a selected object using the Drawing Object dialog box

Fig. 25.13
Resize an object by dragging its selection handles, or use the Drawing Object dialog box when you want to set precise measurements for an object's size.

Troubleshooting

I tried to resize an object, but it moved instead.

You didn't drag a selection handle. To resize an object, drag it by a selection handle, not by a side. Dragging an object by its side moves it.

Drawing and Reshaping Freeform Shapes and Polygons

The freeform tool is very versatile. With it, you can draw a curve, a squiggle, a jagged line, a straight line, or a closed polygon (see fig. 25.14). A completed freeform or polygon is composed of any combination of line segments—straight or curved—connected by nodes (small black squares that appear when you reshape the freeform). For example, a stop-sign-shaped polygon is composed of eight straight sides with eight connecting corners.

Fig. 25.14
A freeform shape or polygon is composed of line segments connected by nodes.

Tip
Use the Freeform tool to trace complex drawings that you import from another software program. You can then modify the drawing in Word and delete the original image.

When you draw a freeform shape, lines appear in the selected line color or style; closed polygons appear with the fill you selected, and are bordered in the line color or style you selected.

Only one constraint key works with freeform shapes and polygons. Hold the Shift key as you draw to keep your straight line segments perfectly vertical, horizontal, or at a set angle.

To draw a freeform shape or polygon, follow these steps:

1. Click the Freeform button and move the mouse arrow to the page, where it turns into a crosshair for drawing. Double-click the Freeform button if you want to draw more than one freeform shape or polygon.

2. Draw your shape using one of these techniques:

   To draw a shape composed of straight line segments, click the left mouse button to start the shape, move the crosshair to the end of the first line segment and click again, and continue moving the crosshair and clicking to define each line segment.

   Or, to draw a curved shape, click and hold the left mouse button to start the shape; then drag the crosshair in a curving fashion to draw.

   Or, to draw a composite shape, including straight and curved line seg-ments, click and hold the left mouse button when you want to draw a curved line segment, and click once when you want to draw a straight line segment.

3. Complete your shape in one of two ways:

   For an open shape or a line, double-click the mouse button when you finish drawing. (If you selected a fill color or pattern, Word connects the last and first points and fills the shape; select None as your fill color and pattern if you want just a line.)

   Or, for a closed shape, click once on the beginning point of your shape.

You can reshape a freeform shape or a polygon in two ways. When the shape is selected as it is after you draw it, you can drag its corner handles, as you do any shape, to stretch it into a different size and shape. Or you can reshape it by dragging any of the nodes that connect its segments.

Reshaping a freeform line is amazing the first time you see it done. After you draw a freeform shape and then click the Reshape button, you find that the shape is composed of small lines connected by movable handles called *nodes*. You can drag any of these nodes to change the shape.

As you reshape a freeform or polygon object, you can add or delete nodes. Adding a node in between two existing nodes can give you another node with which to smooth a curve. Deleting a node will make a line straighten to join the nodes on either side of the deleted node.

V

Publishing with Graphics

To reshape a freeform or polygon object, complete the following steps:

1. To display the nodes linking the individual line segments, select the freeform or polygon object (see fig. 25.15, left), and then click the Reshape button.

2. Move the pointer to a node. When it turns into a crosshair, hold the left mouse button and drag the node to a new location (see fig. 25.15, right). Release when the node is where you want it. Repeat to move other nodes.

3. Click outside the object when you finish.

Fig. 25.15
Use the Reshape tool to rearrange the line segments that comprise a polygon.

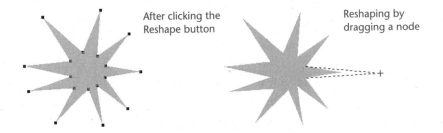

After clicking the Reshape button

Reshaping by dragging a node

To add or delete nodes on a freeform or polygon shape, follow these steps:

1. Display the nodes linking the individual line segments by selecting the freeform or polygon object, and then clicking the Reshape button, or by double-clicking the freeform shape.

2. To add a node, point to the line where you want the node, hold down the Ctrl key, and click the mouse button.

   Or, to remove a node, point to the node, hold down Control, and click the mouse button.

Changing Line Style and Color

Line color is like fill color: it is the color of a line, whether the line stands alone or whether it is the border around the edge of a shape. Line style is either the weight (width) of a line, or it is the appearance of the line, whether it is solid, dotted, or dashed. The weight, or width, of lines is measured in points, and a point is 1/72 of an inch. If you want a hairline-weight line, choose a 1/4-point line; for a line about the width of a pencil line, try a 1-point line. If you want a very thick line, type your own measurement in the Drawing Object dialog box; for example, a 36-point line is about 1/2-inch wide.

Line color and style apply not only to individual lines, but also to the edges around shapes.

To change the color of a line or of the line around a shape, follow these steps:

1. Select the line or shape.

2. Do one of the following things:

Click the Line Color button and select a line color from the palette that appears.

Display the Drawing Object dialog box (choose F_ormat, Drawing Ob_ject, or double-click the line). Select the _Line tab, and select a line color from the _Color drop-down list in the Line group. Choose OK when you're finished.

To change the style of a line or of the line around a shape, follow these steps:

1. Select the line or shape.

2. Do one of the following things:

Click the Line Style button and select a line style from the palette that appears.

Display the Drawing Object dialog box (double-click the line) and select the _Line tab. In the Line group, select a line style from the _Style drop-down list and select or type a line width from the _Weight drop-down list. Choose OK when you're finished.

Removing the Line around a Shape

Often the line around the edge of a shape is a different color from the shape. If you want the object to appear as if it has no line around its edge, you can remove the line or make it the same color as the shape. The shape is slightly smaller if you remove the line.

To remove a line from around a shape or shapes, follow these steps:

1. Select the shape or shapes.

2. Do one of the following things:

Click the Line Color button and select None or the same color as the shape from the palette that appears.

Display the Drawing Object dialog box, select the Line tab, and select None or the same color as the shape from the Line group. Choose OK.

Changing or Removing a Shape's Fill or Pattern

A shape's fill is the color inside a shape, whether it is a rectangle, an ellipse, an arc, or a freeform shape. It is also the color inside a text box or a callout. You can also change the pattern, and the color of the pattern, that fills a shape. Patterns include *screens,* or percentages of a color, as well as many designs.

To change or remove a shape's fill or pattern, follow these steps:

1. Select the shape or shapes.

2. Do one of the following things:

Click the Fill Color button and select a fill color from the palette that appears. To remove the fill, select None.

Display the Drawing Object dialog box, select the Fill tab, and select a fill color from the Color palette, a fill pattern from the Patterns drop-down list, and the color of the pattern from the Pattern Color drop-down list. To remove the fill, select None from the Color palette. Choose OK when you finish.

Creating Shadowed Lines and Shapes

Tip

To create a drop-shadow for an arc or freeform, duplicate the shape, offset it from the original by a little, layer it behind the original, and change it to black.

You can instantly add a black drop-shadow to a line or shape. The black shadow appears below and to the right of the object you draw. As shown in figure 25.16, drop-shadows add an interesting three-dimensional effect to lines, rectangles, and ovals (drop-shadows cannot be automatically applied to arcs or freeforms).

To create a drop-shadow, follow these steps:

1. Select the line or shape you want to shadow.

2. Choose Format, Drawing Object.

3. Select the Line tab.

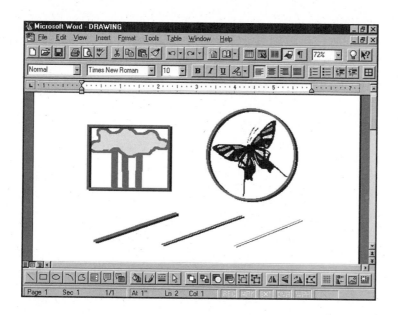

Fig. 25.16
Drop-shadows
create a three-
dimensional effect.

4. Select the Shado<u>w</u> option.

5. Click OK.

Alternatively, choose this option before you begin drawing if you want all
lines and shapes shadowed.

Rotating Shapes and Lines

You can rotate a selected line or shape in 90-degree increments (see
fig. 25.17). Each time you click the Rotate Right button, the object rotates
90 degrees to the right. You can rotate a single selected object or a group of
selected objects.

▶ See "Rotating,
Slanting, and
Arcing Text,"
p. 811

You can rotate a text box or callout, but not the text or picture inside it. Use
WordArt to rotate text.

Fig. 25.17
Each time you
click the Rotate
Right button, the
selected object
rotates 90 degrees
to the right.

To rotate an object or objects, select the object or objects you want to rotate, then click the Rotate Right button.

Flipping Shapes and Lines

Flipping selected objects turns them horizontally (left to right—see fig. 25.18 right) or vertically (top to bottom—see fig. 25.18, left). You can flip a callout, but not the text inside it.

Fig. 25.18

You can flip an object vertically (left) or horizontally (right).

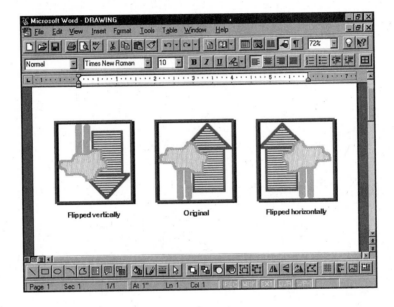

To flip an object or objects, follow these steps:

1. Select the object or objects.

 2. Click the Flip Horizontal button to flip the object or objects from right to left.

   Or, click the Flip Vertical button to flip the object or objects from top to bottom.

Grouping and Ungrouping Lines and Shapes

Grouping objects together fuses them into a single object. When related objects are grouped, they are easier to move and size. You can ungroup objects if you later need to separate them.

Figure 25.19 shows several objects before (left) and after (right) being grouped.

Rectangle
(filled) ———

Text box———

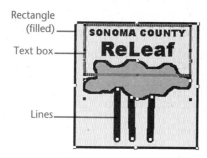

Lines———

——— Freeform (filled)

Fig. 25.19
Grouping objects
fuses them into a
single object.

When you apply commands to grouped objects, they are applied as if the objects were a single object. In some cases, the command may work differently than when you apply it to individually selected objects. For example, when you rotate two separate objects, each rotates around its own center. When you rotate two objects that are grouped as one, however, they rotate around the group's center. The effect is different. Other changes you make, such as fill and line color, apply the same to individual objects as they do to grouped objects.

You can group groups as well as individual objects. You might want to separate the components of a complex drawing into several smaller groups for easier handling.

To group objects, select the objects you want to group, then click the Group button.

If you want to change any individual part of a group, you must first ungroup it. For example, if you want to change the color of one of the objects making up a grouped picture, but not other parts, ungroup the picture first.

To ungroup a group of objects, select the group, then click the Ungroup button.

Tip
You can edit text
even when it is
grouped with
other objects.

Troubleshooting

I ungrouped a group, but I still can't select a certain object.

You can group groups as well as individual objects. Your group probably includes multiple groups; try ungrouping each of them. What appears to be a group may actually be a picture that has been imported from another graphics program. Pictures drawn in Microsoft Draw for Word for Windows 2.0 cannot be ungrouped. They are treated as a single object.

Moving, Copying, Deleting, and Positioning Lines and Shapes

◄ See "Moving, Copying, and Linking Text or Graphics," p. 160

You can easily move an object, or a group of objects, from one part of your drawing to another, or from one part of your document to another. One way to move an object is to drag it to a new location. Another way is to cut it from one place and paste it somewhere else. When you move something a long distance, this method may be the best.

Copying objects enables you to duplicate shapes you want to use again—in the current document, or in another document or even another program.

Delete unwanted objects by selecting them and then pressing the Delete key or choosing Edit, Clear. You can restore them if you immediately choose Edit, Undo.

Like most professional-quality graphics programs, Word offers a scrolling shortcut: when you drag a drawing object to move it, bumping the edge of the screen with the object causes the screen to scroll in that direction. For example, if you drag a circle downward so that it touches the bottom edge of your screen, your screen scrolls downward.

Moving Lines and Shapes

The quickest way to move an object is to drag it to a new position on the page. If you drag to the edge of the screen, the page automatically scrolls. In this way, you can move objects beyond the area of the page that is displayed.

To move longer distances, or to move objects between documents, use Word's cut and paste commands. After an object is cut, you can paste it as many times as you want.

To move an object or objects by dragging, follow these steps:

1. Select the object or objects you want to move.

2. Position the mouse pointer over the object, but not on a selection handle. The pointer should look like the usual arrow pointer and a four-headed arrow.

3. Click and hold the left mouse button, and drag the object to its new location. Release the mouse button when the object is where you want it.

    You can hold the Shift key as you drag to move an object in a straight line.

To move an object or objects long distances using cut and paste, follow these steps:

1. Select the object or objects you want to cut and paste.

2. Choose <u>E</u>dit, Cu<u>t</u>, or click the object with the right mouse button. Select the Cut command from the shortcut menu, press Ctrl+X, or click the Cut button on the Standard toolbar.

3. Position the insertion point where you want to move the object. (Just as with text, you cannot paste a drawing object into a location unless text is already there.)

4. Choose <u>E</u>dit, <u>P</u>aste, or click the screen with the right mouse button. Select the Paste command from the shortcut menu, press Ctrl+V, or click the Paste button on the Standard toolbar.

Another way to move an object is to drag its anchor. For details about object anchors, see the later section, "Positioning Lines and Shapes."

Copying Lines and Shapes

You can use Word's copy and paste commands to duplicate shapes you want to use again—whether in the current document or another document. Until you copy something else, you can paste the shape you copied as many times as you want.

Tip

Quickly duplicate a drawing by holding down the Ctrl key as you drag a copy to a new location.

To copy an object or objects, follow these steps:

1. Select the object or objects you want to copy.

2. Choose <u>E</u>dit, <u>C</u>opy, or click the object with the right mouse button. Select the Copy command from the shortcut menu, press Ctrl+C, or click the Copy button on the Standard toolbar.

3. Position the insertion point where you want to copy the object.

4. Choose <u>E</u>dit, <u>P</u>aste, or press the right mouse button. Select the Paste command from the shortcut menu, press Ctrl+V, or click the Paste button on the Standard toolbar.

Deleting Shapes and Lines

You can easily remove a shape or group of shapes from your drawing.

To delete an object or objects, follow these steps:

1. Select the object or objects you want to delete.

2. Press the Delete key.

You can also remove an object by selecting it and then cutting it using Edit, Cut. Use this technique if you want to paste the object somewhere else.

Aligning Lines and Shapes to Each Other or to the Page

There are two ways you can align objects: to each other (see fig. 25.20, right) or to the page (see fig 25.20, left). When you align objects to each other, they line up on the side you specify: left, right, top, or bottom; or they line up at their centers. Similarly, when you align objects to the page, they line up to the left, right, top, bottom, or center of the page. To align objects to each other, you must select more than one object; however, you can align a single object to the page.

Fig. 25.20

You can align objects to the page (left) or to each other (right).

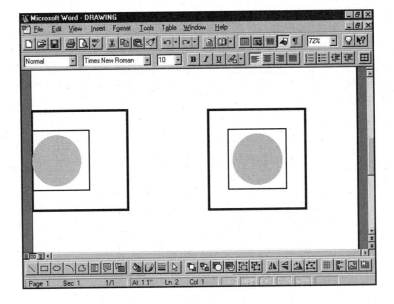

After an object is aligned, you can drag it to move it to another location on the page.

To align objects, follow these steps:

1. Select the objects you want to align to each other, or select the object or objects you want to align to the page.

2. Click the Align Drawing Objects button. The Align dialog box appears.

3. From the Horizontal group, select Left, Center, or Right alignment. Select None if you don't want to align the object or objects horizontally.

4. From the Vertical group, select Top, Center, or Bottom alignment. Select None if you don't want to align the object or objects vertically.

5. From the Relative To group, select Each Other if you selected multiple objects and want to align them relative to each other, or select Page if you selected one or more objects and want to align them relative to the edges of the page.

6. Choose OK.

Positioning Lines and Shapes

There are two ways you can position objects that you draw. You can use the Drawing Object dialog box to specify how far the object should be positioned from the margins, edges of the page, column, or paragraph. Or you can frame an object, and use frame commands to position an object on the page (for details about framing, see the upcoming section, "Framing Objects to Wrap Text around Them"). In either case, you can drag an object after it has been positioned to move it to another location.

To specify an exact position for an object or objects, follow these steps:

1. Select the object or objects.

2. Display the Drawing Object dialog box. (Choose Format, Drawing Object, or double-click the object you want to position.)

3. Select the Size and Position tab.

4. Make selections in these options:

   Select Horizontal and then From, and type or select the distance you want the object to be positioned from the left edge of the margin, page, or column.

   Select Vertical and then From, and type or select the distance you want the object to be positioned from the top of the margin, page, or paragraph.

5. Choose OK.

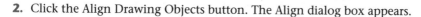

Objects are always anchored to the paragraph nearest to where you draw them. When you move an object by dragging it, the anchor moves to the paragraph nearest to the object's new location—unless you lock the anchor. In that case, the object stays with the paragraph, even if the paragraph moves. Anchors also provide another way you can move objects. If you display the anchors, which appear in the margin, you can drag an object's anchor to a new paragraph, and the object moves to that paragraph.

To lock an object's anchor, follow these steps:

1. Select the object.

2. Display the Drawing Object dialog box (choose Format, Drawing Object, or double-click the object) and select the Size and Position tab.

3. Select the Lock Anchor check box.

4. Choose OK.

To display and move anchors (see fig. 25.21), follow these steps:

1. Choose Tools, Options, and select the View tab.

2. In the Show group, select the Object Anchors check box.

3. Select an object to display its anchor.

4. Drag the anchor to another paragraph to move the anchor.

Fig. 25.21
Objects are anchored to paragraphs; you can move objects by dragging their anchors to a new paragraph.

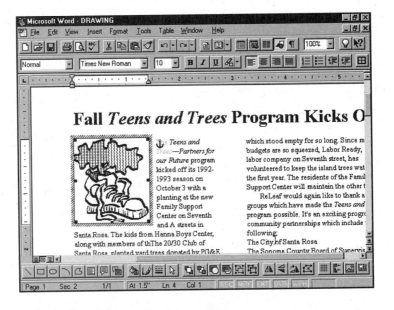

Including Text or Another Picture in a Drawing

You can include either text or a picture created in another application in a drawing or in your document using two tools from the Drawing toolbar—the Text Box button and the Create Picture button. In a text box, you can include text or a picture. In a picture container, you can insert a picture. A text box is more versatile, because you can format, move, flip, rotate, or layer it using buttons on the Drawing toolbar.

There are other ways to include pictures in your document or put text in a box: for example, you can use Insert, Picture or Insert, Object to insert a picture, and you can frame text to put it in a box. But there are some advantages to using the Drawing toolbar. First, you can include text as part of your drawing. Second, you can move a text box to the layer behind the text. Third, you can use the other buttons on the Drawing toolbar to quickly format text boxes.

Figure 25.22 shows a drawing that includes text.

◀ See "Inserting Pictures into Your Document," p. 702

◀ See "Inserting Picture Objects into Your Document," p. 706

Fig. 25.22
Text is sometimes an important part of your drawing.

V

Publishing with Graphics

Inserting Text Boxes

A *text box* is a graphic box with text inside it. It is filled with the fill color you've selected and edged with the line color and style you selected. Like any drawing object, it floats freely on the page, so you can drag it to move it to a new location. You can resize or reshape it; the text inside rewraps to fit the new size or shape.

Text inside a text box is the same as regular text in Word. You can edit it, align it, format it, cut and paste it, or copy it just like any other text. Use Word's normal editing and formatting commands and shortcuts to edit and format text inside a text box. A text box does not automatically resize when you add more text; you must manually resize the text box if you insert more text than you can see (see the earlier section, "Resizing a Line or Shape").

You can also insert pictures created in other applications in text boxes by choosing Insert, Picture.

Because text boxes float freely on the page, you can position them anyplace: in a margin, in the text, or beneath the text. Because of their freedom of placement, text boxes—whether they contain text or inserted pictures—can be very useful with desktop publishing projects. The starburst and word SALE in figure 25.23 are contained in a text box.

Fig. 25.23

Text boxes can be placed anywhere on the page—even behind text.

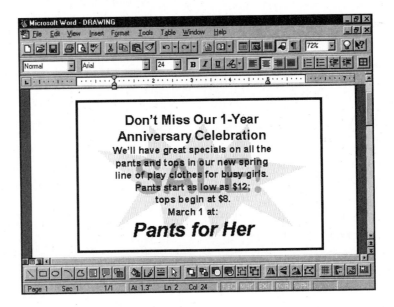

To draw a text box, follow these steps:

1. Click the Text Box button. The mouse pointer becomes a crosshair.

2. Move the crosshair where you want to start drawing your text box.

3. Click and hold the mouse button, and drag from one corner to the opposite corner where you want the text box.

   Hold down the Shift key if you want a square text box.

4. Release the mouse button.

When you release the mouse button, a flashing insertion point appears in the text box, indicating that you can begin typing text. Type continuously; the text wraps when you reach the margin. If you type more text than will fit in the box, the box contents scroll so that you can see what you are typing; the full contents may not be visible. If you later decide to change the size or shape of the text box, the text inside wraps to fit the new shape.

Although you can rotate or flip a text box, you can't rotate or flip the text inside it. Use WordArt to rotate text and create many other special text effects.

▶ See "Rotating, Slanting, and Arcing Text," p. 811

When you see the flashing insertion point, you can use <u>I</u>nsert, <u>P</u>icture to insert a picture inside the text box.

> **Note**
>
> If you want text in your document to wrap around text in a box, you must use a frame rather than a text box. With no object selected, click the Insert Frame button, then drag the crosshair to insert an empty frame. An insertion point flashes in the top left corner of the frame. Type and format your text, then move the framed text wherever you want it—text in your document will wrap around it. You can also insert a picture into a frame.

◀ See "Framing Text," p. 728

Inserting Picture Containers

You can create a picture composed of several different objects by drawing in a picture container. In this way, you don't have to group your objects into a whole drawing: they are already grouped in the picture container.

You can also insert pictures into a picture container and add to them using Word's drawing tools.

To create a picture in a picture container, follow these steps:

1. Click the Create Picture button. The Picture window appears (see fig. 25.24).

2. Draw objects inside the rectangular drawing window. If you want, you can insert a picture by choosing <u>I</u>nsert, <u>P</u>icture or <u>I</u>nsert, <u>O</u>bject. Or, you can type text.

   To shrink the picture container's borders to fit the object inside the container, click the Reset Picture Boundary button in the Picture toolbar.

3. Choose Close Picture.

Fig. 25.24

A picture container groups drawing objects. It can also include text, as well as pictures or objects that you insert.

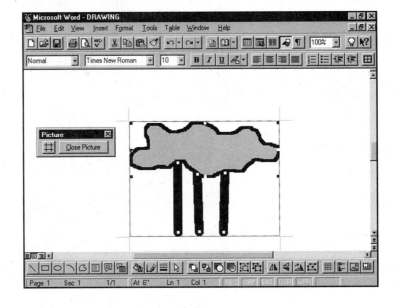

Tip

If you close the Picture toolbar by clicking the Close Picture button, you must redisplay it to return to your document. Choose View, Toolbars, Drawing.

To edit an object drawn in a picture container, double-click it to redisplay the Picture window.

Troubleshooting

I inserted a picture I created in CorelDRAW! in a picture container, but I can't move it around on the screen, and the line color won't change.

Click the Frame button to frame the picture container if you want to move it around on the page. Use Format, Borders and Shading, or the Borders toolbar, to change the line around the edge of a frame. Alternatively, insert the picture in a text box rather than a picture container. Use a text box to hold your picture if you want to use drawing tools to change the line color and style or the fill color, or if you want to move the picture to the layer behind the text.

Adding and Changing Callouts

Callouts are a very handy addition to any document in which you include illustrations that need some explanation. Callouts are a special type of text box that include a pointer which you can accurately aim at any location on the document. You can include text or an inserted picture in a callout.

Like text boxes, callouts appear in the fill and line colors that you've selected, and in the line style you've selected. If you want a callout to appear as text only, select None as your fill and line colors. You can change, move, and layer callouts like any drawing object.

A special formatting command exists for designing and pointing your callout. It allows you to very accurately specify how the callout looks and how it's attached to the text.

Figure 25.25 shows how callouts can clarify your document.

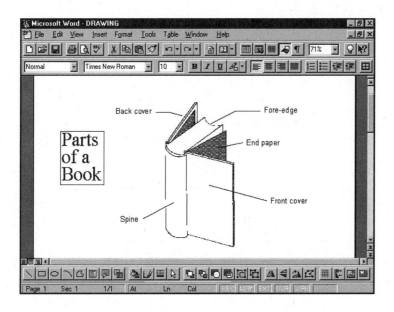

Fig. 25.25
Callouts help explain illustrations in your document.

V

Publishing with Graphics

Inserting a Callout

When you insert a callout, you draw a line from where you want the callout to point, to where you want the callout text.

To insert a callout, follow these steps:

1. Click the Callout button.

2. Move the crosshair to the place in your document where you want the callout to point.

3. Click and hold the mouse button, and drag to where you want the callout text.

4. Release the mouse button.

5. Type the callout text.

Changing a Callout

You can apply all the same colors and line styles to a callout as you do to any object you draw. You can move a callout to a different layer.

Besides these formatting features, callouts also have a special dialog box for changing the callout's specifications. You can determine how many segments comprise the callout line, and what their angles are; you can determine how the callout line is attached to the callout text; and you can determine whether there is a border around the callout text.

To format a callout, follow these steps:

1. Select the callout you want to format.

2. Click the Format Callout button to display the Format Callout dialog box (see fig. 25.26).

Fig. 25.26

You can determine many aspects of a callout's appearance using the Format Callout button.

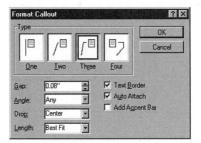

3. In the Type group, select one of the four callout types shown: One, Two, Three, or Four. Types One and Two use a straight line; type Three uses a two-part line; type Four uses a three-part line.

4. Select from among these additional options (not all options are available for all callout types):

Select This Option	For This Effect
Gap	Type or select the distance between the callout line and the callout text.
Angle	Type or select the angle at which you want the callout line. It can be Any, or a degree.

Select This Option	For This Effect
Drop	Type or select the position where you want the callout line attached to the callout text: attached at an exact distance from the top, or attached at the Top, Center, or Bottom.
Length	Type or select the length you want the callout line: Best Fit, or measured precisely.
Text Border	Select this check box if you want a border around the text (it appears in the selected line color and style).
Auto Attach	Select this check box if you want the callout line at the bottom of the callout text (rather than at the top) when text is to the left of the callout line.
Add Accent Bar	Select this option to include a vertical line next to the callout text.

5. Choose OK.

The selections you make in the Format Callout dialog box apply to the current callout and the next callouts you create.

Note

You can display the Format Callout dialog box by displaying the Drawing Object dialog box (double-click the callout), selecting the Size and Position tab, and then clicking the Callout button. Use this method to format many aspects of the callout at once—its fill, line, size and position, and callout style.

Rearranging a Drawing's Layers

Word has three layers you can work with, giving you great flexibility in how you can use pictures. The text layer is where text appears—it's the layer you're accustomed to working with in a word processing program. Uniquely, Word has two additional layers: the drawing layer above the text and the layer behind the text. You can move any object, or your entire picture, between these layers.

V

Publishing with Graphics

When an object or picture is in the drawing layer above the text, it obscures text, as shown on the left in figure 25.27. To move objects into the text layer, you must frame them; then text wraps around the framed object as shown in the center of figure 25.27. When you move an object behind text, you can see it through the text, as the right side of figure 25.27 illustrates.

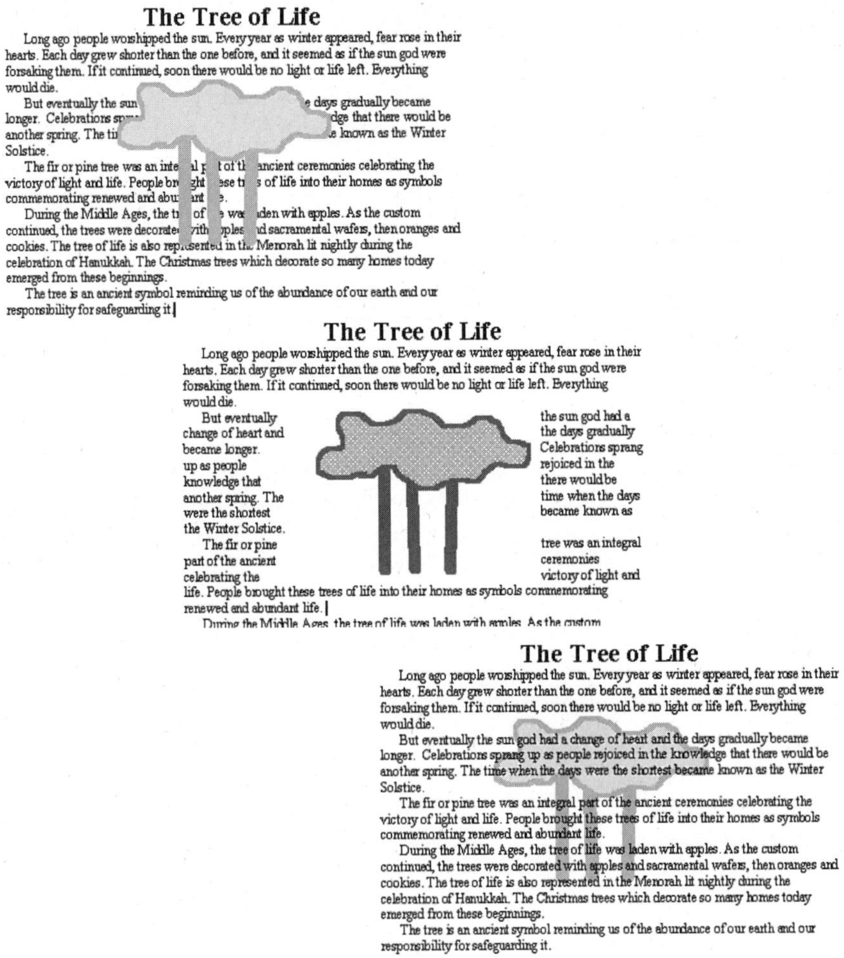

Fig. 25.27

An object in the drawing layer obscures text (left). You must frame an object to wrap text around it (center). You can see through the text to an object layered behind the text (right).

The Tree of Life

Long ago people worshipped the sun. Every year as winter appeared, fear rose in their hearts. Each day grew shorter than the one before, and it seemed as if the sun god were forsaking them. If it continued, soon there would be no light or life left. Everything would die.

But eventually the sun ... e days gradually became longer. Celebrations sp... dge that there would be another spring. The ti... e known as the Winter Solstice.

The fir or pine tree was an inte... l p... t of th... ancient ceremonies celebrating the victory of light and life. People br... ght ...ese tr... s of life into their homes as symbols commemorating renewed and abu... nt ...e.

During the Middle Ages, the t... of ... we... den with apples. As the custom continued, the trees were decorate... ith ...ples... d sacramental wafers, then oranges and cookies. The tree of life is also rep...sented in th... Menorah lit nightly during the celebration of Hanukkah. The Christmas trees which decorate so many homes today emerged from these beginnings.

The tree is an ancient symbol reminding us of the abundance of our earth and our responsibility for safeguarding it

The Tree of Life

Long ago people worshipped the sun. Every year as winter appeared, fear rose in their hearts. Each day grew shorter than the one before, and it seemed as if the sun god were forsaking them. If it continued, soon there would be no light or life left. Everything would die.

But eventually | the sun god had a
change of heart and | the days gradually
became longer. | Celebrations sprang
up as people | rejoiced in the
knowledge that | there would be
another spring. The | time when the days
were the shortest | became known as
the Winter Solstice.

The fir or pine | tree was an integral
part of the ancient | ceremonies
celebrating the | victory of light and
life. People brought these trees of life into their homes as symbols commemorating renewed and abundant life.

During the Middle Ages, the tree of life was laden with apples. As the custom

The Tree of Life

Long ago people worshipped the sun. Every year as winter appeared, fear rose in their hearts. Each day grew shorter than the one before, and it seemed as if the sun god were forsaking them. If it continued, soon there would be no light or life left. Everything would die.

But eventually the sun god had a change of heart and the days gradually became longer. Celebrations sprang up as people rejoiced in the knowledge that there would be another spring. The time when the days were the shortest became known as the Winter Solstice.

The fir or pine tree was an integral part of the ancient ceremonies celebrating the victory of light and life. People brought these trees of life into their homes as symbols commemorating renewed and abundant life.

During the Middle Ages, the tree of life was laden with apples. As the custom continued, the trees were decorated with apples and sacramental wafers, then oranges and cookies. The tree of life is also represented in the Menorah lit nightly during the celebration of Hanukkah. The Christmas trees which decorate so many homes today emerged from these beginnings.

The tree is an ancient symbol reminding us of the abundance of our earth and our responsibility for safeguarding it.

When you first draw an object, it appears in the drawing layer on top of the text. Within this drawing layer, objects are layered—one on top of the other, with the most recently drawn on top. You can move objects in front of or behind one another within the drawing layer.

There are four separate tools on the Drawing toolbar for rearranging layers: two for moving objects in front of and behind other objects in the drawing layer, and two for moving objects behind or in front of the text layer.

To move an object or drawing into the text layer, you must frame it. Framing an object is a good idea when you want to wrap text around a drawing or an object. An unframed drawing object remains in the layer above or below the text, but text does not wrap around it.

Like most procedures in Word, a simple rule applies when you're moving objects in front of or behind each other, or between the layers in the document: select and do. Select the object you want to move, and then click the button that moves it to the layer where you want it. You can select and rearrange a single object or multiple objects.

Moving Objects in front of or behind Each Other

Each new object you draw appears on top of other objects in the drawing layer. You can select any object and move it to the top of all the other objects, or beneath all the other objects. If you have several objects to arrange, think about the order in which they are to appear. Select the top object and move it to the back, then select the second object and move it to the back, and so on through all the objects. When you're finished, you've moved the last object furthest back, and the objects are in the right order.

To move objects in front of or behind each other, follow these steps:

1. Select the object or objects you want to move.

2. Select one of the following buttons:

   Click the Bring to Front button to move the object(s) to the front of all the other objects in the drawing layer.

   Click the Send to Back button to move the object(s) behind all the other objects in the drawing layer.

Layering Objects below or above the Text

You can move any single object, or your entire drawing, below the text. You can then see the drawing through your text. Use this technique to create interestingly shaped backdrops for your text (rather than the simple square boxes or shading that Format, Borders and Shading allows). You can even use this technique to create a watermark, by placing a drawing in your document's header so that it appears on every page.

◀ See "Creating Headers and Footers," p. 417

V

Publishing with Graphics

To select an object that is behind the text layer, click the Select Drawing Objects button and then click on the object with the selection arrow.

Remember, when you first draw objects, they appear in the drawing layer on top of the text.

To move an object or objects behind the text layer, follow these steps:

1. Select the object or objects.

2. Select one of these buttons:

 Select the Bring in Front of Text button to move the object(s) in front of the text layer.

 Select the Send Behind Text button to move the object(s) behind the text layer.

Framing Objects to Wrap Text around Them

 If you want text to wrap around an object or picture you draw, you must frame it. You can use Insert, Frame to do this, but it's easiest to just use the Insert Frame button on the Drawing toolbar. After a drawing object is framed, you can choose Format, Frame to assign the framed object a fixed position or size, or to remove the frame.

◀ See "Wrapping Text around a Frame," p. 750

When you frame a drawing object, text automatically wraps around it.

You can also insert an empty frame and type text or insert a picture inside it. Use this technique when you want text in your document to wrap around text in a box (you can't frame a text box) or when you want to insert a picture that you plan to frame anyway (it saves a step over inserting and then framing a picture container).

You must choose Format, Borders and Shading, or use the Borders toolbar, to add color to a frame.

To frame an object or objects, follow these steps:

1. Select the object or objects.

 2. Click the Insert Frame button.

To insert an empty frame, follow these steps:

 1. Click the Insert Frame button. When you move the mouse pointer onto the document, it becomes a crosshair.

2. Drag the crosshair to draw the size of the frame. An insertion point flashes in the top left corner of your frame; use it to type text or insert a picture.

To remove a frame from an object or text, follow these steps:

1. Select the frame.

2. Choose F<u>o</u>rmat, Fra<u>m</u>e. The Frame dialog box appears.

3. Choose <u>R</u>emove Frame.

Chapter 26

Creating Banners and Special Effects with WordArt

Words can serve as more than abstract symbols that we read for meaning. Words sometimes work as graphics that not only convey meaning, but also attract attention and create memorable images. You see examples of words used as graphics every day: pull-quotes in magazines lighten a page of text and attract attention to important points; logos turn words into symbols that you recognize without even reading; decorated words embellish the mastheads in newsletters; special text effects add interest to advertisements.

With WordArt, you can turn ordinary words into graphics. You can pour text into a shape, flip or stretch letters, condense or expand letter spacing, rotate or angle words, or add shading, colors, borders, or shadows to text. By combining WordArt effects, you can create hundreds of interesting designs.

The following list contains just some of the tasks you learn to do in this chapter:

- Apply text treatments such as fonts, styles, and sizes

- Apply special effects such as rotation, slanting, shaping, and arcing

- Apply colors, borders, and shading

- Apply typographic aids such as aligning and adjusting character spacing

You can use WordArt with a mouse or your keyboard—either way, you can create great graphics.

Figures 26.1 through 26.3 show some examples of finished WordArt objects.

Fig. 26.1
WordArt created
this newsletter
banner. The words
"ReLeaf" and
"News" are two
separate objects,
framed together.

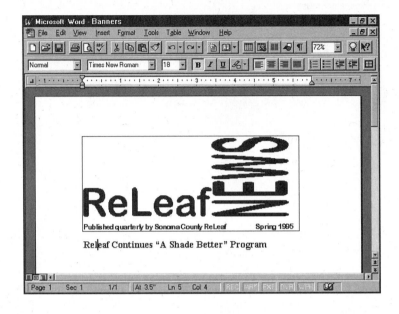

Fig. 26.2
WordArt created
this logo, which
can be used for
stationery.

Fig. 26.3
WordArt created
this simple motto
for use on a flyer.

What You Need to Know about WordArt

WordArt is an OLE-based add-in program that comes free with Word for
Windows 95 (OLE stands for *object linking and embedding*). Because of the OLE
technology, WordArt objects you insert in your document remain linked to
the WordArt program. You can edit WordArt objects easily; the image in your

Word for Windows document updates to reflect the edit changes. Because WordArt is built into Word for Windows, you can't run WordArt by itself—you can run it only from within Word for Windows (and other Windows programs that support OLE). Further, you can't create a separate WordArt file—WordArt images are part of your Word for Windows file.

You must install WordArt before you can use it. You may have installed WordArt when you installed Word. (WordArt is installed if it is listed in the Object Type list in the Object dialog box.) If you didn't install WordArt when you initially installed Word, you can install it now. You must use your original Word disk or CD-ROM to install WordArt.

▶ See "Embedding Data," p. 986

▶ See "Linking Documents and Files," p. 993

Creating a WordArt Object

After you start WordArt, creating a WordArt object is a two-part process: you type the text to be included in the image, and then you add whatever special effects you want. At any time before you close WordArt, you can change the text or the special effects. You never leave your document when you work with WordArt—you create your WordArt object directly on the page of your document, using WordArt commands and buttons.

A WordArt object behaves the same as any other picture that you insert into a Word document. You insert it at the insertion point, and the object moves with the text that surrounds it. You can size it, crop it, or add a border to it.

Because WordArt graphics are based on text, fonts are the raw materials you have for creating WordArt objects. Windows comes with some fonts, such as Arial and Times New Roman. Your printer may contain other fonts, and you can purchase additional fonts to install on your computer. Any font installed on your computer is available for use in WordArt.

◀ See "Inserting Pictures into Your Document," p. 702

Starting WordArt

Because WordArt is an OLE-based program that works only within other programs, it doesn't look like other programs. When you work with WordArt in Word, WordArt does not appear in a window of its own; instead, WordArt menus and buttons replace the Word menus and buttons.

◀ See "Formatting Characters and Changing Fonts," p. 251

To start WordArt, follow these steps:

1. Position the insertion point where you want the WordArt object to appear in your document.

2. Choose Insert, Object. The Object dialog box appears (see fig. 26.4).

V

Publishing with Graphics

Fig. 26.4
To start WordArt,
select it in the
Object dialog box.

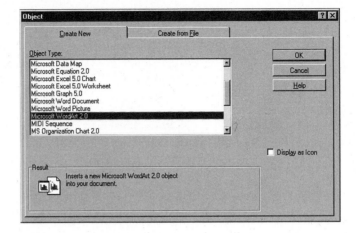

3. Select the Create New tab.

4. From the Object Type list, select Microsoft WordArt 2.0.

5. Choose OK.

When you have started WordArt, you see the screen shown in figure 26.5. You enter and edit the text of your WordArt image in the Enter Your Text Here dialog box. As you edit your text and add special effects, you see the results of your work in the shaded box in the working area of your page (when you start WordArt, this shaded box contains the words Your Text Here).

Fig. 26.5
This is how your
screen looks when
you first start
WordArt. You can
watch your image
develop as you
create it.

Entering and Editing the Text

When you start WordArt, you can type as much text as you want in the Enter Your Text Here dialog box. The size of the WordArt image is limited by the size of your page. By default, a new WordArt object is two inches wide, and as tall as the text you type.

You can watch your WordArt image change in the shaded box as you enter text and add special effects. The shaded box marks the spot where your finished WordArt image appears in your document.

To enter and edit text to be used in the WordArt object, follow these steps:

1. Select the existing text in the Enter Your Text Here dialog box. The text you type replaces the selected text. Press Enter when you want to start a new line.

2. Choose the Update Display button to see your new text in the shaded box on your page.

Understanding WordArt's Commands, Lists, and Buttons

WordArt's special effects are available through commands in the WordArt menus and through lists and buttons on the WordArt toolbar. The following table describes the unique commands and buttons contained in WordArt (they are described also in the section "A Description of WordArt Special Text Effects," in WordArt Help). WordArt's commands and buttons are described in detail later in this chapter, in the "Adding Special Effects" section.

Table 26.1   WordArt Commands and Buttons

Menu Command	List or Button	Description
Edit, Edit WordArt Text		Selects text in Enter Your Text Here dialog box. You can do the same by dragging across the text.
Format, Spacing Between Characters		Increases or decreases spacing between characters. Turns kerning on or off.
Format, Border		Adds a border, in your choice of width and color, around edges of each letter.
Format, Shading		Applies shading or pattern to text, in color or in black and white.

(continues)

Table 26.1 Continued

Menu Command	List or Button	Description
Format, Shadow		Adds a shadow to each letter, in a selection of styles and colors.
Format, Stretch to Frame		Stretches text vertically and horizontally to fit box the text is in.
Format, Rotation and Effects		Rotates text or applies different effects, depending on the shape applied. You can slant straight text, or change the arc of curved text.
	Shape list	Lists all shapes you can pour text into.
	Font list	Lists fonts on your computer. All are available in WordArt.
	Font Size list	Lists font sizes, measured in points (there are 72 points per inch). The Best Fit option fits the font to the size of the box.
		Applies bold formatting to text.
		Applies italics to text.
		Makes all letters the same height, regardless of case.
		Flips each letter on its side side (90 degrees, counter-clockwise).
		Selects alignment of text within WordArt frame (centered text is the default).

Exiting WordArt

When your WordArt image is complete, exit WordArt by clicking the working area of your page somewhere outside the Enter Your Text Here dialog box or the WordArt image. When you exit WordArt, the Enter Your Text Here dialog box disappears, the Word menus return, and your WordArt image appears in your document.

Adding Special Effects

When you add a special effect to a WordArt image, the image changes immediately and you instantly see the result of each effect you choose. You can experiment with different effects and get quick feedback about how they look.

◀ See "Including Text or Another Picture in a Drawing," p. 789

You can add many different types of special effects to create a WordArt image. All the effects apply to the text rather than to the border or background of the text. You can combine the effects to develop a look of your own. Figure 26.6 shows just a few of the special effects you can achieve with WordArt.

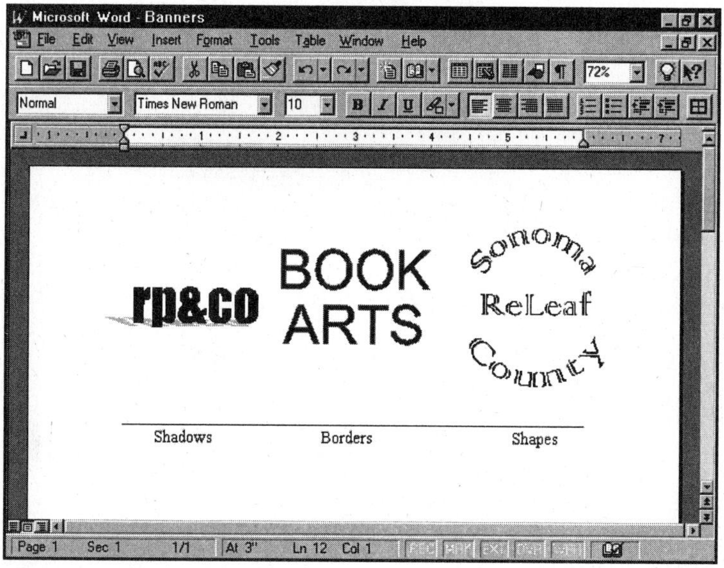

V

Publishing with Graphics

Fig. 26.6
You can create many special effects with WordArt.

What You Need to Know about WordArt Effects

The effects you apply in WordArt apply to all the text in the Enter Your Text Here dialog box. You cannot apply an effect to just a few of the letters in the dialog box.

Choosing some of the commands or buttons displays a dialog box from which you make selections. To remove the effect, choose the same command or button and select a different option.

Shaping the Text

By applying one special WordArt effect—pouring your text into a shape—you can create an interesting sign or logo. WordArt's toolbar includes a Shapes list that displays a grid of different shapes. When you select one of these shapes, the text in the Enter Your Text Here dialog box "pours" into that shape.

Some shapes produce different results, depending on the number of lines of text you are shaping. The circle shape, for example, turns a single line of text into a circle, but turns multiple lines of text into a vertical half circle. The button shape turns three lines into a button, but turns a single line into an arch. Experiment to get the result you want.

To shape text, follow these steps:

1. Start WordArt, and type text in the Enter Your Text Here dialog box.

2. Choose the Shapes list (see fig. 26.7).

3. Select the shape you want.

Fig. 26.7
By selecting one of these shapes, you can create an interesting sign or logo.

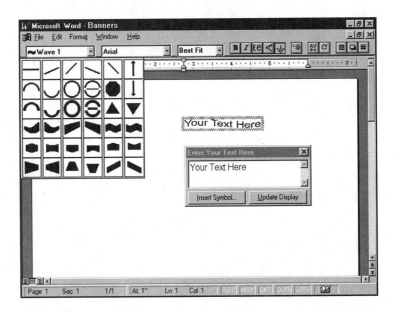

Changing the Font or Font Size and Inserting Symbols

You can change the *font* (the letters' style) or size of the font in a WordArt object by selecting from lists in the WordArt toolbar. You can use the same fonts in WordArt that you use in Word.

The default WordArt font size is Best Fit. This setting fits your text into the standard two-inch WordArt frame. If you select a smaller or larger font size, the size of the WordArt frame changes to fit your text.

Because you can use only one font per WordArt image, your symbol selections depend on the font you are using. By inserting a symbol, you can access symbols contained in your font that are not shown on the keyboard. The Windows TrueType fonts, Arial and Times New Roman, for example, include copyright symbols, fractions, and accented letters.

To change the font or font size, follow these steps:

1. Start WordArt, and type text in the Enter Your Text Here dialog box.

2. Select a font from the Font list in the WordArt toolbar.

3. Select a font size from the Font Size list in the WordArt toolbar. Select Best Fit if you want WordArt to choose the size that best fits the WordArt frame. If the size you want is not listed, type it in the Font Size box.

To insert a symbol, follow these steps:

1. Start WordArt, and type text in the Enter Your Text Here dialog box.

2. Position the insertion point where you want the symbol to appear.

3. Choose the Insert Symbol button. The Insert Symbol dialog box appears (see fig. 26.8).

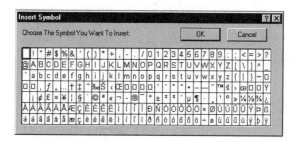

Fig. 26.8
The Insert Symbol dialog box gives you access to symbols not shown on the keyboard.

4. Select the symbol you want to insert.

5. Choose OK.

Applying Bold, Italics, or Even Caps

You can apply bold and italicized character formats in WordArt just as you do in Word. WordArt also enables you to make all the letters in your text the same height, regardless of case (see fig. 26.9). Each of these three effects—Bold, Italic, and Even Caps—toggles on and off through buttons on the toolbar. To apply Even Caps, for example, you click the Even Caps button; to remove this effect, you click the button a second time.

Fig. 26.9
Bold and Italics are the same in WordArt and Word, but the Even Caps effect is unique to WordArt.

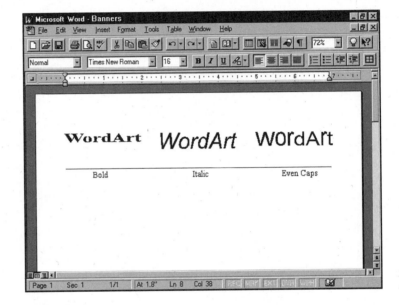

Flipping and Stretching Letters

By flipping letters, you create a different effect than that obtained by rotating the entire text—the Flip effect flips each individual letter (see fig. 26.10). By stretching letters, you stretch them to fit the WordArt frame (by default, a two-inch square frame), as shown in figure 26.11. Although you can change the size of letters in a WordArt image by changing the size of the WordArt frame (see the later section, "Editing a WordArt Object"), stretching text is the only way to lengthen it vertically.

Fig. 26.10
These are examples of flipped text.

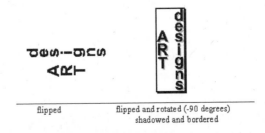

flipped   flipped and rotated (-90 degrees)
                          shadowed and bordered

ART ART

Normal text   Stretched

Fig. 26.11
This is an example
of stretched text.

The Flip and Stretch buttons toggle on and off on the WordArt toolbar; click the appropriate button to choose the effect, and click it again to remove the effect. You can stretch text also by choosing a menu command; like the button, the menu command toggles on and off.

Rotating, Slanting, and Arcing Text

The Rotation and Effects command or button enables you to rotate your WordArt image, slant the letters, change the angle of the arc, or reduce the height of the letters. The Special Effects dialog box that you see when you choose this command or button changes, depending on the shape you have selected for your image. You can rotate and slant images that you have poured into noncircular shapes. You also can rotate and change the arc or letter height for images you have poured into circular shapes. Figure 26.12 shows some of the effects you can achieve with the Rotation and Effects command or button.

V

Publishing with Graphics

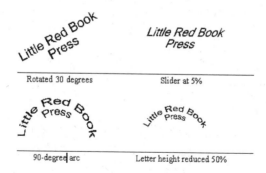

Rotated 30 degrees   Slider at 5%

90-degree arc   Letter height reduced 50%

Fig. 26.12
You can change
the angle, arc, or
height of letters.

To rotate, slant, or arc text, follow these steps:

1. Start WordArt, and type text in the Enter Your Text Here dialog box.

2. Click the Rotation and Effects button, or choose F_ormat, R_otation and Effects. The Special Effects dialog box appears (see fig. 26.13).

Fig. 26.13
If you have selected a circular shape, you can change rotation, arc, angle, and letter height (left); if you have selected some other shape, you can change the rotation or use Slider to change the slant (right).

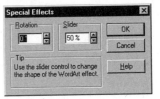

3. To rotate your WordArt image, select Rotation and select a rotation degree. For example, 90 degrees rotates the text to a vertical position, reading from bottom to top.

4. To slant the text, select Slider and select a percent. 100% angles the text backward; 50% is normal; 0% angles the text forward (similar to italics).

5. To change the angle of the arc, select Arc Angle and select a percent. The default, 180 degrees, is a half-circle; 90 degrees is a quarter-circle.

6. To reduce the letter height, select Reduce Letter Height By and select a percent. The default, 50%, reduces the letter height by half; 100% makes the letters very small.

7. Choose OK.

Aligning the Text

By default, text in a WordArt image is centered; however, WordArt offers other text-alignment options. You can change the text's alignment to the left or right. You can also *stretch justify* it to stretch the letters to fit the WordArt frame, *letter justify* it to space the letters out to fit the frame, or *word justify* it to space the words to fit the frame. These alignment effects are shown in figure 26.14.

Fig. 26.14
You can align and justify text six ways.

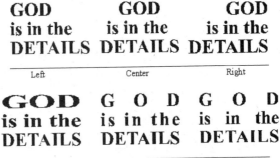

To align text, follow these steps:

1. Start WordArt, and type text in the Enter Your Text Here dialog box.

2. Click the Alignment button on the toolbar. A list of alignment options appears (see fig. 26.15).

3. Select the alignment style you want.

| ✓ Center |
| Left |
| Right |
| Stretch Justify |
| Letter Justify |
| Word Justify |

Fig. 26.15
You can align text to the center or a side of the WordArt frame, or justify it to fill the frame.

Adjusting Spacing between Characters

Kerning means adjusting the spacing between character pairs, and WordArt gives you the option of turning on kerning to optimize the spacing between certain adjacent letters. In general, kerning tightens the spacing between letter pairs such as *AV* and *Td*. If your type is any larger than normal reading size, kerning can make your type more readable.

Tracking adjusts the spacing between all letters. In WordArt, you can loosen or tighten the tracking, or set it to an exact percent of normal (see fig. 26.16).

Tracking controls letter spacing	Tracking controls letter spacing	Tracking controls letter spacing
Very tight	Normal	Very loose

Fig. 26.16
You can tighten or loosen tracking to adjust spacing between characters.

To adjust the spacing between letters and words, follow these steps:

1. Start WordArt, and type text in the Enter Your Text Here dialog box.

2. Click the Spacing Between Characters button or choose Format, Spacing Between Characters. The Spacing Between Characters dialog box appears (see fig. 26.17).

3. Select a tracking option: Very Tight (60% of normal), Tight (80%), Normal (100%), Loose (120%), or Very Loose (150%). Or select Custom and select a percent of normal.

V

Publishing with Graphics

Fig. 26.17
You can control the precise spacing between characters in your WordArt image.

4. Select the Automatically <u>K</u>ern Character Pairs option if you want WordArt to automatically kern characters. Deselect (clear) the option to turn off kerning.

5. Choose OK.

Adding Borders

◀ See "Shading and Bordering Paragraphs," p. 323

When you apply borders in a WordArt image, you apply them to the characters, not to the frame around the edge of the image. (To border the frame, exit WordArt, select the WordArt image, and choose the Format Borders and Shading command. Apply the border in a contrasting color to create interesting characters (see fig. 26.18).

Fig. 26.18
Apply borders of different widths and contrasting colors to create a neon-like effect.

To add or remove a border, follow these steps:

1. Start WordArt, and type text in the Enter Your Text Here dialog box.

2. Click the Borders button or choose F<u>o</u>rmat, Bord<u>e</u>r. The Border dialog box appears (see fig. 26.19).

3. Select a border thickness (width): Hair<u>l</u>ine, <u>T</u>hin, N<u>o</u>rmal, <u>M</u>edium, <u>W</u>ide, or <u>E</u>xtra wide. Select <u>N</u>one to remove a border.

4. Select <u>C</u>olor, and select a border color from the list box.

5. Choose OK.

Fig. 26.19
You can select borders of varying thickness and color.

Adding Color, Shading, or a Pattern

Colors, shading, and patterns fill each character. Patterns look best on text that is big and bold. For both shades and patterns, you can choose a foreground and background color. To change the color of text, simply select a different foreground color in the solid foreground pattern.

To add a pattern, follow these steps:

1. Start WordArt, and type text in the Enter Your Text Here dialog box.

2. Click the Shading button, or choose Format, Shading. The Shading dialog box appears (see fig. 26.20).

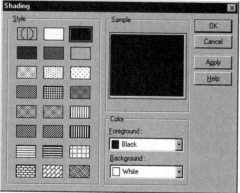

Fig. 26.20
The Sample box in the Shading dialog box shows you how your selections look.

3. From the Style group, select a pattern style. The top three options in this group are (from left to right): clear, background color, and foreground color.

4. Select Foreground and Background colors from the lists. Look at the Sample box to see the effects of your choices.

5. Choose Apply to see the effects of your choices on your text without closing the Shading dialog box, or choose OK or press Enter to close the dialog box.

Follow these steps to add color to text:

1. In WordArt, click the Shading button or choose Format, Shading.

2. In the Style group, select the solid background option (top middle) and select the color you want from the Background list.

   Or, select the solid foreground option (top right) and select the color you want from the Foreground list.

3. Choose Apply to see the effect of your choice on your text without closing the Shading dialog box, or choose OK or press Enter to close the dialog box.

Follow these steps to add shading to text:

1. In WordArt, click the Shading button or choose Format, Shading.

2. In the Style group, select a shading option (the second and third rows are dotted shading patterns; the fourth row includes patterns small enough to work as shading).

3. Select the shading color you want from the Foreground list, and select White from the Background list.

4. Choose Apply to see the effect of your choice on your text without closing the Shading dialog box, or choose OK or press Enter to close the dialog box.

Adding Shadows

Like borders, shadows apply to the letters in your WordArt image, not to the edge of the WordArt frame. (To add a shadowed border, exit WordArt, select the WordArt image, and choose Format, Borders and Shading. You can add many different types of shadows to your letters, in a variety of colors.

◄ See "Shading and Bordering Paragraphs," p. 323

You can add a shadow by using either the Shadow button or a command. To choose a color for a shadow, however, you must display the Shadow dialog box (see fig. 26.21). To display the Shadow dialog box, either click More in the Shadow palette displayed when you click the Shadow button (see fig. 26.22), or choose Format, Shadow. Text remains black, unless you change its color by using the Shading button or command (refer to the "Adding Color, Shading, or a Pattern" section, earlier in this chapter).

Fig. 26.21
By choosing
For̲mat, Shadow,
you can choose
both shadow style
and color.

Fig. 26.22
Choose from the
shadow styles
shown.

Editing a WordArt Object

You can edit a WordArt object in several ways. You can change the image itself by restarting WordArt and editing the text or choosing different special effects. In this section, you learn how to select your WordArt object and re-start WordArt.

◀ See "Formatting Characters," p. 254

◀ See "Working with Pictures," p. 712

Many other methods of editing WordArt objects also are available to you. You can resize, crop, move, or copy a WordArt image by using the same techniques you use for any inserted picture. These techniques are covered in "Working with Pictures" in Chapter 23, "Inserting Pictures in Your Document." You can insert a WordArt object in a text box that you draw by using the Drawing toolbar (see "Including Text or Another Picture in a Drawing" in Chapter 25, "Drawing with Word's Drawing Tools"). By framing and positioning a WordArt object, you can move it freely on the page and wrap text around it. You can add a caption (see Chapter 31, "Adding Cross-References and Captions"). Later in this section, table 26.2 provides an overview of how to use these techniques to edit your WordArt object.

Shortcuts for adding a border or caption or for framing your WordArt object are included in the WordArt shortcut menu. You can display that menu by clicking the WordArt object with the right mouse button.

◀ See "Moving and Positioning Frames," p. 738

You must select a WordArt image before you edit it. In some cases, selecting the WordArt object is part of the process of editing; for example, you can double-click the WordArt image to select the image and start WordArt for editing. In other situations, you must select the WordArt object before you can edit it. A WordArt object selected with the mouse appears with square selection handles on all sides and corners; selected with the keyboard by holding down the Shift key, and pressing an arrow key to cross the graphic, the object appears reversed.

V

Publishing with Graphics

◀ See "Working with Pictures," p. 712

When you change a WordArt image, you can use WordArt in the usual way (displaying the Enter Your Text Here dialog box and replacing the Word menus and toolbar with WordArt menus and buttons), or you can display WordArt in a dialog box. The WordArt 2.0 dialog box is shown in figure 26.23.

Fig. 26.23
Open the WordArt dialog box to edit your WordArt object.

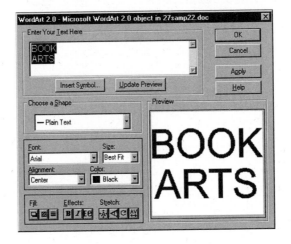

◀ See "Working with Pictures," p. 712

To edit a WordArt object, do either of the following:

■ Select your WordArt object and choose Edit, WordArt Object. From the menu that opens, choose Edit to display WordArt in the usual way, or Open to display the WordArt 2.0 dialog box.

■ Or, click your WordArt object with the right mouse button to display the shortcut menu. Select Edit WordArt to edit your image in the usual way, or select Open WordArt to edit your image by using the WordArt dialog box.

Table 26.2 shows an overview of different ways to edit a WordArt object.

Table 26.2 Techniques for Editing a WordArt Object—An Overview

To	Do This
Move a WordArt object	Select it and drag it to a new location.
Copy a WordArt object	Select it and choose any Copy command or shortcut; or, drag it while holding down the Ctrl key.
Paste a WordArt object	Position the insertion point where you want the graphic, and choose any Paste command or shortcut.
Resize a WordArt object	Select and drag a corner selection handle for proportional resizing; drag a side handle for nonproportional resizing.
Crop a WordArt object	Select the object and hold Shift while dragging any selection handle.
Crop or resize a WordArt graphic	Select and choose Format, Picture.
Frame a WordArt object	Select and choose the Insert Frame command, or click the graphic with the right mouse button and select Frame Picture.
Position a WordArt object	Frame the graphic and choose Format, Frame.
Border a WordArt object	Select and choose Format, Borders and Shading, or click the graphic with the right mouse button and select Borders and Shading.
Add a caption to a WordArt object	Select and choose the Insert Caption command, or click the graphic with the right mouse button and select Caption.

◀ See "Including Text or Another Picture in a Drawing," p. 789

▶ See "Adding Cross-References and Captions," p. 917

V

Publishing with Graphics

Chapter 27

Graphing Data

With Microsoft Graph, you can create informative and impressive charts for your Word for Windows 95 documents. You can turn an overwhelming table of numbers into a chart that shows important trends and changes. You can relegate the detailed numeric table to a location where it doesn't slow down communication. Microsoft Graph is not just a small charting application; it has the capability of Microsoft Excel, the most capable Windows spreadsheet, graphics, and database program.

Microsoft Graph is a separate program that embeds charts and their data into Windows applications such as Microsoft Word for Windows.

Charts embedded into a Word for Windows document contain both the chart and the data that creates the chart. You cannot save the chart or data separately.

In this chapter, you learn to do the following:

- Create charts

- Edit charts

- Add items, such as legends and titles, to a chart

- Change the chart type

- Change the size of a chart

- Format datasheets

Creating a Chart

Figure 27.1 shows a Word for Windows document enhanced by a chart. Charts are created from data entered into a *datasheet*, a spreadsheet-like view of the data, displayed in rows and columns, in its own window.

Fig. 27.1
A Word for Windows document can be enhanced by a chart.

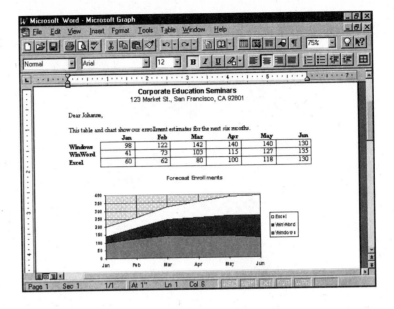

With Microsoft Graph, you can create any of 14 chart types in Word for Windows, using several methods. The text and numbers in the datasheet can be entered in any of the following ways:

■ Selected from a table in the Word for Windows document

■ Typed into Microsoft Graph

■ Copied in from any Windows document

■ Imported from a Microsoft Excel, Lotus 1-2-3, or text file

■ Read in from an existing Microsoft Excel chart

To start Microsoft Graph, follow these steps:

1. Position the insertion point where you want the chart to appear in your document.

2. Choose Create, New, and select the Create New tab in the Object dialog box.

3. Select Microsoft Graph 5.0 from the list in the Object Type list box.

4. Click OK.

   Microsoft Graph opens in the active document window, with default data in the datasheet and chart (see fig. 27.2). The chart reflects the data in the sample datasheet.

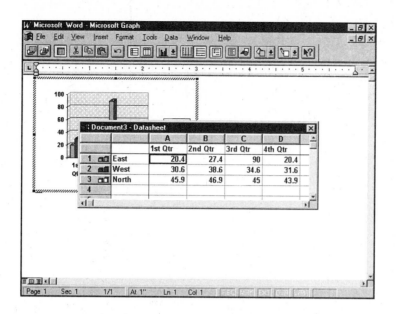

Fig. 27.2
When Microsoft Graph is open, the Word toolbars disappear, and the Microsoft Graph Standard toolbar appears.

> **Note**
>
> You can add the Insert Chart button to the toolbar with Tools, Customize. Select Insert from the Categories box, click the Chart button, and drag it onto the toolbar. Click Close. Click the Insert Chart button to start Microsoft Graph.

You can change the data in the Microsoft Graph datasheet in many ways. Select and change the data in the datasheet to change the chart. You can also add or remove chart items, such as legends, arrows, and titles, or change the appearance or position of selected chart items or data in the sheet.

When you are finished making changes, click outside the chart to return to your document. Microsoft Graph closes and the Word toolbar reappears.

Using the ChartWizard to Create a Chart from a Table

The ChartWizard displays a sequence of dialog boxes that guides you through creating a chart (see fig. 27.3). You quickly complete tasks that take longer when you make the same selections from menus and toolbars. The ChartWizard lets you specify the chart type, the format, and how you want the data in the chart plotted. The data you use in your chart comes directly from a table in your Microsoft Word document.

Fig. 27.3

Word displays the ChartWizard, a series of dialog boxes that guides you through creating a chart, using the data you inserted in your table.

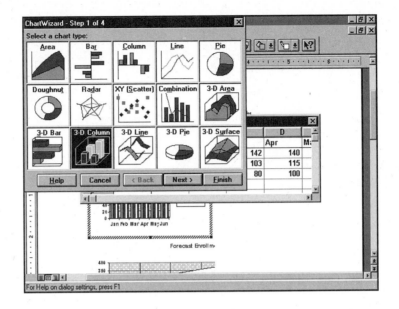

To use the ChartWizard, follow these steps:

1. Use the Table feature to insert and format a table, and then choose Table, Select Table to select the entire table.

◀ See "Creating Tables," p. 506

2. Choose Insert, Object, Create New.

3. In the Object Type list box, choose Microsoft Graph 5.0, and then choose OK.

4. Specify a chart type in the Select a chart type group and click the Next button.

5. Specify a format for the chart type and click the Next button.

6. Specify how you want the data plotted and click the Next button.

7. Add a legend, a chart title, and a title to each axis if you want, and click Finish.

The completed datasheet and chart, superimposed over the original table, appear (see fig. 27.4).

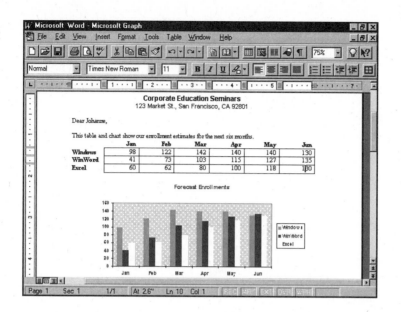

Fig. 27.4
This chart was created from the table with the ChartWizard.

Using the Microsoft Graph Datasheet

Microsoft Graph plots data points from the datasheet as *markers* in the chart. Markers appear as lines, bars, columns, data points in X-Y charts, or slices in a pie chart. With the Microsoft Graph default settings, a row of data points appears in a chart as a *series* of markers; a series of values appears in the chart connected by a line, or as bars or columns of the same color. In figure 27.5, for example, the row labeled East corresponds to one line in the 3-D line chart.

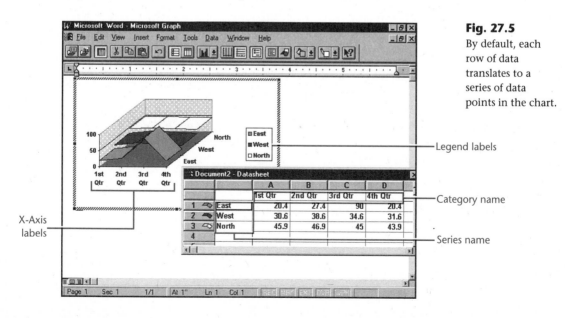

Fig. 27.5
By default, each row of data translates to a series of data points in the chart.

X-Axis labels

Legend labels

Category name

Series name

Tip
Display the datasheet by choosing <u>V</u>iew, <u>D</u>atasheet. Graphics display in either the row or column headers to show which contains the data series.

In this default orientation, known as Series in Rows, the text in the first row of the datasheet becomes the *category names* that appear below the *category (X) axis* (the horizontal axis). The text in the left column becomes the *series names*, which Microsoft Graph uses as labels for the legend. (The *legend* is the box that labels the colors or patterns used by each series of markers.) If you change orientation and want to return to the default orientation, choose <u>D</u>ata, Series In <u>R</u>ows.

If your data uses the reverse orientation on the datasheet, so that each data series goes down a column, you must choose <u>D</u>ata, Series In <u>C</u>olumns. When you use that command, Microsoft Graph takes the category names (x-axis labels) from the left column of the datasheet and the series names (legend labels) from the top row (see fig. 27.6).

Fig. 27.6
A data series can show column orientation.

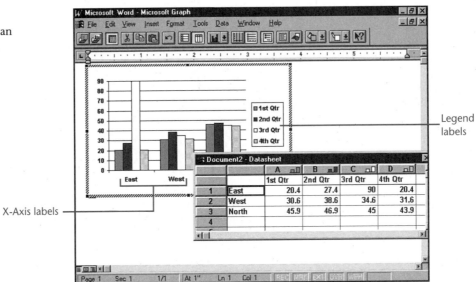

Legend labels

X-Axis labels

When you create a Microsoft Graph chart, be sure that you have text for each series name (legend labels), text for each category label (x-axis), and a number for each data point.

Copying Data from Word for Windows or Other Applications

You can copy data from applications and paste it into the datasheet to create a chart. You can create a chart, for example, from a series of text and numbers aligned on tabs in Word for Windows, or you can copy a range of cells from a Microsoft Excel worksheet. ("Importing a Microsoft Excel Chart," later in this chapter, describes how to import a range from Microsoft Excel or use a Microsoft Excel chart as a basis for a Microsoft Graph chart.)

You must use tabs to separate data and text in a word processing document if you want to copy the information into separate datasheet cells. Figure 27.7 shows a Word for Windows document with the data and labels separated by right-align tabs.

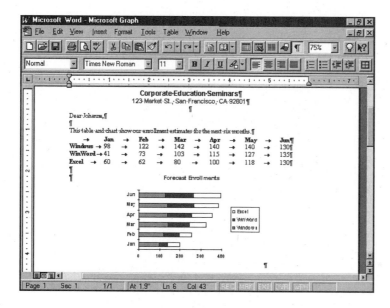

Fig. 27.7
You can separate data and labels by tabs, and create a chart from them.

To copy data from a document or Microsoft Excel worksheet, and create a chart, follow these steps:

1. Select the tabbed data or range of Microsoft Excel cells.

2. Choose Edit, Copy.

3. Position the insertion point where you want the chart, and then choose Insert, Object. Select Microsoft Graph 5.0 from the list, and then choose OK.

4. Activate the datasheet and erase all existing data by selecting it and choosing Edit, Clear, All or by pressing the Delete key.

5. Ensure that the top-left cell in the datasheet is selected, and then choose Edit, Paste.

   The data is pasted into the datasheet, and the chart updates.

Tip
You can select the entire datasheet by clicking the Select All button located at the top-left intersection of the column and row headings.

6. Format, modify, or size the chart and datasheet as necessary.

7. Click outside the chart to return to the document.

   The chart is inserted at the insertion point.

Importing Worksheet or Text Data

You may want to use data you have in an ASCII text file, or in a Microsoft Excel or Lotus 1-2-3 worksheet, for a chart. You can save time by importing this data directly into the Microsoft Graph datasheet.

To import data into the datasheet, follow these steps:

1. Erase all unwanted data from the datasheet, and then select the cell where you want to position the top-left corner of the imported data. If you are importing an entire chart's worth of data, select the top-left cell of the datasheet.

2. Choose Edit, Import Data or click the Import Data button. The Import Data dialog box appears (see fig. 27.8). Find and select the file from which you want to import data.

Fig. 27.8

The Import Data dialog box.

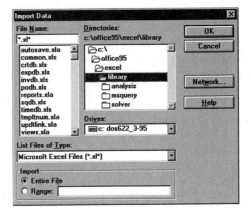

3. Specify Entire File or Range to indicate a range, such as **A12:D36**, or a range name in the Import group. (Refer to your spreadsheet program for information on naming a range.)

4. Choose OK.

To import data from a worksheet, you must have the worksheet converter files loaded. If they are not loaded, run the Word for Windows or Microsoft Office Setup program. Select the options to install the converters you choose without reinstalling all of Word for Windows. You must use your original Word for Windows or Microsoft Office installation disk to load the converters.

Importing a Microsoft Excel Chart

With Microsoft Excel, you can create mathematical models that generate charts, and you can link the charts to Word for Windows documents. If you change the Excel worksheet that contains your mathematical model, you change the chart. These changes are reflected in the Word for Windows document.

Importing a Microsoft Excel chart into Microsoft Graph to embed the chart into the Word for Windows document has other advantages. Because embedded charts keep the data with the chart, another person can update the chart without using Microsoft Excel or the original Microsoft Excel worksheet. Links are not broken if the source worksheet or chart in Microsoft Excel is renamed or moved to a different folder.

▶ See "Linking Documents and Files," p. 993

To import a Microsoft Excel chart and the chart's related data, follow these steps:

▶ See "Embedding Data," p. 986

1. Position the insertion point where you want the chart; start Microsoft Graph 5.0 by choosing Insert, Object, selecting Microsoft Graph, and clicking OK.

2. Choose Edit, Import Chart. The Import Chart dialog box appears (see fig. 27.9).

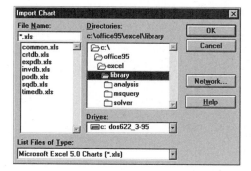

Fig. 27.9

The Import Chart dialog box allows you to import a Microsoft Excel 4 chart sheet saved with an XLS file extension. You also can import the first chart in a Microsoft Excel 5 or Excel 95 workbook.

3. Select the drive, folder, and file name of the Microsoft Excel chart, and then choose OK. Choose OK to confirm that overwriting any data in the chart is OK.

The chart must be on its own sheet in the workbook.

V

Publishing with Graphics

The chart opens in Microsoft Graph, and the associated data appears in the datasheet. Data series that were in rows in Microsoft Excel are in columns in the Microsoft Graph datasheet, but the chart is correct.

Entering Data to Create Overlay Charts

Overlay charts overlay one two-dimensional chart type with another. (You cannot combine 3-D chart types.) By combining chart types, you can clearly display the relationships between different types of data or data with widely different scales.

One way to create a combination chart is to choose Format, AutoFormat. First, double-click the chart to start Microsoft Graph, and choose Format, AutoFormat; select Combination in the Galleries list box. Then select one of the combination chart formats in the Formats box, and choose OK.

You can also create an overlay chart from existing charts by selecting a data series (line, bar, or column) whose chart type you want to be different from the other data series, and choosing Format, Chart Type. Make sure that the Selected Series option is selected in the Chart Type dialog box, then select the desired chart type for that series, and choose OK. This method is the one to use if you've already customized a chart, because choosing Format, AutoFormat will destroy the custom formatting.

Tip

Choose Format, AutoFormat to quickly combine chart types to create an overlay. See "Using AutoFormat on a Chart Type," for more information about using AutoFormat.

When you have more than one chart type in a chart, each chart type forms a *series group*. Each series group appears as a selection at the bottom of the Format menu. You can select the group from the Format menu and make changes to how that series group appears. For example, if your chart contains a column group, then you could choose Format, Column Group and change the columns on the chart from side-by-side to stacked columns. Only the column portion of the chart would be affected.

To add a secondary axis for that data series, select the series in the chart and choose Format, Selected Data Series. Select the Axis tab, then select the Secondary Axis option and choose OK. The secondary axis can be formatted separately from the primary axis, so, for example, you can adjust the scale on this axis to match the data it represents.

Editing the Datasheet

Working in the datasheet is similar to working in a Word for Windows table or a Microsoft Excel worksheet. You can edit cellular data directly in a cell or in an editing box.

Selecting Data

To move and select cells in the datasheet, you use many of the same techniques used in Microsoft Excel. If you are using a mouse, you can use the scroll bars to scroll to any location on the datasheet. You can select parts of the datasheet by using the following methods:

- To select a cell, click it.

- To select multiple cells, drag the mouse across them.

- To select a row or column, click its header.

- To select multiple rows or columns, drag across the headers.

- To select all cells in the datasheet, click in the blank rectangle at the top-left corner, where row and column headings intersect.

If you are using the keyboard, use the keys shown in the following tables to move the insertion point, or to select cells and their contents:

To Move	Press
A cell	Arrow key in the direction to move
To first cell in row	Home
To last cell in row	End
To top-left data cell	Ctrl+Home
To lower-right data cell	Ctrl+End
A screen up/down	Page Up/Down

To Select	Press
A cell	Arrow key to cell you want
A range (rectangle) of cells	Shift+arrow key or F8 (enters Extend mode). Arrow key, and then F8 (exits Extend mode)
A row	Shift+space bar
A column	Ctrl+space bar
The datasheet	Shift+Ctrl+space bar, or Ctrl+A
Undo selection	Shift+Backspace

Tip
Select the entire worksheet contents and press Delete to erase the entire worksheet.

V

Publishing with Graphics

Replacing or Editing Existing Data

The easiest way to replace the contents of a cell is to select the cell by moving to it or by clicking it, and then typing directly over the cell's contents. When you press Enter or select a different cell, the change takes effect.

To edit the contents of a cell, select the cell by moving to it or by clicking it. Press F2, the Edit key, or double-click the cell. You can edit the cell's contents as you would edit text in a document. After you finish editing, press Enter.

Inserting or Deleting Rows and Columns

Microsoft Graph expands the chart to include data or text you add in rows or columns outside the originally charted data. If you add rows or columns of data and leave blank rows or columns, Microsoft Graph does not include the blank rows or columns as part of the chart.

To insert rows or columns in the datasheet, select the rows or columns you want to insert, and then choose Insert, Cells. Rows or columns are inserted, depending on what you selected. To delete rows or columns, select what you want to delete, and choose Edit, Delete. The shortcut keys for inserting and deleting are Ctrl++ (plus) and Ctrl+– (minus), respectively. (Use the plus and minus keys on the numeric keypad only.) If you do not select an entire row or column, a dialog box appears and asks you to select whether you want to affect the rows or columns that pass through the selected cells.

Including and Excluding Data from a Chart

When you add data or text to the datasheet, Microsoft Graph immediately redraws the chart, even if the data you've added is not adjacent to other data in the table. This redrawing is inconvenient if you want to add a row or column of data to the table, but not include the data in the chart.

To include or exclude a row or column with the mouse, double-click the row or column heading. The double-click toggles the row or column between being included and being excluded. Excluded rows or columns are grayed.

To include or exclude a row or column with the keyboard, select the entire row or column and then choose Data, Include Row/Col, or Data, Exclude Row/Col.

Changing Data by Moving a Graph Marker

Microsoft Graph enables you to move column, bar, lines, or X-Y markers on 2-D charts. As you move the data point, the corresponding data changes in the datasheet—a convenient feature for smoothing a curve so that it matches real-life experience, or for "fudging" numbers so that they fit the results you want.

To change values on the datasheet by moving markers on the chart, follow these steps:

1. Open the worksheet and chart. Activate the chart. The chart must be a two-dimensional column, bar, or line chart.

2. Click the column, bar, or line marker you want to change one time to select the data series, then click it a second time to select the data point. A black handle appears on the marker.

3. Drag the black handle to the new height. When you drag the black handle, a tick mark on the vertical axis moves, showing you the value of the new location.

4. Release the mouse when the marker is at the location you want.

The corresponding data in the datasheet changes.

◀ See "Selecting Text," p. 141

◀ See "Moving, Copying, and Linking Text or Graphics," p. 160

Changing the Chart Type

When Microsoft Graph first opens, the chart it displays is a 3-D column chart. Many different chart types are available. You select the chart type appropriate for the data you want to graph.

Try to choose the appropriate chart type before you begin customizing. To change the chart type after you customize, follow the procedure described in the "Customizing an Existing Chart Type" section, later in this chapter.

Selecting the Original Chart Type

When you build charts, you can use any of the 103 predefined chart formats. The easiest way to create charts is to select the predefined chart closest to the type you want. Then you can customize the predefined chart until it fits your needs.

To use a predefined chart, follow these steps:

1. Choose Format, Chart Type. The Chart Type dialog box appears (see fig. 27.10).

Fig. 27.10
To select the chart type you want from the Chart Type dialog box, double-click the box containing that type.

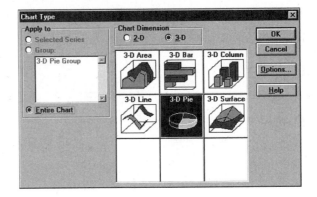

2. Select the group to which you want to apply your selection in the Apply To group.

3. Select 2-D or 3-D from the Chart Dimension box. Examples of each chart type are illustrated directly below the Chart Dimension box.

4. Click a chart type from the samples.

5. Choose the Options button to see additional subtypes of the chart type you selected.

6. Choose OK.

Customizing an Existing Chart Type

You can save yourself work by deciding on the type of chart you want before you customize it. Use the Format, Chart Type command or click the Chart Type button to try different types of charts, and then customize the one you decide to use. If you change the chart type after you customize a chart, you may lose some of your custom selections.

To customize a chart type, follow these steps:

1. Activate the chart and choose Format, Chart Type or click the Chart Type button. The Chart Type dialog box appears, with the options appropriate to the active chart type available.

2. Select, in the Apply To group, the portion of the chart to which you want to apply the new type.

3. Select the Chart Dimension (2-D or 3-D), and then select the chart type.

4. Click Options to display the Format Column Group dialog box (see fig. 27.11). The options available are appropriate for the type of chart that is active. They include Subtype, Options, and Axis.

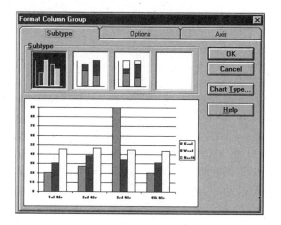

Fig. 27.11
Use the Format Column Group dialog box to change subtypes, add special lines and bars, and change other options.

5. Choose OK.

Using AutoFormat to Change a Chart Type

Instead of applying formatting yourself, you can save time by applying an autoformat. Choose one of the built-in autoformats, or create your own custom autoformat and use it on future charts. Autoformats are similar to templates and are based on chart types. They can include legends, gridlines, data labels, colors, and other formatting characteristics. The look of the chart changes as soon as you apply an autoformat, but the data does not change. You cannot alter the formatting used by the autoformats.

To apply an autoformat to a chart, follow these steps:

1. Double-click the chart you want to format to start the Microsoft Graph program.

2. Choose Format, AutoFormat, or right-click the chart and choose AutoFormat from the shortcut menu.

3. Select Built-in or User-Defined from the Formats Used box. Choose User-Defined to choose a custom autoformat. (See the following section, "Creating a Custom AutoFormat," for more information.)

4. Select the chart type you want from the Galleries list box.

5. Select the autoformat you want to apply from the Formats box.

6. Choose OK.

Creating a Custom AutoFormat

If you have formatted a chart to create a look you want to use again, you can add the custom format to the AutoFormat Gallery and apply it to future charts.

To create your own custom autoformat, follow these steps:

1. Create a chart and format it, using the techniques described later in this chapter.

2. Activate the formatted chart.

3. Choose Format, AutoFormat, or right-click the chart and choose AutoFormat from the shortcut menu.

4. Select User-Defined from the Formats Used group.

5. Choose the Customize button, and then choose Add. The Add Custom AutoFormat dialog box appears.

6. Type the Format Name and a Description for the new autoformat.

7. Choose OK and then click Close. The new listing appears in the Formats box in the AutoFormat dialog box when you select User-Defined.

Formatting the Datasheet

The proper formatting of your datasheet is important for reasons other than ensuring the ease and accuracy of data entry. The format of dates and numbers in the datasheet controls the format of dates and numbers in the chart.

 In Microsoft Graph, the datasheet disappears when you are editing the chart. To display the datasheet, choose View, Datasheet or click the View Datasheet button.

Adjusting Column Widths in the Datasheet

Depending on the number format of a cell, when a number is too large to fit in a cell, the cell may fill with # signs. To adjust column width with the mouse, move the pointer over the line separating the column headings until the pointer changes to a two-headed arrow. Drag the column separator line to the column width you want, and release the mouse button.

To adjust column width with the keyboard, select cells in the columns you want to adjust, then choose Format, Column Width. The Column Width dialog box appears. Type a number representing the width of the column, and then choose OK.

You can return column widths to their standard setting by choosing the Use Standard Width check box in the Column Width dialog box. Choose Best Fit to set the column to the minimum width required to display the current cell contents. You must change it again later if you change the cell contents.

Formatting Numbers and Dates

Microsoft Graph has many predefined numeric and date formats. You can choose from these formats to format the datasheet and chart, or create your own custom formats.

The format of the first data cell in a series defines the numeric or date format for that series in the chart. You can even enter a date such as **12-24-95** as a label for a category axis. You can then format the cell with a different date format (such as **d-mmm**, so that the date appears as 12-Dec).

To format data cells, follow these steps:

1. Select the data cell or range you want to format. You can select entire rows or columns at one time.

2. Choose Format, Number. The Number Format dialog box displays a list of numeric and date formats.

3. Select from the list the numeric or date format you want to apply to the selected data cells.

4. Choose OK.

The following table gives examples of the different formats:

Format	Entry	Result
#,###	9999.00	9,999
#,###.00	9999.5	9,999.50
$#,###	9000.65	$9,001
0.00 ;(0.00)	5.6	$5.60
0.00 ;(0.00)	-9.834	($9.83)

(continues)

Tip

Double-click the right border of the column heading to set the column to the minimum width required to display the widest entry in the column.

V

Publishing with Graphics

Format	Entry	Result
mmm	12	Dec
dd	6	06
yy	1991	91
hh:mm AM/PM	6:12	06:12 AM

Custom Formatting of Numbers and Dates

◀ See "Formatting Characters," p. 254

◀ See "Formatting Field Results," p. 602

If the format you need is not in the Number Format list, you can create your own custom formats by typing them in the Code text box. Use the same characters as those used in the predefined formats. After you create a custom format, it appears at the bottom of the Number Format list so that you can reuse it. *Special Edition Using Excel for Windows 95,* published by Que, contains detailed information about creating custom formats.

Adding Items to a Chart

You can add many items to your Microsoft Graph charts—such as titles, legends, and arrows—that make the charts more informative and easier to read.

Adding to existing Microsoft Graph charts in a Word for Windows document is easy. With a mouse, double-click the chart. With the keyboard, select the chart by moving the insertion point next to the chart, and then pressing Shift+left- or right-arrow to move across the chart. After the chart is selected, choose Edit, Object, Edit.

Microsoft Graph opens and loads the chart, after which you can use any of the procedures described in this chapter to modify your chart or data. If the datasheet is not open, choose View, Datasheet or click the View Datasheet button.

When you select an item that you've added to your chart—a title, for example—black handles appear around the item, and you can move or resize it.

Adding Titles and Data Values

You can use the Insert menu to add or delete most items to or from a chart. To add a title or data label to a fixed location on a chart, for example, follow these steps:

1. Choose <u>I</u>nsert, <u>T</u>itles. The Titles dialog box appears (see fig. 27.12).

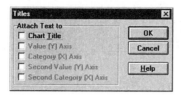

Fig. 27.12
The Titles dialog box allows you to choose from several different kinds of titles.

2. Select one of the check boxes.

3. Choose OK.

   Depending upon the option you choose in step 2, a default title of Title, X, Y, or Z appears at the appropriate location in the chart.

4. While that default title is selected, type the title text you want to use. Press Enter to move to a second line. Edit using normal editing keys.

5. To finish the text, press Esc or click outside the text.

   To remove fixed text, select the text and then press the Delete key or choose <u>E</u>dit, Cl<u>e</u>ar.

To attach numbers or labels that move with the data point in a bar, column, or line chart, follow these steps:

1. Choose <u>I</u>nsert, <u>D</u>ata Labels to display the Data Labels dialog box.

2. Select the Show <u>V</u>alue or Show <u>L</u>abel option. If you are working with a pie chart, the Show <u>P</u>ercent and Show Label <u>a</u>nd Percent options are available.

3. Choose OK.

To delete data point values or labels, select them and press Delete, or choose Insert, <u>D</u>ata Labels, and select <u>N</u>one.

Adding Floating Text

You can use *floating text* to add comment boxes or to create boxes for embellishing or covering parts of a chart.

To add floating text, make sure that no other text is selected, and then type the text. You don't have to choose a command; just type and then press Esc. Your text appears in a floating box. To move or resize the box, click it to display the black handles. Then resize the box or drag it to a new location.

> **Note**
>
> You can insert a text box by clicking the Text Box button and then typing the contents. Click the text box to select and move or resize it.

To use the keyboard to select text so that it can be formatted, hold down the shift key while you press the arrow keys until the text you want formatted is enclosed by black or white handles. You cannot use the keyboard to move floating text.

To edit the text in a floating text box, click the text to select it, and then click where you want the insertion point. If you are using the keyboard, you must retype the text. To delete a floating text box, select the text and then press the Delete key, or use Edit, Clear, All.

Adding Legends, Arrows, Gridlines, Trendlines, and Error Bars

To add a legend, choose Insert, Legend or click the Legend button. The legend that appears is enclosed in black handles. To move a legend, select it, choose Format, Selected Legend, and select the Placement tab. Choose an option in the Type group and choose OK. Or, drag the legend to a new location and release it.

To change the labels in the legend, change the series labels in the datasheet.

To add arrows to your charts, choose View, Toolbars, select the Drawing toolbar, and choose OK (see fig. 27.13). Use the Arrow tool to place an arrow in your chart. Arrows have black handles at either end so that you can resize them. To move an arrow, drag with the pointer on the arrow's shaft.

Fig. 27.13
Choose View, Toolbars to display any or all of the toolbars available in Microsoft Graph 5.0.

To add gridlines to a chart, choose Insert, Gridlines. The Gridlines dialog box that appears has check boxes for major and minor vertical and horizontal gridlines. To delete gridlines, clear the check boxes for the gridlines you don't want. You can also click the Vertical Gridlines and Horizontal Gridlines buttons on the Standard toolbar.

To add axes, choose Insert, Axes. The Axes dialog box appears, from which you control whether an axis is visible. A checkmark in the box indicates that the axis will display.

Trendlines indicate direction in a data series. With Microsoft Graph 5.0, you can add trendlines to data series in area, bar, column, line, and xy (scatter) chart groups. (Check Microsoft Graph's Help for information about the types of trendlines from which you can select, and how to do it.) You can add a trendline by choosing Insert, Trendline.

Error bars indicate the range of uncertainty of the data in a data series. With Microsoft Graph 5.0, you can add error bars to data series in area, bar, column, line, and xy (scatter) chart groups. (Check Microsoft Graph's Help for information about types of error bars, and how to add them.) You can add an error bar by choosing Insert, Error Bars.

Formatting the Chart and Chart Items

After you select a predefined chart format and add chart items, you can customize your chart. You can change the colors, patterns, and borders of chart items; the type and color of the fonts; the position and size of some chart items; and you can add lines, arrows, titles, legends, and floating text. By selecting an axis and then a format command, you can change the scale and the appearance of tick marks and labels. You also can rotate 3-D charts and create picture charts, in which pictures take the place of columns, bars, or lines.

Customize charts by selecting an item in the chart, and then choosing a format command, as in the following steps:

1. Select the chart item you want to customize by clicking it or by pressing an arrow key until the chart item is selected.

2. Choose the Format menu and a formatting command to format the item. A dialog box appears that provides choices for the type of formatting you want to apply or change.

3. Select the changes you want to make from the dialog box.

4. Choose OK.

As a shortcut, you can double-click any chart item—such as an arrow, bar, or chart background—to produce that item's Format dialog box. You can choose from several tabs, which vary depending on the item you selected. Each tab contains many options for formatting each item on a chart.

Sizing Your Chart

Charts look best in Word for Windows if you resize them in Microsoft Graph. Resizing the chart in Word for Windows changes the size, but does not correct text placement, readjust the scale, and so on.

Change the size of the chart as you would change the size of any window. You can drag its borders or corners with the mouse. You can choose the Size command from the Document Control menu, press Alt+- (hyphen), and then press the arrow keys to resize the window. Make the chart's window the size you want the chart to be when you paste it into the Word for Windows document. (The Document Control menu is the icon located at the top-left corner of the document window, or to the left of the File menu when the document is maximized.)

Changing Patterns and Colors

To add patterns or colors to an item, select the item, choose Format, and the command for that item at the top of the menu, and then select the colors, patterns, shading, and line widths you want for the item. With a mouse, double-click an item to display the item's Format dialog box. Or, click the Color or Pattern button in the Standard toolbar. You can also press Ctrl+1 to open the Format dialog box for the selected item.

To return to the default colors, patterns, and borders, select the chart items you want to change, right-click the items and choose the appropriate Format command, and then select the Automatic option for the specific item in the Format dialog box.

Formatting Fonts and Text

Every datasheet is formatted with a single font, size, and style. You can use a different font, size, or style, however, for each text item in the chart.

To change an item's font, size, or style, select the item, and then choose Format, Font. Select a font, size, or style. With a mouse, double-click the item, and then choose the Font tab. The Font tab of the Formatting dialog box looks like other Font dialog boxes in Word for Windows. It enables you to select from three types of character backgrounds:

- Automatic applies an opaque background if the color beneath the text matches the text color; otherwise, it applies a transparent background.

- Transparent makes the area behind the chart text transparent.

- Opaque applies a solid color behind the chart text.

To rotate or align text, such as the text on an axis, double-click the axis to display the Format Axis dialog box. Click the Alignment tab, select the text orientation you want, and choose OK.

Formatting Axes

Microsoft Graph automatically scales and labels the axes, but you can select any axis and change its patterns, scale, font, number format, or alignment.

To format an axis, follow these steps:

1. Double-click the axis you want to format.

   Or, select the axis you want to format, and choose Format, Selected Axis. The Format Axis dialog box appears.

2. Select the tab(s) you want, and make changes.

3. Click OK.

Rotating 3-D Charts

You can rotate the angle of your 3-D chart to display the chart's best view. To rotate a 3-D chart, follow these steps:

1. Choose Format, 3-D View. The Format 3-D View dialog box appears (see fig. 27.14).

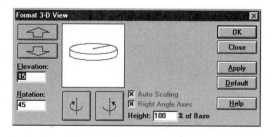

Fig. 27.14
Changing the values of Elevation and Rotation in the Format 3-D View dialog box affects the wire frame sample chart.

V

Publishing with Graphics

2. Change the Elevation or Rotation by clicking the large up and down arrows, or by typing values into the text Elevation or Rotation boxes.

3. When the wire-frame sample is oriented so that you can see the view of the chart as you want it to be, choose OK.

The Apply button enables you to apply the new orientation to the chart and keep the dialog box open—a helpful feature when you want to experiment. Click the Default button to return to the original orientation.

Exiting or Updating Graphs

◀ See "Formatting Characters," p. 254

◀ See "Moving and Positioning Frames," p. 738

◀ See "Sizing Frames," p. 747

As soon as you click outside the chart, Microsoft Graph closes and you return to your document window. You cannot save the chart and data separately—they must be saved as embedded objects in the Word for Windows document.

To update or modify the chart, double-click it to restart Microsoft Graph.

> **Note**
>
> You can convert charts created in earlier versions of Microsoft Graph to 5.0. Open the document that contains the chart you want to convert. Choose Edit, Object, then choose Convert. Select Convert To, then Microsoft Graph 5.0. Choose OK.

> **Note**
>
> If you are familiar with charting in Microsoft Excel, use what you learned in Microsoft Excel to learn about Microsoft Graph. For more detailed information on Microsoft Graph, refer to *Special Edition Using Excel for Windows 95*, published by Que. Many of the descriptions, tips, and tricks used in this best-selling book apply to Microsoft Graph.

Part VI

Handling Large Documents

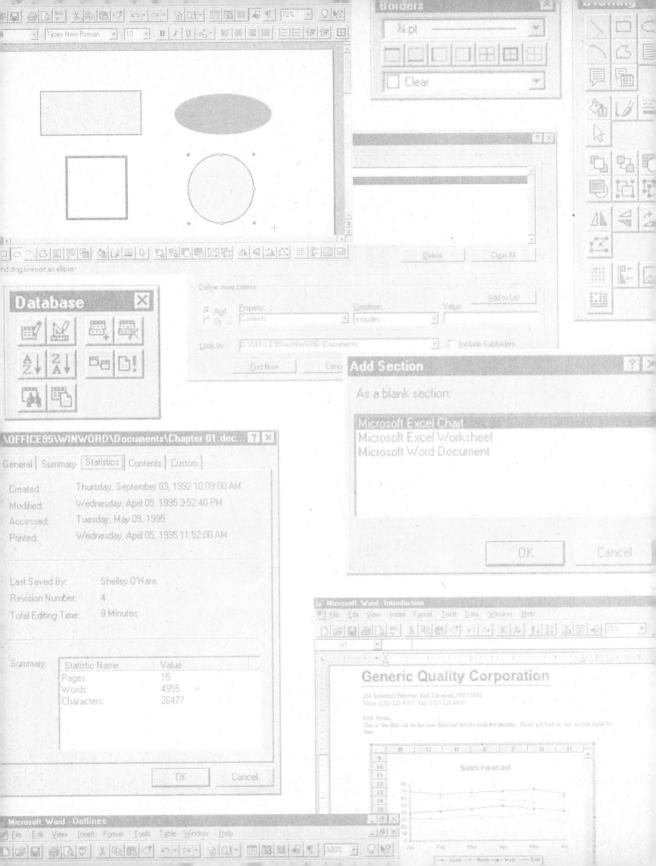

Chapter 28

Inserting Footnotes and Endnotes

Footnotes and endnotes have long been a staple of academic treatises—supplying additional information about a topic in the text or providing a reference. Footnotes and endnotes save you from having to clutter the text of your document with every piece of information you have. Instead, you can include parenthetical or reference information as a footnote or endnote listing. Because each note is referenced in the text, finding this extra information when you need it is easy.

In this chapter, you learn the following:

- The difference between footnotes and endnotes

- How to insert a footnote or endnote

- How to manage footnotes or endnotes with the ability to find, delete, copy, or move them

- How to convert a footnote to an endnote, and an endnote to a footnote

- How to apply custom formats, numbering, and positioning to footnotes or endnotes

What You Need to Know about Inserting Footnotes and Endnotes

Inserting, editing, and formatting footnotes and endnotes is easy in Word. Basically, a footnote consists of two parts: a footnote reference in the text (usually a superscripted number after the text), and the footnote at the bottom of the page, isolated from the body text by a separator line. An endnote is similar, except that the entry for an endnote appears at the end of the section or document, set apart from the text by a separator.

The process of creating footnotes and endnotes involves two basic steps:

1. Insert the note reference to mark the location in the document where a footnote or endnote is referred to. The note reference usually is a number.

2. After Word inserts the note reference, type the note entry (customizing the separator if you prefer). The note entry is the text information that appears in the footnote or endnote.

Several options are available for specifying where footnotes and endnotes appear, the type of separator line that is used, and the style of numbering used for the reference numbers. Figure 28.1 shows examples of footnotes being placed in a document.

Fig. 28.1
You can add footnotes to a document to provide additional information or to indicate references.

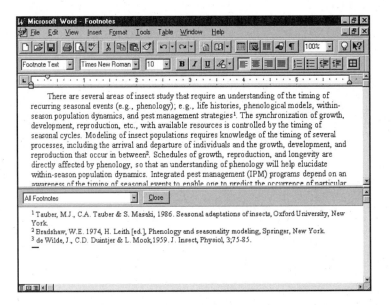

Inserting Footnotes and Endnotes

When you insert a footnote or endnote, Word for Windows inserts a reference mark in the text at the current insertion point. The reference mark is usually a sequential number that identifies the note you are adding. You are then given the opportunity to type the text that the reference mark refers to.

If you are in Normal view, a pane opens at the bottom of the window. In that pane, you can type either a footnote or an endnote, depending on the type of note you selected. If you are in Page Layout view, Word moves the insertion point to the bottom of the page for footnotes, or to the end of the document for endnotes. Entering footnotes and endnotes becomes as visual and as easy as if you were manually writing in a notebook. But Word automatically adjusts the page lengths, because footnotes fill up the page. Endnotes at the end of the document are continually pushed to the last page as your document gets longer.

Note

Footnotes usually make a document more difficult to read because they clutter the bottom of each page. However, many academic institutions require footnotes in their papers, probably because it makes grading easier for teaching assistants. (They don't have to work as hard if they can see that you crammed your paper full of someone else's thinking.) Endnotes are more frequently used in scholarly publications because they do not interfere with reading, but they do make the research accessible for those who need more information.

To create a footnote or endnote, follow these steps:

1. Position the insertion point after the text where you want to insert a reference mark.

   Word inserts the reference mark at the insertion point, unless you have selected text, in which case it positions the mark before the selection.

2. Choose Insert, Footnote. The Footnote and Endnote dialog box appears (see fig. 28.2).

3. Select either the Footnote or the Endnote option.

4. Accept the default AutoNumber to have Word number your footnotes. For custom reference marks, see "Changing the Appearance of Reference Marks" later in this chapter.

5. Choose OK. Word displays the note pane (Normal view) or the bottom margin (Page Layout view) so that you can type your footnote.

6. Type the text of your footnote or endnote.

VI

Handling Large Documents

Fig. 28.2
In the Footnote and Endnote dialog box, you choose the type of note and how it should be numbered.

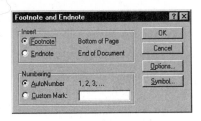

If you're in the Normal view of your document, you type in a special note pane, which appears when you choose OK in step 5. At this point, the screen is divided into two parts: the text of your document on top showing the note reference, and the note pane below showing the note entry (see fig. 28.3).

Fig. 28.3
The note pane is at the bottom of the screen when you work in Normal view.

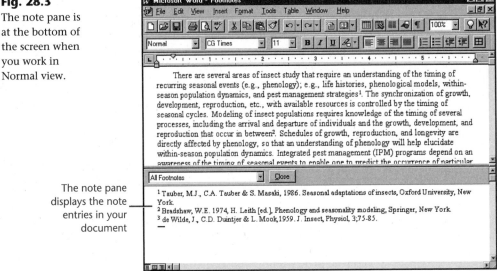

The note pane displays the note entries in your document

If you're in the Page Layout view of your document, you don't see the note pane. Instead, you type the note directly on the page (see fig. 28.4). If you are entering a footnote, you type at the bottom of the page. If you are entering an endnote, you type at the end of the document.

7. If you are in Normal view, leave the note pane visible and press F6 or click the document to move back to the document window. You can also click the document to move the insertion point. Or close the note pane by choosing the Close button or View, Footnotes (which is turned on when you insert a footnote).

Or, if you are in Page Layout view, you can use Shift+F5 (the Go Back key) to return to where you inserted the reference. You can use the mouse to click at any location in the document.

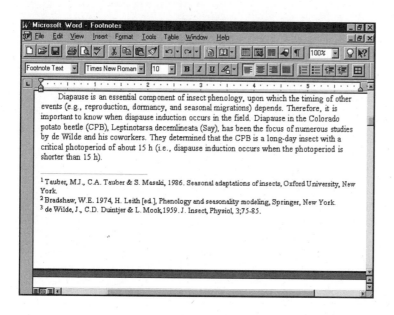

Fig. 28.4
You type footnotes directly on the bottom of the page when in Page Layout view.

Inserting Multiple References to a Single Note

You can insert multiple references to the same footnote or endnote. For example, you can refer to the same footnote text several times in a document without having to repeat the footnote text.

To insert an additional reference to a note that has already been inserted in your document, follow these steps:

1. Position the insertion point where you want to insert the reference mark, and choose Insert, Cross-Reference.

2. Select either Footnote or Endnote from the Reference Type list box; then select either Footnote Number or Endnote Number from the Insert Reference To list box.

3. Select the footnote or endnote you want to refer to in the For Which Footnote or For Which Endnote list box.

4. Choose the Insert button and then click Close.

5. Select the reference mark you just inserted and choose either Footnote Reference or Endnote Reference from the Style drop-down list on the

Tip

Insert a footnote with Alt+Ctrl+F. Insert an endnote with Alt+Ctrl+E.

VI

Handling Large Documents

Formatting toolbar to apply the correct formatting to the reference mark.

> **Note**
>
> You can insert a cross-reference to another note within the text for a note, using the procedure just described.

▶ See "Adding Cross-References," p. 917

Changing the Appearance of Reference Marks

In the preceding procedure, it is assumed that footnotes and endnotes use the default numbering scheme. You set default numbering by selecting the AutoNumber option when creating a footnote or endnote. Footnotes are automatically numbered using Arabic numerals (1, 2, 3, and so on), and endnotes are numbered using Roman numerals (i, ii, iii, and so on). With this option selected, footnotes are renumbered when additional footnotes are added, deleted, moved, or copied.

You can create footnotes or endnotes with a custom reference mark. To use a custom reference mark when you create the note, select the Custom Mark option from the Footnote and Endnote dialog box.

In the Custom Mark text box, you can type up to 10 characters, such as asterisks or daggers; or you can choose the Symbol button and select a symbol from the Symbol dialog box. Custom reference marks are not automatically updated, but custom reference marks don't interfere with any automatically numbered footnote references already in your document.

To change an existing reference mark, follow these steps:

1. Select the mark.

2. Choose Insert, Footnote

3. Type a new mark in the Custom Mark text box.

4. Choose OK. Word displays the footnote pane (in Normal view, choose Close to close it) or the bottom margin (in Page Layout view, press Shift+F5 to return to your document).

Editing and Viewing Footnotes and Endnotes

Research papers, theses, and technical documents are rarely completed in a single pass. They usually require multiple rewrites and, after review, usually require additional footnotes or endnotes. To make changes, you need to know how to view and edit existing footnotes and endnotes.

Viewing Footnotes and Endnotes

If you choose to leave the note pane open, it will scroll along with the document to display the notes that correspond to the note references displayed in the text.

Word offers some handy shortcuts for viewing existing notes. If you have a mouse and are in Normal view, you can open the note pane by double-clicking any note reference in your document, and you can close the pane and move back to the note reference by double-clicking the reference mark for any note entry in the note pane. You can also open the note pane by holding down the Shift key while you drag the split bar down. (The *split bar* is the narrow gray button above the up arrow in the right scroll bar.) Close the pane by dragging the split bar back up or by double-clicking the split bar.

Once you have opened the note pane, you can switch between viewing footnotes and endnotes by selecting either All Endnotes or All Footnotes from the drop-down list at the top of the pane.

You can also choose <u>V</u>iew, <u>F</u>ootnotes to view footnotes and endnotes. When you are in Normal view, choosing this command will open the note pane. When you are in Page Layout view, a dialog box appears if your document has both footnotes and endnotes, giving you a choice to view either the footnote or endnote area.

Formatting and Editing Footnotes and Endnotes

Footnote and endnote text can be formatted and edited just like any other text. You can use the ruler, toolbars, and menu commands for formatting notes. The default point size is 10 points for the note text and eight points for the reference mark.

To change the formatting of all your footnotes by redefining the Footnote and Endnote Reference and Footnote and Endnote Text styles, follow these steps:

Tip

Use shortcut menus displayed with the right mouse button to quickly format in the note pane.

▶ See "Creating Cross-References," p. 920

VI

Handling Large Documents

1. Choose Format, Style, and select the style you want to change from the Styles list.

2. Choose Modify, and then choose the appropriate command from the Format submenu.

3. Make the desired formatting changes in the dialog box that is displayed and choose OK. Repeat these steps for any other formatting changes you want to make.

◄ See "Using Word for Windows Standard Styles," p. 348

4. Choose OK, and then choose Close.

Finding Footnotes

If you are in Page Layout view, you can double-click the number to the left of a footnote or endnote reference to return to where you inserted the reference. You can return to the note associated with a reference by double-clicking the reference mark. This method enables you to quickly move back and forth between the document and the note while in Page Layout view. You can edit notes in Page Layout view just like any other text; simply scroll to the note and make the desired changes.

To locate notes, follow these steps:

1. Choose Edit, Go To, or press F5 to display the Go To dialog box.

2. Select either Footnote or Endnote in the Go to What list box, enter the number of the note you want to find in the text box.

3. Choose the Go To button.

◄ See "Using Find and Replace," p. 197

To find the next or previous note, leave the text box blank and click either Next or Previous. Choose Close to close the Go To dialog box.

You can also choose Edit, Find to locate notes. Choose Edit, Find, position the insertion point in the Find What text box, and click Special. Select either Endnote Mark or Footnote Mark from the list and click Find Next repeatedly until you find the note you are looking for. Choose Cancel to close the Find dialog box.

Deleting, Copying, and Moving a Footnote or Endnote

To delete, copy, or move a footnote or endnote, work with the reference mark—not the actual note text. If you delete, copy, or move the actual note text, the reference mark is left in place where it was originally inserted. When you delete, copy, or move a reference mark, Word automatically renumbers all numbered notes.

To delete a footnote or endnote, you must select the reference mark for the footnote and press Delete or Backspace. Deleting the note's text leaves the reference mark in the text.

If you want to remove all the footnotes or endnotes in a document, choose Edit, Replace, and click Special. Select Endnote Mark or Footnote Mark from the list, clear any contents in the Replace With text box, and choose Replace All. Choose Close to close the Replace dialog box.

> **Caution**
>
> Be careful when deleting text that contains footnotes or endnotes. If you select and delete text that contains a footnote marker, you also delete the footnote or endnote.

To copy or move a note by choosing either Edit, Copy or Edit, Cut, follow these steps:

1. Select the reference mark for the note you want to move.

2. If you want to copy the note, choose Edit, Copy. You can also click the Copy button in the Standard toolbar.

   If you want to move the note, choose Edit, Cut. You can also click the Cut button in the Standard toolbar.

3. Position the insertion point at the new position where you want the note reference.

4. Choose Edit, Paste. You can also click the Paste button in the Standard toolbar.

To copy or move a note with the mouse, follow these steps:

◀ See "Moving,
Copying, and
Linking Text
or Graphics,"
p. 160

1. Select the reference mark for the note you want to move.

2. To move the note, drag the selected note reference to the new location and release the mouse button.

   To copy the note reference, hold down the Ctrl key and drag and drop the note reference to the location you want to copy it to.

Converting Footnotes and Endnotes

So you've worked and slaved to get an article written for the *Arabian Rain Forest Review*, and it's finally complete. After waiting for three weeks, you get a letter stating that if you resubmit the article by tomorrow, it will be published. But you used footnotes, and they want you to redo your article with endnotes. Because you typed it with Word, you don't have a problem; you can convert existing footnotes to endnotes, or endnotes to footnotes. You can convert all the notes in a document or individual notes.

To convert all notes, follow these steps:

1. Choose Insert, Footnote.

2. Click the Options button to display the Note Options dialog box; then click the Convert button.

3. Select one of the options in the Convert Notes dialog box (see fig. 28.5).

Fig. 28.5
Use the Convert Notes dialog box to convert footnotes to endnotes, or endnotes to footnotes.

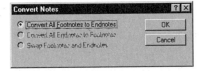

4. Choose OK to close the Convert Notes dialog box, choose OK to close the Note Options dialog box, and then click the Close button to close the Footnote and Endnote dialog box.

To convert individual notes, follow these steps:

1. Choose View, Normal if you are not already in Normal view.

2. Choose View, Footnotes.

3. Select All Footnotes or All Endnotes in the view drop-down list at the top of the note pane.

4. Select the note you want to convert in the note pane.

5. Click the right mouse button to display the shortcut menu.

6. Choose either Convert to Footnote or Convert to Endnote.

Customizing Note Settings

You can override the default note settings to suit your particular needs in several ways. You can customize the separator—the line that separates notes from the document text and from each other if they continue across more than one page. You also can add a continuation notice specifying that a note continues on the next page.

By default, footnotes appear on the bottom of the page on which their reference marks appear. If you want, you can specify that footnotes are printed directly beneath the document text if the text on a page does not extend to the bottom. Endnotes normally appear at the end of the document. You can specify that they instead appear at the end of each section in a document.

Finally, you can change the numbering scheme for notes. You can change the starting number for notes or choose to have note numbering restart on each page or at the beginning of each section, rather than having the notes numbered sequentially from the beginning of the document. You can also change the number format used for footnotes and endnotes.

> **Note**
>
> Word's footnote style is not necessarily the acceptable style for academic institutions. Many universities use Turabian (the author of a manual) as a standard for theses and dissertations. Turabian indents the first line of footnotes and double-spaces between footnotes, for example. You may need to edit the footnote reference and text styles.

Customizing Note Separators

Footnotes and endnotes are separated from the text in a document by a *separator*. When a footnote continues from one page to the next, Word inserts a *continuation separator* line between the document text and the continued footnote.

VI

Handling Large Documents

To customize separators, follow these steps:

1. Choose View, Normal if you are not already in Normal view.

2. Choose View, Footnotes.

3. Select either All Footnotes or All Endnotes from the view drop-down list at the top of the pane.

4. To edit the separator line, select Footnote Separator or Endnote Separator from the view drop-down list.

   The default is a two-inch line. You can keep the line, delete it, or add characters before or after the line. You can change the characters that are used as the separator or use graphics characters if you want.

5. To edit the continuation separator line, select Footnote Continuation Separator or Endnote Continuation Separator from the view drop-down list.

   The Continuation Separator is the separator between the document text and the remainder of a note that continues across more than one page. Word proposes a margin-to-margin line. You can edit this line the same way as the separator line.

6. Choose the Close button or press Alt+Shift+C to close the note pane.

To reset the default settings for the note separators, follow steps 1– 4 in the preceding procedure, choose the Reset button and click Close.

A *continuation notice* is text that explains that footnotes or endnotes continue on the next page. You can add a continuation notice in the note pane.

To add a continuation notice, follow these steps:

1. Choose View, Normal if you are not already in Normal view.

2. Choose View, Footnotes.

3. Select either All Footnotes or All Endnotes from the view drop-down list at the top of the pane.

4. Select either Footnote Continuation Notice or Endnote Continuation Notice from the view drop-down list.

5. Type the text you want to use for the continuation notice.

6. Choose the Close button or press Alt+Shift+C to close the note pane.

To view the text, switch to Page Layout view. You can only edit the continuation text in the note pane. To reset the default settings for the continuation notice, follow steps 1 through 4 in the preceding procedure, choose the Reset button, and then click Close.

Placing Footnotes

You can specify where the footnotes or endnotes you create are to appear in your document. Traditionally, footnotes appear at the bottom of the page. Word for Windows places them at the bottom margin, below the footnote separator. You can change the placement so that footnotes appear immediately below the text in a document.

Endnotes normally appear at the end of a document. You can choose to have endnotes appear at the end of each section in a document, provided that the document is divided into sections.

To change the position of footnotes, follow these steps:

1. Choose Insert, Footnote.

2. Choose the Options button. The Note Options dialog box appears (see fig. 28.6).

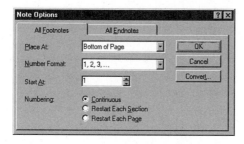

Fig. 28.6
Select the position of notes in the Note Options dialog box.

VI

Handling Large Documents

3. Select either the All Footnotes or All Endnotes tab.

4. Select one of the following options from the <u>P</u>lace At drop-down list:

Option	Function
Bottom of Page	Places footnotes at the bottom margin of the page on which the footnote references appear (the default setting)
Beneath Text	Prints footnotes after the last line of text. This style is handy when the text is much shorter than a page.
End of Section	Prints the endnotes at the end of the section
End of Document	Prints endnotes at the end of the document

5. Choose OK and then choose the Close button.

Figure 28.4, shown earlier in this chapter, demonstrates a document with the footnotes placed at the bottom of the page, just below the document text. Figure 28.7 shows the same document with the endnotes collected at the end of the document.

Fig. 28.7

A document in Page Layout view shows endnotes collected at the end of the document.

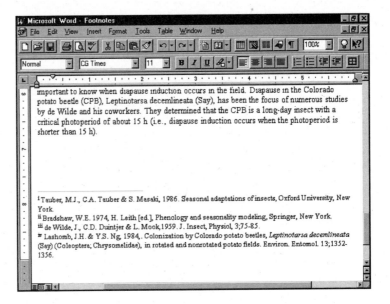

If you specify endnotes to appear at the end of each section, you can choose to print the endnotes at the end of the current section, or you can save them for a later section. Place the insertion point in the section in which you want to suppress the endnotes. Choose <u>F</u>ile, Page Set<u>u</u>p, and select the <u>L</u>ayout tab.

Select S̲uppress Endnotes to save endnotes for the next section, or clear Suppress Endnotes to include the endnotes with the current section.

Customizing Numbering

You can change how you number your footnotes. To customize the numbering of footnotes, follow these steps:

1. Choose I̲nsert, Footn̲ote.

2. Choose the O̲ptions button. The Note Options dialog box appears.

3. Select either the All F̲ootnotes or All E̲ndnotes tab.

4. To change the starting number, type a new number in the Start A̲t text box, or scroll the spin box arrows to select a new number.

5. Select one of the following Numbering options:

Option	Result
C̲ontinuous	Numbering is continuous from beginning to end of document.
Restart Each S̲ection	Numbering is restarted in each section of the document.
Restart Each Pa̲ge	Numbering is restarted on each page of the document (available only for footnotes).

6. Choose OK and then click Close.

VI

Handling Large Documents

Chapter 29

Creating Indexes and Tables of Contents

Imagine trying to locate a specific topic in a long reference book with no table of contents, trying to get information from a long technical document without a good index, or trying to remember where you saw a useful chart or table in a book with no list of figures. Word for Windows is equipped with powerful tools for creating these reference aids. This chapter shows you how to build references for a document.

In this chapter, you learn how to do the following:

■ Create, format, and edit index entries, and then compile and format an index

■ Use a concordance file to automatically create index entries

■ Create and format a table of contents based on heading or other styles, and create table of contents entries based on any text

■ Create tables of figures, or other tables based on figure captions, within any text

Creating Indexes

An index, such as the one found at the end of this book, lists topics covered in a book or document and provides the page numbers where you can find the topics. Without an index, your readers will have difficulty locating information in a long document or one that is filled with references.

In Word for Windows, creating an index involves two steps:

■ You must identify in the document each entry you want indexed.

■ You must collect these entries into an index.

Word for Windows has the capability to create simple indexes, such as the following:

```
Printing, 5, 12, 25
Publishing, 37, 54, 68
```

Word for Windows also can create indexes that use subentries so that specific topics are easier to locate:

```
Printing
        Envelopes, 37, 39
        Merge, 43-45
```

If you need more in-depth or complex indexing, Word for Windows is capable of creating indexes that include different characters such as separators, unique formatting, and multiple levels of subentries:

```
Printing
        Conversion, See WordPerfect conversion
        Envelopes: 37, 39-42
        Mail Merge
                Data document: 54-62
                Main document: 50-55, 67, 72
```

Creating Index Entries

Identifying an entry, such as a word, to be included in your index can be as simple as selecting the word and choosing a command. As an alternative, you can position the insertion point where you want the entry referenced, choose a command, and type the word to index. This second method gives you the flexibility to decide how the topic will appear in the index.

> **Note**
>
> When creating index entries, you should select the entire word or phrase to be indexed. Remember that you can select entire words by double-clicking the word or by moving to the beginning of the word and pressing Shift+Ctrl+right arrow.

To create an index entry in your document, follow these steps:

1. Select the word or words to index, or position the insertion point where you want the entry.

2. Choose Insert, Index and Tables. Word for Windows displays the Index and Tables dialog box.

3. Click the Index tab to display the indexing options, if they are not already displayed (see fig. 29.1).

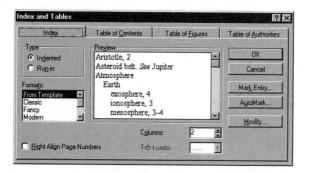

Fig. 29.1
Use the Index and Tables dialog box to create index entries and compile indexes.

4. Click the Mark Entry button. Word for Windows displays the Mark Index Entry dialog box.

   The Mark Index Entry dialog box includes the selected word or words (see fig. 29.2). If no word or words are selected, type the index entry.

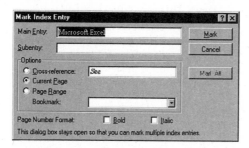

Tip
You can also open the Mark Index Entry dialog box by pressing Alt+Shift+X.

Fig. 29.2
Create an index entry in the Mark Index Entry dialog box.

Note

If the selected text contains a colon (:), Word for Windows prefaces the colon with a backslash (\). If you type text that contains a colon, you must preface the colon with a backslash yourself. As you learn in "Creating Multiple-Level Index Entries" later in this chapter, the colon has a special meaning in an index entry. The backslash character tells Word for Windows to ignore the colon's special meaning and instead to include the colon in the index entry text.

VI

Handling Large Documents

5. In the Main Entry text box, make no change if the index entry looks the way you want it; or type and edit the index entry as you want it to appear in the index.

6. Select among the index entry options:

   Select Cross-reference to create a cross-reference index entry. Cross-reference index entries are described later in the section "Creating Cross-Reference Index Entries."

   Select Current Page to have the index entry refer to the current page only.

   Select Page Range, and type or select the name of a bookmark from the drop-down list if you want the index entry to refer to the range of pages spanned by the bookmark. (See this chapter's "Including a Range of Pages" section.)

◀ See "Marking Locations with Bookmarks," p. 157

7. Select among the Page Number Format options:

   Select Bold to print the index page numbers for this entry in boldface text.

   Select Italic to print the index page numbers for this entry in italic text.

8. Choose Mark to mark only this entry for inclusion in the index.

   Or, you can choose Mark All to have Word for Windows search the entire document and mark all index entries that match the text in the Main Entry text box for inclusion in the index. Mark All is only available if you have preselected text in the document.

   The Mark Index Entry dialog box remains open after you mark the index entry, whether you choose Mark or Mark All. To create additional index entries, scroll your document and select additional text, or move the insertion point to where you want the next index entry and type the entry directly into the Main Entry text box, repeating steps 5 through 8.

9. Choose Close to close the Mark Index Entry dialog box.

Repeat these steps for every index entry in your document.

Note

To add character formatting to the index entry—formatting that will be evident in the compiled index—select text in the Main Entry or Subentry text boxes, and use the character formatting shortcut keys. If you want the main index entry to be in bold, for example, select all the text in the Main Entry text box and press Ctrl+B to apply bold character formatting. When the index is compiled, this entry appears in bold.

Including a Range of Pages

As you create an index, you probably will want to reference a range of pages for an index entry, as in the following example:

◄ See "Formatting Characters and Changing Fonts," p. 251

```
Desktop Publishing, 51-75
```

To do this, you must first select the range of pages and assign a bookmark to the selection. Then, when you insert the index entry, you use the bookmark name in the Bookmark text box (part of the Page Range option) to indicate the range of pages for the entry.

You need to use a range name to mark the span of pages (rather than an actual number of pages), because editing, insertions, and deletions may move the topic so that it spans different pages than those whose numbers are typed. By using a bookmark, Word for Windows calculates the new location of the bookmark so that the index will be up-to-date.

◄ See "Marking Locations with Bookmarks," p. 157

To reference a range of pages, first create the bookmark by following these steps:

1. Select the pages you want to reference in the index entry.

2. Choose Edit, Bookmark.

3. Type a name of up to 40 characters in the Bookmark Name text box.

4. Choose Add.

Now create the index entry, and use the bookmark to describe the page range involved in the reference by following these steps:

1. Position the insertion point where you want to insert the index entry.

2. Choose Insert, Index and Tables.

VI

Handling Large Documents

3. Select the Index tab to display the Index options, if necessary.

4. Click the Mark Entry button.

5. In the Main Entry text box, make no change if the index entry looks the way you want it, or type an index entry.

6. Select Page Range, and type the bookmark name in the text box or select it from the drop-down list.

7. Select other options as necessary.

8. Click Mark to create the index entry. The Mark Index Entry dialog box remains open.

9. Choose Close to close the Mark Index Entry dialog box.

Note

You can also select text and set bookmarks after you open the Mark Index Entry dialog box. Open the Mark Index Entry dialog box, and then use the usual procedure to set a bookmark; the Mark Index Entry dialog box stays open.

Customizing Index Entries

When you select the Mark Entry option of the Index and Tables dialog box, enter index text, and choose Mark or Mark All, you actually are entering a hidden field code that looks like {XE} into the document at a point directly after the insertion point or the selected text. These field codes are a powerful feature that can help you automate Word for Windows and customize the results of some commands, such as Insert, Index and Tables.

Tip
You can also display hidden text in {XE} fields by clicking the Show/Hide ¶ button on the Standard toolbar or by pressing Ctrl+Shift+*.

To see the hidden text of the field codes inserted by the Mark Entry option after choosing Insert, Index and Tables, choose Tools, Options and then select the View tab. Select Hidden Text from the Nonprinting Characters group, and choose OK. The hidden text in the index field is now displayed at all times. Deselect this check box when you want to hide the {XE} field text.

Some examples of field codes for index entries are as follows:

Field Code	Result in Index
{XE "Printing"}	Printing, 56
{XE "Printing Envelopes" \r "PagesEnv"}	Printing Envelopes, 72-80
{XE "Printing Envelopes" \b \i}	Printing Envelopes, 56

You can modify and edit these codes to give them more capabilities or formatting than is built into Insert, Index and Tables, Mark Entry. The section "Formatting an Index" later in this chapter covers formatting in detail.

Index entries appear in the compiled index capitalized exactly as they are in the {XE} index entry fields. If your document contains index entries for the words *computer* and *Computer*, Word for Windows creates a separate entry in the finished index for each word. If you want only one entry for both words, you must edit the text in the {XE} field to have the same capitalization.

Assembling a Simple Index

After you create an entry for each index entry or subentry you want collected into an index, you can compile the index. Follow these steps to create your index:

1. Position the insertion point where you want the index.

    If you are creating an index for a master document, choose View, Master Document to switch to Master Document view, and make sure that the insertion point is not in a subdocument.

2. Turn off the display of hidden text and field codes so that the document will be repaginated properly as the index is created.

3. Choose Insert, Index and Tables.

4. Click the Index tab to display the index options, if they are not already displayed (see fig. 29.3).

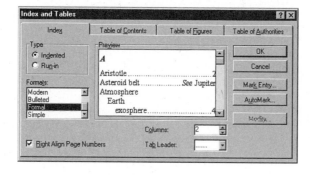

Fig. 29.3
You can compile an index with the Index and Tables dialog box.

VI

Handling Large Documents

5. Choose from two types of indexes: indented or run-in. Select Indented to indent subentries under major entries in the index, as in the following example:

```
Printing
    Envelopes, 56
```

Select Run-in to include subentries on the same line as their major entries, with words wrapping to the next line if necessary, as in the following example:

```
Printing: Envelopes, 56
```

6. Select among seven Formats for the index; a sample of the format you select is shown in the Preview box.

   If you select Custom Style, the Modify button is enabled. Click Modify to adjust the style of the text used in the index. Word for Windows displays a standard Style dialog box, except that style editing is limited to the Index Heading and Index styles 1 through 9.

◄ See "Applying, Copying, and Removing Styles," p. 354

7. Set the number of columns in the index in the Columns spin box.

8. Use the Right Align Page Numbers check box to turn on or off the right alignment of page numbers.

   If Right Align Page Numbers is selected, the Tab Leader list box is enabled.

9. Select the leader style (none, dots, dashes, or a solid line) in the Tab Leader list box.

10. Choose OK. Word for Windows repaginates the document and compiles the index. Figure 29.4 shows a sample index.

Fig. 29.4
This figure shows a sample index.

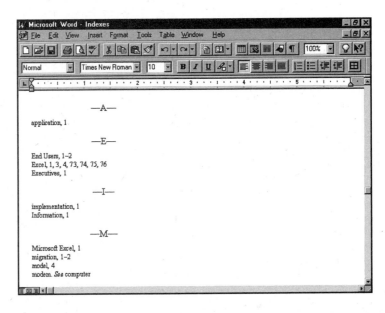

When you use Insert, Index and Tables to compile an index, you are actually inserting a hidden field code, {INDEX}. Chapter 20, "Automating with Field Codes," describes field codes in detail; the following example shows the field code for the index shown in figure 29.4:

```
{INDEX \h "A" \c "2" }
```

To view the INDEX field code, place the insertion point in the index and press Shift+F9. Press Shift+F9 while the insertion point is in the field to again view the index's text.

◀ See "A Reference List of Field Codes," p. 616

If you choose Custom Style for your index, no index heading to separate the index entries (such as separating the A's from the B's) is included in the index. If you want to include a heading in an index with a custom style, you must manually add the \h code to the {INDEX} field code. In the preceding index field code example, the "A" after the \h indicates that the index heading should contain the letter of the alphabet for the index entries below that heading. To edit the INDEX field code, place the insertion point in the index and press Shift+F9 to display the field code, then edit the text in the field code as you would any other text. To display the index with the new heading, follow the instructions for updating indexes later in this chapter.

Formatting an Index

You can change the appearance of an index by formatting the index and by formatting individual index entries.

Formatting an Index Using Styles

The easiest and fastest way to change the character and paragraph formatting of an index is to use styles. Word for Windows supplies automatic styles for index entries: Index heading, Index 1, and so on, through Index 9. *Index heading* is the style Word for Windows uses to format the letters at the beginning of each section of an index. In figure 29.4, the index heading style has been changed to add a border over the index heading paragraph, so that a line is drawn between sections in the index. To redefine a style, choose Format, Style.

◀ See "Changing Styles," p. 368

VI

Handling Large Documents

Note

You can access several formatting options for indexes by using switches in the INDEX field. For example, you can use the \h switch to specify which characters are used to separate index headings. Or with the \e switch, you can change the characters used to separate the index text from the page numbers (the default is a comma plus a space). To add these switches, place the insertion point over the index, and press Shift+F9 to display the INDEX field (or choose Tools, Options; select the View tab, and select the Field Codes check box). Next, type the desired switches.

◀ See "Inserting Field Code Switches or Bookmarks," p. 598

Formatting an Index Directly

You also can format the index directly, using the F<u>o</u>rmat menu commands, Formatting toolbar, and the ruler. If you update your index, however, you will lose all direct formatting changes. For this reason, you should redefine the styles for your index to make formatting changes, or only apply formatting directly to an index that you have fixed as text by unlinking the {INDEX} field.

Formatting Index Entries

You can also apply character formatting to individual index entries by directly formatting the text in the {XE} index entry field. Any character formatting you apply to text in the index entry field is applied to that index entry as Word for Windows compiles the index. The character formatting in the index entry field is applied to the text for that entry, in addition to any formatting dictated by the index style. Character formatting applied directly to text in the {XE} field is unaffected if you update or replace the index.

You can apply character formatting to individual index entries in two ways:

- You can format the text in the Mark Index Entry dialog box as you create the index entry.

- You can edit the index entry field itself.

◀ See "Formatting with Keyboard Shortcuts," p. 258

To format the text as you create the index entry, select text in either the Main <u>E</u>ntry or <u>S</u>ubentry text boxes, and use the character formatting shortcut keys. To make an entry appear in italics, for example, select the text in the Main <u>E</u>ntry text box, and press Ctrl+I.

To edit the {XE} index field itself, click the Show/Hide ¶ button on the Standard toolbar so that hidden text and printing codes are displayed, or choose <u>T</u>ools, <u>O</u>ptions, <u>V</u>iew to display H<u>i</u>dden text. Select all or part of the text in the {XE} field, and use the Formatting toolbar or F<u>o</u>rmat, <u>F</u>ont to apply character formatting as you would with any other text.

> **Note**
>
> If you chose <u>I</u>nsert, Page N<u>u</u>mbers to have Word for Windows display chapter numbers with page numbers (for example, 4–27), the chapter numbers are also shown with the page numbers in your index.

Updating or Replacing an Index

If you later add index entries to your document and want to update your index, move the insertion point within the {INDEX} field code (or the text that results from the code), and then press F9 (the Update Field key). Word for Windows updates the index, adding any new index entries and updating the page numbers for all index entries. Any formatting changes that you made to the index by redefining index styles or formatting individual index entries is kept; any formatting that you performed directly on the index text is lost.

Occasionally, you may want to completely replace an index, especially if you have made extensive changes in a document, or if you want to completely change the appearance of the index. To replace an index, place the insertion point within the {INDEX} field code (or the text that results from the code), and then choose Insert, Index and Tables as you would for compiling a new index. After you choose OK to begin compiling the index, Word for Windows asks whether you want to replace the existing index. Respond Yes to replace the selected index, and Word for Windows compiles a new index, replacing the existing index. If you respond No, then Word for Windows still compiles a new index, but adds another {INDEX} field to the document.

Caution

If you choose Insert, Index and Tables to replace an index or to compile more than one index, Word for Windows resets all the index styles (Index Heading and Index 1 through 9) to have the characteristics of the index format you choose in the Index and Tables dialog box. If you want to keep any changes you have made to the index styles, press the F9 (Update Fields) key to update an index instead of replacing it.

Deleting an Index

To delete an index, select the index and press Delete. You can select the entire index quickly by clicking the mouse button in the left margin over the section break at either end of the index. To select and delete an entire index quickly using the keyboard, place the insertion point to the left of the first entry, press F8, press the down-arrow key once, and press Delete. Another alternative is to choose Tools, Options to display field codes, select the {INDEX} code, and press Delete.

Fixing an Index as Text

An index is actually created with a hidden field code, {INDEX}. As long as the field code is there, you can quickly update the index by selecting the code and pressing F9.

In some cases, you may want to change the field code to its text result so that the index cannot be changed or updated. You may want to fix the field code so that you can reformat the index without losing formatting if someone selects the document and presses F9 to update other fields, or so that you can save the document to another word processing format while preserving the index.

To fix the INDEX field code so that it changes to text, select the index or field code so that the entire index is selected. This is most easily done by dragging across one end of the index, which causes the entire index to be selected. Then press Shift+Ctrl+F9, the Unlink Field key combination.

Creating Multiple-Level Index Entries

If you have ever looked up a topic in an index and found the topic listed with a dozen or so page numbers, you know the value of a multiple-level index. When you expect to have several occurrences of a topic, you can help your reader by using categories and subcategories to divide the topic into more specific references. In Word for Windows, these entries are called *multiple-level index entries*, and they're easy to create.

The following is an example of the difference between a regular and a multiple-level index:

Index Type	Result
Regular	Computers, 1, 6, 17, 25, 33–37, 54
Multiple-level	Computers hard disk drives, 6 modems, 17 processor types, 33–37, 54 software, 1, 25

To create a multiple-level index entry, follow these steps:

1. Position the insertion point where you want the index entry, or select the text you want indexed.

2. Choose Insert, Index and Tables.

3. Click the Index tab to display the index options, if necessary (refer to fig. 29.3).

4. Click Mark Entry. Word for Windows displays the Mark Index Entry dialog box (refer to fig. 29.2).

5. In the Main Entry text box, type the name of the main category, or edit the selected text until the main category item appears as how you want it.

6. Type the name of the subcategory in the Subentry text box.

   If you want to create sub-subentries, separate each subentry level in the Subentry text box with a colon (:).

7. Select other options as needed, and click Mark.

   The Mark Index Entry dialog box remains open so that you can scroll through your document and create additional index entries. Repeat steps 5 through 7 for each index entry with a subentry.

8. Choose Close when you are finished creating index entries.

Follow this procedure for each index entry and subentry. To create the following multiple-level index entry, for example, you would type **Computers** in the Main Entry text box, and **Hard disk drives** in the Subentry text box (refer to step 6):

```
Computers
       Hard disk drives, 54, 65
```

You also can create sub-subentries, as in the following example:

```
Computers
       Hard disk drives
              Maintenance, 54
              Performance, 65
       Processors, 102
```

All the preceding sub-subentries were made with **Computers** in the Main Entry text box and the following text in the Subentry text box:

```
Hard disk drives:Maintenance
Hard disk drives:Performance
Processors
```

Notice how each subentry level is separated from the previous level by a colon (:). You can have up to nine levels of subentries. The index entry fields for these entries would look like this:

```
{XE "Computers:Hard disk drives:Maintenance" }
{XE "Computers:Hard disk drives:Performance" }
{XE "Computers:Processors" }
```

Creating Cross-Reference Index Entries

You can choose Insert, Index and Tables to create cross-reference indexes. A *cross-reference index* gives the reader information such as

```
Modem, see Computers
```

VI

Handling Large Documents

To create a cross-reference index entry, follow these steps:

1. Select the word or words to index, or position the insertion point where you want the entry.

2. Choose Insert, Index and Tables. Word for Windows displays the Index and Tables dialog box.

3. Click the Index tab to display the indexing options, if necessary.

4. Click the Mark Entry button. Word for Windows displays the Mark Index Entry dialog box.

   The Mark Index Entry dialog box includes the selected word or words (refer to fig. 29.2). If no word or words are selected, type the index entry.

5. In the Main Entry and Subentry text boxes, make no change if the index entry and subentry look the way you want; or type and edit the index entry and subentry as you want them to appear in the index.

6. Select Cross-reference, and type the cross-reference topic in the Cross-reference text box.

7. Select among other options as needed, and click Mark to mark only this entry, or Mark All to mark all words in the document matching the Main Entry.

   The Mark Index Entry dialog box remains open so that you can scroll through your document and create additional index entries. Repeat steps 5 through 7 for each index entry.

8. Choose Close when you are finished creating index entries.

Repeat these steps for each index entry. As with all other index entries, Word for Windows inserts an {XE} field code each time you mark an index entry. If you view the cross-reference index field, you will notice that it includes a special switch—\t—to create the cross-reference entry. The text preceding the \t switch is the index entry, and the text that follows the \t switch is the cross-reference text. The following line shows a cross-reference INDEX field:

```
{XE "Graphics" \t "See Desktop Publishing" }
```

The preceding index entry field produces the following entry in the compiled index:

```
Graphics. See Desktop Publishing
```

Automatically Creating Index Entries

If you have a large number of index entries to create or you want to standardize the capitalization of your index entries, you can have Word for Windows create index entries for you. To automatically create index entries, you must first create a concordance file containing the words or phrases you want to index and their corresponding entries and subentries. After you create the concordance file, you can select the AutoMark option after choosing Insert, Index and Tables to mark the index entries. You can add index entries to your document automatically or manually, in any combination.

Creating a Concordance File

The *concordance file* is a Word for Windows document file containing a single two-column table, and no text outside the table. The first column of the table contains the words and phrases you want to index, and the second column of the table contains the entry and subentry that should appear in the index for the indexed word or phrase.

◄ See "Creating Tables," p. 506

To create a concordance file, follow these steps:

1. Choose File, New, or click the New button to create a new document file.

2. Choose Table, Insert Table, and then choose OK. Word for Windows inserts a two-column table into the document. You can also click the Insert Table button to create a two-column table.

3. In the first column of the table, type the word or words you want to index.

◄ See "Adding or Deleting Cells, Rows, or Columns," p. 529

4. In the second column of the table, type the text you want to appear in the index for each entry.

   To create an index subentry, separate each subentry level with a colon, as described earlier in this chapter for multi-level indexes. You cannot use a concordance file to create cross-reference index entries.

5. Perform steps 3 and 4 for each word or phrase you want to index, adding additional rows to the table, as necessary. See Chapter 16, "Creating and Editing Tables," for more information about tables.

6. Save and close the concordance file.

Creating Index Entries from a Concordance File

To create index entries from the concordance file, follow these steps:

1. Turn off the display of hidden text, if necessary. Click the Show/Hide ¶ button on the Standard toolbar, or choose Tools, Options. Select the View tab, then deselect Hidden Text.

2. Choose Insert, Index and Tables.

3. Click the Index tab to display the index options, if necessary.

4. Click the AutoMark button. Word for Windows displays the Open Index AutoMark File dialog box (see fig. 29.5), which operates like the standard Open dialog box.

Fig. 29.5

Select the concordance file to automatically create index entries.

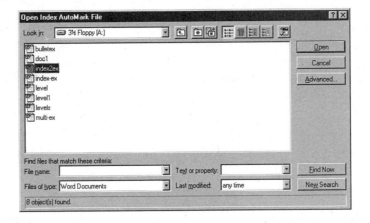

5. Select the disk drive and directory, as necessary, and then select the concordance file you want to use.

   If the concordance file you want is not listed, use the List Files of Type list box to change the files displayed in the File Name list, or try another disk or folder.

6. Choose Open.

   Word for Windows searches through your document, and inserts an index entry at every location where a word or phrase matches a word or phrase in the first column of the table in the concordance file.

◄ See "Marking Locations with Bookmarks," p. 157

After inserting the index entries, create the index as described in "Assembling a Simple Index" earlier in this chapter. If you later make changes in the concordance file, choose Insert, Index and Tables, AutoMark again. Word for Windows adds any new index entries and updates any existing index entries to reflect changes in the concordance file.

Creating Tables of Contents

A table lists selected items included in your document, along with their page numbers. Building a table of contents at the beginning of a document is probably the most common use of this feature. You also can create tables of figures, photos, tables, or other items. Figure 29.6 shows one of the types of tables of contents you can create.

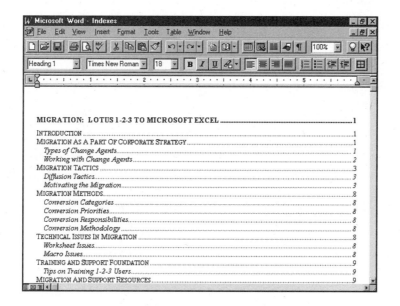

Fig. 29.6
Word for Windows can create tables of contents in many formats and for different items.

You have two ways to create a table of contents: by using heading styles, or by using special table of contents entry fields. The easiest way to create a table of contents is to collect heading styles.

◄ See "Choosing a Formatting Method," p. 337

Creating a Table of Contents Using Outline Headings

If you know you want a table of contents, you may want to format your document headings by using the built-in heading styles, heading 1, heading 2, and so on. When you compile a table of contents, Word for Windows recognizes these heading styles and uses the text with those styles to create the table of contents. Word for Windows provides nine heading levels, heading 1 through heading 9. You choose which heading levels to use when you create a table of contents.

VI

Handling Large Documents

The heading styles used to create tables of contents or lists are the same heading styles used automatically when you create an outline. If you prefer to work with Word for Windows' Outliner, you may want to outline your document before or as you write, and then use the outline headings to create your table of contents. Chapter 19, "Organizing Content with an Outline," describes how to create and use outlines.

Before you can create a table of contents, you must apply heading styles to each heading you want to list in a table of contents. (To create a table of figures or other table, see the "Creating Special-Purpose Tables" section later in this chapter.) To apply heading styles, move the insertion point into the text and then use one of the following methods, which are listed in order of complexity, beginning with the easiest:

- Select the desired heading style from the style list box in the Formatting toolbar.

- Press Alt+Shift+left arrow or Alt+Shift+right arrow to change a paragraph into a heading style and move it to a higher or lower style.

- Choose Format, Style, select the desired heading style from the Styles list, and choose OK.

You can apply heading styles as you type the headings, using either the mouse or keyboard methods.

To create a table of contents from headings formatted with heading styles, follow these steps:

1. Position the insertion point where you want the table of contents to appear in your document.

   If you are creating a table of contents for a master document, choose View, Master Document to switch to Master Document view, and make sure that the insertion point is not in a subdocument.

2. Turn off the display of hidden text and field codes so that the document will be repaginated properly as the table of contents is created.

3. Choose Insert, Index and Tables.

4. Click the Table of Contents tab to display the table of contents options, if necessary (see fig. 29.7).

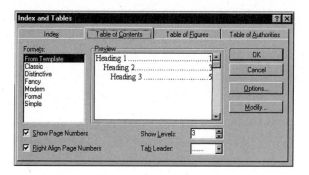

Fig. 29.7
Create a table of
contents with the
Index and Tables
dialog box.

5. Select among seven For**m**ats for the table of contents; a sample of the format you select is shown in the Pre**v**iew box.

   ◄ See "Applying
   Paragraph
   Styles," p. 355

   If you select From Template, the **M**odify button is enabled. Click **M**odify to adjust the style of the text used in the table of contents. Word for Windows displays a standard Style dialog box, except that style editing is limited to TOC styles 1 through 9. The TOC styles are used for each of the heading styles; TOC1 for heading 1, and so on.

6. Select **S**how Page Numbers to turn the display of page numbers on or off.

7. In the Show **L**evels text box, set the number of heading levels to show in the table of contents.

8. Use the **R**ight Align Page Numbers check box to turn the right alignment of page numbers on or off.

   If **R**ight Align Page Numbers is selected, the Ta**b** Leader list box is enabled.

9. Select the leader style (none, dots, dashes, or a solid line) in the Ta**b** Leader list box.

10. Choose OK. Word for Windows repaginates the document and compiles the table of contents.

Figure 29.6, shown earlier, shows a table of contents built from heading styles.

When you choose **I**nsert, Inde**x** and Tables to create a table of contents, you are inserting a hidden field code, {TOC}. Field codes are described in detail in Chapter 20, "Automating with Field Codes." The following example shows the field code for the table of contents shown in figure 29.6. To view the table of contents field code, place the insertion point in the table of contents and press Shift+F9. Press Shift+F9 while the insertion point is in the field to view again the table of contents text:

```
{TOC \o "1-9" }
```

In this table of contents field, the \o switch tells Word for Windows to create the table of contents from outline headings; the numbers enclosed in quotation marks after the switch indicate the range of heading levels to include in the table of contents.

> **Note**
>
> Create a table of contents early in your work, so that you can use it to navigate through your document. If you put the table of contents at the end of the document, you can press Ctrl+End to go to the end, check the table of contents to identify the page number you want, and then choose Edit, Go To (or press F5) to quickly go to that page.

Creating a Table of Contents Using Any Style

◀ See "Creating Styles," p. 358

You may want to create a table of contents or some other table for a document that does not contain heading styles, or you may want to include references to items that have a style other than one of the heading styles. You can create a table of contents based on any styles used in the document.

To create a table of contents that includes entries based on styles in addition to (or instead of) the built-in heading styles, follow these steps:

1. Turn off the display of hidden text and field codes so that the document will be repaginated properly as the table of contents is created.

2. Position the insertion point where you want the table of contents to appear in your document.

   If you are creating a table of contents for a master document, choose View, Master Document to switch to Master Document view, and make sure that the insertion point is not in a subdocument.

3. Choose Insert, Index and Tables.

4. Click the Table of Contents tab to display the table of contents options, if necessary (refer to fig. 29.7).

5. Choose Options. The Table of Contents Options dialog box appears (see fig. 29.8).

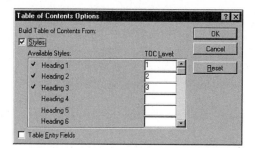

Fig. 29.8
The Table of
Contents Options
dialog box enables
you to choose
which items are
included in the
table of contents.

6. To create a table of contents that contains *only* entries compiled from certain styles, select the Styles check box so that there is a check mark in the box, and deselect Table Entry Fields so that there is a check mark in the box.

   Or, to create a table of contents that contains entries compiled from headings or other styles *as well as* from table entry fields, select Styles and Table Entry Fields so that there is a checkmark in both check boxes.

   The next section of this chapter describes how to create a table of contents based on table entries.

7. For every style in the Available Styles list that you want included in the table of contents, type the table of contents level for that style in the corresponding TOC Level text box. You can use levels 1 through 9.

   If you don't want a style included in the table of contents, make sure that its TOC Level text box is empty.

8. Choose OK to accept the options you set. Word for Windows closes the Table of Contents Options dialog box.

9. Set any other options in the Index and Tables dialog box, as necessary.

10. Choose OK to compile the table of contents. Word for Windows closes the Index and Tables dialog box and creates the table of contents.

Creating a Table of Contents Using Any Text

You may want to include references to items that don't have headings or other styles. In those cases, you can insert a table of contents field code, along with a descriptive entry, at the beginning of each appropriate section in your document (or wherever you want the listing to be referenced in the table of contents). Word for Windows then can collect these fields and descriptions into a table of contents.

VI

Handling Large Documents

Marking Table of Contents Entries

To insert table of contents fields into your document, follow these steps:

1. Position the insertion point where you want the table of contents entry.

2. Choose Insert, Field.

3. Select Index and Tables in the Categories list.

4. Select TC in the Field Names list.

5. Position the insertion point in the Field Codes box, leaving one space after the TC entry.

6. Type an opening quotation mark ("), type the text of the table of contents entry, and type a closing quotation mark (").

   To create the first entry in the table of contents shown in figure 29.6, for example, type the following in the Field Codes box (the \l switch is explained in step 7):

   TC "MIGRATION: LOTUS 1-2-3 TO MICROSOFT EXCEL" \l 1

7. Type a space, a backslash, and the letter **l** (as shown in the entry line).

8. Type a space and then type the number for the level at which you want this entry to appear in the finished table of contents. You can specify levels 1 through 9.

◀ See "Inserting Field Codes," p. 597

9. Choose Options to add additional switches to the TC entry; otherwise, skip to step 11.

10. Select the desired switch in the Switches list, choose Add to Field to add the switch to the TC field, and then type any additional text needed for the switch in the Field Codes text box.

11. Choose OK to close the Field Options dialog box.

12. Choose OK to insert the table of contents entry and close the Field dialog box.

Repeat these steps for each table of contents entry you want. The field codes you insert will not be visible in your document unless you have turned on the Hidden Text option in the View tab of Tools, Options. You can also click the Show/Hide ¶ button or press Ctrl+Shift+*.

> ## Note
>
> You can bypass Insert, Field by using the Insert Field key combination, Ctrl+F9. Position the insertion point where you want the table of contents entry, press Ctrl+F9 (a pair of field characters will appear), and type
>
> ```
> TC "text" switches
> ```
>
> where *text* is the text you want to appear in the table of contents and *switches* is the \l switch and level number, followed by any of the optional field code switches you want to use.

Editing Table of Contents Entries

You can edit a table of contents entry as you would any other text in your document. Any character formatting that you apply to the text in the table of contents entry will also appear in the finished table of contents. To display the table of contents entry text, use the Show/Hide ¶ button on the Standard toolbar to display the hidden text, or choose Tools, Options, View to turn on the display of Hidden Text.

To collect {TC} field codes into a table of contents, follow these steps:

1. Turn off the display of hidden text and field codes so that the document will be repaginated properly as the table of contents is created.

2. Position the insertion point where you want the table of contents to appear in your document.

3. Choose Insert, Index and Tables.

4. Click the Table of Contents tab to display the table of contents options, if they are not already displayed (refer to fig. 29.7).

5. Choose Options. The Table of Contents Options dialog box appears (refer to fig. 29.8).

6. To create a table of contents that contains *only* entries compiled from table entry fields, select the Styles check box and Table Entry Fields so that there are check marks in both boxes.

   Or, to create a table of contents that contains entries compiled from headings or other styles *as well as* from table entry fields, select Styles and Table Entry Fields so that there is a check mark in both check boxes.

> **Tip**
> Creating tables of contents based on styles is described earlier in this chapter.

7. Choose OK to accept the options you set. Word for Windows closes the Table of Contents Options dialog box.

8. Set any other options in the Index and Tables dialog box, as necessary.

9. Choose OK to compile the table of contents. Word for Windows closes the Index and Tables dialog box and creates the table of contents.

Troubleshooting

Table of contents entries created from any text don't appear in the compiled table of contents.

Table of contents entries you created from any text (by creating a {TC} field) are included in the compiled table of contents only if you select the Table Entry Fields check box in the Table of Contents Options dialog box, or if the \f switch is in the {TOC} field. To correct this problem, do one of the following:

- Replace the table of contents by following the instructions in the section "Updating, Replacing, or Deleting Tables of Contents and Other Document Tables," later in this chapter. Make sure that you click the Options button and then select the Table Entry Fields check box in the Table of Contents Options dialog box.

- Manually edit the {TOC} field, adding the \f switch to the field, and then update the table of contents as described in the section "Updating, Replacing, or Deleting Tables of Contents and Other Document Tables," later in this chapter.

The page numbers for entries in the table of contents are incorrect.

If you make extensive changes to a document, the pagination of your document may change, so that the page numbers in a table of contents no longer match the actual page numbers of the heading or table of contents entry. If you compile a table of contents while hidden text is displayed, your document may not paginate correctly. To correct the page numbers in your table of contents, update the table of contents as described in the section "Updating, Replacing, or Deleting Tables of Contents and Other Document Tables," later in this chapter.

Creating Special-Purpose Tables

◄ See "A Reference List of Field Codes," p. 616

With Word for Windows, you can create not only tables of contents, but also tables of figures, photos, charts, equations, tables, or any other items. These tables usually appear in a document after the table of contents.

You can create tables of figures or other special-purpose tables in two ways:

■ By compiling the special purpose tables based on the style of the text

■ By manually inserting the table entries into the document

Using Styles to Create Special-Purpose Tables

The easiest way to assemble tables of figures or other special-purpose tables is to use the Figure Caption, Equation, and other styles built into Word for Windows. If you choose Insert, Caption to create all your figure captions, for example, you can easily build a table of figures.

▶ See "Creating Captions," p. 923

To create a table of figures, equations, or tables based on one of Word for Windows' caption styles, follow these steps:

1. Position the insertion point where you want the table of figures to appear in your document.

   If you are creating a table of figures for a master document, choose View, Master Document to switch to Master Document view, and make sure that the insertion point is not in a subdocument.

2. Turn off the display of hidden text and field codes so that the document will be repaginated properly as the table of figures is created.

3. Choose Insert, Index and Tables.

4. Click the Table of Figures tab to display the table of figures options, if necessary (see fig. 29.9).

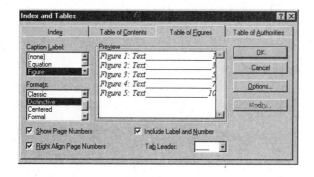

Fig. 29.9
Create a table of figures with the Index and Tables dialog box.

VI

Handling Large Documents

5. Select the appropriate caption in the Caption Label list.

6. Select among the Formats for the table; a sample of the format you select is shown in the Preview box.

If you select From Template, the Modify button is enabled. Click Modify to adjust the style of the text used in the table of figures. A standard Style dialog box appears.

◄ See "Applying, Copying, and Removing Styles," p. 354

7. Select Show Page Numbers to turn the display of page numbers on or off.

8. Use the Right Align Page Numbers check box to turn the right alignment of page numbers on or off.

   If Right Align Page Numbers is selected, the Tab Leader list box is enabled.

9. Select the leader style (none, dots, dashes, or a solid line) in the Tab Leader list box.

10. Choose Options if you want to change the style on which the table of figures is based (otherwise, skip to step 12). The Table of Figures Options dialog box appears (see fig. 29.10).

Fig. 29.10
The Table of Figures Options dialog box enables you to choose how the table of figures is built.

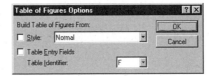

11. To create a table of figures that contains *only* entries compiled from a selected style, select the Style check box so that there is a check mark in the box, and then select the style in the list box. Also, deselect Table Entry Fields if there is a check mark in the box.

    Or, to create a table of figures that contains entries compiled from the selected style *as well as* from table entry fields, select Styles and Table Entry Fields so that there is a check mark in both check boxes. Next, select the text style in the Style drop-down list box, and select the table identifier in the Table Identifier drop-down list box.

    Creating a table of figures based on table entries and table identifiers is described in the next section of this chapter.

12. Choose OK. Word for Windows repaginates the document and compiles the table of figures.

When you choose Insert, Index and Tables to create a table of figures, you are actually inserting the same {TOC} hidden field code used to create a table of contents. A table of figures is really just a special variety of table of contents. The following is an example of the field code for a table of figures:

```
{TOC \c "Figure" }
```

In this example, the \c switch tells Word for Windows to create the table by using the text in paragraphs marked with {SEQ} fields. The text enclosed in quotation marks after the switch indicates which items to group together in the same table. {SEQ} fields are the hidden codes inserted by choosing Insert, Caption. If you choose Insert, Caption to insert a figure caption, for example, the following code is inserted into the document:

```
{SEQ Figure \* ARABIC }
```

Using Any Text to Create Special-Purpose Tables

Another way to collect special tables is to use field codes instead of (or in addition to) styles. These field codes do the following three things:

◀ See "Inserting Field Codes," p. 597

- They mark the spot in the text you want to reference by page number.

- They include the text you want to appear in the table.

- They include an identifier that defines into which table they should be accumulated.

▶ See "Creating Captions," p. 923

You can type these field codes directly into a document or choose Insert, Field to insert them. The field codes you insert look similar to the following:

```
{TC "Automated publishing" \f p}
```

In the command, TC is the field code, "Automated publishing" is the text that appears in the table, and the \f switch indicates that the table will be built from fields. The p is an identifier that associates this entry with other entries with the same identifier. This entry will be accumulated in a table with other field codes that have the p identifier.

The letters you use are up to you. The code for tables, for example, could be simply t. Following are some examples of how you might group items in different tables:

Item	Field Code Identifier
Charts	c
Figures	f
Lists	l
Pictures	p
Tables	t

To insert field codes that mark what will be included in tables, follow these steps:

1. Position the insertion point on the page where you want the table to reference.

2. Choose Insert, Field.

3. Select Index and Tables in the Categories list.

4. Select TC in the Field Names list.

5. Position the insertion point in the Field Codes box, leaving one space after the TC entry.

6. Type an opening quotation mark ("), type the text of the table entry, and type a closing quotation mark (").

7. Press the space bar once, and type \f, (the f indicates that the table is being built from fields).

8. Press the space bar to insert a space, and then type a single-character list identifier, such as **g**, for graphs. Use the same single-letter character for all items to be accumulated in the same table.

◀ See "A Reference List of Field Codes," p. 616

9. Click the Options button to add additional switches to the TC entry. Choose OK to close the Field Options dialog box.

10. Choose OK to insert the table entry and close the Field dialog box.

Repeat these steps for each entry you want. The field codes you insert do not appear in your document unless you turn on the Hidden Text option in the View tab after choosing Tools, Options. Your TC field code should look similar to the following:

```
{TC "Graph Showing Learning Retention" \f g}
```

Another, and often quicker, way to enter the field code is to position the insertion point, press Ctrl+F9 to insert the field code braces {}, and then type the code and text inside the braces.

To create a table that accumulates all the items belonging to a single identifier, such as f for figures or g for graphs, follow these steps:

1. Turn off the display of hidden text and field codes so that the document repaginates using only the text that will print.

2. Position the insertion point where you want the table to appear.

3. Choose Insert, Index and Tables.

4. Click the Table of Figures tab to display the table of figures options, if the options are not already displayed (refer to fig. 29.9).

5. Choose Options. Word for Windows displays the Table of Figures Options dialog box (refer to fig. 29.10).

6. To create a table that contains *only* entries compiled from table entry fields, select the Style check box and Table Entry Fields so that there are no check marks in both boxes.

   Or, to create a table that contains entries compiled from a selected style *as well as* from table entry fields, select Style and Table Entry Fields so that there is a check mark in both check boxes, and select the style in the Style list box. (Creating tables based on styles is described earlier in this chapter.)

7. Select the table identifier in the Table Identifier list box, (for example, g for graphs).

8. Choose OK to accept the options you set. Word for Windows closes the Table of Figures Options dialog box.

9. Set any other options in the Index and Tables dialog box, as necessary.

10. Choose OK to compile the table. Word for Windows closes the Index and Tables dialog box and creates the table.

◀ See "A Reference List of Field Codes," p. 616

If you display the resulting field code, it should appear similar to the following:

```
{TOC \f G \c}
```

The preceding {TOC} field produces a table from any TOC fields that contain the G identifier. By using different list identifiers, you can include multiple tables for different entries in a document (for example, charts, graphs, lists, and so on).

Creating a Table of Authorities

If you work with legal documents, you are familiar with tables of authorities. A *table of authorities* lists where citations occur in a legal brief; the citations can be references to cases, statutes, treatises, constitutional provisions, and so on.

To create a table of authorities, you first create the citation entries in your document, and then compile the table of authorities.

Creating Citation Entries

To create citation entries in your document, follow these steps:

1. Select the citation text, or position the insertion point where you want the entry.

2. Choose Insert, Index and Tables. The Index and Tables dialog box appears.

3. Click the Table of Authorities tab to display the table of authorities options, if necessary (see fig. 29.11).

Fig. 29.11
The Index and Tables dialog box shows the Table of Authorities options.

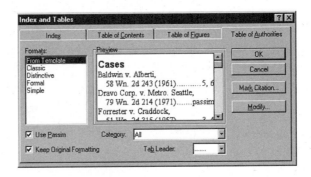

Tip
You can also open the Mark Citation dialog box by pressing Alt+Shift+I.

4. Click the Mark Citation button. Word for Windows displays the Mark Citation dialog box.

The Mark Citation dialog box includes the selected citation in both the Selected Text box and the Short Citation text box (see fig. 29.12). If no citation is selected, type the citation entry.

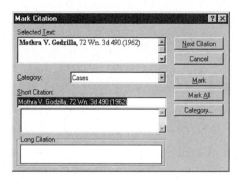

Fig. 29.12
Create a citation
entry in the Mark
Citation dialog
box.

5. In the Selected Text box, edit the text so that the long form of the citation entry looks the way you want it to appear in the table of authorities.

   You can use any of the character formatting shortcut keys (such as Ctrl+B) to apply formatting to the text in the Selected Text box, and press Enter to add line breaks to the text.

6. Select the citation category in the Category list box.

7. Edit the text in the Short Citation text box so that it matches the short citation form you use in your document. Because Word for Windows searches for and marks short citations in your document by matching the text in the Short Citation text box, be sure that capitalization, punctuation, and abbreviations are the same.

8. Click Mark to mark only this entry for inclusion in the table of authorities.

   You can also choose Mark All to have Word for Windows mark the current citation and then search the entire document and mark all long and short citations that match your entries in the Mark Citation dialog box.

   The Mark Citation dialog box remains open after marking the citation, whether you choose Mark or Mark All.

9. To create additional citation entries, scroll your document and select additional text, repeating steps 5 through 8.

   You can also choose Next Citation to have Word for Windows search your document for common abbreviations used in legal citations ("in re," "v.," "Ibid.," or "Sess."). Then repeat steps 5 through 8.

10. Choose Close to close the Mark Citation dialog box.

Repeat these steps for every citation entry in your document.

Editing Citation Entries

After you create a citation entry, you cannot edit it by choosing Insert, Index and Tables. Instead, you must edit the text in the hidden field code that is inserted in the document directly after the selected text whenever you create a citation entry in the Mark Citation dialog box.

Tip
You can also display hidden text in {TA} fields by clicking the Show/Hide ¶ button on the Standard toolbar.

To see the hidden text of the field codes inserted by the Mark Citation option, choose Tools, Options, and then select the View tab. Select Hidden Text from the Nonprinting Characters group, and choose OK. The hidden text in the index field is now displayed at all times. Deselect this check box when you want to hide the {TA} field text.

Edit and format the hidden text in the citation entry field the same way you would any other text in your document.

Assembling a Table of Authorities

After you create an entry for each citation you want collected into the table of authorities, you can compile the table. Follow these steps to create your table of authorities:

1. Position the insertion point where you want the table.

If you are creating a table of authorities for a master document, choose View, Master Document to switch to Master Document view, and make sure that the insertion point is not in a subdocument.

2. Turn off the display of hidden text and field codes so that the document will be repaginated properly as the table of authorities is created.

3. Choose Insert, Index and Tables.

4. Click the Table of Authorities tab to display the index options, if necessary.

5. Select among four Formats for the table of authorities; a sample of the format you select is shown in the Preview box.

If you select From Template, the Modify button is enabled. Click Modify to adjust the style of the text used in the index. Word for Windows displays a standard Style dialog box. (Refer to Chapter 11, "Using Styles for Repetitive Formats," for more information on editing styles.)

6. Select the Use Passim check box (so that a check mark is in it) to substitute the term *passim* whenever a citation has five or more different page numbers.

7. Select the Keep Original Formatting check box to have the citation appear in the table of authorities with the same formatting it has in the document text.

8. Select the tab leader style (none, dots, dashes, or a solid line) you want to use for the page numbers in the Tab Leader drop-down list box.

9. In the Category drop-down list box, select the category for this table of authorities. The All selection includes all the other categories in a single table.

10. Choose OK. Word for Windows repaginates the document and compiles the table of authorities:

When you choose Insert, Index and Tables to compile a table of authorities, you are inserting the {TOA} hidden field code. To view the index field code, place the insertion point in the index and press Shift+F9. Following is an example of a typical field code for a table of authorities:

```
{TOA \h \c "1" \p}
```

Customizing Citation Categories

You can change Word for Windows' predefined citation categories, or add your own categories.

To customize the citation categories, follow these steps:

1. Choose Insert, Index and Tables. The Index and Tables dialog box appears.

2. Click the Table of Authorities tab to display the table of authorities options, if necessary.

3. Click the Mark Citation button. The Mark Citation dialog box appears.

4. Click the Category button. The Edit Category dialog box appears (see fig. 29.13).

5. In the Category list, select the category you want to change. Word for Windows permits up to 16 categories, and only predefines the first seven. The remaining categories in the Category list are simply numbered 8 through 16.

Fig. 29.13
Create customized
citation categories
in the Edit
Category dialog
box.

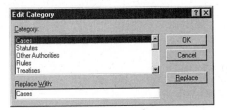

◀ See "Format-
ting with
Keyboard
Shortcuts,"
p. 258

6. Type the new category name in the Replace With text box.

7. Click the Replace button to change the category name.

8. Repeat steps 5 through 7 for each category you want to customize.

9. Choose OK to close the Edit Category dialog box.

Updating, Replacing, or Deleting Tables of Contents and Other Document Tables

You can easily update, replace, or delete any table of contents, table of figures, table of authorities, or other tables you create by choosing Insert, Index
and Tables.

Updating Document Tables

As you add text to or delete it from a document, you also add or delete various table entries. If you add new headings to a document, additional figures,
or other items, you will need to update the various tables in your document.

To update any table of contents or other table, follow these steps:

1. Place the insertion point in the table's field code (or the text resulting
   from it).

2. Turn off the display of hidden text, so that the document will paginate
   correctly as the table is updated.

3. Press F9, the Update Fields key. Word for Windows displays a dialog
   box similar to the one shown in figure 29.14 (the exact title of the
   dialog box depends on the type of table you are updating).

4. Select Update Page Numbers Only if you have only added text to or
   deleted it from the document, without adding or deleting table or
   citation entries.

You could also select Update Entire Table if you have added or deleted table or citation entries in the document.

5. Choose OK.

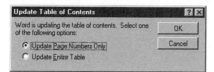

Fig. 29.14
Word for Windows asks you how extensive the table update should be.

If you choose to update a table, any formatting you applied to the table by editing the styles used by the table will be unchanged. If you formatted the table directly, then updating page numbers leaves that formatting in place, but updating the entire table causes the formatting to be replaced by the style formatting.

Tables that have been unlinked so that their text is fixed cannot be updated; instead, you must re-create the table if you want an updated version.

Replacing Document Tables

Occasionally, you may want to completely replace a table of contents or other table, especially if you have made extensive changes in a document, or if you want to completely change the appearance of the table. To replace a table of contents or other table, place the insertion point in the table's field code (or the text that results from the code), and then choose Insert, Index and Tables as you would for compiling a new table of contents, table of figures, or table of authorities. After you choose OK to begin assembling the table, Word for Windows asks whether you want to replace the existing table. Respond Yes to replace the selected table; Word for Windows compiles a new table, replacing the selected one. If you respond No, then Word for Windows still compiles a new table, but adds another table field ({TOC} or {TOA} field) to the document.

Deleting Document Tables

To delete any table of contents, table of figures, or table of authorities, just select the table and press Delete, or choose Tools, Options to turn on the view of field codes, and then delete the table field.

VI

Handling Large Documents

Limiting Tables of Contents and Other Tables

◀ See "Editing Fields," p. 601

If you need to create a table of contents or other table for part of a document, you need to modify the field codes with switches. To modify the field codes, choose Tools, Options, select the View tab, and then select Field Codes so that you can see the {TOC} or {TOA} field codes. Type the switches inside the field code braces, as shown in the following table. After modifying the field code, you must update the entire table as described in the preceding section of this chapter.

Switch	Argument	Use
\b	bookmarkname	{TOC \o \b NewIdeas} The table of contents that is built is only for the area named NewIdeas. The \o indicates that the table of contents is built from heading styles.
\o	"1–4"	{TOC \o "1-4"} The table of contents is built from a limited selection of heading styles, Heading 1 through Heading 4.

Formatting Tables of Contents and Other Tables

◀ See "Editing Fields," p. 601

◀ See "A Reference List of Field Codes," p. 616

▶ See "Inserting Tables of Contents, Indexes, and Cross-References," p. 950

If you format a table of contents, table of figures, or other table by using the format commands or the Formatting toolbar and ruler, that formatting will be lost if you update the entire table (updating page numbers only does not affect formatting). You can use two methods to format tables of contents, tables of figures, or other tables so that formatting is not lost when tables are updated:

- Apply formatting to the table by editing the styles used by the table.

- Use switches that are inserted in the TOC or TOA field to add or preserve formatting.

The following two sections explain these methods in detail.

Formatting with Styles

Each level in a table of contents has a specific style—TOC1, TOC2, and so on. By redefining these styles, you can change the format of the table of contents, and that new format will still be used when you update the table of contents. For a table of figures or authorities, you change the formatting of the Table of Figures and Table of Authorities styles.

This method of changing styles is useful if you want to format one level of the table of contents differently from other levels. For example, you might want the first level of the table, TOC1, to be in bold 12-point Times Roman without tab leaders (dots or dashes before the page number), and all other levels to use the Normal font with tab leaders.

Word for Windows' original TOC (Table of Contents) styles are based on the Normal style, with added indents, so that your table of contents will resemble the rest of your document. To redefine the TOC, Table of Figures, or Table of Authorities styles, choose Format Style, and use the Styles list to select the style you want to redefine (such as TOC1 for the first level of table of contents entries). Next, click the Modify button to open the Modify Style dialog box, which gives you options for redefining styles.

Click the Format button and select the font, border, and other formatting options for the style you want to change. After making the formatting changes to the style, choose OK; Word for Windows applies the changes in style to all text in your document that uses that style. When the original Style dialog box reappears, continue to redefine styles, or click the Close button.

Formatting with Field Code Switches

The second method of formatting a table of contents or figures so that formatting is preserved when you update the table employs switches you include with the TOC field code. You can use many switches to format the entire table of contents or figures.

◄ See "Inserting Field Codes," p. 597

To make changes, first display the field codes by choosing Tools, Options, selecting the View tab, and then selecting the Field Codes check box (so that it has a check mark in it). Add your switch(es) inside the field code braces to tell Word for Windows how you want the table formatted after it updates. For example, if the TOC field code appears as

```
{TOC \fG \* charformat}
```

the entire table of graphs uses the formatting applied to the first letter of the TOC. In this case, the bold and italic on the letter T apply to the entire table. The * charformat switch applies the formatting of the first character in the field code to the entire result.

VI

Handling Large Documents

◄ See "Editing Fields," p. 601

◄ See "A Reference List of Field Codes," p. 616

Some useful switches are in the following table:

Switch	Argument	Use
*	charformat	{TOC \o * charformat} Applies formatting of first character in field code to entire result of field. For example, changes the fonts of the entire table of contents.
*	mergeformat	{TOC \o * mergeformat} Retains formatting in field results that you applied manually. Formatting of updated results applies on a word-for-word basis. For example, changes the tab leader throughout the table of contents.
*	upper	{TOC \f t * upper} Changes all characters in the table of contents to uppercase.
*	lower	{TOC \f g * lower} Changes all characters in the table of contents to lowercase.
*	firstcap	{TOC \o * firstcap} Changes all words in the table of contents to use a capital for the first letter.
*	roman or * ROMAN	{TOC \o * roman} Changes numbers in the table of contents to Roman numerals. *roman* produces iv; *ROMAN* produces IV.

After making changes in the TOC field, you must select the field and press F9 (Update) to see the results of the changes. ❖

Chapter 30

Tracking Revisions and Annotations

Because you don't work in a vacuum, Word for Windows 95 is ready to work with other people, too—right on your computer screen. Using revision marks and annotations can eliminate errors and time spent transferring changes from paper to computer. Soon after you start using these features, you may wonder how you ever did without them.

Whether you work in a group or alone, revision marks keep track of changes made to a document. Each piece of added or deleted text is marked with the date, time, and reviewer's name. In effect, revision marks create an automatic history of the review process. Even if an edited document did not have revision marks turned on, you can create them by comparing the document to the original.

Word for Windows lets you use annotations just as you would jot notes in the margin, without worrying about these comments accidentally appearing in a final draft. Annotations enable you and other reviewers to include comments and questions in a special window, marked by the reviewer's initials and attached to the text being commented on.

This chapter helps you maintain your documents and manage changes made within a workgroup. You learn how to do the following:

- Mark revisions and edits so that they are easy to see and can be accepted or rejected

- Compare two documents for changes

- Annotate a document with remarks or notes that do not print with the main document

Using the Revision Marks Feature

Revising a document is often a job shared by several people. For example, several co-workers might work together to produce an annual report, or more than one editor might review a book. If a revised document has no marks, it can be hard to find everything that was changed or who did the changes. Revision marks show where the document has been changed and by whom, allowing the originator to accept or reject any of the changes.

Adding revision marks is simple. Before someone makes revisions, turn on revision marking. Revisions to the document are then marked automatically as the reviewer makes changes (see fig. 30.1).

Fig. 30.1

With revision marking turned on, you can see exactly what additions and deletions a reviewer has made. The MRK indicator in the status bar tells you that revision marking is on.

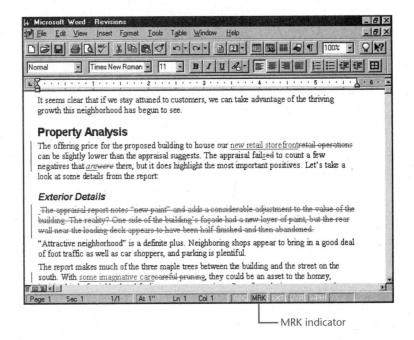

MRK indicator

When you view revision marks, you get a general idea of how much has changed in your document, as well as the details of specific words and letters that were edited. You can also hide revision marks to see exactly what the document would look like if you accepted the changes.

Marking Revisions

When revision marking is turned on, revision bars appear in the margin next to any lines where text has been inserted or deleted. Revision marks indicate the actual text that has changed—inserted text is underlined, and deleted text has strikethrough formatting. The section "Customizing Revision Marks," later in this chapter tells how you can change these marks.

Before you turn on revision marking, you should save a copy of the original document. This can help later if you need to merge revisions from several reviewers or compare a reviewed file to create revision marks.

To mark revisions in the active document, follow these steps:

1. Choose <u>T</u>ools, Re<u>v</u>isions. The Revisions dialog box appears (see fig. 30.2). You turn on revision marking in the Revisions dialog box.

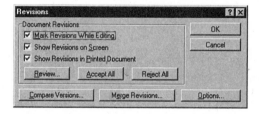

Fig. 30.2
A check mark indicates that an option is turned on in the Revisions dialog box.

2. Select the <u>M</u>ark Revisions While Editing check box.

3. If you do not want to be distracted by revision marks while reviewing a document, deselect the Show Revisions on <u>S</u>creen check box.

4. Choose OK.

To turn off revision marking, choose <u>T</u>ools, Re<u>v</u>isions, and deselect the <u>M</u>ark Revisions While Editing check box.

While revision marking is turned on, any text inserted in the document or deleted from it is marked. If you move a selection of text, two sets of marks appear: the text you moved appears as deleted (strikethrough) text in its original location and as inserted text in its new location. If you delete text marked as inserted, the text simply disappears. Only original text appears in strikethrough format when you delete it.

Tip
Double-clicking the MRK indicator in the status bar, shown in figure 30.1, is a shortcut to display the Revisions dialog box.

> **Note**
>
> You can turn on revision marking for all documents at once, if they are based on the NORMAL.DOT template. Open the NORMAL.DOT template, choose <u>T</u>ools, Re<u>v</u>isions, select the <u>M</u>ark Revisions While Editing check box, and save the template. You can also deselect the Show Revisions on <u>S</u>creen and Show Revisions in <u>P</u>rinted Document check boxes to hide revision marks until you actually review the revisions.

VI

Handling Large Documents

Showing Revisions

When a document comes back from your reviewers or you return to a document after editing it yourself, you can look over the changes. If revision marks are not visible in the document, choose Tools, Revisions and select the Show Revisions on Screen check box.

The document now appears with revision bars in the margin, marking where text has been inserted or deleted. If multiple reviewers made revisions, each reviewer's changes appear in a different color. If you want to continue tracking revisions but without seeing revision marks, choose Tools, Revisions, and deselect the Show Revisions on Screen check box.

By default, Word prints documents with revision marks showing. To print a document without revision marks, choose Tools, Revisions, and deselect Show Revisions in Printed Document.

> ### Note
>
> If you customize your user information, you can keep track of your own editing sessions separately. For each session you want to distinguish, choose Tools, Options, select the User Info tab, and change the Name text box. For example, start with First Draft, then use Style Review for another editing session, and then use Final Draft. Each set of revisions appears in its own color, and the Review Revisions dialog box shows those names. Be sure to restore your original name later, because other Word for Windows features use this information.

Accepting or Rejecting All Revisions

Word for Windows makes using or discarding revisions easy. To incorporate all the revisions marked in the document, choose Tools, Revisions, and Accept All. When prompted to accept the revisions, answer Yes and choose Close. All the deleted text disappears, the inserted text is incorporated into the document, and revision bars are removed.

Rejecting all revisions means restoring your document to its contents before it was reviewed. To reject all revisions, choose Tools, Revisions, and Reject All. When prompted to reject all revisions, answer Yes and choose Close. Inserted text disappears, deleted text is restored, and revision bars are removed.

You can undo these commands. As a safety measure, save your file with a new name before you accept or reject all revisions. You then have a copy of original and revised drafts for later reference or comparison. Remember that any formatting changes made by reviewers remain, whether you accept or reject revisions, unless you are accepting deletions.

Accepting or Rejecting Individual Revisions

You'll probably want to use some but not all of the revisions made to your document. You can look through the document, jumping directly from revision to revision, and choose whether to accept or reject each change.

To accept or reject individual revisions, follow these steps:

1. Choose Tools, Revisions.

2. Click the Review button. The Review Revisions dialog box appears (see fig. 30.3).

    In the Review Revisions dialog box, you can review all revision marks, and see which reviewer made a revision and when.

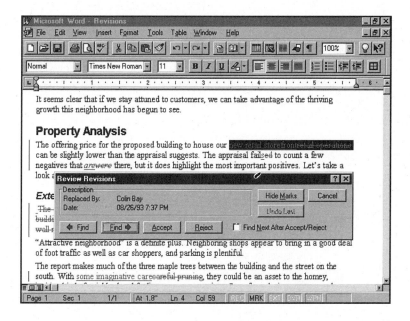

Fig. 30.3
The Review Revisions dialog box helps you move through your document to examine the revisions.

3. Click one of the Find buttons to find either the next or the previous revision in the document and to show which reviewer made the change and when.

4. Click the Accept button to keep the change, or the Reject button to discard it. If the Find Next After Accept/Reject check box is selected, Word immediately finds and selects the next revision.

5. If you change your mind, click the Undo Last button to restore the most recent revision that you accepted or rejected.

6. Click one of the Find buttons to locate the next revision.

While the Review Revisions dialog box is on-screen, you can click anywhere in the document to edit the text, or you can select another revision to display information about it. To see what the revision would look like if accepted, choose Hide <u>M</u>arks. Then choose Show <u>M</u>arks to display the revision marks again.

> **Note**
>
> A quick way to locate only revisions marked as inserted text is to choose <u>E</u>dit, <u>F</u>ind, select the Fi<u>n</u>d What text box, and press Ctrl+N for New. To search for anything except inserted text (including deleted text and unchanged text), select the Fi<u>n</u>d What text box and press Ctrl+N twice for Not New. Choose <u>F</u>ind Next to locate the text.

Customizing Revision Marks

Usually, revision bars in the margins appear black, the revision mark for inserted text is an underline, deleted text has a line through it, and changes made by up to eight reviewers are marked in different colors. (If you have more than eight reviewers, Word for Windows reuses the earlier colors.) You can customize each of these marks to your liking. For example, you can mark deleted text as a subdued color, such as light gray, and inserted text as green.

To customize revision marks, follow these steps:

1. Choose <u>T</u>ools, <u>O</u>ptions, and select the Revisions tab. You can also choose <u>T</u>ools, Re<u>v</u>isions, and then click the <u>O</u>ptions button to display the tab shown in figure 30.4.

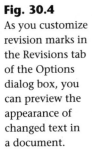

Fig. 30.4
As you customize revision marks in the Revisions tab of the Options dialog box, you can preview the appearance of changed text in a document.

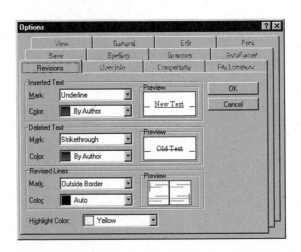

2. Select styles from the Mark list boxes under Inserted Text, Deleted Text, and Revised Lines.

3. If you do not need color to distinguish reviewers, select a color from the Color list boxes under Inserted Text and Deleted Text.

4. If you want revisions to be highlighted, select a color from the Highlight Color list box.

5. Choose OK.

If you select By Author under Color in the Inserted Text and Deleted Text sections, each reviewer's changes appear in a different color for up to eight reviewers. The Revised Lines options specify the appearance of the revision bars in the margins of your document.

Protecting Documents for Revisions

Protecting a document for revisions ensures that revisions are being tracked. If a reviewer turns off revision marking in your document, you could have a good deal of extra work finding where revisions are and who made them. For increased security, you can add a password so that only you can unprotect the document.

When a document is protected for revisions, Word for Windows tracks all revisions and does not allow revision marks to be removed by accepting or rejecting them. Reviewers can add annotations as well as revise the document directly. For more information, see "Using Annotations," later in this chapter.

◀ See "Protecting and Unprotecting a Form with a Password," p. 664

To protect a document for revisions, follow these steps:

1. Choose Tools, Protect Document. The Protect Document dialog box appears (see fig. 30.5).

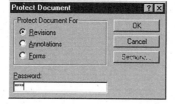

VI

Handling Large Documents

Fig. 30.5
Use the Protect Document dialog box to ensure that your document is not changed without your knowledge.

2. Select the Revisions option.

3. If you want to keep other users from unprotecting the document, type a password in the Password text box.

4. Choose OK. If you entered a password, Word for Windows prompts you to reenter the password for confirmation.

5. Reenter the password and choose OK.

Caution

It's easy to forget passwords. If you don't remember the password you use, you will not have access to the file. You might want to jot down the name of the document and the password you assign to it for future reference.

◄ See "Sending Documents Electronically," p. 247

To unprotect a document, choose <u>T</u>ools, Un<u>p</u>rotect Document. While the document is protected for revisions, any revisions made to the document will be tracked until it is unprotected, and you cannot choose to accept or reject any revisions. If you defined a password, you must enter it before the document can be unprotected. If you are using the routing feature of Word for Windows, you can protect the document when you add a routing slip.

Merging Revisions and Annotations

Several different reviewers may have worked on separate copies of a document instead of routing the same copy. If so, filtering through all the revision marks and annotations in multiple files can be tedious. To make the work easier, you can combine all the changes into the original document and see them together. You need the original document and any revised documents from it.

To merge revisions and annotations, follow these steps:

1. Open one of the revised documents.

2. Choose <u>T</u>ools, Re<u>v</u>isions.

3. Click the M<u>e</u>rge Revisions button. The Merge Revisions dialog box appears.

4. Select the original unrevised document and choose <u>O</u>pen.

5. Repeat these steps for each revised version of the document that you want to merge into the original.

Word for Windows merges the revision marks and annotations into the original document, where you can see and evaluate them in one place.

Troubleshooting

I don't have any revision marks in my document.

You can see revision marks only if revision marking was turned on while the document was being edited. Choose Tools, Revisions, click the Review button, and then click the Find button. If no revision marks are found, you can add them by comparing your document with the original version of the file. See "Comparing Documents," later in this chapter.

I see a revision bar in the margin but no revision marks.

There may be revision marks inside hidden text, field codes, or annotations. To see these, choose Tools, Options, select the View tab, and then select the Field Codes and Hidden Text check boxes.

I need to see the reviewer name and time information in the Review Revisions dialog box.

Information about each revision appears only after you find the revision. Choose one of the Find buttons to search for revisions.

I can't turn off the option for tracking revisions.

If the document is protected for revisions, the Mark Revisions While Editing check box is grayed. To turn off this option, choose Tools, Unprotect, asking the document's author for the password if necessary.

Comparing Documents

You can pinpoint revisions by comparing the current document to an earlier version. When you compare two documents, Word applies revision marks to your current document wherever it differs from the earlier version. The two documents you're comparing must have different names or locations on the disk.

◄ See "Sending Documents Electronically," p. 247

To compare two versions of a document, follow these steps:

1. Open the document in which you want to see revisions.

2. Choose Tools, Revisions. The Revisions dialog box appears. You can choose options from the Document Revisions section of the dialog box to determine how the revisions appear.

3. Click the Compare Versions button. The Compare Versions dialog box appears.

VI

Handling Large Documents

4. Select a file to which you want to compare the current file.

5. Choose <u>O</u>pen. Word for Windows compares the two documents and, based on the options you selected on the Revisions tab, marks any revisions that appear in the current document.

You can select or reject any of the revisions by using the following options in the Revisions dialog box:

Choose This	To Do This
<u>R</u>eview	Display each revision mark so that you can accept, reject, or ignore it. The Review Revisions dialog box provides these options.
<u>A</u>ccept All	Leave the selection unchanged and remove the revision marks.
Re<u>j</u>ect All	Reverse all changes and remove revision marks.

Using Annotations

Revisions are useful for tracking editing changes in a document, whereas annotations are best for attaching comments to a document. Because annotations are linked to specific parts of a document, they are just like notes scribbled in the white space—except that annotations are more convenient.

You may have had the experience of printing a final copy of a document and then noticing a note to yourself that you forgot to delete. The annotation feature takes care of that problem by keeping comments separate from the rest of your text; they aren't printed unless you specifically decide to print them. Annotations are the ideal place to store questions and notes to yourself or to an author whose work you're reviewing.

Inserting Annotations

When you insert an annotation, Word marks the location in the document and opens the Annotations pane. Here, you can type your comments and even format them.

To insert an annotation, follow these steps:

1. Select the word or passage you want to comment on, or position the insertion point in the text.

2. Choose <u>I</u>nsert, <u>A</u>nnotation, or press Alt+Ctrl+A to insert an annotation mark and open the Annotations pane (see fig. 30.6).

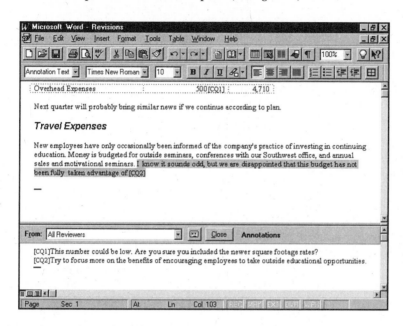

Fig. 30.6
The Annotations pane shows the reviewer's initials and the text of the annotation.

3. Type your annotation in the Annotations pane. You can use font and paragraph formatting just as you normally would.

The annotation mark contains the reviewer's initials and a number—for example, [CQ1]. Annotations are numbered in sequence. In the Annotations pane, a corresponding mark precedes the annotation text.

To close the Annotations pane, click the <u>C</u>lose button or double-click any annotation mark in the pane.

Adding Audible Annotations

The Insert Sound Object feature in Word 95 enables you to add sound annotations, providing your computer has sound equipment installed. You can record an annotation, or use a prerecorded sound file, and insert it in the appropriate location in your document.

To insert a sound annotation, follow these steps:

1. Select the word or passage to which you want to add sound, or position the insertion point at the end of the text.

VI

Handling Large Documents

2. Choose <u>I</u>nsert, <u>A</u>nnotation, or press Alt+Ctrl+A to insert an annotation mark and open the Annotations pane.

3. If you want to include text with the voice annotation, type your annotation in the Annotations pane. You can use font and paragraph formatting just as you normally would.

4. Position the insertion point at the end of the annotation text, then click the tape icon in the annotations pane. The Sound Object sheet appears. It uses VCR-like controls.

5. Click the Record button, the red circle, and say your message into the computer's microphone.

6. Click <u>F</u>ile, E<u>x</u>it & Return to Document.

A speaker icon appears in the annotation pane. Double-clicking the speaker icon will play the voice annotation you recorded. To edit the sound object, click it once, then choose <u>E</u>dit, Wave Sound <u>O</u>bject, <u>E</u>dit. To delete it, click it once, then press Delete.

To close the Annotations pane, click the <u>C</u>lose button or double-click any annotation mark in the pane.

Finding and Viewing Annotations

There are several ways to display annotation marks in a document. When the Annotations pane is open, annotation marks always appear. Because annotation marks are formatted as hidden text, they appear also when hidden text is showing (when you choose <u>T</u>ools, <u>O</u>ptions, View and select H<u>i</u>dden Text from the Nonprinting Characters group). Finally, you can show annotation marks by clicking the Show/Hide ¶ button on the Standard toolbar.

To find a specific annotation mark, follow these steps:

1. Choose <u>V</u>iew, <u>A</u>nnotations. The Annotations pane appears.

2. Choose <u>E</u>dit, <u>G</u>o To to display the Go To dialog box. In the Go To dialog box, you can go to a particular reviewer's next annotation or type the number of an annotation (see fig. 30.7).

3. Select Annotation from the Go to <u>W</u>hat list box.

4. If you want to find a specific reviewer's annotation, type or select the person's name in the <u>E</u>nter Reviewer's Name box.

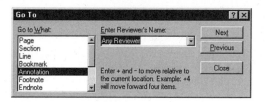

Fig. 30.7
The Go To dialog
box includes the
Annotation
option, which lets
you go directly to
the annotion you
choose.

5. If you want to find a specific annotation, type a number in the Enter
Reviewer's Name text box. For example, type **3** for the third annotation
or **+2** for the second annotation after the current selection.

6. Click the Next or Previous button. The Next button changes to Go To if
you type a number rather than select a reviewer's name.

> **Note**
>
> If you don't need to specify the reviewer, you can find annotations quickly by
> choosing Edit, Find and then selecting Annotation Mark from the Special
> drop-down list. The Annotations pane appears automatically when an annota-
> tion is found. (This pane does not appear when you choose Go To.)

When you select an annotation in the Annotations pane, Word for Windows
highlights the corresponding document text. This is why it's most useful to
select the text in question when you insert annotations. You can adjust the
size of the Annotations pane by dragging the split box—the short, gray button between the vertical scroll bars of the document and Annotations panes.

Including or Deleting Annotations

An annotation often consists of comments or questions about the selected
text. If the annotation contains suggested text, however, you can easily move
the text into your document. Simply select the text in the Annotations pane
and drag it into your document. Similarly, you can copy the text by holding
down the Ctrl key while dragging. (If you cannot drag the text, choose Tools,
Options, select the Edit tab, and then choose the Drag-and-Drop Text Editing
check box.)

> **Note**
>
> You can easily remove all annotations at once. Choose Edit, Replace, choose Annota-
> tion Mark in the Special drop-down list or type ^a in the Find What text box, leave
> the Replace With text box empty, and click the Replace All button.

VI

Handling Large Documents

If several reviewers added annotations to separate copies of an original document, you can merge all the annotations into the original document for convenient evaluation. To merge annotations, see "Merging Revisions and Annotations," earlier in this chapter.

Protecting Documents for Annotations Only

At times, you might want reviewers to comment on your document but not to change it directly. You can allow annotations (but no revisions) by protecting your document for annotations.

To protect a document for annotations, follow these steps:

1. Choose Tools, Protect Document, and select the Annotations option.

2. If you want to keep others from unprotecting the document, type a password in the Password text box.

3. Choose OK. If you entered a password, Word prompts you to reenter the password for confirmation.

4. Reenter the password and choose OK.

No changes except annotations can be made to the document until it is unprotected, and menu commands that could make changes are unavailable. When anyone tries to edit the document, a beep warns the user that the document is protected. A message appears in the status bar saying, `This command is not available because the document is locked for edit.`

To unprotect a document, choose Tools, Unprotect Document. If you defined a password, you must enter it and choose OK before the document can be unprotected.

Printing Annotations

To get a printed copy of an annotated document, you can either print just the annotations or print them at the end of the document.

To print annotations only, follow these steps:

1. Choose File, Print.

2. Select Annotations from the Print What drop-down list box.

3. Choose OK.

Word prints the contents of the Annotations pane, adding the page number where each annotation mark occurs in the document.

◀ See "Finding and Replacing Special Characters," p. 208

To print a document with annotations, follow these steps:

1. Click the Options button in the Print dialog box.

◀ See "Controlling Printing Options," p. 244

2. Select the Annotations check box, which automatically selects the Hidden Text check box, and choose OK.

3. Select Document from the Print What list box.

4. Choose OK.

Because annotation marks in a document are formatted as hidden text, all hidden text is printed. The annotations are printed at the end of the document, along with the page number of the accompanying annotation mark.

Troubleshooting

When I try to delete an annotation comment, the annotation mark doesn't go away.

To delete an annotation, select the annotation mark in the document text and press Backspace or Delete. You must select an annotation mark first, before pressing Backspace or Delete, because it is a special nontext character.

I don't remember deleting an annotation, but now it's gone. Why?

If you delete the text surrounding an annotation mark in the middle of a document, the mark is deleted, even if the mark is not visible.

I need to change the initials in an annotation mark.

The initials are taken from the User Info tab of the Options dialog box. If you change your initials there, future annotations will contain the new initials.

VI

Handling Large Documents

Chapter 31

Adding Cross-References and Captions

Cross-references and captions greatly simplify the job of creating complex or illustrated documents. *Cross-references* refer to text or objects in some other part of your document, or in another document. *Captions* label and number illustrations and tables in your document. You can update cross-references and captions automatically, so that when you insert them you can be sure they remain accurate.

In this chapter, you learn to use cross-references and captions in order to do the following:

- Cross-reference headings, bookmarks, and page numbers in the current document or in related documents

- Label pictures, tables, and other illustrations

- Add captions automatically when you insert objects

Understanding Cross-References and Captions

Cross-references and captions simplify your job when you create a document, and they also make your reader's job easier. Cross-references give readers quick access to related information in other parts of your document; captions provide consistent and accurate labeling for the illustrations and tables that augment text.

Figures 31.1 and 31.2 show examples of a cross-reference and a caption.

Fig. 31.1
Both the section title and the page number are cross-references. If either changes, the text on this page reflects that change.

Cross-reference ——

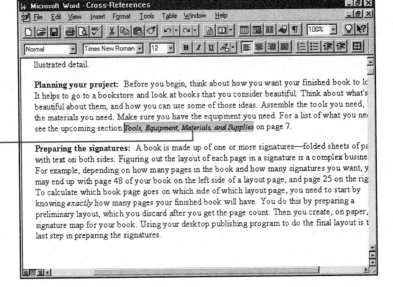

Fig. 31.2
Word numbers captions automatically.

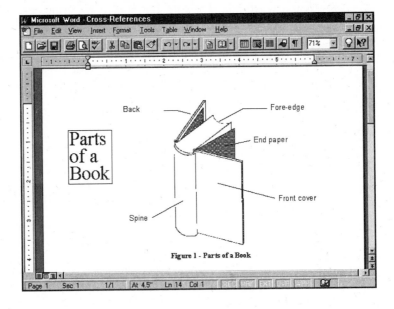

Because cross-references and captions are fields, Word can update them automatically whenever you print the document. (*Fields* are hidden text that perform special functions, such as linking parts of a document together.) Alternatively, you can update fields yourself by selecting them and pressing F9. If you have included page numbers in cross-references throughout your document, for example, and you subsequently add text (so that page numbers change), the cross-references update to show the new page numbers. Or if you include automatically numbered captions for figures and then add more figures, Word renumbers existing figures.

In a cross-reference, the entire text (except any text you type yourself) is a *field result.* In a caption, however, only the chapter and caption number are fields. For example, in a caption reading *Figure 1,* the word *Figure* is not a field result, but the number *1* is.

As a rule, you see the results of fields in your document; they look like text (see fig. 31.3). If you choose Tools, Options, however, and on the View tab, select Field Codes in the Show group, you see a code inside braces—the field code—instead of text (see fig. 31.4). Deselect this option to see the result of your field, rather than the code.

◀ See "Understanding the Basics of Fields," p. 589

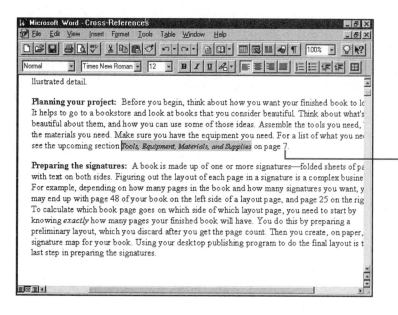

Fig. 31.3
The cross-reference field code result in text can be formatted or edited.

Field Result

Fig. 31.4

You can choose Tools, Options, the View tab, and the Field Codes option to display field codes.

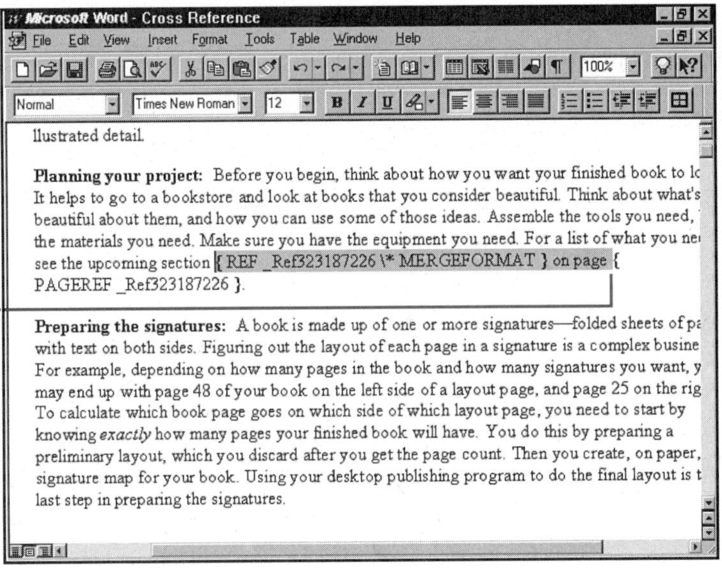

Field codes appear within braces

```
Microsoft Word - Cross Reference
File   Edit   View   Insert   Format   Tools   Table   Window   Help
Normal        Times New Roman    12    B  I  U
```

Illustrated detail.

Planning your project: Before you begin, think about how you want your finished book to lo
It helps to go to a bookstore and look at books that you consider beautiful. Think about what's
beautiful about them, and how you can use some of those ideas. Assemble the tools you need,
the materials you need. Make sure you have the equipment you need. For a list of what you nee
see the upcoming section { REF _Ref323187226 * MERGEFORMAT } on page {
PAGEREF _Ref323187226 }.

Preparing the signatures: A book is made up of one or more signatures—folded sheets of pa
with text on both sides. Figuring out the layout of each page in a signature is a complex busine
For example, depending on how many pages in the book and how many signatures you want, y
may end up with page 48 of your book on the left side of a layout page, and page 25 on the rig
To calculate which book page goes on which side of which layout page, you need to start by
knowing *exactly* how many pages your finished book will have. You do this by preparing a
preliminary layout, which you discard after you get the page count. Then you create, on paper,
signature map for your book. Using your desktop publishing program to do the final layout is t
last step in preparing the signatures.

Creating Cross-References

A cross-reference refers the reader to information in another part of your document (or another document that is part of the same master document). You have the option of including page numbers in cross-references. If the content or location of the information changes, you can update the cross-reference to reflect those changes.

You can cross-reference several types of information, including headings formatted with Word's built-in heading styles (Heading 1 through Heading 9), page numbers, footnotes and endnotes, captions, and bookmarks. When you apply a cross-reference in your document, Word finds the referenced information and inserts that information at the cross-reference. If you cross-reference a heading, for example, Word inserts the text of that heading at the location of the cross-reference. If you cross-reference a page number, Word inserts the correct page number.

Cross-references generally contain two types of text: text that you type, and the cross-reference information that Word inserts. You may type, for example, the words **For more information see page** and then insert a cross-reference to a page number.

You can include multiple references within a single cross-reference in your document. For example, you may want your cross-reference to read: "For more information see X on page Y," with Word filling in both a heading title and a page number.

Adding Cross-References

Because cross-references contain two kinds of text—the text you type and the cross-reference itself—creating a cross-reference is a two-part process. You type the introductory text and then insert the cross-reference. In many cases, you insert two cross-references—one for a title and one for a page number. Word leaves the Cross-reference dialog box open so that you can insert as many cross-references as you need.

When you use the Cross-reference dialog box, you make three choices for each cross-reference you insert. This process involves narrowing down your options. First you select the general category of your cross-reference; for example, you select Heading because your cross-reference is based on one of Word's built-in heading styles (Heading 1 through Heading 9). You next select what part of that heading you want to reference: the heading text, the page number where that heading appears, or the heading number (if you have included heading numbering). Finally, you select the specific heading you want to reference—the Cross-reference dialog box lists all the headings. Each reference type (Heading, Bookmark, Footnote, and so on) has specific options.

Caution

Before you can insert a cross-reference, you must mark the item you want to reference. You can use a heading style, bookmark, footnote, endnote, or caption to mark a location. If you have not marked locations in one of these ways, the lists in the Cross-reference dialog box will not display items for you to cross-reference.

To add a cross-reference, follow these steps:

1. Type the introductory text preceding the cross-reference. For example, type **"See the following page."** Leave the insertion point where you want the cross-reference to appear.

2. Choose Insert, Cross-Reference. The Cross-reference dialog box appears (see fig. 31.5).

Fig. 31.5

The Cross-reference dialog box stays open while you complete your cross-reference.

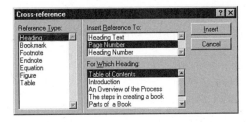

3. In the Reference Type list, select the type of item you want to reference.

   For example, select Heading if you want to cross-reference to a title or subtitle formatted with a heading style.

4. In the Insert Reference To list, select the information about the item that you want to reference.

   The list varies, according to which reference type you have selected. For example, if you had selected Heading as the Reference Type, you could reference the heading's text title, the page number of the heading, or the heading number.

5. In the For Which Heading list box, select the specific item you want to reference.

   Word lists all the items of the selected type that it finds in your document. If you had selected Heading as the Reference type, you would see a list of all headings in the document.

6. Click Insert to insert the cross-reference.

7. If you want to add additional text in your document before closing the Cross-reference dialog box, click in your document and type the text. Then you can repeat steps 3–6 to insert an additional cross-reference. Choose Close when you are finished. (Close appears after you insert a cross-reference.)

Cross-Referencing Another Document

To include a cross-reference to another document, both documents must be part of a master document. *Master documents* are used to create a large document from many smaller subdocuments. To insert a cross-reference, choose View, Master Document, and in Master Document view, insert cross-references in the usual way (see the earlier section, "Adding Cross-References"). When you are in Master Document view, the Cross-reference dialog box lists all the headings, bookmarks, and so on that are contained in the documents linked to this master document.

Updating Cross-References

You can update cross-references and captions by simply selecting them and pressing the F9 key. To update all the cross-references in your document, select the entire document and press F9. Cross-references update automatically when you print your document.

Formatting Cross-References

In your document, a cross-reference looks like text (even though it is a field result), and you can edit it just like text. When the insertion point is inside a cross-reference field, the entire cross-reference is highlighted. The field is selected, but the text is not. Within the highlighted field, however, you can select text and edit it using any of Word's usual editing techniques. When you cross-reference a heading, for example, you may want it to appear in italic. After you insert the cross-reference, select the text in the usual way and apply italic using a command or shortcut. For more information about selecting fields, see the section "Editing and Deleting Cross-References and Captions," later in this chapter.

Creating Captions

Captions help readers reference the illustrations you include in your document. In Word, a caption includes a label, a number, and (optionally) a chapter number. A caption may read, for example, `Figure 7` or `Table II-ii`. You can type additional text after the label and number.

When you create a caption, you can select from a list of preexisting labels such as `Figure` or `Table`, or you can create your own labels. You can select from a list of predefined numbering styles, such as `1 2 3`, `A B C`, or `I II III`. You can place a caption above or below your illustration.

You can include captions in your document in one of two ways. You can instruct Word to include a caption each time you insert a particular type of object; for example, you may want a caption for each picture you insert. Or you can select an object and create a caption for it manually.

Captions update automatically when you insert additional captions in your document. The first caption you insert, for example, may read `Figure 1` and the second `Figure 2`. If you insert a new caption between Figure 1 and Figure

Tip
You can include a cross-reference in a header or footer. You may want to include a cross-reference, for example, which displays the title of a chapter inside a header.

◀ See "Understanding the Basics of Fields," p. 589

◀ See "Marking Locations with Bookmarks," p. 157

◀ See "Creating Numbered Headings," p. 566

VI

Handling Large Documents

2, the new caption is numbered `Figure 2` and the previous Figure 2 becomes `Figure 3`.

Word formats captions with the Caption style. The style that follows Caption is Normal; therefore, when you press Enter after inserting a caption, Word automatically sets the next paragraph's style to Normal. You can change the formatting of the Caption style by using Format, Style, or by defining a new Caption style by example. For details, see Chapter 11, "Using Styles for Repetitive Formats."

Captions work well with cross-references. You can create a cross-reference to any type of caption. If the caption number or label changes, you can update the cross-reference to reflect that change. (For information about updating, see the earlier section, "Creating Cross-References.")

Inserting Captions Manually

You can insert captions manually for figures, tables, objects, and even text. Use this technique when the illustrations are already inserted in your document, or when you include various types of illustrations (pictures and tables, for example), and you want them to have a consistent labeling and numbering scheme.

A caption always includes a label and number, but you also can add text to further explain your illustrations. For example, you may want a caption to read `Table 1 Summary of Annual Sales`. For each type of label you include, Word creates a separate numbering sequence. If you already have inserted Figure 1 and Figure 2, for example, and then insert a caption with the label `Table`, the caption reads `Table 1` rather than `Table 3`.

To insert a caption manually, follow these steps:

1. Select the object for which you want a caption.

2. Choose Insert, Caption. The Caption dialog box appears (see fig. 31.6).

Fig. 31.6
Captions include labels and numbers, and you can add additional text as well. In this example, Figure is the label and 1 is the number.

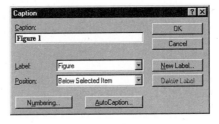

3. With the insertion point after the proposed label and number in the Caption text box, type any additional text you want in your caption.

4. You can select a different label from the Label list box. Word numbers each type of label separately.

5. You can select a different location for your caption—above or below the selected item—from the Position list box. Figure 31.7 shows a caption placed below an illustration.

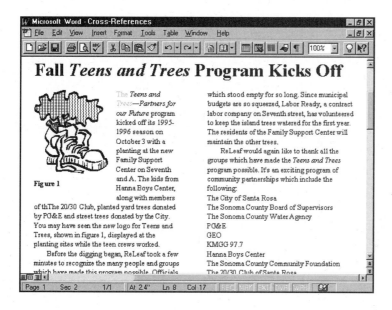

Fig. 31.7
Word inserts the caption above or below the selected item.

6. Choose OK.

When you return to your document after inserting a caption, the insertion point flashes at the end of the caption. The caption is formatted with the Caption style. Press Enter to start a new paragraph formatted with the Normal style.

> **Note**
>
> Because captions are formatted with a style, be sure to put them on a line by themselves; otherwise the entire paragraph where you insert the caption is formatted with Caption style.

VI

Handling Large Documents

Inserting Captions Automatically

If you plan to insert many illustrations of a certain type in your document, you can specify that Word include a caption for each one. If you intend to illustrate your document with many pictures, for example, you can have Word include a caption for each picture. You determine what label Word uses in the captions.

You can include automatic captions for as many different types of objects as you want. The captions either can share a label (and thus share a numbering scheme), or captions for each type of object can have a unique label and a separate sequence of numbers. If you want to add explanatory text after an automatic caption, position the insertion point at the end of the caption and type the text.

Insert automatic captions before you begin inserting your illustrations. If you insert automatic captions after you have inserted some of your illustrations, select the existing illustrations and add their captions manually (see the earlier section, "Inserting Captions Manually," for information on this procedure). If the manually and automatically inserted captions use the same label, Word updates the caption numbers to keep them sequential.

To include automatic captions, follow these steps:

1. Choose Insert, Caption.

2. Click the AutoCaption button. The AutoCaption dialog box appears (see fig. 31.8).

Fig. 31.8
You can use automatic captions for many types of objects.

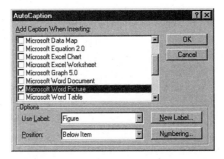

3. In the Add Caption When Inserting list, select the type of object for which you want Word to add automatic captions. Select several types of objects if you want them all to have the same label and numbering scheme.

4. Select Options for the type of object you selected. From Use Label, select the type of label for the object; from Position, select Above Item or Below Item.

   To create a unique label, choose New Label (for details, see the next section, "Creating New Caption Labels"). To change the numbering style or include chapter numbers, choose Numbering (see the "Changing Caption Numbering" later in this section).

5. Repeat steps 3 and 4 to add automatic captions for additional types of objects. By first selecting the object (step 3) and then selecting options (step 4), you can create a separate label and numbering scheme for each type of object for which you insert automatic captions.

6. Choose OK.

Creating New Caption Labels

You can create a new caption label at any of three times when working in your document: when you insert the caption manually, when you insert automatic captions, or after you have inserted your captions.

When you create a new label, Word adds it to the list of existing labels; the new label is available the next time you create a caption.

To create a new label for a manual caption, follow these steps:

1. Select the object for which you want a caption and choose Insert, Caption.

   > **Note**
   >
   > You can't drag across an existing label in the Caption box to select it; to change a label, you must choose Insert, Caption, and then select a caption from the Label list box or create a new one by choosing New Label.

2. Choose New Label. The New Label dialog box appears (see fig. 31.9).

3. In the Label text box, type the text of the label you want. Choose OK to close the New Label dialog box.

4. Choose OK to close the Caption dialog box.

Fig. 31.9

Create your own
label by typing it
in the Label box.

Your new label appears in the Caption list box of the Caption dialog box, as
shown in figure 31.10.

Fig. 31.10

Your new label
appears in the
Caption text box.

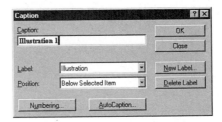

To create new labels for automatic captions, follow these steps:

1. Choose Insert, Caption.

2. Click AutoCaption to display the AutoCaption dialog box (refer to
   fig. 31.8).

3. From the Add Caption When Inserting list box, select the object type
   for which you want automatic captions.

4. Click New Label.

5. In the Label box, type the text of the label. Choose OK to exit the New
   Label dialog box.

6. Choose OK.

Changing Caption Labels

You can change the labels for captions you already have inserted in your
document. When you change the label for an existing caption, all captions
with that label-type change. If you change Figure to Table, for example, all
the captions labeled as Figure change to Table.

To change labels for existing captions, follow these steps:

1. Select a caption with the label type you want to change. If you want to
   change all captions with the label Figure to the label Table, for example, select one *Figure* caption.

2. Choose Insert, Caption.

3. Select a different label from the Label list, or choose New Label and create a new label.

4. Choose OK.

Deleting a Caption Label

When you create new caption labels, they are added to the list of existing labels. You can delete these new labels from the list, but you can't delete Word's built-in labels (like Figure and Table). To delete the label, choose Insert, Caption, select the label from the Label list, click Delete Label, and then choose Close.

If you delete the label from an existing caption, the caption number remains, and the numbering scheme for that label type is unchanged. To learn about editing captions, see the section "Editing and Deleting Cross-References and Captions" later in this chapter.

Changing Caption Numbering

You can change the caption numbering style for manual or automatic captions when you insert the captions. Alternatively, you can change the numbering style for existing captions in your document. When you change the caption numbering style, the change affects all captions with the same label type as the caption you changed.

To change caption numbering when you insert captions, follow these steps:

1. For manual captions, select the object for which you want to insert a caption and choose Insert, Caption. In the Caption dialog box, click Numbering.

   For automatic captions, choose Insert, Caption. In the Caption dialog box, click AutoCaption. Select the type of object for which you want automatic captions, then choose Numbering. The Caption Numbering dialog box appears (see fig. 31.11).

2. To change the style of the numbers, select an option from the Format drop-down list. For example, select 1, 2, 3; or a, b, c; or A, B, C; or i, ii, iii; or I, II, III.

3. Choose OK to return to the previous dialog box.

VI

Handling Large Documents

4. Choose OK to return to your document.

Fig. 31.11
You can change
the format of the
caption number,
and you can
include chapter
numbers in your
captions.

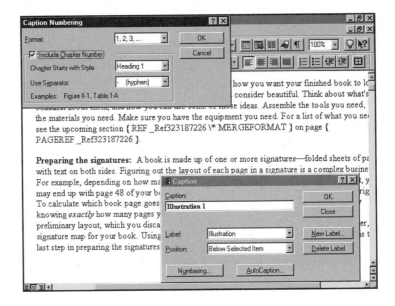

To change caption numbering style for existing captions, follow these steps:

1. Select a caption of the label-type whose numbering style you want to change. For example, if you want to change all the "Figure 1-*x*" captions to "Figure A-*z*" captions, select a single "Figure 1" caption.

2. Choose Insert, Caption.

3. In the Caption dialog box, click Numbering.

4. Select a different numbering style from the Format list.

5. Choose OK to return to the Caption dialog box.

6. Choose Close to return to your document.

All captions using the same label-type reflect your new numbering style.

Including Chapter Numbers in a Caption

In a caption, you can include the current chapter number, if you format your chapters with one of Word's built-in heading styles (Heading 1 through Heading 9), and if you have selected a heading numbering style. A caption with a chapter number may read, for example, Figure 1A or Table II:ii.

This technique works well with a document containing several chapters. In a document containing only one chapter, all the chapter numbers are the same.

To include chapter numbers in your captions, follow these steps:

1. Format all chapter titles and subheadings with built-in heading styles: Heading 1 through Heading 9. Be sure to format the title of each chapter as Heading 1.

2. Choose Format, Heading Numbering. In the Heading Numbering dialog box, select a heading numbering style. Choose OK.

3. For manual captions, select the object for which you want to insert a caption and choose Insert, Caption. In the Caption dialog box, choose Numbering.

   For automatic captions, choose Insert, Caption. In the Caption dialog box, choose AutoCaption. Select the type of object for which you want automatic captions, then choose Numbering.

4. In the Caption Numbering dialog box, select the Include Chapter Number option.

5. In the Chapter Number Ends With list box, select the lowest level of heading you want to include in your caption number. If you want only the chapter number, for example, select Heading 1 to get a caption such as `Figure 1-3`. If you want to include the chapter and first subheading number, however, select Heading 2 for a caption such as `Figure 1.2-3`.

6. In the Use Separator list, select the punctuation you want to separate the chapter number and the caption number. Options include a hyphen, a period, a colon, or an em dash (a wide hyphen).

7. Choose OK to return to the previous dialog box.

8. Choose OK to return to your document.

Formatting Captions

The Caption format style is the Normal style, with the addition of bold and a line space before and after the paragraph. You can reformat all your captions automatically by making changes to the Caption style. Alternatively, you can select the caption and apply manual formatting. Because most captions are a

Tip

You also can change numbering by selecting a captioned object, rather than a caption. If you use this technique, close the Caption dialog box by choosing Close in step 4 rather than OK. If you choose OK, you add an extra caption.

VI

Handling Large Documents

single line (and therefore, a single paragraph), you can apply paragraph formatting commands such as indentations and alignment, as well as text formatting commands such as italic or another font.

Editing Captions

You can edit captions in several ways. You can change their labels or numbering styles, as described in the previous sections, "Changing Caption Labels" and "Changing Caption Numbering." You can format captions, as described in the previous section, "Formatting Captions." You can update captions, as described in the upcoming section "Updating Captions."

You also can edit caption text. Editing a caption's text does not affect other captions of the same type. You can add text to the end of a caption called Figure 1, for example, and no other Figure captions are affected. You also can edit the field portion of a caption; that edit also does not affect other captions of the same type. To learn how to edit the field, see the section "Editing and Deleting Cross-References and Captions" later in this chapter.

Updating Captions

When you insert new captions using a label you previously have used in your document, Word includes the correct sequential caption number. Word renumbers existing captions when you insert a new caption between existing captions.

When you delete or move something a caption references, however, you must update it by selecting it and pressing F9. To update all the captions in your document at once, select the entire document and press F9.

Framing a Caption with Its Object

When you move an object for which you have inserted a caption, the caption does not move with the object. If you want the object and caption to move together, frame them as a single object. When an object and caption are framed together, you can use the mouse to drag them anywhere in your document.

To frame an object and its caption, follow these steps:

1. Select the object and its caption.

2. Choose Insert, Frame.

   Or, click the Insert Frame button on the Standard or Drawing toolbar.

Alternatively, you can frame the object and *then* insert its caption—the caption is included automatically inside the frame.

Editing and Deleting Cross-References and Captions

Cross-references and captions are fields; by default, you see in your document the result of the fields. You may see, for example, a cross-reference such as `Editing Cross-References` or a caption such as `Figure 3`. If you display fields, however, rather than field results, you see field codes, such as

`{REF _Ref270669594\* MERGEFORMAT }`

or

`{ SEQ Figure \* ARABIC }`

Word uses fields so that it can update cross-references and captions if the information changes.

You can edit either the field result or the field code. Editing the field result is the same as editing text, however; the next time the field code is updated, the editing will be lost unless you unlock the results as described in Chapter 20, "Automating with Field Codes." You also can edit the field code when it is displayed. You may want to edit the field code as a quick way of changing a reference or as a means of inserting a special formatting. Chapter 20 describes in detail editing field codes and adding formatting switches. Many cross-references and captions also include normal text preceding or following the field. Edit this text using Word's usual text-editing techniques; for details, see Chapter 5, "Editing a Document."

The key to editing a cross-reference or caption is in selecting and displaying the field code that creates the cross-reference or caption. To make selecting a field code easier, you can set viewing options to shade data from field codes.

To shade any data from field codes, follow these steps:

1. Choose Tools, Options and select the View tab.

2. Select one of the following items from the Field Shading drop-down list:

Select This	To Get This Action
Never	Field codes and results are never shaded.
Always	Field codes and results are always shaded.
When Selected	Field codes and results are shaded only when they are selected or the insertion point is in the field code.

3. Choose OK.

You can switch the entire document between field codes and results by pressing Alt+F9.

To edit or format a field result, move the insertion point within the field result. If the Field Shading option is on, the field results turn light gray (see fig. 31.12). Select the text you want to edit or format. Figure 31.13 shows selected text within a field result.

Fig. 31.12
A field result appears with light shading when the insertion point is inside and Field Shading is turned on.

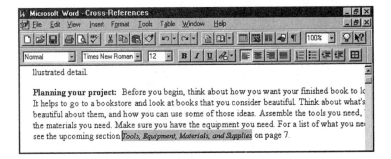

Fig. 31.13
This field result shows darker selected text that can be edited or formatted.

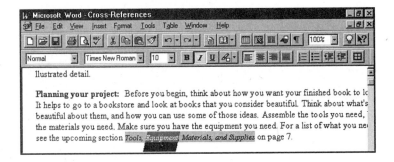

To delete a field code and its result, select across one field code marker or across the entire field result. The entire field result will turn darker (see fig. 31.14). Press the Delete key. It is easier to select and delete field codes if you display the field codes rather than field results.

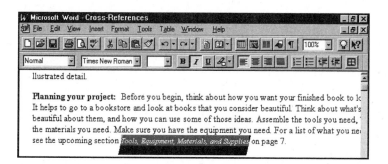

Fig. 31.14
Selecting the entire field result displays the entire result with dark shading. The field code can be deleted at this point.

To update the field, select it and press F9. To update a field, you either can highlight it by positioning the insertion point inside it, or you can select it by dragging across it. ❖

Tip
To select quickly the next field following the insertion point, press F11. To select the field prior to the insertion point, press Shift+F11.

VI

Handling Large Documents

Chapter 32

Assembling Large Documents

You can work with any size document in Word for Windows 95, but several considerations dictate the most efficient approach to working with large documents. Large documents, as well as documents with many graphics, fields, bookmarks, and formatting, consume more memory and disk space. They can be slow to load, save, and work in, depending on how much memory you have and the speed of your computer.

Most of this chapter focuses on using master documents to work with large documents, because this is the most efficient and flexible way to manage large documents. However, you also learn how to break a large document into individual files and treat these files separately. You learn how to create tables of contents and indexes that span the information contained in these individual files.

Documents of 20 or fewer pages give the best performance in Word for Windows. If your documents are significantly larger than 20 pages, you can segment the documents into multiple files and rejoin them using the techniques described in this chapter.

In this chapter, you learn to do the following:

- Create a master document
- Work with a master document
- Work with subdocuments
- Insert tables of contents, indexes, and cross-references in long documents

Understanding the Components of a Large Document

Although you can break a document into smaller documents and work with and print these smaller files individually, there are many advantages to combining these smaller subdocuments into a master document, and using Word for Windows powerful master document feature to organize and work with the large document. When you work in Master Document view of a large document (see fig. 32.1), it's like working with an outline, so it is much easier to move around the document and to organize the document using the same techniques you use to organize an outline (see Chapter 19, "Organizing Content with an Outline"). There are also several tools in the Master view that you can use to manage the subdocuments in a master document.

Fig. 32.1

You can use Master Document view to manage a large document.

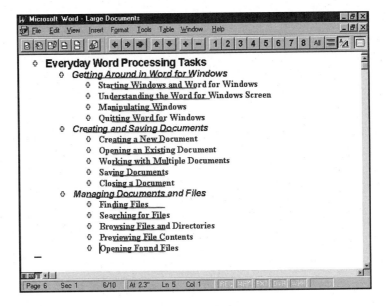

You can work with two views in the master document. Master Document view is similar to Outline view (refer to fig. 32.1), and enables you to organize your document using the same techniques you use to organize an outline with the buttons on the Outlining toolbar. Using the buttons on the Master Document toolbar, you can move and delete entire subdocuments, insert new subdocuments, combine subdocuments, and demote a subdocument so that it becomes part of the master document text. If you need to work with one of the subdocuments, you can quickly open it from the master document.

To view the entire document to edit and format it, you can switch to Normal view. In Normal view, you can work with the document just as if it were a single document. You can add a table of contents, index, and cross-references just as in any other document. You need to be in Normal view when you want to print the document. You can print in the Master Document view if you want to obtain an outline of your document.

When you switch to Normal view for the master document, it's just like working on a single document, so you can use the standard procedures for adding page numbers, tables of contents, indexes, and cross-references, while avoiding the complications of trying to accomplish these tasks using individual files. You can print the master document just as you would any file, so you don't have to open and print each individual file. When necessary, you still can work with the individual subdocuments. For example, when you want each subdocument to have its own header and footer, you work with the documents individually. Also, different people can work on the individual subdocuments in a master document. Then you can open the master document to pull together all the subdocuments and make editing changes that affect the whole document—for example, adding a table of contents and an index—and print the entire document all at once.

Another technique covered is choosing Insert, File to insert a document into the master document. The inserted source documents become part of a master document, as if they were created there. This is useful for creating contracts or proposals by inserting paragraphs saved on disk. The inserted material is not linked back to the source. There are two disadvantages to this method. If a source document changes, you must change the master manually. Also, the master document can become as large and as slow as if you had typed a large document.

Creating a Master Document

There are three ways to create a master document. You can create a master document from scratch by entering an outline for your document, using one of the heading levels to indicate the beginning of each subdocument. You then create the subdocuments from the headings, using one of the buttons on the Master Document toolbar. You can also create a master document from an existing document or combine several documents into a master document. The three ways of creating a master document are discussed in the following sections.

Whatever method you use to create your master document, you must work in Master Document view and use the built-in heading styles (Heading 1 through Heading 9) for the headings in your outline. You can use the promote and demote buttons on the Outlining toolbar to create your headings; Word for Windows automatically uses the heading styles. You can also apply the heading styles using the Style box on the Formatting toolbar.

Creating a New Master Document

You create a new master document in a blank document using Master Document view. To create a new master document, follow these steps:

1. Open a new document.

2. Choose View, Master Document.

   When you switch to the Master Document view, the Outlining and Master Document toolbars appear at the top of the screen (see fig. 32.2). A Master Document View button appears to the left of the horizontal scroll bar so that you can easily switch between Normal, Page Layout, Master Document and Outline views. These buttons are used to promote and demote outline headings and work with subdocuments. Table 32.1 summarizes the functions of the individual buttons on the Outlining and Master Document toolbars.

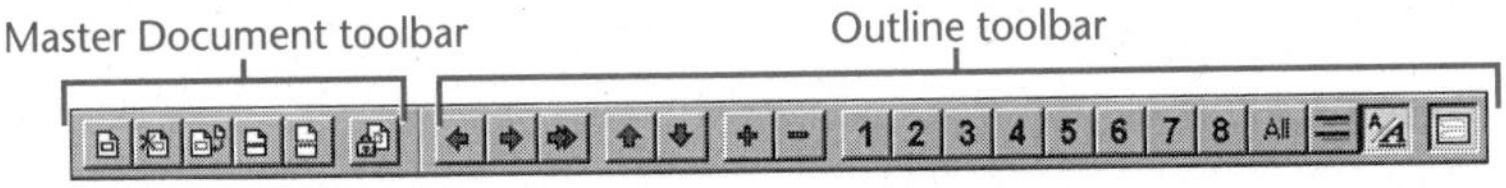

Fig. 32.2
The Outlining and Master Document toolbars help you view and manage your long documents.

Table 32.1 Outline and Master Document Toolbar Functions		
Button	**Name**	**Function**
	Promote	Promotes the heading (and its body text) by one level; promotes body text to the heading level of the preceding heading
	Demote	Demotes the heading by one level; demotes body text to the heading level below the preceding heading
	Demote to body text	Demotes a heading to body text and applies the Normal style
	Move Up	Moves the selected paragraph(s) before the first visible paragraph that precedes the selected paragraph(s)

Button	Name	Function
	Move Down	Moves the selected paragraph(s) after the first visible paragraph that follows the selected paragraph(s)
	Expand	Expands the first heading level below the currently selected heading; repeated clicks expand through additional heading levels until body is expanded
	Collapse	Collapses body text into heading, then lowest level headings into higher level headings
	Show Heading	Displays all headings and text through the lowest level number you click
	Display All	Displays all text if some is collapsed; displays only headings if all text is expanded
	Show First Line Only	Toggles between showing all the body text in an outline and only the first line of text
	Show Formatting	Toggles between showing normal character formatting in Outline view and Normal view
	Master Document View	Toggles between showing Outline and Master Document view
	Create Subdocument	Creates subdocuments from selected outline items
	Remove Subdocument	Removes the selected subdocument, leaving the text in the master document
	Insert Subdocument	Inserts the file selected in the Insert Subdocument dialog box into the master document
	Merge Subdocument	Merges selected subdocuments into one subdocument

(continues)

VI

Handling Large Documents

Button	Name	Function
	Split Subdocument	Splits the selected portion of a subdocument into another subdocument
	Lock Document	Locks and unlocks the file for the selected subdocument

Table 32.1 Continued

3. Type an outline for the master document.

   You can use the buttons on the toolbar to promote and demote headings as you enter your outline. Decide on a heading level that designates the beginning of a subdocument. For example, you might use **Heading Level 2** to indicate the beginning of each subdocument.

4. Select the headings you want to create your subdocuments from.

   You can select as many headings as you want, but you must be sure that the first heading in the selection is the same level as the one you are using to indicate the beginning of subdocuments, as shown in figure 32.3.

Fig. 32.3
The first heading level in your selection should be the level you want to convert to subdocuments.

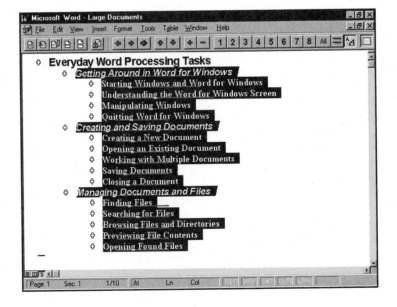

5. Click the Create Subdocument button on the Master Document toolbar.

Word for Windows divides the master document into subdocuments: one subdocument for each heading level that you designate as the subdocument heading. Each subdocument is enclosed in a box and a subdocument icon appears in the upper-left corner of the box, as shown in figure 32.4.

6. Save the master document.

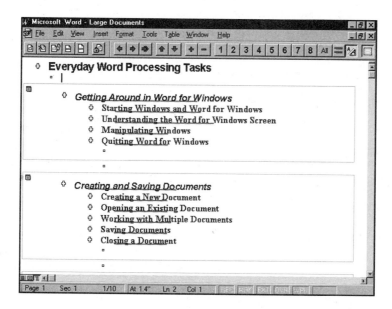

Fig. 32.4
Word for Windows creates a sub–document for each subdocument heading level.

When you save the master document, Word for Windows automatically saves each of the subdocuments as a file. Word for Windows assigns a file name to each subdocument, using the first characters in the heading for the subdocument. For example, the file names for the subdocuments created from the outline shown in figure 32.3 are GETTING.DOC, CREATING.DOC, and MANAGING.DOC. Word for Windows uses numbers or other characters in the file name if the file names based on the headings conflict with other files.

VI

Handling Large Documents

> **Caution**
>
> If you decide to rename a subdocument or save it in a different location on your hard disk, be sure to do it while you are in the master document; then save the master document again. First, you must open the subdocument from within the master document. To do this, double-click the subdocument icon in the upper-left corner of the box enclosing the subdocument. Then choose File, Save As to save the subdocument with a new name or in a new location. This keeps the links between the master document and the subdocuments from being broken.

Creating a Master Document from an Existing Document

If you already created a document, you can convert it to a master document. To do so, use the Outlining toolbar in Master Document view to set up headings in the document, and then create subdocuments from these headings, as described in the previous section.

To create a master document from an existing document, follow these steps:

1. Open the document you want to convert to a master document.

2. Choose View, Master Document.

3. Use the buttons on the Outlining toolbar to assign heading levels to your document and to rearrange the headings, if necessary.

◀ See "Creating an Outline," p. 575

4. Complete steps 4–6 as outlined in "Creating a New Master Document" earlier in this chapter.

Building Your Master Document by Inserting Subdocuments

You can insert subdocuments into an existing master document. Use this method as a way of adding new documents at a specific location in your master document.

You also can insert subdocuments into a normal document, which changes the normal document into a master document. Use this method as a quick way of changing a normal document into a master document.

To insert an existing document into a normal or master document, follow these steps:

1. Open a new document or an existing master document.

2. Choose <u>V</u>iew, <u>M</u>aster Document.

3. Move the insertion point where you want to insert the document.

4. Click the Insert Subdocument button on the Master Document toolbar.

5. In the File <u>N</u>ame text box, type the name of the file you want to open, or select the file you want to open from the File <u>N</u>ame list in the Insert Subdocument dialog box.

   The file is inserted into the master document with its original file name. Word for Windows uses the formatting from the master's documents template if it is different from the subdocument's template. The original formatting is preserved in the subdocument file if you open it separately.

Troubleshooting

I selected the headings that I wanted to convert to subdocuments and clicked the Create Subdocument button, but my subdocuments did not divide as I intended.

The key to creating subdocuments from the headings in a master document is to make sure that when you select the headings you want to create subdocuments from, you select all of the headings you want to convert to subdocuments. You also need to make sure that the first heading in the selection is assigned the heading level you want to use to begin all subdocuments. For example, if the first heading in the selection is assigned Heading Level 2, all sections beginning with Heading Level 2 will be converted to subdocuments.

 See "Creating an Outline," p. 575

Working with the Master Document

When you have set up your master document, you can use Master Document and Normal views to work with the document. In Master Document view, you can view the overall structure of the document, and reorganize the sections in the document. For example, it is very easy to reorder the subdocuments that make up the master document by using the mouse and the buttons on the Outlining toolbar. You can also open the individual subdocuments in Master Document view. You should work in Master Document view when you need to make changes that affect the overall document.

In Normal view, you can work with the document just as if it were a single document. You can format the document and add page numbers, tables of contents and other tables, indexes, and cross-references. When you switch to Normal view, each subdocument that makes up the master document is a

VI

Handling Large Documents

section (see Chapter 13, "Formatting the Page Layout, Alignment, and Numbering"). You can apply section formatting to these sections. For example, you can set up different headers and footers in the individual sections.

Formatting the Master Document

Tip
To ensure consistency when you or a team are writing large documents, read Chapter 6, "Using Templates and Wizards for Frequently Created Documents," and Chapter 11, "Using Styles for Repetitive Formats."

Formatting a master document is no different than formatting a single document. You can create templates, styles, and AutoText for the master document and format all or any part of the master document. If a subdocument is based on a different template than the master document, the master document's template styles override the subdocument styles. If you open a subdocument file outside of the master document, the original template styles will still be in effect.

To insert headers and footers that are the same for the entire master document, set them up in the master document. If you want different headers and footers for the individual subdocuments, set them up in each subdocument. You can also modify the page numbers, margins, and other section-level formatting within subdocuments, and insert new section breaks within a subdocument. When you insert an existing file into a master document, any section formatting in that document is maintained. This helps if you already set up headers and footers in the individual documents you combine to create a master document and you want to maintain those headers and footers in the master document.

◀ See "Moving, Copying, and Linking Text or Graphics," p. 160

Another benefit of working in the master document is that you can move text and graphics among subdocuments without opening the individual subdocuments. You can even use the drag-and-drop technique for moving text and graphics from one subdocument to another. You need to be in the Normal view of the master document to move text and graphics.

Printing a Master Document

Printing a master document is as simple as printing a single document. The ability to print an entire long document at once is one of the advantages that a master document has over working with individual files. To print the entire document, you must be in Normal view. You can then choose File, Print to print the document.

To print an outline of your document, switch to Master Document view. You can then collapse or expand the outline to include exactly the heading levels you want to include in your outline and print the outline.

Sharing a Master Document

One advantage of using a master document to manage a long document is that several users can work together on the subdocuments of the master document at the same time. Word for Windows has a locking feature that allows anyone to open a master document. While locking is on, you can only edit the subdocuments which you created. However, you will be able to read the subdocuments created by others. Word for Windows uses the AUTHOR field in the summary information of a subdocument to determine the author of a subdocument.

◄ See "Opening an Existing Document," p. 79

Word for Windows allows you to unlock any locked document. For this reason, if you want to provide absolute protection for a document against changes, use the techniques described in Chapter 3, "Creating and Saving Documents," to apply password protection to the document. Also, you will not be able to work on a subdocument if another user on the network already opened that document. See Chapter 3 for more information on opening documents on a network.

◄ See "Saving a Document," p. 91

To lock or unlock a subdocument, follow these steps:

1. Select the subdocument you want to lock or unlock.

2. Click the Lock Document button on the Master Document toolbar.

A padlock icon appears just below the subdocument icon when a subdocument is locked (see fig. 32.5).

Padlock icon ──

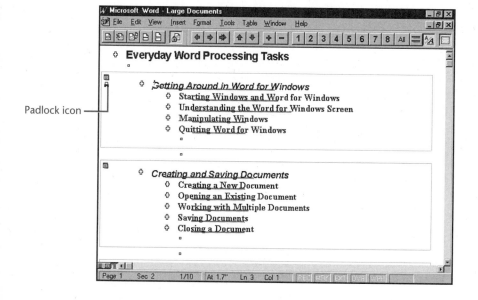

Fig. 32.5
The padlock icon in a subdocument indicates that the subdocument is locked against changes.

VI

Handling Large Documents

Troubleshooting

I am able to open a subdocument outside of the master document and then edit and save it, but whenever I open the same subdocument from within the master document, I am unable to edit and save it.

The reason for this is that the subdocument has been locked in the master document. If you look just below the subdocument icon for the subdocument you are trying to work with, you will see a padlock symbol, which indicates that the subdocument is locked. When you open a locked subdocument, it is opened as a read-only document and cannot be edited and saved with the same name. To unlock the subdocument, locate the insertion point anywhere in the subdocument and click the Unlock Subdocument button, the last button on the Master Document toolbar (refer to fig. 32.2).

Working with Subdocuments within the Master Document

You can work with subdocuments in the Master Document view of a master document. You can open a subdocument from within a master document if you need to edit the subdocument. You can also rearrange the order of subdocuments, and merge, split, or remove subdocuments.

Opening Subdocuments from within a Master Document

You can quickly open a subdocument when you are in the master view of a document. This is handy if you need to edit the subdocument. To open a subdocument, open the master document, switch to Master Document view, and double-click the subdocument icon for the subdocument you want to open. If you make any editing changes in the subdocument, be sure to save it. When you do, the changes are saved in both the subdocument and the master document.

Rearranging Subdocuments in a Master Document

When you work in a master document, it is easy to rearrange the order of the subdocuments in the master document by using the same methods you use to move the contents of an outline. You can move headings within a subdocument or move entire subdocuments.

To move a subdocument within a master document, follow these steps:

1. Click the subdocument icon to select the entire subdocument.

2. Drag the subdocument to the new location.

   A gray line appears on-screen as you drag the selection. Drag the gray line to the point where you want to move the selection and release the mouse button.

   Or, you can hold down the Alt+Shift keys and use the ↑ and ↓ keys to relocate the subdocument.

You can also move individual headings within a subdocument by using the same techniques.

◄ See "Promoting and Demoting Headings," p. 577

Splitting, Merging, and Deleting Subdocuments

If a subdocument becomes larger than you would like, you can split it into subdocuments. Or you can merge smaller subdocuments into one large subdocument.

To split a subdocument, follow these steps:

1. Open the master document and switch to Master Document view.

2. Position the insertion point where you want to split the document.

3. Click the Split Subdocument button on the Master Document toolbar.

4. Save the master document so that Word for Windows will save and name the new subdocument.

To merge two or more subdocuments, follow these steps:

1. Open the subdocument and switch to Master Document view.

2. If necessary, move the subdocuments you want to merge next to each other.

3. Select the entire contents of the subdocuments you want to merge.

4. Click the Merge Subdocument button on the Master Document toolbar.

5. Save the master document to save a new file for the merged subdocuments. Word for Windows uses the file name of the first subdocument.

To remove a subdocument from a master document, follow these steps:

1. Open the subdocument and switch to Master Document view.

2. Click the subdocument icon to select the subdocument you want to remove.

◄ See "Promoting and Demoting Headings," p. 577

VI

Handling Large Documents

3. Press Delete to remove the subdocument and its contents from the master document. When you delete a subdocument, the subdocument file is still stored on the hard drive.

4. Click the Remove Subdocument button on the Master Document toolbar to remove the subdocument and retain the text in the master document.

Caution

To delete a subdocument from a master document, do so while in Master Document view. If you simply delete the file from your hard disk, when you try to open the master document you will get an error message informing you that the subdocument is missing.

Inserting Tables of Contents, Indexes, and Cross-References

◀ See "Creating Cross-References," p. 920

When you work with a master document, one of the advantages is that you can use the same techniques you use in a single document to create tables of contents and other tables, indexes, and cross-references. To insert a table of contents or index into a master document, open the master document and switch to Normal view. Then use the normal methods for inserting the table of contents or index (see Chapter 29, "Creating Indexes and Tables of Contents"). You also must be working in Normal view of the master document to insert cross-references that make references across documents. When you update tables of contents, indexes, or cross-references, be sure to do so from within the master document to avoid error messages.

Troubleshooting

When I work on a subdocument containing cross-references, I get many error messages. The same is true of the subdocument that contains my table of contents and index.

To work on cross-references and tables of contents and indexes, you must be in the master document. This is because cross-references, tables of contents, and indexes make references across documents. To replace the error messages in your subdocuments, open the master document, select the text containing the error messages, or position the insertion point anywhere in a table of contents or index, and press F9. The fields used to return this information will be updated.

Working with Individual Files

Another technique for assembling large documents is to print the smaller documents separately. For large documents that would overload memory if they were inserted or linked into one large master document, this technique is preferable.

When you use this technique, you must set the starting numbers for pages, paragraphs, footnotes, and so on, for each individual file to maintain sequential numbering across the larger document. You must also use {RD} (Referenced Document) field codes for creating tables of contents and indexes. The table of contents and index are created in a separate document, and an {RD} field code is inserted for each of the individual files that make up the document. You cannot use cross-references across files when you work with individual files.

Setting Starting Numbers

To set the starting numbers for the individual files, start with the first file in the series. Repaginate the file, and then note the number of the last page and of any other sequentially numbered items, such as paragraphs, lines, footnotes, and items numbered using the {SEQ} fields (tables or figures, for example). Next, open the second file in the series and use the appropriate commands to set the starting numbers for each sequentially numbered item in that document. Follow this procedure for each of the individual files. To save time and to minimize the possibility that you have to repeat the process of setting starting numbers, carry out this procedure after all editing changes have been made.

To set the starting page numbers, follow these steps:

1. Choose Insert, Page Numbers.

2. Select the Format option.

3. Type or select the appropriate page number in the Start At text box (one higher than the number of the last page in the preceding file).

4. Choose OK and then choose Close.

To set the starting footnote numbers, follow these steps:

1. Choose Insert, Footnote.

2. Click the Options button.

3. Type or select the appropriate number in the Start At text box (one higher than the number of the last footnote in the preceding file).

4. Choose OK and then choose Close.

To set the starting line numbers, follow these steps:

1. Choose File, Page Setup.

2. Select the Layout tab.

3. Select the Line Numbers option.

4. Select the Add Line Numbering option.

5. Type or select the appropriate line number in the Start At text box (one higher than the number of the last line in the preceding file).

6. Select the Continuous option in the Restart Field.

7. Choose OK twice.

To set the starting number for paragraphs, follow these steps:

1. Select the group of paragraphs you want to renumber.

2. Choose Format, Bullets and Numbering.

3. Select the Numbered tab and choose the Modify option.

4. Type the appropriate number in the Start At text box (one higher than the number of the last numbered paragraph in the preceding file).

5. Choose OK.

To set the starting numbers of items numbered using the SEQ field, follow these steps:

1. Choose Tools, Options and select the View tab.

2. Select the Field Codes option and choose OK.

3. Find the first {SEQ} field and type **\r** followed by the appropriate number (one higher than the last number in that sequence of items).

4. Repeat step 2 for each sequence in the document.

> **Note**
>
> See Chapter 20, "Automating with Field Codes," for information on using the {SEQ} field code to create a sequentially numbered series of items. Also, you can learn how to insert chapter numbers using the {SEQ} code in "Inserting Chapter Numbers," later in this chapter.

Creating Chapter Numbers

When you print the individual documents separately (not linking in a master document), you must insert the chapter number. To do so, you add the chapter number to the header or footer next to the page number code. The entry in the header or footer for Chapter 2, for example, might look like this:

```
2-{page}
```

If the order of the chapters changes, you must edit the chapter numbers that appear in the header or footer to maintain the proper sequencing.

Inserting Chapter Numbers

In documents assembled in a master document, you can use the {SEQ} field to print chapter numbers with the page numbers.

First you must put an {SEQ} field at the beginning of each chapter, as in the following steps:

1. Open the first subdocument in the master document.

2. Move the insertion point to the beginning of the subdocument.

3. Press Ctrl+F9 to insert a pair of field characters, {}.

4. Type **SEQ *identifier* \h** in the brackets.

   Identifier is a name you assign to the sequence (here, a chapter). The \h code hides the result of the field so that it is not displayed in the document. The identifier may be a name such as WordBook. Use this identifier for all chapters in the same master document or book.

5. Repeat this process at the beginning of each subsequent chapter.

Now use this {SEQ} field to create a chapter/page number combination in each subdocument. For the first source document included in your master document, follow these steps:

1. Choose <u>V</u>iew, <u>H</u>eader and Footer.

2. Position the insertion point where you want the chapter and page numbers to appear in the header or footer.

3. Press Ctrl+F9, and type **SEQ *identifier***.

4. Use the arrow key to move the insertion point outside the field bracket, and type a dash or the character you want to separate the chapter number from the page number.

5. Click the page button to insert a page field code.

   The entry in the header or footer will look similar to the following:

   ```
   {seq WordBook}-{page}
   ```

6. Click the Close button.

7. Save the file.

◄ See "Under-
standing the
Basics of
Fields," p. 589

You must set the starting page number for the second and subsequent files in the series of files included in the master document. When you use a master document to assemble a large document, you usually do not have to set the starting page numbers because Word for Windows automatically assembles the final document into one file and numbers the pages sequentially. When the page numbering includes the chapter number, however, the page numbers have to restart at 1 for each chapter. See "Setting Starting Numbers," earlier in the chapter, for instructions on how to set the starting page number.

To set the page numbering in each subsequent chapter, follow these steps:

1. Choose Insert, Page Numbers.

2. Click the Format button.

3. Type or select **1** in the Start At text box.

4. Choose OK twice.

In the individual files, the {SEQ} field that outputs the chapter number always results in the number 1. When you assemble the master document, however, and the SEQ fields are updated, a sequence of chapter numbers results.

Printing Individual Files

After you set the starting numbers for each of the files, you can print them individually. To print several documents with one command, choose Find, Files or Folders from the Windows 95 start button. When you choose this command, Word for Windows finds all the files in the path specified in the Find: All Files dialog box. You can edit this path if necessary. To find all the files in the path and print them, follow these steps:

1. Click the Start button in the taskbar at the bottom of the screen.

2. Move the mouse pointer over the Find command, and click Files or Folders. The Find: All Files dialog box appears.

3. Type the name of the files in the Named edit box.

4. Choose the location of the files from the Look In list, and then choose Find Now.

5. Press and hold down the Ctrl key and click the name of each file you want to print.

   Or, you can press Shift+F8 and use the arrow keys to move to the file you want to print. Press the space bar to select the file. Repeat this step for each file you want to print.

6. Choose File, Print.

Creating a Table of Contents

When you print the smaller documents separately, you must insert {RD} fields to create indexes and tables of contents. The {RD} fields are inserted into a document separate from the individual documents. Insert one {RD} field for each separate file that makes up the larger document. You then choose Insert, Index and Tables to create the index and table of contents from the document containing the RD fields. This document then contains only the index and table of contents, not the text of the documents. You can print the table of contents and index separately and combine it with the larger document.

To create a separate index or table of contents, follow these steps:

1. Open a new file to contain the RD fields.

2. Press Ctrl+F9, the Insert Field shortcut key.

3. Type **rd** followed by a space and the name and path of the first file that makes up the document. If the files are all in the current directory, you do not need to include the path (**rd chapt1.doc**, for example). Use the full path name if the files are located in different directories. Use a double backslash where a single backslash normally is used in a path name.

4. Use the arrow keys to move outside the field and press Enter to start a new paragraph.

5. Repeat steps 2–4 for each of the files that makes up the document.

6. Position the insertion point where you want to locate the table of contents and choose Insert, Index and Tables to create a table of contents.

7. Press Ctrl+Enter, the page break key, to separate the table of contents and index.

8. Position the insertion point where you want to locate the index, and choose Insert, Index and Tables to create an index.

◀ See "Creating Tables of Contents," p. 879

9. Choose Insert, Page Numbers to set the appropriate page numbers for the table of contents and index.

To set separate starting page numbers for the table of contents and the index, you must insert a section break between them. Choose Insert, Break, select the Next Page option, and choose OK.

Figure 32.6 illustrates the field code view of a document set up to print the table of contents and index for a book.

Fig. 32.6

{RD} fields are used to create a table of contents.

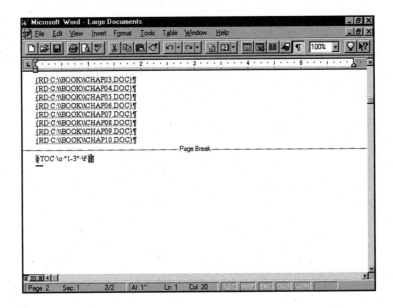

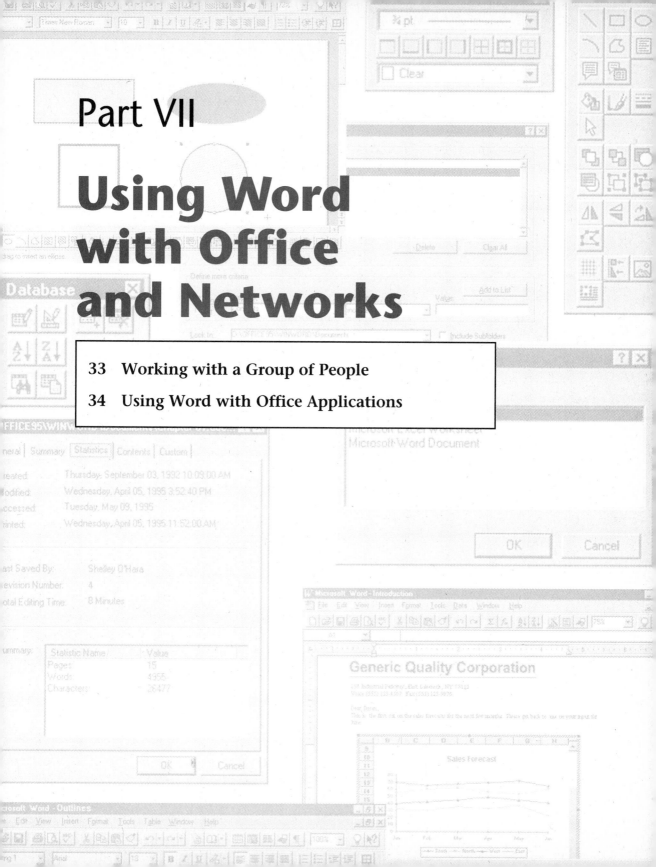

Part VII

Using Word with Office and Networks

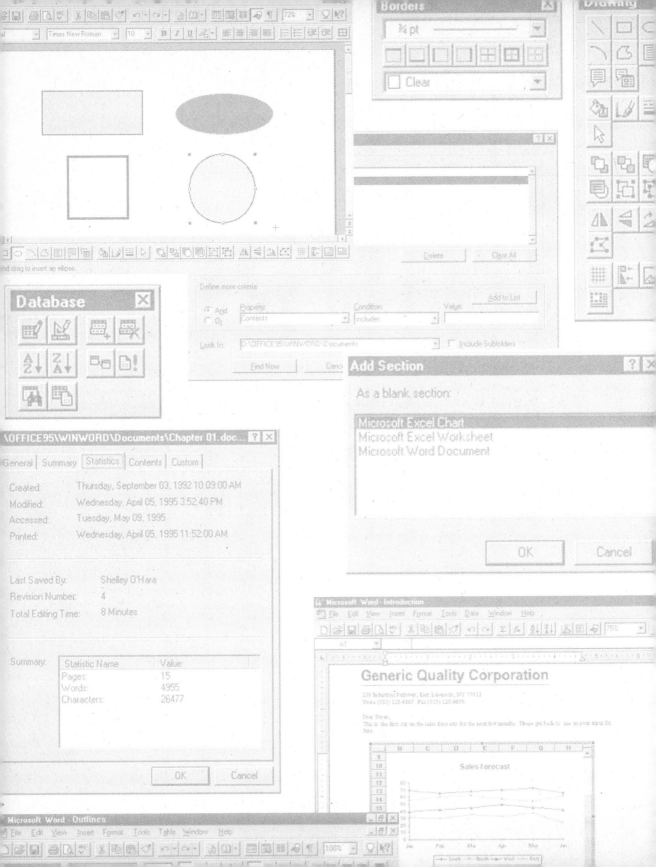

Chapter 33

Working with a Group of People

One of the fastest growing segments of the computer industry is networking. By connecting people's computers and giving them access to corporate data, companies are finding that people work more productively and accurately. In addition, they can complete projects much faster.

Because most projects involve groups of people working on the same or similar documents, it is important that you become familiar with how to use Word and other Microsoft Office applications with groups of people. This chapter shows you how you can edit and revise documents as a group. Rather than routing paper copies and then trying to compile changes, you can use Word and your networking software to accept revisions, keep track of who made what recommendations or changes, and then accept or delete changes. Coupled with electronic mail (or e-mail), you will find that you can quickly send Word documents to co-workers over a local network or to clients through a commercial online service. You can even fax a document from within Word.

In this chapter, you learn the following:

■ How to share binders that contain documents from different Microsoft Office applications

■ How to do group editing and revision on one document

■ How to send a Word document as e-mail

■ How to use Word as an e-mail editor

■ How to send a fax from within Word

Using Binders for Group Projects

Almost any project involving many people also involves many documents created by more than one application. When you are faced with projects that generate reports with many different documents, you should use Microsoft Binder to compile the documents into collated reports and to organize related documents.

▶ See "Using Microsoft Binder to Group Documents," p. 1003

Microsoft Binder enables you to bind together documents from different Microsoft applications into a single large document. You can edit any document from within Binder so that you do not need to continually open and close different applications.

Sharing a Binder on a Network Using My Briefcase

If you are connected to a network, you can share a binder that you have created with other users on the network using My Briefcase. To share a binder using My Briefcase, follow these steps:

1. Move the binder file to a shared folder on your network.

2. Inform those users who will be working with the binder that they should copy the binder to their local My Briefcase. Each user can now open the briefcase copy of the binder and work on it.

3. To update the briefcase, choose Briefcase, Update All.

    When the Update All command is issued, the changes in the user's copy of the binder are copied to the network copy, and any changes in the network copy of the binder are copied to the user's copy.

Editing and Revising as a Group

If you are working on a network, you can make your documents available to other users on the network so that they can review them. To make the document available to other users, simply put a copy of the document in a shared folder. However, to protect the document against permanent changes being made by other users, you must first prepare the document for review. You can protect the document so that other users cannot change the text but can add comments, called *annotations*. Annotations appear in a separate pane and are identified by the user's initials. Another option is to allow the user to make revisions, but the revisions are marked so that they are not incorporated into the document until you choose to do so. You can identify who made each revision and the time and date they were made. Word uses a

VII

different color to mark each user's revisions. For extra protection, you can attach a password to the document so that other users cannot unprotect the document and make changes that are not tracked.

To prepare a document for review by others, follow these steps:

1. Open the document you want to send out for review.

2. Choose Tools, Protect Document.

3. To allow tracked revisions to be made, select Revisions.

4. To allow comments to be added to the document but no changes to be made, select Annotations.

5. To keep other users from turning off the protection you have selected, add a password.

   Be sure to remember the password, or you will not be able to unprotect the document.

6. Click OK.

> **Note**
>
> With Word's new highlighting feature, you can highlight text that you want to call to the attention of other users before you send out the document for review. You can also have each reviewer use a different color highlight to mark text they want to bring to your attention. You can use the Find command to locate any highlighted text in a document. See "Highlighting Text" in Chapter 9, "Formatting Characters and Changing Fonts," for more information on how to use this feature.

◀ See "Using the Revision Marks Feature," p. 902

Sending Faxes and Electronic Mail with WordMail

If you have a modem and have Office 95 installed, you can fax and e-mail your Word documents directly from your computer. Word comes with WordMail, and in conjunction with Microsoft Exchange, you can fax and e-mail documents. WordMail is a built-in feature of Word for Windows 95. It enables Word to act as a fax and e-mail editor. Microsoft Exchange is a universal communication's manager that is part of Windows 95. Microsoft Exchange takes care of both fax and e-mail transmissions. Together WordMail and Microsoft Exchange make a powerful package.

The benefit of using WordMail as your e-mail editor is that you can use all the editing and formatting power of Word to improve the layout and appearance of your e-mail messages. You can, for example, format characters and paragraphs, create numbered lists, highlight important text using the Highlight tool in Word and add borders and tables to your messages.

To use Microsoft Exchange you must install and configure Microsoft Exchange for use with your fax/modem and the e-mail systems to which your computer connects. Microsoft Exchange is an optional program that you have a chance to install when you installed Windows. If Microsoft Exchange is not available on your computer you can rerun Windows 95 Setup and choose to install it. Microsoft Exchange includes a wizard that will guide you through initially configuring it. For additional help, see Chapter 24, "Using Microsoft Exchange," in Que's *Special Edition Using Windows 95*.

Microsoft Exchange sends documents via fax or e-mail. It decides how to send your document depending upon which Microsoft Exchange Profile you have selected and which fax and communication numbers are available to the recipient.

Part of Exchange is a Personal Address Book, where you can store names, addresses, phone numbers, fax numbers, and different e-mail telephone and identification numbers.

Choosing to Use WordMail

If you decide to use WordMail as your e-mail editor, be aware that many of the formatting features that you can use in Word will not appear in Microsoft Exchange or other e-mail editors. This means that the recipients of your e-mail messages must also use Word as their e-mail editor to display all the WordMail formatting in your messages, such as tables, borders, and highlighting.

> **Note**
>
> Microsoft advises users that they should have at least 12M of memory to use WordMail as their e-mail editor. Also, if you are using Word to edit documents and you switch over to your e-mail system in which you are using WordMail, Word will run very slowly. Before you switch to WordMail, close all dialog boxes in Word.

To choose WordMail as your e-mail editor, follow these steps:

1. Open the Start menu, click <u>P</u>rograms, then Microsoft Exchange.

2. Choose Co<u>m</u>pose, <u>W</u>ordmail Options.

3. Select Enable <u>W</u>ord as Email Editor.

4. Click OK.

Using WordMail as your e-mail editor is no different from using Word to create documents. To learn how to send, read, reply to, and forward e-mail messages, see the online Help in Microsoft Exchange.

Choosing Your Microsoft Exchange Profile

Before sending a message, you will need to select the profile that you want to use in Exchange. The profile specifies how a message will be sent, whether by Microsoft Fax, Microsoft Mail, Microsoft Network Online Service, or through another communication service. The profile also stores information required for each communication medium. For example, a profile that includes fax will include the type of fax/modem used and your fax telephone number for use on the return line of the fax. If you specify Microsoft Mail, you will need to specify the path to your postoffice, your name, and your password. You can define different profiles for your communications and give each profile a name.

If the profile you select has multiple communication methods available, Microsoft Exchange will try more than one medium. It will use the different e-mail or fax addresses that are listed in the address book for an individual. If you want to restrict Exchange so that it only sends a fax, for example, then you should create a profile that has fax as the only available communication method. When using this profile, Exchange will only look at the fax numbers in the different address books.

Caution

You may want to specify different profiles for different types of communications. If Microsoft Exchange has trouble keeping your fax and e-mail messages separate, create a separate profile for each. When you want to send a fax, use the profile you have set up for only faxes. When you want to send an e-mail, use the profile that contains only e-mail information.

To specify your Microsoft Exchange profile, follow these steps:

1. Prepare the document that you want to send. Save it with the name you want it sent with.

2. Choose File, Send to display the Choose Profile dialog box shown in figure 33.1.

Fig. 33.1

Select a Microsoft Exchange profile to specify the media and configuration to be used to send your messages.

3. Select the profile you want from the Profile Name drop-down list, then choose OK.

4. If your chosen profile involves a medium (such as e-mail) that requires a password, you will be prompted for a password, as shown in figure 33.2.

Fig. 33.2

Enter passwords that are needed by the profile you choose.

Tip

To define a new profile, choose New and follow the wizard that guides you through creating a new profile.

5. Enter the password and choose OK. The WordMail window appears, as shown in figure 33.3.

To address and send your document, follow the steps in the next section beginning with step 3.

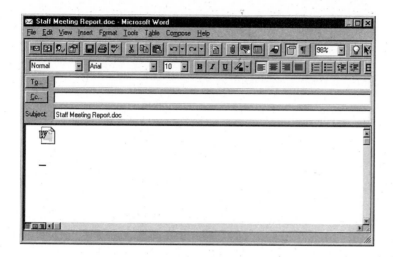

Fig. 33.3
Your Word document appears as an icon in the WordMail document. You can type and format additional information in the document.

Sending and Addressing Your Message

Once you have specified a Microsoft Exchange profile, you will have far fewer dialog boxes to complete when sending a message. If you have previously selected a profile, follow these steps to send and address your Word document:

1. Prepare the document that you want to send. Save it with the name you want it sent with.

2. Choose File, Send.

   Your document appears in the WordMail document as an icon (refer to fig. 33.3). This icon is your workbook embedded as an OLE object.

3. Type and format the WordMail document as you would in any Word document. Almost all Word features and formatting abilities are available.

4. To address your document, click the To button in WordMail to display the Address Book dialog box shown in figure 33.4.

5. Choose an address book from the Show Names drop-down list.

   You may have different address books available from the Personal Address Book, Postoffice Address List, Microsoft Network, and so forth. Depending upon the transmission methods available in the profile you selected, Microsoft Exchange will use the appropriate fax or e-mail address and password from the Address Book.

Tip

Unlike most e-mail editors, WordMail enables you to create well-formatted documents using most of Word's formatting capabilities.

Fig. 33.4
From the Address Book, you can select which address book you want to use, as well as who will receive a message and who will receive a copy.

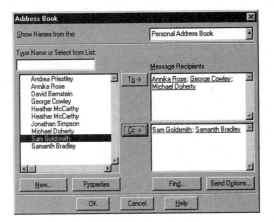

6. To send an original document, click a name in the Type Name list and then click the To button. To send a copy, click the Cc button. Figure 33.5 shows a completed Address Book.

Fig. 33.5
You can add names to either list. To remove a name, right-click it and choose Cut.

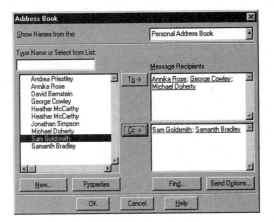

7. Choose OK to close the Address Book and return to WordMail. Figure 33.6 shows a document with To and Cc addressing as well as a short note to accompany the workbook.

8. To send your e-mail or fax message, choose File, Send.

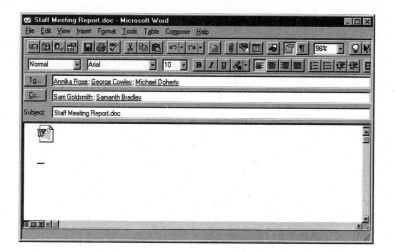

Fig. 33.6
You can type notes
or entire Word
documents to go
with your
embedded
workbook.

Routing a Message

An alternative to sending a document from Word is to *route* the document.
Routing a document from Word gives you more control over who gets the
document and when they get it. When you route a document, you fill out a
routing slip, indicating who you want to receive the document and in what
order. You may, for example, want a department head to receive and revise
the document first, before it is sent on to a project manager and then to key
personnel working on the project. If you want, you can choose to have everyone on the list receive the document at the same time. You can also request
that the document be returned to you when everyone on the routing list has
seen it.

To add or edit an existing routing slip that specifies who will see your document, and in what order they will see it, follow these steps:

1. Prepare your document and save it with the name you want it to have
   when sent.

2. Choose File, Add Routing Slip. If this document already has a routing
   slip, the command will be File, Edit Routing Slip. The Routing Slip dialog box appears, as shown in figure 33.7.

3. Click the Address button to display the Address Book dialog box shown
   in figure 33.8.

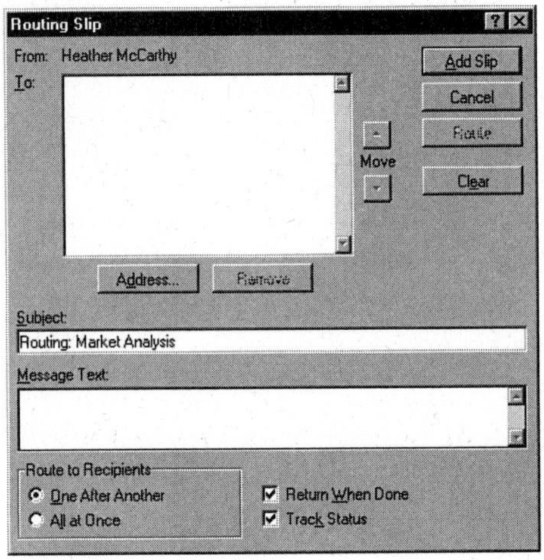

Fig. 33.7
The routing slip specifies who sees your document and in what order they see it.

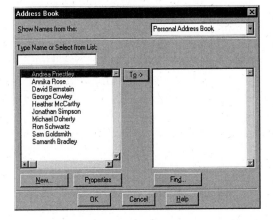

Fig. 33.8
From the Address Book dialog box, select who you want to see your document.

4. Select the address book you want to use from the Show Names list. For each name you want on the routing list, click a name in the Type Name list, then click To. Choose OK when your recipient list is complete.

   The Routing Slip dialog box, shown in figure 33.9 reappears.

5. To move a name in the To list up or down in the order in which it will be received, click the name, then click the up or down Move buttons.

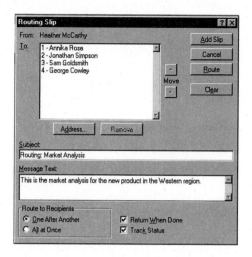

Fig. 33.9
After adding
recipients to the
routing slip, you
can change the
order in which
they will receive
the document.

6. If you want recipients to receive the document in the order shown,
   select the Qne After Another option. For everyone to receive the document simultaneously, select the All at Once option.

7. Choose Route to immediately send the document to the list of recipients. Choose Add Slip to attach this slip to the document so that it can
   be sent later.

If you choose to add the routing slip to your document, you can send it at
a later time. To send a document that already has a routing slip attached,
follow these steps:

1. Choose File, Send to display the Routing Slip dialog box, shown in
   figure 33.10.

2. Select the Route document option to send to the recipients on the slip.
   Select the Send copy of document option to send the document independent of the routing slip.

3. If you chose the Route document option, the document is routed. If
   you chose the Send copy of document option, your document appears
   in WordMail ready for addressing.

Fig. 33.10
After routing
slips have been
attached, you can
send to addressees
on the routing slip
or to an individual
recipient.

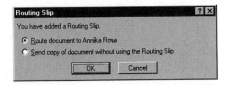

> **Note**
>
> Sending and routing documents is a very efficient way to allow other users to review
> your documents, add comments, and make revisions that you can then incorporate
> into your document. You can use WordMail's revision and annotations features in
> conjunction with e-mail to send out a document for review by other users, collecting
> the revisions and annotations from each user and then getting the document back to
> incorporate these revisions and annotations. Word will automatically track these
> revisions and annotations.

Opening E-Mail

To open e-mail or faxes that you receive, minimize applications so that you
can see your desktop. Then follow these steps:

1. Double-click the Inbox icon on the desktop.

2. New mail in the Inbox appears in bold type. Double-click new mail to
   read it.

3. If a document contains an icon for embedded data and your system has
   an application that can read that type of data, double-click the embedded icon. An application that can read the data will open and display
   the icon's contents.

Chapter 34

Using Word with Office Applications

One of the unique advantages of Windows applications is their capability to exchange and link information easily with other Windows applications. With Word for Windows 95, you also can import or link to files from many DOS applications, such as Lotus 1-2-3, AutoCAD, or dBASE. Through the use of Microsoft Query, you even can insert or link your Word documents to data found in an SQL server or mainframe. Figure 34.1 shows a letter with an embedded Microsoft Excel chart.

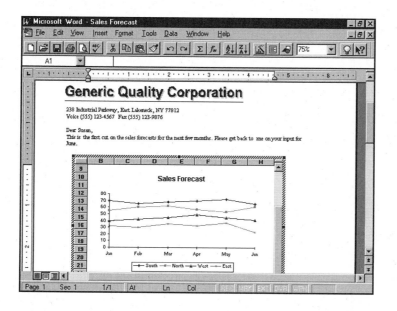

Fig. 34.1
Word documents can have data linked or embedded from other Windows applications like this chart from Microsoft Excel.

If you are used to working with a single application, the value of linking, embedding, or pasting data may not be immediately apparent to you. After you begin to link, embed, or paste data, however, you will see how tasks involving multiple applications come together to produce a single integrated document. You can use Word for Windows with other applications, for example, to do the following:

■ Create mail-merge data documents from a mailing list file kept in dBASE or Microsoft Excel, or from a network or mainframe file

■ Create sales projections, financial analyses, inventory reports, and investment analyses with worksheets and charts in Microsoft Excel or Lotus 1-2-3 for Windows, and link or embed these charts and tables into Word for Windows documents

■ Produce proposals and contracts that include designs from major drafting programs

■ Produce advertising or marketing materials that include artwork created in different Windows or DOS drawing and design applications

In this chapter, you learn the following:

■ How to open frequently used applications, documents, and folders with the Office Shortcut Bar

■ The advantages and disadvantages of pasting, linking, or embedding data from other applications

■ The available data formats

■ How to embed and then convert all or part of data from an OLE 1.0 or OLE 2.0 application into a Word document

■ How to link all or part of a file into a document so that changes in the source file appear in the Word document

■ Bind together documents from different applications using the Microsoft Binder

Using the Microsoft Office Shortcut Bar for Multi-Application Users

The Microsoft Office Shortcut Bar is a very handy tool for people who frequently use more than one Windows application. The Office Shortcut Bar, shown at the top of figure 34.2, enables you to open or switch between Office applications, open documents and templates, add tasks, schedules, or contacts to Schedule+, and much more. It takes up little room on your screen, yet it can save you a lot of time during the day.

The Office Shortcut Bar is only available with the Microsoft Office 95 suite of applications. However, you can use the Office Shortcut Bar with Windows applications beyond those in Office 95.

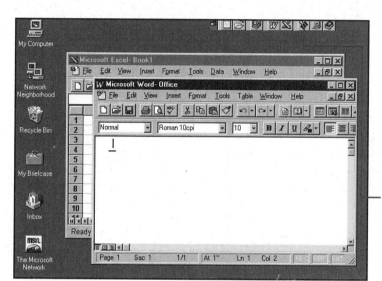

Fig. 34.2
The Microsoft
Office Shortcut Bar
shown at the top
edge of the screen
will save you time
if you frequently
use multiple
applications.

Microsoft Office
Shortcut Bar

Opening the Office Shortcut Bar

If you do not see the Microsoft Office Shortcut Bar open on your desktop, then click the Start button, choose Programs, Microsoft Word, and then click the Microsoft Office Shortcut Bar item. The Office Shortcut Bar appears at the top of your screen as you see in figure 34.2.

Like other Microsoft toolbars, you can drag this toolbar to other locations on-screen by dragging one of the background areas between menu bar buttons. When the toolbar is away from a screen edge, it appears as a floating toolbar that you can resize by dragging an edge. You can customize the shortcut bar so that it remains over the top of other windows.

Understanding the Buttons on the Office Shortcut Bar

You can place many applications, files, and folders on the Office Shortcut Bar. Figure 34.3 shows a few of the more commonly used buttons. In the next section you will learn how to customize the Office Shortcut Bar.

Tip
If you select the
Auto Fit into Title
Bar area check box
when you customize the Office
Shortcut Bar, it
stays neatly out of
the way in the title
bar of maximized
applications.

Fig. 34.3
You can drag the Office Shortcut Bar in the background areas between buttons or resize it by dragging an edge.

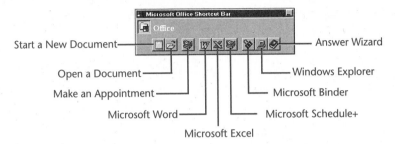

Opening Documents and Applications from the Office Shortcut Bar

The Office Shortcut Bar is a very quick and convenient way to open applications, documents, and even folders that you use frequently. As a result of customizing, when you click a document button, you open that document into the appropriate application. When you click an application button, you open the application. And when you click a folder button, you open that folder into a single My Computer window. What makes this feature even more convenient is that you can create your own custom toolbars out of the contents of any folder on your computer. The contents of the folder show up as buttons on your custom toolbar.

If you want to start a new document using a template from any Office application, you can store that template in one of the folders underneath C:\MSOFFICE\TEMPLATES. The template then displays when you click the Start a New Document button. Figure 34.4 shows the dialog box that displays folders and templates found under the TEMPLATES folder. You can open any of these templates to start a new document and load it into the appropriate application.

Customizing the Office Shortcut Bar

Tip
If you have a document or folder that you use frequently, add it to the Office Shortcut Bar.

You can customize much of the Office Shortcut Bar. One of Word's most valuable customizing features is the ability to add or remove applications and tasks. You can customize how the bar appears and whether it displays over other applications or disappears. You can add other Windows toolbars to the Office Shortcut Bar. And you can change the folder in which Office looks for templates.

To change the location (whether it displays over other applications) and appearance of the Office Shortcut Bar, follow these steps:

1. Right-click in the background area between buttons on the Office Short-cut Bar. Click <u>C</u>ustomize. The Customize dialog box displays.

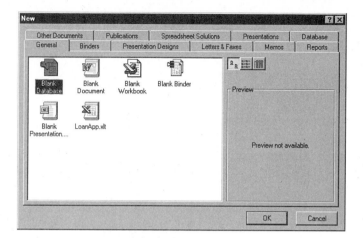

Fig. 34.4

The New dialog
box enables you to
open templates
that come with
Office or templates
that you add.

2. Click the View tab to display the View options, as shown in figure 34.5.

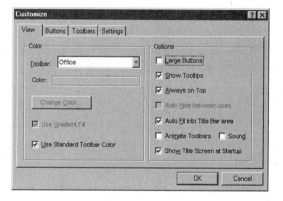

Fig. 34.5

You can customize
how Office
Shortcut Bar
appears and
whether it stays
on top of applica-
tions.

3. To change the Office Shortcut Bar colors, select one of these options:

Option	Description
Toolbar	Selects which toolbar's background color you want to change.
Change Color	Changes the color of the selected toolbar.
Use Gradient Fill	Shades toolbar color from dark on left to light on right. Solid when check box is cleared.
Smooth	Smoothes the image.
Use Standard Toolbar Color	Returns toolbar background to the standard gray background.

(continues)

Option	Description
Large Button	Shows buttons in a larger size. Appropriate for high-resolution monitors.
Show Tooltips	Displays the names of buttons when the pointer pauses over buttons.
Always on Top	Keeps the Office Shortcut Bar on top of other active applications.
Auto Hide Between Uses	Hides the Office Shortcut Bar so that only a thin gray line at the screen edge is shown. Moves the pointer to the line at the screen edge to display the Office Shortcut Bar.
Auto Fit into Title Bar area	Fits the toolbar into the title bar of maximized applications. The Always on Top option must be selected as well.
Animate Toolbars	When multiple toolbars are in the shortcut bar area, clicking the icon of another toolbar slides the new buttons into the display.
Sound	Enables sounds.
Show Title Screen at Startup	Displays the Microsoft Office Shortcut Bar title screen when the shortcut bar starts.

   4. Click OK.

Adding Buttons for Applications, Documents, or Folders

To add applications, documents, or folder buttons to the Office Shortcut Bar, follow these steps:

   1. Right-click in the background area between buttons on the Office Short-cut Bar. Click Customize. The Customize dialog box displays.

   2. Click the Buttons tab to display the Buttons options, as shown in figure 34.6.

   3. Select Office from the Toolbar list.

   4. Select the tasks or applications you want to add to the Office Shortcut Bar from the Show these Files as Buttons list box. A check mark shows selected items.

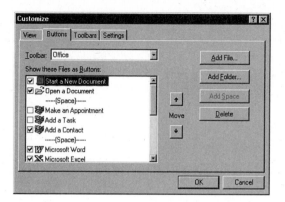

Fig. 34.6
You can add new
tasks and applica-
tions to the
toolbar through
the Buttons view.

5. Modify the Office Shortcut Bar with the following options and buttons:

Option	Description
Add File or Add Folder	Click to add your own application, document, or folder in front of the selected button. Select the file or folder you want to add from the Add File or Add Folder dialog box that displays. When you select a file button, you open the application and load the document. When you select a folder button, you open the folder in a My Computer window.
Add Space	Add a space in front of the selected button, which appears to the left of the button on the toolbar.
Delete	Delete the selected button. You will be prompted when you leave the dialog box to confirm that you want the button deleted.
Move	Move the selected button up or down the list. This moves the button left or right on the Office Shortcut Bar.

6. Click OK.

Adding Additional Toolbars to the Office Shortcut Bar

You can add additional toolbars to the Office Shortcut Bar. These toolbars can
include Microsoft Network as well as items that appear on your desktop, or
they can include applications in the PROGRAMS or ACCESSORIES folders.
In fact, you can make the contents of any folder into a toolbar.

Tip
The contents of
any folder can
become a toolbar
on the Office
Shortcut Bar.

Although many toolbars can be stored in the Office Shortcut Bar, only one toolbar displays at a time. To see the toolbar that you want, click the button in the Office Shortcut Bar that represents the toolbar you want displayed. The buttons for that toolbar will replace the buttons that are currently displayed.

If you want to create a custom toolbar that will display in the Office Shortcut Bar, you must first create a folder. Give the folder a name that you will recognize as a toolbar. In this folder, you must place the items that you want to appear on the toolbar, such as application files, documents, or folders. Instead of placing actual files and folders in the toolbar folder you are creating, place shortcuts to the real files and folders. Shortcuts have the advantage of automatically updating if the files they represent move. If you delete the toolbar folder, only the shortcuts will be deleted, not the actual files and folders.

To add custom toolbars to the area that is normally occupied by the Office Shortcut Bar, follow these steps:

1. Right-click in the gray area between buttons on the Office Shortcut Bar. Click Customize. The Customize dialog box displays.

2. Click the Toolbars tab to display the Toolbars options, as shown in figure 34.7.

Fig. 34.7
You can display desktop and Start menu items in the Office Shortcut Bar.

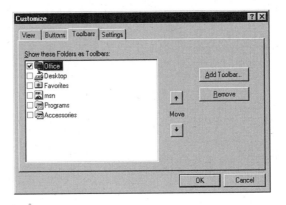

3. Select a toolbar that you want to add to the Office Shortcut Bar.

4. Move the toolbar icons by selecting the toolbar in the list and then clicking the Move arrows.

5. Click the <u>A</u>dd Toolbar button to create custom toolbars from the contents of your own folders. The Add Toolbar dialog box in figure 34.8
appears. Click the <u>B</u>rowse button to select the folder that you want as a
toolbar. If you want a new toolbar that does not exist as a folder, enter
its name in the <u>C</u>reate box. Click OK.

Buttons for the documents and applications within a folder will appear
in your custom toolbar. When you click a button, you load the document or open the application.

6. Click OK.

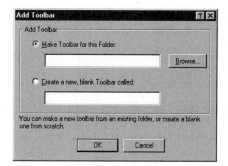

Fig. 34.8
Display the
contents of your
own folders as
toolbars on the
Office Shortcut
Bar.

Setting Up Custom Templates for the Office Shortcut Bar

The Office Shortcut Bar will display templates that belong to Office applications. When you double-click one of these templates from the OFFICE template folder, the template loads into the appropriate application. You can
customize the Office Shortcut Bar so that it looks for templates in the folder
that you specify.

To change the location where the Office Shortcut Bar looks for template files,
follow these steps:

1. Right-click in the gray area between buttons on the Office Shortcut Bar.
Click <u>C</u>ustomize. The Customize dialog box displays.

2. Click the Settings tab.

3. Select the item that you want to modify from the list, and then click
the <u>M</u>odify button. Enter the new location for that template or item.
Click OK.

4. Click OK.

Choosing to Paste, Link, or Embed Data

> **Note**
>
> This chapter includes references to source and destination documents. The *source* is the file on disk or document in an open application that supplies data. The *destination* is the document that receives the data.

You can look at the various methods of exchanging data in many different ways: you can evaluate whether the source of the data is a file or an active application; you can evaluate whether you are exchanging text or graphic data; or you can evaluate which of the different procedures you can use.

Word for Windows provides the following primary methods for exchanging data:

- *Embedded Data.* The source data is encapsulated and inserted within the Word for Windows document. The data is contained within the Word document as an integral unit.

  Advantage: The data, such as a Microsoft Excel worksheet or chart, is stored within the Word for Windows document. You do not need to be concerned with broken links, renaming files, or sending linked files with the document, because it is all self-contained. Editing is done by simply double-clicking the embedded data, which then starts the source application and loads the data.

  Disadvantage: Do not use embedded data when you want to be able to change one source file and have many destination documents change. Each file containing embedded data must be updated individually. The original source and the embedded data are not linked. Word files containing embedded data can be very large.

- *Linking Data.* The source data is located in a source file on disk or in a Windows application.

  Advantage: Users can update the linked data when they open the Word document or while the document is open. Links may be live, so that a change in one document is immediately reflected in another document. Changes to the source document are available to all linked documents, so updating multiple destination documents is easy.

Disadvantage: The source data is updated by starting the source application and manually opening the source file and editing it. When you ship a Word document with links to other files, the other files and applications must be available.

■ *Pasting Data.*   The source data is converted to text or a graphic and inserted into Word.

Advantage: The source data takes up less storage than embedded data. There is no link—the information appears as a *snapshot*. The source application does not have to be available.

Disadvantage: The source data cannot be edited or updated; it must be re-created.

■ *Inserting or importing from a file.*   The source data remains in a file on disk separate from the Word document. Updating the Word document is done manually, or it can be automated through a macro. The source application does not need to be available to the user's computer, but a converter file that will convert the source file must be installed in Word.

Advantage: You do not need the source application because Word for Windows converts the file or graphic while inserting it. Changes to the source document may affect multiple destination documents.

Disadvantage: Changes to the data will be lost when you update the inserted file.

Use the following commands for exchanging data:

Command	Action
File, Open and conversion	Use this command if the data is in a disk file, and you transfer large amounts of non-graphic data infrequently. Use this command to load text files or worksheets as new Word for Windows documents.
Insert, File	Use this command if the data is in a disk file and you need only portions of the file, or if you want to insert the file within an existing Word for Windows document. Data can be brought in unlinked or linked to the disk file (source). Updates from the source on disk can be controlled automatically or manually.

(continues)

Command	Action
Insert, Picture	Use this command for a graphic in a disk file. You can bring in graphics unlinked or linked to the source file. Updates from the source on disk can be controlled automatically or manually. This is described in Chapter 23, "Inserting Pictures in Your Document."
Insert, Object	Use this command to embed an object from another Windows application. Objects package all the data that you select and place it within the Word document. You do not need to be concerned with links to external files. You can edit data in objects.
Insert, Database	Use this command to paste or link database information, like that used for mailing lists or product information, into your Word document. The database information can be from many different personal computer or network databases.
Edit, Paste	Use this command to paste data into a Word document that you may have copied from a running Windows application.
Edit, Paste Special without linking	Data can be pasted in numerous different formats including as a picture, unformatted text, formatted text, or an embedded object. You must re-paste the data to update it.
Edit, Paste Special with linking	Data can be pasted in numerous different formats. The formats include picture, unformatted text, formatted text, or an embedded object. Data is linked to the source. When the source changes, you can update the data.

Note

Before Word for Windows exchanges data with files or applications that use a data format other than Word for Windows or text, you must install the appropriate file converter. Before you can open dBASE files or insert ranges from a Microsoft Excel worksheet, for example, you must install the dBASE and Microsoft Excel converter files. If you did not install the converter files when you installed Word for Windows, you can rerun the Word for Windows or Office 95 installation program, and you can install them without completely reinstalling Word for Windows. You will need your original installation disks.

What You Need to Know about Data Formats

When you link data or embed an object, you have a choice of the form in
which the data is stored. The data from the source can appear in the Word for
Windows document in different forms such as tabbed text, a formatted table,
a picture, or a bitmap, depending on the source application. Microsoft Excel
data, for example, can appear in a number of forms. If you copy a range of
Microsoft Excel cells and then use Edit, Paste Special to paste them into a
Word for Windows document, you see the following alternatives in the Data
Type dialog box:

■ *Object.* The data is an embedded object with all data stored in the object
inside the Word document. No link is maintained with the source
document.

■ *Formatted Text (RTF).* Text transfers with formats. Worksheets appear
formatted as tables. You can edit or reformat data.

■ *Unformatted Text.* Text does not contain character or paragraph formatting. Worksheets appear as unformatted text with cells separated by
tabs. You can edit or reformat data.

■ *Picture.* Pictures, text, database, or worksheet ranges appear as a picture.
You can format them as pictures, but you cannot edit text in Word for
Windows. Unlinking changes them to drawing objects.

■ *Bitmap.* Pictures, text, or worksheet ranges appear as a bitmapped picture. You can format them as pictures, but you cannot edit text in Word
for Windows. Resolution is poor.

Exchanging Data through Files

One of the easiest ways to bring large amounts of textual or numeric data
into Word for Windows from another Windows or DOS application is to
choose File, Open.

Chapter 3, "Creating and Saving Documents," describes how to change the
Files of Type drop-down list box to the All Files (*.*) option. This option lists
all files so that you can see and open non-Word for Windows files. If you
installed the appropriate file converter, Word for Windows will open and
convert the file simultaneously.

Transferring Data with Copy and Paste

The simplest way to transfer small amounts of data or graphics from one application to another is to copy and paste in the same way that you move text or graphics within a document.

To copy from one Windows application to a Word for Windows document, follow these steps:

1. Select the text, cells, or graphic in the document that contains the original text or graphic.

2. Choose Edit, Copy.

3. Click the Word for Windows button on the taskbar or press Alt+Tab until Word is selected, then release the keys.

   If the taskbar is not visible, press Ctrl+Esc.

4. Position the insertion point where you want the data to appear in the document.

5. Choose Edit, Paste.

Text is pasted into the document as formatted text; Microsoft Excel worksheet cells or ranges paste in as a table; graphics paste in as a bitmapped picture. None of them are linked to their source document, but if you double-click a pasted picture, the appropriate drawing program on your computer will activate and load the picture.

Using Scraps to Transfer Data

When you are using Word with Windows 95, you will find a new way to store and transfer data. You can use your mouse to select a part of a document and drag it to the desktop, where it becomes a scrap. A *scrap* is a file or portion of a file that you store on the desktop. You can use this scrap whenever and wherever you want, dragging it back into a document in the same application in which you created it or into a document in another application. You can use the scrap as many times as you want, and the scrap will remain on the desktop until you delete it. Scraps offer two major advantages over the Clipboard:

■ You can store as many scraps as you want on the desktop, while the Clipboard can hold only one piece of information at a time.

■ Scraps remain on the desktop even when you shut off your computer. Whatever is in the Clipboard disappears when you shut off your computer, unless you make the effort to save each clipping to a file.

> **Note**
>
> You can only use scraps with applications that support OLE 2.0.

To create a scrap, follow these steps:

1. Make sure that a part of the desktop is visible outside the window of the application you are working in.

2. Select the part of your document that you want to create a scrap from.

3. Drag the selection to the desktop with the right mouse button.

4. To create a scrap on the desktop and leave the selection in the original document, choose Create Scrap Here from the shortcut menu.

   Or, to move the selection from the document to a scrap on the desktop, choose Move Scrap Here.

The data you selected appears as a scrap on your desktop. To use the scrap in another document, which can be in the same application in which it originated or in another application, drag the scrap into the document and drop it where you want to insert it.

You can also drag scraps into a folder. You can, for example, create a new folder on your desktop for storing scraps and then drag scraps into this folder. If you work with a lot of scraps, folders can help you organize them. To create a folder on the desktop, right-click the desktop and choose New, Folder. Type a name for the folder and press Enter. Now you can drag-and-drop scraps into this folder. To use the scraps, double-click the folder to open a window showing its contents and drag-and-drop scraps from the folder into your documents.

As with any icon, you can change the text that appears beneath the icon for a scrap. To change the text, click the icon once to select it and then a second time to edit the icon name. (Pause briefly before the second click or you will open the application for the scrap.) Type in a new name and press Enter.

To delete a scrap, right-click the scrap and choose Delete.

Dragging Data between Applications

When you are working in Windows 95, you can use the mouse to copy information from one application to another, as long as both applications support OLE 2.0. With the mouse, transferring information becomes a simple drag-and-drop operation.

To copy information between applications with the mouse, follow these steps:

1. Select the part of the document that you want to copy to another application.

2. Drag the selection into the window for the receiving application and drop it where you want to insert the information.

   Or, if the window for the receiving application is not activated (visible), drag the selection onto the button for the receiving application in the taskbar, still holding down the mouse button. When the application is activated, drop the selection where you want to insert it in the receiving application.

Embedding Data

When you need to include information from a Windows application in your Word document and you want a copy of the information to go with the Word document, then you should use an embedded object. *Embedded objects* take the data from the source application and embed it into the Word document. If recipients of the Word document want to edit the embedded data, they can use their copy of the source application to make changes.

If you have worked with the WordArt or Microsoft Graph applications, you are familiar with embedded objects and how they work. Although these programs are applets (small applications), other major applications with OLE capabilities can embed their data into Word for Windows documents.

Consider the following advantages of embedding objects:

■ File management and the tracking of source documents is not a problem—the source data goes with the Word document.

■ Linked data is not destroyed when a source document cannot be found during an update.

■ Updating an embedded object is done in the source application. If the source application is OLE 1.0 compliant, then the source application starts and loads the data. If the source application is OLE 2.0 compliant, you can edit the data without leaving the Word document.

Consider the following disadvantages to embedding objects:

■ The recipient must have the source application to edit the embedded object. However, you can convert the embedded object if the appropriate conversion filter has been installed.

■ The Word for Windows document becomes large, containing the Word for Windows document as well as all the embedded data.

Creating an Embedded Object

You can embed data in two ways. Both methods produce the same results. You can create completely new data and then embed it, all in the same action, or you can insert an existing file as an object. After you embed the data, it is referred to as an object.

Applications that enable you to embed data work in two different ways. Applications using OLE 1.0 run and activate the source application you selected and display a blank document in which you can create your embedded object. Applications that use OLE 2.0 leave Word active on the screen. Word's menus and toolbars change to reflect the application you selected. You are still, however, looking at the full Word document.

Figure 34.9 shows how WordArt appears when you insert a WordArt object. Because WordArt uses OLE 2.0, it enables you to work within the Word document. While a WordArt object is active in the Word document, Word's menus and toolbars change to those of WordArt.

Embedded objects appear as field codes when you display field codes. To see field codes, select the document and then press Shift+F9. The following shows some of the embedded objects you may see:

```
{ EMBED MSWordArt.2 \s }
{ EMBED MSEquation.2 }
{ EMBED Word.Document.6 }
<CE>{ EMBED Package }
```

Fig. 34.9
Some Windows
applications
enable you to
create or edit an
object while you
remain in the
Word document.

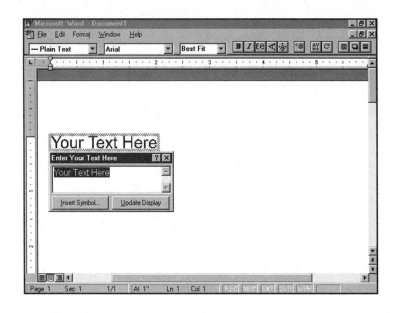

Creating a New Object

To create a new object and embed it, follow these steps:

1. Position the insertion point in the destination document where you want to insert the object.

2. Choose Insert, Object.

3. Select the Create New tab. The tab lists the types of objects you can embed (see fig. 34.10).

Fig. 34.10
From the Create
New tab of the
Object dialog box,
select the type of
data you want to
embed into your
Word document.
The Result box
describes the type
of object.

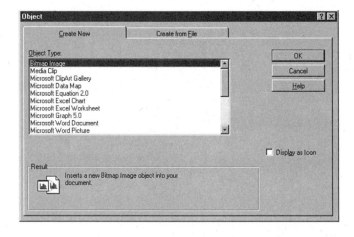

4. From the Object Type list box, select the type of object you want to insert.

5. Select the Display as Icon check box if you want the embedded object to appear as an icon in the Word document. In most cases, you will not select this check box.

6. Click OK.

Create the data you want contained in the object. If a blank worksheet opens, for example, create the worksheet. If a blank drawing window appears, draw the object.

Embedding New Objects

To embed the new object after you have created it, use one of the following methods:

- If you are working in an OLE 2.0 application—one where Word's menus have changed—click outside the object or use the method described in the application's manual or Help file to update the object and close the application.

- If you are working in an OLE 1.0 application, one where the application appears in a separate window, do one of the following:

  Choose File, Close and Return to Document if you are editing a Word document embedded in a Word document.

  Or, choose File, Exit and respond with Yes if you want the destination document updated.

  Or, choose File, Update to update the embedded object but keep the application and object open.

An object appears in the Object Type list box only if the application you use to create the object is registered with Windows and is capable of producing OLE objects.

Select the Display as Icon check box if you believe that the embedded data will take up too much room in the document. Data that appears as an icon displays an icon related to the application that created the data. When it is on-screen, the user can double-click the icon to read the actual data or see the graphic. Although the icon takes up less space on-screen, it still consumes the same amount of memory as a normally embedded object.

Embedding an Existing File or Object

To embed a file that already exists, follow these steps:

1. Position the insertion point in the destination document where you want to insert the object.

2. Choose Insert, Object.

3. Select the Create from File tab, as shown in figure 34.11.

Fig. 34.11

From the Create from File tab of the Object dialog box, select the file you want to embed. The Result area describes the type of object.

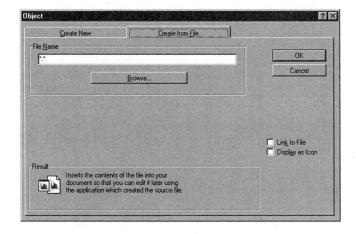

4. Click the Browse button to open the Browse dialog box.

5. Change to the drive and folder containing the file you want to insert. If you need to find the file, use the commands and text boxes at the bottom of the dialog box to search for the file.

6. Select the file from the file list box and click OK.

7. Select the Display as Icon check box if you want the embedded file to appear as an icon on-screen and in print. Icons take up less screen space but the same amount of memory. You can read the contents of an icon by double-clicking it.

8. Click OK.

The data you embed appears as a single object in the document. If you select the object, you will see it enclosed by black handles. You can edit that object at any time by double-clicking the object.

Embedding Part of a File

The preceding two methods required that you embed an entire file. The following method describes how to embed a portion of a file—for example, a range from an Excel worksheet. This example requires only as much memory as the range requires, so the Word document will be smaller.

To create an embedded object that is part of a file, follow these steps:

1. Position the insertion point in the destination document in which you want to insert the object.

2. Activate the application containing the data and select the portion of the data you want to embed. If you are using a Windows spreadsheet such as Excel, you select the cells you want to embed. If you are using a Windows database such as Access, you select the data you want to embed.

3. Choose Edit, Copy or its equivalent in the application.

4. Switch to Word by clicking the Word button on the taskbar.

5. Choose Edit, Paste Special.

6. Select the object listed at the top of the As list in the Paste Special dialog box.

7. Click OK.

The embedded data appears as a single object in your document. When it is not selected, it appears either as normal text or a graphic. When the object is selected, you can see the object surrounded by black handles. Double-click the object to edit it, using its source application.

Editing Embedded Objects

Embedded objects are easy to edit. With the mouse, simply double-click the embedded object. With the keyboard, select the object by moving the insertion point to one side of the object and pressing Shift+arrow key across the object. After you select the object, choose Edit, Object at the bottom of the Edit menu. From the submenu, choose Edit. If the object's application is not open, it opens; if it is open, the application activates. The object then loads so that you can make changes.

To exit the object after you edit or format it, use the same procedures used to exit when you created the object:

- If Word's menus changed when you edited the object, click in the Word document to return to Word and embed the object.

- If the object's application opened in a separate window, do one of the following:

  Choose File, Close and Return to Document if you are editing a Word document embedded in a Word document.

  Or, choose File, Exit and then choose Return to close the application and update the embedded object.

  Or, choose File, Update to update the embedded object but keep the object's application and object open.

Converting Embedded Objects

One problem you may face when exchanging files with others in your workgroup is receiving an embedded object you cannot open or edit. Suppose, for example, that you receive a Word document that contains an embedded Excel worksheet, but you do not have Excel. You can still work with this file, read the Excel worksheet, and even edit the worksheet.

> **Note**
>
> If you want to read or edit the embedded object, you do not need the object's application, but you must have installed the converter required to convert that application's files. You can install these converters at any time by rerunning Setup and using your original Word or Office disks or CD-ROM.

To convert an embedded object into a different format, follow these steps:

1. Select the embedded object by clicking it or by moving the insertion point to one side, and then pressing Shift+arrow key. Black handles appear around the object when it is selected.

2. Choose Edit, Object from the bottom of the Edit menu.

3. Choose Convert from the submenu. The Convert dialog box appears.

4. Select the Convert To option if you want to permanently convert the object to another format. Select the Activate As option if you want to temporarily convert the object so that you can read or edit it. The object is stored back into the document in its original format.

5. Select the type of conversion you want from the Object Type list box.

6. Click OK.

If you must return the Word document to its original creator, but you need to read or edit the object for which you do not have an application, use the Activate As option in the Convert dialog box. This converts the object only while you are reading or editing it. After you close the object, it is converted to its original format and stored back in the document. Using the Activate As option enables the original document creator to reopen the object using the original application that created it.

Troubleshooting

Double-clicking an embedded object opens a different application than I expected.

Double-clicking an embedded object normally opens the application that created that object. If that application is not on your hard disk, but an application that can read that file is on your hard disk, the substitute application that is available will open.

My file contains an object for which the original application is not available. I need to edit the object.

If the proper conversion files were installed in Word, you can convert the object from its current format into the format of an available application. You have a choice of leaving the object in its new converted format or only converting temporarily. To learn more about converting objects, refer to "Converting Embedded Objects" earlier in this chapter.

Linking Documents and Files

Linking data between applications enables one document to show the changes that occur in another document. This capability can be very useful in many business situations. For example, you may have an engineering proposal that is constructed from a standard Word template. The drawings within the template, however, are linked to graphics files and the cost estimates and schedules are linked to worksheet files. When you open the proposal in Word, or at any time, you can update the linked data so that the graphics, cost estimates, and schedules are always current.

There are two ways to link files. You can link the entire file using Insert, File, or you can link data between Windows applications with Edit, Paste Special.

Linking creates a communication channel between two open Windows applications. Data can be sent through this channel when information in the source changes, or when you manually request an update.

Linking Documents to Entire Files

If you need to include in your Word for Windows document a graphic or portions of a file or worksheet, you should become familiar with the methods for inserting files and importing graphics. Linking to files on disk has these advantages:

- The data resides in a disk file.

- All or part of a word processing, worksheet, or database file can be inserted and linked.

- Only a source file on disk is required. The source application need not be open or even on the system.

- The operator controls when the file or graphic data updates. This feature enables you to "freeze" the data in the destination document until you want an update.

- Files and graphics from DOS applications can be linked into Word for Windows documents.

Linking to files has the following disadvantages:

- Renaming or moving a source file can disturb the link. You then must edit the link so that the Word for Windows document can find it.

- Editing an inserted picture can break its link and change the graphic into an embedded object.

To link into your document a file or a portion of a file that is on disk and for which you have an installed converter, follow these steps:

1. Position the insertion point in the destination document at the place where you want the source data to appear.

2. Choose Insert, File. The Insert File dialog box opens (see fig. 34.12).

3. Change to the folder containing the source file. Select the file you want to insert from the file list box. If you do not see the file, change the File of Type to All Files (*.*).

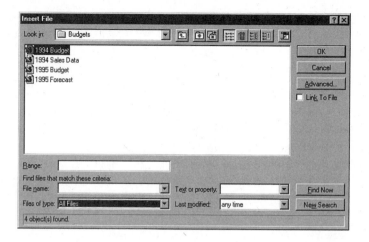

Fig. 34.12
Link a file or
portion of a file
into your docu-
ment using Insert,
File.

4. To insert a portion of the file, type the name (for Microsoft Excel files), the bookmark (for Word for Windows files), or the range name (for 1-2-3 files) in the Range text box.

5. To link rather than insert the source document into the target document, select the Link to File check box.

6. Click OK.

If you are inserting a worksheet file and did not enter a range name, a dialog box appears from which you can select to insert the Entire Worksheet or select from the list of named ranges in the worksheet. When you later update the inserted worksheet by selecting it and pressing F9, you again will have an opportunity to select the range to be updated.

> **Note**
>
> If you are inserting an Excel 5 or later version worksheet, you will also be given the chance to select a specific worksheet from the workbook you select in the Open Worksheet dialog box. Select the sheet you want to open, select the name or cell range in that sheet, and then click OK.

Inserting a file without linking enters data as though it were typed. Worksheets are entered as Word for Windows tables.

If you select the Link to File check box, a link is created to the source document, using an INCLUDETEXT field code.

> **Note**
>
> Before you can use Insert, File to insert data into a document, you must have saved the source document to disk.

Linking Documents to Part of a File

Edit, Paste Special is a useful command, primarily when you want to link two Windows applications and use features in a source application to update data or graphics in your Word for Windows document. You might use the command if you have a financial worksheet and charts in Microsoft Excel, for example, and the results and charts are part of an integrated Word for Windows report. You need to be able to work in Microsoft Excel and use its functions and its links to mainframe data. When the worksheets and charts change, however, the changes should pass immediately to the integrated report in Word for Windows, where you can print them.

Following are some advantages to using links created by Paste Special:

- You can link a single source document to many destination documents. Changes in the single source are available to all the destination documents.

- The data resides in the source application's document. You can use the source application and all of its features to update the source document.

- The data or graphic is not embedded in the Word for Windows document—only the result is shown—so the document is much smaller than a document with embedded data.

- You can bring in all or part of a word processing, worksheet, or database file.

- Updates can be done automatically whenever the source data changes, or they can be done manually when you request them.

Following are some disadvantages to using links created by Paste Special:

- Renaming or moving a source file can disturb the link. You must edit the link so that the Word for Windows document can find the source file.

- The source application and file must be on disk and available to Word for Windows if you want to edit the data or graphic.

■ Not all Windows applications can link data.

■ Automatic updates can slow down computer response time.

Creating Links with the Copy and Paste Special Commands

Creating a link between Word for Windows and a Windows application is as easy as copying and pasting. When you give the paste command, you create a link that updates automatically.

> **Note**
>
> If you copied data from a source application, but Edit, Paste Special does not enable you to link, that source application may not be able to create linked data.

To copy a range or a portion of a document and link it into the Word document, follow these steps:

1. Position the insertion point in the Word document where you want the linked data or graphic to appear.

2. Activate the source application and document, and make sure that the source is saved with the file name it will keep.

3. Select the portion of the source document you want to link.

4. Choose Edit, Copy, or click the Copy button on the Standard toolbar.

5. Activate the Word document.

6. Choose Edit, Paste Special.

7. Select the Paste Link option.

8. From the As list box, select the type of data format you want in the document.

9. Click OK.

You can use any of the following methods to resolve the problem of a lost link:

■ Reconnect the link if you know where the original data file has moved or its new name. This is usually the best and easiest solution if you can still find the original file. Reconnecting a link is described in "Reconnecting Links When Names or Path Names Change" later in this chapter.

Troubleshooting

When the link is updated, an error message appears that says `Error! Not a valid Filename.`

This error occurs when the link cannot find the source file that is supposed to contain the source data, which could be caused by the source file being deleted, renamed, or moved to another folder. First, choose Edit, Undo to restore the last linked data instead of displaying the error message. Do not save the document to the original file name until you fix the problem.

■ Delete the linked data producing the error and re-create it with a new source. This is the best solution if you cannot find the original file and you need a link to a source file in another application.

■ Lock a link so that the image of the last data is maintained and the field code that creates the link is kept for possible future use. This enables you to use the last image or text from the source data, while preserving the link field code in case you later find or re-create the source document. Locking a link is described in "Locking Links to Prevent an Update" later in this chapter.

◄ See "Creating a Master Document," p. 939

■ Freeze the text or image from the last link so that the text or data is like a normal unlinked graphic or text in the document. When you *freeze* linked data, you are undoing the link to the source document, but maintaining the text or graphic image in your Word document. The field code that maintained the link is deleted. To freeze linked data as it appears currently in the document, see "Converting Linked Data to Fixed Data" later in this chapter.

Managing Links

Keeping track of the many links found in a large or complex document can be a difficult task. You can, however, choose Edit, Links to make the job easier. When you choose Edit, Links, the Links dialog box, shown in figure 34.13, opens and displays a list of all the links, their type, and how they update. From the buttons and check boxes, you can update linked data, open linked files, lock links to prevent changes, cancel the link, change a link between automatic and manual, or change the file names or folders where the linked data is stored.

Fig. 34.13
The Links dialog
box enables you to
update, unlink, or
protect links. If
the source file
moves or is
renamed, you can
relink to the
source using the
Links dialog box.

Passing Linked Documents to Other Computer Users

If you want to change the linked data in your document, you must have the
source document the link is connected to as well as the application that created the data. When you give a document containing links to other users,
make sure that you give them the source documents. They will need the
source application if they want to make edits in the original data.

Reducing the Size of a Linked File

The linked data that appears in your Word document is actually a representation of the real data that exists in a source document. This image, however,
still requires memory. If your document displays a link to a large graphics file,
the representation of the graphics file alone can be very large.

You can reduce the size of a file containing links by not storing the graphic
representation; instead, you store only the field codes that describe the links.
When the document opens, these field codes reestablish the link to the
source document and regenerate an image in your Word document.

The advantage to storing only the link is that you can significantly reduce
your Word document file size if your document contains links to large graphics. The disadvantage to storing only the links is that documents with large
files take longer to load as you re-create the images, and links that you cannot re-create will appear as rectangular placeholders on-screen.

To store a document as a reduced size file, follow these steps:

1. Choose Edit, Links.

2. Select the link you want stored as a link field without the graphic
   image.

3. Deselect the Save Picture in Document check box.

4. Click OK.

Opening the Source Document

In your Word for Windows document, you can edit linked data such as text or numbers just as though you typed them in the document. When you update the link, however, your changes disappear. To change linked data so that it remains, you need to edit the source document. The source application and source document must be open when you edit the link.

To open a source document that may be closed, follow these steps:

1. If you want to open a file specific to one link, select the linked data.

2. Choose Edit, Links to display the Links dialog box (refer to fig. 34.13).

3. From the Source File list box, select the link you want to open. If you selected linked data in Step 1, the link you want to open is already selected.

4. Choose the Open Source button. The source application opens.

5. Make your updates, edits, or formatting changes to the source document.

6. If you have made all the changes you want, save and then close the source document.

If the link is automatic, the Word for Windows document updates immediately. If the link is manual, you must update the linked data to see the change. Update linked data by selecting it and pressing F9.

Caution

When you rename or move a source file, make sure that the destination document is open; save the destination document after renaming or moving the source file. This step is recommended because the {LINK} field in the destination document stores the file and path name of the source file. You can see these names by selecting linked data and pressing Shift+F9. If you rename or move the source file while the destination document is closed, the {LINK} field will not be able to update itself to the new file or path name. If you accidentally lose a link, you can reconnect the link by using the technique described in "Reconnecting Links When Names or Path Names Change" later in this chapter.

> **Note**
>
> To preserve manually applied formatting during an update to linked data, use the
> * mergeformat and * charformat field switches described in Chapter 20, "Au-
> tomating with Field Codes." To preserve wide titles in a table, do not merge cells to
> give a title extra width in a cell. Instead, change individual cell widths to allow space
> for a wide title.

Converting Linked Data to Fixed Data

To convert linked information to text or a graphic, select the linked information and then press Shift+Ctrl+F9 to unlink. The information changes into
text, a picture, or a bitmap—as if you had pasted it and not paste-linked it.
You can also select the link, choose Edit, Links, choose the Break Link button,
and then confirm with Yes.

Updating Links

To update individual links in a document so that the destination file receives
new information, select the linked text or graphic, and then press F9. To
update links selectively without scrolling through the document, choose Edit,
Links. When the Links dialog box appears, select the links you want to update (use Ctrl+click to select multiple links), and then choose the Update
Now button.

When you want to update all the links in an entire document, select the
entire document by pressing Ctrl and clicking in the left boundary, or press
Ctrl+5 (numeric pad). Then press the F9 key or choose Edit, Links and choose
the Update Now button.

Changing Links between Automatic and Manual

Using Edit, Paste Special creates an automatic link; pasted data normally updates immediately when the source information changes. This automatic
updating process can slow your computer's operation if changes are frequent.
If you do not need to see immediate changes, however, you can change an
automatic link to a manual link.

To change between manually or automatically updated links, follow these
steps:

1. Select the linked data or graphic.

2. Choose Edit, Links.

3. From the Update options at the bottom of the dialog box, you can choose <u>M</u>anual to update a link by manually selecting it and pressing F9. Or, choose <u>A</u>utomatic to automatically update a link when the source data changes.

4. Click OK.

To update a manual link, select the linked information and press F9. To prevent a link from updating, lock the link, as described later in "Locking Links to Prevent an Update."

Reconnecting Links When Names or Path Names Change

If a source's location, file name, or range name changes, you must update the field code that creates the link to reflect the new folder and file name. To update a linking field, choose <u>E</u>dit, Lin<u>k</u>s, select the link you need to edit, and then choose the Cha<u>n</u>ge Source button to display the Change Source dialog box (see fig. 34.14). From this dialog box, you can select or type a new file name, path name, or item. (The item is a range name in a worksheet or bookmark in a Word document.)

Fig. 34.14
You can reconnect source files to the destination even if you have moved or renamed the source file.

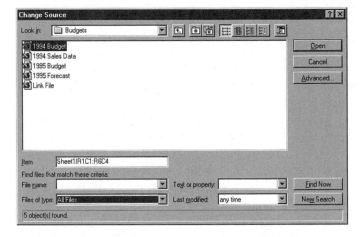

If you are familiar with the operation and editing of field codes as described in Chapter 20, "Automating with Field Codes," you can display the field code for the link and edit the file name, path name, and item name directly. Remember that you need two backslashes to separate folders in a path name within a field code.

Locking Links to Prevent an Update

You may want to prevent accidental updating of a link by locking the field. When the field is locked, its data will not change. The linking field code is preserved, however, so that at a later time you can unlock the field and update the linked data.

To lock a field, follow these steps:

1. Select the field you want to lock.

2. Choose Edit, Links, select the Locked check box, and click OK.

To unlock a locked field, follow these steps:

1. Select the field you want to lock.

2. Choose Edit, Links, deselect the Locked check box, and click OK.

◀ See "Updating, Unlinking, or Locking Fields," p. 613

Using Microsoft Office Binder to Group Documents

One of the great advantages to working in Windows with Office 95 is having the ability to create documents that use material from different applications. For example, a proposal to a client may contain material from Word, Excel, and Project. The proposal may begin with a letter of introduction, followed by answers to the bid request, and include documents containing project specifications, worksheets containing budget and resource items, charts showing costs and resource loading, as well as Gantt or Pert charts showing project management.

Prior to Office 95 and Windows 95, most people worked with each of these documents separately, storing, printing, and collating them as individual files. A few people tried linking or embedding everything into a Word document. The Binder enables you to work with the files involved in a project as though they are a single bound document. Within one window you can work with documents from many different Office 95 applications. As you switch between documents, the menus and toolbars change to reflect the application that created the document. You can easily switch between documents, insert new documents, print the entire project with contiguous page numbers, and store or e-mail the binder as a single file.

Creating a New Binder

You can start a new binder to group together documents from any Microsoft
Office compatible applications, such as Word and Excel. Creating a new
binder consists of opening a new, blank binder and adding documents from
compatible applications to the binder. Each document you add becomes a
section in the binder. You can also create a new binder based on one of the
templates that comes with Binder.

To create a new binder, open the Start menu and select _P_rograms and
Microsoft Word; then choose Microsoft Binder. The Binder window opens
with a blank binder, as shown in figure 34.15. If Binder is already open, use
its menu to choose _F_ile, _N_ew Binder. Click OK to open a new, blank binder.

Fig. 34.15

When you first
open Microsoft
Office Binder, you
are presented with
a new, blank
binder to which
you can add
documents.

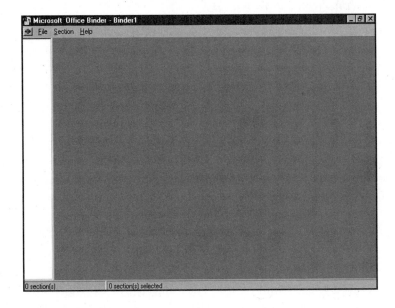

Opening an Existing Binder

Tip

To open a file in
the Open Binder
dialog box,
double-click the
file in the list box.
This selects the file
and closes the
dialog box in one
step.

To open a binder that already exists on your computer, follow these steps:

1. In the Binder window, choose _F_ile, _O_pen Binder.

2. Select the drive and folder containing the binder file in the Open
   Binder dialog box.

3. Select the binder file in the File list box.

4. Choose _O_pen.

> **Note**
>
> Each time you open an existing or new binder, a new binder window opens. Unless you want to work on more than one binder at a time, you should close the binder you are working on before you open another binder, or you may end up with several binder windows open at the same time, using up your computer's memory unnecessarily.

Adding Documents to a Binder

Whether you are starting a new binder from scratch or working with an existing binder, the procedures for adding a new document to a binder are the same. You can add both new and existing documents to a binder. This gives you the flexibility to build your binder from new and old material. You can, for example, add an existing document from Microsoft Word, and then add a new document from Microsoft Excel. You can then work in the new worksheet from within the Binder.

> **Note**
>
> You can add a portion of a document into a binder by dragging the selected portion from the Office application into the left pane of the binder. Position the pointer in the left pane where you want the document and release the mouse button.

To add an existing document to a binder, follow these steps:

1. Select the document in either My Computer or Windows Explorer.

   If the left pane is not visible in the Binder window, click the double-headed arrow to the left of File on the menu bar.

2. Drag-and-drop the document on the left pane of the Binder window at the location in the binder where you want the document to be added.

An icon representing the document will appear in the left pane, and the document itself will appear in the right pane (see fig. 34.16). The document becomes a section in the binder. The menu bar and toolbar for the document's application will also appear, allowing you to work on the document from within the Binder (refer to fig. 34.15).

Fig. 34.16

When you add an existing document to a binder, an icon representing the document appears in the left pane of the binder, and the document itself appears in the right pane.

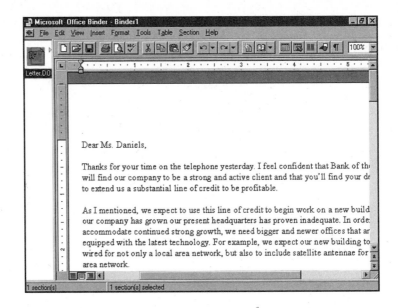

To add a new document to a binder, follow these steps:

1. Choose <u>S</u>ection, <u>A</u>dd to display the Add Section dialog box (see fig. 34.17).

Fig. 34.17

Select the type of document you want to add as a section to a binder in the Add Section dialog box.

2. Select the type of document you want to add to your binder from the list box and click OK.

The new, blank document appears as a section in the binder, and the menu and toolbars for the documents application appear (see fig. 34.18). An icon representing the document appears in the left pane of the Binder, with a section name assigned to it, for example, Section 1. The icon for a section indicates with which application the section's document is associated. You can work on the document from within the Binder.

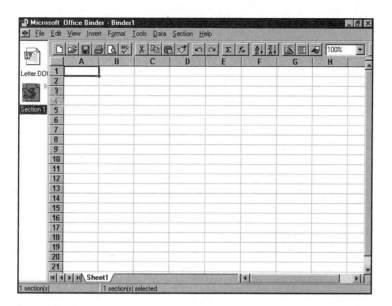

Fig. 34.18
When you add a
new document to
a binder, a blank
document is
inserted as a
section in the
binder, and the
menu and toolbars
for the document's
application
appear.

> **Note**
>
> To quickly add a new document after an existing document in a binder, select the
> existing document and click the right mouse button in a blank area of the left-hand
> column. Choose Add from the shortcut menu, select the type of document you want
> to add from the Add Section dialog box, and then click OK.

Selecting a Binder Document

When you want to work with, move, copy, or delete a document in a binder,
you must select it first. You can even select multiple documents to carry out
an action on more than one document at the same time.

To select documents, follow one of these steps:

- To select a single document, click the document's button in the left
  pane of the Binder.

  If the left pane is not displayed, click the double-headed arrow to the
  left of File in the menu bar.

- To select two or more documents that appear consecutively in the left
  pane of the Binder, click the first document's icon, hold down the Shift
  key, and then click the last document's icon.

■ To select two or more documents that do not appear consecutively in the left pane, click the first document's icon and while holding down the Ctrl key, click the icons for the other documents.

■ To select all the documents in a binder, choose <u>S</u>ection, Select All.

After you have chosen the Select All command, you must choose <u>S</u>ection, Unselect All to unselect the documents.

Moving a Binder Document

You can use the mouse or <u>S</u>ection, <u>R</u>earrange to reorder the documents in a binder. You can also move a document from one binder to another, or even from a binder to a folder in My Computer or Windows Explorer.

To move a document with the mouse, drag the icon for the document to where you want it in the left pane of the binder. If the left pane is not visible, click the double-headed arrow to the left of <u>F</u>ile in the menu bar.

To move a document with a menu command, follow these steps:

1. Choose <u>S</u>ection, <u>R</u>earrange to display the Rearrange Sections dialog box (see fig. 34.19).

Fig. 34.19

Move sections around in a binder using the Re-arrange Sections dialog box.

2. Select the section you want to move in the Reorder <u>S</u>ections list box.

3. Choose the Move <u>U</u>p or Move <u>D</u>own button to move the section to its new location.

4. Click OK.

To move a document from one binder to another, open both binders. Size and arrange the Binder windows so that the left panes in each window are visible. Select the document in the left pane of the source binder and drag-and-drop it to where you want it in the left pane of the destination binder.

If you want to move a document out of a binder into a folder, you can drag-and-drop it from the Binder window. To move the document, select it in the left pane and drag-and-drop it on the destination folder in My Computer or Windows Explorer with the right mouse button. When the shortcut menu appears, choose <u>M</u>ove Scrap Here.

Copying a Binder Document

You can use the mouse or choose <u>S</u>ection, Du<u>p</u>licate to make a copy of a document in a binder.

To copy a document with the mouse, follow these steps:

1. Select the document in the left pane of the Binder window.

   If the left pane is not visible, click the double-headed arrow to the left of <u>F</u>ile in the menu bar.

2. Drag-and-drop the document to where you want to insert a duplicate copy with the right mouse button.

3. When the shortcut menu appears, choose <u>C</u>opy Here.

To copy a document with a menu command, follow these steps:

1. Select the document you want to duplicate in the left pane of the Binder window.

2. Choose <u>S</u>ection, Du<u>p</u>licate to open the Duplicate Section dialog box.

3. Select the section after which you want the duplicate to be created in the list box.

4. Click OK.

To create a copy of a binder document in a MY COMPUTER or WINDOWS EXPLORER folder, drag-and-drop the document from the left pane of the Binder window to the destination folder with the right mouse button. When the shortcut menu appears, choose <u>C</u>reate Scrap Here.

Renaming a Binder Document

To rename a document in a binder, double-click the name under the document, type the new name, and then press Enter. Or select the document you want to rename, choose <u>S</u>ection, <u>R</u>ename, type the new name, and then press Enter.

Tip

After you select the document you want to duplicate in the left pane of Binder, right-click the document and choose Add to open the Duplicate Section dialog box.

Deleting a Binder Document

To delete a document from a binder, right-click the document, click Delete, and then click OK when the confirmation dialog box appears. Or you can select the document and choose Section, Delete.

Hiding and Displaying Binder Documents

Tip

Double-click the name of the document you want to unhide in the Unhide Sections dialog box. This selects the file and closes the dialog box in one step.

You can hide a document if you do not want it to appear in the binder for some reason, and do not want to delete it. To hide a document, select it and then choose Selection, Hide. To unhide a document, choose Section, Unhide, select the document in the Unhide Sections dialog box, and then click OK.

Saving Binder Sections as Documents

You can save a section that you have added to a binder as a separate document. To save a binder section as a document, follow these steps:

1. Select the document in the left pane of the Binder window.

   If the left pane is not visible, click the double-headed arrow to the left of File in the menu bar.

2. Choose Section, Save As File to display the Save As dialog box.

3. Select the folder where you want to save the file.

4. Enter a name for the document in the File Name text box.

5. Click OK.

Unbinding a Binder into Separate Documents

You can unbind a binder so that its component parts are saved as separate files. When you unbind a binder, the original binder file remains intact.

To unbind a binder into its component documents, follow these steps:

1. Either in My Computer or Windows Explorer, locate the binder file on your hard disk.

2. Select the file and click the right mouse button.

3. Choose Unbind.

Caution

You cannot unbind documents if one of the documents in the binder is open.

The documents that make up the binder are saved as separate files in the same folder that the binder file is in.

Viewing a Document in Its Application

If you want to view a document in a binder in its original application, select the document in the left pane of the Binder window and choose Section, View Outside. The original application will open along with the selected document. To return to the Binder, choose File, Close and then Return To.

Printing and Collating from Multiple Applications

You can print all or selected sections of a binder using the File, Print Binder command. To print selected sections, select the sections you want to print using the methods outlined in "Selecting a Binder Document," earlier in the chapter.

To print a binder, follow these steps:

1. Choose File, Print Binder.

2. To print the entire binder, make sure that you have selected the All Sections option. To print just the selected sections, select the Selected Section(s) option.

3. Specify the number of copies in the Number of Copies spinner box.

4. Select the Collate option if you want to collate multiple copies.

5. Select Consecutive in the Numbering Group if you want to number the pages in the binder consecutively from first to last page.

   Or, select Restart Each Section if you want page numbering to start at 1 for each section (document) in the binder.

6. Click OK.

To print a single document in a binder, select the document in the left pane of the Binder window. Choose Section, Print, select the desired options in the Print dialog box, and then click OK.

Using Binder Templates for Repetitive Documents

Templates are like blueprints that serve as the basis for creating a new binder. When you open a new binder based on a template, the basic parts of the template are already in place, saving you the trouble of creating the binder from scratch. When you save the binder, the original template on which the binder is based remains intact.

Using Binder's Built-In Templates

Binder comes with four templates that you can use as a foundation for new binders that you create. These templates already contain sections for some of the typical binders that you may create for your business needs. After you open the template, you fill in your own information in each of the binder sections. The four templates that come with Binder are Client Billing, Meeting Organizer, Proposal and Marketing Plan, and Report. Figure 34.20 shows the Client Billing template. Notice that there are five sections in the binder, consisting of Microsoft Word and Excel documents.

Fig. 34.20

The Client Billing template that comes with Microsoft Office Binder includes sections for a fax cover sheet, cover letter, invoice, time card, and materials card.

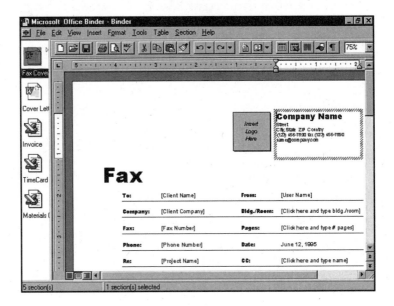

To start a new binder based on a Binder template, follow these steps:

1. Choose File, New Binder.

2. Select the Binders tab.

3. Click OK.

Now you can fill in your own information in each binder section and save the file using File, Save Binder.

Creating a New Binder Template

If you have created a binder that you want to use as the basis of additional binders that you will create in the future, you can save the binder as a template. Before saving the binder as a template, you should delete any information that you do not want repeated in new binders based on the template.

To save a binder as a template, follow these steps:

1. Choose File, Save Binder As.

2. In the Save As dialog box, select the OFFICE folder, then the TEMPLATES folder, and finally, the BINDERS folder.

3. Select Binder Templates from the Save As Type drop-down list.

4. Click OK.

When you want to start a new binder based on this template, select the template from the Binders tab of the New Binder dialog box. ❖

Part VIII

Customizing with Word

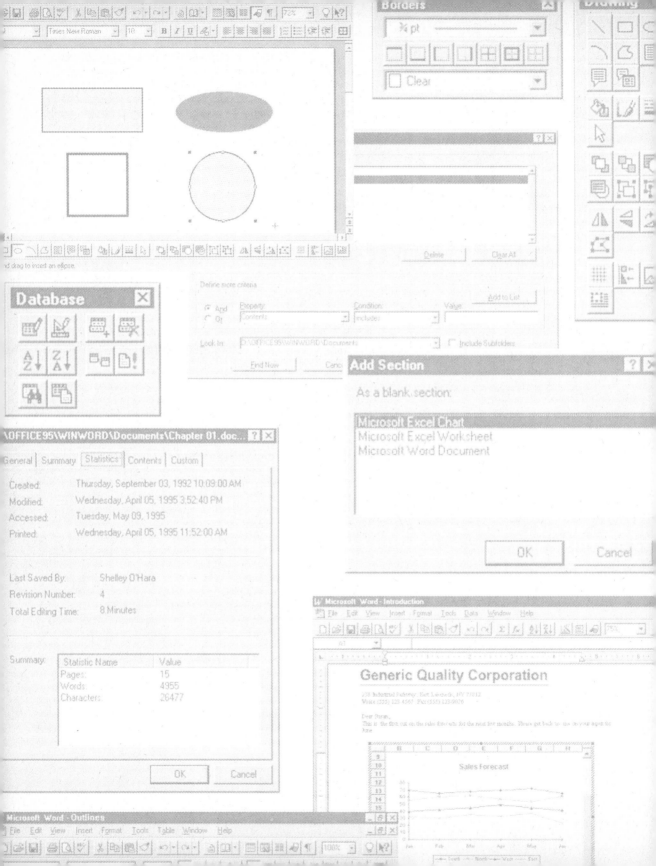

Chapter 35

Customizing and Optimizing Word Features

As you use Word for Windows 95, you might want to customize it to fit the way you work or to make trade-offs between increased performance and features. Other chapters have shown you how to customize Word features such as menus, toolbars, and shortcut keys. But there are many other ways in which you can customize Word. This chapter contains suggestions and options to help you fine-tune Word and customize it for the way you work.

In this chapter, you learn about the following:

- Improving the performance of Word for Windows
- Optimizing memory usage
- Starting Word or documents automatically
- Customizing the workspace and display
- Personalizing the mouse

Note

To follow the examples in this chapter, it is assumed that Word for Windows has been installed in the C:\MSOFFICE\WINWORD folder. If you have installed Word in a different folder, please substitute your Word folder's name in the following examples.

Customizing Commonly Used Features

Other chapters of this book discuss techniques for customizing many Word for Windows features. The following list indicates some commonly customized features and the chapters in which they are discussed:

If You Want to Customize	Refer To
Dictionary	Chapter 7, "Using Editing and Proofing Tools"
Document on startup	Chapter 6, "Using Templates and Wizards for Frequently Created Documents"
Documents that are frequently used	Chapter 6, "Using Templates and Wizards for Frequently Created Documents"
Font on startup (default font)	Chapter 9, "Formatting Characters and Changing Fonts"
Menus or commands	Chapter 36, "Customizing the Toolbar, Menus, and Shortcut Keys"
Page settings on startup	Chapter 13, "Formatting the Page Layout, Alignment, and Numbering"; Chapter 6, "Using Templates and Wizards for Frequently Created Documents"
Paragraph settings on startup	Chapter 10, "Formatting Lines and Paragraphs"; Chapter 6, "Using Templates and Wizards for Frequently Created Documents"
Procedures or commands	Chapter 37, "Recording and Editing Macros"
Screen display	Chapter 2, "Getting Started in Word for Windows"
Shortcut keys	Chapter 36, "Customizing the Toolbar, Menus, and Shortcut Keys"
Toolbars	Chapter 36, "Customizing the Toolbar, Menus, and Shortcut Keys"

Improving the Performance of Word for Windows

Depending on the work that you do and the capability of your computer, Word for Windows may not perform as fast as DOS-based word processors.

80386 computers, minimum RAM memory, large graphics files, and long tables can make Word perform more slowly. You can make a number of trade-offs, however, to improve the speed of Word for Windows.

Modifying Word for Windows Settings

You can improve Word's performance by choosing certain options within Word for Windows. Significant performance improvements also can be made by increasing the memory available to Windows or by increasing the effective speed of your computer's hard disk.

To improve Word's performance from within Word for Windows, follow these steps:

1. Choose Tools, Options. The Options dialog box appears (see fig. 35.1).

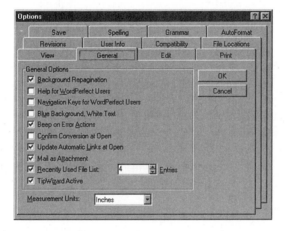

Fig. 35.1
You can use the Options dialog box to customize many Word for Windows options.

VIII

Customizing with Word

2. Select the tab listed in the first column of the following table; then select or deselect the option or check box to make the performance trade-offs you want:

Tab	Option or Check Box	To Improve Performance
View	Picture Placeholders	Select for faster performance; pictures display as empty rectangles on-screen.
General	Background Repagination	Deselect for better performance; page break markers and automatic page numbering aren't correct until you repaginate.

(continues)

Tab	Option or Check Box	To Improve Performance
General	Update Automatic Links At Open	Deselect to open files faster; linked data is not correct unless the individual link (or the entire document) is updated.
Print	Draft Output	Select to print faster on dot-matrix printers; the document does not use the fonts shown on-screen. Some character formatting may be lost.
	Background Printing	Deselect to work faster on-screen; you cannot print while you work.
Save	Allow Fast Saves	Select to save more quickly by saving only the changes made to documents; files become larger and cannot be converted by other programs when saved with fast save.
	Always Create Backup Copy	Deselect to save more quickly; no duplicate copy (file extension BAK) is made during saves.
	Automatic Save Every	Deselect to avoid being interrupted by timed saves to disk; no periodic saves are made unless you remember to make them yourself.

3. Choose OK.

4. Select Print TrueType Fonts as graphics.

5. Choose OK.

You also can gain a few percentage points of performance by limiting the type or number of fonts you use. Use one or both of the following methods to improve performance by way of font selection:

- Do not use several different fonts within a single document. This guideline is in keeping with a general rule of desktop publishing which suggests that no more than three fonts should be used in a document.

- Use TrueType fonts sparingly. TrueType fonts slow computer and printer performance slightly. Instead, use the built-in fonts provided by the currently selected printer.

Printer fonts appear in the Font list of the Font dialog box (choose Format, Font) with a miniature printer to the left of their names.

To make sure you do not use TrueType fonts, follow these steps:

1. Click the Start button on the Windows desktop and then choose Settings, Printers to open the Printers folder.

2. Select the printer and then choose File, Properties. The printer's Properties dialog box appears.

3. Click the Fonts tab.

> **Note**
>
> The Fonts tab only appears on laser or similar printers that use soft fonts or hand cartridge fonts. Dot matrix users won't see a Fonts tab.

Your document becomes printer specific when you use printer fonts, so you might want to use styles when formatting. Doing so makes it easier to change fonts throughout the document if you have to change printers.

Managing System Memory

Having more memory available can make Word run faster and enable you to work more efficiently in larger or more complex documents. You can get a significant improvement in performance by increasing your computer's memory to more than 8M of memory.

You also can improve performance (although the gains are not as significant) by making the proper selections of Word features and using wise file and application management practices. The following tips also can help you improve performance:

- Exit all applications that are not being used while you are working in Word for Windows. Other applications also require memory.

- Close unneeded documents in Word or data files in other open Windows applications. Each document and application requires a portion of Windows' limited system resources memory.

- Use the Disk Defragmenter program that comes with Windows 95, to consolidate your hard disk so that information can be read and written more quickly. Start this program by opening the Start menu, then clicking Programs, Accessories, System Tools, and then Disk Defragmenter. Disk fragmentation occurs normally as you save and delete files. As time

VIII

Customizing with Word

passes, files are saved in pieces scattered over the disk to make the best use of available space. Unfortunately, this process slows down read and write operations. Defragmenting reorganizes information on the disk so that each file is stored in a single contiguous location.

■ Do not create large documents exceeding 30 to 50 pages in length. Instead, create smaller documents and link them together into a master document using the techniques described in Chapter 32, "Assembling Large Documents."

Starting Word or Documents on Startup

◀ See "Controlling Printing Options," p. 244

◀ See "Linking Documents and Files," p. 993

If you use Word for Windows as your primary Windows application, you might want it to run or load as an icon each time you start Windows. This section explains how to do that, as well as how to create icons in the Windows Explorer that will start Word or load a specified document.

Starting Word or Documents when Windows 95 Starts

To start Word when Windows 95 starts, you need to add Word to the Startup folder. You can do this by following these steps:

1. Open the Start menu, and click Settings, and then Taskbar. Choose the Start Menu Programs tab from the Taskbar Properties sheet, as shown in figure 35.2.

Fig. 35.2

Start programs or documents on startup through the Start Menu Programs tab. You can also add programs to the Start menu.

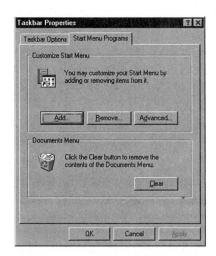

2. Click the <u>A</u>dd button to display the Create Shortcut dialog box.

3. Click the B<u>r</u>owse button to display the Browse dialog box. To start Word when Windows 95 starts, open the folder containing Word 95 and double-click the Microsoft Word file. If you want to start a document on startup, open the folder to the document and double-click the documents file. The Browse dialog box will close.

4. Click the Next button to display the Select Program Folder dialog box.

5. Select the Startup folder, as shown in figure 35.3.

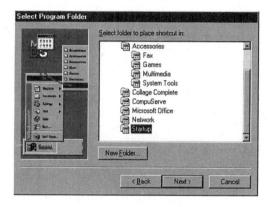

Fig. 35.3
Select the Startup folder if you want your document or application to start when Windows 95 starts.

VIII

Customizing with Word

6. Click the Next button to display the Select a Title for the Program dialog box.

7. Type the name you want to use to represent Word or the document. Click the Finish button to return to the Taskbar Properties sheet.

8. Choose OK.

The next time you start Windows 95, the Word program or Word and the document you selected will open automatically.

To stop a program or document from loading automatically, reopen the Start Menu Programs tab from the Taskbar Properties sheet. Click the <u>R</u>emove button. Open the Startup folder in the Remove Shortcuts/Folders dialog box. Select the program or document you no longer want to start up and click the <u>R</u>emove button. Choose Close and OK.

Creating Desktop Shortcut Icons for Word or Documents

You can get quick access to Word or to a Word document from your desktop by adding a shortcut icon to your desktop for that file. Double-clicking a shortcut icon to Word will open Word. Double-clicking a shortcut icon to a Word document will open Word and load the document.

To create a shortcut icon to Word or a document, follow these steps:

1. Open My Computer or Windows Explorer.

2. Open the folder containing the application or document file for which you want to create a shortcut.

3. Drag the file to the desktop using the right mouse button. When you release the right mouse button a shortcut menu displays.

4. Choose Create Shortcut(s) Here.

This will create a shortcut icon to the file you specified.

> **Note**
>
> If you have too many shortcut icons on your desktop, you can create a shortcut folder in which to store them. Right-click the desktop, choose New, and choose Folder. Type a new name and press Enter. You can drag and drop your shortcut icons into the folder. To get at an icon in the folder, just double-click the folder.

Delete shortcut icons by clicking them and then pressing the Delete key.

Customizing the Start Menu to Include Word or Documents

Tip
To quickly add Word to the highest level of the Start menu, drag Word's application file from the Explorer or My Computer window and drop it on the Start button.

The contents of the Start menu can be customized. You can add a list of applications you use frequently, and then start those applications directly from the menu. By adding programs or documents to the Start menu you avoid having to display additional menus.

To add Word or a document to the Start menu, follow these steps.

1. Right-click a gray area between buttons on the taskbar. Choose Properties.

   You can also open the Start menu and choose Settings, Taskbar.

2. Click the Start Menu Programs tab (refer to fig. 35.2).

3. Click the Add button to display the Create Shortcut dialog box.

4. Click the Browse button to display the Browse dialog box. This dialog box looks very similar to an Open File dialog box.

5. Find and click the file that starts the program or document file you want to add to the Start menu. Click the Open button once you have selected the file.

   You can limit the displayed files to program files by selecting Programs from the Files of Type list box at the bottom of the dialog box. For example, if you wanted to start Word, you would open the MSOFFICE folder, open the WINWORD folder, and then click WINWORD. Most program files use an EXE extension.

6. Click the Next button to display the Select Program Folder dialog box (refer to fig. 35.3).

7. Select the folder that corresponds to the location on the Start menu where you want the program to appear. Choose Next.

   For example, if you wanted the program you selected to appear at the top of the Start menu, you would select the Start Menu folder. If you wanted the program to appear as an item on the Programs menu, then you would select the Programs folder.

8. Type the name or words you want to appear on the Start menu in the edit box. Choose Finish.

> **Note**
>
> If you frequently copy files to the same folders, put Shortcuts to those folders in the WINDOWS\SENDTO folder. The Shortcuts to the folders will then show up under the Send To command on the menu that appears when you right-click a file.

To remove a program from the Start menu, you follow a similar process:

1. Display the Taskbar Properties sheet as described earlier in this chapter.

2. Click the Start Menu Programs page.

3. Click the Remove button to display the Remove Shortcuts/Folders dialog box.

4. Select the shortcut or folder you want to remove from the Start menu.

VIII

Customizing with Word

5. Click the <u>R</u>emove button to remove the file or folder.

6. Remove additional items or choose Close. Choose OK when you return to the Taskbar Properties sheet.

Clearing the Documents List on the Start Menu

The Start menu contains a Documents item that shows a list of recently used documents. At times this list may become too long or you may want to clear the list so documents are easier to find. To clear the documents from the Documents menu, follow these steps:

1. Display the Taskbar Properties dialog box.

2. Select the Start Menu Programs tab.

3. Click the <u>C</u>lear button in the Documents Menu area of the dialog box.

4. Choose OK.

Making Menus, Toolbars, and Shortcut Keys Globally Available

If you find that a template has menus, toolbars, and shortcut keys that you use frequently, you can make them available without using the Organizer to transfer them to the NORMAL.DOT template. (The Organizer is a feature described in Chapter 6, "Using Templates and Wizards for Frequently Created Documents.") Instead, copy the template file (DOT extension) containing these features into the \WINWORD\STARTUP folder. The template files are usually located in the \MSOFFICE\TEMPLATE folder.

Make sure you copy a template into the StartUp folder. If you move a template out of the Template folder, it will not appear in the New dialog box when you choose <u>F</u>ile, <u>N</u>ew.

Customizing the Workspace and Display

If you work at your computer a lot, even small things like customizing screen colors or arranging screen elements can help you reduce stress. Refer to

Chapter 36, "Customizing the Toolbar, Menus, and Shortcut Keys," for more information.

To change the display or your Word for Windows workspace, follow these steps:

1. Choose Tools, Options. The Options dialog box appears.

2. Select the tab listed in the first column of the following table. Then select or deselect the associated option or check box depending on your display preferences:

Tab	Option or Check Box	To Change
View	Status Bar	The appearance of the status bar at the bottom of the screen
	Horizontal Scroll Bar Vertical Scroll Bar	The appearance of the or horizontal or vertical scroll bars. Remove them if you use only the keyboard
General	Recently Used File List	The number of files shown under the File menu listed as having been recently opened
	Measurement Units	The units used on the ruler (choice of inches, centimeters, points, or picas)
	Beep on Error Actions	The status (on/off) of the audible beep that sounds for each error
	Blue Background, White Text	Changes to a white-on-blue screen, reducing the eye strain caused by reading a black-on-white screen
File Locations	File Types	The location of files used by Word. Select the file type and choose the Modify button. You can change the locations for Documents, ClipArt Pictures, User Templates, Workgroup Templates, User Options, AutoSave Files, Dictionaries, and StartUp

VIII

Customizing with Word

3. Choose OK.

Customizing Mouse Settings

You can customize the mouse to operate more slowly; you also can switch the button actions between left and right sides.

To customize the mouse, follow these steps:

1. Start the <u>C</u>ontrol Panel found in the <u>S</u>ettings group on the Start menu.

2. Start the Mouse program.

3. Change any of the following options:

Buttons	<u>D</u>ouble-click speed	The speed with which you must double-click for a double-click to be accepted. Use the slow setting while learning.
Buttons to Buttons	<u>R</u>ight-handed/ <u>L</u>eft-handed	Swaps the right and left mouse button. Use for operating the mouse from the opposite hand.
Motion	Pointer <u>s</u>peed	The speed of the on-screen pointer moves with respect to your movement of the hand-held mouse. Use the slow setting while learning.
	Sh<u>o</u>w pointer trials	Produces a shadowed trail of mouse pointers that makes the pointer easier to see on LCD paneldisplays (used in laptop computers).

4. Choose OK.

5. To close the Control Panel, click the Close button in the top-right corner.

Many of the newer mice have additional customizing options available (such as changing the size of the pointer or reversing the color of the pointer). These options, if available, appear in the Pointers page of the Mouse Properties sheet.

Customizing Word for the Hearing- or Movement-Impaired

Windows applications can be made more accessible for users with unique needs, whether those needs are for hearing, vision, or movement.

The hearing impaired can contact Microsoft Sales and Service on a text telephone at 800-892-5234. Technical support is available on a text telephone at 206-635-4948.

> **Caution**
>
> Accessibility options are not installed with a normal Windows 95 installation. You can reinstall Windows 95 from your original disk or CD-ROM and select the custom installation option that will enable you to select Accessibility options.

Windows 95 includes numerous options for people who find it difficult to use the keyboard, require larger fonts, or need visual cues and warnings rather than sounds. To access these options in Windows 95, follow these steps:

1. Click the Start button and choose Settings, Control Panel.

2. Double-click the Accessibility Options icon. The Accessibility Properties dialog box appears.

3. Make your selections.

4. Where applicable, click the appropriate settings buttons to enable hot keys and set related properties.

5. Click OK.

The accessibility properties dialog box include the following tabs:

Tab	Description
Keyboard	Make the keyboard more tolerant and patient. Select Use StickyKeys if you need to press multiple keys simultaneously but are only able to press keys one at a time. Select Use FilterKeys to ignore short or repeated keystrokes. Select Use ToggleKeys to make a sound when you press Caps Lock, Num Lock, and Scroll Lock.
Sound	Provide visual warnings and captions for speech and sounds. Select Use SoundSentry to make Windows use a visual warning when a sound alert occurs. Select Use ShowSounds to display captions instead of speech or sounds.

(continues)

VIII

Customizing with Word

Tab	Description
Display	Enables colors and fonts that can be read easily. Select Use High Contrast to use color and font combinations that produce greater screen contrast.
Mouse	Control the pointer with the numeric keypad. Select Use MouseKeys to use the numeric keypad and other keys in place of the mouse. The relationship of keys to mouse controls appears in the table that follows.
General	Turn off accessibility features, give notification, and add an alternative input device. Use Turn Off Accessibility features after idle for to set Windows so accessibility features remain on at all times, or are turned off after a period of inactivity. Notifications options indicate when a feature is turned on or off. Support SerialKey Devices enables Windows to receive keyboard or mouse input from alternative input devices through a serial port.

Some of these accessibility features could be difficult for a disabled person to turn on or off through normal Windows procedures. To alleviate this problem, Windows includes special *hotkeys*. Pressing the keys or key combinations for the designated hotkey turns an accessibility feature on or off, or changes its settings. The following table gives the hotkeys for different features:

Feature	Hotkey	Result
High-contrast mode	Left-Alt+left-Shift+ Print Screen pressed simultaneously	Alternates the screen through different text/background combinations
StickyKeys	Press the Shift key	Turned on or off five consecutive times
FilterKeys	Hold down right Shift key	Turned on or off for eight seconds
ToggleKeys	Hold down Num Lock key	Turned on or off for five seconds
MouseKeys	Press left-Alt+ left-Shift+Num Lock simultaneously	Turned on or off

MouseKeys can be very useful for portable or laptop computer users and graphic artists as well as for people unable to use a mouse. Graphic artists will find MouseKeys useful because it enables them to produce finer movements than those done with a mouse. Once MouseKeys is turned on you can produce the same effects as a mouse by using these keys:

Action	Press This Key(s)
Movement	Any number key except 5
Large moves	Hold down Ctrl as you press number keys
Single pixel moves	Hold down Shift as you press number keys
Single click	5
Double click	+
Begin drag	Insert (Ins)
Drop after drag	Delete (Del)
Select left mouse button	/
Select right mouse button	-
Select both mouse buttons	

Chapter 36

Customizing the Toolbar, Menus, and Shortcut Keys

Part of the power of Word for Windows 95 comes from its flexibility; you can change its shape to fit your work habits. You can create menus, toolbars, shortcut keys, and buttons that allow you to do things your way. You can add Word commands that don't normally appear on the menu or toolbar. You can even assign macros that you create to commands, buttons, or short-cut keys.

In this chapter, you learn how to:

- Find and store customized features
- Add, remove, and rearrange toolbar buttons
- Assign Word's built-in commands or your macros to a toolbar button
- Transfer toolbars to other templates
- Add or remove menus or commands
- Create custom shortcut keys or custom toolbars

Caution

Custom key assignments, menus, and toolbars combined with Word for Windows' easy-to-create macros enable you to build a word processor tailored to the work you do. This capability also holds a danger: you have the potential to modify the global

(continues)

(continued)

menus and keyboard assignments so much that Word for Windows becomes difficult for other people to use. For this reason, you probably should assign your menus, toolbar buttons, and key assignments to templates rather than assigning them globally.

Understanding Where and When Customizing Occurs

You have the ability to assign one of Word's built-in commands or one of your macros to a menu command, toolbar button, or shortcut key. However, unless you know a few rules about assigning commands and macros, you may cause conflicts. When conflicts occur, a different command or macro than the one you expected will run. When you assign a macro to a command, button, or shortcut key, it can be a global assignment or specific to a template.

Global assignments—assignments that apply to *all* documents—are stored in the NORMAL.DOT template. Such global assignments may conflict with the custom menus, toolbars, or shortcut keys you create in a template. Suppose, for example, you assign Ctrl+C to a Calculate macro in your Invoice template. Ctrl+C is a global assignment for the Edit Cut command and is stored in NORMAL.DOT. If a document based on your Invoice template is open, which assignment takes precedence? To avoid confusion, Word for Windows follows a strict hierarchy: template assignments always take precedence over the global assignments stored in NORMAL.DOT.

When you create custom menus, toolbars, or shortcut keys, always remember to open a document that uses the template you want to change. Then, in the Customize dialog box, select either NORMAL.DOT or the specific template that should contain the new menu, toolbar, or shortcut key.

Customizing and Creating Toolbars

Word for Windows enables you to customize toolbars and create your own toolbars and tools. Specifically, you can do the following:

- Change any of the supplied toolbars

- Design and edit your own toolbars

■ Draw your own button images

■ Assign a macro, command, font, AutoText entry, or style to a custom toolbar button

> **Note**
>
> You must have a mouse or equivalent pointing device to modify toolbars or create custom buttons.

Adding Buttons

Word offers more than 200 buttons, each with its own built-in commands, that you can add to any toolbar. Adding a button is as easy as dragging the button from a dialog box and dropping it at the desired location on the toolbar. The following example shows how you can add a button to a toolbar.

To add a new button to the toolbar, follow these steps:

1. Make sure that the toolbar you want to change is displayed. If you want the button to appear only when documents that use a specific template are open, open a document that uses that template.

2. Use the right mouse button to click the toolbar, and then choose Customize from the shortcut menu.

3. When the Customize dialog box appears (see fig. 36.1), make sure the Toolbars tab is selected.

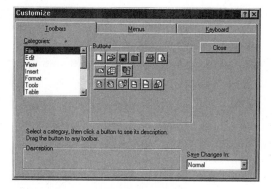

4. Select a button category from the Categories list box; your selection determines the items that appear in the Buttons group.

Tip

You always can return a predefined toolbar to its originally installed condition (see "Reorganizing Buttons" later in this chapter).

VIII

Customizing with Word

Fig. 36.1
Add a button by dragging it from the Customize dialog box and dropping it on a toolbar.

5. If you want this toolbar change to apply only to documents that use a specific template, select that template from the Sa_v_e Changes In drop-down list box. (Remember that a document using that template must be open.) If you want the change to apply to all toolbars in all documents, select the NORMAL.DOT template.

6. Select the button you want by clicking it. A description of its action or command appears in the _D_escription box.

7. Drag the button from the dialog box and drop it onto the toolbar in the location where you want it to appear.

8. Repeat steps 6 and 7 as necessary to add more buttons, and then click Close to close the Customize dialog box.

Tip

If you are unsure of a button's function, simply click the button in the Buttons area and read the description of its function in the _D_escription area.

If you choose All Commands in the _C_ategories list box, the Button group changes to the C_o_mmands list box. You drag commands to the toolbar in the same way that you drag a button. In many cases, Word creates a button image for the new button; however, some of the commands that appear in the _C_ommands list box do not have images. If you drag one of these buttons to a toolbar or document, the Custom Button dialog box appears. This dialog box enables you to select a custom button image or to draw a new image. For further instructions, see "Drawing Your Own New Button Image" later in this chapter.

If you choose Macros, Fonts, AutoText, or Styles from the _C_ategories list, corresponding lists appear, as described in "Assigning a Command or Macro to a Toolbar Button" later in this chapter.

At this point, the Standard toolbar may appear a bit crowded, especially if you are working with a standard VGA screen. You can eliminate this crowding by removing buttons, changing the spacing between buttons and changing the width of a pull-down list (see the next section of this chapter for details). If you have many buttons you want to add, you might want to create your own custom toolbar, a process described in "Creating Your Own Toolbar" later in this chapter.

Tip

To add buttons to a toolbar by moving or copying them from another toolbar, the Customize dialog box must be open.

To move or copy buttons from one toolbar to another, open the Customize dialog box while both the toolbar containing the button you want to copy or move and the toolbar on which you want to place the tool are displayed on-screen. To move the button, drag it from one toolbar to another. To copy the button, hold down the Ctrl key while you drag the button from one toolbar to another.

Reorganizing Buttons

If a toolbar gets crowded, you need to remove buttons, slide buttons left or right (so you can fit more buttons on the bar), or reorganize the buttons.

To return a predefined toolbar to its originally installed condition, follow these steps:

1. Open a document that contains the toolbar you want to reset.

2. Choose View, Toolbars.

3. Select the toolbar(s) you want to reset from the Toolbars list, and then click the Reset button.

4. In the dialog box that appears, select the template in which you want the selected toolbar(s) reset. If you want the reset to apply to all documents, select All Documents (NORMAL.DOT).

5. Choose OK and then choose OK again to close the Toolbars dialog box.

6. Choose Yes when you close the document and are asked if you want to save changes to the template.

To change the width of a drop-down list box, such as the Style drop-down list box, follow these steps:

1. Click the right mouse button while the pointer is positioned on the toolbar, and then choose Customize from the shortcut menu. The Customize dialog box appears with the Toolbars tab displayed.

2. While the Customize dialog box is on-screen, click a drop-down list box, such as Style, Font, or Font Size, on the toolbar.

3. Move the mouse pointer to the right side of the list box. When the double arrow appears, click and drag the arrow left or right to resize the list box (see fig. 36.2).

Fig. 36.2

When the Customize dialog box is open, you can click a drop-down list box and drag it to a new width.

Double arrow pointer—

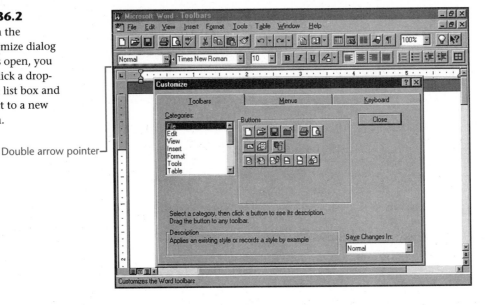

4. Choose Close from the Customize dialog box.

If you want to remove a button from the toolbar, complete the following steps:

1. Click the right mouse button when the pointer is positioned on the toolbar, and then choose Customize from the shortcut menu. The Customize dialog box appears with the Toolbars tab selected.

2. While the Customize dialog box is on-screen, drag the button off the toolbar into the document area.

3. Release the mouse button.

Tip

You can visually group buttons on the toolbar by dragging together buttons in the group and leaving spaces to mark the left and right ends of the group.

You can move groups of buttons left or right to put spacing between groups. To slide a group away from another group, open the Customize dialog box and then click the button at the end where you want to make space. Drag the button one-half button width away from the location for the space; drop the button in the location where it would be if the space existed.

To reorganize a toolbar and move buttons into new locations, follow these steps:

1. Click the right mouse button when the pointer is positioned on the toolbar, and then choose Customize from the shortcut menu. The Customize dialog box appears with the Toolbars tab selected.

2. While the Customize dialog box is on-screen, drag a button to a new location between two existing buttons (place the center of the button you're moving between the buttons that appear on either side of the desired location).

3. Release the mouse button.

Creating Your Own Toolbar

If you need to add many new buttons, you might want to create your own toolbar. This technique is especially useful for creating a toolbar designed to work with documents that use a specific template. For example, you may want to create a custom toolbar to work with your Invoice template. Its tools and their arrangement may be designed specifically for invoicing.

◀ See "Creating Styles," p. 358

To create your own toolbar, follow these steps:

1. If you want this toolbar to appear with documents using a specific template, you must begin by opening a document that uses that template.

2. Click the right mouse button when the pointer is positioned on the toolbar and then choose Toolbars from the shortcut menu (or choose View, Toolbars). The Toolbars dialog box appears (see fig. 36.3).

VIII

Customizing with Word

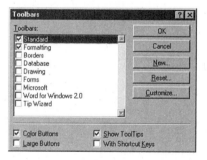

Fig. 36.3
Create a new toolbar by clicking the New button and typing the new toolbars title.

3. Click the New button to display the New Toolbar dialog box (see fig. 36.4).

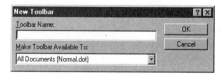

Fig. 36.4
Type your custom toolbar's name and select the template in which it should be stored.

4. Type the title for the toolbar in the Toolbar Name text box. The name can be up to 255 characters in length and can contain spaces.

5. From the Make Toolbar Available To drop-down list box, choose the template (and the set of documents using that template) with which the toolbar should appear. Select All Documents (NORMAL.DOT) if you want the toolbar to be available at all times.

6. Choose OK. The Customize dialog box appears with the Toolbars tab selected. Your new toolbar appears at the top left of the screen; initially it is only large enough for one button.

7. Drag the buttons you want from the Customize dialog box to the new toolbar.

8. Choose Close after you finish. The new toolbar contains the tools you copied onto it.

You also can create a toolbar quickly by displaying the Customize dialog box and dragging one of the tools onto your document. The toolbar that appears is called Toolbar 1, Toolbar 2, or the next sequentially numbered toolbar name.

In either case, the name of your new toolbar now appears at the bottom of the Toolbars list box in the Toolbars dialog box. You can treat it like any other toolbar.

To delete a custom toolbar, follow these steps:

1. Click the right mouse button while the pointer is positioned on the toolbar.

2. Choose Toolbars from the shortcut menu or choose View, Toolbars.

3. Select your custom toolbar from the Toolbars list and then click the Delete button.

4. Respond with Yes to confirm you want to delete it.

5. Choose OK to close the Toolbars dialog box.

Assigning a Command or Macro to a Toolbar Button

You provide yourself with fast access to frequently used Word commands by placing standard commands as buttons on the toolbar. But Word for

Windows also enables you to accomplish some other useful goals by putting buttons of your own making on the toolbar. With custom tools you can do the following:

- Run Word commands that are not on menus or buttons

- Run your macros

- Change fonts

- Insert AutoText

- Apply styles

You even get to select or draw an image for your custom buttons!

You can save time later by looking through the global list of Word for Windows commands now. Take the time to scan through the commands listed in the All Commands category on the Toolbars tab of the Customize dialog box. Many of these commands are very useful. Most of them perform a function for which you normally would have to choose a command and make a selection from a dialog box. Creating buttons for them can save you time.

To assign a command or macro to a button on the toolbar, follow these steps:

1. Display the toolbar to which you want to add the button.

2. Click the right mouse button while the pointer is positioned on the toolbar, and then choose Customize from the shortcut menu. Or choose View, Toolbars to display the Toolbars dialog box and then click the Customize button.

3. Select either All Commands, Macros, Fonts, AutoText, or Styles from the Categories list.

4. Drag one of the commands, macros, AutoText names, or styles from the central area onto your toolbar.

   If a button image exists for this command or style, a button with that image will appear on the toolbar. If a button image does not exist for the command or style you dragged, the Custom Button dialog box appears (see fig. 36.5). Your custom buttons can contain a text label, an image, or an image that you draw.

▶ See "Recording Macros," p. 1054

VIII

Customizing with Word

Fig. 36.5

Create custom buttons by using the Custom Button dialog box.

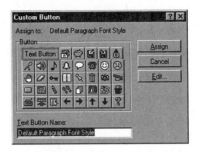

5. Choose one of the predrawn buttons, type a text label, or draw your own button image, as described in "Creating Custom Button Images," the next part of this section.

6. Click the Assign button and then choose Close in the Customize dialog box.

Creating Custom Button Images

When you add your own button that does not have an image, you have the opportunity to create the button image.

To create custom buttons for your toolbar, follow these steps:

1. Drag and drop the item from the Customize dialog box to the toolbar. The Custom Button dialog box appears.

2. Choose one of the following options:

   Text Button. Type the label in the Text Button Name box that you want to appear within the button.

   Images. Click an image if you want to use that face on the button.

3. Choose Assign if you want to use the text label or the button image as it is. If you want to draw your own button image, see "Drawing Your Own Button Images" later in this section.

4. Choose Close in the Customize dialog box.

Troubleshooting

I'm wasting time reselecting and redrawing icons. What do I do?

If you have buttons that you need occasionally and you don't want to reselect or redraw them every time you need them, create a toolbar used for storage. Drag copies of buttons you think you might need again onto this toolbar. If you need one of these buttons later, just display the storage toolbar you created. Then open the Customize dialog box and drag a copy of the needed button to an active toolbar. To drag a copy, press the Ctrl key while dragging.

Drawing Your Own Button Images

To draw a custom button image, follow these steps:

1. Perform the steps given earlier in "Creating Custom Button Images," but do not click the Assign button in step 3.

2. If you want to modify a button image that appears in the Button group, select that image. If you want to start drawing with a clear background, click the Text Button image.

3. Click the Edit button to display the Button Editor dialog box. If you selected a button image to edit, it appears in the Picture box (see fig. 36.6).

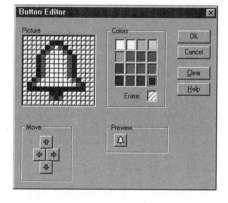

Fig. 36.6
Draw custom button faces by clicking a color and then dragging in the Picture box. Use the Move buttons to reposition your drawing on the button.

4. Use the Button Editor to draw a button image in the Picture box.

   Click a color and then click or drag in the Picture box to paint. Click the Erase color and then drag over the Picture to erase cells. Watch the

Preview box to see what the tool looks like at its actual size. Click the Move buttons to reposition your drawing within the button.

5. Choose OK to accept the drawing and paste it onto the button.

6. Choose Close to close the Customize dialog box.

Transferring Toolbars with the Organizer

At times, you will want to transfer a toolbar from one template to another. You or a coworker might create a template that has a toolbar you can use in another template. It's easy to transfer toolbars between open templates.

To transfer toolbars between two open templates, follow these steps:

1. Open a template containing the toolbar you want to copy. Also open the template that you want to receive a copy of the toolbar.

◄ See "Changing a Template," p. 186

2. Unprotect the templates if they are protected by choosing Tools, Unprotect Document. You cannot transfer from or to a protected template.

3. Activate the template from which the toolbar will come.

4. Choose Tools, Macro. The Macro Dialog box appears.

5. Click the Organizer button in the Macro dialog box; select the Toolbars tab (see fig. 36.7).

Fig. 36.7
Select a toolbar from any open template and copy it to any other open template.

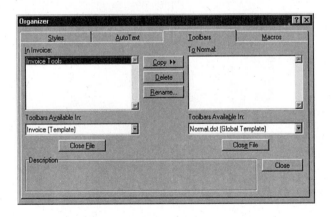

6. From the Toolbars Available In drop-down list box, select the template containing the toolbar.

7. In the right side of the Organizer, select from the Toolbars Available In drop-down list box the template you want to receive a copy of the toolbar.

8. In the left side of the Organizer, select from the In *TemplateName* list box the toolbar you want copied.

9. Click the Copy button. The toolbar is copied from the template on the left side to the template on the right side.

10. If you want to copy additional toolbars, return to step 6. If you are finished, click the Close button. When you return to the documents and close them, you are prompted to save the templates and the changes to their toolbars.

Customizing the Menu

Word offers far more commands than you would ever want on the menu at a single time. But you can put any of Word's commands on an existing or custom menu. In fact, you can also add to the menu any macro, style, font, or AutoText that you want to be readily available. You can add these features to the menus associated with a specific template or to the global menus associated with the NORMAL.DOT template.

Adding Commands to Menus

You can add a command to any predefined menu or custom menu that you build. To make your menus easier to use, you can also add separator lines between groups of commands, and you can place a new command anywhere on the menu.

To add a command to a menu, follow these steps:

1. Before you customize a menu, open any document to change the global menu or open the specific template to change the menu associated with that template.

2. Choose Tools, Customize, and then select the Menus tab in the Customize dialog box (see fig. 36.8).

3. Select from the Save Changes In drop-down list box the template you want the custom menu attached to (select NORMAL.DOT for the global menu).

4. Select from the Categories list box the type of feature you want to add.

VIII

Customizing with Word

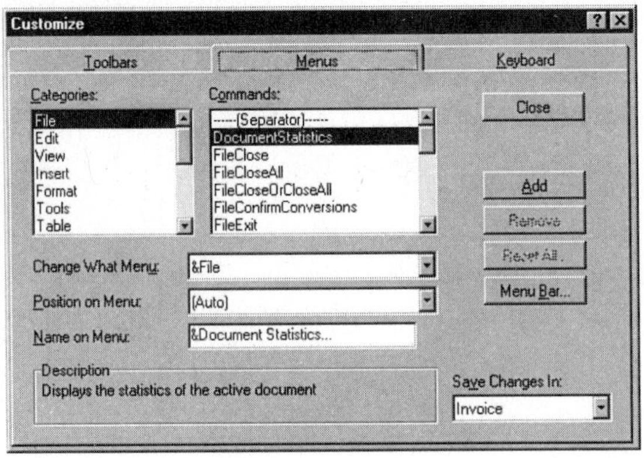

Fig. 36.8

You can add to Word's menus any of hundreds of commands or your own macros, styles, and AutoText.

5. Select from the list box at the top center the specific item you want to add. Depending on the choice you made in step 4, this item could be a command, style name, macro name, AutoText, or font name.

   If you want to add a separator line between groups of related commands on a menu, select the choice

   `------(Separator)------`

Tip

Notice that you can even add commands to shortcut menus.

6. Select from the Change What Menu drop-down list the menu to which you want to add the command.

7. Select from the Position on Menu drop-down list the location for the new command. Here are your choices:

   Auto. Word attempts to group new commands.

   At Top. New command placed at top of menu.

   At Bottom. New command placed at bottom of menu.

   (Existing Command). New command placed below the selected command.

8. Type the name of your command in the Name on Menu box.

   Type an ampersand (**&**) before the letter you want underlined as the hot key. Pick a letter that hasn't been used before in that menu. Word makes a recommendation for the command's name, but you do not have to accept it. You can edit the recommended name.

9. Click Add or Add Below.

10. Return to step 3 to add more commands, or choose Close.

> **Caution**
>
> It's very easy to click the Close button instead of the Add button, because in most dialog boxes, you choose OK or Close after you finish. If your new command doesn't appear on the menu, try the procedure again, making sure that you click Add or Add Below before closing the dialog box.

The macro description, displayed in the Description area at the bottom of the dialog box, appears in the status bar at the bottom of the screen when the newly added command is selected on the menu.

Removing or Resetting Commands

To remove a predefined or custom command from a menu, follow these steps:

1. Open a document with a menu containing the command you want to remove.

2. Choose Tools, Customize, and then select the Menus tab.

3. Select from the Save Changes In drop-down list box the template for this document (select NORMAL.DOT if the menu is available to all documents).

4. Select the menu containing the command you want to remove from the Change What Menu drop-down list box.

5. Select from the Position On Menu drop-down list box the command you want to remove. Commands appear in the list in the same order in which they appear on the menu.

6. Click the Remove button.

7. Continue removing items if necessary, or choose Close if you are finished.

Notice that when you remove a command, the other commands on the menu move up. Press the Esc key if you decide not to remove a command and want to return the pointer to normal.

VIII

Customizing with Word

To restore menus to the original configuration provided by Word for Windows, follow these steps:

1. Open a document containing the menu you want to restore.

2. Choose Tools, Customize, and then select the Menus tab.

3. Select from the Save Changes In list box the template that contains the menu.

4. Click the Reset All button.

5. Respond Yes when asked to confirm that you want to reset the menu in that template.

6. Choose Close to close the Customize dialog box.

Adding or Removing Menus

When you create templates designed for a specific type of work, you may want to remove menus that are not needed. In some cases, fewer menus means fewer training and support problems. You can remove entire menus and add your own menus that contain custom commands.

To add a custom menu, follow these steps:

1. Open a document that uses the template that is to contain the added menu.

2. Choose Tools, Customize, and then select the Menus tab.

3. Select from the Save Changes In drop-down list, in the lower-right corner, the template to contain the new menu.

4. Click the Menu Bar button. The Menu Bar dialog box appears.

5. Type the name of the new menu in the Name on Menu Bar text box. Type **&** (ampersand) before the activating letter or hot key.

6. Select from the Position on Menu Bar list box the menu you want to appear to the left of your menu (see fig. 36.9).

   Or choose (First) to place the new menu at the far left end of the menu bar, or (Last) to place the new menu at the far right end of the menu bar.

7. Click the Add or Add After button.

Fig. 36.9
From the Menu Bar
dialog box, you
can remove entire
menus or add new
menus for your
custom com-
mands.

8. Return to step 4 to add more menus, or choose Close to return to the Customize dialog box.

9. Continue to add commands to the new menu from the Customize dialog box, or choose Close to return to the document.

Note

You may accidentally (or purposefully) delete the Tools menu or the Tools Customize command. You are then faced with that sinking-in-the-pit-of-the-stomach feeling because you seem to have no way to reset the menu (it looks like you can't get to the Customize dialog box). But there is a way! Choose View, Toolbars, or click the right mouse button on a toolbar; then choose Customize. When the Customize dialog box appears, select the Menus tab and restore the menu or command you deleted.

To remove a menu, follow the procedure described previously to select the template and display the Menu Bar dialog box. Select the menu from the Position on Menu Bar list box and then click the Remove button. Respond Yes to confirm deleting the menu and its menu items.

Restore menus to their original display by selecting the template containing the menu from the Save Changes In drop-down list box and then clicking the Reset All button. Respond Yes to confirm that you want to reset the menus. Click Close to return to the template.

Assigning Commands and Macros to Shortcut Keys

Shortcut keys enable you to perform routine operations quickly without moving from the keyboard to the mouse. You should consider assigning shortcut keys to frequently used menu options.

Many of Word for Windows' commands and options are assigned to shortcut keys in the global template, NORMAL.DOT. Pressing Ctrl+B, for example,

◀ See "Inserting
Frequently
Used Material,"
p. 151

applies boldface to selected text. These key combinations are global; they work with all documents unless they have been deleted.

If you did not assign a key combination to a macro when it was created, you can assign it using the following procedure.

To assign key combinations to Word's predefined commands, your own macros, styles, fonts, or AutoText, follow these steps:

1. Open a document that uses the template that you want to contain this shortcut keystroke.

2. Choose Tools, Customize, and select the Keyboard tab (see fig. 36.10).

Fig. 36.10
Assign shortcut keys to almost any of Word's features to increase your work efficiency.

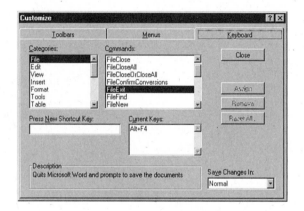

3. Select from the Save Changes In drop-down list box the template you want to contain the shortcut.

4. Select from the Categories list box the type of feature.

5. Select a specific feature from the list box at the top center of the dialog box.

Check the Current Keys list box to see if the command you have selected has an existing shortcut key. It may already have one assigned.

6. Select the Press New Shortcut Key box, and then press the shortcut key combination you want. To enter a combination, you must press a letter while holding down an individual key or combination of the Ctrl, Alt, and Shift keys (Ctrl+Alt+Q, for example). Remove a key combination from the edit box by pressing the backspace key.

Tip
You can create double-keystroke combinations, such as Alt+B,F, by pressing Alt+B, releasing them both, and then pressing F.

Caution

If the keystroke combination you press in step 6 has already been assigned, you see the command it has been assigned to under the title `Currently Assigned To:` on the left side of the dialog box. (This message only appears while you are assigning a keystroke.) Combinations that have not been assigned display `[unassigned]`.

---

7. Click the <u>A</u>ssign button.

8. Continue to make more shortcut key assignments, or choose Close.

To return to the default keyboard assignments, display the Customize dialog box and select the <u>K</u>eyboard tab. Select the template containing the shortcut keys you want removed; then choose the Re<u>s</u>et All button. Choose <u>Y</u>es to confirm that you want to reset the key assignments for the selected template. Word for Windows restores the original shortcut keys for that template. ❖

Chapter 37

Recording and Editing Macros

Word for Windows macros enable you to automate frequent procedures and command choices with minimal effort. The easiest way to create a macro is to record your keystrokes and commands with the macro recorder. You also can modify recorded macros or write them directly—once you know WordBasic, the programming language included with Word for Windows. You can test and modify your macros using the Word for Windows macro editor.

You can assign your macros or Word for Windows built-in commands to buttons in your documents, buttons on toolbars, custom menu commands, or new shortcut keys. You can turn Word for Windows into a word processor specially designed to handle the work you face or the industry you are in.

In some word processors, all automation must be done with macros. Word for Windows is more powerful and flexible. Word for Windows also gives you styles, AutoFormats, Style Gallery, field codes, and AutoText entries to make your work easier.

In this chapter, you learn how to:

- Record macros

- Save macros for use with any document or for use with a specific document

- Run macros that are global or specific to a template

- Edit macros that you have recorded

- Display an input dialog box and enter the typed information anywhere in your document

- Run macros automatically

Using Word's Built-In Automation Features

Many of the tasks performed by macros in other word processors can be done more efficiently with the macro features shown in the following table. It is much faster and more manageable to use these built-in features than it is to program in WordBasic. In some cases, you may need to "bind" together features in the table into a procedure, or you may need to create a custom process. That is when you should use a macro. The built-in features that will help you automate Word are the following:

Feature	Function
Style	Manually applies a collection of formats. Redefining the collection of formats in a style changes the appearance of the style throughout the document
AutoFormat	Automatically applies styles to documents that have a consistent layout
Style Gallery	Displays a list of named document types. Selecting from the list shows you what your document will look like using this predefined layout and style
Field codes	Automates entries such as the current date or filling a form
AutoText	Repeats frequently used text, tables, or pictures

Recording Macros

Macros can be recordings of keystrokes and commands or sophisticated programs you build. Even simple recorded macros can significantly improve your work efficiency. Some of the simple tasks and procedures you can easily automate with a macro include the following:

- Opening, selecting, and updating a document filled with field codes

- Adding custom zoom or edit buttons to the toolbar

- Creating a shortcut key to toggle table gridlines on or off

- Opening and arranging collections of files that are used together

- Removing styles or heading levels

- Opening a document and immediately moving to the last location edited

- Opening a document and immediately switching to outline view

- Storing different display and work settings so you can switch between them easily

- Copying selected data from the active sheet to the end of a second document

- Requesting data from the user, checking it, and entering it in a book-mark (a hidden location placeholder)

◀ See "Marking Locations with Bookmarks," p. 157

- Reformatting the active document to meet prerecorded layout and print settings

Deciding How Your Macro Will Work

Before you create a macro, you need to decide whether it affects a specific portion of the document, the currently selected portion, or the entire document. If the macro always affects a specific part of a document, insert bookmarks in the document that name the specific text or graphic so that the macro can find these parts easily. If you want a macro to work on whatever is selected when you run it, make your selection before you begin recording the macro.

You also must decide whether you want to make a *global macro* (a macro that can be used with any document) or a *template macro* (a macro that can be used only with documents based on that template).

Specifying Where Macros Are Stored

Macros are stored in three different ways—as commands, global macros, or template macros. *Commands* are built-in macros stored within the Word for Windows program, WINWORD.EXE. Many of these built-in macros are menu commands, such as <u>F</u>ile, <u>N</u>ew. Many of these commands do not exist on the menu but are useful when added to a shortcut key or toolbar button, or used within one of your macros. Macros that you record or write are stored as a *global* or *template* macro. Global macros are stored in the NORMAL.DOT template and are available to all documents and templates. Template macros are stored in a specific template and are available to only those documents based on that template.

VIII

Customizing with Word

You can ensure that a macro is available in all documents by declaring it as a global macro. If you store too many macros as global macros, however, you clutter your NORMAL.DOT file with macros used for a specific purpose or for a specific document. You should save macros designed for a specific purpose with the appropriate template. Save macros as global macros only when they need to be shared by many documents.

When you record your macro, you will be given the opportunity of selecting whether the macro will be a global macro, stored in NORMAL.DOT and available to all documents, or whether it will be stored in a specific template and available only to documents based on that template. Should you change your mind later about where you want the macro stored, you can use the Organizer, described later in this chapter, to copy the macro from one template to another.

Preparing to Record a Macro

Before you record a macro, there are a few things you may want to do first. This preparation is something that becomes automatic after you have recorded a few macros, but if you are new to the process, running through the following checklist can prevent you from having to re-create the macro many times. You should consider the following items in the order they are described:

1. Practice the procedure you want to record and know the order in which you want to choose commands or select items.

2. Decide whether you want the macro to be global, so any document can use it, or to be template-specific, so only documents based on that template can use it.

3. Decide on a macro name that is descriptive but does not include spaces or unusual characters. It must begin with a letter.

4. Decide how you want to run your macro. Macros can be run by choosing Tools, Macro; a button on the document; a toolbar button; a custom menu command; or a shortcut key. Macros also can be run automatically when you open or close a document, or start or exit Word.

5. Open a document of the type in which you want to use the macro. If you want the macro available to all documents, the document should be based on NORMAL.DOT. If you want to use the macro only with documents from a specific template, open a document based on that template. You can see which template a document is based on by choosing File, Templates.

The template you want your macro stored in must be open before you start recording. This does not mean you have to open the DOT file that contains a template. Opening a document based on a template automatically opens the template and hides it.

Prepare the document as it would be when you want the macro to run.

Decide whether you want to select the text or object and then run the macro, or if you want the macro to make the text and object selections. The first case enables you to use the macro on items you select manually. In the second case, the macro will always try to find the same text or object.

Decide how you want to move or make selections during the recording. Some of the most frequent ways of recording moves and selections are:

■ Naming a location by choosing Edit, Bookmark before the recording starts. During the recording you can then select or return to that named location by choosing Edit, Go To.

■ Moving to a relative or specific position in the document by choosing Edit, Go To and any move code described in Chapter 5, "Editing a Document." You can use locations such as **P12L2** (page 12, line 2).

■ Moving to the last edited location by pressing Shift+F5.

■ Moving to the beginning of the document by pressing Ctrl+Home.

■ Moving to the end of the document by pressing Ctrl+End.

■ Selecting the entire document by choosing Edit, Select All or pressing Ctrl+A.

■ Not selecting anything, so the macro affects whatever is selected when you run it.

Tip
Before you start recording your macro, make sure the appropriate template is open.

VIII

Customizing with Word

What Gets Recorded

Before you record a macro you need to understand what is recorded while the recorder is on. This will help keep you from recording unwanted changes, help you when you need to delete actions from a recorded macro and will help you set up Word prior to starting the macro recorder.

Dialog boxes are only recorded if you choose OK. The settings for all options in the dialog box are recorded. If you don't want some of the options to change when the macro runs, then you must edit the macro and remove the dialog options you don't want changed. (This is easy if you read this chapter.)

Dialog boxes that contain tabs, such as Tools, Options, only record the contents of a tab when you choose OK in that tab. For example, if you want to record Save, View, and Edit options, you must choose Tools, Options for each set of options, select the options, and then choose OK. You must do this once for each set of options.

Some items, such as the Ruler, toggle between on and off. The macro recorder records a single statement, ViewRuler. If the Ruler is already on, then ViewRuler turns the Ruler off. If the Ruler is off, then ViewRuler turns the Ruler on. That means that running a recorded macro could actually turn off the Ruler when you wanted it to stay on.

Some macro statements, such as ViewNormal, only record when you change to them. If you are in Page Layout view and switch to Normal view, the ViewNormal statement is recorded. But, if you are already in Normal view and you select View, Normal, nothing is recorded.

Recording a Macro

◀ See "Moving and Scrolling with the Keyboard," p. 136

Mouse actions are limited while the recorder is on. You can choose commands, but you cannot move or select within the document. If you are unfamiliar with using the keyboard to select or move, see the list of keyboard methods in the previous section.

To record a macro, follow these steps:

1. If you plan to use the macro with a template, open a document based on that template. If you plan to make the macro global, open any document.

2. Choose Tools, Macro, and then click the Record button. Alternatively, if the Macro toolbar is already displayed, click the Record button. The Record Macro dialog box appears (see fig. 37.1).

Fig. 37.1
Type macro names that begin with a letter and are as many as 80 characters in length.

3. Type the macro's name in the Record Macro Name text box.

   Enter a descriptive name. Macro names must begin with a letter and can be as many as 80 characters long. Do not use spaces. A combination of uppercase and lowercase letters is best (PrintEnvelope, for example).

4. If you want to assign the macro to a button on a toolbar, a command on a menu, or a shortcut key combination, choose one of the buttons in the Assign Macro To area. You can assign the macro, and you can also run it by choosing Tools, Macro. If you want, you can assign or reassign macros after the macro has been created.

◀ See "Assigning Commands and Macros to Shortcut Keys," p. 1049

5. Select the template in which to store your macro from the Make Macro Available To drop-down list box. This list only shows templates for documents that are open.

6. Enter a description in the Description text box to help you remember what the macro does. This description appears in the Macro dialog box and in the status bar.

7. Click OK.

The REC indicator in the status bar changes to bold, the Macro Recording toolbar appears at the top left of the document window, and the mouse pointer changes to resemble a pointer attached to a cassette tape. The recorder is on and is recording all your commands and keyboard actions.

If you want to pause the macro momentarily so you can check commands or the document, click the Macro Pause button in the Macro Recording toolbar. Click the button a second time to restart macro recording.

Complete the process you want to record. If you make a mistake, choose Edit, Undo as you normally would. If you are working in a dialog box, choosing Cancel prevents the dialog box from being recorded. Text that has just been typed and is backspaced out is not recorded.

To stop the recording, choose Tools, Macro, then click the Stop Recording button to turn off the macro recorder. Choose Close to close the Macro dialog box. If you are using the mouse, you can click the Stop button on the Macro Record toolbar.

VIII

Customizing with Word

Recording a Sample Macro

Tip

The macro re-
corder does not
record commands
used inside appli-
cations like
Microsoft Excel or
Microsoft Graph.

The following procedure illustrates how easily you can record a macro. Follow
these steps to record a macro that sets up Word for Windows screens and
options for the way you might want to work. This type of macro is convenient when many people use the same computer, but each person prefers
different custom settings. Running the macro enables you to quickly restore
toolbar, view, and other settings.

Before starting the recorder, set up Word for Windows so the commands and
options you choose will be recorded. An earlier section in this chapter, "What
Gets Recorded," describes some rules about preparing to record.

To make sure this macro records your toolbar selections, makes the transition
to normal view, and turns the Ruler on, prepare Word for Windows. Hide all
toolbars by choosing <u>V</u>iew, <u>T</u>oolbars and deselecting the checked toolbars.
Turn off the Ruler with <u>V</u>iew, <u>R</u>uler.

To turn on the recorder and name your macro, follow these steps:

1. Open a document. Because this will be a global macro attached to
   NORMAL.DOT, any document will do.

2. Choose <u>T</u>ools, <u>M</u>acro, and click the Rec<u>o</u>rd to display the Record Macro
   dialog box.

3. Type **MyWorkspace** in the <u>R</u>ecord Macro Name text box.

4. Skip the Assign Macro To group. You can use the methods in Chapter
   36, "Customizing the Toolbar, Menus, and Shortcut Keys," to assign the
   macro at a later time.

5. Select the All Documents (NORMAL.DOT) item from the Make Macro
   Available To drop-down list.

6. Enter **Changes Word to my workspace settings** in the <u>D</u>escription
   text box, shown in figure 37.2.

Fig. 37.2
The Record Macro
dialog box enables
you to name the
macro, store it in a
template, and
assign it to a
toolbar, menu, or
keystroke.

7. Click OK.

The macro recorder is now on, and the Macro Recording toolbar appears on-screen. Follow the next steps to record the MyWorkspace macro:

1. Choose View, Normal to set the screen to Normal view.

2. Choose View, Ruler to display the ruler that you had previously turned off.

3. Choose View, Toolbars and select the Standard, Formatting, and Drawing check boxes. Deselect the Macro Record check box, which is on because you are recording a macro. (This hides it so you are not able to use it to pause or stop the macro.) Choose OK.

4. Choose View, Zoom, and then enter **85** in the Percent spinner box. Choose OK.

5. Choose Tools, Options, and select the Edit tab. Select the Typing Replaces Selection and the Drag-and-Drop Text Editing check boxes.

6. Select the Save tab. Select the Allow Fast Saves check box and deselect the Automatic Save Every __ Minutes check box. Choose OK to record your selections for this tab.

7. Choose Tools, Macro, click the Stop Recording button, and finally choose Close.

To save the macro, choose File, Save All. If you attempt to close a document attached to a template and that template contains an unsaved macro, you will be asked whether you want to save changes to the template.

Your macro is now stored in the NORMAL.DOT template, so it is available no matter which document is active. Keep the MyWorkspace macro you just recorded; you will use it when you learn how to edit a macro.

Troubleshooting

I recorded a macro, but after restarting Word, the macro is no longer available.

This problem may be caused by two things. You may have forgotten to save the macro, or you may have stored the macro in a template that is not available when

(continues)

(continued)

you restart Word. To make sure you save a macro after recording it, choose <u>F</u>ile, Save All. When you are asked whether you want to save changes to the template, respond by clicking Yes. The second problem occurs if you save the macro to a specific template rather than saving it to the NORMAL.DOT template. Macros that are stored in a specific DOT file are only available when a document based on that template (DOT file) is open.

While recording a macro, I chose the wrong command.

◄ See "Marking Locations with Bookmarks," p. 157

◄ See "Creating a New Template," p. 188

If you are in a dialog box while the recorder is on, click the Cancel button or press Esc to close the dialog box. None of your selections in the dialog box will be recorded. If you have already completed a command or closed a dialog box, then choose <u>E</u>dit, <u>U</u>ndo, and the last command will be removed from the macro. If too many commands have been chosen to use <u>E</u>dit, <u>U</u>ndo, use the editing techniques at the end of this chapter to remove the incorrect macro statement from the recording. Remember which command you want removed. The macro statement you want to remove will have a similar name.

When you run the macro, you may notice some errors. Later, you will be able to edit the macro.

Running a Macro

After you record a macro, you should test it. Save your document so that if the macro doesn't do what you wanted, you can recover your document and edit it.

The following list describes the ways you can run a macro:

- Select the macro from the Macro dialog box, and then click the <u>R</u>un button.

- Create an Auto macro that runs when you open or close a document, or start or exit Word for Windows.

◄ See "Inserting Field Codes," p. 597

- Click a {MACROBUTTON} field code in a document. {MACROBUTTON} field codes display a button in a document that runs a macro.

- Click a standard or custom button in a toolbar.

- Choose a custom command from a menu.

■ Press a shortcut key combination.

■ Run the macro under the control of another macro.

■ Run the macro under the control of a Dynamic Data Exchange (DDE) command.

The Auto macros are described in this chapter in the section, "Automating a Template." Creating custom tools, buttons, commands, and shortcut keys is described in Chapter 36, "Customizing the Toolbar, Menus, and Shortcut Keys."

You can run a global macro at any time because NORMAL.DOT is always available. If you want to run a macro that is stored in a specific template, you must have an open document that is based on that template.

◄ See "Using Templates as a Pattern for Documents," p. 178

To run a macro, follow these steps:

1. Activate a document on which the macro is designed to work. If the macro is designed to work with items preselected, select those items.

2. Choose Tools, Macro to display the Macro dialog box (see fig. 37.3).

Fig. 37.3
A shortcut for running the macro is to double-click its name in the Macro dialog box.

3. Select from the Macros Available In drop-down list the location of the macro—All Active Templates, NORMAL.DOT (global template), or Word's built in commands.

4. Select or type the macro or command name in the Macro Name list box.

5. Click the Run button.

VIII

Customizing with Word

◄ See "Transfer-
ring Template
Contents Using
the Organizer,"
p. 182

◄ See "Assigning
a Command
or Macro
to a Toolbar
Button,"
p. 1040

◄ See "Adding
Commands
to Menus,"
p. 1045

If you assigned your macro to a shortcut key, menu command, or tool, you
also can run a macro by following step 1 in the preceding steps, and then
pressing the macro shortcut key, choosing the command, or clicking the tool.

Troubleshooting

*My macro does not appear in the Macro Name list of the Macro dialog box—what
happened to it?*

Make sure a document based on the template that contains your macro is open. Or
open a new blank document based on that template. Choose the name of this document or template from the Macros Available In drop-down list of the Macro dialog
box. If you want the macro to be available at all times, use the Organizer to transfer a
copy of the macro out of its current template into the NORMAL.DOT template.

Editing a Macro

The steps recorded by your macro are stored on a macro document as
WordBasic statements. You can see this document and edit these statements
much like a normal document. By editing a macro, you can remove commands recorded by mistake, modify recorded commands, or make your
macros more efficient.

You can view or edit your recorded macro, MyWorkspace, by following these
steps:

1. Choose Tools, Macro.

2. Select from the Macros Available In drop-down list where the macro is
   stored. (The MyWorkspace macro just recorded was stored in
   NORMAL.DOT and is global.)

3. Select or type the name in the Macro Name text box or list box.

4. Click Edit.

Figure 37.4 shows the newly recorded macro, MyWorkspace, in the macro
editing window.

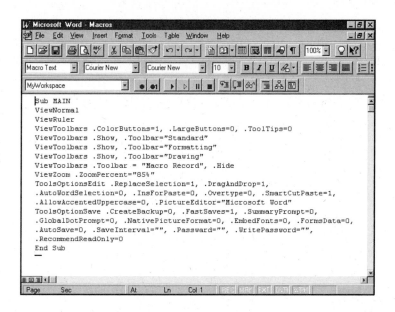

Fig. 37.4
Editing a macro uses the same editing techniques as a normal document. Macro statements match the command and options you chose during the recording.

When you open a macro for viewing or editing, Word for Windows displays the Macro toolbar at the top of the screen. The buttons on the bar are helpful when you troubleshoot macros.

The title bar shows the name and context of the macro being displayed—`Global: MyWorkspace`. The macro begins with the words `Sub MAIN` and ends with `End Sub`. All macros within WordBasic are considered *subroutines* (subprograms) that run under Word for Windows.

In your recording, you started by choosing View, Normal. Notice that the first statement is `ViewNormal`. Each statement that follows describes a command you chose.

Each item that follows ToolsOptionsEdit and ToolsOptionsSave corresponds to a selection in a list, edit box, option button, or check box. Notice that the items following these commands name an item in the dialog box. A `0` (zero) value indicates that a check box is not selected; a `1` indicates that it is selected.

When you are in the macro editor, use standard Word for Windows editing procedures and menu commands to edit, type, or delete macro statements and functions. You can tab to indent lines. Tabs are found in fixed locations, and you cannot format the characters in the macro code.

Tip
You can get help and a greater explanation on any of these WordBasic statements by clicking within the statement and pressing F1.

VIII

Customizing with Word

The capability to edit macros is useful even if you only record macros and never program in WordBasic. With simple edits, you can correct typographical errors, delete commands, copy macros or parts of macros from one document or template to another, and reorganize a macro by cutting and pasting.

◀ See "Selecting Text," p. 141

While a macro is open, the Macro toolbar remains on-screen. You can switch between macro windows and other document windows like you would change between any Word for Windows documents; choose the document from the Window menu, click an exposed portion of a document window, or press Ctrl+F6 to toggle between documents.

To close your macro editing window, activate the macro's window, and choose the document control menu icon by pressing Alt+- (hyphen). Choose Close. This closes the window and keeps the macro in memory. (It does not save the macro to disk.) If you choose File, Close instead, you close the macro window and the document containing the macro.

Saving a Macro

◀ See "Using Templates as a Pattern for Documents," p. 178

◀ See "Transferring Template Contents Using the Organizer," p. 182

Your new macro is stored in memory but is not automatically saved to disk. You can lose your macro if you forget to save it. Template macros must be saved before you close the template to which they are attached; global macros are saved automatically before you exit Word for Windows. Just as you save preliminary versions of documents every 15 minutes or so, occasionally save versions of your macros to protect against accidental deletion.

To save a macro to disk, choose File, Save All. The Save All command goes through your open templates and documents, including any macros you opened to view or edit, and determines whether they have been newly created or changed. Word for Windows prompts you to specify whether to save the changes to the document and to the template. If you close a document that has unsaved macros in its template, then you are given a chance to save the macros to the document. If you attempt to exit Word and there are global macros that have not been saved to the NORMAL.DOT template, and the Prompt to Save Normal Template is selected in Tools, Options, Save, you will be asked if you want to save those macros.

Modifying Your Macros

After you learn how to record macros that perform small tasks, you should learn how to modify your recorded macros so they handle special situations, prompt the user for data entries, or operate automatically when you open or close documents. And none of these changes requires learning how to program.

If you do want to learn how to program, you may want to learn more about WordBasic. WordBasic is the language in which macros are recorded. If you go beyond what this chapter teaches, you can learn how to write your own custom dialog boxes, control other Windows applications, and much more. But for now, this is the place to learn how to make your recorded macros even better.

When the macro recorder is on, every time you choose a command, tool, or shortcut key, Word stores a WordBasic statement in a macro document. That WordBasic statement is the equivalent of choosing the command. In most cases, you can read the statement and tell immediately which command is being referenced. Some of them are obvious, such as Bold, PasteFormat, or InsertTableOfContents.

One of the most familiar features of the Word for Windows program is its reliance on the dialog box to store information from the user. A dialog box is composed of one or more dialog elements: scrolling lists, check boxes, text boxes, option buttons, and so on. When you make a selection in a dialog box, Word for Windows stores the selections as a WordBasic statement in a macro that resides in a template. If you are familiar with how this dialog information is stored, you can modify it or delete unnecessary parts.

Understanding Dialog Recordings

Each time your record information from a dialog box in Word for Windows, all the information in the dialog box is stored in the macro document. The dialog box information is stored in the following format:

```
CommandName.Argument1 = Value, .Argument2 = Value,...
```

In this convention, `CommandName` is the menu and command that, when chosen, displays the dialog box. These are known as WordBasic *statements*. A statement runs a Word for Windows command. Each argument, such as `.Argument1`, corresponds to an element within the dialog box—for example, the name of a check box. The value for each argument describes the condition of that argument—`1` or `0` if a check box is selected or cleared, for example, or text enclosed in quotes for the contents of an edit box. For example, the Font tab of the dialog box from the F<u>o</u>rmat, <u>F</u>ont command is recorded as follows:

```
FormatFont .Points = "11", .Underline = 1, .Color = 0,
➥.Strikethrough = 0, .Superscript = 0, .Subscript = 0,
➥.Hidden = 0,
➥.SmallCaps = 0, .AllCaps = 0, .Spacing = "0 pt",
➥.Position = "0 pt", .Kerning = 0, .KerningMin = "", .Tab = "0",
➥.Font = "Times New Roman", .Bold = 1, .Italic = 0
```

The statement `FormatFont` describes the dialog box. Each element of the dialog box follows this. For example, `.Points = "11"` means that the point size was set to 11. Notice the `.Font`; this shows you which font was selected. Check boxes are recorded as `1` for selected and `0` for deselected. Notice that the `.Bold` check box is selected, but the `.Italic` check box was not.

The recorded macro is a straightforward guide to the user's selections within the dialog box. Each option in the dialog box is represented by an item in the recorded macro.

Dialog item names are preceded with a period, text values are enclosed in quotation marks, and selected or cleared values for Bold, AllCaps, and so on, are identified by a `0` for clear and a `1` for selected. When an item (`.Color`, for example) requires the user to choose from among several values in a list, the number of the selected value is stored in the argument. Auto is the first choice in the `.Color` list box, so the `.Color` item's value is 0.

Using What You Want from a Recording

There are two very simple edits you can make to your recorded macros that can improve them. (Editing is described earlier in this chapter.) Using the previous WordBasic code as an example, you can edit the line to change the action of the statement. If the code was originally:

```
FormatFont .Points = "11", .Underline = 1, .Color = 0,
➥.Strikethrough = 0, .Superscript = 0, .Subscript = 0,
➥.Hidden = 0, .SmallCaps = 0, .AllCaps = 0, .Spacing = "0 pt",
➥.Position = "0 pt", .Kerning = 0, .KerningMin = "", .Tab = "0",
➥.Font = "Times New Roman", .Bold = 1, .Italic = 0
```

you can change the size of the font to 14 by changing the argument `.Points = "11"` to **.Points = "14"**. Or you can make the font different by editing the font argument to be **.Font = "Arial"**.

Check boxes that are selected in a dialog box such as .Bold = 1, can be deselected by changing their corresponding argument to a 0, such as .Bold = 0.
The value for an item selected from a list becomes the number of that item in
the list. (Remember counting starts at 0.) For example, instead of the color
being Automatic, which is the first (or 0) item, you could edit the .Color
argument to use the fourth color, so the argument would appear as

```
.Color = 3.
```

An important concept is that a statement only changes the listed arguments
following the statement. For example, if you use the previous FormatFont
statement on selected text, all the recorded characteristics of the text will be
changed. Even if you only wanted the bold to be recorded, you actually
record all the items in the dialog box. When you run this recording on text
with the Bookman font, the .Font statement changes the font to Times New
Roman—even though you only wanted bold.

The solution is to record the entire dialog box, then delete the arguments you
do not want changed when the macro runs. For example, if you want your
recording to only change the bold characteristic, you should edit the statement to look like

```
FormatFont .Bold = 1
```

Prompting for Input

One of the things you will probably want to add to your recorded macro is
the ability to request an entry from the user. WordBasic has a very simple
statement, InputBox$, that displays a pre-built dialog box for data entry.

The easiest way to create a data entry macro is to create a template that contains bookmarks at the locations where data will be inserted. When the user
chooses File, New and opens a new document based on the template, all the
appropriate text and graphics will be there, as well as the bookmarks that
indicate where the macro should insert entries. If you want to duplicate the
following code, you should create a document, then choose Edit, Bookmark
to put two bookmarks in. The first bookmark is named TextLocation and
marks where a name will be inserted. The second bookmark is NumberLocation
and marks where a number will be inserted. Save this document as a
template.

VIII

Customizing with Word

Close the template you have just created and choose File, New to open a new document based on that template. Turn on the macro recorder and name the new macro **InputData**.

To create a base recording you can modify, follow these steps while the macro recorder is on:

1. Press Ctrl+Home to move the insertion point to the beginning of the document.

2. Choose Edit, Go To, select Bookmark from the Go to What list box, select TextLocation from the Enter Bookmark Name list box, and choose Go To. The insertion point should move to the TextLocation position.

3. Choose Close to close the Go To dialog box.

4. Type a name.

5. Choose Edit, Go To, select Bookmark from the Go to What list box, select NumberLocation from the Enter Bookmark Name drop-down list box, and choose Go To. The insertion point should move to the NumberLocation position.

6. Choose Close to close the Go To dialog box.

7. Type a number.

8. Choose Tools, Macro, click the Stop Recording command, and choose Close. You also can click the Stop button on the Macro Record toolbar.

Your recording has produced a basic macro that you can now modify. You can edit your macro by choosing Tools, Macro, selecting the InputData macro from the Macro Name list, and then clicking the Edit button. Your macro code should look similar to the following code:

```
Sub MAIN
StartOfDocument
EditGoTo .Destination = "TextLocation"
Insert "Name"
EditGoTo .Destination = "NumberLocation"
Insert "10"
End Sub
```

Moving to Specific Locations in a Document

In the following procedures, you learn how to modify your recorded macro to produce the macro shown in the upper window of figure 37.5. This macro asks the user to type a name into an Input box and then inserts the name at the bookmark, `TextLocation`. The macro then asks the user to type a number into an Input box. The number comes from the Input box as text, so it must be converted back to a number (`Val`). It is then multiplied by 1.2, converted back to text (`Str$`), and the number is finally inserted at the bookmark `NumberLocation`.

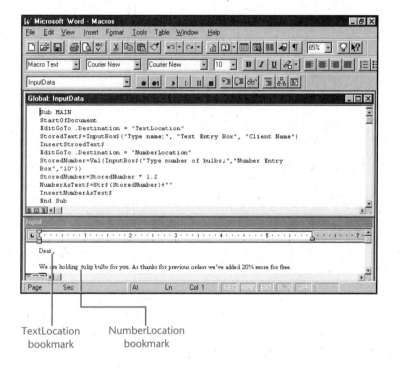

TextLocation
bookmark

NumberLocation
bookmark

Fig. 37.5

The macro in the upper window displays dialog boxes that prompt for data. The macro then inserts the data at the correct locations in the letter in the lower window.

This macro uses an Input box to ask the user for an entry. Figure 37.6 shows the first input box displayed by the macro in figure 37.5. The `InputBox$` statement uses the following layout:

```
InputBox$(Prompt$[,Title$][,Default$])
```

where `Prompt$` is text in quotes that tells the operator what to enter. `Title$` (optional) is text in quotes that is used as a title for the Input dialog box. `Default$` is the optional text in quotes that will appear in the edit box when the dialog box appears. Choosing OK without making an entry results in the default. If the user clicks Cancel, an error occurs that can be trapped for with an `On Error` statement.

Fig. 37.6

Use the `InputBox$` statement to add a dialog box to your recorded macro.

The first part of the code asks for and inserts a name:

```
StartOfDocument
EditGoTo .Destination = "TextLocation"
StoredText$ = InputBox$("Type name:", "Text Entry Box",
➥"Client Name")
Insert StoredText$
```

The `StartOfDocument` statement moves the insertion point to the beginning of the document. The `EditGoTo` was the recorded move to the bookmark named `TextLocation`. The text that the user types into the Input box will be stored in the text variable `StoredText$`. A *variable* is a name that can hold information for later use. The `$` at the end of the variable means that it will only hold text values. What the user typed is then inserted at the current insertion point by the `Insert` statement.

The second part of this example asks for a number. The number is then multiplied by 1.2 and inserted in the document:

```
EditGoTo .Destination = "NumberLocation"
StoredNumber = Val(InputBox$("Type number of bulbs:",
➥"Number Entry Box", "10"))
StoredNumber = StoredNumber * 1.2
NumberAsText$ = Str$(StoredNumber) + " "
Insert NumberAsText$
```

Working with a number takes a little more work because `InputBox$` returns a number as text, which will not work with math. To convert this number as text into a true number, the `InputBox$` statement is put inside a `Val` statement. This produces a true number that is stored in the variable `StoredNumber`. The amount in `StoredNumber` is multiplied by 1.2 and then stored back into the same variable `StoredNumber`. `StoredNumber` then gets converted back into text and has a blank space added to the end. The resulting number as text is now stored in `NumberAsText$`, which gets inserted by the `Insert` statement.

Notice that WordBasic automatically created a numeric variable from the word StoredNumber as soon as it was used. Text variables are created by ending the variable name with **$**. (WordBasic does have the ability to dimension variables at the beginning of each module.)

The finished macro looks like this:

```
Sub MAIN
StartOfDocument
EditGoTo .Destination = "TextLocation"
StoredText$ = InputBox$("Type name:", "Text Entry Box",
➡"Client Name")
Insert StoredText$
EditGoTo .Destination = "NumberLocation"
StoredNumber = Val(InputBox$("Type number of bulbs:",
➡"Number Entry Box", "10"))
StoredNumber = StoredNumber * 1.2
NumberAsText$ = Str$(StoredNumber) + " "
Insert NumberAsText$
End Sub
```

Automating a Template

You may want some macros to run automatically at certain times. To run a macro automatically, you only need to give them a special name. Table 37.1 describes Word for Windows' five Auto Macros.

Table 37.1 Running Macros Automatically

Macro Name	Function
AutoExec	Global macro that runs when you start Word for Windows. For example, the macro could change to a selected directory, prompt the user for preferences, or prompt for a document or template to start up in.
AutoExit	Global macro that runs when you exit Word for Windows. For example, it closes applications that Word for Windows macros opened, or automatically opens another application.
AutoNew	Global or template macro that runs when you create a new document based on the template containing AutoNew. For example, it displays an instruction message to help new users or update arguments in a new document.

(continues)

Table 37.1 Continued	
Macro Name	**Function**
AutoOpen	Global or template macro that runs when you open an existing document. For example, it updates arguments in an existing document, or automatically inserts text from a specified file.
AutoClose	Global or template macro that runs when you close a document. For example, it saves a changed document to a predetermined file name.

To prevent an automatic macro from running, hold down the Shift key when you perform the action that starts the macro. To prevent AutoOpen from running when you open a document, for example, hold down the Shift key while you click the OK button in the Open dialog box.

As table 37.1 indicates, automatic macros are especially useful for performing operations that set up a document when it opens. A handy use of the AutoNew macro, for example, is to update all fields in a document when you open a template for that document. This is especially useful for templates containing date and time fields and {FILLIN} field codes. The macro to update an entire document might appear as follows:

```
Sub MAIN
      EditSelectAll
      UpdateFields
      StartOfDocument
End Sub
```

This macro is useful when saved as an AutoNew macro with a template used for forms and containing field codes such as {fillin}. When a new document opens from a template having this macro, each field code is updated. For example, all the {fillin} input boxes are displayed in order.

Tip

You can learn more about WordBasic by recording macros, then pressing the F1 key as described here to learn about the statements and functions involved in your recording.

Getting Help on Macros

Word for Windows contains extensive help for macros. You can choose Help, Microsoft Word Help Topics, Contents to see the index of major help topics. To get an overview and detail on specific procedures, double-click the book icon next to WordBasic Reference and then double-click a subtopic.

You also can get information about a specific macro statement or function. For example, you may have recorded a macro and need to know which argument values are appropriate to turn a dialog option on or off. To find out about a specific macro statement, function, or argument, choose Tools, Macro to select a macro, and then change to the edit window. Move the insertion point into the macro statement or argument you need information about, and then press F1 (Help). Figure 37.7 shows the help screen for the InputBox$ macro statement and function. The numeric values that can be used or returned by Bold are shown.

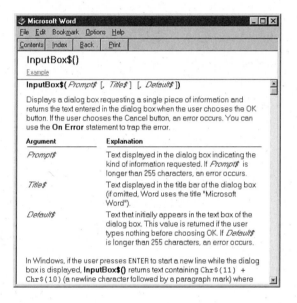

Fig. 37.7

Help for the currently selected WordBasic statement appears when you press F1. To display InputBox$ help as shown here, move the insertion point into InputBox$ and press F1.

Part IX

Techniques from the Pros

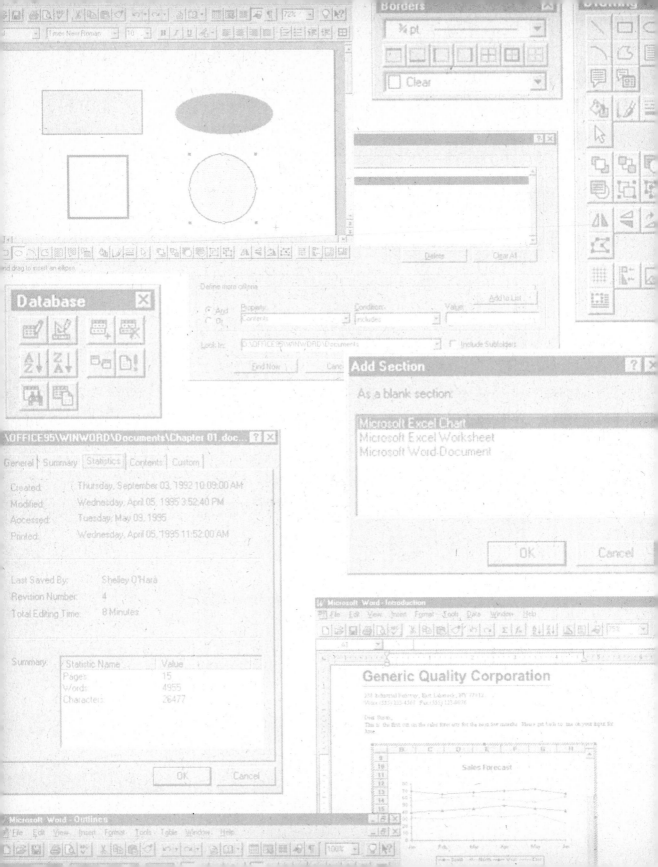

Chapter 38

Desktop Publishing

Karen Rose is the owner and publisher of *Little Red Book Press*, publishers of hand-bound books. She has taught for the University of California, Berkely Extension, and Sonoma State University.

In the years since word processing and desktop publishing programs have both come to be widely used, the two have grown more and more alike. Word processing programs have gained graphics capabilities. Desktop publishing programs have gained text editing capabilities. But until now, no one program really served both needs—the need to work powerfully with text and the need to incorporate graphics and illustrations easily.

Word for Windows successfully bridges the narrowing gap between word processors and desktop publishers. It has the very powerful text handling capabilities that serious publishers need, but at the same time it has surprisingly sophisticated graphics capabilities as well. And like all desktop publishing programs, what Word for Windows cannot do graphically, it can import from other specialized programs.

As you venture into the world of desktop publishing, keep in mind that desktop publishing is not a single skill—rather, it is the successful and creative use of many different skills. Throughout this chapter, you see examples of how you can use Word for Windows as a desktop publishing program, and you read about the

Techniques from the Pros

by Karen Rose

skills you need to do similar projects yourself. You also see references to earlier chapters in this book where you can learn more about the skills you need. But to become a successful desktop publisher, first become familiar with Word's basic features and capabilities. Learning these features makes your publishing job easier. Figure 38.1 shows you only some of the many capabilities Word offers in desktop publishing.

Fig. 38.1

This multiple-column newsletter shows some of Word's desktop publishing features.

In this chapter, you learn how to incorporate Word for Windows desktop publishing capabilities into your documents, particularly the following:

- Produce typeset-quality text using any font available on your printer or computer, in scalable sizes ranging from unreadable to bigger than the page

- Lay out text in columns and vary the number and style of columns throughout your document

- Incorporate lines, boxes, and shading

- Draw pictures directly on the page and layer them in front of or behind the text

- Manipulate text into a graphic form

- Insert into your publication illustrations created in other graphics programs

- Drag text and other objects freely on the page, with text wrapping around them

- Use templates and wizards to save time when you produce periodicals and styles to ensure consistent formatting throughout a publication

- Use Word for Windows to create publications including newsletters, catalogs, brochures, stationery, business cards, manuals, price lists, advertisements—anything that needs to make a visual impact on readers

Tools to Help You Work

Word for Windows includes many tools you can use as you're designing and developing a publication. You use them to help you work faster and more efficiently. The following sections describe these tools in more detail.

Working in Different Views

Normally, while you're working on a publication, you work in the Page Layout view so that you can see all the page elements (lines, columns, positioned graphics, and so on) and how they will print.

In Page Layout view, use the page size drop-down list on the Standard toolbar or choose View, Zoom to set the page size. The Page Width option is a good working size because you see the whole width of the page, but at a readable size (on most screens). Whole Page shows you the entire page from top to bottom—switch to this view frequently to see how your page is shaping up as a whole. If your publication includes facing pages, select Two Pages so that you can see how your pages look side by side; after all, that's what the reader sees when she opens your publication. All page layout views are completely editable.

◀ **See** "Controlling Your Document's Appearance On-Screen," p. 123

To select the Page Layout view, choose View, Page Layout. (If the horizontal scroll bar is displayed, click the Page Layout View button to switch to Page Layout view.) To hide everything on the screen except your page, choose View, Full Screen. Press Esc or click the Full Screen icon to return to the normal page.

Using the Toolbars

Word for Windows provides many different toolbars you can use to help you work more quickly. Each toolbar contains tools, or buttons, that you can click for quickly executing a command. Choose View, Toolbars or click the right mouse button in a toolbar to show a list of the toolbars you can display.

Using Templates

If you use the same layout over and over, create a template to save formatting and any text and graphics that you use each time. Newsletters are good candidates for templates: you can include the nameplate, headers and footers, styles for formatting, columns, mailers, postal indicia, mastheads, and anything else you use each issue. Templates save you the time of re-creating the issue from scratch each time. See the section, "Maintaining Consistent Formatting," later in this chapter.

You use a template each time you choose File, New.

Using Wizards

◀ **See**
"Using Wizards to Guide You," p. 191

Word for Windows includes Wizards that create instant awards, calendars, fax cover sheets, memos, newsletters, and more. Wizards include all the formatting and graphics needed in a publication—you just supply the text. Use them when you need a quick design. To use a Wizard, choose File, New and select a template that ends with the word Wizard. Wizards are described in Chapter 6, " Using Templates and Wizards for Frequently Created Documents."

Using Styles

◀ **See**
"Formatting a Document Automatically," p. 339

When you use repetitive formatting, format with styles. A style is a set of remembered formatting characteristics, such as font and size and text alignment. Word for Windows includes many built-in styles, but you can create your own. Styles are easy to apply, and when you format with styles, you can make global formatting changes instantly by simply changing the style. The quickest way to apply an existing style is to choose it from the drop-down list of styles on the Formatting toolbar. You can select from a gallery of pre-designed styles by choosing Format, Style Gallery and selecting one of the templates or wizards listed.

Spelling and Grammar Checkers

◀ **See**
"Checking Your Spelling," p. 211

◀ **See**
"Checking Your Grammar," p. 219

Professionals don't let their work go out the door with mistakes. Always use Word for Windows spelling checker and use the grammar checker when you're unsure about wording. Don't let the spelling checker substitute for careful proofreading, however; it doesn't catch misused words (such as to, too, and two, or there, their, and they're). But remember, we all make mistakes sometimes, and making mistakes isn't the end of the world.

To check spelling, choose <u>T</u>ools, <u>S</u>pelling or press F7. To check grammar, choose <u>T</u>ools, <u>G</u>rammar.

Automatic Corrections

If you're prone to certain spelling and grammar mistakes, or if there are particular replacements you'd like Word to automatically make for you, you can use Word's AutoCorrect tool as you type. Options include capitalizing the first word in a sentence, changing straight quotes to smart (typesetting) quotes, replacing certain characters with others, and correcting misspellings. To choose these options, choose <u>T</u>ools, <u>A</u>utoCorrect and select the options you want from the customizable list.

◀ **See** "Correcting Spelling Errors as You Type," p. 154

You also can have Word correct your spelling as you type. To check your spelling automatically, choose <u>T</u>ools, <u>O</u>ptions and select the Spelling tab (or choose <u>T</u>ools, <u>S</u>pelling, <u>O</u>ptions). Select <u>A</u>utomatic Spell Checking.

Laying Out the Page

Your publication's page layout includes the size of its pages, page orientation, and margins. These global choices are among the first you make as you start to assemble your publication.

Paper Size

You can design your publication to use a standard paper size, such as letter or legal. Or you can select a custom paper size. To select paper size, choose <u>F</u>ile, Page Set<u>u</u>p, then select the Paper <u>S</u>ize tab and make your selections.

◀ **See** "Determining Paper Size and Orientation," p. 432

- Select a standard size paper for newsletters, flyers, stationery, reports, catalogs, and brochures. Be aware of what sizes of paper your printer can accommodate.

- Choose a custom paper size to create invitations, business cards, envelopes, and other items that are smaller than usual. Most laser printers include a manual paper feed for printing custom paper sizes.

If your printer can't print on the size of paper you want to use for your project, check with a local service bureau to see if they have a printer with the capabilities you need. Then set up your project for the size you want, and take your file to the service bureau to print.

Paper Orientation

Word for Windows can print your publication vertically on the page, called *portrait orientation*, or horizontally, called *landscape orientation*. Paper orientation applies to any page size. To select paper orientation, choose File, Page Setup, select the Paper Size tab, and select either Portrait or Landscape.

- Use portrait orientation for most publications, such as newsletters and catalogs.

- Use landscape orientation to create two-fold (three-panel) brochures like the one in figure 38.2, signs, and horizontally oriented advertisements.

Fig. 38.2

This two-fold brochure was created using landscape orientation. Each of the brochure's two pages is divided into three columns of equal lengths.

ReLeaf needs your support.

Please help us continue our work of planting trees and teaching people about the importance of trees by sending your tax-deductible contribution to:

Sonoma County ReLeaf
P.O. Box 14806
Santa Rosa, CA 95402

Sonoma County ReLeaf
P.O. Box 14806
Santa Rosa, CA 95402

printed on recycled paper

Plant a tree, cool the globe.

Sonoma County
ReLeaf
A plan of action:

- For our communities
- For our neighborhoods
- For our schools

THE GREENHOUSE EFFECT:
HOW YOU CAN DO YOUR PART

The greenhouse effect is slowly but dangerously heating up our planet. It's going to take some lifestyle changes, including energy conservation, to help reverse the buildup of carbon dioxide in our atmosphere.

SONOMA COUNTY RELEAF
INVITES YOU TO DO YOUR PART:

- PLANT drought-tolerant trees on the southeast, southwest, or south sides of your home.
- ORGANIZE your neighbors to plant trees on your street.
- DRIVE a fuel-efficient car.
- CARPOOL or use public transit whenever possible.
- WALK or ride a bicycle for short trips.
- SWITCH off lights and air conditioning whenever possible.
- LOWER your thermostat to 68 degrees.
- RECYCLE glass, aluminum, and paper to save energy and trees.
- COMPOST your yard waste and kitchen scraps to reduce trash.

FOR MORE INFORMATION CALL:
Sonoma County ReLeaf
(707) 539-4119

California ReLeaf is a grassroots effort to plant and care for 20 million trees in towns and cities throughout the state by the year 2000.

Sonoma County ReLeaf as part of this statewide campaign has the following objectives:

- To educate about the implications of the global warming trend.
- To participate in the California ReLeaf campaign by planting thousands of trees around our homes, offices, shopping centers, streets, and highways.
- To encourage people through the act of planting a tree to enact their commitment to caring for our environment and the future of our earth.

Enclosed is my contribution to Sonoma County ReLeaf. Contributions will support tree plantings, community outreach, and education.

- ❏ $25
- ❏ $50
- ❏ $100
- ❏ $ ___

All contributions are tax-deductible. Make checks payable to ReLeaf:

ReLeaf/Friends of the Urban Forest
P.O. Box 14806
Santa Rosa, CA 95402

Please send me information on the following:

- ❏ Tree list and how to plant and maintain trees.
- ❏ Global warming fact sheets.
- ❏ How to organize neighborhood tree plantings.
- ❏ Energy conservation information.

Name _____
Address _____
City _____
State _____ Zip _____
Phone _____

Margins

Margins are the distance between text and the edges of the page. You can set top, bottom, left, and right margins for any size page. To set margins, choose File, Page Setup, select the Margins tab, and set your margins.

◀ **See**
"Setting Margins," p. 400

In any type of publication, margins may be your most important tool in creating unified white space on the page—whenever possible, be generous with your margins. Don't crowd the page.

Also, don't vary margins arbitrarily from page to page in your document.

Facing Pages for Newsletters, Catalogs, Magazines, and Books

You see facing pages when you open a magazine or book: the left and right pages face each other. To create facing pages, select mirror margins. Instead of left and right margins, you set inside and outside margins. Very often the inside margin is wider than the outside margin—both for design and to accommodate binding. To select facing pages, choose File, Page Setup, select the Margins tab, and select the Mirror Margins option.

- Use facing pages to create a newsletter, magazine, catalog, book, or any other type of publication that you plan to print on both sides of a sheet of paper and for which you want wider inside margins.

- When you're using mirror margins, position page numbers on the outside edges of each page.

Binding Gutters for Extra Margin Width

Even if you're not using facing pages, you can add extra space to the gutter for binding. If you add extra space on facing pages, you add it to inside edges; on regular pages, you add space to the left edge. Gutters don't change your margins but rather are added to margins. Gutters make the printing area of your page narrower, however. To add gutters, choose File, Page Setup, select the Margins tab, and select the gutter width you want using the Gutter option.

- Use gutters in any document in which you need extra margin space for binding. Examples include price lists, training manuals, and reports.

- Consider adding extra gutter width any time you design with facing pages.

Changing the Page Layout within a Document

◀ **See**
"Dividing a
Document into
Sections,"
p. 414

You can vary page layout options such as margins, headers and footers, number of columns, page numbers, and even page size and orientation within a single document. Any time you want to make these changes, you must insert a section break. A new section can start on the same page, the next column, the next page, or the next odd- or even-numbered page. To insert a section break, choose Insert, Break and select an option from the Section Breaks area. You can use a section break to do any of the following:

- To separate a one-column nameplate from the three-column text of a newsletter.

- To separate an envelope and letterhead, each with unique margins, in a single document.

- To start each new chapter in a book; this way each chapter will start on a right-facing page.

- To separate a report into sections so that each section can have unique headers and footers, or unique page numbering.

Look at figure 38.5, which shows an example of how a section break divides a newsletter into two-column and three-column sections.

Including Headers and Footers

◀ **See**
"Creating
Headers and
Footers,"
p. 417

Headers and footers appear in the top and bottom margins of each page in your document. They can include any font in any size, as well as illustrations, lines and boxes, automatic page numbers, the date or time, and even chapter numbers. You can format headers and footers using any of Word for Windows formatting commands. To add headers and footers, choose View, Header and Footer. You can use headers and footers in any of the following ways:

- In any type of multipage publication, including newsletters, books, reports, catalogs, price lists, and much more.

- To repeat text or graphics consistently on every page.

- Headers and footers can be different from section to section, or on the first page of a document. On a newsletter, for example, you usually want the first-page headers and footers to be different from those on remaining pages.

Positioning Text and Graphics in the Margins

Usually text is confined to the space between margins on your page—with the exception of headers and footers. But sometimes you want text and graphics to appear in the left or right margin of your page. You can use text in the margin if you frame the text or graphic and then position it in the margin. If you position a framed object so that it is only partially inside a margin, text on the page wraps around it. To frame text or an object, select it and choose <u>I</u>nsert, <u>F</u>rame. To position a framed object, drag it with the mouse or select it and choose F<u>o</u>rmat, Fra<u>m</u>e.

◀ **See**
"Positioning a Frame in a Margin," p. 745

Use text in the margin when you want to:

- Give emphasis to pull-quotes, sidebars, and illustrations in a newsletter by positioning them outside the regular text.

- Create an ad, flyer, or résumé with an illustration or big headline that extends across both the margin and text, with text wrapping around it.

Designing with Text

Text is the primary building block of most publications, because most publications are meant to be read. Although decisions about text may seem simple, they are important to your design.

Consistency is the first rule in working with text on the page: make your titles, headings, subheadings, pull-quotes, captions—any text you use regularly in your publication—consistent from use to use.

Selecting the Font

Windows comes equipped with two TrueType fonts that you use often in your desktop publishing projects: Times New Roman, a serif font; and Arial, a sans serif font. Your printer may include additional fonts, and you may purchase still others. Any fonts you've installed in Windows are available in Word for Windows, but even if you have only Times New Roman and Arial, you have enough variety for desktop publishing. To change fonts, position the insertion point where you want a new font to begin, or select existing text, and then choose F<u>o</u>rmat, <u>F</u>ont (or right-click on selected text and choose Font from the shortcut menu). Or select a different font from the fonts drop-down list box on the Formatting toolbar.

◀ **See**
"Changing Fonts," p. 263

Remember these simple design rules when you choose a font:

- *Serifs* are the small strokes at the ends of letters, and in general, fonts are either *serif* fonts or *sans serif* (without serifs) fonts. If your publication includes paragraphs of text to read, a serif font like Times is best—the serifs carry the eye from letter to letter and make reading easier. If you have a big, bold headline to be seen from a distance, a sans serif font like Arial is a better choice.

- Mix fonts but use only two or three (at most) per publication. Set body copy in Times New Roman, for example, and headlines in Arial.

- Use unusual or decorative fonts only when you have an unusual purpose. Use them sparingly.

- Make readability your primary consideration when you select a font.

Selecting the Font Size

◀ **See** "Changing Font Size," p. 265

With TrueType, you can make letters as tiny or as big as you want—from 1 to 1,638 points (non-TrueType printer fonts may be limited in size). Use 72-point type to create a one-inch letter. To change font size, position the insertion point where you want a new font size to begin, or select existing text, and then choose Format, Font (or right-click on selected text and choose Font from the shortcut menu). Or select a different size from the font size drop-down list box on the Formatting toolbar.

Follow these design rules when choosing a font size:

- Text for reading should be between 9 and 11 points for most fonts (although readability varies considerably among fonts, so print a sample before you decide). Text for subheadings and headlines should be from 14 points and up.

- If your publication includes titles, headings, and subheadings, size them consistently throughout your publication (an easy way to size headings is to use styles—see "Maintaining Consistent Formatting" later in this chapter). Be sure you have enough difference in the size of body text, subheadings, headings, and titles so that the reader can tell which is which at a glance.

Choosing Text Styles and Color

You can apply bold, italic, bold italic, and other styles to most fonts (you may not be able to choose these styles for some specialty fonts). You also can apply color to text—you see it in color on-screen, but you need a color printer to print color. To change font color, position the insertion point where you want a new color to begin, or select existing text, and then choose F̲ormat, F̲ont (or right-click selected text and choose Font from the shortcut menu).

◀ **See**
"Changing Character Colors,"
p. 273

Here are some thoughts to remember when choosing text styles and colors:

- Use text styles sparingly and meaningfully. Save bold for headlines and subheadings in a publication or for big headlines in flyers and ads. Reserve italics for titles and occasional emphasis. Use all caps rarely; small caps is a better design choice (all caps are hard to read and were used for emphasis or contrast when people used typewriters, not computers capable of producing typeset-quality output).

- Color is useful in publications that are never printed but rather are used on-screen or in a presentation that you project in front of an audience. In an ad or flyer or to create a banner or newsletter nameplate, try dark or light gray. Make the text big to compensate for the loss of contrast when text is lighter than black.

Using Typesetting Characters

Special typesetting characters take the place of a typewriter's straight quotation marks and double dashes, and they're easy to insert in Word for Windows. Instead of a double dash, use an em dash (—). Instead of straight quotation marks, use opening and closing quotation marks. To insert typesetting characters, choose I̲nsert, S̲ymbol and select the S̲pecial Characters tab.

◀ **See**
"Inserting Special Characters and Symbols,"
p. 281

Remember these things when you type your publication:

- An *em dash* is the width of your point size—if your text is 10 points, an em dash is 10 points wide. Use it to indicate a pause. An en dash is half the width of your point size; use it between numbers or times (for example, "from 9-12 p.m.").

- Always use "typesetting" quotation marks in a publication, rather than straight quotation marks. Typesetting quotation marks curve inward toward the text (see fig. 38.3). Use an opening quotation mark at the beginning of a quote and a closing quotation mark at the end; both single and double quotation marks are available. To save time, turn on "smart quotes" (Word's name for typesetting quotation marks) by choosing Tools, AutoCorrect and selecting Change "Straight Quotes" to 'Smart Quotes.'

Fig. 38.3

Always use typesetting quotation marks in a publication.

"Eat your peas," she said.
regular quotation marks

"Eat your peas," she said.
typesetting quotation marks

- Word for Windows includes other special characters, such as trademark (™) and register mark (®), that you should use when appropriate. If you'll use them a lot, have Word insert them for you automatically by choosing Tools, AutoCorrect and selecting Replace Text as You Type.

Controlling the Letter Spacing

◀ **See**
"Adjusting Character Spacing," p. 276

Word for Windows automatically controls the spacing between letters, and usually Word's setting is fine. You optionally can expand or condense spacing (called *tracking* when you use it on all your text), and you can turn on *kerning*, which adjusts the spacing between letter pairs. Usually, kerning reduces the space between adjacent letters like *AV* or *Yo* that may be too far apart with normal spacing. In Word for Windows, you can turn on automatic kerning, or you can kern letter pairs individually. To change letter spacing, select the text, and then choose Format, Font. Select the Character Spacing tab.

Here are some suggestions for when to use letter spacing:

- Turn on automatic kerning for type larger than body copy size—usually greater than 10 points.

- Kern headlines as needed. To kern individual letter pairs, position the insertion point between the two letters and condense the spacing as needed.

- For large headlines, select the entire headline and condense the spacing slightly, until it looks tight but not crowded.

- Sometimes you can condense, or track, text slightly to make it fit on a line when space is tight.

- Use expanded type only for special effects.

Using Titles, Headings, and Subheadings

Appropriate titles, headings, and subheadings help guide readers through text. When you see a title, you know an article is about to begin. When you see a subheading, you know a new concept is starting. These "meaning markers" are invaluable to readers.

Here are some hints about making your document more readable with headings and subheadings:

- Format titles, headings, and subheadings consistently. In your newsletter, for example, make the titles of all feature articles 24-point bold; make less important titles 18 points bold; and make subheadings 12-point bold.

- For titles, headings, and subheadings, choose a font that contrasts with the body copy font. A sans serif font, such as Arial, is a good choice.

- Use styles to maintain consistent formatting.

Determining Alignment and Justification

Text can be left-aligned, centered, right-aligned, or justified (aligned to both margins). To align text, select the text or position the insertion point inside the paragraph you want to align and choose Format, Paragraph. Select the Indents and Spacing tab and make a selection from the Alignment drop-down list box. Or, select the Align Left, Center, Align Right, or Justify button on the Formatting toolbar.

◀ **See** "Formatting a Document Automatically," p. 339

Here are some tips about using alignment effectively:

- Left-aligned text is the best choice for body copy. It is easiest to read because the reader's eye knows exactly where to go to start a new line.

- Use centered text sparingly—for invitations, logos, and, occasionally, headlines.

- Use right-aligned text only when you have a specific reason to do so, such as in tables, or in a header or footer on a right-facing page.

- When you use justified text (even on both sides), Word for Windows must increase the spacing between words. Be sure to use hyphenation with justified text to avoid gaping spaces between words. Choose Tools, Hyphenation to use automatic hyphenation.

Adjusting Line and Paragraph Spacing

◀ **See**
"Adjusting Line
and Paragraph
Spacing,"
p. 317

In Word for Windows, you can add extra space before and after paragraphs, and you can adjust the spacing between the lines in a paragraph. In typographical terms, the spacing between lines is called *leading* (pronounced "ledding"). You can adjust line spacing, or leading, by lines ("1.5 lines" or "double") or by some specified amount ("At Least" or "Exactly"). If you specify an amount, you measure it by points, the same way font size is measured. Normal leading for 10-point type, for example, is 12 points; to increase leading, you increase line spacing to a larger point size. To adjust line and paragraph spacing, choose Format, Paragraph and select the Indents and Spacing tab. Make selections from the Spacing group.

Here are some ideas for using line and paragraph spacing effectively:

- Add spacing before subheadings to help them stand out from the rest of your text.

- Add spacing after paragraphs instead of pressing Enter twice each time you finish a paragraph. Often half a line of extra spacing looks better than a whole line. If you need to change the spacing later, you can select all the paragraphs and make the change quickly.

- Use styles to apply line spacing consistently in your document.

- Increase line spacing (leading) when lines in your paragraph are longer than about 40 characters. Long, tightly spaced lines are hard to read because the reader's eye gets lost as it travels back to the left margin.

- Increase line spacing for graphical effect in pull-quotes, invitations, flyers, and other occasions when you're using type decoratively.

Keeping Text Together

Word for Windows breaks text at the bottom of a page regardless of whether the page ends at the beginning of a paragraph or between the lines of a two-line subheading. You can prevent unwanted breaks, however. To keep text together, select the text and choose Format, Paragraph. Select the Text Flow tab.

Use these options to control text flow:

- Select the Widow/Orphan Control option to prevent single lines at the beginning of paragraphs from appearing at the bottom of a page, or single lines at the end of a paragraph from appearing at the top of a page. Widows and orphans are bad form in any publication.

- Select the <u>K</u>eep Lines Together option when you don't want a paragraph to break between two pages.

- Select the Keep with Ne<u>x</u>t option when you want a subheading to stay with the paragraph that follows it.

Maintaining Consistent Formatting

Styles are one of word processing's greatest inventions (one that is shared by most desktop publishing programs). A *style* is simply a set of remembered formatting commands that you can apply instantly and change globally. Styles are invaluable to desktop publishers because they save time, enforce consistent formatting, and allow for experimentation. Styles are often included in templates. You can create or apply a style by choosing <u>F</u>ormat, <u>S</u>tyle.

◀ **See**
"Formatting a Document Automatically," p. 339

Here are some ideas for using styles in your publication:

- Use styles to format body copy, subheadings, headings, titles, pull-quotes, tables, lists—just about everything. You save time creating your publication because you have to invent your formatting only once. And your publication benefits from a consistent appearance.

- Use styles to experiment with design. If you format your whole publication with styles, you can change formatting throughout your publication just by changing the style. If you don't like the change, try something else.

- Use Word for Windows built-in heading styles to format anything you may later want to collect into tables, lists, or cross-references. You can change the style—you just have to keep the name.

Indenting Paragraphs

Don't press Tab to indent the first line of every paragraph. Instead, create an automatic indent. It saves time because each new paragraph you create is indented automatically. You can create indents by using the ruler or the Paragraph dialog box. To indent paragraphs, select the paragraph and choose

◀ **See**
"Setting Indents," p. 306

Format, Paragraph. Select the Indents and Spacing tab and make selections from the Indentation area. Or select the paragraph and drag the indentation markers on the horizontal ruler.

Here are some hints about indenting paragraphs:

- Don't make paragraph indents too deep—0.5 inches is too deep for most paragraphs. Try 0.25.

- Use hanging indents to create lists.

Creating Lists

◀ **See**
"Creating Bulleted Lists," p. 549

Word for Windows includes two tools to help you make lists quickly and attractively: the Bulleted List button and the Numbered List button. Both are on the Formatting toolbar.

Here are some ideas about creating lists:

◀ **See**
"Creating Numbered Lists," p. 555

- Always use a hanging indent to create an itemized list. You can get a hanging indent by clicking the Bulleted or Numbered List button, by using the Bullets and Numbering dialog box, by using the ruler, or by using the Paragraph dialog box.

- Customize lists by using dingbats rather than bullets. Choose Insert, Symbol to insert a special character.

◀ **See**
"Starting Paragraphs with a Drop Cap," p. 278

Using Text as Graphics

◀ **See**
"Creating a WordArt Object," p. 803

Text becomes a graphic when you use it as a logo (see fig. 38.4), as a newsletter nameplate, as a drop cap, or any time you make it decorative rather than expository. You can change text to a graphic in many ways in Word for Windows: by using WordArt, by creating a drop cap, by enclosing it in a border or shading it, or even just by making it big and setting it apart from the rest of your text. To create a drop cap, select the first letter of a paragraph and choose Format, Drop Cap.

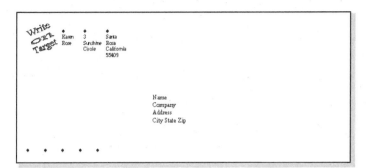

Fig. 38.4

This letterhead and stationery set uses text as graphics in two ways: the "Write on Target" logo is created in WordArt, and the diamond-shaped dingbats are inserted symbols.

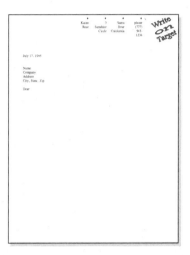

Here are some ideas about creating a graphic effect with text:

■ Use text as a graphic when you don't have any other illustrations for your publication. Drop caps, pull-quotes, and boxed text all can relieve a long expanse of unbroken text and add interest to the page.

■ Use WordArt to create logos, signs, and banners. Also use it for simpler purposes—such as rotating or stretching text, or adding a simple drop-shadow.

■ Frame text when you want to move it freely on the page, with other text wrapping around it.

■ Use the Drawing toolbar to group text with objects. Use these creations to illustrate your publication or to attract attention in an ad.

Working with Columns

◄ **See**
"Creating Columns," p. 380

Many published documents are formatted with columns. Columns are usually easier to read than full-width text—studies show that the optimal line length for reading is about one and one-half to two alphabets. And columns make a page look more graphical than uninterrupted text because they create blocks of text surrounded by white. Because text and white space are two of the primary building blocks in desktop publishing, columns often are an early design decision.

You can create two types of columns in Word for Windows: snaking (or newspaper-style columns) and side-by-side columns. You create snaking columns by using a formatting command, and you create side-by-side columns by using a table.

Figure 38.1 earlier in this chapter shows a newsletter created with newspaper-style columns. Figure 38.6 later in this chapter shows a two-column ad created as a table (side-by-side columns).

Creating Snaking, Newspaper-Style Columns

◄ **See**
"Understanding Sections," p. 382

◄ **See**
"Creating Columns of Equal Width," p. 385

◄ **See**
"Creating Columns of Unequal Width," p. 387

You commonly see snaking columns in newsletters, magazines, brochures, and newspapers—wherever text is continuous from one column to the next. Columns can be any width you want—and they can be the same width or different widths. You can control the space between columns, and you can add lines between columns. To create columns, position the insertion point inside the section you want formatted as columns and choose Format, Columns. Or select the number of columns you want using the Columns button on the Standard toolbar.

Here are some hints about using columns effectively:

- The width of a column is the length of a line. For best readability, lines of text should be one and one-half to two alphabets wide.

- If columns are wide (thus, lines are long), add extra spacing between the lines.

- The narrower the column, the less space you need between columns. Be sure to include enough space so that the columns remain visually separate.

- Word for Windows includes an option for creating columns of different widths. Use this option for an asymmetrical appearance, but use it consistently in your publication. In a layout with facing pages, mirror uneven columns on left- and right-facing pages.

- Include lines between columns to add a graphic effect to pages and to separate columns. Don't let the lines "outweigh" the text—their weight (thickness) should be in proportion to the text. Smaller text and narrower columns need a thinner line than larger text or wider columns.

- If text is justified, the edges of columns form a visual line. You probably don't need lines between these columns, unless you want to create a multiline effect.

- Columns are an excellent basis for creating an underlying grid structure around which you can design your document.

- If you position illustrations or framed text on a page of columns, size it to equal one or more column widths. If you have a three-column layout, make pictures one column or two. If you have a six-column grid, however, in which you use three columns of text, pictures can be in multiples of half a column.

- To override columns, frame text and position it so that it crosses columns. Text in the columns wraps around a frame.

Controlling Column Length

You usually determine column length by page length, but you can control the length of columns in three ways: by balancing columns at the end of a publication, by forcing text to start at the top of the next column, and by inserting a section break so you can have different numbers of columns on a page (see the next section for details).

◀ **See** "Balancing Column Lengths," p. 396

Here are some ideas about using balanced columns:

- Balance columns when you don't have enough text to fill the page—your half page of text should be in columns of equal length. Balance columns by inserting a section break at the end of the text. Use this technique on the last page of a newsletter, for example.

- Force a new column to start by inserting a column break or by inserting a continuous section break and formatting it as a new column. Use this technique for creating brochures or any other design that requires columns to be a specific length. The two-fold brochure shown in figure 38.2 uses column breaks to keep the columns even.

Varying the Number of Columns in a Publication

◀ **See**
"Understand-
ing Sections,"
p. 382

In Word for Windows, you can create snaking columns in your whole document, or in *sections*. In many publications, you see a first section with only
a single column—the title—followed by another section with multiple columns—the text. Insert a section break wherever you want to format different
parts of the document with different numbers or styles of columns (see
fig. 38.5). To insert a section break, position the insertion point where you want
the break and choose Insert, Break. Select an option from the Section Breaks
area.

Fig. 38.5

Section breaks make
it possible for you to
format a publication
with varying
numbers and styles
of columns.

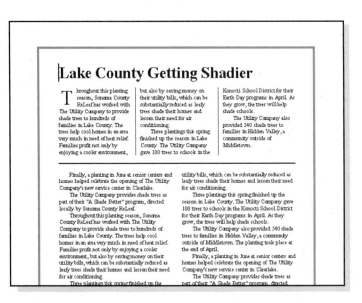

Here are some ideas how you can use section breaks effectively:

- Use a section break after a title when you want a one-column title followed
  by multicolumn text.

- Insert a section break wherever you want to start new column formatting.

- Insert two continuous section breaks when you want two sections with
  different numbers or styles of columns separated by a blank line. If you
  want a horizontal line to separate two sections with different numbers of
  columns, insert three continuous section breaks, with the middle section
  formatted as a single column including one paragraph with a single-line
  border.

Creating Side-by-Side Columns

With short paragraphs of text that you want to appear side by side, a table may be a better formatting choice than columns. You can format a table so that borders appear or do not appear. To create a table, choose Table, Insert Table, or click the Insert Table button on the Standard toolbar.

◀ **See** "Creating Tables," p. 506

Here are some instances when tables can be useful:

■ Use a table to create side-by-side columns of numbers or data.

■ Use tables when you need to do extensive formatting with borders or shading, and need flexibility about where the borders and shading appear, as in a form.

■ Use a table to format text inside a frame into columns.

Creating Sideheads

Headings and subheadings usually appear above text, but your design may place them to the side of paragraphs instead. You can use frames to create sideheads. To create a sidehead, select the sidehead text and frame it by choosing Insert, Frame or by clicking the Insert Frame button on the Drawing toolbar. Then position the sidehead in the margin by selecting it and choosing Format, Frame.

◀ **See** "Positioning a Frame in a Margin," p. 745

Here are some hints about using sideheads:

■ Set wide margins and position framed subheadings in the margins to create sideheads. Using this technique you can create the illusion of a two-column layout, with only the subheads in one column.

■ Use sideheads when you want to create a simple design with a light look—sideheads contribute to a light look by using wide margins.

■ Use styles to format and position sideheads so that they have a consistent appearance.

Incorporating Illustrations

Illustrations are an important building block in most publications. They can take many forms: photographs that you scan or for which you leave a blank space, pictures that you insert from other programs, clip art, drawings that you create in Word for Windows using the Drawing toolbar, and even text that is transformed into an illustration.

Including Photographs

◀ **See**
"Inserting Pictures into Your Document," p. 702

You can include photographs in your publication in two ways. You can scan photographs and insert them as pictures, or you can leave a blank space where you manually paste a photo after you print your publication. To insert a scanned photo, choose Insert, Picture. To create a blank frame, make sure nothing is selected and choose Insert, Frame. Then drag the crosshair to create the blank frame.

Here are some tips about using high-quality photos in your publication:

- Unless you have a high-resolution scanner and printer, photos print at poor resolution. Include scanned photographs in your publication when you don't need high-quality output or when you have the equipment to produce high-quality output.

- If you don't have the equipment but need high-quality output, use a service bureau to scan your photos and print your pages. Use your own equipment for proofing before you get a final high-quality print.

- If you are going to reproduce your publication in quantity using a commercial offset printer, insert an empty frame for photos and have a typesetting shop or your printer make halftones. Paste the half-tones onto your printed originals before you take them to the commercial printer for duplication. You can create a blank space by inserting an empty frame as a placeholder.

Creating Illustrations in Other Programs

You can use graphics programs to create illustrations that you include in a Word for Windows publication (see 38.6). The program can be as simple as Windows Paint or as sophisticated as Aldus Freehand or CorelDRAW!—as long as the program is compatible with Word for Windows or can create a file in a format compatible with Word for Windows. To include an illustration in your document, choose Insert, Picture or Insert, Object.

Fig. 38.6

Illustrations are an indispensable part of some desktop publishing projects, such as this ad.

Here are some hints about creating and inserting illustrations:

- When you need illustrations beyond the scope of what Word for Windows can produce, create them in programs other than Word and insert them into your Word for Windows document.

- If you aren't an illustrator yourself, hire one to prepare drawings for your publication. Art students may be more affordable than professionals if your budget is limited.

- Find out which graphics formats are compatible with Word for Windows by choosing Insert, Picture and reading the file types in the Files of Type drop-down list box. Install filters for other formats by running the Word for Windows Setup program.

Adding Captions

Some experts say that people look first at pictures and second at captions in your publication. Word for Windows makes including captions easy, and it even numbers them for you automatically. To add a caption, choose Insert, Caption.

◀ **See**
"Including a Caption in a Frame,"
p. 733

Here are some hints about using captions:

- Include descriptive captions for your illustrations.

- Frame captions together with illustrations if you want to move them freely on the page as a unit.

Sizing and Cropping Illustrations

◄ **See**

"Resizing and Cropping Pictures," p. 713

In Word for Windows you can size an inserted illustration proportionally or nonproportionally. You can crop, or cut away the edges of, an illustration. You can crop a selected illustration by holding down Shift while you drag a selection handle.

Here are some suggestions about improving your illustrations by sizing or cropping them:

- Illustrations should be in proportion to the text—and to each other—in your publication. Don't let illustrations overpower text. Make an important illustration larger than a less important illustration.

- Size illustrations to fit within your layout grid—if you have a four-column grid, illustrations may be one, two, three, or even four columns wide but not half a column or one and one-half columns wide.

- Crop illustrations to focus on what's important about them—you don't have to use the whole photo if it's not relevant.

Knowing Where to Position Illustrations

If your publication is divided into columns, use them as a design grid.

Here are some suggestions about where to place illustrations:

- Position illustrations on your grid. Often you can position them by aligning them to a column or margin.

- Place important illustrations above the fold in newsletters and magazines (usually above the horizontal center of the page).

- Pos tion illustrations as close as possible to the text they illustrate.

Drawing in Word for Windows

You can use the Word for Windows Drawing toolbar to create surprisingly sophisticated illustrations right in your publication. You can create drawings in your document by displaying the Drawing toolbar (choose View, Toolbars and select the Drawing toolbar) and using any of its drawing tools. For details, see Chapter 25, "Drawing with Word's Drawing Tools."

◀ **See**
"Drawing and Changing Shapes and Lines," p. 759

Here are some ways you can use Word's drawing tools:

- If you're artistic, use buttons on the Drawing toolbar to create simple or sophisticated illustrations for your publication.

- Use Word for Windows drawing tools to create lines and boxes that you can move freely on the page. You can click the Rectangle button, for example, to draw a border around the edge of a page.

- Click the Align Drawing Objects button to center a border on the page. To duplicate a border on all pages, create and copy it on the first page, and paste it on the remaining pages, centering it vertically and horizontally relative to each page.

- Share drawings you create in Word for Windows with other Word documents, or even with other programs in Windows, by copying and pasting them.

Repeating Graphics on Every Page

Include graphics that you want to repeat on every page in headers or footers. The graphics do not have to be confined to the space within the top and bottom margins. To create headers or footers, choose View, Header and Footer. With the insertion point inside the header or footer pane, choose Insert, Picture to insert an existing picture, or use drawing tools to create a drawing. Alternatively, choose Insert, Object to create a WordArt logo or other graphic.

◀ **See**
"Creating Headers and Footers," p. 417

Here are some ideas for repeating graphics:

- Use headers and footers to create rules that appear at the top and bottom of every page in a publication. Rules can appear by themselves or in conjunction with text.

- Create a *watermark* by placing a large graphic in a header, setting it to overlap the margin, and moving it into the layer behind the text layer. A watermark can be any graphic that appears behind text on the page. It should be a light enough color that you can read text through it.

Creating Transparent Graphics

◀ **See**
"Layering Objects below or above the Text," p. 797

Any drawing that you create with Word for Windows drawing tools you can layer behind text. This way you can read text through the drawing. Display the Drawing toolbar and draw objects to create transparent graphics.

Here are some ideas about using transparent graphics:

■ If you want to read text through a drawing, create the drawing using buttons on the Drawing toolbar and send it to the layer behind the text by clicking the Send to Back button.

■ Use transparent graphics to create eye-catching illustrations for ads and flyers. Use them under big, bold text.

Creating Logos with WordArt

◀ **See**
"Creating a WordArt Object," p. 803

WordArt enables you to manipulate text in ways that turn text into a graphic. You can pour text into a shape, rotate it, flip it, stretch it, border it, shadow it, and much more. To create a WordArt logo, choose Insert, Object and select the Create New tab. Select Microsoft WordArt 2.0 from the Object Type list. For details about using WordArt, see Chapter 26, "Creating Banners and Special Effects with WordArt."

Here are some uses for WordArt logos:

■ Use WordArt to create logos for business identity materials—letterhead, business cards, envelopes, brochures, and anything else you need (refer to fig. 38.4)

■ Use WordArt to rotate text; for example, rotate a newsletter's nameplate so that it's vertical, and position it on the left side of the front page of the newsletter (fig. 38.1 shows a nameplate with WordArt-rotated text).

■ Use WordArt in combination with drawing tools to create advertising graphics.

◀ **See**
"Inserting Pictures into Your Document," p. 702

◀ **See**
"Inserting Picture Objects into Your Document," p. 706

Using Ready-Made Computer Art

Many companies sell computer *clip art*—pictures on a disk that you can insert into your publication. You can buy specialized collections of clip art related to topics such as business, sports, seasons, and other subjects. Look in the back of desktop publishing magazines for ads selling clip art and call the companies you're interested in for samples. Windows includes a good collection of clip art images that you can use with Word. To insert an illustration from the Windows clip art collection, choose Insert, Picture and select a file from the CLIPART subfolder located within the MSOFFICE folder. Word for Windows contains another collection of clip art—choose Insert, Object, click the Create New tab, and select Microsoft ClipArt Gallery.

Here are some ideas about using clip art:

- Use clip art with restraint. Many designers don't use it at all because it looks too "canned."

- Use clip art as the basis for creating your own illustrations. Size it, crop it, color it, or use it together with other art to create something unique.

Wrapping Text around Graphics (and Other Text)

The capability to wrap text around graphics and other text is one of the primary features that makes Word for Windows a desktop publishing program. In Word for Windows, you can frame any graphic or block of text and wrap the text of your publication around it. You also can border, shade, or color a frame.

◀ **See**
"Wrapping Text around a Frame," p. 750

Framing and Moving Text and Objects

When you frame text or an object, you can move it anywhere on the page. You can move it by dragging it with the mouse, or you can position it relative to some anchor on the page, such as a margin or column. By default, text wraps around a frame (if at least one inch is available for text). To frame an object, select it and choose Insert, Frame. To position a frame, select it and choose Format, Frame and make selections from the Horizontal and Vertical groups.

◀ **See**
"Moving and Positioning Frames," p. 738

Here are some tips about using frames:

- Even though you can move frames anywhere, design within your column grid. For example, if you have a four-column newsletter, make a pull-quote one or two or three columns wide.

- For precision, use the Frame dialog box to position frames relative to some anchor on your grid, like a column edge or margin.

- In a template, create frames for repetitive blocks of text such as a teaser box on the front page of a newsletter. Then just change the contents each issue.

- Use a frame when you want to position something in a margin. If the framed object overlaps body copy, text wraps around it. Use this technique to create sideheads, for example.

- You can use a frame when you want a story in a newsletter to override columns (see fig. 38.7). If you want a two-column-wide story in a three-column layout, for example, create a frame the width of two columns and position it relative to the left or right margin.

Fig. 38.7

When you want text to override columns, frame it.

The Tree of Life

Long ago people worshipped the sun. Every year as winter appeared, fear rose in their hearts. Each day grew shorter than the one before, and it seemed as if the sun god were forsaking them. If it continued, soon there would be no light or life left. Everything would die.

But eventually the sun god had a change of heart and the days gradually became longer. Celebrations sprang up as people rejoiced in the knowledge that there would be another spring. The time when the days were the shortest became known as the Winter Solstice.

The fir or pine tree was an integral part of the ancient ceremonies celebrating the victory of light and life. People brought these trees of life into

The tree is an ancient symbol reminding us of the abundance of our earth and our responsibility for safeguarding it.

their homes as symbols commemorating renewed and abundant life.

During the Middle Ages, the tree of life was laden with apples. As the custom continued, the trees were decorated with apples and sacramental wafers, then oranges and cookies. The tree of life is also represented in the Menorah lit nightly during the celebration of Hanukkah. The Christmas trees which decorate so many homes today emerged from these beginnings.

The tree is an ancient symbol reminding us of the abundance of our earth and our responsibility for safeguarding it.

Framing and Grouping Items Together

See
"Framing Objects Together," p. 733

When you want to group items so that they behave as a single item, frame them together. You either can select existing items—such as a picture and its caption—and then add a frame, or you can create a frame and insert objects or type text inside it. Items that are framed together move as a unit on the page, and text wraps around them.

If you're working with buttons on the Drawing toolbar, use the Group button to group items such as drawings and their callouts. You can move drawings you create and group using the Drawing toolbar anywhere on the page, but you must frame them if you want text to wrap around them.

If you want to frame an inserted picture together with callouts (which you create using the Drawing toolbar), insert the picture in a text box, create the callouts, and then group the picture and callouts. Although you cannot frame the individual items together, you can frame the group.

To frame objects together, select them and choose Insert, Frame or click the Insert Frame button on the Drawing toolbar. To group drawing objects, select them and click the Group button on the Drawing toolbar.

Here are some suggestions for when you can frame items together:

- Frame illustrations and their captions together so that they stay together.

- Frame pictures and callouts together so that they move easily as a unit.

- In a newsletter, frame together the items needed to create a mailer on the back page. Then position the frame at the bottom margin. A table provides a good skeleton for organizing the items in a mailer and can be framed (refer to fig. 38.1).

Using Lines, Boxes, and Shading

Lines, boxes, and shading can add graphic interest to a publication, even if you don't have any illustrations to use. In Word for Windows, lines, boxes, and shading apply to selected paragraphs and frames. You can add lines and boxes around inserted pictures or WordArt images, but you cannot shade an inserted picture or WordArt image.

◀ **See**
"Shading and Bordering Paragraphs," p. 323

Many of the examples shown throughout this chapter incorporate lines, boxes, and shading.

Putting Information in a Box

You can select a paragraph or group of paragraphs and add a box around them. The box is as wide as the margins or column; if you want it narrower, indent the paragraph. To box text, select it and choose Format, Borders and Shading. Select the Borders tab and select Box, or create your own box using the Border area.

Here are some tips for using boxed text:

- Add a box around important text in a newsletter. It can be as little as a pull-quote or as much as several paragraphs of information.

- Don't crowd text with a box. Include enough space between the box and the text inside it and surrounding it.

- Don't let the box outweigh the text. If text is small, use a lightweight (thin) line. Use heavy lines only when they don't overpower the text.

Lines above and below Paragraphs

Lines, or rules, above paragraphs can serve as text separators—complementing, or sometimes even replacing, subheadings, or dividing stories in a newsletter. To place lines above and below text, select the text and choose Format, Borders and Shading. Select the Borders tab and create lines by clicking at the top and bottom of the sample box in the Border area. Select a line style from the Style list.

Here are some ways to use lines with text:

- Use lines above and below paragraphs the same way you use text—consistently. If you include a 2-point line above some subheadings, include one above all. If you place lines above and below some pull-quotes, use them with all pull-quotes.

- Keep lines in proportion to the text surrounding them and in proportion to your overall design. Don't use big, bold lines in a publication with a light appearance; don't use skinny little lines with a big, heavy headline in an ad.

Including Lines between Columns

◀ **See**
"Adding a Line between Columns," p. 389

In the Columns dialog box, you can select an option to add lines between columns. The lines extend from the top of the section to the bottom of the longest column in the section. Use this option, rather than the drawing tools or the Borders and Shading dialog box, to include lines between columns. To add lines between columns, position the insertion point in the text that is formatted as columns, choose Format, Columns, and select the Line Between option.

Here are some ideas for using lines:

- Don't crowd the page. Make sure the space between columns is wide enough to comfortably accommodate the lines.

- If text is justified, its edges create a visual line. You may not need lines between the columns as well.

Shading and Coloring Paragraphs

◀ **See**
"Shading and Bordering Paragraphs," p. 323

With the Borders and Shading dialog box, you can add shading or a color behind paragraphs. You can blend foreground and background colors to create just about any hue imaginable. To shade or color text, select it and choose

Format, Borders and Shading. Select the Shading tab and select an option from the Shading list box.

Here are some ideas for using shading in your publication:

- Shading and coloring are good techniques for adding emphasis to important paragraphs or for setting sidebars apart from the rest of the text. Shading adds color to a page and can give it a graphical appearance without illustrations.

- Be sure text is readable through the shading. For most text, 20 percent is as dark as you should shade a paragraph. Before finalizing this choice, however, print a few samples to see how shading looks and how it works with the text size you plan to use.

- You can create "reverse" type by formatting text as white and adding a black or dark background. Don't reverse small type or large quantities of text. Reversed text is best in a sans serif font and usually looks best in bold style.

- You can create horizontal gray or patterned bars by formatting a blank line in your text with shading.

- Don't even think about placing a pattern behind text—it makes the text unreadable.

Printing Your Publication

Printing means two things to a publisher: printing an original from your own printer, and printing quantities of your publication, usually done by a copy shop or commercial offset printer.

◀ **See** "Printing the Current Document," p. 239

For some publications, all printing is accomplished on a laser printer.

Many desktop publishers have laser printers for typeset-quality output at 300 dots per inch (dpi), or even more. Some people have lower resolution printers, and some have higher resolution or color printers. But no matter what type of printer you have, you still can create attractive publications. If your own printer cannot do the job, service bureaus can do it for you. Call any local commercial printer, typesetting shop, or Quick Print shop for names of shops that can print your original.

Most publications go outside your office for duplication in quantity. This approach has many advantages—saving time, saving wear and tear on your laser printer, printing in a larger format than your own printer can accommodate, printing in color, and binding your publication.

Understanding Your Own Printer's Capabilities

Because most publications end up on paper, a printer is an important tool for desktop publishers. Get to know yours: What is its printing resolution? What fonts does it contain? How do shaded areas look when printed? How fast or slow is it? Do large publications stall it? Does heavy paper jam it? Do you have easy access to your printer? Before you even begin your design, consider your printer's capabilities. If they don't meet your needs, try to find outside resources for printing your final publication and use your own printer for drafts.

Printing an Original for Outside Duplication

If you're printing limited quantities of a publication, you don't need to add color, you don't need a larger size than your printer can accommodate, and you don't need high-quality photographs, you might be able to use your printer to print final copies of your publication. Many publishers use their laser printers to print a single original of their publication and then take the original to a copy shop or commercial offset printer for duplication. You need to use real laser paper, not copier paper, to print from a laser printer.

If you print only an original, invest in a ream of good-quality, smooth, bright white paper that is heavier than the bond weight paper you use day to day. Print your original on this good-quality paper. It holds up well and provides a good surface for pasting on any illustrations you must add before you take your publication to the printer.

Find out from your commercial printer how to present your artwork—if your print job is a newsletter, you may need to create printing spreads of facing pages, paste on noncomputer illustrations, and add a tissue overlay on which you mark areas to be printed in color. Do any final paste-up before you take your original to the printer.

Getting Your Printing Job Typeset

◀ See
"Sending
Documents
Electronically,"
p. 247

Any printer available in Windows is available to Word for Windows; that also includes typesetting equipment. If your publication is very high-quality—a magazine to be printed on glossy paper or an ad to go in a national magazine—you may want your text printed at higher resolution than is available on most laser printers. Many typesetting service bureaus can print Word for Windows documents at resolutions beginning at 1200 dots per inch (compared to 300 dpi for most laser printers). The price is generally per-page.

If you want typeset output, call typesetters in your area to find out whether they can take a disk containing a Word for Windows document or how you can save your document so that they can print it. Be sure you understand how they need the file—what format, what disk size—before you take your file to them. You may be able to install the printer your typesetter is using and print to a file to create a file for the typesetter. To print to a file, choose File, Print and select the Print to File option.

Typesetters generally offer two options: printing a positive or a negative image. Sometimes you can save money or time with a negative rather than a positive because commercial offset printers must convert to a negative before going to press anyway. Work closely with commercial printers to find out what they need before you have your publication typeset.

Hints on Creating the Desktop Publishing Examples in This Chapter

Throughout this chapter you see examples of projects desktop published using Word. Read this section to find hints about how these examples are created.

"ReLeaf News" Newsletter

The four-column, two-page newsletter shown in figure 38.1 employs many of Word's desktop publishing capabilities.

The top of the newsletter's first page, where the graphic and nameplate, the subtitle, and the title of the first article appear, is a single column. A continuous section break follows, then the format changes to four columns.

The graphic was hand-drawn and scanned; the word news in the nameplate was created in WordArt. The graphic was inserted at the left margin; the word ReLeaf begins at a left tab; news is framed and positioned at the right margin. For design consistency, the graphic is sized to be the same width as one column, the nameplate is as wide as three columns.

The "teaser" box in the left column of the first page is framed, aligned to the left edge of the column, and positioned at the bottom of the page. Keeping the frame narrow prevents it from obscuring the column line to its right. A column break follows the first column.

The boxed text on the back page is framed and positioned at the center of the page. The frame is sized to be the width of two columns.

At the end of the newsletter text (on the second page) is a continuous section break, and single-column formatting follows. The newsletter's mailing box is created as a two-column table which is framed and positioned at the bottom of the page.

This newsletter has a template, which includes much "placeholder" text that changes with each issue. For example, the title of the first story, the "teaser" box, and a few lines of text for the first story are all included in the template as "placeholder" text which is retyped for each issue. Because only a few lines of the main story are included in the template, the template is only a single page, and the mailer thus appears on page 1, overlapping the teaser box.

Creating a Two-Fold Brochure

The two-fold brochure shown in figure 38.2 fits perfectly into a business envelope when folded.

The brochure set up in landscape orientation, with three equal columns. The spacing between the columns is double that of the left and right margins, to accommodate the fold.

Column breaks at the bottom of each column force text to start at the top of the following column. A new page section break separates the two pages.

Two alternative methods for creating this brochure include inserting a section break between columns (by choosing Format, Columns, Start New Column), and setting the brochure up as a three-column, one-row table (one table for each page).

The box that appears around each panel is made consistent by drawing it once (using the Rectangle button on the Drawing toolbar), and duplicating it for the other panels. The boxes are sent to the layer behind the text.

WordArt is used to rotate text on the brochure's mailing panel.

The horizontal lines following the name and address on the donation form are created as a right-aligned tab with a solid-line leader.

Letterhead and Envelope

The letterhead and envelope shown in figure 38.4 are created as a template which can be used again and again.

The template has two pages, with a "next page" section break between the pages. The first page, the envelope, is landscape orientation, 9.5 inches wide and 4.125 inches high. The second page, the letterhead, is portrait orientation, letter size.

The graphics and text comprising the letterhead and the return address on the envelope are contained in headers and footers (different on each page) so they don't interfere with typing. Margins are set wide enough to accommodate them.

The logo is created in WordArt. The diamond-shaped bullets are Wingding symbols.

Both the envelope and letterhead include formatted dummy text. The letterhead also includes an automatically-updating date field in the first line.

"A Day at the Races" Ad

The ad shown in figure 38.6 is based on a table, which provides a convenient working structure.

The page is set up in landscape orientation, with margins that leave the working area the size of the ad. A two-column, two-row table is the size of the page.

The picture in the top left cell was drawn using Word's Drawing toolbar. It has a box around it.

The race schedule in the bottom left cell uses right-aligned tabs with dot leaders.

The headline in the top right cell uses a large (but not bold) font with reduced line spacing—often a good idea for large, multiline headlines. Letter spacing is adjusted to make all lines the same length.

The text in the bottom right cell uses increased line spacing, and includes a ten percent shaded background.

The table is formatted with a border around the outside, and crop marks are drawn using the Line button on the Drawing toolbar. ❖

Chapter 39

The Power of Field Codes

Christine Solomon has been developing business applications with Microsoft Office since 1989, when she developed her first Excel-based application. She is author of *Developing Applications with Microsoft Office* (published by Microsoft Press), and founder of the BusinessMedia Group, which uses Microsoft Office to build publishing tools.

Word provides many tools for companies trying to improve productivity by decreasing the time it takes to produce complex documents. Templates (explained in Chapter 6, "Using Templates and Wizards for Frequently Created Documents") are one such tool; fields are another. *Fields*—also called field codes—are built-in Word functions designed to automatically track and display a variety of information, from page numbers to the results of equations.

This chapter includes five examples that show how to use Word's fields to automate elements that often appear in business documents, such as information in headers and footers, spreadsheet-like evaluation of information in tables, and automated retrieval of data from an external database such as Access.

In this chapter, you learn how to:

- Edit fields
- Use fields to create custom headers and footers
- Use fields to evaluate conditions and make decisions
- Use fields to track document information

Techniques from the Pros

by Christine Solomon

- Use sequence fields to create numbered lists
- Use Word's database field to report data stored in Access

Editing Fields

Tip
Before editing text inside fields, choose Tools, Options. Select the AutoFormat tab and clear the Straight Quotes with 'Smart Quotes' check box.

Understanding how to edit fields is key to using Word's 68 fields to produce complex documents more efficiently. There are two ways to edit fields:

- Using the Field dialog box
- Editing the fields directly in the document

In many cases I use both methods: I use the Field dialog box when I first create a field, and I edit the field directly in the document later when I'm refining the field's content and formatting.

The Field Dialog Box

◀ **See**
"Creating a Template Based on an Existing Document," p. 190

The Field dialog box (available through Insert, Field) provides a dialog box interface for selecting and formatting fields. Figure 39.1 shows the Field Options dialog box for the PRINTDATE field. Most fields provide such a dialog box, which includes the field's built-in formatting options (also called switches) and, in some cases, a list of the document's bookmarks. (Some fields refer to bookmarks and require that you add one; others let you choose whether to add a bookmark or another reference, such as a table cell.)

Fig. 39.1

One way to edit fields is to choose Insert, Field, select the field type, and then click the Options button. Use the Add to Field and Undo Add buttons to edit the field, or type in the text box.

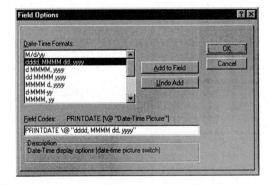

Editing Fields in the Document

The View tab of the Options dialog box (available by choosing Tools, Options) provides a Field Codes check box. When this box is selected, Word displays the actual fields in your document, rather than their results. This lets you edit the field codes directly. (To toggle between fields and their results, press Alt+F9.) Figures 39.2 and 39.3 show the difference between displaying field codes and field results.

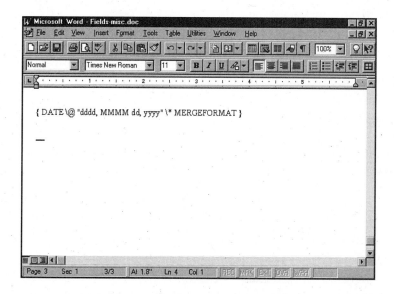

Fig. 39.2

Another way to edit fields is to choose Tools, Options, select the View tab, and then check the Field Codes box. When this box is selected, you see field codes in your document.

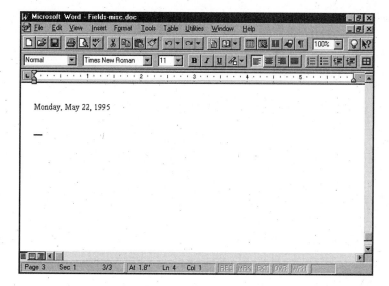

Fig. 39.3

When the Field Codes box on the View Tab of the Tools, Options command is clear, you see the field result rather than the code.

Using Fields in Templates to Create Custom Headers and Footers

You can add fields to templates to create a more automated environment. For example, companies often add the PRINTDATE field, the FILENAME field, and the NUMPAGES field to a header or footer in a template so that documents based on that template show this information automatically. The PRINTDATE field shows the time and date documents were printed, which helps distinguish multiple versions of a document. The FILENAME field shows the name of the electronic version of the printed document, which makes it easier to locate that document on a computer. The NUMPAGES field shows the total number of pages in a document. Figure 39.4 shows a document header containing the FILENAME field, and figure 39.5 shows a document footer containing the PRINTDATE and NUMPAGES fields.

Fig. 39.4

This document header uses the FILENAME field with the /p switch to provide the path.

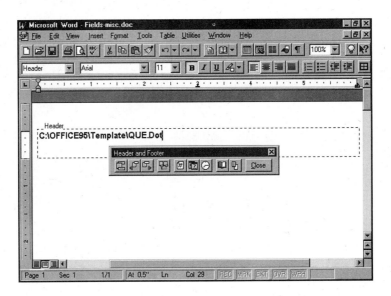

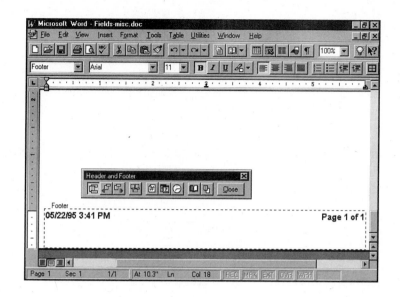

Fig. 39.5

This document footer uses the PRINTDATE field with a custom date and time format, and the NUMPAGES field.

Adding Fields to Templates

To add the FILENAME to the header in a template and the PRINTDATE and NUMPAGES fields to the footer, follow these steps:

1. Choose File, New, and then select the Template option.

2. Click OK.

3. Choose View, Header and Footer.

4. In the header, choose Insert, Field, select the Document Information category, and then select the FILENAME field.

5. Click the Options button, select Title Case from the General Switches tab, and then click the Add to Field button.

6. Choose the Field Specific Switches tab, select the \p switch, and then click the Add to Field button. Choose OK. Choose OK again to continued.

7. Switch to the footer. Choose Insert, Field, select the Date and Time category, and then select the PRINTDATE field.

8. Click the Options button, select the MM/dd/yy h:mm AM/PM format, and then click the Add to Field button. Choose OK.

9. Choose OK again to close the Field dialog box. When you're finished, the field code should look like this:

```
{ PRINTDATE @ "MM/dd/yy h:mm AM/PM" \* MERGEFORMAT }
```

10. Press Tab twice to position the cursor at the right margin in the footer. Type **Page**, enter a space, and click the Page Numbers button on the Header and Footer toolbar to insert a PAGE field.

11. Enter a space, type **of**, enter a space, and then choose Insert, Field, select the Document Information category, and then select the NUMPAGES field. Choose OK. Click the Close button to close the toolbar. When you're finished, the page information should look like this:

```
Page { PAGE } of { NUMPAGES  \* MERGEFORMAT }
```

Creating Custom Date and Time Formats

You can edit date and time fields to create custom formats. For example, although Word provides more than a dozen date and time formats, it doesn't provide this format:

Monday, May 22, 1995 10:20 AM

To create this format, you have to edit the field and add the necessary date and time codes. These codes, which are nearly identical to those used by Excel, are listed in table 39.1. The code for the complete date and time stamp used in the example is

```
dddd, MMMM dd, yyyy h:mm AM/PM
```

Table 39.1   Date and Time Codes

Code	Result
Months	
MMMM	January–December
MMM	Jan–Dec
MM	01–12
M	1–12

Code	Result
Days	
dddd	Monday–Sunday
ddd	Mon–Sun
dd	01–07
d	1–7
Years	
yyyy	1904–1999
yy	04–99
Hours	
hh	01–12
h	1–12
Minutes	
mm	01–60
m	1–60
Seconds	
ss	01–60
s	1–60

To customize the date and time format for the PRINTDATE field so that it shows a complete date and time stamp, follow these steps:

1. Choose Insert, Field, select the Date and Time category, and then select the PRINTDATE field.

2. Click the Options button, select the MM/dd/yy h:mm AM/PM format (which is reasonably close to the desired format), and then click the Add to Field button. Choose OK. Choose OK again to continue.

3. In the document, choose Tools, Options, select the View tab, and then select the Field Codes check box. Choose OK.

Tip

The *
MERGEFORMAT
switch preserves
any manual
formatting you
may have ap-
plied to a field's
result when you
update the
field.

The field code looks like this:

```
{ DATE \@ "MM/dd/yy h:mm AM/PM" \* MERGEFORMAT }
```

4. Edit the field code just as you would regular text. When you're done, the field code should look like this:

```
{ DATE \@ "dddd, MMMM dd, yyyy h:mm AM/PM" \* MERGEFORMAT }
```

Using Fields to Evaluate Conditions and Make Decisions

You can use the IF field and a nested = field to evaluate certain conditions in your document automatically and help make decisions. For example, many companies use Word tables to maintain lists that sales staff use for mailings, phone calls, or targeted promotions. By adding fields to these lists, you can flag companies that meet certain criteria automatically, such as sales greater than $5 million. Figure 39.6 shows the results of one such spreadsheet-like list.

Fig. 39.6

This table uses the
IF field and a nested
= field to flag
companies that
have sales greater
than $5 million
automatically as
HIGH priority.

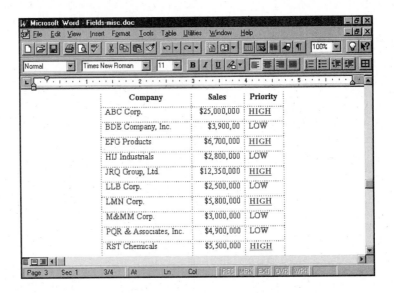

Company	Sales	Priority
ABC Corp.	$25,000,000	HIGH
BDE Company, Inc.	$3,900,00	LOW
EFG Products	$6,700,000	HIGH
HIJ Industrials	$2,800,000	LOW
JRQ Group, Ltd.	$12,350,000	HIGH
LLB Corp.	$2,500,000	LOW
LMN Corp.	$5,800,000	HIGH
M&MM Corp.	$3,000,000	LOW
PQR & Associates, Inc.	$4,900,000	LOW
RST Chemicals	$5,500,000	HIGH

To work with data in tables, you have to understand the codes Word uses to refer to table cells. These codes are listed in table 39.2.

Table 39.2   Field Codes for Referencing Table Cells

Reference This Cell...	Using This Field Code...
Immediately to the left	{ =SUM(LEFT) }
Immediately to the right	{ =SUM(RIGHT) }
Immediately above	{ =SUM(ABOVE) }
Immediately below	{ =SUM(BELOW) }

To create a table that provides spreadsheet-like evaluation of information, follow these steps:

1. Create a table with an extra column, and then enter data into that table. This example assumes that you have set the table up so that the condition that you want to evaluate (such as sales) is immediately to the left of the extra column.

2. In the first row of the extra column, create a field. Because this field is highly customized, it makes sense to create it from scratch, bypassing Insert, Field. To do this, press Ctrl+F9 to insert a pair of field characters. Type **IF**, and then insert another pair of field characters. Inside this second pair of field characters, type **=SUM(LEFT)** to refer to the table cell to the left of the one containing the field.

3. Reposition the cursor to the right of the second pair of field characters and type the condition that you want to evaluate, such as **> 5,000,000** or **<= 10,000,000**.

4. After the condition that you want to evaluate, type the text that you want to appear when the condition is true, such as **HIGH**. Notice that you should format this text just as you want it to appear in the document. In this case, I formatted **HIGH** red, bold, and underlined so that high priority companies stand out clearly.

5. After the text that appears if the condition is true, type the text that appears when the condition is false, such as **LOW**.

   The field should now read:

   ```
   {IF { = SUM(LEFT)} > 5,000,000 HIGH LOW}
   ```

Tip

You can use these conditional operators: = (equals), < (less than), > (greater than), <= (less than or equal to), or >= (greater than or equal to).

Tip
Press Alt+F9 to toggle between field results and field codes.

6. Copy this field into each of the cells in the last column, select the entire document, and then press F9 to update the fields. The following example shows what your finished table might look like with field codes on.

Company	Sales	Priority
ABC Corp.	$25,000,000	{IF { = SUM(LEFT)} > 5,000,000 **HIGH** LOW}
BDE Company, Inc.	$3,900,000	{IF { = SUM(LEFT)} > 5,000,000 **HIGH** LOW}

Using Fields to Track Key Document Information

You can use fields such as NUMWORDS, SAVEDATE, and LASTSAVEDBY to track key information about business documents that will be published:

- *NUMWORDS*. Tracks the number of words in a document, to alert authors when they've exceeded the maximum word count.

- *SAVEDATE*. Records the date and time that the document was last saved, to help provide version control when more than one person writes and edits documents.

- *LASTSAVEDBY*. Records the user name of the person who last saved the document, as a version-control device. (Set the user name through the User Info tab after choosing Tools, Options.)

Tip
These fields can control a document's length and facilitate version control.

Figure 39.7 shows a table at the start of a document which summarizes this key information automatically. You can incorporate such a table as part of the template on which your business documents are based. (See "Using Fields in Templates to Create Custom Headers and Footers" earlier in this chapter for an example showing how to add fields to templates.)

Fig. 39.7

You can add the NUMWORDS, SAVEDATE, and LASTSAVEDBY fields to templates to track key information about business publications in order to control their length and facilitate version control.

To create a summary table that tracks the number of words in a document and records pertinent information regarding the last save, follow these steps:

1. Create a table in a template to hold the summary information.

2. To add the NUMWORDS field to the table, choose Insert, Field, select the Document Information category, and then select the NUMWORDS field.

3. Click the Options button, select 1 2 3... from the Formatting category, select #,##0 from the Numeric Formats category, and then click the Add to Field button. Choose OK. When you're finished, the field code should look like this:

   ```
   { NUMWORDS \# "#,##0" \* MERGEFORMAT }
   ```

4. To add an IF field to evaluate whether the word count exceeds the limit, press Ctrl+F9 to insert a pair of field characters. Type **IF**, and then insert another pair of field characters.

5. Inside this second pair of field characters, type **NumWords**. Reposition the cursor to the right of the second pair of field characters and type the condition that you want to evaluate, such as **> 1,500**. Next, type the text that you want to appear when the condition is true, such as **OVER**. Last, type the text that appears when the condition is false, such as **OK**. When you're finished, the field code should look like this:

   ```
   { IF { NUMWORDS }  > 1,500 OVER OK }
   ```

6. To add a SAVEDATE field to record the last date and time that the document was saved, choose <u>I</u>nsert, Fi<u>e</u>ld, select the Date and Time category, and then select the SAVEDATE field.

7. Click the <u>O</u>ptions button, select M/d/yy h:mm AM/PM from the Date-Time Formats category, and then click the Add to Field button. Choose OK. When you're finished, the field code should look like this:

```
{ SAVEDATE \@ "M/d/yy h:mm AM/PM" \* MERGEFORMAT }
```

8. To add a LASTSAVEDBY field to record the name of the user that last saved the document, choose <u>I</u>nsert, Fi<u>e</u>ld, select the Document Information category, and then select the LASTSAVEDBY field. Choose OK. When you're finished, the field code should look like this:

```
{ LASTSAVEDBY  \* MERGEFORMAT }
```

9. Select the entire document and press F9 to update the fields. The following example shows what your finished table might look like with field codes on:

Word count (MAX: 1,500)	{ NUMWORDS \# "#,##0" * MERGEFORMAT } words; Your word count is { IF { NUMWORDS } >1,500 <u>OVER</u> OK }
Last saved	{ SAVEDATE \@ "M/d/yy h:mm AM/PM" * MERGEFORMAT } by { LASTSAVEDBY * MERGEFORMAT }

Using "Sequence" Fields to Automatically Number Multiple Lists

You can use SEQ fields (called "sequence" fields) to track and number items in multiple lists. For example, figure 39.8 shows a document that uses SEQ fields to number both figures and tables. If you add a few lines of WordBasic code, you can create a handy macro that manages numbered lists better than Microsoft's own Bullets and Numbering feature, because it lets you add multiple paragraphs to each numbered item automatically.

Fig. 39.8

You can use the SEQ field to track and number items in multiple lists, such as figures, tables, or even to-do lists.

Table 1.				
	1990	1991	1992	1993
Product A	$12,000,900	$13,450,000	$16,800,900	$19,800,000
Product B	$12,999,999	$14,500,000	$15,890,000	$17,300,200

Table 2.				
	1994	1995	1996	1997
Product A	$20,000,000	$21,550,000	$22,800,000	$23,800,800
Product B	$18,000,000	$19,560,000	$20,800,900	$22,500,500

Figure 1.

To use SEQ fields to track and number items in multiple lists, follow these steps:

1. Create a SEQ field for the first list. To do this, choose Insert, Field, select the Numbering category, and then select the SEQ field.

2. Following SEQ in the Field Codes text box, type a word that identifies the list. For example, you might use **Figure** to identify a list of figures, **Table** to identify a list of tables, or **Key** to identify a list of key points that the reader needs to consider. Choose OK. When you're finished, the field code should look like this:

   ```
   { SEQ Figures \* MERGEFORMAT }
   ```

3. Repeat the first step for each separate list that you want to number.

4. To add a SEQ field to an item, copy and paste the field that contains the correct identifier. To update the SEQ fields, select the entire document and then press F9 to update the fields.

Tip
Click the Options button to see the formatting options available for the SEQ field, such as numbers (1 2 3...), letters (a b c...), and ordinal numbers (1st 2nd 3rd...).

Creating a Macro to Automatically Insert and Update SEQ Fields

Macros (introduced in Chapter 37, "Recording and Editing Macros") are the ultimate form of automation, allowing you to customize Word's behavior completely. To create a macro that automatically inserts SEQ fields into your document and updates them, follow these steps:

1. Choose Tools, Macro; type a one-word name for the macro, such as Sequencer; select NORMAL.DOT (Global Template) from the Macros Available In list; and then click the Create button.

2. Type the text listed. Note that every macro starts with Sub MAIN and ends with End Sub. Note, too, that text starting with an apostrophe is explanatory text used by the programmer, not by the macro itself.

3. When you finish typing the macro, choose File, Save to save it.

4. To test the macro, switch to a document and press the blue right arrow button on the toolbar (the ToolTip is labeled Start). If there's an error in your macro, Word displays a message box to that effect. When you switch to your macro, you will see the error formatted in red. Compare the error with the following macro code, and then retype the offending line.

This macro inserts SEQ fields into your document:

```
Sub MAIN
'Change mouse pointer to hourglass.
    WaitCursor 1

'Turn off screen redraw.
    ScreenUpdating 0

'Mark cursor location when macro is invoked
'so you can return to it at the end.
    EditBookmark "BackToHere"

'Build SEQ field code using the InsertField command.
'Remember that Figure can be any identifier you like.
    InsertField .Field = "SEQ Figure \* MERGEFORMAT"

'Select the entire document.
    EditSelectAll

'Update all fields in document.
    UpdateFields

'Return to the starting point.
    EditGoTo .Destination = "BackToHere"

'Delete the bookmark that the code added.
    EditBookmark "BackToHere", .Delete

'Turn on screen redraw.
    ScreenUpdating 1
```

◀ **See**
"Customizing
and Creating
Toolbars,"
p. 1034

```
        'Return mouse pointer to standard.
            WaitCursor 0
        End Sub
```

5. After you test the macro, you can add it to a toolbar by choosing <u>V</u>iew, <u>T</u>oolbars, or a shortcut key using <u>T</u>ools, <u>C</u>ustomize.

Tip
Press Ctrl+F6 to switch from the macro to a document.

Using Word as a Reporting Engine for an Access Database

You can use the DATABASE field to create and automatically update reports from an Access database, or from any other ODBC database. *ODBC* is the acronym for *Open Database Connectivity*, which is Microsoft's standard interface for communicating with databases. Figure 39.9 shows a report generated from an Access database using the DATABASE field.

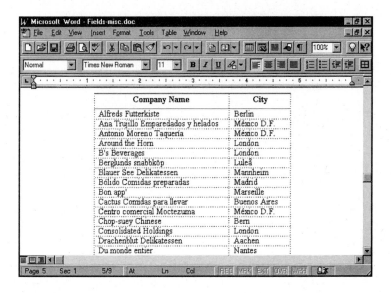

Fig. 39.9

When you use the DATABASE field to create a report from a database, such as Access, you can update that report by putting the cursor anywhere in the table and then pressing F9.

To use Word as the reporting engine for an Access database, follow these steps:

1. Use the ODBC Manager, an application that you can install when you install Word, to set up a data source for the database you want to use. When you start the ODBC Manager, the Data Sources dialog box opens (see fig. 39.10).

Fig. 39.10

The main dialog box for the ODBC Manager lets you set up data sources (or databases) that you can later access from Word or Excel.

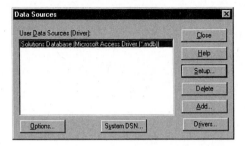

2. Click the Add button to create a new data source.

3. In the Add Data Source dialog box, choose the Microsoft Access Driver (*.MDB) and then choose OK. This opens the ODBC Microsoft Access 2.0 Setup dialog box (see fig. 39.11). Type a name for the database in the Data Source Name text box, and type a description of the database in the Description text box.

Fig. 39.11

To set up ODBC data sources, attach an ODBC driver (such as the Microsoft Access driver) to a data-base (such as NWIND.MDB) and then give this driver/database combination a name (such as **Northwind Database**).

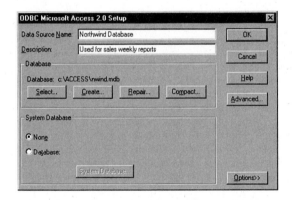

4. Click the Select button to locate the database you want to use. For this example, I used the sample database NWIND.MDB that comes with Access. Choose OK. Click the Close button to exit the ODBC Manager.

5. In Word, choose Insert, Database. The Database dialog box appears (see fig. 39.12).

6. From this dialog box, click the Get Data button to select the database you want to use.

7. After selecting a database, Word prompts you to confirm the data source, and then displays a list of the tables that the database contains. Select the table that you want to use for the report. For this example, I used the Customers table. Choose OK to return to the Database dialog box.

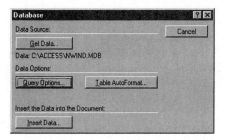

Fig. 39.12

Choosing Insert, Database opens the Database dialog box, which lets you select a database, query that database, and then insert the results of the query into Word.

8. In the Database dialog box, click the Query Options button to query the database and retrieve the specific data you want. The Query Options dialog box contains three tabs: Filter Records (for selecting data that meets specific criteria), Select Fields (for selecting which fields of data display in the report), and Sort Records (for ordering data). For this example, I selected the Select Fields tab to choose two fields for the report (Company Name and City), and then I sorted the records alphabetically by Company Name. Choose OK to return to the Database dialog box.

9. In the Database dialog box, click the Insert Data button. In the Insert Data dialog box, select the option labeled All and the Insert Data as Field check box. Choose OK.

Caution You must insert data as a field to update the report automatically.

---

10. Your report now appears in a Word table. Press Alt+F9 to see the field code. The field in my example looks like this:

```
{ DATABASE  \d "C:\\ACCESS\\NWIND.MDB" \c "DSN=Northwind
Database;DBQ=C:\\ACCESS\\NWIND.MDB;
DefaultDir=c:\\ACCESS;Description=Used for sales weekly reports;
DriverId=25; FIL=MS Access;MaxBufferSize=512;
PageTimeout=600;UID=admin;
" \s "SELECT 'Company Name', 'City' FROM 'Customers'
ORDER BY 'Company Name'" \h }
```

Tip
If you format the table that contains the report, add * **MERGEFOR-MAT** to the end of the field code to preserve the formatting when you update the data.

Using the Database Field and Custom SQL Statements to Create Complex Database Reports

As of this writing, the Insert, Database command lets you generate reports for only one table. To generate reports that present data from multiple tables, add a more complex SQL statement to the field. *SQL*, an acronym for *Structured*

Query Language, is the language that ODBC uses to communicate with databases. The DATABASE field uses SQL to indicate which data to retrieve from the database, and you identify SQL statements in the field by preceding them with the \s switch. The previous example used the following SQL statement:

```
\s "SELECT 'Company Name', 'City' FROM 'Customers'
ORDER BY 'Company Name'"
```

Note that the SQL statement itself is enclosed in double quotation marks ("). The database's table and field names are enclosed by single quotation marks (').

To use Word to generate complex database reports, you need to add appropriate SQL statements to the DATABASE field. If you don't know SQL, you can use Access or Microsoft Query (an application that comes with Microsoft Office) to create the SQL statements you need. The process is similar in both cases:

1. Create a query using Access or Microsoft Query. (Like Word, Microsoft Query requires that you set up an ODBC data source.)

2. Click the SQL button on the toolbar in either Access or Microsoft Query to display the SQL statement used behind the scenes to generate the query.

3. Copy the SQL statement and paste it into the Word field.

4. Edit the SQL statement into a form Word recognizes. This includes such things as deleting references to the database and ensuring that accent characters enclose field names.

For example, I created the following SQL statement in Microsoft Query to generate a report from the NWIND.MDB database listing the products bought by each customer:

```
SELECT Customers.'Company Name', 'Product List'.'Product Name'
FROM c:\ACCESS\NWIND.Customers Customers,
c:\ACCESS\NWIND.'Order Details' 'Order Details',
c:\ACCESS\NWIND.Orders Orders,
c:\ACCESS\NWIND.'Product List' 'Product List'
WHERE Orders.'Customer ID' = Customers.'Customer ID'
AND 'Order Details'.'Order ID' = Orders.'Order ID'
AND 'Product List'.'Product ID' = 'Order Details'.'Product ID'
ORDER BY Customers.'Company Name'
```

To use this statement in Word, I deleted all references to C:\ACCESS\NWIND, and I deleted every duplicate reference to Tables and Field. I also added accent characters around all tables—for example, around Orders. The edited field follows:

```
\s "SELECT Customers.'Company Name', 'Product List'.`Product Name`
FROM 'Customers', 'Order Details', 'Orders', 'Product List'
WHERE Orders.'Customer ID' = Customers.'Customer ID'
AND 'Order Details'.'Order ID' = Orders.'Order ID'
AND 'Product List'.'Product ID' = 'Order Details'.'Product ID'
ORDER BY Customers.'Company Name'"
```

Figure 39.13 shows the report that this SQL statement produces.

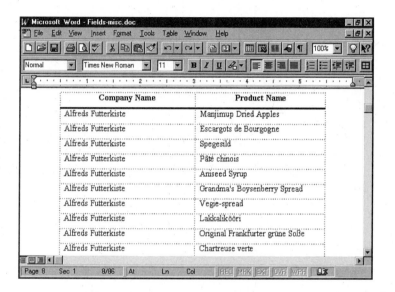

Fig. 39.13

You can edit the SQL statement used in the DATABASE field to produce complex reports showing data from multiple tables. For example, this report shows data from NWIND.MDB'S Customers and Product List tables.

Chapter 40

Creating Online Help and Manuals

Ted Kennedy is vice president of franchise services for MOLLY MAID. Prior to MOLLY MAID, he was a software developer with extensive experience in Microsoft Access. While at MOLLY MAID he used Microsoft Access, Microsoft Word, and Doc-To-Help to develop the Custom Care System and Franchisor Customer Information System, FranCIS. MOLLY MAID is the only company to have won the Windows World Open competition twice—in 1994 and 1995.

Developing first-class documentation and online help is not an easy task, but it is much easier than it used to be! My goal in this chapter is to describe how I have used two tools to dramatically reduce the time and work involved in this once-odious task. These tools are Microsoft Word and Doc-To-Help by WexTech Systems.

In this chapter I will give you a background of

- How MOLLY MAID benefited from online documentation

- Why MOLLY MAID chose Doc-To-Help to create its written and online documentation

- How Doc-To-Help operates

Techniques from the Pros

by Ted Kennedy

Let me first give you some background on the company MOLLY MAID, the needs we had for documentation and online help, and how we were able to satisfy those needs in a rapid and cost-effective manner.

Background on MOLLY MAID

MOLLY MAID is a national franchising organization and the world leader in residential maid service franchising, with 150 franchisees in the United States. About two new franchises are added every week.

One of the most important tasks for any franchisor is supporting its franchisees. At MOLLY MAID we knew we couldn't afford a huge staff, but we saw early on that we could leverage technology to provide a superior level of support to our franchisees, especially using Microsoft Windows and Office. We use all the components of Office to dramatically increase our productivity.

This productivity gain through technology is the primary reason why MOLLY MAID won the Windows World Open in both 1994 and 1995. The Windows World Open is a custom software development contest sponsored by Microsoft and *ComputerWorld* Magazine, and MOLLY MAID is the only company to have ever won the contest twice.

Many people ask me what MOLLY MAID is doing in the world of high-tech computer applications, and how it ever won the Windows World Open. This company won because our applications were developed quickly and had tremendous impact on the company. The Windows World Open focuses on the bottom-line: the fanciest applications don't win—the most cost-effective ones do. Our 1995 entry, for example, won against another application which had taken *100 times* longer to develop. Figure 40.1 shows the opening screen of the MOLLY MAID online help system. Our competitor's application was definitely more sophisticated and more complicated, but we run our entire company on our application, and it was developed in a much shorter time. This is the goal of technology use in a company: productivity, efficiency, and bottom-line results.

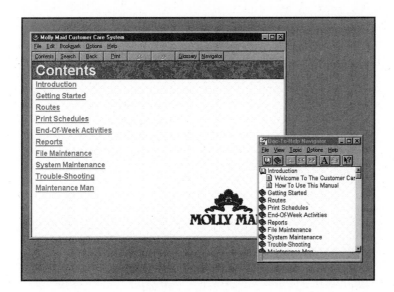

Fig. 40.1

Molly Maid Help File with Doc-To-Help Navigator and Watermark.

Why Does MOLLY MAID Need Documentation?

You may be thinking, "What's so complicated about cleaning houses that you need computer systems and documentation?" The truth is that almost any business gains a competitive advantage by properly using computer technology and by documenting its systems and procedures.

For example, our franchise owners save 10–20 hours per week using our MOLLY MAID Customer Care System™, which schedules customers and employees, computes payroll, prints work schedules, and so on. This is a tremendous timesaver for them, but it takes knowledge to operate the system properly, and we have to teach them. This is why documentation is so important: it helps our franchisees learn the system more quickly and use it properly, and decreases our training and support load. In addition, it increases the perceived quality and value of the software to the franchisees, and helps them train new office personnel much more quickly.

Besides documenting our proprietary computer systems, documentation is extremely important for the broader systems and procedures used by our franchisees. There are seven manuals which cover everything from starting the business to reselling it, personnel hiring to personnel firing, negotiating car leases to settling insurance claims, and so on. This documentation is important because it clearly defines the MOLLY MAID system, both for us and for our franchisees, and helps us to continually revise and fine-tune the MOLLY MAID system.

At MOLLY MAID, we seek to continuously improve the way we run every part of our business. Having all our manuals in electronic form makes it possible to properly document this rapidly-evolving business. The manuals are revised whenever a change is made in any component of the system (almost every week), and re-issued once a year.

When Does Your Company Need Online Help?

Many people wonder when it is best to use written manuals and when online help is more effective. In my experience, written manuals are always necessary, though in an office environment where many people are working together, only one set of manuals may be needed.

Online documentation and help is most effective when:

- Users have easy access to computers

- The documentation is used primarily as a reference (as opposed to sitting down and reading the whole manual)

The obvious "perfect case" is when the documentation is for a computer program. The user by definition has access to a computer and frequently needs to look up a particular piece of information about how the program works. In many cases, online documentation can help people with work that is not computer-related. For example, company procedures that change frequently or procedures that require many cross-references can be enhanced with online documentation. In these cases, the computer is used only as a means of running the reference source.

Written documentation today is far more common than online help, but this situation is rapidly changing. I see it changing for two reasons: computers are virtually everywhere (so more and more people have easy access to them), and online help is addictive, especially when it is context-sensitive. It is easy and fast to use—much faster than written documentation and usually much more helpful.

I have done serious development in Microsoft Access for three years, but I have never read the Access 2.0 manual. I read the Access 1.0 manual because I was new to the product and the help was not complete, but during my use of Access

1.0, I became so addicted to online help that I stopped using the manual. By the time version 2.0 came out, I didn't even bother to read the manual—I just went straight to the Help file.

Context-sensitive help can dramatically reduce support costs, if Help is well-designed and the users understand how easy it is to use. Online help is much easier to use than a written manual, and context-sensitive help is much easier to use than regular help.

MOLLY MAID has two categories of documentation:

- *Documentation for our software programs.* This is distributed both in written form and as context-sensitive online help. Users read the manual when they are first getting started to get a broad overview of the software's capabilities. Then they use online help for ongoing reference.

- *Documentation for our broader systems and procedures.* This is distributed only in written form. Because the computer is a much-used resource for a franchisee, it is often not available when needed, and the manuals are sometimes needed on the road, where it is not practical to have a computer.

So far, this pattern has been best for us. As computers become even more common, we may move toward converting more of the documentation into help files, but at the present time this would not be very usable by our franchisees.

In the future, more and more information will be stored and distributed electronically. The Help file format is especially attractive for this, because it allows quick look-up of topics, and enables the user to jump between related topics with a single mouse click.

Development Tools for Documentation and Online Help

MOLLY MAID uses two tools to develop documentation and online Help: Microsoft Word and Doc-To-Help from WexTech Systems. We chose Word because it is a solid word processor which integrates well with the other Microsoft Office components, and we chose Doc-To-Help for three reasons:

- It is easy to use.

- It helps develop first-class manuals.

- It easily converts manuals to online help.

Doc-To-Help is used both to write manuals which are converted into online help, and to write manuals which are in printed form. It is very helpful to us in both situations.

The remainder of this chapter explains how we have used Word and Doc-To-Help to create our documentation. I do not pretend to be a Word or Doc-To-Help power user; in fact, I probably use less than half the features in either program. You don't have to be a power user to get a lot out of both these programs.

How Doc-To-Help Works with Word

Doc-To-Help is almost seamlessly integrated with Microsoft Word. In fact, until you open a file using a Doc-To-Help template, you don't even know it's there. After you initially configure a Doc-To-Help document, the only apparent difference is in the expanded menu options and the Doc-To-Help toolbar. The Doc-To-Help toolbar is shown in figure 40.2.

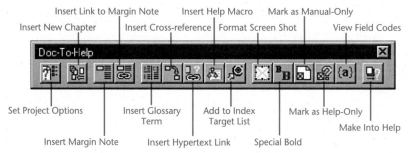

Fig. 40.2

The Doc-To-Help toolbar makes the most used functions readily available.

Simply speaking, Doc-To-Help does three things for you:

- It provides a set of very useful and easy-to-use templates.

- It automates several of Word's more sophisticated features.

- It converts documents to help files by keying in on Word constructs and translating them into help file constructs.

Templates

Doc-To-Help comes with a great set of templates. The one I have used is the Standard Manual template (D2H_NORM.DOT). There are several others, but I liked this one right away, and stuck with it for virtually all my work. When you open a new file (choose File, New), you have the choice of several Doc-To-Help templates. All the template file names begin with D2H. When you choose a template, you get a document with formatting built right into it. Each document contains many different Word styles, a title page, a table of contents, a glossary, and an index. You are coached through the creation of all these elements by the Doc-To-Help Set Project Options dialog box.

Automating Word Features

The document created by Doc-To-Help incorporates several of Word's more sophisticated features. In fact, I have learned more about Word from Doc-To-Help than from any other single source. When I started my first Doc-To-Help document, I thought, "This Doc-To-Help does some very cool stuff," only to discover later that I was using a standard Word feature at that point.

Converting Documents to Online Help

As I mentioned earlier, if you want to create good-looking manuals quickly, Doc-To-Help is great. It helps you do impressive work in very little time. But if you want to create online help, this is where Doc-To-Help *really* shines.

◄ **See**
"Using Word for Windows Standard Styles," p. 348

Doc-To-Help works in a simple but elegant way: it helps you construct a Word document containing many standard Word styles and several special styles. Doc-To-Help then uses a set of rules for translating those styles into Help file components.

◄ **See**
"Applying, Copying, and Removing Styles," p. 354

For example, Doc-To-Help redefines four Word heading styles (Heading 1, Heading 2, Heading 3, and Heading 4). When converting your document to a help file, each of these headings becomes a help file topic.

After you grasp the concept that Doc-To-Help converts Word's styles into elements of a help file, creating a first-class manual and first-class help is quite easy. The tricky part is to always think on two planes. For any given portion of your document, you must ask yourself, "How will this look in the printed manual?" and simultaneously, "How will this look in online help?"

In writing the documentation, I encountered limitations here and there. These limitations mainly arose when a section of the document needed to be treated one way in the hard-copy document and another way in online help. Doc-To-Help does provide ways to handle differences between hard-copy document and online help—it allows "Manual Only" and "Help File Only" designations—but it seemed easier to just alter my preferences a bit. In every situation where a conflict appeared, the time saved using Doc-To-Help outweighed subtle restrictions to creativity.

Creating Your First Document

Let's walk through the process of creating a document using Doc-To-Help. This will not be a Doc-To-Help tutorial and will not fully equip you to use Doc-To-Help, but will add some additional perspective and give you a few hints which can save a lot of time.

Create a Test Document First

The fastest way to become familiar with Doc-To-Help is to create a small part of your document and work it all the way through to completion (including the creation of online help if desired). That is, create a brief chapter using every level of heading, add a graphics image if you will be using one, and add some regular text (Doc-To-Help calls it Body Text). See how the different styles behave, and especially notice how it is all translated into online help. This is the most valuable time you will invest in learning Doc-To-Help. If you make a mistake on a small document, it is easy to fix. If you format something so that it looks great in the printed document but unsatisfactory in online Help, it is easy to change.

I unfortunately did not do this on my first project. I created a rather large document before converting it to online help, before I really understood some of Doc-To-Help's features and limitations. I spent considerable time fixing errors and reformatting large portions of my document.

Pay Attention to the Granularity of Your Help File

The *granularity* of your help file refers to how much text is found under each help topic. Help topics with many pages of text are hard to use. It takes too long to find the desired information, and the user quickly tires of reading endless text. On the other hand, help topics with one sentence on each screen are also hard to use. The reader must constantly click to get to the next screen.

Keep in mind that Doc-To-Help will translate each Heading 1, 2, 3, and 4 into a separate Help topic. This means that if you use the Heading 3 style for a list of points within a Heading 2 section, each of those Heading 3 points will be a separate Help topic. I did this in my very first manual (after typing in approximately 100 pages of text), and had to go back and substantially reformat large sections.

It will take some experimentation, but ideally you want each help topic to be one or two screens long. This brings the user quickly to the information they need with a minimum of switching between screens. To achieve this, you must use the heading styles within your document in a disciplined and carefully planned manner.

Working with the Template to Customize the Format

For the MOLLY MAID manuals, I needed to add an extra line to the footers which Doc-To-Help supplies on every page, and reduce the distance from the footer to the edge of the paper. After working tediously through one completed manual and changing the footers in each section, I said to myself, "There must be a better way." I discovered, after some experimentation, that the best way to customize your document is to create a new template based on a Doc-To-Help template, but modified to your exact specifications. Then whenever you create a new document (and whenever you add a new chapter to the docu-ment), the formatting will automatically come out the way you want.

I copied the file D2H_NORM.DOT into another DOT file, and then in each section I added the desired line to the footers and changed the distance from the footer to the edge of the page. After the modification, the footer looked like this (for an odd-numbered page):

```
Molly Maid Doc-To-Help Manual      Chapter Title  •  7

Copyright ©1995, Molly Maid, Inc. Proprietary and Confidential Information
```

Because I also wanted the manual printed on two sides, the even numbered pages had to look like this:

```
8   •   Chapter Title Molly Maid Doc-To-Help Manual
```

```
Proprietary and Confidential Information Copyright© 1995, Molly Maid, Inc.
```

(Notice how the copyright notice and the Proprietary and Confidential Information switch sides, as do the document title and the page number).

To have this effect reproduced throughout our manuals, I had to create a second page in each section of the template (by pressing Ctrl+Enter) and specifically format the even page footer as shown above. After this was done, these footers were automatically created in each new manual and added to every new chapter.

Making alterations to the Doc-To-Help templates is quite easy to do, but be sure to create a new template file and save your changes to that file.

Creating Your First File

◄ **See**
"Creating a New Template," p. 188

Doc-To-Help's documentation makes it very clear that each Doc-To-Help document must be in its own folder. This is necessary because Doc-To-Help creates a DOC2HELP.INI file which saves settings specific to each document. If you try to have more than one Doc-To-Help document in a folder, Doc-To-Help becomes confused, because the two documents will attempt to share the same DOC2HELP.INI file. I make a practice of always naming the folder exactly the same as the Doc-To-Help document it contains (so if I want to create a document called "M," I first create a folder named "MANUAL," and then within that I create a file called "MANUAL.DOC").

Set up your folder with the proper name, bring up Word, choose File, New and choose the appropriate D2H template. As soon as you choose the template, the Doc-To-Help Set Project Options dialog box appears (see fig. 40.3).

You may at first be puzzled by some of the options—unless you have thoroughly read the manual and studied the tutorial. Don't be afraid to experiment; you can change any of these options later. Just choose the options which seem best and proceed.

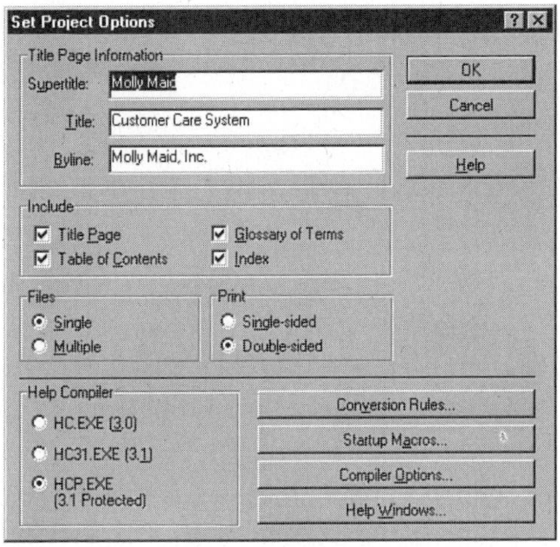

Fig. 40.3

In the Set Project Options dialog box, you specify some of the major options for the document.

Doc-To-Help sets up the document for you, and you can just start typing. For the first two chapters, you must replace the titles "Chapter 1" and "Chapter 2." After that, you must use Insert, New Chapter to create additional chapters.

The main rule to follow when using Doc-To-Help is this: whenever changing the structure of a document, use a Doc-To-Help menu choice whenever possible. Do not make a structural change directly unless you have no other option, because you will almost certainly mess something up.

For example, when adding a new chapter, choose Insert, New Chapter from the menu. Do not simply choose the Heading 1 style and start typing. If you simply choose the Heading 1 style for a new paragraph, it *looks* like you have created a chapter, but you really haven't!

Or, if you decide that you don't want a glossary of terms, don't delete that section directly. While Doc-To-Help is much more accommodating than it used to be about users tinkering with the structure of their documents, you'll get more consistent and reliable results if you use Doc-To-Help's Set Project Options dialog box. Choose Format, Set Project Options, and deselect the Glossary of Terms check box. Doc-To-Help removes the Glossary of Terms section.

> **Note**
>
> The Set Project Options dialog box which appeared when you first created your document is the same one which appears when you choose Format, Set Project Options, and enables you to change any of the choices you made when you originally created the document.

Doc-To-Help relies very heavily on the structure of the Word document when translating the document into online help. If this structure is altered, Doc-To-Help will not be able to create online help properly.

Caution Don't change the document structure; specifically, don't add or delete sections except to delete chapters which you wish to remove entirely.

Adding Graphics to Your Document

Graphics can add a lot of power to both your documents and your online help, but they also add a tremendous amount to the size of the document and help files. Graphics is another area where experimenting with a small document really helps. When I created my first manual, I boldly captured shots of entire screens and dropped them in my Word document. Then, to my horror, I noticed that Word slowed to an absolute crawl and I discovered that my file, which used to be 100K was now 3.5M—after only four screen shots. I had to radically re-think my approach and I ended up using small segments of screens. In general, you will want to use small graphics in your documents and online Help. Large graphics take up too much room and slow performance dramatically.

WexTech Systems offers another product called "Quicture" for use with Word; it stores graphics images in separate files, and puts only a placeholder in Word. This dramatically increases the speed with which Word manipulates your file. but does result in a proliferation of files (one for each image). It is a very good product, and makes it practical to put large amounts of graphics in a Word file. Keep in mind that your help file will eventually contain all the images, and if the images are very large, the help file will also be very large.

Translating Your Document into Online Help

If you have properly constructed your Word document, translating it into online Help is very easy. You simply choose Format, Make Into Help, and Doc-To-Help takes it from there. You are given the option of checking for errors before converting the document to help; you should definitely do this after any session in which the document structure was changed. After you've checked the document, the conversion process takes place.

At this point, if you have a long document, you begin to want a faster machine, because the conversion process can take awhile. This is another reason it is advisable to start with a small document and experiment. Converting long documents to online help on anything less than a 90 MHz Pentium is a lesson in patience.

As I mentioned earlier, the trickiest issue in creating a good basic help file is the granularity of the help topics. Try to chunk topics into small readable sections no larger than one or two screens. If you have the document structured properly for this, your help files look pretty good with very little effort.

Advanced Features

Both Word and Doc-To-Help have many more features than I have used, so I will mention some of them but not attempt to cover them in detail. The Doc-To-Help documentation is good, and the tutorial walks you through many of its features.

Indexing

A good index is great to use, but very difficult to create. Doc-To-Help makes it rather painless for you to create a basic index, but creating a full-blown sophisticated index is a lot of work, even with Doc-To-Help.

The most challenging concept to master in working with indexes is the difference between the Index Target and the Index Tag. Let me see if I can make it easier for you:

- An *Index Target* is a word or phrase which occurs one or more times in your document to which you would like Index Tags to point.

  You first specify an Index Target, and then specify one or more Index Tags associated with that target.

- An *Index Tag* is a word or phrase in the index which points to Index Targets.

  Every Index Target has a Default Index Tag which is the Index Target word or phrase itself. In addition, an Index Target can have multiple Index Tags pointing to it.

  An Index Tag can point to multiple Index Targets.

When Doc-To-Help builds your index, it scans your document once for every Index Target you have specified, and finds each occurrence of that word or phrase. It then creates an index entry for every Index Tag associated with that Index Target.

Here is an example. Let's say you have an Index Target consisting of the phrase `Doc-To-Help` (that is, this phrase occurs several times in your document, and you want index entries pointing to the places where it occurs). You want an entry in your index (an Index Tag) called "Doc-To-Help" which points to the places where the phrase `Doc-To-Help` occurs in your document. This is pretty obvious, and this Index Tag is called the *Default Index Tag*.

However, you may want another entry (another Index Tag) called Writing Tools which also points to the places where Doc-To-Help occurs in your document. Thus, for every occurrence of the phrase `Doc-To-Help` in your document, you would have two index entries. If `Doc-To-Help` and `Writing Tools` occur on page 10, your index would contain the following entries:

	Page
Doc-To-Help	10
Writing Tools	10

Let's say you also have an Index Target which consists of the word `Word`. Let's assume that you want three Index Tags pointing to the places where `Word` occurs: "Word," "Writing Tools," and "Word Processors." If `Word` occurred on page 8, your index would now contain the following entries:

	Page
Doc-To-Help	10
Word	8
Word Processors	8
Writing Tools	8, 10

The last entry `Writing Tools` is indexed on both pages 8 and 10. On page 8, it is indexed for the Index Target "Word." On page 10, it is indexed for the Index Target "Doc-To-Help."

This feature is tricky to grasp at first, but is very powerful. It enables you to put phrases you think will come to the reader's mind in the index, and have them point to phrases you have used in your document.

Doc-To-Help has more indexing options which I have not used, but that enable you to create very sophisticated indexes. In my experience, the basic index creation functions were quite adequate and took a lot less time. Creating a full-blown index is a major undertaking and can take a lot of time.

Margin Notes

Margin notes add a lot to the look of a manual and translate very well into online help. Adding a Margin Note is a two-step process: inserting the note and linking the note to some text.

If you just insert the note, it looks great on your document, but if you fail to link the note to some text, it will not become a pop-up definition in your online help. You don't link the note to the whole paragraph, but to a phrase within the paragraph (usually just one or two words). In your help file, this phrase will appear in green with the standard dotted underline, and when the user clicks it, the margin note will appear as a pop-up definition (see figs. 40.4 and 40.5).

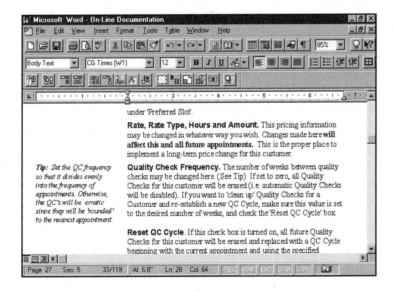

Fig. 40.4

Margin notes appear to the side of body text in printed documentation.

Fig. 40.5

A margin note is converted into a pop-up definition in the help file.

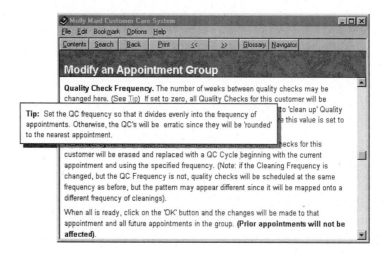

Cross-References and Hypertext Links

Doc-To-Help enables you to easily insert cross-references into your document. Note that the part of your document to which you are referring must first be defined either by being formatted in a heading style, by being a bookmark, or by being one of several other special Word constructs (footnote, endnote, and so on). This is a very useful feature, and translates especially well into Help, where the cross references become hypertext links (on which the user can click to instantly jump to that part of the Help file). To create the links, use the Insert Hypertext Link dialog box shown in figure 40.6.

If you want to create a hypertext link in your help file but *not* have it appear in your document, you can do that, too. In this case, the links can only refer to headings (not to bookmarks and the like). This makes sense because in the help file you must jump to a *topic*, and the headings in your document are translated into topics in your help file.

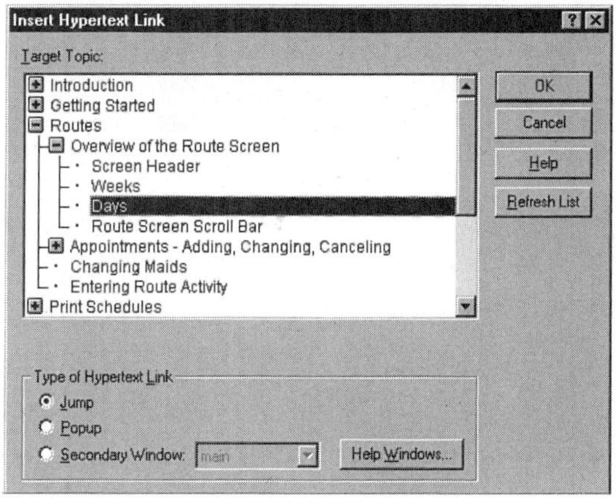

Fig. 40.6

Use the Insert Hypertext Link dialog box to link between a phrase you select and a heading, bookmark, or other construct.

Context-Sensitive Help

Context-sensitive help is one of my favorite things. It enables users to get help on the specific part of a computer program in which they are working. Using Doc-To-Help to create it is easy. I won't go into the details (which are covered quite well in the Doc-To-Help manual), but let me give a few tips.

Make your help context-sensitive to the screen level. That gives the user 99 percent of the benefit and saves you a lot of time. If you try to make it context-sensitive to the field level, you will find yourself in an editing nightmare, especially as you make changes to your application in the future.

Begin by opening a Word file and listing all your screens, grouping them in logical fashion, then assigning them *context numbers*. Leave spaces in the numbering sequence so that future screens can fit logically. I grouped my screens by my menu structure: all screens accessed by the first Main Menu button were put in the 1000–1999 range, all screens accessed by the second Main Menu button were put in the 2000–2999 range, and so on. Save this Word file separately, and use it to assign the Help Context ID numbers in your software application and to assign Map Numbers in your Doc-To-Help file.

If you try to create context-sensitive help without this type of document, you will quickly find yourself confused. It will also be difficult to update your help.

Other Advanced Features

Doc-To-Help gives you tools to add some very powerful effects to your help files without extra work. These include things like hot-spots, graphics, and many more.

It also enables you to create Help Macros, which can turn a Help file into something like a Personal Program Manager. You can jump to other Help files, launch Windows applications, or even play sound and video files.

I have only dabbled in these advanced features, and can't give much advice beyond what is contained in the Doc-To-Help manuals. These advanced features can help you create some world-class Help files.

Hyperformance Tools

WexTech Systems has also created some Doc-To-Help add-ons called Hyperformance Tools. These include:

- *Doc-To-Help Navigator.*   An interactive table of contents that makes the Help file much more accessible to the user and author.

- *256-Color Bitmap Support.*   Allows your help systems to go beyond the 16-color limitation of the Windows Help engine.

- *Watermarks.*   Spice up your help system by adding a watermark to your topic screens. (Note that Doc-To-Help does not "lighten" your graphic to make it a watermark—you have to do that yourself before you insert it.)

- *Setup Wizard.*   Enables you to create a customized installation program for your Help system's end-users. This gives the installation process a professional touch and enhances the value of your Help system.

- *Context Remapping Utility.*   Enables you to easily display and remap the Context Map Numbers in your Help system. This is a very useful utility for updating your Help files if your application is upgraded. The Context Mapping Utility is shown in figure 40.7.

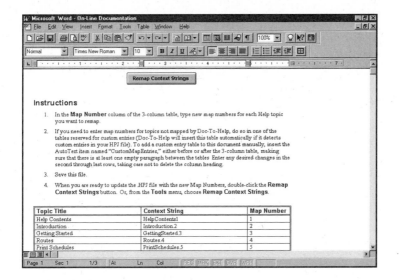

Fig. 40.7

Doc-To-Help
Context Mapping
Utility enables you
to track how
context-sensitive
items are related.

Conclusion

Writing manuals and developing online help is rarely an enjoyable task. I have found, however, that using Microsoft Word and Doc-To-Help has made the task much easier and at times almost enjoyable.

Doc-To-Help gives you a solid and productive framework within which to operate, whether you are creating a manual, online help, or both. You don't have to tinker with designing styles, figuring out how they interact, designing footers, and so on. It's all in the program, and you can just start using it. As far as creating help files goes, it is hard to imagine the process being any easier.

For me, the bottom line is always quality and productivity. For our latest winning entry in the Windows World Open, it took me less than two days to write a professional-looking 50-page manual and convert it into first-class online help. Without Word and Doc-To-Help, there's *no way* I could have done this, or even come close.

Doc-To-Help Ordering Information

To order Doc-To-Help, call WexTech Systems at (800) 939-8324 or write to them at 310 Madison Avenue, Suite 905, New York, NY 10017. ❖

Publishing on the Web with Word's Internet Assistant

Imagine more than 35,000 computers connected over a network spanning 72 countries. Imagine more than four million people being able to read pages of information from these computers—pages that contain text, graphics, sound, and motion pictures. Any of these people can read the text of proposed government legislation, download graphics files of paintings from the Louvre, or retrieve databases of information about business, science, and medicine. And anyone who uses Word for Windows 95 and the Internet Assistant and is willing to pay a fee between $15 and $100 per month can publish their own documents on the Web.

With the use of the Internet Assistant, you will be able to create your own Web pages that contain text, graphics, and hyperlinks to other pages on the Web. You also can create interactive forms and graphics. Your Web pages can ask readers to select option buttons, check boxes, items from a drop-down list, or type into a text edit box. Readers can fill out forms, order products or information, or respond to your surveys.

What Is Microsoft's Internet Assistant?

Microsoft's Internet Assistant software makes it easy for you to create your own Web pages for the World Wide Web or for use over your own network. The Internet Assistant even includes a Web browser that enables you to view

Web pages if you have an Internet connection. One of the things that makes the Internet Assistant so easy to use is that anyone who is familiar with Word for Windows will be able to easily view or create pages on the Web.

Microsoft's Internet Assistant for Word for Windows is a free add-on to Word for Windows 95. Internet Assistant contains software that enables you to:

- Browse through pages on the World Wide Web

- Create your own Web pages using the HTML editor

- Convert Word's DOC files to HTML files that will appear as pages on the Web

- Create Word DOC files containing Web hyperlinks that can be used as Web pages

- Create your own web of hyperlinked DOC files on any network

- Download files from the Internet using FTP

An additional piece of software available free from Microsoft is the Word Viewer. The Word Viewer enables users who do not have Word for Windows to view and print Word's DOC files retrieved from the Web.

> **Note**
>
> The figures in this appendix represent Internet Assistant for Word 6 for Windows. At the time this book went to press, Internet Assistant for Word for Windows 95 was not available for testing. Our best estimate is that the initial releases of Internet Assistant for Word for Windows 95 will be very similar to the figures and capabilities described in this appendix.

What Are Web Pages?

A Web page is a simple ASCII text document. When opened inside Web browser software such as Internet Assistant, Mosaic, or Netscape, that simple text document becomes a gateway to the Internet.

The page can include graphics as well as text. You can link any text or graphic on your Web page to any document on your computer or any Internet or Web site. A Web page includes any or all of the following elements:

- Text

- Text formatting codes

- Headings, levels 1 through 6

- Lists—bulleted, numbered, or glossary

- Addresses

- Divider lines, called *horizontal rules*

- Images, sounds, and animations

- Hyperlinks to other locations in the same document, other documents, or other documents on the Web

- Interactive form fields such as check boxes, text edit fields, and drop-down lists

Figure A.1 shows an example of a Web page in Internet Assistant that illustrates some of the elements you can put on a page. In Internet Assistant, you format or insert graphics or hyperlinks by selecting styles, choosing menu commands, or clicking buttons, just as you do when you create a Word document. The commands you select insert styles or codes into the Word document. When the Internet Assistant saves a document, Word's styles and codes are converted into HTML codes that are understood by the World Wide Web. HTML is the *HyperText Markup Language*. It is the *lingua franca* for World Wide Web documents.

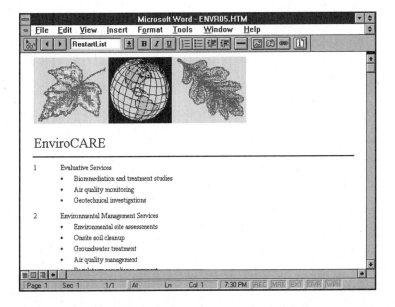

Fig. A.1
A Web page in Internet Assistant illustrates many of the design elements you can include in a page.

When you save the document you are working on, Internet Assistant examines the styles you have applied and inserts HTML *tags* where appropriate. These tags are codes that are interpreted by World Wide Web browsers. The file is then saved as a text document with the tags. Figure A.2 shows the HTML file from figure A.1 opened as text so the HTML tags are visible. The figure shows the upper part of the <BODY> area.

Fig. A.2

This is the same Web page that you see in figure A.1. Here it's shown as text so you can see the HTML tags.

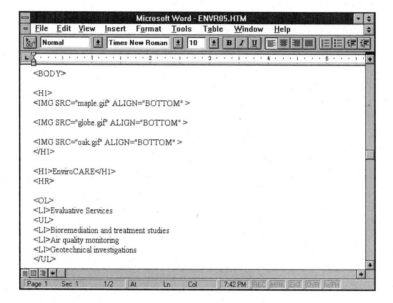

What Design Features Are Available in HTML?

Documents retrieved from the World Wide Web are viewed through the use of *browser* software. Although the HTML tags are standardized, each browser interprets them slightly differently.

The HyperText Markup Language includes simple formatting capabilities. HTML commands enable you to format documents with the following design features:

- Use variable font sizes to create headings that enable the user to find information quickly.

- Use bold, italic, and underline to emphasize text.

- Use bulleted or numbered lists to make information more accessible. Web browsers support multiple levels of bullets as well as numbered lists. Indent commands allow bulleted items with multiple lines of text to flow and wrap correctly.

- Create tables for numeric or text columns using monospaced characters.

- Use horizontal rules to separate areas with a horizontal line.

- Insert graphics to enliven the Web page.

- Add hypertext to create links that enable you to jump to other locations on the Web.

HTML does impose limitations to the design of the display. Keep in mind the following limitations as you design a Web page:

- Text cannot wrap around graphics the way you frequently see in newsletters or magazines, but graphics can be inserted on the same line as text. A line of text normally appears following an image and is aligned with the bottom of the image. You also can choose center or top alignment. (Text alignment always appears at the bottom when documents are viewed in the Internet Assistant.)

- Multiple columns of text like those that appear in newspapers are not possible in HTML documents.

- Only left-aligned text is available. You cannot use center-, full-, or right-aligned text. Newer versions of HTML will be able to align text.

- Interactive forms with data entry fields are available in HTML.

Downloading Internet Assistant and the Word Viewer for Free

Internet Assistant for Word for Windows 95 will be available for free approximately 60 days after the release of Word for Windows 95.

You can download the Internet Assistant and Word Viewer from Microsoft's World Wide Web server located at

www.microsoft.com

or from Microsoft's FTP site at

ftp.microsoft.com

At the time this book was printed, you could reach the Internet Assistant and Word Viewer hyperlinks that download the software through the What's New hyperlink on the **www.microsoft.com** home page.

At the time of this writing, the URL to the Internet Assistant is

ftp://ftp.microsoft.com/deskapps/word/winword-public/ia/

The URL to download the Word Viewer is

ftp://ftp.microsoft.com/softlib/mslfiles/

Caution

Make sure you download and install the version of Internet Assistant and Word View designed for Word for Windows 95. The 16-bit versions designed for Word 6 for Windows will not work with Word for Windows 95.

Understanding the Internet Assistant

Internet Assistant works within Word for Windows 95. If you already use Word for Windows, you will find Internet Assistant very familiar—many of the commands and methods of operation are the same. If you are new to Word for Windows but familiar with other Windows applications, you should be able to pick the skills necessary to create and format a Web page in a very short time.

Understanding the Edit and Browse Views

Internet Assistant displays documents in two different views, Browse view and Edit view. Browse view enables you to link to the World Wide Web and display documents. You will normally use it while you are browsing through pages on the World Wide Web. While you are in Browse view, the menus display commands appropriate to browsing the Web. The Standard and Formatting toolbars change in Browse view and display buttons designed to help you browse the Web.

You will use Edit view to create new Web pages or edit existing Web pages. While in Edit view, menus change to present commands for formatting and creating Web pages. Also, the Standard and Formatting toolbars change to present buttons with tasks appropriate to editing and revising.

Browsing the World Wide Web

The World Wide Web links together many resources that exist on the Internet. When you use the World Wide Web, you jump among locations (thousands of computer hosts), system applications, and information formats (files and documents).

There are three ways to retrieve Web pages using Internet Assistant. You can manually type a *URL*, or *uniform resource locator*, into a dialog box and let the browser retrieve the page; you can click a text or graphic hyperlink that retrieves a page; or you can click a link that has been saved in a history or list of favorite places.

Manually Entering a URL

To manually enter a URL, follow these steps:

1. Click the URL button or choose File, Open URL. The Open URL dialog box appears (see fig. A.3).

2. Type the new URL. Be sure to type it accurately.

3. Click OK.

The new Web page may take anywhere from a few seconds to a minute or more to load and display.

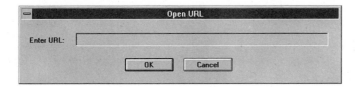

Fig. A.3
The Open URL dialog box enables you to type the URL for the next document that you want to view.

Entering and Formatting Web Pages

Pages you read on the Web are usually well-formatted, well-presented displays. Since the page creator cannot know what type of computer or terminal the reader will use, the publisher cannot use text with specific formatting information, such as fonts and point sizes to produce these documents. To assure that everyone sees documents with approximately the same formatting text, codes are inserted into a document that describe how the document should be formatted, where hyperlinks are and where they are connected to, and which graphics should be displayed. This method of inserting formatting codes in the document allows the viewer's browser to create the best display it can on the viewer's terminal or computer. These text codes that are inserted compose the HyperText Markup Language, HTML. The text codes, known as tags, are automatically inserted by Internet Assistant as you create your Web pages.

Using Internet Assistant to Create Web Pages

One of the beauties of using Internet Assistant is that you already know how to use the commands and buttons of Word. You don't have to know HTML tags to create a Web page. You simply format with Word styles or click toolbar buttons. When you save your document, Internet Assistant automatically converts the Internet Assistant styles to their HTML tags. Internet Assistant inserts HTML tags that are syntactically correct, significantly reducing errors.

Preparing an HTML Document

You can create a Web page by opening a new HTML document, by editing an existing Web page, or by converting a Word DOC file into an HTML file.

If you want a new blank page on which to work, you should open the HTML template. To create a Web page, use the Web page template called Html. When you open the Html template, Word's menus change to give you commands appropriate for HTML editing. The Standard toolbar changes to a toolbar appropriate to HTML editing. This template includes styles for creating Web pages.

You apply Html styles in the same way you apply styles in any Word document. When you save the document, Internet Assistant converts the styles to their HTML equivalents.

To create a new Web page document, follow these steps:

1. Choose File, New.

2. Select Html from the list of templates, then choose OK to open a new HTML document.

The following sections will give you some feel for how to format different parts of an HTML document.

Entering Headings

Text that you want displayed as large titles or topic headings should be formatted with Heading formats. HTML supports six heading levels, Heading 1,H1 through Heading 6,H6. The attributes assigned to each heading level depend on the browser you are using. For example, Internet Assistant displays all Heading 1 elements in Arial, 14-point bold text, while Lynx uses all caps and centers Heading 1 items. As you create headings, remember that you cannot control the font, point size, and other attributes—only the relative visual importance given to headings.

> **Note**
>
> It is a good idea to use only the first three heading levels. You cannot be sure that other users' browsers will display the lower level headings well enough to distinguish that they are headings.

Emphasizing Text

HTML includes two categories of tags for emphasizing text: logical and physical. *Logical tags* let you format text based on your overall design, rather than specific details. The interpretation is left to the browser to most effectively display the text. You select the Emphasis, HP1, EM style, for example, to add emphasis to text, and the browser will make it stand out more than the plain text.

Physical tags, on the other hand, enable you to specify your intentions exactly. If you use bold, italic, or underline commands, that is how the text will display—no guessing involved. Most browsers do not support the underline format, but nearly all support bold and italic. To apply any of these character formats, select the text and click the appropriate button in the Formatting toolbar.

Formatting Lists

One way to efficiently present information is by using lists. Internet Assistant provides you with three methods of formatting lists in your Web pages. Three listing tools may not seem like much, but with those three tools you can actually create distinctive formatting within the limitations of HTML. Internet Assistant provides several styles that support HTML's listing features.

Creating Ordered Lists

Clicking the Number button in Internet Assistant is the same as in Word for Windows. Just click it, and Internet Assistant adds the HTML tag for numbering. Numbering is automatic, so each successive time you add a paragraph, its number increments by one.

Indentation in Internet Assistant is also set automatically with the style and can be increased or decreased by clicking the Increase or Decrease Indent buttons. Use numbers and bullets together to create more effective designs (see fig. A.4).

Fig. A.4
You can nest bullets within numbers to enhance Web page design.

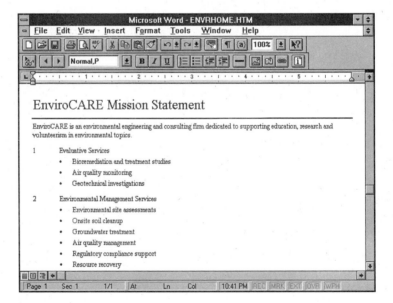

Creating Unordered Lists

Bullets can make information easier to sort through. You can use bullets alone or combine them with numbers as shown in figure A.4. You add a bullet to a paragraph by applying the List Bullet, UL style. Indentation is automatically set. The HTML tag <UL> is automatically inserted at the beginning of text and </UL> inserted at the end of the bulleted text.

Entering Tables as Preformatted Text

You can use the Preformatted, <PRE> style to align text into columns or tables without much fear that HTML will mess up your handiwork. Preformatted text displays in a nonproportional font such as Courier with all of your carriage returns and spacing intact. The Preformatted, <PRE> style automatically adds tab stops to the ruler.

Inserting Graphics

One of the first things that people will judge about your Web page is whether it is visually appealing. You can make your pages more appealing by adding graphics to them. Figure A.5, for example, shows three graphics placed side-by-side that are used as banners and blue 3-D balls that are used as bullets for the text.

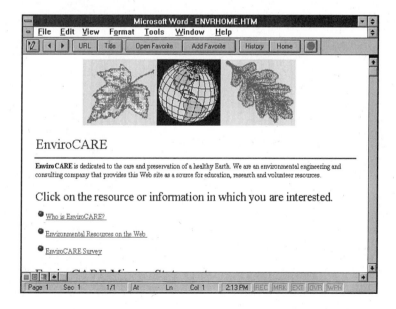

Fig. A.5
Use graphics as banners, anchors for hyperlinks, or bullets.

Using Graphics in a Web Page

Graphics are not inserted directly into a Web page as they are in Word documents. Instead, a link to a graphics file is inserted into the Web document. This link describes where to locate the graphics file that should be displayed when the document is retrieved. The browser that displays the Web document can display the Web page with only its text for improved performance, or display the combined text and graphics. Newer browsers such as Internet Assistant and Netscape retrieve and display the text in a document first, and then retrieve the graphics. This two- or three-pass retrieval enables you to begin reading the text in a document while graphics are being retrieved.

Graphics files that are used in Web documents and recognized by the Internet Assistant use two file formats, the Graphics Interchange Format (GIF) that is familiar to CompuServe users, and the JPEG format, a more compressed format. Many high-level drawing programs for Windows can save their graphics in GIF and JPEG formats.

To insert a graphic into your Web page, follow these steps:

1. Position the insertion point where you want the graphic to appear.

2. Choose Insert, Picture or click the Picture button. The Insert Picture dialog box appears, as shown in figure A.6.

Fig. A.6

The Insert Picture dialog box inserts graphics from GIF and JPEG file formats.

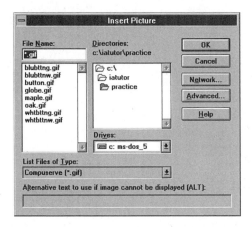

3. In the Alternative Text to Use if Image Cannot Be Displayed box, type the phrase you want displayed if the browser cannot display graphics or the graphic file cannot be found.

4. If you want to align text that follows the graphic on the same line, click the Advanced button to display the Advanced Picture Options <IMG> dialog box, shown in figure A.7.

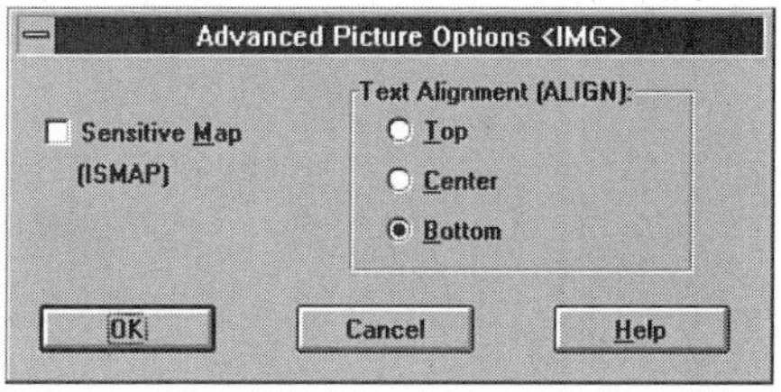

Fig. A.7
You can align text that follows the graphic on the same line.

5. Select whether you want the text that follows on the same line as the graphic to align with the Top, Center, or Bottom of the graphic. Choose OK after your selection.

The ISMAP check box is used to enable readers to click portions of a graphic and send the mouse coordinates back to the Web site where different actions can take place. It is useful for creating interactive maps or graphical menus.

6. Select the file type, GIF or JPEG, from the List Files of Type list box.

7. Select the directory containing the graphics files, then select the file from the File Name list box. Click OK to insert the picture.

The graphic will appear in the Web page at the location of the insertion point. If the graphic does not display correctly, select the text or graphic that does appear and click the Picture button in Edit view. The Insert Picture dialog box will reappear and show the current links and text attributes. Check that they correctly describe the graphic you want.

Creating Hyperlinks to Documents and Files

Most Web documents are hypertext and hypermedia documents. The browser software you use to view Web documents enables you to click a hypertext link and jump to another document on another computer. The hypermedia link enables you to click a link and view motion video or hear sound. Hypertext and hypermedia are important concepts in Web publishing. In this appendix, you will learn how to create your own hypertext and hypermedia links.

Understanding the Importance of Hypertext and Hypermedia

Hypertext refers specifically to computer-based documents in which you move from one place in a document to another or between documents in a nonlinear or nonsequential manner. This means that you don't access information in a traditional beginning-to-end fashion. With a book, for example, you normally begin reading at page one and move page by page, chapter by chapter, to the end. In a nonlinear computer document, you move nonsequentially through the document. Words, phrases, and icons in the document become links that enable you to jump at will to a new location in the document or even to a new document.

Hypermedia is a natural extension of hypertext. In hypermedia, links connect to visuals such as graphics or photographs, audio messages, or video, as well as to text.

The documents and information that comprise the *hyperspace* on the Web are often linked by different authors. The process is similar to placing a footnote in a document; the footnote can automatically open the resource to which it refers. Hypermedia authors use HTML to create hypertext and hypermedia links. With the Internet Assistant, you don't need to know HTML to create most hypermedia documents. You only need to learn a few Internet Assistant toolbar buttons or commands.

Creating Hypertext Links

One of the defining features of any hypertext document is the link it includes (also known as *hyperlink*). Links are simply references to other documents. But they aren't just stated references like "see pages 2-3 for more information." They are actual live links, where you can activate the link and cause the referenced item to appear on your screen. When someone writes a hypertext document, he or she can insert links to other documents that have information relevant to the text in the document.

There are two parts to a hypertext link. One part is the reference to the related item (whether it's a document, picture, movie, or sound). In the case of the Web, the item being referenced could be within the current document or anywhere else on the Web.

The second part of a hypertext link is the *anchor*. The author of a document can define the anchor to be a word, group of words, picture, or any area of the reader's display. The reader may activate the anchor by pointing to it and clicking with a mouse (for a graphical-based browser) or by selecting it with arrow keys and pressing Enter (for a text-based browser).

The anchor appears differently, depending on the browser software you are using. If it is a color display, anchor words may be a special color, and anchor graphics may be surrounded by a colored box. Internet Assistant displays text anchors in blue, underlined text, and graphical anchors outlined in blue. On a black-and-white display, anchor words may be underlined, and anchor graphics may have a border drawn around them. On a simple terminal, anchor words may be in reverse video (and, of course, there would be no graphics!).

When you click the anchor, your browser fetches the item referenced by the anchor. This may involve reading a document from your local disk, or going out on the Web and requesting that a document be sent from a distant computer to yours. The reference indicates what type of item is being retrieved (HTML document, sound file, and so on), and your browser tries to present the material to you in the appropriate format.

Internet Assistant supports three types of HTML links:

- To any named location within the current HTML document

- To any other HTML document stored locally or on the Internet

- To any non-HTML document (pictures, binary files, text, and so on) stored locally or on the Internet

You create an anchor in Edit view in the HyperLink <A> dialog box. This dialog box includes three tabs from which you can select (see fig. A.8): To Bookmark, To URL, and To Local Document. Each type of link you create with Internet Assistant provides the opportunity to choose a graphic to display as the anchor for the hyperlink you are creating. In addition, you can select from a set of Advanced options.

Tip
One way to identify an anchor in some browsers is to watch the pointer. Your pointer may change to another shape when it passes over an anchor. The pointer does not change in Internet Assistant.

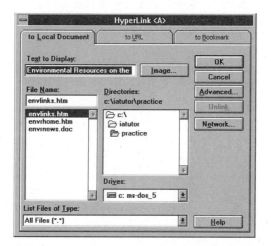

Fig. A.8
The HyperLink <A> dialog box shows you various links you can establish.

Creating Links to Files on the World Wide Web

The most exciting type of hypertext link provided in Internet Assistant links your Web page to the World Wide Web. Anytime you link to a document located on a Web server, you must include the full path name, known as the URL.

To add a hypertext link to another Web Page, follow these steps:

1. Display your Web document in Edit view. Select a word or image you want to use as an anchor if it is already in place.

2. Click the HyperLink button or choose Insert, HyperLink. The HyperLink <A> dialog box displays.

3. Click the to URL tab. The To URL dialog box appears, as shown in figure A.9.

Fig. A.9

You can create a hyperlink that jumps to a file on your local drive or network.

4. If you want to link to text and you did not select text in step 1, type the text you want to appear as hypertext in the Text to Display edit box. Click OK.

5. If you want to link to a graphic image and you did not select one in step 1, click the Image button and select a graphic file from the dialog box. Click OK.

6. (Optional) Click the Advanced button and enter any desired modifications. Click OK.

7. In the Type a URL edit box, type the full URL for the document to which you want to link. For example,

   http://www.mcp.com/

8. Click OK.

You return to the document, and the anchor is displayed in blue and underline (text) or blue outline (image), indicating that it is now an anchor.

Dragging and Dropping Links

Internet Assistant in Word 95 has the powerful capability of creating shortcuts to Web pages. This enables you or others to quickly reconnect to the same document on the World Wide Web.

To create a shortcut to your Web document, follow these steps:

1. Display a Web document in the Internet Assistant. Arrange Word's window so that you can see part of the desktop.

2. Select all or part of the Web page. With the right mouse button, drag the selection onto the desktop and drop it.

3. Choose Create Shortcut(s) Here from the shortcut menu.

A shortcut icon will appear on the desktop. You can double-click this shortcut to reload the document and reconnect to that URL on the World Wide Web.

Another powerful technique is to select a Web document or select its file and use the right mouse button to drag it into a document you will give or send to someone. Again, choose Create Shortcut(s) Here from the shortcut menu. If the other person also has Internet Assistant for Word for Windows 95, he or she will be able to double-click the shortcut and load the same Web page and reconnect to the same URL.

Creating Interactive Web Forms and Maps

World Wide Web pages can do more than just present information. They can also interact with the reader. Interactive Web pages enable readers to request additional information, sign up for electronic newsletters, purchase products, and even request information or link to other pages by clicking points on a map or graphical menu. Interactive maps enable readers to click a geographic area of interest on a map or click an area within a graphical toolbar or menu.

With the Internet Assistant, you can add most interactive fields using a command or toolbar button. The few interactive form fields that are not supported by Internet Assistant can be inserted manually.

Figure A.10 shows one example of a very simple interactive form you can build with the Internet Assistant.

Fig. A.10
Internet Assistant enables you to build interactive Web pages that return entered data to a Web server.

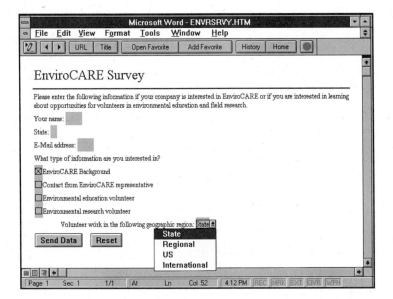

Publishing Microsoft Office Documents on the Web

The World Wide Web offers incredible potential for easily linking information throughout the world, but the HTML language used to create pages on the Web does not yet offer the robust formatting and embedded data capabilities of Word for Windows documents. However, you can create Word for Windows documents and display them on the Web. These DOC files can contain sophisticated formatting as well as embedded data from other Windows applications. With a few simple Word commands, you can create DOC files for the Web, like the one shown in figure A.11, that include embedded Excel data, multiple column formatting, and more.

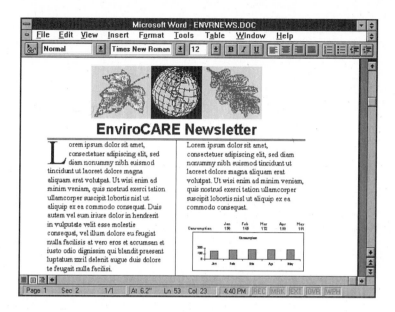

Fig. A.11
You can display
Word documents
on the Web that
contain rich
formatting and
embedded data.

Word for Windows documents on the Web can be accessed and read by anyone connected to the Internet with the Internet Assistant. For those on the Web who do not use the Internet Assistant, Microsoft has created Word Viewer, which is free. While the Word Viewer does not give a reader all the features of Word, it does enable someone with a Mosaic browser to retrieve, read, and print DOC files that are on the Web.

While HTML files on the Web have opened a new world of communication, they do not look as professional as printed materials, nor do they have a great amount of data content. By using DOC files on the Web in place of HTML files, you can create documents that have all the elements and aesthetics of magazines, posters, or newsletters. With Word's capability to embed data in a DOC file, you can also include data that gives them another dimension. Instead of just surface content and appeal, the user can double-click and actually read and use data embedded from other applications. For example, you can embed an Excel chart that, when double-clicked, loads the chart and its data into Excel where you can expand the chart view, change the chart type, or analyze the numeric data that created the chart. The capabilities of DOC files on the Web go far beyond the simple text and graphic formatting available through HTML files. ❖

Index of Common Problems

(continues)

If you have this problem...	You'll find help here...
Graphics	
Can't select a certain object after ungrouping the object	p. 783
Can't draw small shapes	p. 773
Frame extends from margin to margin when you frame multiple lines with paragraph end marks	p. 735
Nothing appeared on-screen when you tried to draw a shape	p. 772
Object didn't change after you modified the object	p. 767
Object you tried to resize moved instead of resizing	p. 776
Picture you inserted in a picture container cannot be moved on-screen	p. 792
Selection box you drew around objects would not select all the objects	p. 767
Working with Large Documents	
Annotation disappears, but you don't remember deleting it	p. 915
Annotation mark doesn't go away when you try to delete an annotation comment	p. 915
Can't change the initials in an annotation mark	p. 915
Can't turn off the option for tracking revisions	p. 909
Page numbers for entries in the table of contents are incorrect	p. 886
Reviewer's name and time information doesn't appear in the Review Revisions dialog box	p. 909
Revision bar appears in the margin, but no revision marks display in the document	p. 909
Revision marks don't appear in your document	p. 909
Subdocument containing cross-references displays many error messages	p. 950
Subdocuments did not divide as you intended	p. 945
Table of contents entries created from text don't appear in the compiled table of contents	p. 886

(continues)

If you have this problem...	You'll find help here...
Special Features	
Document contains an object for which the original application is not available, and you need to edit the object	p. 993
Double-clicking an embedded object opens a different application than you expected	p. 993
Drag and drop doesn't work with table cells you have selected	p. 518
Error message `Error! Not a valid Filename` appears when you update a link	p. 998
Field results you edited are lost when you print the document	p. 601
First field isn't selected when you open a new form	p. 653
Insert Rows and Insert Columns commands do not appear in the Table menu when you try to insert rows or columns in a table	p. 532
Printed form data doesn't line up with the form filed on the preprinted form	p. 668
Customizing Word	
Chose the wrong command while recording a macro	p. 1062
Custom toolbar buttons you use often take too long to reselect and redraw	p. 1043
Macro doesn't appear in the Macro Name list of the Macro dialog box	p. 1064
Macro you recorded is no longer available after restarting Word	p. 1061

Index

X-Y-Z

Broaden Your Mind And Your Business With Que

Copyright 1995 © Macmillan Computer Publishing–A Simon & Schuster Company

Complete and Return this Card
for a *FREE* Computer Book Cat

Thank you for purchasing this book! You have purchased a superior computer book
expressly for your needs. To continue to provide the kind of up-to-date, pertinent cov
you've come to expect from us, we need to hear from you. Please take a minute to co
and return this self-addressed, postage-paid form. In return, we'll send you a free cata
all our computer books on topics ranging from word processing to programming and th
internet.

Mr. ☐ Mrs. ☐ Ms. ☐ Dr. ☐

Name (first) ☐☐☐☐☐☐☐☐☐☐☐ (M.I.) ☐ (last) ☐☐☐☐☐☐☐☐☐☐☐☐☐☐☐

Address ☐☐☐☐☐☐☐☐☐☐☐☐☐☐☐☐☐☐☐☐☐☐☐☐☐☐☐☐☐☐

☐☐☐☐☐☐☐☐☐☐☐☐☐☐☐☐☐☐☐☐☐☐☐☐☐☐☐☐☐☐

City ☐☐☐☐☐☐☐☐☐☐☐☐ State ☐☐ Zip ☐☐☐☐☐ ☐☐☐☐

Phone ☐☐☐ ☐☐☐ ☐☐☐☐ Fax ☐☐☐ ☐☐☐ ☐☐☐☐

Company Name ☐☐☐☐☐☐☐☐☐☐☐☐☐☐☐☐☐☐☐☐☐☐☐☐☐

E-mail address ☐☐☐☐☐☐☐☐☐☐☐☐☐☐☐☐☐☐☐☐☐☐☐☐

1. Please check at least (3) influencing factors for purchasing this book.

Front or back cover information on book .... ☐
Special approach to the content .... ☐
Completeness of content .... ☐
Author's reputation .... ☐
Publisher's reputation .... ☐
Book cover design or layout .... ☐
Index or table of contents of book .... ☐
Price of book .... ☐
Special effects, graphics, illustrations .... ☐
Other (Please specify): _____ ☐

2. How did you first learn about this book?

Saw in Macmillan Computer Publishing catalog .... ☐
Recommended by store personnel .... ☐
Saw the book on bookshelf at store .... ☐
Recommended by a friend .... ☐
Received advertisement in the mail .... ☐
Saw an advertisement in: _____ ☐
Read book review in: _____ ☐
Other (Please specify): _____ ☐

3. How many computer books have you purchased in the last six months?

This book only .... ☐   3 to 5 books..................... ☐
2 books .... ☐   More than 5..................... ☐

4. Where did you purchase this book?

Bookstore .... ☐
Computer Store .... ☐
Consumer Electronics Store .... ☐
Department Store .... ☐
Office Club .... ☐
Warehouse Club .... ☐
Mail Order .... ☐
Direct from Publisher .... ☐
Internet site .... ☐
Other (Please specify): _____ ☐

5. How long have you been using a computer?

☐ Less than 6 months   ☐ 6 months to a year
☐ 1 to 3 years   ☐ More than 3 years

6. What is your level of experience with personal computers and with the subject of this book?

	With PCs	With subject of book
New	☐	....
Casual	☐	....
Accomplished	☐	....
Expert	☐	....

Source Code ISBN: 0-7897-0084-0

wing best describes your

...t ....

alog

written
erage ...OO ....
mplete
og of ...... Medical Professional ....
e ...... tor/Trainer ....
...... nician ....

...ed/Student/Retired ....
...ase specify): _____

:h of the following best describes the area of company your job title falls under?

...inting ....
...neering ....
...nufacturing ....
...erations ....
...Marketing ....
...Sales ....
Other (Please specify): _____

9. What is your age?

Under 20 ....
21-29 ....
30-39 ....
40-49 ....
50-59 ....
60-over ....

10. Are you:

Male ....
Female ....

11. Which computer publications do you read regularly? (Please list)

_____
_____
_____
_____
_____
_____
_____
_____
_____
_____

Comments: _____
_____
_____

Fold here and scotch-tape to mail.